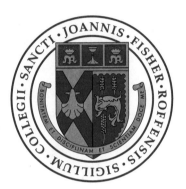

THE NEW

LEXINGTON
PRESS

New Perspectives on International Industrial/Organizational Psychology

New Perspectives on International Industrial/ Organizational Psychology

P. Christopher Earley
Miriam Erez
Editors

Foreword by Sheldon Zedeck

The New Lexington Press
San Francisco

Substantial discounts on bulk quantities of The New Lexington Press books are available to corporations, professional associations, and other organizations. For details and discount information, contact the special sales department at (415) 433–1740; Fax (800) 605–2665.

For sales outside the United States, please contact your local Simon & Schuster International Office.

The New Lexington Press Web address: http://www.newlex.com

Manufactured in the United States of America on Lyons Falls Turin Book. This paper is acid-free and 100 percent totally chlorine-free.

Library of Congress Cataloging-in-Publication Data

New perspectives on international industrial/organizational psychology
    / P. Christopher Earley, Miriam Erez, editors. — 1st ed.
        p.   cm. — (The New Lexington Press management and
    organization sciences series)   (The New Lexington Press social and
    behavioral sciences series)
      Includes bibliographical references and index.
      ISBN 0-7879-0936-X (alk. paper)
      1. Psychology, Industrial.   2. Organization—Research.
    I. Earley, P. Christopher.   II. Erez, Miriam.   III. Series.
    IV. Series: The New Lexington Press social and behavioral sciences
    series.
    HF5548.8.N474   1997
    158.7—dc21   97-13596

FIRST EDITION
HB Printing 10 9 8 7 6 5 4 3 2 1

A joint publication in
The New Lexington Press
Management and Organization Sciences Series
and
The New Lexington Press
Social and Behavioral Sciences Series

Frontiers of Industrial and Organizational Psychology

SERIES EDITOR

Sheldon Zedeck
University of California, Berkeley

EDITORIAL BOARD

Walter C. Borman
University of South Florida

Ann Howard
*Leadership Research Institute and
Development Dimensions International*

Daniel R. Ilgen
Michigan State University

Allen I. Kraut
Baruch College

Elaine D. Pulakos
Personnel Decisions Research Institutes, Inc.

Denise M. Rousseau
Carnegie-Mellon University

Contents

Foreword

The Society for Industrial and Organizational Psychology established the *Frontiers of Industrial and Organizational Psychology* series in 1982, in part, to advance the scientific status of the field. The series was specifically designed so that each volume would deal with a single topic considered to be of major contemporary significance in the field. The volume editor, a leading contributor to the topic, takes responsibility for the development of the volume with a particular goal of presenting cutting-edge theory, research, and practice in chapters contributed by individuals doing pioneer work on the topic. Each volume is aimed at the interests of members of the Society for Industrial and Organizational Psychology—researchers, practitioners, and students. Volumes are published on a timely basis rather than a fixed schedule, though at a projected rate of one volume per year.

The first editor of the series was Raymond Katzell, who was followed by Irwin Goldstein. I began my term as series editor in May 1993. The practice of choosing volume topics and editors that I am following is the one successfully established by my predecessors. Specifically, the choice of topics and volume editors is determined by the *Frontiers* series editorial board; there is considerable exchange between the board and the volume editor in the planning stages of each volume. Once the volume is under contract, the series editor works with the volume editor to coordinate and oversee the activities between the board, the publisher, the volume editor, and the volume authors.

Under the excellent leadership and guidance of the premiere editor, Raymond Katzell, three major volumes were developed and published: *Career Development in Organizations,* edited by Douglas T. Hall (1986); *Productivity in Organizations,* edited by John P. Campbell and Richard J. Campbell (1988); and *Training and Development in Organizations,* edited by Irwin L. Goldstein (1989). Under the equally excellent stewardship of Irwin Goldstein, four additional volumes were published: *Organizational Climate and Culture,* edited by Benjamin Schneider (1990); *Work, Families, and Organizations,* edited by Sheldon Zedeck (1992); *Personnel Selection in Organizations,* edited by Neal Schmitt and Walter Borman (1993), and *Team Effectiveness and Decision Making in Organizations,* edited by Richard A. Guzzo and Eduardo Salas (1995).

Since my term began, the series has added two volumes: *The Changing Nature of Work,* edited by Ann Howard (1995), and *Individual Differences and Behavior in Organizations,* edited by Kevin Murphy (1996). The success of the series is evidenced by the high number of sales (approximately 29,000 copies have been sold), by the excellent reviews written about the volumes, and by the frequent citation of volumes and chapters in scholarly papers.

New Perspectives on International Industrial/Organizational Psychology, edited by P. Christopher Earley and Miriam Erez, continues the tradition of publishing volumes designed to move the field forward and to present new thinking and approaches. The general purpose of this volume is to provide divergent perspectives on industrial and organizational topics that cross cultures and national origins. Many scholars have acknowledged the rapid environmental changes that are occurring within the global marketplace. This globalization presents us with challenges in understanding cultural differences in workers' needs, values, and norms and in the human resource practices and management related to these workers. This volume attempts to enhance our understanding by focusing on the nature of the employee-organization relationship. The authors of the primary chapters in each subsection explore their topics from the perspective of the employee-organization relationship and, in particular, look at how the relationship between the two changes as a function of culture and national origin. The goal is to present new conceptual frameworks that can be used by researchers to study employee-organization relationships across cultural boundaries.

An interesting twist in this volume is that it establishes pairings of researchers for most of the topics covered. Within each topic subsection, one chapter is written by an author (or authors) designated as the primary contributor(s). A second author (or authors) then explores the primary contribution from another perspective, one that includes the second author's own research background, knowledge, and culture. Thus the chapters within each subsection are complementary, providing several perspectives on common topics of interest to researchers. The volume's ultimate goal is to enhance our understanding of the role culture and national origin play in influencing employees' reactions to organizational practices.

Volume editors Chris Earley and Miriam Erez have done an excellent job in identifying the topics, selecting a diverse group of authors, and working with those authors to develop a focused volume that is sure to direct our research for many years to come. The society owes Earley and Erez and their chapter authors a considerable debt of gratitude for undertaking such an ambitious volume. We anticipate that this volume will serve as an important stimulus for researchers seeking to move forward in understanding behavior in today's environment.

The production of a volume such as this one requires the cooperation and efforts of many individuals. The volume editors, the volume chapter authors, and the series editorial board all played an obvious major role. They deserve our sincere appreciation and thanks for devoting their time and efforts to a task that is undertaken for the sole purpose of contributing to our field, without any remuneration whatsoever. Also to be thanked is Cedric Crocker, editor of the Jossey-Bass Business & Management Series, and his colleagues at Jossey-Bass, especially Cheryl Greenway, who had the chore of working with editors from two different continents and sent the manuscript into production without a hitch.

April 1997   SHELDON ZEDECK
                                        University of California, Berkeley
                                        Series Editor

Preface

A major impetus for this volume was the ever increasing demand on industrial and organizational researchers to understand the dynamics of organizational phenomena. Despite our inherent need to understand the potential limits to generalization of our theories and frameworks, misunderstanding persists about the theoretical and practical significance of modern organizational research. Despite the seemingly obvious constraint that any international or cross-cultural context places on research frameworks and findings, researchers proliferate the literature with findings based on single cultural contexts but do not ask the critical question, is the finding generalizable to other cultures? Our research literatures, riddled with incomplete views of the entire cultural phenomenon under their gaze, are like the proverbial blind man's description of an elephant.

As the editors of this book, we collected chapters with the purpose of providing the interested reader with divergent perspectives on a wide variety of industrial and organizational research topics. Thus we have chosen a focus on a person's relationship to his or her work organization as the fundamental building block of each chapter. We have also chosen this path because much of the work described in the international and cross-cultural organizational literature is in its infancy, and our hope is that this book will act as both a reference and a starting point for researchers interested in conducting further work of this type. In fact the diversity reflected in this book by people who have already committed significant time and energy to the study of organizations from an international perspective suggests that a substantial new direction for the field of industrial and organizational psychology is being born.

Research in the field of I/O psychology is embarking on an exciting new adventure by exploring the employee-organization relationship across country and cultural boundaries. For a number of years there has been ample evidence that various work methods were differentially effective in various cultures, but practitioners were able only to speculate why such differentiation occurred. It has been dissatisfying to explain comparative findings with such panacea platitudes as "we are just different" or "the social system prevents techniques from transferring." It is our belief, and hope, that the approaches presented in this book will enhance practitioners' and researchers' understanding of the role culture plays in shaping individuals' reactions to organizational practices, and will enable them to predict which practices will be most effective in a given cultural context.

Acknowledgments

Many individuals contributed to the creation of this book, and needless to say, the chapters reflect the accumulation of many scholars' efforts. As we developed the core concept behind this volume, our thinking was influenced by a number of people, including Elaine Mosakowski, Lyman Porter, and Harry Triandis. We are grateful to our home institutions and colleagues for their continued support as we worked on this book, and Christopher Earley also wishes to thank both the University of California, Irvine, and the London Business School for support during the completion of this book. We are particularly grateful to C. J. Farrar, whose administrative efforts in the role of managing editor enabled us to track contributors from a dozen countries and across four continents. We also extend a strong thanks to series editor Sheldon Zedeck and to the members of the review panel for the Society of Industrial and Organizational Psychology. Through their comprehensive and timely feedback, we were able to create a coherent vision for this volume of the *Frontiers* series.

We would like to thank the editorial staff at Jossey-Bass as well for their patience and help in shaping chapter drafts into a rigorous presentation. Our particular thanks go to Cheryl Greenway, who bore most of the burden of a sometimes awkward U.S.–Israel connection that slowed the book's completion.

Finally, we would like to thank our doctoral students who have stimulated our thinking about international, cross-cultural, and intercultural issues. We continue to develop in part because our students never cease asking what scholars mean by intercultural and cross-cultural organizational research.

April 1997

P. CHRISTOPHER EARLEY
Irvine, California, U.S.A.

MIRIAM EREZ
Technion City, Haifa, Israel

The Authors

P. CHRISTOPHER EARLEY received his Ph.D. degree (1984) in industrial and organizational psychology from the University of Illinois, Urbana–Champaign. He is the Corporate Partners Research Professor of Management at the University of California, Irvine. His research interests include intercultural and international aspects of organizational behavior such as the relationship of cultural values to workgroup dynamics, the role of face and social structure in organizations, and motivation across cultures. His recent publications include the books *The Transplanted Executive* (with Miriam Erez, 1996) and *Culture, Self-Identity, and Work* (with Miriam Erez, 1993), the article "East Meets West Meets Mideast: Further Exploration of Collectivistic and Individualistic Work Groups" (*Academy of Management Journal,* 1991), and the chapter "A Framework for Understanding Experimental Research in an International and Intercultural Context" (with Elaine Mosakowski, in *Handbook of International Management Research,* 1995).

MIRIAM EREZ is professor of industrial and organizational psychology and dean of the faculty of industrial engineering and management at the Technion-Israel Institute of Technology. Her research focuses on two major areas: first, work motivation, with an emphasis on participation in goal setting and its effect on performance quantity and quality, and second, cross-cultural organizational behavior, with an emphasis on the differential effect of motivational techniques across cultures. She is a Fellow of the APA and of the Society for Industrial and Organizational Psychology. She serves on the editorial board of *Organizational Behavior and Human Decision Processes* and *The Academy of Management Journal,* and she is the associate editor of *Applied Psychology: An International Review.* She is the president-elect of the Division of Organizational Psychology, International Association of Applied Psychology.

Ram N. Aditya is completing his doctoral dissertation in social and organizational psychology at Temple University. He has worked for several years as a management professional in the corporate sector in India. He is currently engaged in a number of research projects on methodological issues as well as in social and organizational psychology with an emphasis on leadership and managerial behavior. Aditya is a member of the coordinating team of the GLOBE project—a worldwide, cross-cultural study of leadership involving 58 countries and over 140 investigators, initiated by Robert House.

Neil Anderson is senior lecturer in occupational psychology and course director of the MSc. degree in occupational psychology at Goldsmiths College, University of London, and has been visiting professor at the Universities of Minnesota and Hangzhou. He is founding editor of the *International Journal of Selection and Assessment* and former associate editor of the *Journal of Occupational and Organizational Psychology.* He has coauthored or edited five books, and his work has appeared in several scholarly journals including the *Journal of Applied Psychology,* the *Journal of Organizational Behavior,* the *Journal of Occupational and Organizational Psychology,* and the *International Journal of Selection and Assessment.* His research interests span recruitment and selection, organizational and workgroup socialization, innovation at work, and organizational climate. Some of his ongoing research projects are also examining the structure and psychometric properties of popular "Big Five" measures of personality, telephone-based interview decision making, and cognitive aspects of organizational socialization.

Rosario Martinez Arias is senior professor of psychometrics and research methods at the Complutense University of Madrid, where she is the head of the Department of Methodology of Behavioral Sciences. She received her Ph.D. degree in psychology from Complutense University. At present, she is researching and writing on decision-making processes, evaluation, and psychometric methods. She has published several books and coauthored papers and articles in a large number of Spanish and international journals, such as *Personality and Individual Differences* and *European Psychologist.*

Richard D. Arvey is a professor of industrial relations at the University of Minnesota. He received his Ph.D. degree in industrial and organizational psychology from the University of Minnesota, and he has taught at the Universities of Tennessee and Houston. He has also been a visiting professor at the University of California, Berkeley, and more recently at the University of California, Irvine. He conducts research in the areas of staffing, training and development, job satisfaction and morale, and other related topics in organizational behavior. He is interested in cross-cultural research issues, particularly those that pertain to human resource management.

Zoe I. Barsness is an assistant professor in the Department of Management at Texas A&M University. She received her Ph.D. degree in organizational behavior from Northwestern University. Her current research focuses on the changing meaning of organizational membership and the impact of flexible work arrangements on individuals and groups within organizations. Her other research interests include cross-cultural research methodologies, the influence of diversity on group processes and effectiveness, organizational culture and commitment, negotiation, and alternative dispute resolution procedures.

John W. Berry is a professor of psychology at Queen's University, Kingston. He received his Ph.D. degree (1966) from the University of Edinburgh. He has been a lecturer at the University of Sydney for three years, a Fellow of the Netherlands Institute for Advanced Study, and a visiting professor at the Université de Nice and the Université de Genève. He is a past secretary-general, past president, and Honorary Fellow of the International Association for Cross-Cultural Psychology and a former associate editor of the *Journal of Cross-Cultural Psychology*. He is senior editor of the *Handbook of Cross-Cultural Psychology* and the author or editor of over twenty books in the areas of cross-cultural and social and cognitive psychology. He is particularly interested in the application of cross-cultural psychology to public policy and programs in the areas of acculturation, multiculturalism, immigration, health and education.

Dharm P. S. Bhawuk is an assistant professor in the School of Management at the University of Hawaii, Manoa. He obtained his Ph.D. degree (1995) from the University of Illinois. He also holds a Bachelor of Technology degree in mechanical engineering from the Indian Institute of Technology, Karagpur, India, and an M.B.A. degree from the University of Hawaii. He has edited one book and has published half a dozen papers in refereed journals, as well as ten book chapters.

Michael Harris Bond was born in the year of the monkey (1944) in Toronto, Canada. His first introduction to foreign cultures was to study Latin for six years at a British-model private school. He received his Ph.D. degree from Stanford University, where he never heard about culture but encountered a lot of it on the freeways and the beaches of California. Having married an adventurous lady and become a Baha'i, he has spent the last twenty-five years of his professional life raising a family and crafting a career as a cross-cultural psychologist in the Orient. He is currently a professor of psychology at the Chinese University of Hong Kong and is revising his text *Social Psychology Across Cultures* with his colleague-in-culture, Peter Smith. He lifts weights, listens to Gregorian chants, reads "with his eyes hanging out," and strives to find the same in the others, everywhere.

Jeanne M. Brett received her Ph.D. degree (1972) in industrial and organizational psychology from the University of Illinois. After teaching at the Universities of Michigan and Illinois, she joined the faculty of the Kellogg Graduate School of Management in 1976. In 1989, she became the first DeWitt W. Buchanan, Jr., Professor of Dispute Resolution and Organizations. She is also founder and director of Northwestern University's Dispute Resolution Research Center. In 1990, she held a faculty appointment at the Institute d'Administration des Entreprises, Université de Droit, d'Économie et des Sciences d'Aix-Marseille, and she frequently teaches in the annual International Teachers Program held by a consortium of European business schools. Her research has taken her from the Appalachian coalfields, where she has studied alternative dispute resolution techniques, to the headquarters of Fortune 500 corporations, where she has examined work and family issues ranging from relocation to the advancement of female managers. She is the author of more than fifty articles and three books. *Getting Disputes Resolved: Designing Systems to Cut the Costs of Conflict* received the 1988 Center for Public Resources Award for excellence and innovation in alternative dispute resolution.

Helen De Cieri lectures in the Department of Management and Industrial Relations at the University of Melbourne, Australia. She holds a Ph.D. degree from the University of Tasmania. Her research interests are in the fields of international human resources and expatriate management, and her work has been published in Australian and international refereed journals and monographs. She is also the editor of the *Asia Pacific Journal of Human Resources.*

Peter J. Dowling received his Ph.D. degree from Flinders University of South Australia. He is the Foundation Professor of Management at the University of Tasmania. He has also held teaching appointments at Monash University, the University of Melbourne, and Cornell University. His research interests are in the areas of international human resources and strategic management.

Cristina B. Gibson is assistant professor of management at the University of Wisconsin, Madison. Prior to joining the UW–Madison faculty, she was most recently with the Graduate School of Management at the University of California, Irvine, where she completed her Ph.D. degree (1995) in organizational behavior. Her research interests include social cognition, the impact of culture and gender on work behavior, communication and interaction in groups, and international management. Her recent research projects investigate work team performance in Indonesia and Hong Kong and the effective implementation of teams in multinational corporations in Puerto Rico, the Philippines, and Western Europe. Her research has appeared in the *Journal of International Business Studies, Advances in International Comparative Management,* and *Journal of Managerial Issues.* She is also a former director of research for the Reed Group, a consulting firm that designs and implements programs for the improvement of leadership skills and employee morale in Fortune 500 corporations.

George B. Graen is an internationally recognized consultant, researcher, and educator in international industrial and organizational psychology, and a professor of international leadership and management at University of Cincinnati. In 1989, he received a grant from the Cleveland Foundation to establish the Center for the Enhancement of International Competitiveness at the university, and as director of that center, he manages professional consulting services and conducts research studies for private and public clients worldwide. Specializing in international leadership and work design issues, his professional consulting clientele includes major Fortune 500 companies. He has published over one hundred scientific articles, papers, technical reports, chapters, and books. Graen is a Fellow of the American Psychological Association. For the last two years, he and his cross-cultural research and consulting team have been engaged in a project to understand joint venture businesses in China, Hong Kong, and Taiwan. He is director of the West Lake Center for International Joint Venture Research and Training in Hangzhou, China.

Tove Helland Hammer is a professor of organizational behavior at the New York State School of Industrial Labor Relations at Cornell University. She received her Ph.D. degree (1973) in industrial and organizational psychology from the University of Maryland. Her research interests are the evaluation of worker participation programs and forms of employee stock ownership, leadership effectiveness in trade unions, and the effects of management values on employment relations and organizational change. She is editor of the *Industrial and Labor Relations Review*.

Jean F. Hartley is principal research Fellow at the Warwick Business School, University of Warwick. She received her Ph.D. degree in organizational psychology from Manchester University and has held previous appointments at the Universities of London, Sheffield, and Manchester. Her current research interests are transformational change in the public sector and psychological aspects of employment relations. She is the coauthor of *Employment Relations: The Psychology of Influence and Control at Work* (with Geoffrey Stephenson) and has published two other books and numerous articles and chapters on organizational psychology and on industrial relations.

John R. Hollenbeck is a professor of management at the Eli Broad Graduate School of Business Administration at Michigan State University. He received his Ph.D. degree (1984) in management and organizational behavior from New York University. He serves or has served on the editorial boards of the *Journal of Applied Psychology, Academy of Management Journal, Organizational Behavior and Human Decision Processes, Journal of Management,* and *Personnel Psychology.* The first recipient (1992) of the Ernest J. McCormick Award for early contributions to the field of industrial and organizational psychology, he also received the 1987 Teacher-Scholar Award at Michigan State University. His research focuses on self-regulation theories of work motivation, employee separation and acquisition processes, and team decision making and performance.

Robert J. House holds the Joseph Frank Bernstein endowed chair of organizational studies at the Wharton School of the University of Pennsylvania. He received his Ph.D. degree (1960) in management from Ohio State University. He has been a visiting professor at the University of Michigan, the Massachusetts Institute of Technology, the University of New South Wales, the University of Southern California, and Suffolk University, and a visiting scholar at Concordia University, the Chinese University of Hong Kong, and Stanford University. He is Fellow of the Academy of Management, American Psychological Association, and Society for Industrial and Organizational Psychology. House is the author of six books and approximately one hundred articles in management and social science journals. He is a cofounder of the Organizational Behavior Division of the Academy of Management, *Leadership Quarterly,* and MESO, an organization devoted to the integration of micro and macro organizational behavior theory and research. House's current research concerns the distribution and exercise of power in complex organizations, the nature and effects of outstanding leadership, the role of personality variables in complex organizations, and cross-cultural investigation of organizational and leadership practices.

Chun Hui is an assistant professor in the Management of Organizations Department at Hong Kong University of Science and Technology. He received both his M.A. degree in social psychology and his Ph.D. degree in organizational behavior and human resource management from Indiana University at Bloomington. His research interests include leadership, conflict management, selection, and performance appraisal. He is also developing an active program of research on comparative management, with a special focus on Chinese management. He has published in management and social psychology journals.

Daniel R. Ilgen is the John A. Hannah Professor of Psychology and Management at Michigan State University, a position he has held since 1983. He received his Ph.D. degree (1969) in psychology from the University of Illinois. Throughout most of the 1970s and early 1980s, he was on the faculty at Purdue University in the Department of Psychological Sciences. His research has focused on work motivation, performance feedback, and performance of teams that are hierarchically structured and are composed of members with differing expertise. This research has been published in a wide variety of journals, including *Journal of Applied Psychology, American Psychologist, Organizational Behavior and Human Decision Processes, Personnel Psychology,* and *Academy of Management Journal.* He currently serves as associate editor of *Organizational Behavior and Human Decision Processes.*

Maddy Janssens is an associate professor of human resource management at Katholieke Universiteit Leuven in Belgium. She received her M.S. degree in organizational behavior from Northwestern University and her Ph.D. degree in psychology from Katholieke Universiteit Leuven. She has been a visiting professor at INSEAD in France, and she has published in international journals in the areas of expatriate management and cross-cultural methodology. Her current research topics include commitment and human resource management practices, the transferability of human resource management practices across cultures, language in international management, and diversity in transnational teams.

Boris Kabanoff is a professor at the Queensland University of Technology, Brisbane, Australia, and head of the university's School of Management. Prior to this appointment, he was at the Australian Graduate School of Management of the University of New South Wales. He received his Honours degree in psychology from the

University of Queensland and his Ph.D. degree in industrial and organizational psychology from Flinders University in South Australia. He has received best paper awards from the International Association for Conflict Management and the Academy of Management. His major research interests lie in the application of computer-aided text analysis to a number of issues within organizational behavior and industrial and organizational psychology. He is the editor of the organizational behavior area of the *Australian Journal of Management,* special issues editor for the *Journal of Organizational Behavior,* and a member of the editorial board of the *Asia Pacific Journal of Human Resources.*

Kenneth S. Law received his Ph.D. degree in human resource management from the University of Iowa. He has worked in the Australian Graduate School of Management of the University of New South Wales in Sydney, and currently holds an appointment in the Department of Management of Organizations of the Hong Kong University of Science and Technology. His major research interests are methodological issues in human resource management research and also such human resource management content issues as compensation and personnel selection. Most recently, he has been working on such organizational behavior issues as organizational justice perceptions and management in Chinese contexts.

Jeffrey A. LePine is a doctoral student in organizational behavior at Michigan State University. He received his M.A. degree (1993) in management from Florida State University. His primary research interests include the effects of trait, ability, and cultural differences in role assimilation, team development, and performance. His other research interests include feedback interventions and their effect on learning and motivation in team settings and individual differences in information-processing strategies.

Kwok Leung is professor and chairman in the Department of Psychology of the Chinese University of Hong Kong. He holds a Ph.D. degree from the University of Illinois. He is currently an associate editor of the *Journal of Cross-Cultural Psychology.* He is a coeditor of *Innovations in Cross-Cultural Psychology* and a coauthor of *Methods and Data Analysis for Cross-Cultural Psychology.* His research interests include justice and conflict resolution, cross-cultural psychology, and cross-cultural research methodology.

Zhiang Lin teaches organizational theory and organizational behavior courses at the Hong Kong University of Science and Technology. Born in Shanghai and educated in both China and the United States, Lin earned his Ph.D. degree (1994) in organizations and policy analysis from Carnegie Mellon University. His research centers around macro organizational issues including relationships among organizational design, environment, and performance; institutions and groups in cross-cultural settings; integration of computational modeling and empirical data for organizational theory building and testing; organizational learning and adaptation; and management of high-risk organizations. His work has been published in refereed journals including *IEEE Transactions on Systems, Man and Cybernetics; Journal of Mathematical Sociology; International Journal of Intelligent Systems in Accounting, Finance, and Management; Economy and Development* (in Chinese); and *Management Science.*

Anne Louise Lytle is an assistant professor in the Management of Organizations Department at the Hong Kong University of Science and Technology. She received her Ph.D. degree from the Kellogg School of Business at Northwestern University. Her current research interests include the role of culture in negotiation and conflict management.

Sara L. McGaughey is currently undertaking doctoral studies at the University of Tasmania, Australia. She holds an M.B.A. degree from Monash University. Her research interest is internationalization management, with a focus on international human resources and internalization of the firm. Her work has been published in book chapters and in refereed international journals and conference proceedings.

Takao Minami is a professor of organizational behavior and social psychology in the Department of Human Relations and in the Institute for Management and Labor Studies at Keio University, Japan. He also received both his B.A. degree (1967) in psychology and his M.A. degree (1969) in sociology from Keio University. He received his M.A. and Ph.D. degrees (1972 and 1976, respectively) in labor relations from the Institute of Labor and Industrial Relations at the University of Illinois, Urbana–Champaign. In 1989–90, he served as a visiting professor and a Fulbright senior researcher at the institute. He is a member of the board of governors of the Japanese Association of Industrial and Organizational Psychology, the Japanese Society for the Advancement of Organizational Sciences, the Japan Association of Job Stress Research, the Japanese Association of Social Psychology, and the Japanese Psychological Association. His current research interests are in the mentor-protégé relationship and career development in organizations, and the work-family relationship. He has published articles on these topics in Japan and the United States.

José M. Prieto is a professor of work and organizational psychology at the Complutense University of Madrid. He received his Ph.D. degree from Complutense University in 1980. During the 1970s, he worked in human resource management, employed successively by three different national banks. During the 1980s, he researched and published on personnel assessment issues. In 1990, he moved his teaching and research interests to human resource development issues, focusing on the transfer of training and on the design of training materials based on hypertext and hypermedia technologies. (His present contributions and developments are included on his home page [http://www.ucm.es/OTROS/Psyap/].) In 1996, he edited two electronic books in Spanish on the "Evaluation of Training Quality in Private Firms." During the last twenty years, he has published more than 130 papers in Spanish, English, French, and Italian. The last three published in English are a chapter in the *Annual Review of Psychology* (1994), a chapter in *the Handbook of Industrial and Organizational Psychology* (edited by H. C. Triandis, M. D. Dunnette, and L. M. Hough, 1994), and a chapter in the monograph *Applied Psychology: An International Review* (Spring 1994). During the last ten years, he has also lectured in Spanish, English, French, and Italian at universities in Europe and North and South America and at international congresses held in Australia, Japan, and Israel.

Simcha Ronen is professor of organizational psychology and comparative management at Tel Aviv University's Graduate School of

Business Administration. He received his Ph.D. degree in industrial/organizational psychology from New York University. Ronen's research interests include cross-cultural aspects of managerial behavior and employees' work values, selection and training of manpower with managerial potential, and the implementation of organizational change. His work has appeared in several scholarly journals, including *Human Relations, Personnel Psychology, Academy of Management Journal,* and *International Review of Applied Psychology.* Ronen has been a guest lecturer at universities throughout the United States, Europe, and Southeast Asia and has consulted to Fortune 500 companies.

Douglas J. Sego is an assistant professor of management at the School of Business and Management, Hong Kong University of Science and Technology. He received his Ph.D. degree (1994) in organizational behavior from Michigan State University. His primary research interests are in training system evaluation, measurement of the transfer of training, turnover in China, and decision making.

J.B.P. Sinha is a professor of psychology at ASSERT in Patna, India. He received his early education in India and holds a Ph.D. degree in psychology from Ohio State University. He has served on the faculty at Ranchi University, Patna University, and the A.N.S. Institute of Social Sciences—all in India. Sinha has also been a national lecturer of the University Grants Commission, a national Fellow of the Indian Council of Social Science Research, and visiting professor at universities in the United States and Canada. He is a vice president of the World Association For Dynamic Psychiatry and a executive member of the International Association of Applied Psychology. Sinha has published over 125 research articles in Indian and international journals in the areas of organizational behavior, values, social change, and national development. He has also written or coauthored a number of books including *Development Through Behaviour Modification, The Nurturant Task Leader, Work Culture in the Indian Context,* and *The Cultural Context of Leadership and Power.*

Peter B. Smith is a professor of social psychology at the University of Sussex and director of the Centre for Research into Cross-Cultural

Organisation and Management at Roffey Park Management Institute, Horsham, England. He obtained his Ph.D. degree (1962) from the University of Cambridge. He is currently editor of the *Journal of Cross-Cultural Psychology.*

Kiyoshi Takahashi recently completed his doctoral studies in human resource management at the Industrial Relations Center of the University of Minnesota. He received his B.A. degree (1984) in human relations and his M.A. degree (1986) in sociology from Keio University, Japan. His primary research interests are in staffing, personnel selection, and organizational justice. His plans are to begin his teaching career in Japan in the Department of Management at Nanzan University.

Catherine H. Tinsley is an assistant professor of management at Georgetown University's School of Business, where she continues to pursue questions of negotiations, conflict management, and the cross-cultural applicability of management theories. These interests stem from her experiences with living, negotiating, and trying to navigate conflicts in a foreign culture. She spent two years in Africa learning that her assumptions and fundamental beliefs were generally inapplicable in her village context. After receiving her Ph.D. degree in organizational behavior from Northwestern University, she spent a year as a visiting scholar at the Hong Kong University of Science and Technology, relearning that fundamental assumptions do not necessarily generalize across cultural contexts.

H. C. Triandis is a professor at the University of Illinois, Urbana–Champaign. He was named University of Illinois Scholar in 1987. Triandis received his Ph.D. degree (1958) in psychology from Cornell University. He has published several books, and his *Attitudes and Attitude Change* (1971) has been named a citation classic. He has also published more than eighty book chapters and more than ninety articles and monographs. He has lectured in more than forty countries on all inhabited continents and has received an honorary doctorate from the University of Athens, Greece. The American Psychological Association (APA) named him Distinguished Scientist Lecturer (1994) and also gave him its Distinguished Contributions to International Psychology Award. On the occasion of its centennial year (1992), the APA gave four citations for distinguished contributions to international psychology in the areas of education, practice, public service, and science—Triandis received the science citation. In 1996, the American Psychological Society named him a James McKeen Cattell Fellow.

Mitsuru Wakabayashi is associate director of the Graduate School of International Development at Nagoya University, Japan. He received his Ph.D. degree (1979) at the University of Illinois. He also is a principal scholar in the West Lake Center for International Joint Venture Research and Training in Hangzhou, China, and he is editor of the *Japanese Journal of Administrative Behavior.*

Zhong-Ming Wang is professor of industrial/organizational psychology and management at Hangzhou University in China. He was educated in China, Sweden, and the United Kingdom. He received his doctorate from Hangzhou University in a joint program with Gothenburg University in Sweden. He is currently the dean of the school of management and vice president of Hangzhou University. He is also vice president of the Chinese Ergonomics Society. Wang is associate editor of both the *Chinese Journal of Applied Psychology* and *Chinese Ergonomics* and is on the editorial boards of *International Encyclopedia of Business & Management, Encyclopedia of Psychology, International Journal of Human Resource Management, International Journal of Selection & Assessment, Applied Psychology, Journal of Cross-Cultural Psychology, Journal of Management Development,* and *Journal of Managerial Psychology.* His main research interests include personnel selection and assessment, team process, organizational decision making, leadership, organization development, cross-cultural organizational behavior, and human resource management.

Shinichiro Watanabe is an assistant professor of organizational behavior in the Institute of Policy and Planning Sciences at the University of Tsukuba, Japan. He received his B.A. (1979) and M.A. (1986) degrees in sociology from Keio University, and his Ph.D. degree (1994) in organizational behavior from the School of Industrial and Labor Relations at Cornell University, where he taught organizational behavior courses for three semesters following the completion of his degree. Watanabe has published articles in the United States and Great Britain on work withdrawal behaviors and the job-life satisfaction relationship. He is the recipient, along with T. A. Judge, of the 1993 Outstanding Competitive Paper Award from the Organizational Behavior Division of the Academy of Management for the article "Another Look at the Job-Life Satisfaction Relationship."

Norman S. Wright is an assistant professor of business management at Brigham Young University–Hawaii. His teaching and research interests include organizational behavior in multicultural settings and the international dimensions of business strategy and entrepreneurship.

Sheldon Zedeck is professor of psychology and chairman of the Department of Psychology at the University of California, Berkeley. He received his B.A. degree (1965) from Brooklyn College and his M.A. (1967) and Ph.D. (1969) degrees from Bowling Green State University, all in psychology. He is past president of the Society for Industrial and Organizational Psychology and is the editor of the Frontiers of Industrial and Organizational Psychology series. Among Zedeck's research interests are selection and validation, performance appraisal, assessment centers, test fairness, and work and family issues. His books include *Data Analysis for Research Designs* (with G. Keppel, 1989), and he is editor of *Performance Measurement and Theory* (with F. Landy and J. Cleveland, 1983) and of *Work, Families, and Organizations* (1992).

New Perspectives on International Industrial/Organizational Psychology

CHAPTER 1

Introduction

P. Christopher Earley
Miriam Erez

Most existing models of organizational psychology and work performance have been developed in the United States and Western Europe during the last three decades. These models focus mainly on the individual employee devoid of a general cultural or national context, and they attempt to explain work behavior by looking at individuals' values and goals, expectancies including self-efficacy expectations, and needs satisfaction (Boyacigiller & Adler, 1991). Likewise, the material in U.S. industrial and organizational (I/O) psychology journals dominated by human resource management research topics such as personnel selection and employee performance appraisal has placed a strong emphasis on the individual employee. For example, individual incentive plans have been designed to reinforce individual performance, and differential incentive plans and flexible cafeteria-style benefits have been tailored to satisfy the needs of the individual employee (Cascio, 1989). From a historical perspective, this individualistic focus is explained by the dominant liberal individualist stream in Western psychology, which views the individual as self-contained, with an identity defined apart from the world (Cushman, 1990; Erez & Earley, 1993; Sampson, 1989). As a result of this emphasis on the individual, research has largely ignored cultural and national differences in people's values and beliefs and how these differences may affect work behavior. However, the organizational significance of the rapid environmental changes of the last decade can no longer be ignored. The globalization of the marketplace has had a tremendous impact on employees, on their work motivation and organizational commitment, and on their performances and related outcomes.

This globalization presents us with many new challenges. We must confront cultural differences in people's needs, in norms for work behavior and work values, in human resource management practices, and in managerial decision making. The growing popularity of books by and for practitioners on how to do business with other cultures and peoples (for example, Graham & Sano, 1984) is a testimony to the need for information and to the continuing paucity of relevant research, despite some early thrusts by researchers over two decades ago (for example, Haire, Ghiselli, & Porter, 1966; Hofstede, 1980; Roberts, 1970).

The Purpose of This Book

What seems to be lacking in the existing research literature is an integration of the broader cultural and national contexts in which many people live and work with the existing emphasis on the individual. Our purpose in editing this book is to advance theorizing on international I/O psychology by bringing together cutting-edge perspectives about the influence of employees' cultural and national origins, relating to and augmenting both nontraditional and traditional topics in I/O psychology. More specifically, we have assembled new theories that address whether the relationship of an employee to his or her organization changes as a function of that employee's cultural and national origin, and how it changes.

Perhaps the most fundamental aspect of work is the nature of the employee-organization relationship (EOR). Theorists focusing on topics such as motivation, job attitudes, absenteeism and turnover, and organizational citizenship often turn to the EOR in order to better understand observed phenomena. However, that relationship of employees to their organizations changes as a function of employee culture.

By *culture*, we mean a *shared meaning system* (Shweder & LeVine, 1984): members of the same culture share a common way of viewing events and objects, and therefore they are likely to interpret and evaluate situations and management practices in a consistent fashion. People who are from different cultures or countries and who do not share a common way of interpreting and evaluating situations may well respond dissimilarly to any given organizational intervention. For example, in an individualistic culture such as found in the United States, employees are expected to function autonomously and are often praised for individual initiative. In a collectivistic culture such as found in Japan, employees are expected to function as an integral part of a team and to place the team situation ahead of their personal situation. This difference suggests that an organizational practice capitalizing on group action may be more effective in Japan than in the United States. For example, quality control circles have been successfully implemented in Japan and the Far East but have met with mixed success in the United States (Lawler, 1986). This does not mean that team-based work will never be effective in the United States but that such work should be modified to fit the U.S. culture. For example, teamwork may be effective in an individualistic culture when each team member's personal contributions are identified or when each member is made personally accountable for the team's success.

What have been missing from I/O research literature are the theoretical frameworks people can bring to bear in explaining such patterns, not simply describing them. We have used the nature of the EOR in cross-cultural contexts (and its relation to organizational practices) as the common thread that connects the various chapters of this book. By examining how the EOR changes, practitioners and researchers will better understand how an employee's enacted role may differ vastly across cultural borders and what this might imply about specific work practices.

The study of cultural and national differences in an employee's relationship to an organization also points the way to new topics and ideas. For example, the growing interest in the significance of the work-family relationship was stimulated in part by U.S. observations of Euro-Scandinavian family and work patterns. (This issue is discussed in Chapter Eleven, by Shinichiro Watanabe, Kiyoshi Takahasi, and Takao Minami, and in Chapter Twelve, by Sheldon Zedeck.) The work-family relationship is important to an understanding of a number of domestic and international topics, such as the changing role of women in the workforce and the varying degree to which work and family are seen as distinct. In the United States, work and family are often viewed as separable but frequently at odds with one another. However, in developing countries, work and family tend to overlap: women may undertake craft work at home, and there will be more family businesses and entrepreneurship, which act to develop and strengthen the bonds between family and work. The work-family relationship clearly varies across cultural boundaries, and yet organizational psychology has paid little attention to this topic until recently.

Unfortunately, current theories of organizational psychology lack adequate conceptual frameworks for understanding how culture and I/O psychology are interrelated. That is why our primary focus in this book is the development and presentation of new conceptual frameworks for understanding the moderating effect of nation or culture, frameworks that can be brought to bear by researchers seeking new research topics and directions.

Campbell (1990) proposed that a conceptual model could be improved by any of three means: empirical evaluation, evaluation by experts in the field of study, and analytical evaluation. Using these means to judge the existing frameworks used in cross-cultural I/O psychology, it is clear that these theories are preliminary and that further thinking must be stimulated. People working in this domain themselves have pointed out that current theories of I/O psychology do not provide a conceptual framework for understanding how culture and organizational actions are interrelated (see, for example, Boyacigiller & Adler, 1991).

The lack of research on cross-cultural organizational psychology can be attributed not only to past unawareness of its importance but also to methodological difficulties. Chapters Four, by Jeanne Brett, Catherine Tinsley, Maddy Janssens, Zoe Barsness, and Anne Lytle, Five, by John Berry, and Six, by Douglas Sego, Chun Hui, and Kenneth Law, discuss significant and critical methods concerns and unique difficulties facing the cross-cultural researcher and involving appropriate sampling, effective translations, appropriateness of methods to the culture to be studied, equivalence of measurement, response sets, and so on. Brett and her colleagues argue that no single method is the "best"; rather the effective researcher must be aware of multiple methods and bring them to bear selectively. Roberts and Boyacigiller (1984), using eight criteria for judging the quality of cultural research, found a number of prominent studies to be lacking in a number of respects. Thus a difficulty that researchers now face is understanding what constitutes rigorous, methodologically sound research in cross-cultural I/O psychology.

In summary, then, this book presents new thinking on an employee's relationship to his or her organization in an international and cross-cultural context and as it relates to both theoretical and methodological issues. We bring together new theoretical models of cross-cultural researchers on various topics within I/O psychology with the purpose of stimulating new research agendas, questions, and directions for the field.

General Organization of the Book

In order to stimulate the eclectic and cross-cultural approach we aimed for, we asked our primary contributors to work with colleagues from a different culture but knowledgeable in a similar research topic. In addition, *all* our authors were chosen in part for their specific experience with cross-cultural research. Because we wanted each chapter to stimulate research models and agendas that capture the moderating influence of culture, we did not simply choose an area expert and pair him or her with an area expert from another country when neither might have thought about the relevance of culture as a key variable, In other words, our focus is not simply an overview of I/O research across the globe; rather we seek to advance theory concerning the potential contribution of culture to our understanding of I/O psychology through presenting the thinking of researchers actually conducting cross-cultural research and through pairing these researchers for each topic discussed.

Thus the format for most topics includes, first, a primary chapter that is relatively long and comprehensive. It focuses on the development of a specific theoretical model that looks at the employee-organization relationship in a cultural context. As mentioned earlier, the nature of EOR in a cultural context is the common thread that links the various sections of this book. This primary chapter is followed by a chapter with an extensive commentary about the general topic, the model developed in the primary chapter, and the research questions generated from the model. This commentary, of course, draws upon the second expert's cultural research background and knowledge. This style of exchange avoids the redundancy that can occur when two authors write separate sections on a common topic, and it highlights the cultural differences in the different authors' ideas.

More specifically, because the purpose of this edited book is to present cutting-edge theories of various topics in cross-cultural and international I/O psychology, we took a two-fold approach. First, we asked the primary contributors to examine recent developments within their area of expertise from a cultural perspective and to create a specific theoretical, or conceptual, model that can be used to generate new research streams and advance these developments. Thus these contributors focus on recent changes from a cultural perspective rather than simply reviewing the traditional literature within their area. Second, we invited leading scholars from across the world who are engaged in international and cross-cultural I/O psychology, human resource management, and organizational behavior and in related research. We chose people who would capture divergent viewpoints across their two chapters as well as offer specific expertise. The ideal product from each collaboration is a brief overview of the topic followed by a more specific theoretical advancement drawing on the authors' divergent cross-cultural research perspectives. It was never our intention to have the second chapter for each topic critique the first chapter. The chapter pairs are not competitive but complementary; they build on one another. It is such constructive collaborations, we believe, that will create significant learning for scholars in this field.

The book consists of twelve subsections. Most contain two chapters. However, in two subsections, the second author chose to present his or her ideas within the context of the first author's chapter. In one subsection, there are two additional chapters rather than one. During a seminar taught by Earley, Sego and his colleagues at Hong Kong University of Science and Technology were so taken by Brett and her colleagues' chapter that they posed an interesting extension, which we chose to include as a third chapter for this subsection. It is precisely this type of research energy that we seek to generate with this volume. Finally, after the primary contributor originally invited to write on work values and national identity chose to withdraw from the project, Michael Harris Bond graciously agreed to shift his participation from that of a commentator to that of a primary contributor.

In the first part of this book, the authors focus on theory and method innovations in international I/O psychology research. In Chapter Two, Harry Triandis and Dharm Bhawuk discuss and describe various aspects of culture, with a focus on the interplay of individualism with power distance. Jai Sinha (Chapter Three) extends the discussion to the case of management philosophy in India, including a description of a philosophical orientation not discussed to any significant degree in the Western literature. In Chapters Four through Six, Brett and her colleagues, Berry, and Sego and his colleagues present advances on methods and on the construct of culture, offering various conceptualizations of culture. In Chapter Seven, George Graen, Chun Hui, Mitsuru Wakabayashi, and Zhong-Ming Wang examine the potential of cross-cultural teams of researchers as a means of improving cross-cultural research.

Parts Two through Four focus on new directions for intercultural I/O psychology, covering the general topics of motivation and values across cultures, working across cultural borders, and power relationships.

Part Two addresses work motivation, work values and national identity, and work-family relationships. In Chapters Eight and Nine, Erez examines the Erez-Earley model of culture and self in relation to work motivation, and Earley comments on the importance of self-enhancement, or face, from a motivational perspective. In Chapter Ten, Bond poses a new, and potentially controversial, approach to the study of behavior and values from a cross-cultural perspective, calling for a fundamental rethinking of the existing research emphasis on values. In Chapters Eleven and Twelve, Watanabe and his colleagues examine the significance of diversity and work-family ties, and Zedeck expands on this discussion with some alternative perspectives.

Part Three discusses communication, work teams, individual-union-organization relationships, and international human resource management. In Chapters Thirteen and Fourteen, Cristina Gibson first looks at the nature of cross-cultural communication, using various cultural dimensions as well as cognitive styles, and Zhiang Lin then takes a macro perspective on communication within the organizational context. Chapters Fifteen and Sixteen examine divergent perspectives on teams tied together with a common thread of decision making. Daniel Ilgen, Jeffrey LePine, and

John Hollenbeck present a framework related to their long-term examination of group dynamics and decision making, whereas José Prieto and Rosario Martinez Arias provide a distinctly different historical and sociological framing of team decision making. In Chapter Seventeen, Tove Hammer and Jean Hartley integrate their two perspectives into a common view of the changing nature of the individual-union-organization connection across cultures. In the chapter by Helen De Cieri, Sara McGaughey, and Peter Dowling (Chapter Eighteen), the authors propose an overarching framework for understanding international HRM from a strategic perspective. Richard Arvey and Neil Anderson extend this discussion with an interesting case analysis of HRM practices in South Africa.

Part Four examines power in organizations, focusing on leadership and on negotiation and conflict. In Chapters Twenty and Twenty-One, Robert House, Norman Wright, and Ram Aditya first propose a new leadership framework that integrates core aspects of culture; then Peter Smith offers a new perspective on the role of leadership from a somewhat more general view of cross-cultural research. Chapters Twenty-Two and Twenty-Three provide some updates and new perspectives on reward allocation and negotiation. After Kwok Leung analyzes reward allocation and justice research from a cultural perspective, Boris Kabanoff provides a new way of linking organizational justice issues to culture by refocusing from an individual- to an organization-level analysis.

Finally, in Part Five, Simcha Ronen examines the themes emerging from the various contributions and identifies critical gaps that still exist in the literature (Chapter Twenty-Four). And in Chapter Twenty-Five, we review the various contributions and offer our own integrating theme for understanding what researchers and practitioners can gain from all the new perspectives that this book presents.

References

Boyacigiller, N., & Adler, N. J. (1991). The parochial dinosaur: Organizational science in a global context. *Academy of Management Review, 16,* 262–290.

Campbell, J. P. (1990). The role of theory in industrial and organizational psychology. In M. D. Dunnette and L. M. Hough (Eds.), *Handbook of industrial and organizational psychology* (Vol. 1, 2nd ed., pp. 39–73). Palo Alto, CA: Consulting Psychologists Press.

Cascio, W. F. (1989). *Managing human resources: Productivity, quality of work life, profits.* New York: McGraw-Hill.

Cushman, P. (1990). Why the self is empty: Toward a historically situated psychology. *American Psychologist, 45,* 599–611.

Erez, M., & Earley, P. C. (1993). *Culture, self-identity, and work.* New York: Oxford University Press.

Graham, J. L., & Sano, Y. (1984). *Smart bargaining: Doing business with the Japanese.* New York: Ballinger.

Haire, M., Ghiselli, E. E., & Porter, L. W. (1966). *Managerial thinking: An international study.* New York: Wiley.

Hofstede, G. (1980). *Culture's consequences: International differences in work-related values.* Thousand Oaks, CA: Sage.

Lawler, E. E., III. (1986). *High-involvement management: Participative strategies for improving organizational performance.* San Francisco: Jossey-Bass.

Roberts, K. H. (1970). On looking at an elephant: An evaluation of cross-cultural research related to organizations. *Psychological Bulletin, 74,* 327–350.

Roberts, K. H., & Boyacigiller, N. A. (1984). Cross-national organizational research: The grasp of the blind men. In B. M. Shaw & L. L. Cummings (Eds.), *Research in organizational behavior* (Vol. 6, pp. 423–475). Greenwich, CT: JAI Press.

Shweder, R. A., & LeVine, R. A. (1984). *Culture theory: Essays on mind, self and emotion.* New York: Cambridge University Press.

PART 1

Theory and Method Innovations in International Research

Cultural Values and Meaning

New Approaches to Intercultural and International Industrial/Organizational Psychology

International and Intercultural Research Alliances

CHAPTER 2

Culture Theory and the Meaning of Relatedness

H. C. Triandis
Dharm P. S. Bhawuk

In this chapter we discuss the most overarching of culture theories, namely the theory of individualism and collectivism, and describe its relationship to other theories, especially to Fiske's four kinds of sociality (1990, 1992) and to Rokeach's typology of values and political systems (1973). We then discuss how an understanding of this culture theory allows practitioners and researchers to explain and predict behavior in the workplace. To connect this theory with organizational behavior, we discuss its implications for the analyses of such organizational situations and characteristics as selection, training, motivation (specifically, goal setting), communication, leadership, employee appraisal (specifically, attributions of responsibility), compensation, social exchanges, behavior settings, conflict resolution, and concepts of morality in human resource management.

Individualism and Collectivism

The constructs of individualism and collectivism have been popular in most of the social sciences for about a century. For example, the terms *Gemeinschaft* (community) and *Gesellschaft* (society) in sociology and *relational value orientation* and *individualist value orientation* in anthropology have been used for some time. However, there has not been systematic empirical work at the individual level until relatively recently (Hui & Triandis, 1986; Triandis et al., 1986;

Triandis, Leung, Villareal, & Clack, 1985; Triandis, Bontempo, Villareal, Asai, & Lucca, 1988; Triandis, 1990).

Hofstede (1980) worked with the responses of IBM employees (117,000 protocols) covering a wide variety of occupations and demographic variables in sixty-six countries. He summed the responses of the subjects from each country to several value items and conducted a factor analysis of the mean responses based on a sample size of forty (the number of countries with enough employees to provide stable means). He identified four factors and called one of them *collectivism-individualism. Power distance* is correlated with collectivism. *Masculinity-femininity* and *uncertainty avoidance* have received relatively little attention in the social science literature.

Since then others (such as Bond, 1988, working with the values of college students in twenty-one countries) have found similar factor-analytic results. Triandis et al. (1986) replicated some of Hofstede's results related to individualism and collectivism with fifteen samples from different parts of the world. In a series of studies, they also probed with more items and with a more refined focus on the construct of individualism and collectivism and found seven factors (self-reliance and independence, competition, hedonism, interdependence, family integrity, closeness to in-groups, and sociability), the first three reflecting individualism and the last four collectivism.

In this chapter we present the most recent conceptualization of these constructs, based on Triandis (1995). The reader interested in the development of these constructs is referred to the in-depth discussion in Triandis (1989, 1990). A succinct summary of the construct development can be found in Erez and Earley (1993, pp. 74–96).

Triandis (1995) proposed that collectivism and individualism be conceptualized as polythetic constructs. Just as in zoology one or two attributes define a phylum and additional attributes, in different combinations, define a large number of species, here the main defining attributes tell us we are dealing with collectivism or individualism and several additional culture-specific attributes define different kinds of collectivism or individualism.

The following four defining attributes may be the universal dimensions of the constructs of individualism and collectivism:

1. *Definition of the self.* Collectivists view the self as interdependent with others; this interdependency is accompanied by sharing resources. Individualists view the self as autonomous and independent from groups; decisions to share or not share resources are made individually (Markus & Kitayama, 1991a; Reykowski, 1994). Individualists use individuals as the units of analysis of social behavior, whereas collectivists use groups. Interdependence has been measured by Gudykunst, Matsumoto, Ting-Toomey, Nishida, and Karimi (1994) and Singelis (1994).

2. *Structure of goals.* For collectivists individual goals are usually compatible with in-group goals, whereas for individualists individual goals are often not correlated with in-group goals (Triandis, 1988, 1990; Schwartz, 1990, 1992, 1994; Wagner & Moch, 1986). Yamaguchi (1994) developed a scale that measures emphasis on collective or individual goals.

3. *Emphasis on norms versus attitudes.* The determinants of social behavior among collectivists are primarily norms, duties, and obligations, whereas among individualists they are primarily attitudes, personal needs, perceived rights, and contracts (Bontempo & Rivero, 1992; Davidson, Jaccard, Triandis, Morales, & Díaz-Guerrero, 1976; Miller, 1984, 1994). When predicting behavioral intentions from attitudes and norms across a sample of different behaviors, the relative strength of the beta weights in multiple regression equations can be used as a measure of this aspect (Trafimow & Finlay, 1996).

4. *Emphasis on relatedness versus rationality.* Collectivists emphasize unconditional relatedness whereas individualists emphasize rationality. *Relatedness* refers to giving priority to relationships and taking into account the needs of others, even when such relationships are not advantageous. *Rationality* refers to the careful computation of the costs and benefits of relationships (Kim, Triandis, Kagitcibasi, Choi, & Yoon, 1994b). This distinction parallels the distinction between communal and exchange relationships (Mills & Clark, 1982). Clark, Ouellette, Powell, and Milberg (1987) provide a scale that measures this aspect.

Multimethod measurements of these four facets of collectivism and individualism (Triandis, Chan, Bhawuk, Iwao, & Sinha, 1995; Triandis & Gelfand, in press) show correlations that range between 0 and .70, with a mode at about .40. (Since more than 100 positive correlations were obtained in these studies, we can conclude that the four attributes are correlated.)

The most important difference among different kinds of collectivism and individualism seems to be whether people see themselves as like other people or as very different from other people. That is, a culture's traditions can emphasize the *same* or *different* aspects of the self in relation to others. In cultures that are homogeneous (for example, Japan) people do not want to "stick out." When there is also a tradition of equality, as happens under ideologies such as the ideology of the Israeli kibbutz, people see each other as virtually interchangeable. For example, in many of the kibbutzim every adult takes a parental role toward every child, and everyone cleans dishes, on a rotating schedule. These cultures that emphasize the same aspects of the self are labeled *horizontal* (Triandis, 1995).

In contrast, in societies that are heterogeneous, being different is emphasized. The strongest case is that of India, where differences in skin color (*Varna*) seem to have led to traditions that some groups carry out specific tasks, that is, to the caste ideology (*Varnashram*). This aspect of the Indian culture makes it explicit that differences among people are to be emphasized. Though the secular government of India has abolished the caste system and the Indian constitution does not recognize it, people can become extremely violent (sometimes causing death) against those who dare to cross the caste lines (by eloping with someone from a different caste, for example). It seems that the constitution, the product of an enlightened elite, does not mesh well with the basic culture. These cultures that emphasize different aspects of the self are labeled *vertical.* Another example of a vertical culture is traditional Chinese culture. During a famine, for instance, people got food according to a pecking order: the oldest males had food first, and the youngest females had it last. In Muslim cultures also, although there is a horizontal emphasis among males, there is a vertical emphasis in male-female relationships.

Combining the aspects of horizontal (*same self*) and vertical (*different self*) with the aspects of interdependent and independent self (a defining attribute of individualism and collectivism), gives a 2 + 2 typology, represented by horizontal collectivism (for example, the Israeli kibbutz), horizontal individualism (for example, Sweden and Australia), vertical collectivism (for example, traditional China and India), and vertical individualism (for example, France and corporate relationships in the United States) (Triandis, 1995).

Vertical relations are most common in societies high in Hofstede's power distance; horizontal relations are most common in societies low in power distance. Hofstede's other two dimensions have not received much attention from researchers and therefore are not discussed in this chapter.

Of course, all cultures are vertical to some extent (in Sweden, for example, men still hold most of the important positions), and even in the most vertical cultures, horizontal relationships develop across hierarchies (in India, for example, children of different castes play together, and people walking to a shrine treat each other alike).

Horizontal Versus Vertical Collectivism

Chen, Meindl, and Hunt (1997) were the first to propose a distinction between horizontal and vertical collectivism. Horizontal collectivism displays a sense of oneness with members of the ingroup and social cohesiveness. It corresponds to defining attributes 1 and 4. Vertical collectivism displays a sense of serving the in-group and sacrificing for the benefit of the in-group, doing one's duty, and behaving as expected of a good citizen. It corresponds to attributes 2 and 3.

Chen and his associates arrived at the distinction between vertical and horizontal collectivism through working with Chinese data. They found that Chinese who were vertical collectivists were supportive of the late 1980s economic reforms introduced by the Communist Party, and the horizontal collectivists were opposed (Chen & Meindl, submitted). Presumably, the verticals were more sensitive to the fact that authorities were setting these reforms and were willing to carry out the orders in the tradition of Confucianism (obey your master or superior), whereas the horizontals had taken the party preaching of "equality among all" literally and saw the reforms as creating competition and weakening social solidarity.

An interesting finding for organizations is that horizontal collectivism correlated $-.13$ $(p \sim .05)$ with preference for differential rules for compensation in an organization. This makes sense: if one has a sense of oneness with fellow employees one would not be enthusiastic about differential compensation. Vertical collectivism showed no relationship with this outside variable. However, it did correlate significantly with age and with organizational rank (being a top manager rather than a worker) and seniority. Presumably, those who have power favor the tendency of group members to do what the organization wants them to do because those with power benefit from such behaviors. In short, although this study does not establish the distinction between horizontal and vertical collectivism, it is sufficiently strong to lead us to accept the distinction.

Horizontal collectivism, as mentioned, is found in the Israeli kibbutzim, where members have an interdependent/same self, and a member might say, "I am like all other members of the kibbutz; I am equal in status and linked to others in this kibbutz." The Indians (with their great concern for sticking out, see Triandis, 1972) have a different self. However, until they become old and are allowed to withdraw from life's duties, they have many family obligations and are quite interdependent. In short, they are vertical collectivists, and thus might say, "I do my duties, and I am linked to my family; I am sociable, but I am also unique." Like the Indians the traditional Greeks want to shine and be unique, but they are interdependent with members of their in-groups, especially their families. Research by Georgas (1989) shows that the Greeks, especially the student samples, are shifting toward individualism, but probably of the vertical kind. Similarly, a comparison of the findings of Hofstede's study (1980) with those of Triandis et al. (1986) shows that people in India too are shifting toward individualism. It could be argued that affluence is shifting most cultures toward individualism, at least in some domains.

Kim, Triandis, Kagitcibasi, Choi, & Yoon (1994) described collectivism by focusing exclusively on the horizontal variety, and characterized collectivism by collectivists' concern for collective welfare, harmony, self-cultivation, interdependence, succorance, nurturance, common fate, and social obligation. The value to theorists of the typology of vertical and horizontal collectivism (and individualism) becomes clearer when one notes that if Kim and colleagues had also considered vertical collectivism, they would have observed that many collectivists also subordinate their needs, goals, and aspirations to the requirements of the collective.

Horizontal Versus Vertical Individualism

Data from Sweden (Daun, 1991, 1992) suggest that the Swedes tend to be same self, or horizontal, individualists. Their individualism is shown by their extreme self-reliance and avoidance of long-term relationships with nonkin (for example, many people insist on paying for a cigarette on the spot if they ask for one; living by oneself is highly valued; the elderly do not live with their children; a person staying overnight at a friend's house takes his or her own sheets; voluntarism is high; 87 percent indicate they like to live "as I please").

Their same self is shown by the high value they place on modesty (for example, high social status is desired by only 2 percent of the Swedish population versus 7 percent of Americans and 25 percent of Germans, in comparable polls; personal success is problematic, and eccentrics are strongly rejected). According to a Swedish friend, a much valued concept in Swedish is *Jaentelagen,* which essentially means "avoid sticking out."

Swedes do not like being unique, in contrast to the kind of individualists who want to be distinguished or unique. Middle- and upper-class Americans, for instance, are offended if an experimenter suggests to them that they are "average" (Weldon, 1984; Markus & Kitayama, 1991b). We might conclude that Americans are vertical or different self individualists, accepting inequality. Although in social settings they emphasize equality, in economic and political settings they accept inequalities, especially within large corporations.

The Australians also are largely horizontal individualists. They are self-reliant and obtained high scores on individualism in Hofstede's survey (1980), but they do not like people who stick out. Feather (1994, in press) has developed a scale that measures the inclination of subjects to bring down "tall poppies" and has shown that Australians are rather high on this attitude, though there are complexities, such as whether the tall poppies are good or bad, that must be taken into account (Feather, 1994). He argues that those with low self-esteem are especially likely to want to see the fall of high achievers. Brislin (R. W. Brislin, personal communication with the authors, fall 1993) reports that professionals from other countries giving workshops in Australia are warned to expect to spend about a third of the workshop time defending their credentials.

The Swedes might be independent with a same self, and presumably, they would define themselves by saying, "I am self-reliant, independent; I enjoy life; and I am cooperative and I am just like most other Swedes." The middle- and upper-class Americans would be independent with a different self, especially in large corporations and in matters of income redistribution, and would be define themselves by saying, "I am unique, responsible, distinguished, competitive, pleasure loving, independent; and I do my own thing."

Although very individualist and superficially favoring equality, middle-class Americans in fact find all kinds of subtle ways to pull rank, to be distinguished and unique. Faced with large inequalities in their society, with slums and hunger among a substantial percentage of the population, they are not especially aroused and, unlike the Swedes, are unwilling to pay high taxes to redistribute income.

Any typology is an oversimplification. Each individual is likely to use horizontal (H) or vertical (V), individualist (I) or collectivist (C) elements in defining particular social situations. Triandis and Gelfand (in press), using scenarios in multiple-choice format with each option reflecting one of the four possible patterns (HI, HC, VI, VC), found that Illinois undergraduates were HI across 61 percent of the situations, HC across 24 percent, and VI across only 5 percent. This result is inconsistent with the expectation that Americans will be VI. However, the argument that U.S. samples will be VI is derived from observations of Americans' emphasis on being the best, the behavior of Americans with respect to taxation, and so on. Maybe undergraduates are not a good sample to represent U.S. culture. More research is being planned to clarify this contradiction.

It is important to note the relationship between the typology discussed here and the seven factors of individualism and collectivism identified by Triandis and colleagues. In their study of Illinois students, Triandis and Gelfand (in press) obtained the strength of the horizontal and vertical elements, the individualist and collectivist elements, and the seven factors. They found that on a 9-point scale, vertical individualists were very high on competition (7.0), horizontal individualists were also high (6.1), while both kinds of collectivists were neutral (5.1); on emotional distance from in-groups, all samples were low, but the collectivists were especially low (H 4.1, V 3.3). On family integrity all samples were high, but the collectivists were especially high (H 7.1, V 7.6). On hedonism the vertical individualists were very high (7.0), and the vertical collectivists significantly lower (6.0), with the two kinds of horizontals in between at 6.5. On interdependence, the horizontals were relatively high (6.2) and the verticals relatively low (VI 5.1; VC 5.7). On self-reliance the individualists were high (6.8) and the collectivists lower (5.7). On sociability the collectivists were high (6.6) and the individualists low (5.5). Thus, although the major differences on the seven factors reflect the differences between individualists and collectivists, there are also some differences that reflect the vertical-horizontal side of the typology, with the vertical individualists especially high in hedonism, and the vertical collectivists especially high in family integrity and low in emotional distance from in-groups.

The typology of individualism and collectivism matches conceptually with Fiske's theory of sociality (1990, 1992), Rokeach's theory of values and political systems (1973), and Schwartz's findings (1994) about the structure of values in fifty countries. We now turn to these conceptual correspondences.

Fiske's Four Kinds of Sociality

Fiske (1990, 1992) has identified four basic forms of social behavior: sharing, proportionality, equality, and hierarchy. According to him, these forms occur in every culture, though the specific manifestation of each form can vary with culture.

Fiske calls the first form *communal sharing* (CS); it is the sort of behavior that goes on in families in most cultures. Resources are shared according to need. People take what they need, and no one keeps a record. There are some traditional cultures where the land is owned by everyone. Similarly, in modern cultures a city park is a common property. In addition, identity is shared and includes the group of which one is a member, and one has a strong sense of belonging to that group; people think "we" more than "I" and fear isolation, abandonment, and loneliness. Typical behaviors include nurturance, altruism, caring, selflessness, generosity toward the ingroup, and indifference even hostility toward out-groups; relationships are long-term; decisions take place through consensus; and there is much modeling and imitation. Communal sharing has much in common with collectivism in our typology.

The second form is called *market pricing* (MP). Each person receives resources in proportion to his or her contributions (equity). The more one gives, the more one gets. If one invests twice as much as the next person, one receives twice as much interest. If one spends twice as many years studying for a profession, one's salary should be twice as large. In addition, social behavior depends on the advantages (rewards) and disadvantages (costs) of the relationship. There is much emphasis on achievement and freedom to do your own thing; there is a great concern for the rate of return per unit of time; rational bureaucratic structures are common; the self is defined by occupation; and the greatest good for the greatest number is a strong value. Market pricing corresponds to individualism in our typology.

The third pattern is *equality matching* (EM). Here resources must be distributed equally; tit for tat and total equality are the essence of this pattern. One human one vote, distribution of absolutely equal parcels of land to people at one time in the past of the American West, and so forth are examples of this pattern. In addition, there is much emphasis on reciprocity, justice, and fairness. Equality matching corresponds to the horizontal aspect of our typology.

The fourth form is called *authority ranking* (AR). In this pattern resources are divided according to rank. For example, in the traditional Chinese family if the resource is food the grandfather eats first, selecting the pieces he likes best, then the oldest son, then the other sons eat according to age, then the oldest female can choose, then the other females in descending order of age get what is left. In the United States, if the resource is attention, the president of the United States gets a lot more than the secretaries of the departments, who get more than the managers of smaller units, and so on, and the janitors may get little or no attention, unless they go on strike! In addition, bosses are bossy and followers are obedient; respect, deference, loyalty, and obedience are common. Authority ranking corresponds to the vertical dimension of our typology.

In every culture these four patterns of interpersonal relations can be found, Fiske (1992) argued, but they take culture-specific forms. For example, some people marry for love (CS), some for status (AR), some marry a person who is equal in every way (EM), and some marry the person who offers the best marriage contract (MP). In one culture MP is done with money, in another with cows, and in a third one with curved-tooth pigs. People construct their social behavior by combining these four basic patterns, according to the situation. In general, in collectivist cultures people use CS; in individualist cultures they are more likely to use MP.

An important difference between our theory and Fiske's is that Fiske's patterns of sociality are independent of each other, but we see VI, VC, HI, and HC as unique combinations of C and I, V and H. Nevertheless, the parallelism of the two conceptions is strong, as Figure 2.1 indicates.

Rokeach's Culture and Political Systems

It seems plausible that a particular type of culture would predispose a particular political system. A typology of values and political systems developed by Rokeach (1973) matches our typology. Rokeach asked people to rank order eighteen values, for example, *freedom* and *equality*. He identified people who placed both of these values among their top four or five values, people who placed both among their bottom four or five values, people who emphasized freedom and deemphasized equality, and people who emphasized equality and deemphasized freedom. He then discovered that these four kinds of people favored different political systems: those who were high on freedom and equality were social democrats of the Swedish variety; those who emphasized freedom and placed equality low were Reagan-type free-market republicans; those who emphasized equality and deemphasized freedom favored communism; and those who gave both freedom and equality a low rank

**Figure 2.1. Fiske's Sociality Equated to Vertical
and Horizontal Individualism and Collectivism.**

	Vertical (Different Self) Authority Ranking (AR)	Horizontal (Same Self) Equality Matching (EM)
Individualism (Independent Self) Market Pricing (MP)	VI = MP + AR	HI = MP + EM
Collectivism (Interdependent Self) Communal Sharing (CS)	VC = CS + AR	HC = CS + EM

VI = Vertical Individualism
VC = Vertical Collectivism
HI = Horizontal Individualism
HC = Horizontal Collectivism

were fascists. Rokeach also did content analyses of the speeches of leaders such as Hitler, Lenin, U.S. presidents, and so on and found support for his argument. Specifically, Lenin used the word freedom rarely but the word equality frequently; Hitler used neither word much; American presidents used freedom a lot and equality rarely, and Swedish prime ministers used both words a lot. Rokeach's analysis of values and political systems is represented diagrammatically in Figure 2.2.

It can be argued that the rank order of equality represents the vertical (low equality) and horizontal (high equality) aspects of our typology, whereas the rank order of freedom represents individualism (high freedom) and collectivism (low freedom). Because collectivists are bound by norms and a sense of duty and stress conformity, it seems plausible that they would experience less freedom compared to individualists. Some examples of low freedom among collectivists are norms that children must seek permission from their parents, daughters-in-law from their mothers-in-law, the young from the elderly, and subordinates from their superiors, even for some mundane everyday things that individualists would find it unthinkable to ask permission for.

Figure 2.2. Rokeach's Typology of Political Systems.

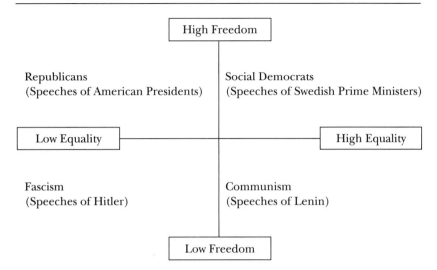

Schwartz's Theory of Universal Values

In a large study of 200 teachers and 200 "others" from more than fifty countries, Schwartz (1992, 1994) identified collectivist clusters of values that he called *conservatism* and *harmony* and individualist clusters that he named *intellectual autonomy* and *affective autonomy*. Conservation and harmony included family security, social order, respect for tradition, honoring parents and elders, security, and politeness. Both kinds of autonomy included being curious, broadminded, and creative and having an exciting and varied life full of pleasures. These value clusters were obtained in every country.

Schwartz's factor analysis obtained two factors that accounted for 73 percent of the common variance. The first contrasted collectivism and individualism. The second contrasted harmony and hierarchy on the one hand with mastery on the other. The relationships among the various value clusters proposed by Schwartz, individualism and collectivism, and the typology discussed earlier is shown diagrammatically in Figure 2.3.

Schwartz's study, which measured *hierarchy* (vertical) and *egalitarian commitment* (horizontal) value clusters as well, tells where a country is located in our typology. For example, in the vertical collectivism cell (see Figure 2.3) are Singapore, the Bulgarian Turks,

Figure 2.3. Schwartz's Theory and Vertical and Horizontal Individualism and Collectivism.

	Values Hierarchy	Values Harmony
Individualism	VI (East Germany)	HI (Italy, France, West Germany)
Collectivism	VC (Singapore, Bulgaria, Turkey, Malaysia)	HC (Slovakia)

VI = Vertical Individualism
VC = Vertical Collectivism
HI = Horizontal Individualism
HC = Horizontal Collectivism

and Malaysia; in the horizontal collectivism cell, Slovakia; in the vertical individualism cell, the former East Germany; in the horizontal individualism cell, France, the former West Germany, and Italy. This outcome for the latter group is different from our theorizing, but it should be remembered that values are only one of many elements of subjective culture. Until further research supports the location of France, Germany, and Italy in the HI cell, we will continue to hypothesize that these countries belong in the VI cell.

Vertical and horizontal collectivism and individualism correspond to different combinations of the kind of self, to Fiske's orientations, to Rokeach's values, to political systems, and to Schwartz's universal value system. Figure 2.4 consolidates the correspondences.

Applications of Culture Theory to Organizations

In this section we discuss the implications of the theory of individualism and collectivism for organizations, organizational issues, and the behavior of people in organizations. We begin our discussion with the implications of culture theory for situation-disposition interaction. We then discuss how culture theory can be used to

Figure 2.4. Vertical and Horizontal Individualism and Collectivism and Other Relevant Conceptualizations.

	Vertical		Horizontal	
	Collectivism	Individualism	Collectivism	Individualism
Kind of self	Interdependent	Independent	Interdependent	Independent
	Different from Others		Same as Others	
Fiske's sociality	Communal sharing Authority ranking	Market pricing Authority ranking	Communal sharing Equality matching	Market pricing Equality matching
Rokeach's values	Low equality Low freedom	Low equality High freedom	High equality Low freedom	High equality High freedom
Political system	Communalism (for example, Panchayat system of Indian village)	Market Democracy (for example, United States, France)	Communal living (for example, Israeli kibbutz)	Democratic Socialism (for example, Sweden, British Labor Party)
Schwartz's theory	Values hierarchy	Values hierarchy	Values harmony	Values harmony

explain or predict selection, training, motivation (specifically, goal setting), communication, leadership, employee appraisal (specifically, attributions of responsibility), compensation, social exchanges, behavior settings, conflict resolution, and concepts of morality in human resource management. Because past research has focused on individualism and collectivism without distinguishing their vertical and horizontal dimensions, we offer many propositions highlighting the similarities and differences between vertical and horizontal collectivism and individualism. A test of these propositions would further an understanding of culture theory and its implications for organizations.

Situation-Disposition Interaction

When an individual is faced with a social situation, that situation "calls forth" one of the four patterns we have been discussing. In some situations the appropriateness of a pattern is very clear; in others it is very unclear and ambiguous. For example, when the in-group is under attack (for example, the CEO wants to downsize the company and eliminate "our" workgroup), in all cultures the probability is that the vertical collectivism pattern will be activated (that is, cognitions and behavioral intentions that favor sacrifice that benefits the in-group become salient). At the funeral of a colleague, the probability that horizontal collectivism (for example, no matter how incompetent the late colleague, we are sad that we lost "one of us") will be activated is high. If the sales department imposes quotas for each salesperson to meet, the probability that the vertical individualist pattern will be activated is high. If the situation calls for a member of an underrepresented group to be on a committee, a horizontal individualist schema is likely to be used (the member is like all other members being represented but will be a self-reliant and independent member of the committee).

The same situation can elicit different behaviors from individualists and collectivists. For example, suppose a person wants to take a trip that will inconvenience many other people. In that situation a person from the modal pattern of vertical collectivism will likely think on duties that cannot be performed during the trip and may decide not to take the trip; an individual from the horizontal collectivism pattern is likely to think about the social support she or he will not be able to give during the trip, and that again may cancel the trip. And both kinds of individualists, feeling sufficiently emotionally detached from the in-group, are likely to suppress such themes and take the trip. Thus, in this kind of ambiguous situation, people's behavior will "match" the modal pattern of their culture. In other words, there is a strong situation-disposition interaction.

However, as suggested earlier, collectivists will not behave in a collectivist way in all situations but only in most, and conversely, individualists will behave as collectivists do in a number of situations. This was shown clearly in a study done in Japan by Caudill and Scarr (1962). They used the scenarios from the Kluckhohn and Strodtbeck questionnaire that measured collaterality (paying attention to peers), lineality (paying attention to those in authority), and individualism (paying attention to one's own internal needs and views). People were asked what they and most people in their culture would do in each scenario. The results showed that each situation produced its own pattern and that the situation was a major determinant of the patterns.

The important point to remember is that people who frequently use a particular cultural pattern are most comfortable doing what that pattern implies. They develop beliefs and attitudes and select norms and values that fit that pattern; they behave according to that pattern and thus develop habits (automatic behaviors carried out without thinking) consistent with that pattern. When they are in a new social situation, to the extent possible they will try to use their habitual behavior pattern. In short, they have developed a "structure of habits" (Triandis, 1980) that fits their cultural pattern and, like the man who has a hammer and tries to use it to do all jobs, will try to use that structure in most situations. If the person is an individualist, overriding the individualist structure of habits requires hard cognitive work. The person must instruct himself or herself to suppress individualist tendencies in situations that require collectivist behaviors. People avoid such hard work, and so they are most likely to use their habitual behavior patterns.

However, the following factors increase the probability that an individual will activate a collectivist cognitive system:

1. The individual knows that most other people in the particular situation are collectivists, and thus the norm of acting as a collectivist becomes salient.
2. The individual is in a collective: for example, the workgroup is defined as a family.
3. The situation emphasizes what people have in common: for example, shared goals.
4. The situation emphasizes that people are in the same collective: for example, people wear the same uniforms.
5. The task is cooperative.

The following factors increase the probability that an individual will activate an individualist cognitive system:

1. Others in the situation are and behave like individualists, which makes individualist norms more salient.
2. The situation makes the person focus on what makes him or her different: for example, the person is dressed very differently from the rest of the group.
3. The task is competitive.

The Attributions That People Make

A major source of misunderstandings in human relationships is that two individuals do not perceive similar causes for a specific behavior. For example, an employee is late for work and perceives the lateness is due to his having missed the bus, but his supervisor perceives the lateness as due to his being lazy. Such nonisomorphic attributions (Triandis, 1975) mean that the same behavior is seen as having very different meanings. More generally, attribution theory can help us improve our understanding of behavior in organizations (Martinko, 1995).

Collectivists tend to attribute events to situations and causes external to the individual more frequently than do individualists; individualists attribute events to internal individual causes more frequently than do collectivists (Morris & Peng, 1994; Newman, 1993). As a result, individualists make the "fundamental attribution error," of overstressing internal relative to external cause of behavior, more frequently than collectivists (Smith & Bond, 1994).

For example, in response to the question "Why did he fail?" individualists are more likely to answer, "He does not have the ability," rather than, "His co-workers did not give him clear instructions." Collectivists are more likely to see the environment as the cause of the failure.

Success is attributed to the help of others among collectivists and to a person's own ability among individualists. Failure is attributed to lack of effort among collectivists, to task difficulty or bad luck among individualists.

Collectivists do not use the Performance equals Ability *times* Effort formulation that is common among individualists (Singh, 1981). They use a Performance equals Ability *plus* Effort formulation. In short, because individualists see performance as a personal quality, if a person has no ability or expends no effort, they see no performance; collectivists see performance as a group quality, and thus it is possible to succeed if one member of the group has ability and the others expend much effort. Effort is a quality that can be changed by the individual, but ability is less changeable. Thus it is much better overall to make effort attributions, and some psychologists, such as Dweck and Leggett (1988), train students to make such attributions, thus helping them improve their performances.

The distinction between horizontal and vertical individualism and collectivism suggests the following propositions about the attribution process:

PROPOSITION 1A: Because vertical collectivists try to be distinguished, they will attribute their own success, or that of their superiors, to stable characteristics of individuals, such as ability, and failure to variable characteristics, such as effort.

PROPOSITION 1B: Vertical collectivists will perceive their subordinates as not especially distinguished and will attribute the success of subordinates to variable characteristics, such as effort, and the failures of subordinates to stable attributes, such as lack of ability.

PROPOSITION 1C: Because horizontal collectivists think of themselves and others as more or less equal, they will attribute to all others the same causes for success and failure that they apply to themselves.

PROPOSITION 1D: Horizontal individualists will attribute success to ability and failure to lack of effort for both themselves and all others.

PROPOSITION 1E: Vertical individualists will attribute success to ability and failure to lack of effort when they think about themselves, but when they think about others they will attribute effort for success and lack of ability for failure.

Goal Setting

The goals of collectivists are role relevant (a collectivist might say, for example, "I must insist that my subordinates do this, because I am their supervisor"), but goals of individualists are personal-need based (an individualist might say, for example, "I must insist that my subordinates do this so that I will feel self-respect").

In general the goals of collectivists are long term, because they see themselves as parts of a chain that includes ancestors (past employees, for instance) and descendants (future employees, for instance). In general the goals of individualists are short term (for example, get a good quarterly report). Also, social loafing, that is, doing less than one is capable of doing when one's performance is not observable, is less likely among collectivists working with in-group members than among individualists (Earley, 1989; Wagner, 1992). The compatibility of in-group and personal goals is likely to be maximal when the in-group is relatively small (for example, the nuclear family) and it decreases as the size of the in-group increases. A clear example of this can be found in the former Soviet Union. The Soviets attempted to make "good communists" out of the population by convincing people to shift their in-group from the family to the communist party. The idea was to make the state's goals the population's personal goals. But it is difficult to identify and develop common goals for an in-group consisting of millions. And it is no surprise that the Soviet system ultimately collapsed, because goals were chronically not met.

The more heterogeneous or affluent the population the more likely it is that the goals of individuals and groups will not be compatible and that individuals will do their own thing, ignoring the group. However, in situations of common threat individuals and groups are likely to have the same goals, and it is easy for collectives to impose their goals. In situations where interdependence is functional (for example, when a major project requires the cooperation of many and will clearly benefit every individual), again individual and collective goals are likely to become compatible. However, in situations where people can do their own thing without any implications for their in-groups, it is very likely that these goals will not be compatible.

The distinction between horizontal and vertical individualism and collectivism suggests the following propositions about the goal-setting process:

PROPOSITION 2A: Collectivists will tend to have group goals that sacrifice group members' individual goals.

PROPOSITION 2B: Horizontal collectivists will expect all group members to have the same goals.

PROPOSITION 2C: Vertical collectivists will expect different goals to operate at each level of the hierarchy.

PROPOSITION 2D: Individualists will select goals by paying much attention to their individual preferences rather than to the goals of their in-groups.

PROPOSITION 2E: Horizontal individualists will expect each group member to have unique goals.

PROPOSITION 2F: Vertical individualists will expect some group members to select goals that will put other group members at a disadvantage.

Motivation

The motive structure of collectivists reflects receptivity to others, adjustment to the needs of others, and restraint of one's own needs and desires. The motive structure of individualists reflects internal needs, rights, and capacities, including the ability to withstand social pressures (Markus & Kitayama, 1991a). Bond (1988) found that the Chinese show a relatively high need for abasement, socially oriented achievement, endurance, nurturance, and order and low levels of need for individual achievement, aggression, and exhibition. Achievement motivation is socially oriented among collectivists and individually oriented among individualists. Yu and Yang (1994) developed separate scales for these two kinds of motivation, and showed that these scales are uncorrelated.

Among collectivists, the welfare of the in-group is of the highest importance, even if the individual members must suffer. In collectivist cultures individuals are expected to value education and self-improvement, obey rules, practice discipline, and respect authority. These values lead to diligence and achievement that will please the in-group. Collectivists will tend to be high in *socially oriented achievement*. One of the typical items of the Socially Oriented Achievement Scale (Yu and Yang, 1994) is "a major goal in my life is to work hard, to achieve something which will make my parents feel proud of me." Those who score high in socially oriented motivation prefer jobs that provide extensive family benefits to jobs that are enjoyable but do not provide such benefits.

The distinction between horizontal and vertical individualism and collectivism suggests the following propositions about motivation:

PROPOSITION 3A: Horizontal collectivists will favor goals that are shared by all group members and reflect socially oriented achievement.

PROPOSITION 3B: Vertical collectivists will favor goals that are different at different levels of the hierarchy and will permit distinction for those at the top of the hierarchy.

PROPOSITION 3C: The goals of individualists will be more heterogeneous than the goals of collectivists.

PROPOSITION 3D: Horizontal individualists will have some socially oriented goals but will not pay much attention to them if they conflict with personal goals.

PROPOSITION 3E: Vertical collectivists will have some personal goals but will suppress them if they conflict with in-group goals.

PROPOSITION 3F: Vertical individualists will emphasize winning in most social situations.

Ronen (1994) has organized the literature on differences in motivation across countries by stressing that in individualist countries challenging jobs, autonomy, advancement, recognition, and earnings are emphasized but in collectivist countries various forms of security and social relationships (with the manager and the coworkers) are emphasized. Future research should explore the implications of these motivating factors for horizontal and vertical individualism and collectivism.

Social Exchanges

Social exchanges have a different character among collectivists than among individualists. Triandis (1990) argued, first, that collectivists "play relationships by ear" and do not expect a clear plan for what is going to happen; individualists are more likely to spell things out ("If I give you this, you will give me that"). Second, the collectivists' time perspective is longer ("If I give you something today, you may reciprocate in two years"). Third, collectivists permit exchanges that are not strictly of equal value and of the same resource (Foa & Foa, 1974) ("If I invite you, I expect a letter of recommendation"). Individualists are more careful to make their exchanges of equal value and the same type of resource ("If I invite you, I expect to be invited back"). Fourth, collectivists regulate their exchanges through empathy (Kitayama, 1993), and individualists regulate them on the assumption that people have stable internal preferences and ought to be given their own chance to choose. "Do you want this or that?" is a common individualist question; "Here is what I know you want" is more typical of collectivists.

Typical items of exchange also vary across cultures. In Turkey, Kagitcibasi (1990) found strong and frequent emotional exchanges among kin members but not many economic exchanges and also found little sharing of economic resources among the members of the middle and upper classes. In lower-class samples, however, she found sharing of economic resources, because without such sharing some members of the in-group will go hungry.

The distinction between horizontal and vertical individualism and collectivism suggests the following propositions about the social exchange process:

PROPOSITION 4A: Among individualists, behavior will be typically described by Fiske's market pricing.

PROPOSITION 4B: Among collectivists, behavior will be typically described by Fiske's communal sharing.

PROPOSITION 4C: Among verticals, behavior will reflect Fiske's authority ranking.

PROPOSITION 4D: Among horizontals, behavior will reflect Fiske's equality matching.

However, some additional factors will be found:

PROPOSITION 4E: In vertical collectivism, if the hierarchy gap between two persons is small, then social exchanges will be based on the other's needs, that is, exchanges will resemble communal sharing. However, if the gap is large, then superiors will give more to subordinates to emphasize the superiors' status, and subordinates will reciprocate by showing respect and deference (they will not try to equal their superiors in returning favors).

PROPOSITION 4F: In horizontal collectivism, social exchanges will be based on the other's needs, that is, exchanges will be guided by communal sharing.

PROPOSITION 4G: In vertical and horizontal individualism, social exchanges will be guided by the computation of a relationship's advantages and disadvantages (keeping a relationship if advantageous; otherwise breaking it), that is, exchanges will be based on market pricing.

Behavior Settings

Collectivists belong to groups as a matter of right, by birth and by marriage, but individualists often have to earn their membership in a group. The result is that collectivists are less likely than individualists to develop skills for entering new groups. Although many collectivists have difficulty getting into and out of a new group, many individualists have few such difficulties (Cohen, 1991). Collectivists usually establish intimate and long-term relationships (Gudykunst, 1983; Verma, 1992). Individualists usually establish nonintimate and short-term relationships.

The typical collectivist recreation group has stable membership, is relatively large (more than three people), and meets frequently. For example, Korean skiers often ski in groups; American skiers ski alone (Brandt, 1974).

The typical individualist recreation group has variable membership, is often small (two or three people), and meets infrequently. The cocktail party, after all, was invented by individualists! The corresponding pattern for collectivists is the stable group that may add a few members in one or another social setting. In short, again, individualists see the individual and collectivists the group as the basic unit of social organization.

The distinction between horizontal and vertical individualism and collectivism suggests the following propositions about behavior settings:

PROPOSITION 5A: Unlike horizontal collectivists, vertical collectivists are used to hierarchical behavior settings, and they will create a hierarchy in a group even if the group started without any hierarchy.

PROPOSITION 5B: Horizontal individualists will try to reduce the hierarchy in behavior settings even if it is natural to have a hierarchy in a particular behavior setting.

PROPOSITION 5C: Vertical individualists will try to create settings (executive dining rooms, special airport lounges for business-class passengers, and so forth) so that people can be distinct from others.

Communication

Collectivists are likely to say, "When you need to use my equipment, if I am not using it go ahead and use it." Individualists are more likely to require that their colleague ask their permission before using the equipment.

During communication, collectivists use "we" a lot and depend on context. Silence is acceptable. Individualists use "I" a lot and emphasize the content of the communication. Silence is embarrassing to individualists and a sign of strength for some collectivists (Iwao, 1993). East Asian collectivists are expected to "read the other's mind" during communication, so that communication is quite indirect and depends on hints, gestures, level and tone of voice, body orientation, use of the eyes, and distance between people's bodies. Many individualists say what is in their mind even if the consequence is that the relationship is hurt.

Collectivists expect social situations to be pleasant and to have few negative elements. Triandis, Marin, Lisansky, and Betancourt (1984), examining data from Hispanic and non-Hispanic samples, found that the Hispanics anticipated higher probabilities of positive behaviors and lower probabilities of negative behaviors in social situations. The researchers called this the *simpatia* cultural script. A person who wants to be *simpatico* (agreeable, pleasant, attractive, noncritical) will behave this way.

Cooperation is more typical of collectivists and competition of individualists. There is evidence that in games where rewards are divided, children from collectivist cultures prefer to maximize joint profit, whereas children from individualist cultures prefer to maximize the difference between in-group and out-group profit (see review by Triandis, 1990).

The interdependence so typical of collectivists is shown in their assumption that if you promote others' goals, these others will attend to your goals. At a banquet in East Asia you are supposed to look after your neighbor's glass, making sure it is always full; then your neighbor will look after your glass, making sure it is always full. Among individualists such assumptions are not found. An individualist looks after his or her own glass.

The distinction between horizontal and vertical individualism and collectivism suggests the following propositions about the communication process:

PROPOSITION 6A: Vertical collectivists and individualists will prefer formal over informal modes of communication, whereas horizontal collectivists and individualists will prefer informal communication.

PROPOSITION 6B: Vertical collectivists and individualists will be harsher with their subordinates (for example, supervisors may yell at subordinates) than horizontal collectivists or individualists.

PROPOSITION 6C: Vertical collectivists and individualists will also expect much more deference from their subordinates in communication.

PROPOSITION 6D: Vertical collectivists will be least likely, vertical individualists will be more likely, and horizontal collectivists and individualists will be most likely to criticize their superiors when the superiors are wrong.

Conflict Resolution

Trubinsky, Ting-Toomey, and Lin (1991) compared Taiwanese and U.S. respondents and found that in conflicts the former were more likely than the latter to use obliging, avoiding, integrating, and compromising styles of conflict resolution as opposed to a confrontational style. Similarly, Ohbuchi and Takahashi (1994) asked ninety-four Japanese and ninety-eight U.S. students to report on their recent conflicts. In a content analysis of 476 episodes, these researchers found that the Japanese were much more likely than the Americans to avoid conflicts. The Japanese were motivated to preserve the relationship. The findings were interpreted as being consistent with theoretical notions about collectivism (Triandis, 1989) and interdependence (Markus & Kitayama, 1991a).

The distinction between horizontal and vertical individualism and collectivism suggests the following propositions about conflict resolution:

PROPOSITION 7A: Horizontal collectivists will be more likely than vertical collectivists to avoid conflict within the in-group.

PROPOSITION 7B: Vertical collectivists will be more likely than horizontal collectivists, vertical individualists, and horizontal individualists to accept mediation by a high-status person.

PROPOSITION 7C: Vertical collectivists and individualists will be more likely than horizontal collectivists and individualists to avoid conflict with their superiors.

Morality

Morality among collectivists is highly contextual and the supreme value is the welfare of the collective. Ma (1988) has provided a Chinese perspective on moral judgment that is somewhat different from the individualist perspective of Kohlberg (1981).

Lying, for example, is an acceptable behavior in collectivist cultures if it saves face or helps the in-group. There are traditional ways of lying that are understood as correct behavior. In traditional Greece, if a person visits another unannounced and the host is not in the mood to receive the visitor, he or she will simply shout through the door, "I am not here." The visitor can, of course, recognize the voice, but this is considered an appropriate way to deal with this situation. Conversely, individualists see lying as breaking a contract, and because contracts are very important to them, this is a serious offense. Trilling (1972) makes the point that when people have a strong sense that they determine who they want to be (as individualists do), they are more likely to seek sincerity and authenticity than when they feel swept along by traditions and obligations (as collectivists characteristically do).

Many observers have emphasized the importance of *face* in collectivist cultures (Hu, 1944; Ho, 1976). A moral person in these cultures behaves as his or her role is specified by in-group members and society. If the individual deviates from such ideal behavior, there is loss of face not only for the individual but also for the whole in-group.

The distinction between horizontal and vertical individualism and collectivism suggests the following propositions about morality:

PROPOSITION 8A: Vertical collectivists will make moral judgments that take social hierarchy into account more than will horizontal collectivists.

PROPOSITION 8B: Horizontal individualists will tolerate much less variation in morality than will vertical individualists.

Leadership

Good leaders among collectivists are warm, supportive, and production oriented (Misumi, 1985). Being first nurturing and then demanding of production is the right way to lead in India (Sinha, 1980). Paternalism is accepted by 80 percent of the Japanese, 51 percent of representative U.S. samples, and around 65 percent in samples from middle-European countries (Hayashi, 1992).

The distinction between horizontal and vertical individualism and collectivism suggests the following propositions about leadership:

PROPOSITION 9A: Horizontal individualists will have the least tolerance for an autocratic leadership style and vertical collectivists the most tolerance.

PROPOSITION 9B: Horizontal collectivists will have more tolerance for an autocratic leadership style than will vertical individualists.

PROPOSITION 9C: Horizontal individualists will prefer the participative leadership style, whereas vertical individualists will prefer a contingency approach to leadership.

PROPOSITION 9D: Vertical collectivists will prefer a nurturing but directing leadership style, whereas horizontal collectivists will prefer a nurturing and nondirecting style of leadership.

Attribution of Responsibility

Studies of attribution of responsibility for a wrongdoing, universally focus on the actor, role position, and social context (Hamilton & Sanders, 1983). Empirical studies done in Japan and India find that samples from these societies give more weight to the latter two factors but that U.S. samples give the first factor most weight. Measures of interdependent construal of the self correlate with emphasis on role position and social context (Singelis & Brown, 1995). In collectivist cultures the collective is responsible for the wrongdoing of one of its members; in individualist cultures only the individual is responsible.

A study of behavior in response to scenarios describing an auto accident involving the subject's father, a stranger, and the subject (Li, 1992) indicated that both Americans and Chinese acted unfairly toward the stranger but that the Chinese were most concerned with protecting their father and the Americans with protecting themselves against accusations of improper action. Yum (1988) identified several Confucian influences on interpersonal relationships in East Asia. Among them were emphasis on reciprocity, a large distinction between in-groups and out-groups, use of intermediaries, and the mixing of social and business relationships.

The distinction between horizontal and vertical individualism and collectivism suggests the following propositions about the attribution of responsibility process:

PROPOSITION 10A: When determining responsibility for wrongdoing, vertical collectivists will attach more importance than horizontal collectivists to the actors, because they focus on individual differences more than do horizontal collectivists. Vertical collectivists will be more inclined to hold superiors responsible for an organizational problem, whereas horizontal collectivists will instead hold the directly concerned person responsible.

PROPOSITION 10B: Horizontal individualists, because of their same self conceptualization, will look at the contextual factors much more than will vertical individualists in determining responsibility for wrongdoing.

Human Resource Management Practices

Culture contains implicit theories of social behavior and acts somewhat like a computer program to control the actions of individuals. Triandis and Vassiliou (1972) predicted, from subjective cultural data, that Greeks and Americans would differ in the way they make employee hiring decisions. Specifically, they predicted that Greeks would give more weight to the recommendations of friends and relatives and Americans would give more weight to the recommendations of neighbors and unknown persons. When files of prospective employees were presented to Americans working in Greece and to Athenian employers, the predictions were supported. More generally, universalist human resource practices (for example, employee selection on the basis of test scores) will be rare in collectivist cultures, and particularist practices (for example, selection on the basis of recommendations) will be more common.

The distinction between horizontal and vertical individualism and collectivism suggests the following propositions about human resource management practices:

PROPOSITION 11A: Collectivists will select people by emphasizing whether they can be trusted and will be loyal; individualists will place all the weight on perceived competence.

PROPOSITION 11B: To take care of in-group interests, vertical collectivist cultures will prefer using interviews for employee selection and use informal channels of communication for circulating information on open jobs. A corollary of this proposition is that when written tests are used for selection in a collectivist culture, the hiring organization will tend to have a third party conduct the examination to avoid in-group pressure on the tester and compromising the selection.

PROPOSITION 11C: In horizontal collectivist and in individualist cultures, the written test and formal channels of communication for advertising job vacancies will be preferred.

Another important human resource management function is promotion. Because vertical individualists and collectivists like to stick out and horizontals do not, it seems plausible that promotions will be very crucial for both vertical collectivists and individualists, whereas in horizontal cultures group promotion will be preferred. Promotion that is also a measure of achievement and individual success is, however, likely to confound the vertical or horizontal tendency. In many collectivist cultures (Japan, for example), promotions are given to all cohorts hired at the same time. In Nepal, too, one of the authors noted that promotion is usually given to a group of people. In the public-sector organizations in India, too, it is not unusual to find that a number of cohorts are promoted at the same time. Group promotions occur in many U.S. schools but are very rare in U.S. industry.

PROPOSITION 11D: In collectivist cultures group promotions will be the preferred method, whereas in individualist cultures individual promotions will be preferred.

Another crucial human resource management function is performance evaluation. Performance evaluations are often used for compensation as well as promotion. Because horizontals think that everyone has the same self, it seems plausible that they would not like to be differentiated through appraisals, whereas verticals would prefer differentiation. This gets further confounded by individualists' desire to relate themselves to their work output and collectivists' desire to maintain group harmony. It seems that the tendency to be individualist or collectivist is stronger than the tendency to be vertical or horizontal. Again, one of the authors noted that in Nepalese public-sector organizations, performance evaluations are not carried out despite a regulation that employees must be evaluated every six months.

PROPOSITION 11E: Performance evaluation is likely to be neglected in collectivist cultures and receive much more attention in individualist cultures.

Employee transfer takes a different hue in a collectivist culture compared to an individualist culture. Because collectivists value their extended family, transfers away from their homes are more of a problem for them than for individualists who feel less encumbered by family considerations. Collectivists, however, can take a transfer if it serves their in-groups (for example, the transfer will bring more resources to the family or provide better education opportunity for children). Transfer, therefore, can become a *power tool* in the hands of managers in collectivist cultures in that it can be used both as a stick and as a carrot.

PROPOSITION 11F: In collectivist cultures transfer is likely to be used more often as an organizational tool by managers than it is in individualist cultures.

Training is yet another important human resource function that may bring out differences between individualist and collectivist cultures.

PROPOSITION 11G: Because collectivist cultures have workers who are more likely to stay with the corporation than do individualist cultures, they will provide more training (for longer periods and for all personnel on a frequent basis) than will individualist cultures.

Because there is not much research evidence to compare human resource practices in individualist and collectivist cultures, tests of these propositions could provide meaningful insight into the differences in human resource practices across cultures. A finer distinction in human resource practices among the vertical and horizontal individualists and collectivists could be built on such research findings.

Support for Sinha's View of India as a Vertical Collectivist Culture

Sinha (Chapter Three) emphasizes that in India the needs of others are taken into account in such personnel decisions as recruitment, appraisal, and training. This is consistent with defining attribute 4 of collectivism. He points out that interviews rather than tests are used in hiring. That is consistent with proposition 11b above. He alludes to decision makers' favoring their in-groups when making such personnel decisions. That is what would be expected from an interdependent self, that is, defining attribute 1 of collectivism.

He suggests that there is elitism in training decisions. That is clearly expected in vertical cultures. Such elitism also occurs in the United States, which we suspect is more vertical than Sweden or Australia. He also points out that resources are amassed not only for one's own use but also for the use of in-group members. His summary of Ganesh's description of Indian organizations reflects the emphasis on what is good for the in-group and on ignoring the out-group that is typical of collectivism.

The work environment is seen differently in collectivist and individualist cultures. In the former, social relationships are the figure and the task is the background; in the latter, the task is the figure and relationships are the background. This is reminiscent of Lebra's finding (1984) that her interviews with Japanese women taught her much about their relationships but little about them; her interviews with American women taught her much about them but little about their relationships.

Sinha mentions that Hindu values emphasize duty and deemphasize hedonism. Such values are central to vertical collectivism, where the individual is supposed to do what is appropriate even if it is distasteful, and consistent with in-group goals, as expressed in defining attributes 3 and 4 respectively.

Finally, Sinha's discussion of ingratiation clearly shows vertical collectivism.

Conclusion

In this chapter we presented the concept of horizontal and vertical collectivism and individualism and discussed its relationship with Fiske's sociality, Rokeach's typology of values, and Schwartz's theory of universal values. We think this typology will become more and more important. Considering the wave of democratization in both Eastern Europe and Asia, we believe vertical collectivism will increasingly shift toward both vertical individualism and horizontal collectivism. The Indian constitution is an example of state intervention in removing the structure (of castes in this case) that supports the vertical structure of that society. This and similar interventions will slowly take their roots in the society, and cultural changes will occur. From this perspective, the typology presented in this chapter is meaningful in that it provides a theoretical basis for tracking shifts from vertical collectivism to individualism. In view of the distinction between horizontal and vertical individualism and collectivism, we suggested some propositions, a test of which will further practitioners' and researchers' understanding of these constructs and their implications for organizational behavior.

References
Bond, M. H. (1988). *The cross-cultural challenge to social psychology*. Thousand Oaks, CA: Sage.
Bontempo, R., & Rivero, J. C. (1992, August). *Cultural variation in cognition: The role of self-concept in the attitude-behavior link*. Paper presented

at the meetings of the American Academy of Management, Las Vegas, NV.

Brandt, V. S. (1974). Skiing cross-culturally. *Current Anthropology, 15,* 64–66.

Caudill, W., & Scarr, H. (1962). Japanese value orientations and culture change. *Ethnology, 1,* 53–91.

Chen, C. C., & Meindl, J. R. *Collectivism and the Chinese enterprise reform: A cultural adaptation perspective.* Manuscript submitted for publication.

Chen, C. C., Meindl, J. R., & Hunt, R. B. (1997). Testing the effects of vertical and horizontal collectivism: A study of reward allocation preferences in China. *Journal of Cross-Cultural Psychology, 28,* 44–70.

Clark, M., Ouellette, R., Powell, M. C., & Milberg, S. (1987). Recipient's mood, relationship type, and helping. *Journal of Personality and Social Psychology, 53,* 94–103.

Cohen, R. (1991). *Negotiating across culture: Communication obstacles in international diplomacy.* Washington, DC: United States Institute of Peace Press.

Daun, A. (1991). Individualism and collectivity among Swedes. *Ethnos, 56,* 165–172.

Daun, A. (1992). Modern and modest: Mentality and stereotypes among Swedes. In A. Sjoegren & L. Janson (Eds.), *Culture and management* (pp. 198–203). Stockholm: Institute for International Business.

Davidson, A. R., Jaccard, J. J., Triandis, H. C., Morales, M. L., & Díaz-Guerrero, R. (1976). Cross-cultural model testing: Toward a solution of the etic-emic dilemma. *International Journal of Psychology, 11,* 1–13.

Dweck, C. S., & Leggett, E. L. (1988). A social cognitive approach to motivation and personality. *Psychological Review, 95,* 256–273.

Earley, P. C. (1989). Social loafing and collectivism: A comparison of the United States and the People's Republic of China. *Administration Science Quarterly, 34,* 565–581.

Erez, M., & Earley, P. C. (1993). *Culture, self-identity, and work.* New York: Oxford University Press.

Feather, N. T. (1994). Attitudes toward high achievers and reactions to their fall: Theory and research concerning tall poppies. In M. Zanna (Ed.), *Advances in experimental social psychology* (Vol. 25, pp. 1–73). Orlando: Academic Press.

Feather, N. T. (in press). Global self-esteem and the fall of high achievers: Australian and Japanese comparisons. In J. Pandey, D. Sinha, & D.P.S. Bhawuk (Eds.), *Asian contributions to cross-cultural psychology.* Thousand Oaks, CA: Sage.

Fiske, A. P. (1990). *Structures of social life: The four elementary forms of human relations.* New York: Free Press.

Fiske, A. P. (1992). The four elementary forms of sociality: Framework for a unified theory of social relations. *Psychological Review, 99,* 689–723.

Foa, U. G., & Foa, E. B. (1974). *Societal structures of the mind.* Springfield, IL: Thomas.

Georgas, J. (1989). Changing family values in Greece. *Journal of Cross-Cultural Psychology, 20,* 80–91.

Gudykunst, W. B. (1983). *Intercultural communication theory.* Thousand Oaks, CA: Sage.

Gudykunst, W. B., Matsumoto, Y., Ting-Toomey, S., Nishida, T., & Karimi, H. (1994, July). *Measuring self construals across cultures: A derived etic analysis.* Paper presented at the convention of the International Communication Association, Sydney.

Hamilton, V. L., & Sanders, J. (1983). Universals in judging wrongdoing: Japanese and Americans compared. *American Sociological Review, 48,* 199–211.

Hayashi, C. (1992). Quantitative social research: Belief systems, the way of thinking, and sentiments of five nations. *Behaviormetrika, 19,* 127–170.

Ho, D. Y.-F. (1976). On the concept of face. *American Journal of Sociology, 81,* 867–884.

Hofstede, G. (1980). *Culture's consequences: International differences in work-related values.* Thousand Oaks, CA: Sage.

Hu, H. C. (1944). The Chinese concepts of face. *American Anthropologist, 46,* 45–64.

Hui, H. C., & Triandis, H. C. (1986). Individualism-collectivism: A study of cross-cultural researchers. *Journal of Cross-Cultural Psychology, 17,* 225–248.

Iwao, S. (1993). *The Japanese woman: Traditional image and changing reality.* New York: Free Press.

Kagitcibasi, C. (1990). Family and socialization in cross-cultural perspective: A model of change. In J. J. Berman (Ed.), *Nebraska Symposium on Motivation, 1989* (pp. 135–200). Lincoln: University of Nebraska Press.

Kim, U., Triandis, H. C., Kagitcibasi, C., Choi, S.-C., & Yoon, G. (Eds.). (1994a). *Individualism and collectivism: Theory, method, and applications.* Thousand Oaks, CA: Sage.

Kim, U., Triandis, H. C., Kagitcibasi, C., Choi, S.-C., & Yoon, G. (Eds.). (1994b). Introduction. In U. Kim, H. C. Triandis, C. Kagitcibasi, S.-C. Choi, & G. Yoon (Eds.), *Individualism and collectivism: Theory, method, and applications* (pp. 1–19). Thousand Oaks, CA: Sage.

Kitayama, S. (1993, October 21). *Culture, self, and emotion: The nature and functions of "good moods/feelings" in Japan and the United States.* Lecture presented at East-West Center, Honolulu. Mimeographed.

Kohlberg, L. (1981). *Essays on moral development.* New York: HarperCollins.

Lebra, T. (1984). *Japanese women: Constraint and fulfillment.* Honolulu: University of Hawaii Press.

Li, M. C. (1992). The effect of group identity on reaction to injustice as a function of individualism and collectivism. *Dissertation Abstracts International, 53,* 2585.

Ma, H. K. (1988). The Chinese perspective on moral judgment and development. *International Journal of Psychology, 23,* 201–227.

Markus, H. R., & Kitayama, S. (1991a). Culture and the self: Implications for cognition, emotion, and motivation. *Psychological Review, 98,* 224–253.

Markus, H. R., & Kitayama, S. (1991b). Cultural variation in the self-concept. In J. Strauss & G. R. Goethals (Eds.), *The self: Interdisciplinary approaches* (pp. 18–48). New York: Springer.

Martinko, M. J. (Ed.). (1995). *Attribution theory: An organization perspective.* Delray Beach, FL: St. Lucie Press.

Miller, J. G. (1984). Culture and the development of everyday social explanation. *Journal of Personality and Social Psychology, 46,* 961–978.

Miller, J. G. (1994). Cultural diversity in the morality of caring: Individually-oriented versus duty-oriented interpersonal codes. *Cross-Cultural Research, 28,* 3–39.

Mills, J., & Clark, M. S. (1982). Exchange and communal relationships. In L. Wheeler (Ed.), *Review of personality and social psychology* (Vol. 3, pp. 121–144). Thousand Oaks, CA: Sage.

Misumi, J. (1985). *The behavioral science of leadership: An interdisciplinary Japanese research program.* Ann Arbor: University of Michigan Press.

Morris, M. W., & Peng, K. (1994). Culture and cause: American and Chinese attributions for social and physical events. *Journal of Personality and Social Psychology, 67,* 949–971.

Newman, L. S. (1993). How individualists interpret behavior: Idiocentrism and spontaneous trait inference. *Social Cognition, 11,* 243–269.

Ohbuchi, K., & Takahashi, Y. (1994). Cultural styles of conflict management in Japanese and Americans: Passivity, covertness, and effectiveness of strategies. *Journal of Applied Social Psychology, 24,* 1345–1366.

Reykowski, J. (1994). Collectivism and individualism as dimensions of social change. In U. Kim, H. C. Triandis, C. Kagitcibasi, S.-C. Choi, & G. Yoon (Eds.), *Individualism and collectivism: Theory, method, and applications* (pp. 276–293). Thousand Oaks, CA: Sage.

Rokeach, M. (1973). *The nature of human values.* New York: Free Press.

Ronen, S. (1994). An underlying structure of motivational need taxonomies: A cross-cultural confirmation. In H. C. Triandis, M. D. Dunnette, & L. M. Hough (Eds.), *Handbook of industrial and organizational psychology* (2nd ed., Vol. 4., pp. 241–269). Palo Alto, CA: Consulting Psychologists Press.

Schwartz, S. H. (1990). Individualism-collectivism: Critique and proposed refinements. *Journal of Cross-Cultural Psychology, 21,* 139–157.

Schwartz, S. H. (1992). Universals in the content and structure of values: Theoretical advances and empirical tests in 20 countries. In M. Zanna (Ed.), *Advances in Experimental Social Psychology* (Vol. 25, pp. 1–65). Orlando: Academic Press.

Schwartz, S. H. (1994). Beyond individualism and collectivism: New cultural dimensions of values. In U. Kim, H. C. Triandis, C. Kagitcibasi, S.-C. Choi, & G. Yoon (Eds.), *Individualism and collectivism: Theory, method, and applications* (pp. 85–119). Thousand Oaks, CA: Sage.

Singelis, T. M. (1994). The measurement of independent and interdependent self-construals. *Personality and Social Psychology Bulletin, 20,* 580–591.

Singelis, T. M., & Brown, W. J. (1995). Culture, self, and collectivist communication: Linking culture to individual behavior. *Human Communication Research, 21,* 354–389.

Singh, R. (1981). Prediction of performance from motivation and ability: An appraisal of the cultural difference hypothesis. In J. Pandey (Ed.), *Perspectives on experimental social psychology in India.* New Delhi: Concept.

Sinha, J.B.P. (1980). *The nurturant task leader.* New Delhi: Concept.

Smith, P. B., & Bond, M. H. (1994). *Social psychology across cultures: Analysis and perspectives.* Needham Heights, MA: Allyn & Bacon.

Trafimow, D., & Finlay, K. (1996). The importance of subjective norms for a minority of people: Between-subjects and within subjects analyses. *Personality and Social Psychology Bulletin, 22,* 820–828.

Triandis, H. C., with Vassiliou, V., Vassiliou, G., Tonaka, Y., & Shanmugam, A. V. (Eds.). (1972). *The analysis of subjective culture.* New York: Wiley-Interscience.

Triandis, H. C. (1975). Cultural training, cognitive complexity, and interpersonal attitudes. In R. W. Brislin, S. Bochner, & W. J. Lonner (Eds.), *Cross-cultural perspectives on learning* (pp. 39–77). Thousand Oaks, CA: Sage.

Triandis, H. C. (1980). Values, attitudes, and interpersonal behavior. In H. E. Howe & M. M. Page (Eds.), *Nebraska Symposium on Motivation, 1979* (pp. 41–133). Lincoln: University of Nebraska Press.

Triandis, H. C. (1988). Collectivism v. individualism: A reconceptualization of a basic concept in cross-cultural social psychology. In G. K. Verma & C. Bagley (Eds.), *Cross-cultural studies of personality, attitudes and cognition* (pp. 60–95). New York: Macmillan.

Triandis, H. C. (1989). The self and social behavior in differing cultural contexts. *Psychological Review, 96*, 506–520.

Triandis, H. C. (1990). Cross-cultural studies of individualism and collectivism. In J. J. Berman (Ed.), *Nebraska Symposium on Motivation, 1989* (pp. 41–133). Lincoln: University of Nebraska Press.

Triandis, H. C. (1995). *Individualism & collectivism.* Boulder, CO: Westview Press.

Triandis, H. C., Bontempo, R., Betancourt, H., Bond, M., Leung, K., Brenes, A., Georgas, J., Hui, C. H., Marin, G., Setiadi, B., Sinha, J.B.P., Verma, J., Spangenberg, J., Touzard, H., & de Montmollin, G. (1986). The measurement of the etic aspects of individualism and collectivism across cultures [Special issue]. *Australian Journal of Psychology, 38*, 257–267.

Triandis, H. C., Bontempo, R., Villareal, M. J., Asai, M., & Lucca, N. (1988). Individualism and collectivism: Cross-cultural perspectives on self-ingroup relationships. *Journal of Personality and Social Psychology, 54*, 323–338.

Triandis, H. C., Chan, D.-K., Bhawuk, D.P.S., Iwao, S., & Sinha, J.B.P. (1995). Multimethod probes of allocentrism and idiocentrism. *International Journal of Psychology, 30*, 461–480.

Triandis, H. C., & Gelfand, M. (in press). Converging measurement of horizontal and vertical individualism and collectivism. *Journal of Personality and Social Psychology.*

Triandis, H. C., Leung, K., Villareal, M., & Clack, F. L. (1985). Allocentric versus idiocentric tendencies: Convergent and discriminant validation. *Journal of Research in Personality, 19*, 395–415.

Triandis, H. C., Marin, G., Lisansky, J., & Betancourt, H. (1984). *Simpatia* as a cultural script of Hispanics. *Journal of Personality and Social Psychology, 47*, 1363–1374.

Triandis, H. C., & Vassiliou, V. A. (1972). Interpersonal influence and employee selection in two cultures. *Journal of Applied Psychology, 56*, 140–145.

Trilling, L. (1972). *Sincerity and authenticity.* New York: Oxford University Press.

Trubiskey, P., Ting-Toomey, S., & Lin, S. (1991). The influence of individualism-collectivism and self-monitoring on conflict styles. *International Journal of Intercultural Relations, 15*, 65–84.

Verma, J. (1992). Allocentrism and relationship orientation. In S. Iwawaki, Y. Kashima, & K. Leung (Eds.), *Innovations in cross-cultural psychology* (pp. 152–163). Amsterdam/Lisse: Swets & Zeitliner.

Wagner, J. A., III. (1992, August). *Individualism-collectivism and free riding: A study of main and moderator effects.* Paper presented at the meeting of the Academy of Management, Las Vegas, Nevada.

Wagner, J. A., III & Moch, M. K. (1986). Individualism-collectivism: Concept and measurement. *Group and Organization Studies, 11,* 280–303.

Weldon, E. (1984). Deindividuation, interpersonal affect, and productivity in laboratory task groups. *Journal of Applied Social Psychology, 14,* 469–485.

Yamaguchi, S. (1994). Empirical evidence on collectivism among the Japanese. In U. Kim, H. C. Triandis, C. Kagitcibasi, S.-C. Choi, & G. Yoon (Eds.), *Individualism and collectivism: Theory, method, and applications* (pp. 175–188). Thousand Oaks, CA: Sage.

Yu, A.-B., & Yang, K.-S. (1994). The nature of achievement motivation in collectivist societies. In U. Kim, H. C. Triandis, C. Kagitcibasi, S.-C. Choi, & G. Yoon (Eds.), *Individualism and collectivism: Theory, method, and applications* (pp. 239–250). Thousand Oaks, CA: Sage.

Yum, J. O. (1988). The impact of Confucianism on interpersonal relationships and communication patterns in East Asia. *Communication Monographs, 55,* 374–388.

CHAPTER 3

A Cultural Perspective on Organizational Behavior in India

J.B.P. Sinha

The role of culture in how people relate to their work environment is clearly exemplified in the Indian industrial organizations that provide a ground for the confluence of Western technology and Indian culture. This chapter examines how the recently transplanted Western forms of industrial organizations, which introduced technologically determined formal systems, rules, and regulations, are being often bypassed, diluted, or integrated by traditional cultural influences in order to get work done effectively at some places and not so effectively at some other places.

In these Indian organizations, such areas of organizational behavior as recruitment, appraisal, training, leadership, power, communication, decision making, conflict resolution, work culture, and so on reflect both collectivist and individualist values that interact but more often just coexist, functioning interchangeably as figure and ground (Tripathi, 1988) in different contexts, primarily because of Indians' context sensitivity and their "engulfing" and balancing mode of thinking (Marriott, 1976). Given these cultural imperatives and the changing industrial scenario, the chapter entertains the possibility that we can use cultural values to build effective organizations.

Note: My thanks to Sarita Singh for assisting in the preparation of this chapter and to ASSERT for allowing me to use its facilities.

The Strands of Cultural Influence

Assuming that culture is the man-made environment (Herskovits, 1955), there are four strands of cultural influence on work organizations in India. First, and relatively recent, is the Indian people's aspiration to build a strong nation. Because of its very weak industrial base at the time of independence in 1947, the country planned and borrowed Western capital and technology particularly to develop a dominant public sector that could (and eventually did) expand the industrial base and provide a lead for other sectors in creating wealth for nation building. Pervasive poverty and a wide gap between the rich and the poor required that the country realize rapid economic growth with equitable distribution of the gains of development. Hence this industrial base was also expected to provide employment, improve conditions of employees, create surplus capacity for future use, promote exports, and manufacture essential goods by subsidizing the costs, and so on. None of these expectations emanated purely from the short-term capitalist motive; rather they were tempered by cultural needs. Therefore they created an impression that employees, their pressing needs and welfare and the like, are the top priority in organizations. This in turn has led employees to construe their organizations in terms not always congruent with organizational profitability. Moreover, the twin goals of economic growth and social justice are readily accepted in national industrial policy.

The second influence emanates from the colonial legacy that carried over to the newly emerging industries. As managers in post-independence India were in short supply, a large number of retired bureaucrats and army officers were hired and those in active service in administration were also deputed. With them, however, they brought the colonial model of bureaucracy, which had an ethos of mistrust of the natives and hence a highly centralized power of decision making. When large power distances, lack of delegation, and pervasive mistrust coexists with the entrepreneurial spirit of capitalism, the two conditions tend to confront each other. The two often coexist in the minds of Indian employees.

These two strands of Western influence have interacted with two Indian strands: traditionally idealized values and their current social variants—operative values—in order to create a highly heterogenous work culture in Indian organizations, where the set of idealized values and the set of operant values often coexist and function as changing figure and ground depending on situational demands. The idealized values are rooted in ancient psycho-spiritual thoughts and are being increasingly retrieved to present a case for "transformation" of management by the Indian ethos (Chakraborty, 1987, 1993). The operant values have evolved from the interaction between the idealized values and India's changing socioeconomic realities. They are manifested in people's current beliefs, practices, and preferences and have been shown to affect organizational behavior (Sinha, 1990a, 1990b).

The Interface of Culture and Technology

Because of the composite influence of these four factors, the industrial organizations in India have remained Western in their formal structure, but that "structure has to be bypassed to keep the system going and to get work done" (Virmani & Guptan, 1991, p. 136).

There are indeed arguments in favor of a culture-free "forceful management action" and professional approach (Khandwalla, 1988, 1992). Khandwalla contended that "to be professional is to be strongly influenced by Western norms of personal growth, personal efficiency, pioneering-innovative motive, etc." (1994, p. 132). In this approach, culture is considered as either a constraint to be overcome or an "incongruent terrain" in which organizations have to "market" their policies and practices such as long-term forecasting, short-term planning, pioneering and innovating products and services, global scanning, using modern communication and informational facilities, and so on. As the industrial scenario comes to include more and more multinationals, the case for forceful professional management is going to be pleaded more forcefully.

Also, sectoral differences in the relative impact of the Western and Indian values are often noticeable. Multinationals and their subsidiaries have been able to stay closer to Western values and make their formal systems work more effectively than have other industrial organizations. Their systems for employee planning, training, placement, appraisal, reward, and so on work reasonably well. In contrast, public-sector organizations are more open to

societal forces and are generally characterized by greater politi-
cization, bureaucratization, procedural rigidity, and vulnerability
to external demands (see reviews by Khandwalla, 1988; Padaki,
1988; Sinha, 1981). The large private-sector companies, too, are
bureaucratized and open to cultural influences; yet many of them
are able to protect their boundaries and inculcate an organizational culture in which social values are likely to be put to the service of high productivity and profit (Sinha, 1990b). The sharpest
contrast to the multinationals' practice is provided by family-owned
firms where the family members occupy all crucial positions and
run the organization in flexible and culture specific ways.

Virmani and Guptan (1991) studied a variety of Indian organizations and concluded that most of the systems of Western management exist in them but are seldom allowed to function the way
they do in the West. The systems for information flow, marketing,
financial management, technological upgrading, planning, recruiting, training, transfer, promotion, appraisal, delegation, grievance handling, and employees participation in management have
all been established. However, familialism, patronage, personalized
relationships, obedience to authority, and a host of other cultural
considerations cause deviations from the way the systems work in
the West. I have reported (Sinha, 1990b) the case of a fertilizer factory where automatic equipment was rendered manual in order to
create more job points and employ more people, causing overstaffing, social loafing, and a soft work culture. At the same time,
I reported another case where a factory did employ more people
than it absolutely needed, on compassionate grounds, but used social values to maintain high productivity and synergetic work culture. In sum, the literature confirms the influence of core cultural
values on work organizations; but that influence can be either positive or negative depending on other factors, which I will deal with
later in the chapter.

Psycho-Spiritual and Social Values

Indian psycho-spiritual values derive from the conceptualization
of *psyche* and *the Ultimate Reality* (*Brahamn*) in traditional Indian philosophy. It is postulated that there is one *Brahamn*, which manifests
in all that is animate and inanimate. The soul, or the psyche, of

individuals has been alienated from *Brahamn* and hence strives to fuse back with Him. The psyche consists of id-like impulses, sensuousness, emotions, and fantasies. And yet it has a built-in disposition to move toward *Brahamn,* a movement attained by the realization of values of controlling the impulses, cultivating "pure mind," doing one's duty, and rising above worldliness.

A number of scholars (for example, Chakraborty, 1987, 1993; Gupta, 1994; Pande & Naidu, 1992; Sharma, in press) have argued that these psycho-spiritual values have a normative role in transforming work organizations. They have reported some evidence that suggests that by practicing *yoga,* meditating, controlling their breathing, and stilling their turbulent minds, workers and managers can rise above their hedonistic and selfish desires, refrain from thinking of material gains only, and view their work as duty rather than an unavoidable burden. If they are so transformed, they are likely to think of what they can contribute to others, including the organization, rather than what they get from others. This *giving* theory of motivation negates the well-established principles of reinforcement and exchange. It is presented as a subjective journey, a pilgrimage, and an inner transformation of mind that is rewarding in itself (Chakraborty, 1993). The essence of the giving theory is not to imitate those who behave in selfish and materialistic ways, but to look within one's own self for guidance and inspiration. In one of the organizations studied, when the employees asked what should they do if their sincere work is ignored while shirkers are getting all kinds of advantages, Chakraborty asserted that they should "think and feel that such work pressure is the divine testing of sincerity and devotion to work" (p. 102).

This approach is based on the assumption that transforming of individual minds is more important than building systems of management that are useless unless "noble ideas" make them work in the right direction. Chakraborty further argues that systems are after all made by individuals; and if several individuals, groups, and departments in an organization start subscribing to the giving view, the organization will certainly get transformed into an effective as well as a satisfying place. He reports cases to show that the changes in managers along these lines not only help them gain self-control and absorb stress but also render them more receptive to others and more prone to form effective teams. These managers also show improved family relations. The evidence, however, is not quite conclusive. It may be that this transformation can be effected in only a few persons and can be quickly counteracted by the more mundane concerns of the majority of employees. Not many organizations are likely to be transformed by the psycho-spiritual values.

Despite the reservations, it seems feasible that psycho-spiritual values still have an important role in balancing the influence of socioeconomic realities by cautioning people not to be guided by expediencies only. The Indian psyche is conceived to be positioned in between the compulsions of reality and the attractions of idealism, and the two jointly give rise to operant social values.

I have previously identified these operant social values as the preference for (1) hierarchy, (2) embeddedness, (3) personalized over contractual relationships, (4) harmony and tolerance, and (5) duty and obligations over hedonism (Sinha, 1990a). Indians tend to arrange things, persons, relationships, ideas, and almost everything hierarchically. Castes, body image, temperament, roles and positions, and so on are all vertically positioned. The larger power distance (Hofstede, 1980), status consciousness, centralization of decision making, need to depend upon a patron, and so on are manifestations of this preference for hierarchy (Sinha, 1990a; Virmani & Guptan, 1991). The colonial contribution of a centralized administration was thus in part a historical continuation of people's existing hierarchical orientation and in part a facilitator of further overcentralization in Indian organizations. In such centralized settings, credit for achievements is attributed to the superior whose blessing and guidance can help a manager advance in a career and whose displeasure can destroy it.

In contrast to Western "individuals," Indians are "dividuals" (Marriott, 1976). They do not possess unalienable components in their identity. In fact they can be better identified with reference to their collectives and in-groups. Indian names often indicate family lineage, caste, and in many cases place of birth. Indians place strong emphasis on maintaining good in-group relationships, cooperating with each other, making sacrifices, caring, and being cared for, and the like. Roland (1988) labeled this behavior preference *affective reciprocity*—an intense emotionality in caring and being cared for without asking. Singh and Paul (1985) called it *affective syndrome.* The affectivity within an in-group is contrasted with indifference, distrust, and even open hostility toward out-group members. Caste conflicts, family feuds, and communal riots are some of the behavioral manifestations.

Discharging one's duty to the relevant others is considered to be more important than doing what one feels like doing. Duty is *dharma*, which means one's religion and that which "holds together"; it is the conduct that maintains order and balance in an otherwise fluid universe (*sansar*). The emphasis in Hindu religion, as stated earlier, is on self-control and containing of impulses and desires. Hence duty consists of appropriate role behaviors, including protecting in-group members and favoring them over others, maintaining respect and obedience for superiors, and loving and caring for juniors and dependents. Maintaining one's face is of course important, but equally important is not letting one's respected superior lose face. If the latter expects it, one can work hard and with dedication without asking for immediate return. Conversely, work for others (*paraya*) is considered to be a favor (McClelland, 1975), which must be exchanged for either a tangible gain or a reciprocal favor.

The Indian preference for harmony and tolerance certainly helps maintain solidarity in in-groups, induces acceptance of asymmetrical gains among in-group members, preempts any defiance—even against an unjust demand—from a subordinate against a superior, allows toleration, protection, and favoring of inefficient and even corrupt in-group members, and similar behavior. Differences and conflicts are likely to be glossed over, unless they cross some limit. Even then, a third-party mediation is preferred over confrontation (Sinha, 1990a).

The five operant social values taken together reflect the presence in the Indian culture of what Triandis and Bhawuk (in Chapter Two) call *vertical collectivism.* M. N. Srinivas (quoted by Marriott, 1976) named this configuration *vertical solidarity.* Other scholars also consider such preferences part of collectivism. For example, Earley (1993) reported that collectivist managers perform poorly when they work with out-group compared to in-group members. Mills and Clark (1982) observed that collectivism is characterized by communal relationships (compared to individualism, which is associated with exchange relationships). Gudykunst (1983) and Verma (1992) found that collectivists tend to maintain long-term relationships. Kidder and Muller (1991) contend that in the collectivist culture of Japan, harmony is taken to be more important than fairness.

Pervasive poverty, inequality, and related problems on the one hand and the colonial legacy of increased overcentralization, mistrust of out-group members, and the like on the other seem to reinforce this vertical collectivism. It seems that an adverse environmental condition requires that the people stick together, cultivate interdependence, and thereby develop collectivist orientations to cope with exigencies. Moreover, there is indeed impressive evidence (Sinha, 1990b; Virmani & Guptan, 1991) that vertical collectivism does affect organizational behavior.

However, managers and workers are also exposed to formal systems of the Western kind and hence are reported to be also influenced by a set of values emanating from Western individualism. Because of this acculturation, they also value freedom, autonomy, challenge, and creativity (Singh, 1979). I have found (Sinha, 1990b) that Indian managers, like their Western counterparts, attach top priority to achievement, advancement, ability utilization, personal development, and peace of mind (this last value is also a typical Indian psycho-spiritual value). It seems that the two sets of values—vertical collectivism and individualism—coexist in Indian organizations. Singh and Das, 1977, have also found that even though managers profess to value freedom, autonomy, and the like, their actual behaviors manifest collectivist orientations, suggesting that the latter are the core values. Parikh (1979) offers a different interpretation. He agrees that Indian managers internalize two sets of values. The first set is acquired from their early socialization and is sustained by collectivist culture. The second set is drawn from Western management education, which is based on the individualist ethos. However, he says that both sets are available to managers and are activated differently in response to situational demands.

The Meta-Cognitive Framework: Context Sensitivity and Balancing

Cultures differ in context orientation—some are quite high while others are low. In the latter, people tend to think in terms of abstract principles and norms (Hall, 1976). Indians, however, are highly sensitive to context in their thoughts and practices (Ramanujan, 1989). They have "associative thinking" (Kedia & Bhagat, 1988). Different *desh, kal,* and *patra* (place, time, and persons respectively) create a variety of contingencies that affect what is considered appropriate or inappropriate, right or wrong. For example, speaking the truth is generally desirable, but it is also desirable not to speak an unpleasant truth (unless one is in an advisory role and the advisee is likely to suffer if he or she is not given a candid opinion). As a result, a gap often exists between public behaviors and private feelings, and as Triandis and Bhawuk (Chapter Two) observe, lying is acceptable when it serves the purpose of saving face or building relationships. Roland (1988) found that Indians can keep important secrets in a much guarded manner and for much longer durations than Americans, even in therapeutic situations.

Context sensitivity tends to render Indians vulnerable to incongruent situational demands that often cause role ambiguities, particularly when duties are variably defined and not aligned with self-interests. Consequently, Indians are likely to engage in "uncertainty avoidance" (Hofstede, 1980). In order to do so effectively, they have developed "encompassing systems" (Dumont, 1970) through which contradictions between thoughts and actions, instead of leading to dissonance and confrontation, are *balanced, accommodated, integrated,* or *allowed to coexist* (Marriott, 1976) in order to cope with situational demands.

The Facets of Organizational Behavior

It is this context sensitivity and balancing that account for the ways pervasive poverty, a high rate of unemployment, and related problems; national aspirations to catch up with the West economically; the colonial legacy; Western forms of organizations and related individualist values; the psycho-spiritual heritage; and the collectivist values interact with each other and differentially influence organizational behavior.

Recruitment, Appraisal, and Training

Pervasive poverty and a high rate of unemployment pressure organizations to employ more people than they require. Employees maneuver the accommodation of family members. Trade union and local political leaders pressure management to hire more and more people on one pretext or another. Contract and casual workers keep agitating till they are "regularized," hired permanently. Some companies have a policy of allowing each employee to register one dependent for a job, irrespective of that person's skills for the jobs available or even of job availability in the first place. Hence most Indian organizations are overstaffed. At some, one-third of the workforce (running into thousands) is an extra burden (Sinha, 1990b). Such overstaffing causes diffusion of responsibility and social loafing (Latane, Williams, & Harkins, 1979), which in turn creates a need to hire more persons for getting work done, this despite the fact that most of these organizations have a planning system to determine the size of the workforce and the procedure for hiring it. Once employed, a worker cannot be fired for shirking work, working irregularly, coming to the factory drunk, or being absent without permission. Workers can be fired only for gross misconduct (for example, assaulting a manager) and even then only after prolonged enquiry. The argument is that firing even a truant worker is depriving that worker's family of its sustenance.

Overstaffing is a more serious problem at the workers' than the managerial level. Managers are hired through a recruitment procedure similar to the one in Western organizations. In large organizations hiring follows entrance examinations, campus visits by recruiting teams, and rounds of individual and group interviews. However, testing of the Western kind is less favored than interviews, which are considered more appropriate for forming an overall impression of the applicants and possibly accommodating their dependents. This is obviously a manifestation of the culture's relationship orientation, which is further revealed in managers' general tendency to gravitate toward their homelands in order to work among their "own" people (their in-groups), even though at times such homeward movement slows down their career progression or interferes with their effective functioning.

Both workers and managers are generally inducted at the lowest levels. There are occasional exceptions at the top levels, but these are resented by insiders. Promotion by seniority is the general rule, although some organizations hire 50 percent of their lowest-level managers directly and promote from inside for the remaining positions. Merit is professed to be important. However, "in the Indian conditions the Western emphasis on merit alone appears to go contrary to the socio-cultural expectation of respect for seniority. Consequently, a loosely defined suitability is put forth that combines in itself the virtues of merit with due deference to seniority" (Virmani & Guptan, 1991, p. 198). Seniors, by the same token, have to make room for younger people: the retiring age is fifty-eight in manufacturing and governmental sectors and sixty in the universities.

Most Indian industrial organizations have a formal appraisal system, but it is seldom used for promotion, placement, or assessment of training needs. The culture does not allow objective appraisal (Sinha, 1985). Because a person and his or her performance are hardly differentiated, an adverse appraisal is misconstrued as the superior's lack of trust in the employee or as some kind of revenge. As a result, the appraisee feels either deflated and depressed or angry and revengeful. When they are done, appraisals are generally all positive, unless a superior is determined to teach a subordinate a lesson (Virmani & Guptan, 1991).

Training suffers precisely because of ineffective appraisals. Practically all Western methods of training are practiced (Khandwalla, 1988), yet persons and methods are selected ad hoc. Those who are not urgently required at work and can most be spared are sent for training. The training institutions, which are not quite known for excellence, solicit participants by evoking personal connections. There is also an air of elitism in training. High-priced programs are arranged for high-level managers and are held in luxurious environments and set up so that trainees use the time more for enjoyment than for learning.

Needs and Work Values

Poverty and weak infrastructural facilities give even those who are not quite poor a sense of scarcity, resulting in a strong need for security, material gains, good physical and service conditions of work, and so on (Khandwalla, 1988; Padaki, 1988). The literature contains enough evidence to show that both workers and managers are *comfort- rather than growth-oriented* and that the meeting of these extrinsic needs is likely to increase their job involvement. Managers, more than workers, desire job challenges, recognition, and appreciation, promotion, and the like. Quite often these seemingly growth-oriented dispositions also implicitly serve the social values of status and prestige. Workers are more concerned about physical conditions of their work than are managers, who care more about the nature of their work (Sinha, 1994b).

The sense of scarcity in combination with the valuing of hierarchy and in-group embeddedness gives rise to a strong need for power that accesses all kinds of resources (Sinha, 1995). Resources are amassed not only for one's own use but also for in-group members' use. They are often used for building up an in-group at the cost of out-groups. This is the reason for the cliques and conflicts based on castes, religion, and language and for little consideration for quality of work or work culture in Indian work organizations that Ganesh (1982) lamented. In sum, the need to build up and maintain in-group relationships takes priority over concern for good work quality.

Weber ([1920] 1958) was the first to argue that the Hindu religion is not conducive to positive work ethic. However, this position has since been rejected (see Sinha, 1994a) owing to the evidence of both a strong and a weak work ethic. Although Indians are said to consider work as a favor (McClelland, 1975) when they are placed in impersonal large organizations, they are also found to work diligently when they are working for themselves or in organizations with which they identify (Sinha, 1990b). In other words, the work ethic in Indian organizations is more a function of the interplay among a number of organizational factors than of early socialization (Rub, 1988).

Leadership and Power

The confluence of Western and Indian cultural influences is clearly manifested in the areas of leadership and power (Sinha, 1995). Four theories deserve mention here. Khandwalla's *pioneering-innovative* (PI) style of management (1983) combines participative style with professional orientation. It is characterized by a commitment to pioneering novel and sophisticated technologies, products, and services; taking high risks; scanning boundaries; and emphasizing creativity and adaptability for excellence. Although its roots are traced to Indian entrepreneurial tradition, PI seems to reflect primarily the Western ethos.

Conversely, Chakraborty's (1993) and Singh and Paul's (1985) views on leadership contain an Indian ethos and are based on the giving theory of motivation. A leader should give unconditional care and affection to subordinates. Such affection is likely to be repaid with subordinates' respect for and dedication to the leader. Thus integrated, leader and followers can form a team with high positive affect and mutual support.

In between these two extremes is my theory of *nurturant task* (NT) leadership (Sinha, 1980). In this view a leader should, first of all, have warmth, affection, care, concern for the growth of subordinates. The leader must guide, direct, and inspire subordinates. This *nurturance* makes subordinates highly receptive to the leader. However, this nurturance cannot be unconditional; it must be contingent on task performance. The leader must keep *the task* as the basis for building *sneh-shradha* (affection-deference) relationships with subordinates. Relationships without a task as their rallying point are likely to drift into sycophancy. The task supplies concrete feedback about who are performing well and who are shirking work. The former have to be rewarded, and the latter have to be reprimanded in order to keep them on track and to get the best out of them. Hence the nurturant-task leader has to restructure the leadership role, becoming a model of the loving, caring, but task-oriented superior. Such a leader helps subordinates grow and assume responsibilities for running the group. Once the subordinates gain experience and skills, the leader delegates authority and encourages the subordinates to participate. Together they grow and mature and create a climate of participation, although the leader's superiority is still acknowledged.

Another integrative theory is given by Singh and Bhandarker (1990). They have borrowed the theory of transformational leadership from the West and given it an Indian spirit: "The cumulative life experiences lead the person to look for a father-figure (symbolically speaking) in the work place for empowering, protection, grooming, and development. In return, the individual develops respect for his superior and demonstrates willingness to accept his authority" (p. 134). Obviously, the authors are referring to nurturance. But then they also incorporate in their description the Western orientations of clarity of mission and the capability to take risks, build teams, and not lose one's balance in the face of calamity (p. 346).

In sum, the four conceptualizations of effective leadership reflect, in varying degrees, both culture specific and universal features. Nurturance and paternalism in the leader and dependency and deference in the subordinates are culture specific; the emphasis on task is by and large universal; the salience of a pioneering and innovative stance, risk taking, system building, and the like are Western ideas. Similarly, the contingency approach and reinforcement principles are of Western origin but are blended with nurturance and paternalism to work effectively.

Studies on power, too, report culture-specific as well as Western ideas. McClelland (1975) contended that Indians, in contrast to Westerners, exert power through giving away important resources. Giving, according to him, is the core theme of Indian culture and is reflected in all sorts of exchanges. Giving obliges the recipient, who has to manage this debt (Blau, 1964). A person who fails to do so is under power pressure. Hence McClelland observed that "renunciation, yielding, and self-sacrifice often serve only to make a strong urge to power" (p. 143). A detailed critique of McClelland's conceptualization is attempted elsewhere (Sinha, 1994a). It will suffice to say here that McClelland is right in saying that giving (*dan*) is central to the Indian exchange and that it does serve as power leverage. However, the processes through which giving renders a person powerful are culture specific.

There are two ways to look at these processes. Control over one's impulses, fleeting emotions, worldly desires, and so on is one of the core Hindu values, earlier described also as an emphasis on duty in contrast to hedonism. Thus a person who gives away important resources, makes self-sacrifices, and so on is raised on the scale of merit and connected to the cosmic power. The weaker ones (who fail to control their impulses) flock around these stronger ones to seek their guidance, thus placing them higher on the power scale. In other words, there exists a vertical collectivist mode of maintaining power relationships in which the less powerful ones are dependent on the more powerful ones for gaining power, the latter feel powerful by serving as patrons and guides.

The second interpretation is based on the collectivist conceptualization of human beings. If X and Y are two independent and autonomous entities (as assumed in individualist cultures), their attempts to influence each other are likely to be resisted, and who has power will depend on who overcomes the resistance more. However, in a collectivist view, X and Y are embedded in a collective and are not separate. Hence X's attempt to use power is not perceived to emanate from an external source and therefore is not likely to be resisted. The more X and Y give to each other, the more they are likely to enhance their perception of power as a non-zero-sum commodity.

This also implies that fierce power struggles are likely to flare up between in-group and out-groups. There is indeed evidence (Sinha, 1995) that in some organizations workers pressure managers to yield to all kinds of legitimate and illegitimate demands but in others they join hands to fight out extraneous forces. The deciding factor is the *quality of relationships*. If managers and workers feel interdependent, and have superordinate goals (the way Sherif's camp boys did; Sherif, 1966), they are likely to share power.

The same is true in interpersonal relationships in an organization. I have reported (Sinha, 1990b) instances of both uses of power in Indian organizations. It has also been found that in between the two extremes, the power game is played in a more manipulative way. Prosocial expressions and persuasion are used liberally to cover up ingratiation and manipulation. This may be one reason that Ansari (1990) found that rationality was the most frequently used power strategy, particularly for realizing common organizational goals, and that ingratiation was the second most popular strategy for influencing one's superiors. For influencing subordinates, rationality was the most popular strategy, personalized help was second, and dependency was fifth. Similarly, Singh-Sengupta (1990) reported that managers and workers employ coercive and referent power bases to influence each other—the former probably for out-group members and the latter for in-group members. It is worth noting that ingratiation in the vertical collectivist culture of India manifests in self-degradation, name dropping, instrumental dependency, and changing one's position in situations (Pandey, 1981)—all of these seem to serve power distance and context sensitivity.

Communication, Decision Making, and Conflict Resolution

There are formalized channels of communication, standardized modes of decision making, elaborate procedures for grievance handling, and clear rules for delegation in most of the large organizations. However, once having adopted these Western systems, the organizations take cultural detours to accommodate employees' habits and values. Decision making is centralized, which often leaves middle- and lower-level managers powerless although it can enhance the top leaders' capacity to quickly mobilize a large number of employees and function effectively. Communication flows through in-group members and tends to leave out-groups in the dark (Pandey, 1989). It generally travels downward and seldom sideways or upward (Singhal, 1973). Upward communication is generally "adjusted to the status, moods, and the reactions of the superiors, the nature of interpersonal relationships, and the social and professional relationships in the organization" (Sinha, 1994a, p. 749).

Despite elaborate multitier procedures for grievance handling, an interesting cultural feature is that the top manager has to have an open-door policy and be available to any employee who wants to bypass or has exhausted all procedures of grievance handling and who now wants to request redress or mercy. The open-door policy is reported to have a positive impact on the employees who feel affinity with the top.

All methods of conflict resolution are practiced in Indian organizations (Sayeed & Mathur, 1980). The specific choice depends again on the quality of relationships. With one's own people, those with whom one feels affinity, conflict is avoided. The more powerful person is expected to show generosity, and the less powerful one is to reciprocate by assuming a humble stance. When a conflict is not resolved in this manner, a third-party mediation is the best way to save face (Thingrajan, 1972). The mediator is likely to ask the person with more resources to yield more. Forcing is avoided at almost any cost. Some forms of forcing are stopping talking suddenly, leaving the room, or wearing a sullen expression (Roland, 1988). One extreme form is suffering overtly (for example, fasting with the intention of fasting unto death or some other threat of suicide). The assumption is that when the two people belong to the same entity, suffering by one will cause guilt and a change of heart in the other.

In contrast, conflict with an out-group member or a stranger can be severe and blown out of all proportion. The caste and communication conflicts in India are phenomenal. In two-person relationships, they may lead to surrender by the less powerful person and persistent and crude exploitative behavior by the more powerful one till the former finds a way to fight back or walk out of the relationship.

Organizational Culture

Because of Indians' context sensitivity, the culture within an organization assumes greater importance in India than in individualist countries. The kind of organizational culture created depends on how an organization handles the confluence of technological requirements and cultural influences. Some multinationals try to seal their boundaries, treating cultural influences as aberrations to be minimized and prevented from surfacing in important organizational behaviors. Employees try to hide their cultural values and tend to imitate their expatriates. Such organizations appear to be technologically determined.

At the other extreme are organizations that for several reasons allow cultural forces to overwhelm organizational domains and render them socially determined. Members construe the organization in terms that serve their individual and group interests. Work is displaced from center stage by nonwork activities aimed to meet social and personal interests and obligations. Employees do not work hard. They are neither clear about their specific responsibilities nor derive satisfaction from work. They take time off from work in order to meet social obligations. Such organizations are said to have a *soft work culture*. The other extreme can be said to have a *synergetic work culture* (Sinha, 1990b).

Soft and synergetic work cultures relate to organizational systems and practices. The managers in a synergetic work culture believe that the organization rewards hard and sincere work, that work norms are well established and must be conformed to, that necessary support systems are available, and that their individual prosperity hinges on the economic viability of their organization. Social values still operate but are put to the service of a meta-value: *good quality work* (Sinha, 1992).

The critical factors that lead to these two opposite cultures are organizational philosophy and goals, top leadership continuity and the role leadership models, the systems the organization creates and maintains, and the critical events in the life of the organization that lend support to organizational credibility and image. If an organization practices the philosophy of self-reliance, rather than depending on government for protection and doles, both managers and workers consider it important to work effectively, lest their own stars fall from the sky. If the management provides supportive systems and liberal welfare measures contingent on the profitability, the organization cultivates synergetic culture. On the contrary, if an organization succumbs to extraneous forces, drifts to soft options, tries to appease dominant groups and individuals for fear of industrial unrest, and fails to enforce strong work norms, the work culture gets soft, and the organization falls into the hands of self-serving individuals and groups. Both extremes in work culture have been profiled (Sinha, 1990b). In sum, the most critical consideration is whether the social values are allowed to get out of hand, undermine technological requirements, and negate the goals for which an organization is formed or whether the technological and social influences combine to serve the purpose for which an organization was formed.

Conclusion

The evidence supports Triandis and Bhawuk's view (Chapter Two) that Indian culture is *vertical collectivist* and that it influences organizational behaviors to a large extent. However, there is also evidence that many Western principles and formal systems of management have been adopted by many Indian organizations. Consequently, individualist values are also available to Indians, who choose either individualist or collectivist or a combination of the two orientations depending on their construction of situations. Because of their context sensitivity and engulfing mode of thinking, they do not always integrate the two orientations. As the contextual variables seem to foster collectivist orientations, collectivism appears as a dominant influence in shaping organizational behavior more often than individualism.

With the globalization of Indian industry, it is likely that increasing competition and the decreasing role of the state will create a strong compulsion for efficiency and productivity that emanate from and lead to self-reliance. This compulsion is likely to play a critical role in placing *work as the meta-value* (Sinha, 1992). Once that happens, Indians' context sensitivity will likely induce them to reorganize collectivist and individualist values in order to facilitate quality performance. Collectivist values will still percolate in work relationships and there be conducive to high productivity and competitiveness.

References

Ansari, M. A. (1990). *Managing people at work: Leadership styles and influence strategies.* Thousand Oaks, CA: Sage.

Blau, P. M. (1964). *Exchange and power in social life.* New York: Wiley.

Chakraborty, S. K. (1987). *Managerial effectiveness and quality of work life: Indian insights.* New Delhi: Tata McGraw-Hill.

Chakraborty, S. K. (1993). *Managerial transformation by values: A corporate pilgrimage.* Thousand Oaks, CA: Sage.

Dumont, L. (1970). *Homo hierarchicus.* Chicago: University of Chicago Press.

Earley, P. C. (1993). East meets Midwest: Further explorations of collectivistic and individualistic work groups. *Academy of Management Journal, 36,* 319–348.

Ganesh, S. R. (1982). *Quality of life in Indian organizations: An irrelevant view* (Working paper No. 407). Ahmedabad: Indian Institute of Management.

Gudykunst, W. B. (1983). *Intercultural communication theory.* Thousand Oaks, CA: Sage.

Gupta, R. K. (1994). Challenges in developing indigenous theories of organization and management: An Indian perspective. *Indian Journal of Social Work, 25,* 220–236.

Hall, E. T. (1976). *Beyond culture.* New York: Doubleday.

Herskovits, M. J. (1955). *Cultural anthropology.* New York: Knopf.

Hofstede, G. (1980). *Culture's consequences: International differences in work-related values.* Thousand Oaks, CA: Sage.

Kedia, B. L., & Bhagat, R. S. (1988). Cultural constraints in transfer of technology across nations: Implications for research in international and comparative management. *American Management Review, 13,* 559–571.

Khandwalla, P. N. (1983). PI management. *Vikalpa, 8,* 220–238.

Khandwalla, P. N. (1988). Organizational effectiveness. In J. Pandey (Ed.), *Psychology in India: The state of the art* (Vol. 3, pp. 97–216). Thousand Oaks, CA: Sage.

Khandwalla, P. N. (1992). *Organizational designs for excellence.* New Delhi: Tata-McGraw Hill.

Khandwalla, P. N. (1994). The PI motive: A resource for socio-economic transformation for developing societies. In R. N. Kanungo & M. Mendonca (Eds.), *Work motivation: Models for developing countries* (pp. 114–134). Thousand Oaks, CA: Sage.

Kidder, L. H., & Muller, S. (1991). What is fair in Japan? In H. Steensma & R. Vermount (Eds.), *Social justice in human relations.* New York: Plenum.

Latane, B., Williams, K. D., & Harkins, S. G. (1979). Many hands make light the work: The causes and consequences of social loafing. *Journal of Personality and Social Psychology, 37,* 822–832.

Marriott, K. (1976). Hindu transactions: Diversity without dualism. In B. Kapferer (Ed.), *Transactions and meaning: Directions in anthropology of exchange and symbolic behaviour.* Philadelphia: ISHI.

McClelland, D. C. (1975). *Power: The inner experience.* New York: Free Press.

Mills, J., & Clark, M. S. (1982). Exchange and communal relationships. In L. Wheeler (Ed.), *Review of personality and social psychology* (Vol. 3). Thousand Oaks, CA: Sage.

Padaki, R. (1988). Job attitudes. In J. Pandey (Ed.), *Psychology in India: The state of the art* (Vol. 3, pp. 19–91). Thousand Oaks, CA: Sage.

Pande, N., & Naidu, R. K. (1992). *Anasakti* and health: A study of non-attachment. *Psychology and Developing Societies, 4,* 89–104.

Pandey, J. (1981). Ingratiation as social behaviour. In J. Pandey (Ed.), *Perspectives on experimental social psychology* (pp. 157–185). New Delhi: Concept.

Pandey, S. N. (1989). *Human side of Tata Steel.* New Delhi: Tata-McGraw Hill.

Parikh, I. J. (1979). *Role orientation and role performance of Indian managers* (Working paper No. 300). Ahmedabad: Indian Institute of Management.

Ramanujan, A. K. (1989). Is there an Indian way of thinking? An informal essay. *Contributions to Indian Sociology, 25,* 41–58.

Roland, A. (1988). *In search of self in India and Japan: Towards a cross-cultural psychology.* Princeton, NJ: Princeton University Press.

Rub, M. M. (1988). *Antecedent of hard working behaviour.* Unpublished doctoral dissertation, Patna University, Patna.

Sayeed, O. B., & Mathur, H. B. (1980). Leadership behaviour and conflict management strategies. *Vikalpa, 5,* 275–282.

Sharma, S. C. (in press). *Management in the new age.* New Delhi: Wiley Eastern.

Sherif, M. (1966). *Group conflict and group cooperation.* Boston: Houghton Mifflin.

Singh, N. K., & Paul, O. (1985). *The corporate soul: Dynamics of effective management.* New Delhi: Vikas.

Singh, P. (1979). *Occupational values and styles of Indian managers.* New Delhi: Wiley Eastern.

Singh, P., & Bhandarker, A. (1990). *The corporate success and transformational leadership.* New Delhi: Wiley Eastern.

Singh, P., & Das, G. S. (1977). Managerial styles of Indian managers. *ASCI Journal of Management, 7,* 1–11.

Singh-Sengupta, S. (1990). *Emerging patterns of power distribution.* New Delhi: Commonwealth Publishers.

Singhal, S. (1973). Psychology of men at work: Communication and job perception. *Indian Journal of Industrial Relations, 8,* 415–424.

Sinha, J.B.P. (1980). *The nurturant task leader.* New Delhi: Concept.

Sinha, J.B.P. (1981). *Participation in work organizations.* Patna: A.N.S. Institute of Social Studies, Patna.

Sinha, J.B.P. (1985, July). *Cultural bias in appraisal system.* Paper presented at the International Seminar on Selection and Appraisal Systems, New Delhi.

Sinha, J.B.P. (1990a). The salient Indian values and their socio-ecological roots. *Indian Journal of Social Sciences, 3,* 477–488.

Sinha, J.B.P. (1990b). *Work culture in the Indian context.* Thousand Oaks, CA: Sage.

Sinha, J.B.P. (1992, Spring). Social values in the service of meta-value: Work. *Abhigyan,* pp. 18–20.

Sinha, J.B.P. (1994a). Cultural embeddedness and developmental role of industrial organizations in India. In H. C. Triandis, M. D. Dunnette, & L. M. Hough (Eds.), *Handbook of industrial and organizational psychology* (2nd ed., Vol. 4, pp. 727–764). Palo Alto, CA: Consulting Psychologists Press.

Sinha, J.B.P. (1994b). Employees' satisfaction in Visakhapatanam steel plant. Patna: ASSERT.

Sinha, J.B.P. (1995). *The cultural context of leadership and power.* Thousand Oaks, CA: Sage.

Thingrajan, K. H. (1972). Conflict resolution: Indian style. *Indian Management, 11,* 5–11.

Tripathi, R. C. (1988). Aligning development to values in India. In D. Sinha & H.S.R. Kao (Eds.), *Social values and development: Asian perspective*. Thousand Oaks, CA: Sage.

Verma, J. (1992). Allocentrism and relational orientation. In S. Iwawaki, Y. Kashima, & K. Leung (Eds.), *Innovations in cross-cultural psychology*. Lisse, Netherlands: Swets & Zeitlinger.

Virmani, B. R., & Guptan, S. U. (1991). *Indian management*. New Delhi: Vision.

Weber, M. (1958). *The religion of India: The sociology of Hinduism and Buddhism* (H. H. Gerth & D. Martindale, Trans. and Eds.). Glencoe, IL: C.T. Press. (Original work published 1920)

CHAPTER 4

New Approaches to the Study of Culture in Industrial/Organizational Psychology

Jeanne M. Brett
Catherine H. Tinsley
Maddy Janssens
Zoe I. Barsness
Anne Louise Lytle

In this chapter we recognize the legitimacy of a variety of different methods for generating cross-cultural knowledge, and we advocate a proactive approach to developing cross-cultural research design. This approach borrows from different research perspectives rather than limiting itself to a single perspective. Our purpose is to encourage cross-cultural researchers to move beyond the paradigm in which they were trained. By incorporating methods from different paradigms and studying cross-cultural similarities and differences simultaneously, researchers should be able to dramatically increase cross-cultural knowledge.

All strategies of inquiry must construct a research design. An effective research design provides a clear focus on the research question and the purposes of the study (Denzin & Lincoln, 1994). It should identify the kind of information that will best answer the research question and detail the research methods that will be used to obtain and analyze that information (LeCompte & Preissle, 1993). Because cross-cultural research is often subject to alternative explanations, it is especially important for cross-cultural researchers to develop rigorous designs that reduce the potential for alternative explanations.

This chapter is intended to help cross-cultural researchers construct their research designs using a multiperspective approach. We begin with a discussion of the various research perspectives that have been applied to cross-cultural research: the positivist versus interpretative, etic versus emic, local versus general knowledge, similarities versus differences, inductive versus deductive, and quantitative versus qualitative. These perspectives define a multidimensional space from which cross-cultural research design can be constructed. We encourage cross-cultural researchers to move around in this space and to select different perspectives for different aspects of their research. Their choices will depend upon the research question, the cultural groups studied, the researchers' relationship to those groups, the phenomena of interest, and the amount and type of prior research about both the phenomena of interest and the cultural groups.

To aid cross-cultural researchers as they navigate this multidimensional space, we propose two different but equally valid approaches to cross-cultural research. Of course, many different approaches are legitimate. We offer these two to illustrate how different perspectives lead to different choices of methods and techniques. In addition, because we argue for the importance of both similarities and differences in cross-cultural research, each of the two approaches provides for the development of specific cross-cultural hypotheses about similarities and differences that can then be tested for confirmation. The routes by which they achieve this goal differ, yet both highlight the dialectical nature of cross-cultural research and integrate the contributions that apparently contradictory perspectives have to offer to research design.

The first approach extends our previous work, where our purpose was to develop an approach for testing the generalizability of midrange theory across cultures (Lytle, Brett, Barsness, Tinsley, & Janssens, 1995). A midrange theory defines a set of phenomena and the relationships among them and then proposes a causal explanation for those relationships (James, Mulaik, & Brett, 1981; Moore, Johns, & Pinder, 1980). This approach was designed to guide the development of confirmatory midrange cross-cultural social science research and is called the *one-way approach*.

A second approach, called the *n-way approach,* is more closely related to the ethnographic methods advocated by anthropologists and other qualitative researchers. It is primarily inductive, but it may also incorporate a hypothetico-deductive stage.

Next we turn to the different types of cross-cultural research designs and what we can infer about their functional and conceptual equivalence across cultures. First, we discuss three types of cross-cultural hypotheses: culture as a main effect (Type I), culture as a moderator (Type II), and culture as an influence on the meaning of constructs (Type III). Because hypotheses have implications for standards of equivalence, we then discuss three kinds of equivalence—conceptual, structural, and functional—and explain their interrelationship.

Whether researchers use the one-way, *n*-way, or some other approach in generating cross-cultural hypotheses and addressing issues of equivalence, they are selecting research design options from the multidimensional space.

In this chapter we also address more specific technical issues relevant to the implementation of a study design and interpretation of data. We first discuss level of theory and sampling. Decisions about level of theory and sampling are driven by researchers' prior choices concerning the types of cross-cultural hypotheses proposed and the standards of equivalence sought. We then turn to what confirmation or disconfirmation indicates to researchers about the cultural explanation, cultural group profiles, research design, cross-cultural hypotheses, or the sample that they have developed. We conclude by investigating the interactive nature of cross-cultural research—how it opens a dialogue between two or more cultures—and the researchers' role as observer, informant, and translator.

Cross-Cultural Research: A Multidimensional Space

When developing our understanding of cross-cultural research, we realized that a number of dichotomies characterize this research: the positivist versus interpretative perspective, the etic versus emic perspective, local versus general knowledge, similarities versus differences, deductive versus inductive processes, and quantitative versus qualitative methodologies. These dichotomies reflect cross-cultural researchers' ontological, epistemological, and methodological premises. Discussions about the conflict between perspectives populate the cross-cultural literature. In this section, we explore these dichotomies as they helped us to understand the variety of research approaches, goals, questions, and methods that characterize cross-cultural research. We first look at researchers' worldviews—positivist versus interpretative—and the perspectives they consequently adopt vis-à-vis their research subject—an etic, or outsiders' perspective, versus an emic, or insiders' perspective. We then examine how these perspectives facilitate researchers' understanding of the research subject—whether general or local knowledge is generated and how that knowledge influences their research questions, goals, and focus on cross-cultural similarities and/or differences. Next we address the process (inductive versus deductive) and methodological tools (qualitative versus quantitative) that cross-cultural researchers who ascribe to a particular perspective might adopt in order to achieve their goals.

Positivist Versus Interpretive Perspectives

The *positivist* perspective holds to critical realist positions concerning reality and its perception (Cook & Campbell, 1979; Denzin & Lincoln, 1994). Positivists contend that there is an objective reality that can be studied, captured, and understood, whereas post-positivists argue that reality can never be fully apprehended, only approximated (Guba, 1990; Cook & Campbell, 1979). Post-positivism, moreover, though emphasizing the discovery and verification of theories, relies on multiple methods as a way of capturing as much of reality as possible (Denzin & Lincoln, 1994; Cook & Campbell, 1979). Despite their epistemological differences, positivists and post-positivists share a similar methodological orientation, emphasizing the measurement and analysis of causal relationships between variables and the importance of confirmation or disconfirmation of the theory or model tested (Cook & Campbell, 1979; Cronbach, 1989).

The *interpretative* stance, in contrast, focuses on the study of phenomena in their natural settings and dictates that the researcher attempt to make sense of, or interpret, those phenomena in terms of the meanings people bring to them (Denzin & Lincoln, 1994). This perspective maintains there is no single objective reality but rather multiple realities that are socially constructed (Guba & Lincoln, 1994). Interpretivists believe that an understanding of the often uniquely personal constructions of reality that characterize subjects' understanding of the world is best elicited and refined through interaction between researcher and research subjects (Guba & Lincoln, 1994).

These opposing views about the ontological reality of the research subject also exist within anthropology, where cultural realists hold that culture has a concrete reality of its own and cultural nominalists hold that culture exists solely as an inference or abstraction in the mind of the researcher (Rohner, 1984). We borrow from both the interpretive and positivist perspectives. As interpretavists, we accept that there are multiple realities and understand culture to be a social construction *shared* among cultural group members (Guba & Lincoln, 1994, pp. 110–111). We also recognize that this social construction is likely to change over time. Yet although we do not assume a fixed reality, we also adopt a more positivist perspective by arguing that cultures are stable systems in equilibrium. As such, we assert, cultures can be measured by researchers, who can identify cross-cultural similarities and differences by capturing this stability. We reject the extreme perspective that holds that culture is constantly changing and reinventing itself so that measures of culture at one time cannot be compared to measures of the same culture across time or measures of other cultures at the same time. We assert instead that the shared social construction of reality among cultural group members is sufficiently powerful to resist disturbance by measurement or interaction with the researcher. Thus we argue that it is possible to use a confirmatory approach to cross-cultural research. The methods for confirmation, however, may vary widely, and include techniques characteristic of both the positivist and interpretive perspectives.

Etic Versus Emic Perspectives

Often defined simply as the contrast between an outsider's and an insider's perspective, the distinction between etic and emic was much broader in Pike's original formulation (1966). According to Pike, researchers who adopt an *etic* perspective not only study behavior from a position outside the system but also examine the same phenomenon across many cultures for the purposes of comparison. The structure, theory, or model that is compared, moreover, is developed by the researcher and imposed from without on the cultural groups studied. Moreover, the criteria for comparison are considered absolute or universal. In other words, understood from an etic perspective, constructs should be general to all cultures.

The *emic* perspective, that of the insider, adopts a more interpretive frame. In Pike's definition, researchers operating from this perspective attempt to study behavior from within the system. They tend to examine only one culture and to do so in depth. They seek to discover structure within rather than to impose it from without. The criteria they identify are relative to internal cultural characteristics. In other words, constructs are considered unique to each culture rather than general across cultures.

We consider both the etic and emic perspectives to be valid and do not champion one perspective over the other. In fact we believe that many cross-cultural research designs will incorporate elements of both perspectives. Researchers testing etic constructs, for example, may choose to use emic operationalizations of those constructs in some cultures (Janssens, Brett, & Smith, 1995; Lytle, Brett, Barsness, Tinsley, & Janssens, 1995).

General Versus Specific Knowledge

Oftentimes, theorists and researchers have linked *general knowledge* with the etic perspective and *local knowledge* with the emic perspective (Lévi-Strauss, 1963; Turner, 1979). We argue that this pairing is misleading and confusing. Local knowledge is richly detailed knowledge of a particular culture (Geertz, 1983). It is important to recognize, however, that some aspects of local knowledge may be generalizable to other cultures and others may be specific to that culture. Researchers identify local knowledge through intimate study of a particular culture. When they lack other reference points, they may be acutely aware of the varied characteristics of the source culture and yet not know whether some or all of the local knowledge they have identified is universal and therefore generalizes to other cultures. General knowledge is less comprehensive than local knowledge. It identifies only those constructs, characteristics, relationships, or phenomena that are universal across cultures and says nothing about what is unique to a culture.

Additional confusion may arise because the terms etic and emic have been used to define types of knowledge as well as particular approaches to cross-cultural research. In this chapter, when describing these types of knowledge, we have used etic to refer to general knowledge and emic to refer to specific knowledge.

We argue that local and general knowledge are both critical to cross-cultural research. Researchers, whether they begin with the desire to acquire local knowledge or the intention to identify general knowledge, are likely to incorporate features of both in the course of their research. Thus the search for either type of knowledge is certain to enhance understanding not just of local and general knowledge but where these two types of knowledge overlap.

Similarities Versus Differences

Similarities are universals that hold across cultures. Differences are specific information, characteristics, relationships, or phenomena that are unique to one or several cultures and exclude others. Cross-cultural researchers seek to identify *similarities* and *differences* between cultural groups. Their goal is to determine whether their midrange theories and models hold across cultures, and if so what aspects of culture are responsible, and if not why culture causes the observed differences.

Traditionally, many cross-cultural psychologists have sought primarily to identify general laws of human behavior (Triandis, 1972). They have tried to determine whether their midrange theories or models hold across cultures and to detect cognitions, values, motivations, and behaviors that are pan human (see, for example, Triandis, 1978; Kohn, 1989). In contrast, others, including many anthropologists, have asserted that the richness and diversity of human nature can only be fully appreciated through in-depth study of individual cultures, their uniqueness and specificity (Herkovits, 1948; Boas, 1911). More recently, some cross-cultural researchers have argued for less extreme perspectives (Berry, Poortinga, Segall, & Dasen, 1992). They adopt the working assumption that basic psychological processes are likely to be shared across different cultural groups but that manifestations may be influenced by culture. In other words, these theorists assert that basic processes are essentially the same across all cultures but are expressed differently in each culture.

We believe that basic processes may or may not differ and may or may not manifest differently depending on the influence of culture. Consequently, we argue that it is equally important to search for differences as to search for similarities between cultures. Cross-cultural research is inherently comparative, and the goal for cross-cultural researchers should be twofold: to understand the range of variability *and* the uniformity in human behavior (Berry & Dasen, 1974). Thus we feel it is important to incorporate both cross-cultural similarities *and* differences into theoretical models.

Inductive Versus Deductive Processes

Cattell (1988) suggests that the *inductive-hypothetico* method and the *hypothetico-deductive* method are simply two parts of a whole (the *inductive-hypothetico-deductive-experimental-inductive cycle*). Many researchers have generally emphasized the hypothetico-deductive-experimental approach. Starting with a theory, they develop specific hypotheses a priori about the effects of culture on the midrange model and then test these hypotheses to seek confirmation or disconfirmation of the midrange model across cultures (Berry, 1989; Lytle, Brett, Barsness, Tinsley, & Janssens, 1995). The inductive-hypothetico approach has been more characteristic of researchers who tend to adopt an interpretive frame. Using methods such as the case study, ethnography, participant observation, and historical profiles, researchers employing the inductive-hypothetico approach develop theory based on the observation of phenomena.

We believe that many phases of the cross-cultural research process are inherently inductive. As we will discuss in the next section, we assert that researchers will move through several inductive and deductive phases in the course of designing a cross-cultural study. The order in which they move through these phases will differ, however, depending on the information available about the cultural groups targeted and the midrange model or theory being tested.

Quantitative Versus Qualitative Methods

Even a cursory review of the cross-cultural literature reveals that quantitative and qualitative methods are not specific to a particular theoretical perspective or research approach. Both researchers who fall into the positivist camp and those in the interpretative camp use a wide variety of methods. Generally speaking, however, *quantitative* methods such as experimentation, quasi-experimentation, and survey research emphasize the measurement and analysis of causal relationships between variables rather than processes (Denzin & Lincoln, 1994). Researchers adopting these methodologies assume that data collection and analysis capture an objective or apprehendable reality.

Qualitative methods, in contrast, stress interpretive and naturalistic approaches such as the case study, rich description, and participant observation. Researchers adopting such methodologies emphasize that research is value laden. They assume reality is socially constructed and recognize the intimate relationship between the researcher and what is studied and also the situational constraints that shape any inquiry (Denzin & Lincoln, 1994).

Each of these methods is often associated with a particular set of strengths and weaknesses. Because the strengths of qualitative methods often compensate for the weaknesses of quantitative methods and vice versa, we assert that cross-cultural research can benefit from a multimethod approach.

Reconciling the Tensions in Cross-Cultural Research

The two approaches to the design of cross-cultural research that we develop in the next section borrow from each of these dichotomies. We have described these dichotomies because we believe that each of these various perspectives has legitimacy. Furthermore, we maintain that high-quality cross-cultural research incorporates aspects of what appear to be contradictory perspectives. Rather than conceptualizing approaches to cross-cultural research as necessarily etic or emic, focused on revealing general or specific knowledge, identifying similarities or differences, employing an inductive versus deductive logic, or adopting quantitative or qualitative methodologies, we argue that this constellation of dualities defines the multidimensional space of cross-cultural research. Cross-cultural researchers may move around this space depending upon the orientation of the research, the cultural groups studied, the researcher's relationship to those groups, the phenomena of interest, and the amount and type of prior research done on both the phenomena of interest and the cultural groups.

Our purpose in this chapter is to encourage cross-cultural research, not discourage it. Although we lay out ideal models of two different methodological approaches for conducting cross-cultural research, we recognize that many approaches are possible and legitimate. Moreover, we recognize that researchers cannot address all issues in every study they perform; trade-offs will be necessary. Consequently, we seek to provide a framework that allows researchers to evaluate more fully what those tradeoffs are and to guide their choices among them.

Two Approaches to Cross-Cultural Research

In this section, we describe two possible approaches to cross-cultural research: the *one-way* and the *n-way* approach. Although differing in process, these approaches share several important characteristics. Each begins with local knowledge. The one-way starts in one locality—a source culture—with the researchers' rich understanding of their own culture. The *n*-way approach begins in multiple localities, also with the research team members' rich understanding of their respective cultures. In both approaches researchers then proceed to induce the influence of culture on the midrange theory or model of interest. And both approaches ultimately reach a deductive stage, in which specific hypotheses about how and why culture causes the model to be either consistent or different across cultures are developed. Researchers then conclude the process by testing the model across cultures for confirmation or disconfirmation of the cross-cultural hypotheses. Finally, researchers' purpose in either approach is to identify both cross-cultural similarities and differences. Thus both approaches accommodate researchers' desire to know what is universal across a particular universe and what is specific to what universe.

One-Way Approach

The one-way approach to cross-cultural research begins with local knowledge of a midrange theory or model as it operates within a source cultural group. The one-way approach has three goals: (1) to determine what aspects of the theory or model generalize across cultures, (2) to determine what aspects are specific to the source culture from which the local knowledge was derived, and (3) to identify the role of culture in causing these cross-cultural similarities and differences.

The one-way approach follows the inductive-hypothetico-deductive method (Cattell, 1988). It consists of three steps. The researcher defines a research model and a theory of culture, uses them to develop inductively an explanation of how culture affects the model, and then derives cross-cultural hypotheses deductively from the cultural explanation and the cultural profiles of the groups to be studied (see Figure 4.1).

Typically, the model will propose relationships among a set of variables based on some midrange theory (Moore, Johns, & Pinder, 1980; Glazer & Strauss, 1967; Lytle, Brett, Barsness, Tinsley, & Janssens, 1995) developed and tested on a cultural group. A theory of culture serves as a basis for developing an explanation of

Figure 4.1. One-Way Approach.

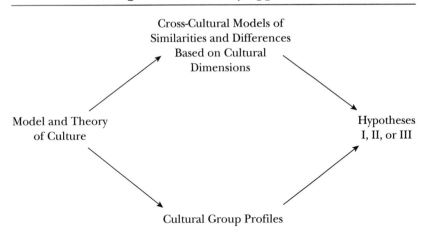

how the model is affected by culture. This theory of culture is also useful in developing profiles of the original cultural group within which the model was developed (*source cultural group*) and the cultural groups (*target groups*) on which the cross-cultural generality of the model is to be tested. The cultural explanation and the cultural profiles provide the basis for the development of hypotheses specifying similarities and differences in the source model as it is moved from one cultural group to another.

Theory of Culture

In Lytle, Brett, Barsness, Tinsley, and Janssens (1995) we developed a theory of culture that can be used as a basis for developing cultural explanations and cross-cultural hypotheses about how and why a model will and will not vary across cultures. In brief, that theory defines culture as a latent hypothetical construct knowable through patterns in its manifestations such as symbols, artifacts, modes of communication, values, behaviors, institutions, and social systems shared among group members. Culture is inherently a group-level construct. It is the unique character of a group—the constellation of characteristics that define the group's unique social identity (Deutsch, 1973).

Culture is a composite construct, consisting of many different latent dimensions. Examples of cultural dimensions include individualist versus collectivist values, associative versus abstractive reasoning, democratic versus autocratic leadership styles, and materialist versus post-materialist economics (see Lytle, Brett, Barsness, Tinsley, & Janssens, 1995, table 1, for definitions). Figure 4.2 represents culture as a collage or union of dimensions. Some cultural dimensions may be broad in scope, others narrow. Some may overlap with certain neighboring dimensions and at the same time be orthogonal to others. Dimensions might correlate differently in different cultures. Some dimensions may be uncorrelated in some cultures. The unique relationships among the cultural dimensions characteristic of a specific group and that group's level on those dimensions define that group's culture.

Cultural dimensions are important because they explain what it is about a cultural group that has an effect on the source model. We proposed further (Lytle, Brett, Barsness, Tinsley, & Janssens, 1995) that cultural dimensions have their effect both because they

Figure 4.2. Culture as Collage.

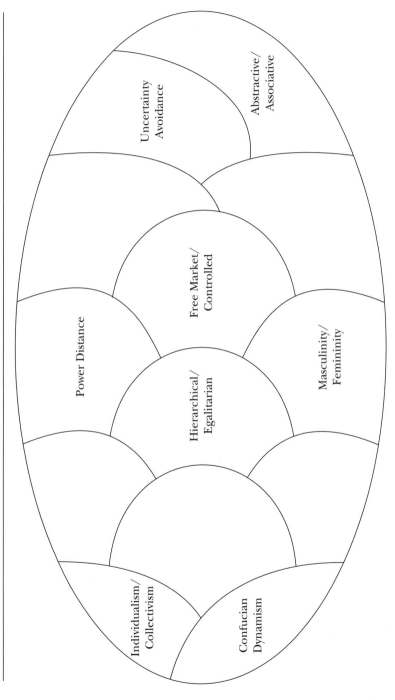

Source: Lytle, Brett, Barsness, Tinsley, & Janssens, 1995, p. 192. Reprinted by permission.

frame and guide the interpretation of experience and provide information about action and because they act as a set of norms that establish appropriate behavior.

Cultural Explanation

The cultural explanation is derived inductively by combining an understanding of the model and an understanding of culture to produce an understanding of the model in a cultural context. The cultural explanation is really a theory of how culture affects the model. We have used the term cultural explanation rather than cultural theory, however, to distinguish this concept from the theory of culture on which the cultural explanation is based. It would be consistent with the inductive-hypothetico-deductive method to call the cultural explanation a hypothesis for it is a proposition about how culture affects the model.

Ideas about a culture's effect on a model may be stimulated in two ways. Researchers may turn to a conceptualization of culture (such as the one in Lytle, Brett, Barsness, Tinsley, & Janssens, 1995) and consider the cultural dimensions that seem likely to affect the variables in the research model. Alternatively, researchers may turn to the cultural groups across which they wish to test the model and consider each group's cultural profile, collecting information about the cultural dimensions that characterize the group, group means on those dimensions, and the relationships among the dimensions.

When starting with cultural dimensions, researchers may study prior research linking cultural dimensions to variables in the model. For example, Leung (1987) reported that the cultural dimension of individualism versus collectivism covaried with cooperation in a negotiation context. Thus researchers testing a model in which cooperation plays a key role would select individualism versus collectivism to use as a cultural explanation. Such prior research or theorizing can identify cultural dimensions likely to be holding the model in place within a cultural group even when that research did not test the model of interest. Where prior research is lacking, researchers may draw upon knowledge of the cultural dimensions or phenomena under investigation to develop their own theoretical rationale to link cultural dimensions conceptually to variables in the model.

Alternatively, researchers may consult prior research on the focal group to construct a cultural profile of it. Because cultural group profiles may include many different cultural dimensions, researchers will need to narrow down the number to those relevant to their model. One approach to selecting relevant dimensions is to consider prior evidence of relationships between cultural dimensions and the model variables. In other words, researchers can ask what cultural dimensions are likely to underlie the model's structure in the source culture.

It may also be useful in narrowing down cultural dimensions to consider the cultural profiles of the other cultural groups in which the model is to be tested. Contrasting the cultural profiles of the source group with the cultural profiles of the target groups may throw into relief cultural dimensions taken for granted in the source cultural group.

The goal of this step of the one-way approach is to identify the cultural dimensions believed to hold the model in place within the source culture and to account for similarities and differences in the target cultures. That goal can be met by considering the links between variables in the model and dimensions of culture or by considering the links between the cultural profiles of groups to be studied and the variables in the model. The cultural dimensions identified in this step provide the basis for hypothesizing about how a model will change when tested in cultures with profiles dissimilar to that of the source culture. They also provide an explanation for exactly why the model will or will not change.

Before specific cross-cultural hypotheses can be developed, a cultural profile of each group to be studied must be developed. Then the researcher develops specific hypotheses about the model for each cultural group as a function of its cultural profile. As we discuss in more detail later, these hypotheses may propose that culture has a main effect on the level of variables in the model (Type I), that culture is a moderator affecting the relationships among the variables in the model (Type II), or that some variables in the source model are not relevant in other cultures or that variables not relevant in the source model are relevant in other cultures and must be accounted for (Type III).

An Example of the One-Way Approach

Janssens, Brett, and Smith (1995) used the one-way approach to generate hypotheses in their study of the cross-cultural viability of a corporate safety policy. They began with a model of factors leading to perceptions of safety level in a plant. The National Safety Council has found that in the United States, management attitudes have a significant impact on workers' perceptions of safety (Ashfahl, 1984). Their model (reproduced in Figure 4.3) was tested on a sample of blue-collar employees from a global corporation's U.S. facility, and validity was confirmed.

Janssens and her colleagues then began to develop a cultural explanation for the model using the Lytle, Brett, Barsness, Tinsley, and Janssens (1995) theory of culture. They first turned to Poole's comparative theory of industrial relations (1986) to begin to identify the dimensions of culture likely to be affecting the variables in their model. Poole's framework holds that environmental factors such as cultural values and social, economic, and legal structures affect the implementation of organizational policies, through management. Janssens, Brett, and Smith (1995) used this general framework to construct a link between outcomes, such as perceptions of safety to cultural values, management styles, and management practices.

They anticipated that their model would be different in different cultural settings despite the organization's corporatewide

Figure 4.3. Janssens, Brett, and Smith's Basic Model.

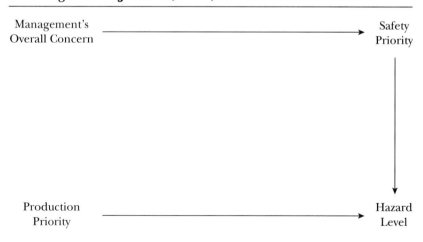

Source: Janssens, Brett, & Smith, 1995, p. 366. Reprinted by permission.

safety policy, because local management practices are a reflection of managers' assumptions about how to manage people. The researchers asserted that three characteristics of culture—the cultural value, individualism versus collectivism; management style, authoritarian versus paternalistic; and management structure, autocratic versus participatory decision making—would account for differences in their model across cultures. This was their cultural explanation.

They next developed cultural profiles of the three cultures in their study with respect to the cultural value, individualism versus collectivism; management style, authoritarian versus paternalistic; and management structure, autocratic versus participatory decision making. From these cultural profiles, they generated specific hypotheses proposing how the model would deviate from its configuration in the U.S. culture in each of the cultures in their study.

Comparison of the One-Way Approach and Berry and Triandis's Approaches

How does the one-way approach relate to other approaches to cross-cultural research in psychology? Berry's three-step process (1969, 1989) and Triandis and colleagues' approach (Triandis with Vassiliou, Vassiliou, Tonaka, & Shanmugam, 1972; Davidson, Jaccard, Triandis, Morales, & Díaz-Guerrero, 1976) are both based on Pike's distinction (1966) between emic and etic research and are widely cited.

Berry's three-step process (literally five steps) begins with local knowledge; the researcher selects a concept that is reasonably well understood and researched in his or her own culture. In step 2, the concept is measured in the second culture, using linguistic and cultural translations; for example, changing references to local places or things in the source culture to recognizable places or things in the target culture. This step is labeled *imposed etic*. The implication is that the construct emic to Culture A is also valid in Culture B and is therefore an etic construct, although there is no step to test the relevance of the construct in Culture B as opposed to being able to measure it. Step 3 is a deliberate attempt to develop an emic understanding of the construct in the second culture. Step 4 is a comparison of the construct emic to each culture. The overlap, if there is any, is labeled in step 5 as *derived etic*.

Triandis and colleagues begin with what they presume to be an etic construct (Hui & Triandis, 1985), which they call a *pseudo etic*. They then develop emic ways of measuring the construct in different cultures (Triandis, 1992). Cross-cultural comparisons are made with a derived etic construct; that is, an etic construct measured emically in each culture.

Both Triandis and Berry have discussed cross-cultural research models in context. Triandis (1972) refers to the geographic environment and the social environment; Berry (1976) to the ecological and sociopolitical context. Both scholars emphasize developing models with micro-mediational chains (Cook & Campbell, 1979) of antecedent contextual variables presumed to be ultimate causes of cultural differences. Triandis (1972) indicated that cross-cultural psychologists' quest to discover the laws that relate major geographic and social features to patterns of behavior will be facilitated by incorporating environmental and social antecedent variables into cross-cultural models. Yoshida (1989), for example, used a demographic homogeneity argument to hypothesize differences between U.S. and Japanese thought processes. He argued that because the United States is demographically diverse, its organizations and managers will focus on what is acceptable. Conversely, in demographically homogeneous Japan they tend to focus on what is desirable.

This emphasis on context contributes to the level of sophistication of cross-cultural research; at the same time, however, it may generate confusion about what factors are cultural and what factors are contextual antecedents of culture. In our view (Lytle, Brett, Barsness, Tinsley, & Janssens, 1995) geography and climate are not culture, but a group's social, political, and economic features are culture. By attributing cross-cultural differences to antecedents in the ecological or sociopolitical context (Berry, Poortinga, Segall, & Dasen, 1992) or to the geographical or social environment (Triandis, 1972), both these scholars deemphasize the explanatory power of culture.

The one-way approach moves beyond the emic-etic distinction of Pike (1966) and the imposed and pseudo etic starting points of Berry and Triandis. It starts with local knowledge, which may be emic, etic, or a combination of both, and seeks to determine what in that local knowledge is specific to the source cultural group and what is general across the source and target cultural groups. In addition its method goes beyond the contextual approach that advocates incorporating environmental and social variables into cross-cultural models. The one-way approach relies on a theory of culture to develop a cultural explanation for cross-cultural similarities and differences, and on that cultural explanation to generate specific hypotheses. The result is a cross-cultural study with specific hypotheses that can be tested.

Triandis (1972) suggested that in the next century researchers may be able to make predictions by relying on information about a cultural group's position on "n variables." We think it is time for the next century to arrive. The goal of the one-way approach is the development of cross-cultural models that rely on information about culture's relation to variables of interest and the cultural profile of groups to predict how variables and relationships between them will be affected by culture. The one-way approach explicitly relies on a theory of culture to develop an understanding of how the model or concept is related to culture. It asks what is it about culture that sustains this model or concept and what would cause the model or concept to change in some way in a different cultural group? In Berry's and Triandis's imposed and pseudo etic approaches, cross-cultural generalities will be identified but without an understanding of what it is about culture that maintains those similarities. Likewise, these approaches can be used to identify cross-cultural differences, but again without a cultural explanation for their existence. A study that incorporates ecological, geographic, or social variables should identify what it is about them that causes cultural group differences. These approaches, however, offer not a cultural explanation but a contextual one. Furthermore, without explicit a priori hypotheses, covariation studies can be used only to study differences not similarities. The strength of the one-way approach is that its hypotheses incorporate both similarities and differences into the same model making explicit a priori predictions about them.

Neither the contextual approach nor the one-way approach develops a fully emic model in the comparison cultures. This is the domain of the n-way approach, discussed in the following section. Because the one-way approach does not develop a fully emic model in comparison cultures, it may not identify a priori constructs that are emic to the model in the comparison cultures. Tests of confirmation (discussed subsequently), or more precisely disconfirmation, will suggest to the researcher that emic constructs may need to be added to the model as it is applied to other cultures.

N-Way Approach

The *n*-way approach to cross-cultural research starts with a research question and a multicultural team of scholars. Team members will have local knowledge of the research question in their source cultures. There are four goals of the *n*-way approach: (1) to determine how the research question should be modeled in each of the source cultures, (2) to identify cross-cultural similarities, (3) to identify cross-cultural differences, and (4) to understand what it is about culture that causes these cross-cultural similarities and differences.

The *n*-way approach consists of five steps, beginning with a research question defined jointly by the members of the research team. Then, in step 2, a local model of the research question is developed for each source culture. In the third step, the researchers engage in a dialogue to create a union model that incorporates all elements from each cultural group's model of the research question, both those that appear to be emic and those that appear to be etic. The fourth step continues the dialogue in order to develop a cultural explanation for the union model, describing why some elements are emic and others etic across the cultures in the study.

These initial four steps are inductive. Some researchers will see the completion of these four steps as a completed cross-cultural study. Others may wish to continue the hypothetico-deductive approach and develop and test specific hypotheses about why culture causes a particular configuration of the research question in each of the multiple source cultures. This would be step 5. The *n*-way approach is illustrated in Figure 4.4.

The *n*-way approach starts with a general research question. This question needs to be stated in terms that allow it to be investigated in each of the source cultures. For example, the GLOBE project, a cross-cultural research project on leadership that was not taking an *n*-way approach, immediately ran into difficulties with the definition of leadership. During a meeting in Calgary, Canada

Figure 4.4. The *N*-Way Approach.

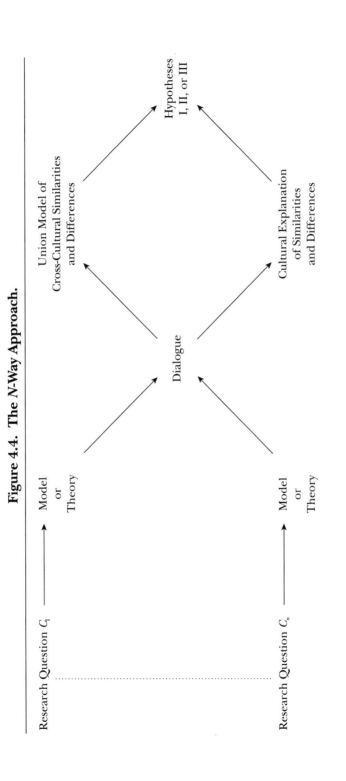

(August 1994), scholars from fifty-four national cultures realized that leadership meant something different in different cultures and that they had to reach agreement on what it was that they were studying. After substantial discussion, they settled on a functional definition that described the effects a leader has on people (rather than the behaviors or characteristics of such a person): "a person who is exceptionally skilled at influencing or enabling me, others, or groups to contribute, support his/her ideas." This definition was to be given to those completing the GLOBE questionnaire. Its purpose was to stimulate all respondents to think about the same role, regardless of the emic meaning of leadership in their own culture.

This example highlights the strength of the *n*-way approach over the one-way approach. The concepts in a one-way model or in an *n*-way research question may not have the same meaning across cultures. Researchers using the one-way approach may find this out as they try to operationalize the model in the target cultures. Researchers using the *n*-way approach will find this out at the first meeting of the *n*-way research team.

In the next step in the *n*-way approach the researchers from each source culture examine the research question (now phrased in etic terms) from an emic perspective. The product of this step is a series of local research models. A local knowledge research model can be developed from reviews of prior research in that culture. However, when there is little applicable prior research, it may be necessary to collect data before a local knowledge model can be developed.

Step 3, another dialogue among the *n*-culture researchers, has multiple activities. First, the researchers share their local models with each other. They then try to understand each other's models, asking each other questions, looking for clarifications, and explaining their interpretations. In trying to understand each other's local models, the researchers are likely to come to a better understanding of their own local models.

After all models are presented and discussed separately, the *n*-culture researchers turn to a discussion of the similarities and differences among the models. The differences may be in relevant variables or different relationships between the variables. Some variables and some relationships among the variables may be emic to a particular source culture. Others will be determined to be etic. The goal of this discussion of similarities and differences is the construction of a union model that incorporates all the variables—both emic and derived etic—relevant to the research question across cultures and also all the relationships among the variables.

The dialogue among the *n*-way researchers then turns to the goal of the fourth step: developing a cultural explanation for the similarities and differences in the models across cultural groups. To accomplish this step, researchers must share a dimensional theoretical perspective of culture. Although the researchers need not agree on which dimensions of culture are the major causal factors, all researchers' perspectives should be included in the cultural explanation. The *n*-culture researchers, moreover, will need to share common conceptual definitions of the cultural dimensions contained in the cultural explanation; for example, they may have to determine what individualism versus collectivism means conceptually. *N*-way researchers may start with cultural dimensions when developing their cultural explanation, or they may start with cultural profiles of the groups to be studied.

These are the primary inductive phases of the *n*-way approach. Some researchers will see the completion of these four phases as a completed cross-cultural study. Others may wish to continue to the hypothetico-deductive phase and, moving on to step 5, may develop specific hypotheses about why culture causes a particular configuration of the research model in each of the multiple source cultures.

The Relation Between the *N*-Way and the One-Way Approaches

Although the *n*-way and one-way approaches have a common goal—to identify how and why a model is similar and different across cultures—their research processes are different.

The one-way approach starts with local knowledge of one cultural group, considers other cultural groups, and asks these questions: what elements of the local knowledge are specific or emic to the source cultural groups? what generalizes across cultural groups? and what is it about culture that causes these similarities and differences? Through the process of generating and testing cross-cultural hypotheses, general knowledge is distinguished from knowledge specific to the source culture. The one-way approach identifies some knowledge that is specific to the target cultures (that is, differences from the source culture). However, it may not identify factors specific to the target cultures that were not part of the source culture's model.

In contrast, the n-way approach has the built-in advantages and disadvantages of working with a multicultural research team. The advantages are that the approach generates a complete view of both general and specific knowledge. It starts with multiple local perspectives on a common research question. Separate local models are developed and are not constrained to variables or models veloped in a single source culture. General knowledge is developed by identifying the similarities among the various local models. Unlike knowledge in the one-way approach, specific knowledge is complete. Instead of one local model tested in multiple target cultures, as in the one-way approach, many local models are compared. Each local model may contain elements specific to its cultural group and only that cultural group. These specific elements cannot be identified in the one-way approach.

There are distinct disadvantages too in working with the n-way approach. Prior to the commencement of the research, the multicultural researchers must agree to, or at least accept, a common research approach. Such acceptance may be extremely difficult to achieve unless the researchers have all had similar training. The n-way approach also assumes equal input from the different researchers into the dialogue. In some cultures, however, researchers may feel that speaking out about their interpretations is rude or presumptuous; researchers from other cultures may feel very powerful and will have a much louder voice in the interpretation of the different local models. Therefore the developed union models will to a certain extent reflect the dynamics of the multicultural team. Another disadvantage is the coordination time and cost associated with the n-way approach. Finally, there may be a tendency to stop this approach short of confirmation.

In addition to their differences in handling specific knowledge, the two approaches also differ in the perspective of the researcher. The one-way approach takes an etic, or outsider, perspective as the principal researcher moves outside the source culture. Although an understanding of the different cultural groups is essential in the one-way approach, cultural outsiders frequently use terms distant from experience and seek etic, or noncontextualized, interpretations (Geertz, 1983). Thus the rich description characteristic of the insider's perspective is likely to be missing.

The *n*-way approach relies on multiple emic perspectives and should provide greater depth of understanding of individual cultures and complete information about cultural uniqueness. The cultural map of the research question should also be more complete when the *n*-way approach is taken because no single culture is the source of the union model or the cultural explanation.

Cross-Cultural Research Designs

In both the one-way and *n*-way approaches, researchers will develop a cross-cultural research design. To this end, the researchers have decided which constructs are important to the phenomena of interest, chosen cultural groups and developed cultural group profiles, determined (induced) which cultural dimensions might relate to the model and the cultural groups, and hypothesized (deduced) specifically how culture will affect the model in the different samples. The result is a cross-cultural research design that consists of the original midrange model plus hypotheses about how culture will influence this model and assertions about equivalence.

Cross-Cultural Hypotheses

Cross-cultural hypotheses can take three different forms, which we (Lytle, Brett, Barsness, Tinsley, & Janssens, 1995) have called Type I, Type II, and Type III. All three types propose cross-cultural similarities and differences. Because hypotheses about similarities and differences have implications for standards of equivalence, we follow the description of the types with a discussion of three different kinds of equivalence—conceptual, functional, and structural—and their interrelationship.

Type I Hypotheses
Type I hypotheses propose that culture has a main effect on the midrange model. In other words, cultural dimensions are hypothesized

to be antecedent constructs, causing mean-level differences in the dependent constructs of the midrange model across cultures. More specifically, it is mean-level differences on the cultural dimension across cultures that cause corresponding mean-level differences on the model constructs.

For example, in examining conflict management behaviors across cultures, Tinsley's research design (1994) included Type I hypotheses. Basing her selection on previous literature on conflict management behavior and culture, she chose four cultural dimensions to explain potential cultural differences in conflict management behavior. Next she identified three different cultural groups that previous anthropological and case-study literature showed to vary on her four cultural dimensions. Finally, she tested specific cross-cultural hypotheses about cultural group differences in conflict management behavior. She argued that differences in the cultural profiles of the groups would lead to group-level differences in the conflict management behaviors across cultures. More simply, she had hypotheses asserting that culture had a main effect on conflict management.

There are two important characteristics of Type I hypotheses. First, the researcher assumes that both the cultural dimensions and the constructs in the midrange model are etic for each of the cultural groups selected. In other words, it is postulated that the constructs in the model are relevant (both valid and explanatory) in all cultural groups. However, although these constructs must be etic, it is possible that they can be operationalized using emic measurements (Triandis, 1992). In short, this part of the model is generalizable across cultural groups. Further, the cultural dimension(s) explaining differences between the cultural groups must be etic. That is, these dimensions have a conceptually equivalent meaning in each of the cultural groups.

Second, Type I hypotheses presume an underlying regularity in the structure of the causal relationship among the constructs across all cultures. Relationships between constructs are hypothesized to be the same in sign and magnitude across all cultural groups. Thus, when hypothesizing about mean-level differences between cultural groups, the researcher is at the same time hypothesizing about relational similarities across cultural groups. The similarities are in terms of construct relevance (the same constructs are valid in all cultures), the structural relationships between and among constructs, and the conceptual equivalence of cultural dimensions. The differences are in terms of mean levels of constructs in the midrange model.

Cross-cultural studies with Type I hypotheses are particularly subject to spuriousness because there are a host of alternative explanations for mean-level differences between two cultural groups (Bontempo, 1993). Significant differences between two cultural groups may be a manifestation of a number of underlying explanations (Cook & Campbell, 1979; Bontempo, 1993; Lytle, Brett, Barsness, Tinsley, & Janssens, 1995) and are not by themselves interesting because they are quite uninterpretable. We do not advocate such research. Rather, we argue for embedding any cross-cultural hypothesis in an elaborated multiconstruct model, in which each cross-cultural hypothesis about mean-level similarities or differences is (1) specified a priori, (2) explained by cultural dimensions, (3) linked to other hypothesized cross-cultural similarities and differences, and (4) tested in three or more cultural groups. Although this elaborated model may be composed of only Type I hypotheses, its high level of specification and complexity make it much harder to confirm than a simple two-sample t test (Popper, 1959). Therefore the researcher can be more confident that confirmatory results are nonspurious and are due to the hypothesized cultural dimensions and not to alternative explanations. (See Lytle, Brett, Barsness, Tinsley, & Janssens, 1995, for further elaboration of this reasoning.)

Type II Hypotheses

Type II hypotheses characterize culture as a moderator. The cultural dimensions moderate, or change, the strength or direction of the relationship between particular constructs in the midrange model. Type II hypotheses predict that the cultural dimensions will cause the relationship between constructs in the midrange model to differ across cultures.

For Type II hypotheses, the constructs in the midrange model and the cultural dimensions are presumed to be etic for all cultures sampled. They are expected to be relevant and have similar conceptual meaning across cultures. Conversely, the relationships between the constructs are expected to vary as a function of culture.

Earley's research (1989) on group processes and outcomes investigated Type II hypotheses. He postulated that the cultural dimension of individualism versus collectivism would moderate the relationship between accountability and social loafing. Thus the meaning of the cultural dimension of individualism versus collectivism and the constructs of accountability and social loafing were assumed to generalize across all cultural groups studied. What was expected to differ across cultures, as a function of each cultural group's level of individualism versus collectivism, was the strength of the relationship between accountability and social loafing.

Type II hypotheses, like Type I, propose both similarities and differences across cultures. Both types of hypotheses also propose that the relevance and meaning of the cultural dimensions and the constructs used to operationalize the phenomena of interest generalize across the cultural groups studied. However, Type I hypotheses propose that variance on the etic cultural dimensions will precipitate mean-level differences in certain constructs within the midrange model. Type II hypotheses, in contrast, propose that variance on the cultural dimension will cause certain constructs in the model to interrelate in different ways.

Type III Hypotheses

Type III hypotheses, unlike Types I and II, propose that different concepts are needed to address the research question in different cultures. Thus Type III hypotheses assert that although some constructs in the proposed midrange model will generalize across cultural groups, emic constructs specific to each cultural group need to be added for the model to be valid in a particular cultural group. Consequently, each cultural group's model needs to be operationalized separately, using some etic and some emic constructs. Furthermore, the need for emic constructs should be explained by reference to cultural dimensions, which themselves need to be etic, as we will explain. Type III hypotheses therefore propose that variance across etic cultural dimensions will cause constructs to emerge as relevant to the midrange model in some cultures but not in others.

Tinsley and Lytle's research (1994) on managerial third-party dispute resolution investigated Type III hypotheses. They examined managerial intervention into organizational disputes and its consequences for disputants' perceptions of fairness and satisfaction with the dispute resolution procedure in the United States and in Mexico. They hypothesized that two managerial behaviors (authoritarianism and facilitation) would be etic and generalize across both cultural groups and that one managerial behavior (paternalism) would be emic and relevant only in Mexico. Given the difference in relevance for the managerial behaviors, the researchers then hypothesized that paternalistic behavior as well as authoritarian and facilitation behavior would affect disputants' perceptions of fairness and satisfaction with managerial dispute resolution procedures in Mexico but that only authoritarian and facilitation behavior would affect perceptions of fairness in the United States. Moreover, both the etic and emic managerial behaviors were hypothesized to be caused by the *same* etic cultural dimensions. The Mexican group's *high* rank on the etic dimensions of collectivism and power distance would cause paternalism to be relevant in that group's model, and the U.S. group's *low* rank on collectivism and power distance would make paternalism an irrelevant construct for the U.S. model. In other words, because of different cultural profiles on the same etic dimensions, the Mexican and U.S. groups exhibited a different set of managerial third-party role behaviors.

Type III hypotheses make cross-cultural research more flexible, as they allow for the inclusion of some emic constructs in the model. There are some constraints, however, on this flexibility. First, not all the constructs in a model can be emic. There must be some etic constructs, or it will be arguable that the researcher is studying different phenomena in different cultures.

Second, the focal constructs in the model should be etic. In other words, the concepts central to the research question must generalize across cultures. As long as they are etic, however, these focal constructs can be either exogenous or endogenous. If, for example, the researcher wishes to study the effects of leadership, then the exogenous leadership construct should be etic across cultures. The effects constructs, in contrast, can be either etic, emic, or mixed. In fact, it is because an effects construct is emic across cultures that the leadership construct must be etic. If the leadership construct were also emic, it would be difficult to argue that the research was indeed comparing the same phenomenon across cultures. Similarly, if the researcher wishes to study the causes of group cooperation, then it is the endogenous group cooperation construct that must be etic across cultures and the exogenous causes constructs that can be etic, emic, or mixed.

Third, as mentioned, the cultural dimensions must themselves be etic if they are to test the cultural explanation by any of the techniques suggested here. Certainly, a cultural dimension, that research has shown to be emic to certain cultures (as Confucian dynamism is emic to Asian cultures, Hofstede & Bond, 1988) can be a valid explanation for model differences between cultures. However, if that dimension is not relevant in one or more of the cultural groups being studied, the cultural explanation based on that dimension cannot be tested using any of the approaches proposed here or in Lytle, Brett, Barsness, Tinsley, and Janssens (1995). These approaches all require that the cultural dimensions underlying the cultural explanation be etic.

Integration of Cross-Cultural Hypotheses

These three types of cross-cultural hypotheses can remain segregated, so a research design may have only one type. Alternatively, they can be mixed in the same cross-cultural research model. Figure 4.5 illustrates a research design that includes only Type I hypotheses. In both cultures A and B the model comprises the same constructs and cultural dimensions, and the interrelationships among the constructs and the cultural dimensions is invariant. The structural parameters in the model in Figure 4.5 are the same in both cultural groups.

Other research designs may include only Type II hypotheses, as depicted in Figure 4.6. Here the model comprises the same constructs, but variance on the cultural dimension causes the interrelationships among the constructs (shown by the structural parameters) to vary across cultures.

Figure 4.7 illustrates a research design that includes only Type III hypotheses. Note that some constructs in the model (Y_2 and Y_3) are emic to their respective cultural group.

Finally, a research design may mix all these different types of cross-cultural hypotheses, as in Figure 4.8. The structural parameter b_{x1-y1} is invariant across cultural groups A and B, although the

Figure 4.5. Research Design with Type I Hypotheses.

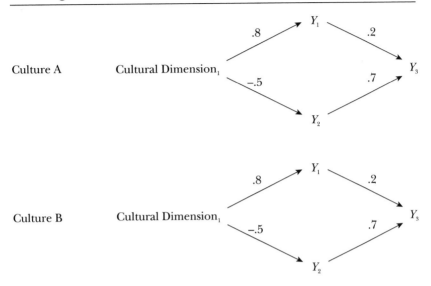

Figure 4.6. Research Design with Type II Hypotheses.

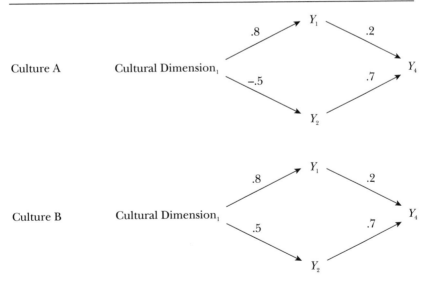

Figure 4.7. Research Design with Type III Hypotheses.

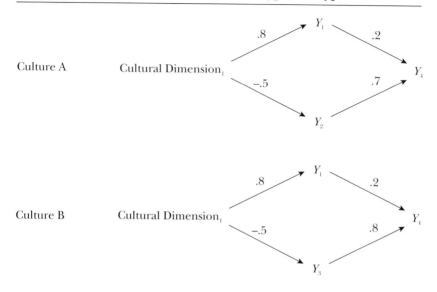

Figure 4.8. Research Design with Mixed Hypotheses.

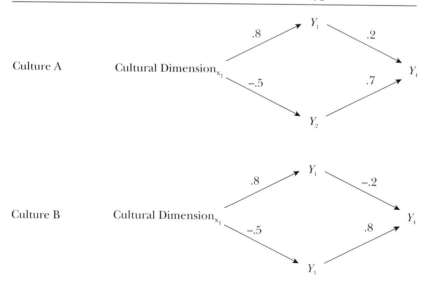

mean levels of Y_1 may be hypothesized to differ across cultural groups, reflecting a Type I hypothesis. Parameter $b_{y_1-y_4}$ changing sign across cultural groups A and B is indicative of a Type II hypothesis. Culture A's model shows a Type III hypothesis: Y_2 mediating the relationship between X_1 and Y_4. In Culture B, Y_3 is the mediator.

Conclusion

Type I, II, and III hypotheses distinguish the elements of the model that are presumed to be culturally relative. The types of hypotheses chosen should be those that best capture the phenomena in each of the cultural groups under investigation. Therefore the choice will depend on (1) the phenomena under investigation, (2) the conceptually related cultural dimensions, (3) the amount and quality of the previous research, and (4) the degree of comparability the researcher wishes to incorporate into the research question. All these parameters will dictate the amount and type of cross-cultural equivalence required by the research design. In the next section we discuss this concept of equivalence in more depth.

Equivalence

Our emphasis on studying both similarities and differences in a complex multiconstruct model has implications for the notion of equivalence. Previous cross-cultural research in psychology relied more on testing constructs rather than full models across cultures and adopted the prerequisite of functional equivalence (Berry, 1969; Berry & Dasen, 1974; Triandis, 1972). In this section, we discuss equivalence in relation to the midrange models that we advocate. We describe three types of equivalence—conceptual, structural, and functional—and then elaborate the distinctions between and relationships among them. We build on the logic of Gerbing and Anderson's two-step approach to model analysis (1992) and distinguish between the measurement and structural level. At the measurement level the operationalization of the different constructs is examined; at the structural level the hypotheses concerning the relationships between the constructs are examined.

Conceptual Equivalence

Conceptual equivalence refers to commonality of meaning across cultures. Hui and Triandis (1985) argue that a construct has conceptual equivalence when it can be meaningfully discussed in a culture. This seems to be a definition of construct validity. For conceptual equivalence, we would go farther than Hui and Triandis (1985) and define a construct as conceptually equivalent in two or more cultures when (1) it can be meaningfully discussed in each culture and (2) it has a similar meaning across all the cultures. Thus a construct that demonstrates conceptual equivalence across particular cultures can be said to be an etic or universal concept for those cultural groups. Conceptual equivalence, however, does not imply that the measurement of the construct must be exactly the same in all cultures (Triandis, 1992). The researcher may use some emic indicators when operationalizing some of these constructs in different cultures.

For example, Hofstede's cultural dimension individualism versus collectivism (1980) appears to be conceptually equivalent in most cultures, an abstract notion that can be meaningfully discussed by researchers from many cultures. Furthermore, this concept has a similar meaning in many different cultural groups. The dimension of Confucian dynamism, in contrast, is not conceptually equivalent in the United States and Hong Kong because it cannot be meaningfully discussed as a concept in the United States (Hofstede & Bond, 1988). The construct of leadership offers another example of nonequivalence. As the GLOBE project has made apparent, this construct tends to refer to organizational leadership in the United States and to political leadership in Asian cultures.

Researchers set different standards for determining similar meaning across all cultures. Although many researchers seek to demonstrate that they are working with etic constructs, there is some disagreement as to how one can confirm whether or not this is the case. Hui and Triandis (1985) discuss a number of approaches including translation equivalence, using, for example, back translation and bilingual responses (Hulin, Drasgow, & Parsons, 1983; Triandis, 1992); metric equivalence (Van de Vijver & Poortinga, 1982), involving, for example, item response theory (Hulin, Drasgow, & Parsons, 1983; Triandis, 1992); internal structural congruence, identifying equivalence by factor analysis, multidimensional scaling, and multisample analysis; combined etic and emic measurement, in which the construct is etic but measurement is emic (Lytle, Brett, Barsness, Tinsley, & Janssens, 1995); and validation by nomological network, showing that the construct is embedded in the same network of constructs in the same manner in each culture. Hui and Triandis advise a multistrategy approach.

We agree that demonstration of the translation equivalence of individual measures is not sufficient when testing midrange models across cultures. Researchers will want to demonstrate equivalence of item convergent and discriminant validity across cultural groups. However, the criterion that all items have equivalent loadings on constructs across cultures is probably too rigid (Peterson et al., in press).

In our previous chapter (Lytle, Brett, Barsness, Tinsley, & Janssens, 1995), we softened this standard by allowing the inclusion of some emic, or culturally specific, items. How many emic items a researcher can use depends on the research model, how well the construct is defined in each culture, and the number and contribution of the other, nonemic items measuring the construct.

In sum, we define conceptual equivalence as the internal coherence of constructs across cultures. We believe that items measuring constructs must demonstrate convergent and discriminant validity across cultures, but we do not restrict measurement to entirely etic indicators. Finally, we restrict our definition of conceptual equivalence to the measurement level, distinguishing it from both structural and functional equivalence, which we discuss in subsequent sections.

Structural Equivalence

Conceptual equivalence refers to the constructs used to build a midrange model, and *structural equivalence* refers to the relationships among the constructs within the model. Structural equivalence refers to the path coefficient between two constructs. A model is said to be structurally equivalent in two cultures when all the path coefficients in Culture A are similar to the corresponding path coefficients in Culture B.

Figure 4.9 illustrates a simple model that is structurally equivalent in cultures A and B. In both cultures the path coefficient

Figure 4.9. Example of Structural Equivalence.

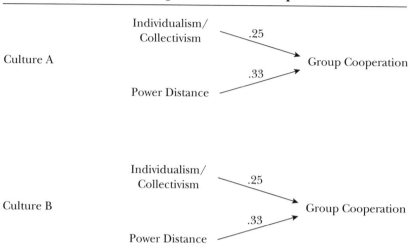

between individualism versus collectivism and group cooperation is .25, the path coefficient between power distance and group cooperation is .33, and the path coefficient between individualism versus collectivism and power distance is zero.

Figure 4.10 illustrates this same three-construct model in cultures A and C; however, this time the model is not structurally equivalent. In both cultures the path coefficient between individualism versus collectivism and group cooperation is still .25, and the path coefficient between individualism versus collectivism and power distance is still zero; yet the path coefficient between power distance and group cooperation is .33 in Culture A and −.50 in Culture C.

Either outcome (path coefficients that are the same or different across cultures) is, in our opinion, equally valid and interesting. As we have stated throughout this chapter, we believe in studying both similarities and differences across cultures. Thus we concentrate our efforts on noting where, when, and in which cultural groups a model is structurally equivalent and where, when, and in which cultural groups it is not. Finding structural equivalence is further support for the constructs' conceptual equivalence (Hulin, Drasgow, & Parsons, 1983). Yet the definition of conceptual equivalence does not rely on structural-level confirmation.

Figure 4.10. Example of Nonstructurally Equivalent Models.

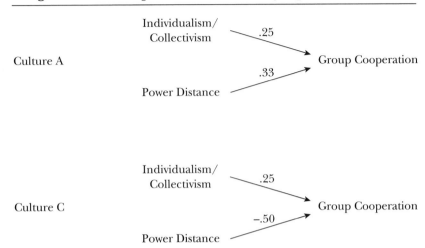

Functional Equivalence

Functional equivalence refers to each construct's placement in the model vis-à-vis other constructs, thereby referring to both the construct and the model. Constructs are defined to be functionally equivalent across cultures when they relate in the same way to the same constructs in their respective models.

Figure 4.11 illustrates the idea of functional equivalence. Here individualism versus collectivism is functionally equivalent to power distance across Cultures A and D. In Culture A, individualism versus collectivism relates to group cooperation with a weight of .25, and in Culture D power distance relates to group cooperation with the same weight. Furthermore, in Culture A the relationship between power distance and group cooperation is zero, and in Culture D, the relationship between individualism versus collectivism and group cooperation is also zero. Thus individualism versus collectivism is functionally equivalent to power distance in Cultures A and D because each construct serves as a causal antecedent to group cooperation in its respective cultural model.

Note, however, that although these constructs are functionally equivalent across Cultures A and D, they are not conceptually equivalent. The construct of individualism versus collectivism in Culture A does not have the same meaning as the construct of

Figure 4.11. Example of Functional Equivalence.

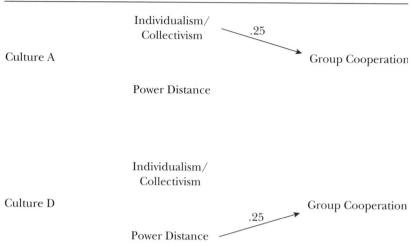

power distance in Culture D. Functional equivalence in no way necessitates conceptual equivalence. Furthermore, the models in cultures A and B are not structurally equivalent. The relationship between individualism versus collectivism and group cooperation is different (.25 in Culture A and zero in Culture D), as is the relationship between power distance and group cooperation (zero in Culture A and .25 in Culture D).

Functional equivalence has been considered a prerequisite for behavioral comparisons across culture (Triandis, 1972). The logic is that aspects of behavior can be compared only when the behavior in question has a similar function in each culture studied. This similarity implies that the behavior developed in response to a common problem shared by the cultural groups, even though the manifest aspects of the behavior may not appear similar (Berry, 1969; Berry & Dasen, 1974; Frijda & Jahoda, 1966).

This emphasis on functional equivalence has been beneficial because it stimulated cross-cultural psychologists to move beyond single construct comparisons across cultures. (An examination of functional equivalence necessitates a multiconstruct approach.) Yet we would leave out the requirement that cross-cultural comparisons must be functionally equivalent. The finding that different behaviors are functionally equivalent across cultures is certainly interesting but is only one part of the universe of interesting cross-cultural research. Indeed, discovering that the same behaviors or constructs serve different functions for their respective cultures is also a legitimate conclusion. What is paramount is discovering what actually exists—where models are similar and different, structurally equivalent, functionally equivalent, both, or neither across cultures. The degree of cross-cultural equivalence should not be a measure of a study's worth. Rather the worth of a cross-cultural research endeavor should depend on the study's ability to provide a cultural understanding of observed cross-cultural similarities and differences.

Relationships Among Types of Equivalence

Conceptual, structural, and functional equivalence are interrelated. A study that demonstrates structural equivalence can do so with constructs that are conceptually equivalent or functionally equivalent. In Figure 4.5, structural equivalence is associated with conceptual equivalence because the constructs that have equivalent parameters across cultures also have the same meaning across cultures. Power distance in Culture A has the same meaning as power distance in Culture B. In Figure 4.7, structural equivalence is associated with functional equivalence because the predictors of the endogenous variable have the same magnitude across cultures; however, these predictor constructs are not conceptually equivalent across cultures. Individualism versus collectivism in Culture A is not conceptually equivalent to power distance in Culture B.

Level of Theory

When making cross-cultural hypotheses, researchers must identify the appropriate *level of theory* for their study. A study's unit of theory is the level to which study findings are generalized (Rousseau, 1985). Unit of theory is sometimes not well understood in cross-cultural research because it is often different from unit of measurement (level at which data are collected) and unit of analysis (level at which data are analyzed).

As we have previously discussed (Lytle, Brett, Barsness, Tinsley, & Janssens, 1995), cross-cultural research is inherently cross-level—the proposed cross-cultural model specifies relationships among variables at different levels, such as the individual and group, individual and organization, group and organization, or organization and society (Rousseau, 1985). Consequently, the researcher developing cross-cultural hypotheses on the basis of previous observations of cultural group differences needs to pay particular attention to the differences between the levels of theory in the research that generated the observed group differences and the level of theory for the new study (Lytle, Brett, Barsness, Tinsley, & Janssens, 1995).

This is important because, as Klein, Dansereau, and Hall (1994) point out, the assumptions that underlie the specification of levels of theory within a study influence the nature of theoretical constructs and hypotheses as well as data collection, analysis, and interpretation. When specifying the level of theory, the researcher implicitly or explicitly predicts that members of the cultural group are homogeneous, independent, or heterogeneous with respect to the constructs of the midrange theory (Klein, Dansereau, & Hall, 1994). Further, in specifying the level of theory, the researcher implicitly or explicitly predicts that the relationships among the theoretical constructs are a consequence of differences between groups, differences between members independent of groups, or differences within groups (Dansereau, Alutto, & Yammarino, 1984). It is critical in cross-cultural research to tie the level of theory explicitly to the cultural group because doing so implies certain assumptions about the characteristics of the group.

For instance, in asserting that group members are homogeneous with respect to a theoretical construct such as individualism versus collectivism, the researcher predicts that all members score similarly on the measure of individualism versus collectivism, that is, that the mean score for the cultural group accurately reflects each individual member's score. When researchers specify that the level of theory is the individual, they are then predicting that group members are independent of the group's influence with respect to the constructs of interest. In this case, the mean score of the cultural group on the cultural dimension of interest would be irrelevant to predicting each individual member's score, and the study is not cross-cultural. Lastly, Klein, Dansereau, and Hall (1994) propose that the level of some theories is neither the individual nor the group but the individual within the group. In this case, the researcher is specifying heterogeneity. When the group is heterogeneous, the group mean can tell the researcher something about the individual, but information about the individual's deviation from the mean is also required. Much cross-cultural theorizing falls into this category: researchers seek to demonstrate cultural effects but may also desire to account for variance in their unit of analysis by including individual (or group) differences. By doing so, researchers recognize that there is more to culture than the stereotypic behavior that would be implied if the level of theory specified homogeneity.

Earley and Mosakowski (1993), for example, assumed heterogeneity when they suggested an alternative procedure of analysis for cross-cultural data, specifying an individual-within-the-group level of theory. If applied to Earley's data (1989) on social loafing, for instance, this type of analysis would have assumed that the degrees to which individuals exhibit collectivist values on the one hand and membership in either a collectivist or individualist culture on the other predicted the extent to which they engaged in social loafing. Using this approach the researcher can maintain a sense of variance attributable to the shared, or cultural, value while measuring constructs at the individual level of analysis. Each group member is assigned a mean value on the cultural dimension along with a difference score representing the deviation of the individual's score from the group's mean score (Earley & Mosakowski, 1993). Although much cross-cultural theorizing specifies heterogeneity, no Type I cultural effects can be assumed unless a difference in between-group means is observed.

Frog Pond Effects

Studies with a mixed level of theory focus on individual scores on an attribute relative to the group average for the same attribute and often describe what are known as *frog pond effects* (Firebaugh, 1980). Central to theories like these is a comparative or relative effect: depending upon the size of the pond the same frog may be perceived to be small (if the pond is large) or large (if the pond is small). The frog pond effect simply means that there are two over-lapping distributions. A subject with a score within the overlapping region will be low in the "high" group and high in the "low" group. An individual who is rated by colleagues as strongly collectivist in a highly individualistic culture, for instance, may be rated as only moderately or weakly collectivist by colleagues in a highly collec-tivist culture. Thus the frog pond effect implies both between- and within-group differences. If there were no differences between cul-tural groups, there would be no frog pond effect.

Because the level of theory in many cross-cultural studies is mixed, researchers need to consider the possibilities of frog pond effects when measuring constructs in the midrange model. The po-tential for frog pond effects indicates the need for metric equiva-lence in measures across groups: subjects' true scores must be measured accurately regardless of the group in which they are lo-cated. This concern is especially applicable to instruments subject to greater interpretation than others. For example, if an inter-viewer were assigned five subjects to rate on collectivism, those rat-ings would be biased by the five subjects interviewed (just as professors often find that they grade papers relative to each other, rather than assigning each paper an objective grade that stands alone). This type of measurement is risky when more than one in-terviewer is involved. In the example just given, the second inter-viewer's ratings will also be affected by the next five subjects, who may not even overlap with the initial subjects in terms of true score, but who will overlap as a consequence of their assigned score. This issue may be best addressed using item response theory (Hulin, Drasgow, & Parsons, 1983; Lytle, Brett, Barsness, Tinsley, & Janssens, 1995, offer in-depth discussion of item response theory and also its application to issues of metric equivalence and cross-cultural research).

Reversal Paradox

Researchers who assign a mixed level of theory to their study must also consider the possibility of the reversal paradox, which might occur when they collect data at the individual level and aggregate it to the collective level (Messick & van der Geer, 1981). Cross-cultural comparisons typically involve the comparison of cultural averages on some measures, thus explaining cultural differences at the level of the cultural group. In this approach cultural group differences on an outcome variable, Y, are explained by cultural group differences on an antecedent variable, X. Leung (1989) asserts, however, that these studies make no assumption regarding the relationship between X and Y within each of the cultures included in the comparison. Consequently, the relationship between the dependent variable Y and the independent variable X within a particular culture at the individual level may not be the same as the relationship between the aggregate Y and the aggregate X across cultural groups. For example, in Figure 4.12 the relationship between the cultural group means suggests a positive relationship between X and Y. Plotted data within the cultural groups, however, indicate a negative relationship between X and Y at the individual level of analysis.

Lincoln and Zeitz (1980), for example, in their study of social service organizations, examined their data at the individual as well as at the organizational level. (The organization-level analysis is analogous to analysis at the cultural group level in cross-cultural

Figure 4.12. Reversal Paradox.

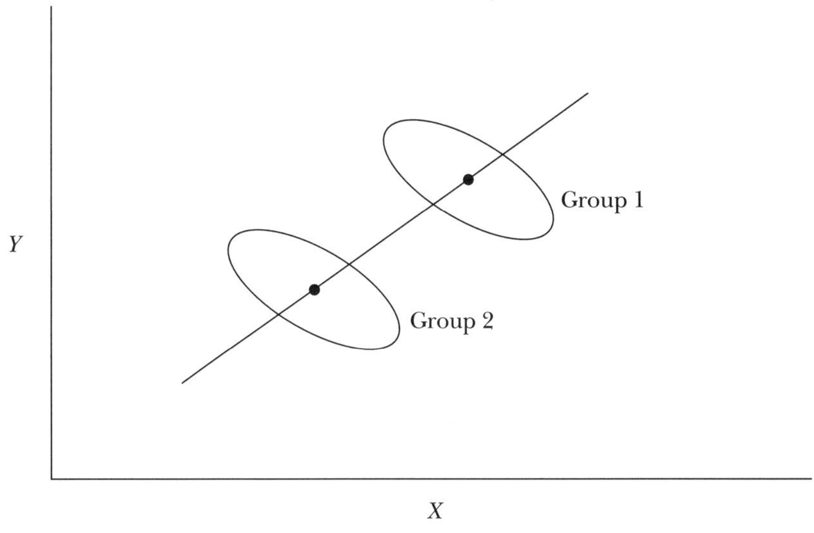

research.) They found that professional status was positively correlated with amount of administrative duties ("administrative intensity") at the individual level. This result is expected, because in social service organizations professional status is often associated with supervisory responsibilities. In the organization-level analysis (in which average scores of professional status and administrative duties from each organization were used), Lincoln and Zeitz reported a negative correlation between professionalization (the average professional status of an organization) and administrative intensity (the average amount of administrative duties in an organization). Thus it is important for the cross-cultural researcher specifying a mixed level of theory to confirm that the hypothesized relationships hold at both the group and individual levels of analysis. If the same relationships do not hold, it may be difficult to confirm the influence of culture on the midrange model. In particular, cross-cultural researchers need to be concerned about the possibility of a reversal when using aggregate data, because they cannot generalize from the cultural group level to the individual level unless they have demonstrated that the hypothesized relationship holds within as well as between groups.

Ecological Fallacy

True reversals may be rare, but Hofstede (1980) points out that within-group correlations are not likely to have the same magnitude as between-group correlations. He comments that in societies in which culture imposes strong norms, there may be so little variance on some values that within-group correlations may be very low. However, between-group correlations may be quite large. The ecological fallacy is to interpret the between-group correlations (ecological correlations in which group mean is the unit of analysis) as if they applied to individuals. Hofstede also points out that the reverse fallacy can occur if correlations based on the individual are used to interpret differences between groups. These issues have been particularly relevant to generalizations made from Hofstede's (1980) and Schwartz's (1992, 1994) studies of cultural values.

Such studies are useful to cross-cultural researchers seeking to profile cultural groups and generate a cultural explanation for differences anticipated in a midrange model. There are fallacy traps here, too, however. The researcher using Schwartz's or Hofstede's studies to profile several cultural groups is using ecological, or group-level, data to distinguish the groups or to develop the cultural explanation. Then, in order to demonstrate that the study's sample is representative of the cultural group on which the hypotheses were based, the researcher collects individual-level value data. (The means on the cultural dimensions in the sample should reflect those of the population.) If the researcher further uses the individual value data in a model that is analyzed at the individual level, the researcher may be disappointed in the magnitude of the correlations, as a result of the ecological fallacy.

Sampling

Consideration of level of theory will not only alert researchers to potential confounds that might occur in cross-level designs; it will also influence their selection of sampling strategy. For example, if researchers assume homogeneity in the cultural groups they have targeted, they should select groups so as to maximize between-group differences and construct their samples within each cultural group so as to minimize within-group variance. If researchers assume heterogeneity in their level of theory, then they should select cultural groups and construct samples so as to maximize both between- and within-group variance. For instance, if researchers anticipate substantial variance in responses on the independent variable from blue-collar workers and managerial workers in each of the cultures studied, then they would want to ensure that their samples in each culture included both blue-collar and managerial respondents. Failure to test empirically the assumptions of the theory regarding the homogeneity, independence, or heterogeneity of the constructs, however, may leave the conclusions of the research open to question and criticism (Klein, Dansereau, & Hall, 1994).

Confirmation

Whether cross-cultural research hypotheses have been developed via a one-way or an *n*-way approach, they are subject to confirmation, the process of assessing the fit between the hypotheses and the data collected from each culture in the study. Prior to data collection, hypotheses are operationalized and samples selected. Once data are collected, they are analyzed for a fit with the hypotheses. When data are consistent with prediction, hypotheses are said to be confirmed. When data are inconsistent with predictions, hypotheses are said to be disconfirmed. Figure 4.13 illustrates the process of confirmation.

Confirmation in cross-cultural research indicates that data from each cultural group were consistent with the cross-cultural hypotheses comparing that group to other groups. Confirmation implies that each step of the cross-cultural research process was consistent: (1) the constructs were operationalized consistently with their conceptualization in the midrange model and were measured appropriately in each cultural group; (2) the samples from which data were collected were representative of the populations of the cultural group on which the hypotheses were based; (3) the fit between the hypotheses and the data was significant. As a result of all these consistencies, the researcher may conclude that the cultural explanation is valid.

It is realistic to expect that some cross-cultural hypotheses in a study may not be confirmed. When a hypothesis is not confirmed, the reason may be buried in any number of places: the inductive profiling of cultural groups, the deduction of hypotheses, the operationalization of constructs, or the sampling. Thus it is useful to build into a cross-cultural study design ways to rule out some potential explanations for disconfirmation. For example, it is important to confirm that samples accurately represent their respective cultural groups. To characterize cultural groups in order to

Figure 4.13. Confirmation.

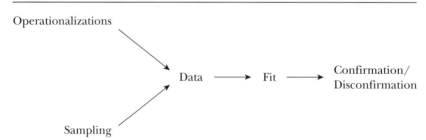

generate cross-cultural hypotheses, it is appropriate for researchers to use whatever data are available, including both individual and group-level measures. Leung (1987), for instance, collected individual-level data on cultural values. He demonstrated that his subjects' values were representative of the cultural groups that he had in mind when developing hypotheses about different preferences for dispute resolution procedures. He was then able to integrate the cultural dimension of individualism versus collectivism into his model and test the micro-mediational chain (Cook & Campbell, 1979) linking cultural group to subjects' cultural values and to their preferences for dispute resolution procedures. Had he no data on cultural values, he still could have tested his hypotheses about the effect of culture on preference for dispute resolution procedures by testing group differences. However, his significant results would be open to criticism that the group differences were due to factors other than the hypothesized dimensions of individualism versus collectivism.

Potential sources for measuring culture without measuring individual differences include anthropological area files, anthropologists' "thick descriptions," political and historical archival sources, surveys of member perceptions, and such qualitative sources as interviews or case studies. Many of these data are likely to be at the group level, however. In testing hypotheses, it is therefore desirable to collect cultural data on subjects in the study. The purpose of such data is to confirm that the groups sampled fit the cultural group profiles deduced from archival information.

Janssens, Brett, and Smith (1995), for example, used archival data to describe the cultural groups in their study of safety perceptions in the United States, France, and Argentina. First, they developed a model of safety perceptions within the corporate headquarters cultural group. Then they consulted Hofstede (1980) and the comparative industrial relations research (Poole, 1986) to identify cultural dimensions manifested in the industrial relations context of individualism versus collectivism, autocratic versus participative decision making, and authoritarian versus paternalistic management style that they thought would account for the differences in the cross-cultural generalizability of their model. Their study would have been able to make a stronger statement about the cultural explanation hypothesized to account for group differences, if they had been able to confirm the cultural profiles that they developed in their study.

Whenever cross-cultural hypotheses are disconfirmed, however, having data on both the dimensions and cultural groups in a study facilitates researchers' ability to identify where their research design erred: whether inaccurate cultural group profiling, a misspecified model, faulty operationalization of theoretical constructs, or inappropriate sampling was responsible for disconfirmation. Consequently, we recommend that researchers provide evidence that samples are representative of the respective cultural groups by collecting data to confirm the characteristics of the cultural profile they have induced.

Research as Interaction: A Dialogue Between Cultures

Whether the result of a one-way or n-way approach, cross-cultural research is always, in some sense, a dialogue between different cultures. In the one-way approach, researchers impose a model developed in one culture on the other cultural groups sampled. The target cultural groups then "reply" by either confirming that the model fits or rejecting its specifications. Upon disconfirmation, researchers are likely to ask why and how the model might be reworked to fit the cultural groups in which it was rejected. Whether they go back to archival sources (ethnographies), informants, or previously collected data, they are again engaged in a dialogue with the target cultural groups. The response that they receive from these groups, moreover, is likely to shape their interpretation of the data and influence the design of their model.

In research that uses an n-way approach, the intercultural dialogue is more explicit. Here researchers from different cultural groups directly communicate with each other concerning the phenomena in the research question, the constructs that most appropriately model those phenomena, the similarities and differences expected across cultures, and the cultural dimensions that might explain these similarities and differences. The n-way approach tends to promote a more complex dialogue because each researcher participates in the process as both informant and observer. In contrast, in the one-way approach researchers from the source culture solicit information from members of the target cultural groups. Members of these latter groups act primarily as respondents, however, having only a limited ability to frame the dialogue or change its course.

Therefore the intercultural dialogue is framed by an etic, or outsider, perspective in the one-way approach. Researchers' emic, or insider, perspective on their own culture contrasts with their etic perspective on the target cultural groups. In the *n*-way approach the interaction between researcher and subject is guided by an emic perspective. The researchers contribute to the dialogue an insider's perspective particular to their own cultures. In collaboration with each other, the research team members then develop an etic, or more generalized, understanding of the research phenomena that is enriched by a clear understanding of the constructs specific to each cultural group included in the study.

Anthropological literature is replete with arguments detailing the pros and cons of each of these perspectives. On the one hand, the etic perspective is thought to be more objective (Lévi-Strauss, 1963), not clouded by the insider's biases (Seeger, 1981; Turner, 1979). On the other hand, the emic perspective is more sensitive to subtleties of each culture (Benedict, 1965) and may elucidate constructs that might otherwise be missed (Geertz, 1983). We feel that the conversational nature of both approaches reconciles the conflict between existing perspectives. Through interaction, both processes move the researchers from a local, emic orientation toward a general, etic position. Local concepts are reviewed and reworked so that a mutual cross-cultural understanding of the constructs' meanings and interrelationships is formed. It is on these mutually developed understandings of concepts' meanings and interrelationships that assertions of cross-cultural similarities and differences are judged. Furthermore, the process of comparing cultures in search of similarities and differences may itself bring researchers closer together simply because they each must transcend their own local worldviews and languages in order to communicate with each other.

The language used in any cross-cultural dialogue must therefore be a meta-language. It must be a medium that transcends the boundaries of each cultural group. Both approaches must use this language. In the one-way approach, the researcher, an outsider, actively seeks emic knowledge specific to each of the target cultural groups. Yet for the researcher to understand this local knowledge, it must be described in a meta-language. Because it is unlikely that local knowledge will naturally be described in a meta-language, someone must translate from local to meta-language—either the outsider researcher, an insider informant, or a previous ethnographer, who may be either insider or outsider.

In *n*-way methodologies, members of the research team, all with an insider's perspective on their own culture, translate their local knowledge into a meta-language in order to engage in dialogue among themselves. Their goal is to discover, through this meta-language dialogue, how much of this local knowledge can be made universal and how much is not translatable and thus must remain local. Furthermore, *n*-way researchers must be willing to work within a common research paradigm and adopt a common theory of culture. The dialogue that leads to their construction of the union model and cultural explanation therefore will probably be preceded by a meta-language dialogue concerning the development of a research paradigm and theory of culture acceptable to all team members.

Thus, whether through *n*-way communication or communication in which one participant takes a more directive role, cross-cultural research necessitates intercultural dialogue using a meta-language and unconstrained by membership in any particular cultural group. This language may focus on general knowledge or local knowledge. But whatever its focus, it should serve to identify both similarities and differences across cultures. A meta-language requires researchers to establish some common ground, moreover, thereby drawing researchers' orientations outward and encouraging them to examine phenomena beyond the traditional parochial boundaries of their own cultures.

Both the one-way and *n*-way approach provide members of a particular culture with knowledge of the similarities and differences of other cultural groups. The interactive nature of these approaches, furthermore, leads to a better understanding of one's own culture. Just as individuals may see themselves more clearly in relation to others, so too can people develop a better understanding of their unique cultural tradition in relation to that of other cultural groups. In this way, cross-cultural research not only expands the breadth of current knowledge but also increases the depth of current knowledge, providing greater understanding of why culture makes a difference.

Conclusion

By its very nature, cross-cultural research is dialectical. Discussions about the conflict between positivist and interpretative perspectives, etic versus emic orientations, general versus local knowledge, similarities versus differences, inductive versus deductive processes, and quantitative versus qualitative methodologies populate the cross-cultural research literature. In this chapter, we explored these dichotomies. We also discussed the contribution each has to offer cross-cultural research.

Our primary purpose, however, has been to open up the research lens for cross-cultural research, to help people who have been trained in a particular research tradition, methodology, or approach to appreciate the value of research methods and techniques they might not otherwise consider. Consequently, what we do in this chapter is recognize the legitimacy of a variety of different approaches to generating cross-cultural knowledge. We argue that cross-cultural researchers should borrow from both positivist and interpretive perspectives, incorporate etic and emic orientations into their study designs, adopt multimethod approaches to their research, and integrate inductive as well as deductive processes into the design and implementation of their studies in their efforts to identify *both* similarities and differences across cultures. By engaging in the sort of cross-cultural dialogue that we feel the one-way, *n*-way, and other approaches encourage, researchers will be better equipped to contribute to people's understanding of themselves and each other, what they share in common and what they do not.

References

Ashfahl, R. (1984). *Industrial safety and health management.* Upper Saddle River, NJ: Prentice Hall.

Benedict, R. F. (1965). *The chrysanthemum and the sword: Patterns of Japanese culture.* Tokyo: Tuttle.

Berry, J. W. (1969). On cross-cultural comparability. *International Journal of Psychology, 4,* 119–128.

Berry, J. W. (1976). *Human ecology and cognitive style: Comparative studies in cultural and psychological adaptation.* New York: Sage/Halsted.

Berry, J. W. (1980). Introduction to methodology. In H. C. Triandis & J. W. Berry (Eds.), *Handbook of cross-cultural psychology* (Vol. 2). Needham Heights, MA: Allyn & Bacon.

Berry, J. W. (1989). Imposed etics–emics–derived etics: The operationalization of a compelling idea. *International Journal of Psychology, 24,* 721–735.

Berry, J. W., & Dasen, P. R. (Eds.). (1974). *Culture and cognition.* London: Methuen.

Berry, J. W., Poortinga, Y. H., Segall, M. H., & Dasen, P. R. (1992). *Cross-cultural psychology: Research and applications.* New York: Cambridge University Press.

Boas, F. (1911). *The mind of primitive man.* New York: Macmillan.

Bontempo, R. (1993, August). *Blindfolded: Culture is not a useful independent variable.* Paper presented at the meeting of the Academy of Management, Atlanta.

Cattell, R. B. (1988). Multivariate method and theory construction. In J. R. Nesselroade & R. B. Cattell (Eds.), *Handbook of multivariate experimental psychology* (2nd ed., pp. 1–20). New York: Plenum.

Cook, T. D., & Campbell, D. T. (1979). *Quasi-experimentation: Design & analysis issues for field settings.* Boston: Houghton Mifflin.

Cronbach, L. J. (1989). *Intelligence, measurement, theory and social policy.* Champagne: University of Illinois Press.

Dansereau, F., Alutto, J. A., & Yammarino, F. J. (1984). *Theory testing in organizational behavior: The variant approach.* Upper Saddle River, NJ: Prentice Hall.

Davidson, A. R., Jaccard, J. J., Triandis, H. C., Morales, M. L., & Díaz-Guerrero, R. (1976). Cross-cultural model testing: Toward a solution of the etic-emic dilemma. *International Journal of Psychology, 11,* 1–13.

Dawson, J.L.M. (1969). Attitude change and conflict among Australian Aborigines. *Australian Journal of Psychology, 21,* 101–116.

Denzin, N. K., & Lincoln, Y. S. (Eds.). (1994). *Handbook of qualitative research.* Thousand Oaks, CA: Sage.

Deutsch, M. (1973). *The resolution of conflict: Constructive and destructive processes.* New Haven, CT: Yale University Press.

Earley, P. C. (1989). Social loafing and collectivism: A comparison of the United States and the People's Republic of China. *Administration Science Quarterly, 34,* 565–581.

Earley, P. C., & Mosakowski, E. (1993). *A framework for understanding experimental research in an international and intercultural context* (Working paper). Irvine: Graduate School of Management, University of California, Irvine.

Firebaugh, G. (1980). Groups as contexts and frogponds. In K. H. Roberts & L. Burstein (Eds.), *Issues in aggregation* (pp. 43–52). San Francisco: Jossey-Bass.

Frijda, N., & Jahoda, G. (1966). On the scope and methods of cross-cultural research. *International Journal of Psychology, 1,* 109–127.

Geertz, C. (1983). *Local knowledge: Further essays in interpretive anthropology.* New York: Basic Books.

Gerbing, D., & Anderson, J. (1992). Monte Carlo evaluations of goodness of fit indices for structural equation models. *Sociological Methods and Research, 21,* 132–160.

Glazer, B. G., & Strauss, A. L. (1967). *The discovery of grounded theory: Strategies for qualitative research.* Hawthorne, NY: Aldine de Gruyter.

Guba, E. G. (1990). The alternative paradigm dialog. In E. G. Guba (Ed.), *The paradigm dialog* (pp. 17–30). Thousand Oaks, CA: Sage.

Guba, E. G., & Lincoln, Y. S. (1994). Competing paradigms in qualitative research. In N. K. Denzin & Y. S. Lincoln (Eds.), *Handbook of qualitative research* (pp. 105–117). Thousand Oaks, CA: Sage.

Herkovits, M. J. (1948). *Man and his works: The science of cultural anthropology.* New York: Knopf.

Hofstede, G. (1980). *Culture's consequences: International differences in work-related values.* Thousand Oaks, CA: Sage.

Hofstede, G., & Bond, M. H. (1988). The Confucius connection: From cultural roots to economic growth. *Organizational Dynamics, 16,* 5–21.

Hui, C. H., & Triandis, H. C. (1985). Measurement in cross-cultural psychology: A review and comparison of strategies. *Journal of Cross-Cultural Psychology, 16*(2), 131–152.

Hulin, C. L., Drasgow, F., & Parsons, C. K. (1983). *Item response theory: Application to psychological measurement.* Homewood, IL: Business One Irwin.

James, L. R., Mulaik, S. A., & Brett, J. M. (1982). *Causal analysis: Assumptions, models, and data.* Thousand Oaks, CA: Sage.

Janssens, M., Brett, J. M., & Smith, F. (1995). Confirmatory cross-cultural research: Testing the viability of a corporation-wide safety policy. *Academy of Management Journal, 38,* 364–382.

Klein, K. J., Dansereau, F., & Hall, R. J. (1994). Levels issues in theory development, data collection, and analysis. *Academy of Management Review, 19*(2), 195–229.

Kohn, J. L. (1989). Cross-national research as an analytic strategy. In M. L. Kohn (Ed.), *Cross-national research in sociology* (pp. 77–102). Thousand Oaks, CA: Sage.

LeCompte, M. D., & Preissle, J. (1993). *Ethnography and qualitative design in educational research* (2nd ed.). Orlando: Academic Press.

Leung, K. (1987). Some determinants of reaction to procedural models for conflict resolution: A cross-national study. *Journal of Personality and Social Psychology, 53,* 898–908.

Leung, K. (1989). Cross-cultural differences: Individual-level vs. culture-level analysis. *International Journal of Psychology, 24,* 703–719.

Lévi-Strauss, C. (1963). *Structural anthropology.* New York: Basic Books.

Lincoln, J. R., & Zeitz, G. (1980). Organizational properties from aggregate data: Separating individual and structural effects. *American Sociological Review, 45,* 391–408.

Lytle, A. L., Brett, J. M., Barsness, Z. I., Tinsley, C. H., & Janssens, M. (1995). A paradigm for confirmatory cross-cultural research in organizational behavior. In L. L. Cummings & B. M. Staw (Eds.), *Research in organizational behavior* (Vol. 17, pp. 167–214). Greenwich, CT: JAI Press.

Messick, D. M., & van der Geer, J. P. (1981). A reversal paradox. *Psychological Bulletin, 90,* 582–593.

Moore, J. F., Johns, G., & Pinder, C. C. (1980). Toward middle range theory: An overview and perspective. In C. C. Pinder & J. F. Moore (Eds.), *Middle range theory and the study of organizations* (pp. 1–16). Boston: Mijhoff.

Peterson, M. F., et al. (1995). Role conflict, ambiguity and overload by national culture: A 21 nation study. *Academy of Management Journal, 38,* 429–452.

Pike, K. L. (1966). *Language in relation to a unified theory of the structure of human behavior.* The Hague: Mouton.

Poole, M. (1986). *Industrial relations: Theory and practice.* Upper Saddle River, NJ: Prentice Hall.

Popper, K. R. (1959). *The logic of scientific discovery.* New York: Basic Books.

Rohner, R. P. (1984). Toward a conception of culture for cross-cultural psychology. *Journal of cross-cultural psychology, 15*(2), 111–138.

Rousseau, D. M. (1985). Issues of level in organizational research: Multilevel and cross-level perspectives. In L. L. Cummings & B. M. Staw (Eds.), *Research in organizational behavior* (Vol. 7, pp. 1–37). Greenwich, CT: JAI Press.

Schwartz, S. H. (1992). Universals in the content and structure of values: Theoretical advances and empirical tests in 20 countries. In M. P. Zanna (Ed.), *Advances in experimental social psychology* (Vol. 25, pp. 1–65). New York: Academic Press.

Schwartz, S. H. (1994). Beyond individualism and collectivism: New cultural dimensions of values. In U. Kim, H. C. Triandis, C. Kagitcibasi, S.-C. Choi, & G. Yoon (Eds.), *Individualism and collectivism: Theory, method, and applications* (pp. 85–119). Thousand Oaks, CA: Sage.

Seeger, A. (1981). *Nature and society in central Brazil: The Suya Indians of Mato Grosso.* Cambridge, MA: Harvard University Press.

Tinsley, C. H. (1994). *The influence of culture on conflict management.* Unpublished doctoral dissertation, Kellogg Graduate School of Management, Northwestern University, Evanston, IL.

Tinsley, C. H., & Lytle, A. L. (1994). *Is mediation best? An examination of managerial dispute resolution in Mexico* (Dispute Resolution Research Center Working paper). Evanston, IL: Kellogg Graduate School of Management, Northwestern University.

Triandis, H. C. (1972). Major theoretical and methodological issues in cross-cultural psychology. In W. J. Lonner Walters (Ed.), *Readings in cross-cultural psychology* (pp. 26–38).

Triandis, H. C. (1978). Some universals of social behavior. *Personality and Social Psychology Bulletin, 4,* 1–16.

Triandis, H. C. (1992). Cross-cultural research in social psychology. In D. Grandberg & G. Sarup (Eds.), *Social judgments and intergroup relations: Essays in honor of Muzafer Sherif.* New York: Springer-Verlag.

Triandis, H. C., with Vassiliou, V., Vassiliou, G., Tonaka, Y., & Shanmugam, A. V. (Eds.). (1972). *The analysis of subjective culture.* New York: Wiley-Interscience.

Turner, T. (1979). The Ge and Bororo societies as dialectical systems: A general model. In D. Maybury-Lewis (Ed.), *Dialectical systems* (pp. 147–179). Cambridge, MA: Harvard University Press.

Van de Vijver, F.J.R., & Poortinga, Y. H. (1982). Cross-cultural generalization and universality. *Journal of Cross-Cultural Psychology, 13,* 387–408.

Yoshida, K. (1989, Fall). Deming management philosophy: Does it work in the U.S. as well as Japan? *Columbia Journal of World Business,* pp. 10–17.

CHAPTER 5

An Ecocultural Approach to the Study of Cross-Cultural Industrial/ Organizational Psychology

John W. Berry

This chapter is essentially a parallel treatment of some of the issues discussed in Chapter Four by Brett and her colleagues. It focuses on the following basic questions in cross-cultural work generally: how shall we approach the study of similarities and differences? how shall we interpret those that are found? and what can we do with them, both scientifically and practically? These three questions are necessarily intertwined and cannot be considered in isolation from one another. My discussion of these questions flows from the theoretical to the methodological to the practical.

Theoretical Issues

At the present time the field of cross-cultural psychology faces three conceptual issues that frame a three-dimensional space within which we all appear to be working (Berry, 1996).

Within and Across

The first issue is where to look for relationships between human behavior and the cultural context in which it was nourished. Quite early on it was evident that certain problems must be faced when studying human behavior across cultures (Frijda & Jahoda, 1966; Berry, 1969). One such issue lies in the common observation that general psychology is both *culture blind* and *culture bound.* That is, general psychology had ignored culture as a possible influence on human behavior, and further, general psychology had taken little account of theories or data from other than Euro-American cultures. The solution to these problems was twofold: to conceptualize and study culture as an important context for human psychological development (a *cultural* approach) and to engage in comparative studies of the influence of features of various cultures on human development (a *cross-cultural* approach).

The emic-etic distinction was prominent in these early writings. The consensus was that *both* perspectives were necessary to the developing field: local knowledge and interpretations (the *emic* approach) were essential, but more than that perspective was required to relate variations in cultural context to variations in behavior (the *etic* approach). These two approaches became elaborated. First came the notion of *imposed etic* (Berry, 1969), which served as the starting point for comparative research because it was obvious that all psychologists necessarily carry their own culturally based perspectives with them when studying other cultures; these perspectives were initial sources of bias (usually Euro-American), to be confronted and reduced as work progressed in the other culture(s). Second came the *emic* exploration of psychological phenomena and the understanding of them in local cultural terms; this approach provided the important culturally based meanings that were most probably missed in the initial *imposed etic* approach to psychological phenomena in various cultures. Third came the notion of the *derived etic,* which might possibly be discerned following extensive use of *emic* approaches in a number of cultures; it was expected that some similarities in psychological phenomena might be derived by the comparative examination of behavior in various cultures (Berry, 1989).

These three concepts, in turn, gave rise to three goals of cross-cultural psychology (Berry & Dasen, 1974): to *transport and test* our current psychological knowledge and perspectives by using them in other cultures (compare the imposed etic approach), to *explore and discover* new aspects of the phenomenon being studied in local cultural terms (compare the emic approach), and to *integrate* what has been learned from these first two approaches in order to generate a more nearly universal psychology, one that has pan-human validity (compare the derived etic approach). The existence of *universals* in other disciplines (for example, biology, linguistics, sociology, and anthropology) provided some basis for the assumption that we would be able to work our way through to this third goal with some success.

Finally, these three goals have become identified with three theoretical orientations in cross-cultural psychology: *absolutism, relativism,* and *universalism* (Berry, Poortinga, Segall, & Dasen, 1992). The *absolutist* position assumes that human phenomena are basically the same (qualitatively) in all cultures: "honesty" is honesty and "depression" is depression no matter where one observes them. From the absolutist perspective, culture is thought to play little or no role in either the meaning or display of human characteristics. Assessments of such characteristics are made using standard instruments (perhaps with linguistic translation), and interpretations are made easily, without taking alternative culturally based views into account. This orientation resembles the *imposed etic* approach.

In sharp contrast, the *relativist* approach assumes that all human behavior is culturally patterned. It seeks to avoid ethnocentrism by trying to understand people in their own terms. Explanations of human diversity are sought in the cultural context in which people have developed. Assessments typically employ the values and meanings that the cultural group under study gives to the studied phenomenon. Comparisons are judged to be problematic and ethnocentric and are thus virtually never made. This orientation resembles the emic approach.

The third perspective, *universalism,* lies somewhere between the first two positions and assumes that basic human characteristics are common to all members of the species (that is, they constitute a set of psychological givens in all human beings) and that culture influences the development and display of these characteristics (that is, culture plays different variations on these underlying themes). Assessments are based on the presumed underlying process, but measures are developed in culturally meaningful versions. Comparisons are made cautiously, employing a wide variety of methodological principles and safeguards, and interpretations of similarities and differences are attempted that take alternative culturally based meanings into account. This orientation resembles the derived etic approach.

Different approaches can be distinguished according to their orientation to this issue of within or across. Although few today advocate a strictly absolutist or imposed etic view, the relativist emic position has given rise to numerous approaches: *ethnopsychology* (Díaz-Guerrero, 1975), *societal psychology* (Berry, 1983), *indigenous psychology* (Enriquez, 1990; Kim & Berry, 1993), and to some extent *cultural psychology* (Shweder & Sullivan, 1993). And the derived etic view has given rise to a *universalist psychology* (Berry, Poortinga, Segall, & Dasen, 1992). A mutual compatibility between the emic and derived etic positions has been noted by many: for example, Berry, Poortinga, Segall, and Dasen (1992, p. 384) and Berry and Kim (1993) have claimed that indigenous psychologies, though valuable in their own right, serve an equally important function as useful steps on the way to achieving a universal psychology using a *cross-indigenous* approach (Enriquez, 1993).

To summarize this first issue, I believe that from the beginning there has been widespread acceptance by most cross-cultural psychologists of the necessity for *both* the *within* and *across* approaches to understanding relationships between cultural context and human experience and behavior. To rephrase my opening comment on this first issue, it is not possible to be *cross-cultural* without first being *cultural;* but to be only *cultural* (or to pretend that it is possible to be so) seriously undermines the possibility of attaining the kinds of general principles to which all sciences aspire.

Culture Contact

The second issue defining the space in which we seem to be presently working is that studies in the general domain of culture and behavior have had to recognize that cultures are not static but change for a variety of reasons. One reason for this view is that when cultures come into contact with each other, *acculturation* occurs. This process involves changes in both *group* or *collective* phenomena (for example, language, politics, religion, work, schooling, social relationships) and *individual* or *psychological* phenomena (for example, identity, beliefs, values, attitudes, abilities). A good deal of early cross-cultural psychological work took place by comparing peoples who were not in contact with each other; indeed, this was a methodological necessity for comparisons requiring independence of cases. However, some early work also took place in situations of intercultural encounters, often as a result of colonization, migration, or the continuation of culturally distinct communities living side by side in plural societies (see, for example, Taft, 1977).

Over the years many cross-cultural psychologists have adopted the view that *both* these kinds of work are legitimate and important ways of understanding human behavior as it is influenced by the cultural context in which it occurs (Berry, 1985). For example, in my own early work, samples were drawn from relatively traditional cultural settings (minimally influenced by Euro-American culture) and from transitional settings (in a process of change as a result of substantial Euro-American contact). Later my *ecocultural framework* (Berry, 1976) explicitly included two major exogenous variables: *ecology* and *acculturation*. The former identified sources of cultural and psychological variation as a collective and individual adaptation to habitat; the latter sought explanation for psychological variations in the historical and contemporary influences stemming from contact with other cultures. One major difference between these two lines of influence is that psychological phenomena during contact may be more difficult to understand and interpret than those in noncontact situations because in the contact setting there are at least two sources of cultural influences; hence comparative studies may be even more important here in order to tease out the relative cultural contributions to psychological phenomena (Berry, Kim, Minde, & Mok, 1987; Berry, 1997a). A second major difference is that opportunities to create new cultural forms may be greater during the process of acculturation.

This interest in psychological phenomena resulting from culture contact has given rise to the suggestion that there could be an *ethnic psychology* or *psychology of acculturation* concerned primarily with group and psychological acculturation phenomena (for example, Berry, 1985; Berry & Annis, 1988). Another field to emerge has been that of *psychologie interculturelle,* studied primarily by French researchers (for example, Retschitzky, Bossel-Lagos, & Dasen, 1989; Clanet, 1990). As intercultural contacts increase, this area of psychology will almost certainly grow in importance.

Culture as Given or Created

The third and final issue (closely related to the *positivist* versus *interpretive* perspective described in Chapter Four) stems from the virtual revolution in anthropology in that field's conception of *culture*. Earlier conceptions of culture included the views that culture was "out there" to be studied, observed, and described; culture was a shared way of life of a group of socially interacting people; and culture was transmitted from generation to generation by the processes of enculturation and socialization. That is, culture was viewed as a *given* that preceded in time the life of any individual member.

This view of culture has had a major influence on thinking in cross-cultural psychology. The main task was to understand how the established culture *influenced* the psychological development of individuals and *guided* their day-to-day behaviors. However, along with more recent cognitive approaches in many branches of psychology, individuals have come to be viewed not as mere pawns or victims of their cultures but as cognizers, appraisers, and interpreters of them (Boesch, 1991). Thus different individuals experience different aspects of their culture and in different ways. One example of this more cognitive orientation is the framework for analyses of cultural contexts (Berry, 1980) in which more subjective and individual *experiential* and *situational* contexts were distinguished from more objective and shared *ecological* and *cultural* contexts.

A sharp contrast to this perspective on the nature of culture is advanced by those adopting a *social construction* perspective (Misra & Gergen, 1993). From this perspective culture is not something that is given but that is being interpreted and created daily through interactions between individuals and their social surroundings. This view is one espoused by those identifying with *cultural psychology*, which has been defined as "a designation for the comparative study of the way culture and psyche make up each other" (Shweder & Sullivan, 1993, p. 498).

This core idea, however, has been a part of the field for some time. There are numerous examples of interactions between context and person (for example, feedback relationships in the ecocultural framework, discussed in the next section of this chapter) and of reaction to contact (as one form of adaptation associated with acculturation) in the cross-cultural approach (for example, Berry, 1976). The reciprocal relationship between person and culture leading to the modification and creation of new cultural forms as a result of acculturation has been of longstanding interest in the field.

An Ecocultural Perspective

My own approach to dealing with culture-behavior relationships has been to develop and assess an *ecocultural model*. This model can accommodate research both within and across cultures, using cultural groups in relative isolation or in contact, and incorporates behavior-to-culture links as well as the more conventional culture-to-behavior influences.

My current version of the ecocultural model (Berry, 1995; see Figure 5.1), in brief, proposes to account for human psychological diversity (both individual and group similarities and differences) by positing two fundamental sources of influence (ecological and sociopolitical) on human behavior. The model proposes a set of *transmission variables* that link these influences to psychological characteristics (through cultural and biological adaptation at the population level and through enculturation, socialization, genetics, and acculturation at the individual level). Overall the ecocultural model considers human diversity (both cultural and psychological) to be a set of collective and individual adaptations to context. Within this general perspective it views cultures as evolving adaptations to ecological and sociopolitical influences, and views psychological characteristics in a population as adaptive to their cultural context as well as to the broader ecological and sociopolitical influences.

Ecological adaptation is, of course, an idea that is fundamental to explaining biological diversity, and from the days of Darwin it has been widely accepted. It has also had an accepted role in explaining cultural diversity; one anthropological approach (that of *cultural ecology*) views many features of a culture as adaptive to some broad givens in the physical environment (such as natural resources, temperature, rainfall, soil quality, and seasonal variations in these givens; Feldman, 1975). It is essential to note that the term

Figure 5.1. An Ecocultural Model for Cross-Cultural Research.

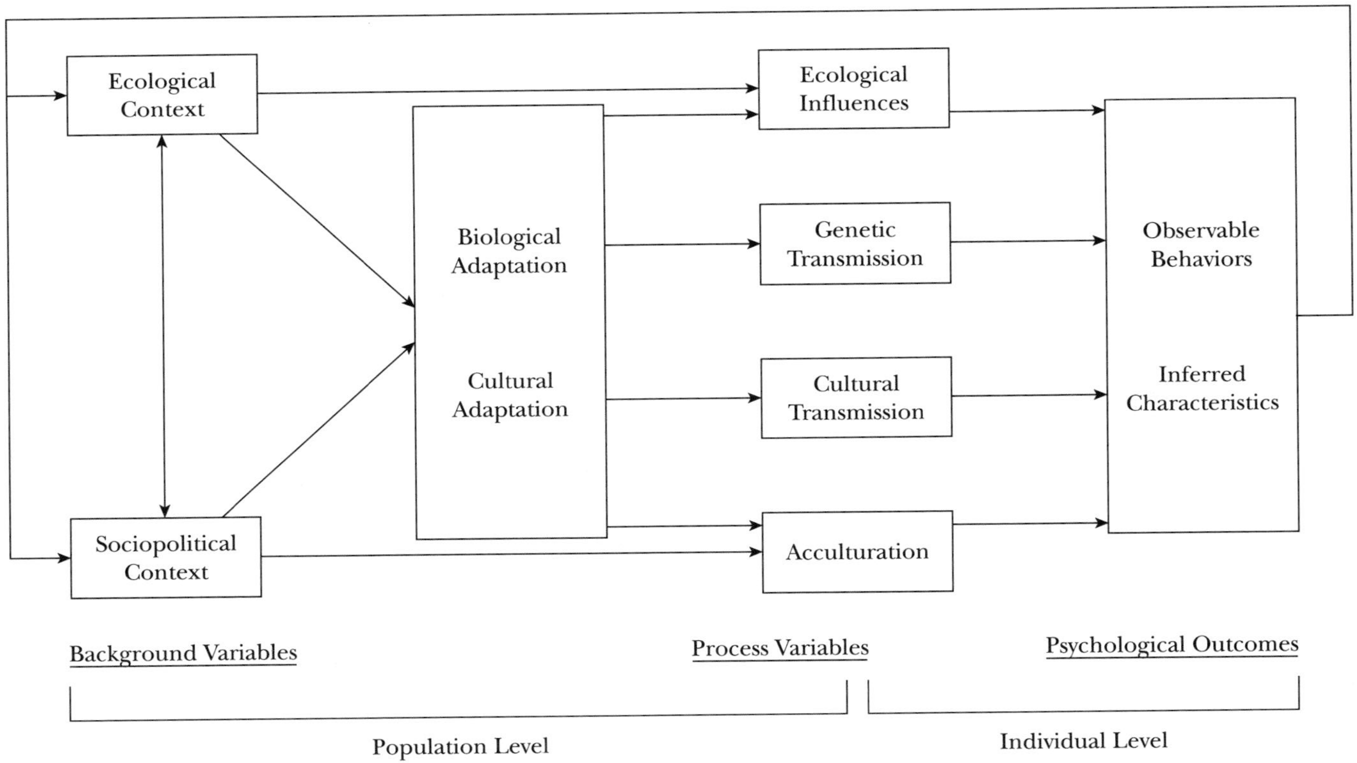

ecological refers to *interactions* between populations and features of the environment and not to a unidirectional determinism from environment to culture.

Many researchers in the burgeoning field of environmental psychology (for example, Brown, Werner, & Altman, 1997) have attempted to specify the links between ecological context and individual human development and behavior. Cross-cultural psychology has tended to view cultures (both a person's own and others the person is in contact with) as differential contexts for development and to view behavior as adaptive to these different contexts.

The ecological approach offers a value-neutral framework for describing and interpreting similarities and differences in human behavior across cultures (Berry, 1994). As adaptive to context, psychological phenomena can be understood "in their own terms" (as Malinowski insisted), and external evaluations can usually be avoided. When two cultural contexts are involved (as in situations of acculturation), psychological phenomena can be viewed as attempts to deal simultaneously with two (sometimes inconsistent, sometimes conflicting) cultural contexts, rather than as pathology in colonized or immigrant cultures (Berry, 1997a).

Methodological Issues: Research Design

With these theoretical and conceptual issues as a foundation, I turn to some methodological issues and propose some standards against which we can judge empirical research (see also Greenfield, 1996; Van de Vijver & Leung, 1996). The starting point is the distinction between the group level and the individual level of analysis outlined earlier. The former provides the context for individual human development and action and is studied primarily through ethnographic methods (including key informant, observational, and archival data sources); the latter is considered to be the psychological outcome for particular individuals (compare the flow from left to right in Figure 5.1). The key methodological issue is how can we demonstrate valid linkages between these two levels?

In the past few decades, most cross-cultural researchers used the "Jack Horner" research strategy, characterized in this rhyme:

Little Jack Horner,
Sat in a corner,
Eating his Christmas Pie,
He stuck in his thumb,
And pulled out a plum,
And said "What a good boy am I" [Horner, 1720].

In other words, this strategy consists of collecting convenient data, deriving some statistical outcomes, and declaring a favored interpretation. The two hallmarks of this strategy are the use of *unguided search* and of *post hoc interpretations.*

In recent years we have moved more and more to a research strategy in which cultural groups that provide *varying contexts* for psychological development and human behavior are *selected* in advance (on the basis of known characteristics based on ethnographic descriptions and national indicators). Individual outcomes are then *predicted,* using some theory that links psychological phenomena to their cultural background. *Independent* conceptualization and measurement of phenomena at the *group* and *individual* levels are required in order to establish nontrivial links between cultural and psychological phenomena (Berry, 1976; Poortinga & Malpass, 1986; Georgas & Berry, 1995).

This alternative to the Jack Horner strategy is portrayed in Figure 5.2. Across the top are various cultural groups, selected because they provide some important variation in the context for psychological development and behavior. Only three are shown here, but in principle many cultures could be included. On the left are the two main levels of phenomena with which we are concerned (group and individual) and some examples of them. The circles represent phenomena of interest to a particular study. The vertical lines indicate some form of influence or cultural transmission that is relevant to the purpose of the study (for example, child socialization, modeling, and schooling). The horizontal lines indicate the cross-cultural comparisons that may be made at the two levels.

In short, within this framework the researcher *identifies* a psychological phenomenon of interest, *selects* cultures that provide varying contexts for the development and display of that phenomenon,

Figure 5.2. A Framework for Designing Cross-Cultural Research Studies.

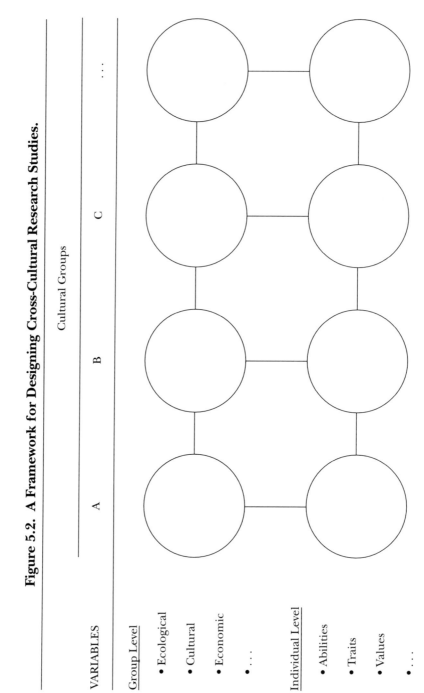

and *predicts* that variations in group-level contexts will have corresponding variations in psychological outcomes. *Independent assessments* of cultural contexts and psychological outcomes are then made.

In order to establish valid linkages between context and outcome, prediction and verification need to be based upon appropriate sampling of the group and individual phenomena of interest. There are four kinds of populations from which samples can be drawn and two types of sampling (*strategic* and *representative*); each sampling strategy has a characteristic goal (to *test* and to *generalize*, respectively) (see Lonner & Berry, 1986; Berry, Poortinga, Segall, & Dasen, 1992, chap. 9).

Considering the two suggested goals first, if the goal of a cross-cultural study is to *test* a particular hypothesized relationship between a cultural and a psychological phenomenon (for example, the relationship between the degree of political stratification in a society and the degree of social conformity among individuals in that society; Berry, 1979), then a few strategically well chosen cultural contexts may suffice. However, if the goal is to produce a *generalization* about such a relationship (perhaps eventually with the status of a universal law), then a representative (and larger) sample would be required.

Considering the four populations from which samples can be drawn, *cultural groups* are typically the largest unit with which we are concerned, although broader *cultural areas* are also of some interest (South Asia or East Europe, for example). In some cases, *societies* or *nation states* are also of interest to a researcher (Georgas & Berry, 1995). The crucial points here are to know and declare the goal of the study (to test or generalize) in advance and to select cultures in order to meet this goal.

Because most groups (whether societies, nations, or cultures) are heterogeneous, the selection of which *communities* within those groups to work with can be crucial. Once again they should be selected according to the goal of the study (to test or generalize) and with all the earlier points in mind (that is, their qualities known in advance).

Individuals may also be a sampling problem in cross-cultural studies. Who can provide a valid test of a prediction and who can be the basis for a generalization may well vary from culture to culture. Variations in a person's status as a *carrier* of the culture are known to exist according to a number of factors (for example, whether the person lives in slavery or freedom and is male or female, schooled or unschooled, oppressed or oppressor). These variations will necessarily render individuals differential exemplars of the hypothesized cultural influence on psychological outcomes.

Finally, *behaviors* sampled should have a known relationship to the population of behaviors nurtured in individuals in the cultures selected (Berry, 1980). Any preselected set of behaviors may or may not match the developed array of behaviors (the *repertoire*) among individuals living in communities that are part of the cultures selected. There needs to be some match between the behaviors the researcher wishes to study and the behaviors actually present in the population.

Combining the views expressed in earlier sections about theoretical and ecocultural approaches with those in this section on research design suggests some comments on the one-way and *n*-way approaches proposed by Brett and her colleagues in Chapter Four. First the one-way approach is rather similar to the imposed etic approach, and the claims made for it do not appear to me to take it beyond the capacity of the combined imposed etic–emic–derived etic approach. The empirical use of this latter approach (see, for example, Berry, 1976, 1979, 1980) started with analyses of ecological and cultural factors as they influenced developing individuals through ecological learning and cultural transmission; these analyses established a basis for predicting psychological outcomes (both similarities and differences) in samples selected in order to test them. The explanatory power of "culture" is thereby enhanced, rather than "deemphasized" as claimed by Brett and her colleagues. Second, the *n*-way approach appears to be a *simultaneous* version of the imposed etic–emic–derived etic approach (which is essentially a sequential and cumulative strategy), but it may also be characterized as a *multiple-emic* approach because it takes a number of local or indigenous meanings into account early in a research project. Overall, though the new distinctions in Chapter Four may elaborate the concrete activities typically carried out using the earlier concepts and practices, I am not convinced that they constitute entirely novel ways of proceeding with cross-cultural research.

Practical Issues: Uses and Applications

There are two main domains within which the fruits of cross-cultural research can be used: scientific and practical. In the scientific domain, cross-cultural information can be used to reflect critically on the *culture-bound* and *culture-blind* discipline within which one works. This is essentially a corrective function, one that both threatens extant knowledge and stimulates new ways in which to view it.

Cross-cultural information can also be used to foster newer and broader generalizations about human behavior and its relationships with cultural factors. I argued earlier that there is no inherent contradiction between the indigenous and universal theoretical perspectives; so too, there is no necessary incompatibility between indigenous and universal data. Indeed, only when we possess a vast array of indigenous knowledge will we have a knowledge base sufficient for us to proclaim universals—or any general statements about human behavior and its relationship to cultural context (Berry & Kim, 1993).

At a practical level, cross-cultural information is of increasing importance both internationally (across cultures, across nation states) and domestically (across cultural and ethnic groups within nation states). Substantially increased effectiveness has resulted from cross-cultural research in such areas as health (Beardsley & Pedersen, 1997), schooling and literacy (Serpell & Hatano, 1997), migration and acculturation (Berry & Sam, 1997), and intergroup relations (Gudykunst & Bond, 1997), as well as in a variety of organizations (Hui & Luk, 1997) and changes to organizations (Berry, 1997b).

A lingering problem, of course, is that much of this scientific work (and thus its potential for application) is largely ignored by those disciplines that would probably benefit most from it. For example, all introductory psychology texts have a chapter called something like "The Biological Bases of Behavior"; none has a counterpart on "The Cultural Bases of Behavior." Some upper-level texts now have a smattering of references, usually very superficial and anecdotal, to studies in "other" cultures. Culture is taken seriously only in those texts and courses that are explicitly devoted to these perspectives, but they are rare and usually marginal to research and practical training in a department or faculty.

In one sense cross-cultural research is not a new approach; many have been researching and practicing cross-culturally for decades. However, it is a new approach in another sense; to most researchers and practitioners, culture is the c-word, mysterious, frightening, and to be avoided. By outlining some of the features of the cross-cultural approach, both theoretical and methodological, I hope that I have made the field more accessible and less threatening to those readers who have until now not accepted the necessity and validity of cross-cultural research.

References

Beardsley, L. I., & Pedersen, P. (1997). Health and counseling. In J. W. Berry, M. H. Segall, & C. Kagitcibasi (Eds.), *Handbook of cross-cultural psychology: Vol. 3. Social behavior and applications* (rev. ed., pp. 413–448). Needham Heights, MA: Allyn & Bacon.

Berry, J. W. (1969). On cross-cultural comparability. *International Journal of Psychology, 4,* 119–128.

Berry, J. W. (1976). *Human ecology and cognitive style: Comparative studies in cultural and psychological adaptation.* New York: Sage/Halsted.

Berry, J. W. (1979). A cultural ecology of social behavior. In L. Berkowitz (Ed.), *Advances in experimental social psychology* (Vol. 12, pp. 177–206). Orlando: Academic Press.

Berry, J. W. (1980). Ecological analyses for cross-cultural psychology. In N. Warren (Ed.), *Studies in cross-cultural psychology* (Vol. 2, pp. 157–189). Orlando: Academic Press.

Berry, J. W. (1983). The sociogenesis of social sciences: An analysis of the cultural relativity of social psychology. In B. Bain (Ed.), *The sociogenesis of language and human conduct* (pp. 449–458). New York: Pergamon.

Berry, J. W. (1985). Cultural psychology and ethnic psychology: A comparative analysis. International Association for Cross-Cultural Psychology presidential address. In I. Reyes-Lagunes & Y. H. Poortinga (Eds.), *From a different perspective* (pp. 3–15). Lisse, The Netherlands: Swets & Zeitlinger.

Berry, J. W. (1989). Imposed etics–emics–derived etics: The operationalization of a compelling idea. *International Journal of Psychology, 24,* 721–735.

Berry, J. W. (1994). An ecological perspective on cultural and ethnic psychology. In E. J. Trickett, R. J. Watts, & D. Birman (Eds.), *Human di-*

versity: Perspectives on people in context (pp. 115–141). San Francisco: Jossey-Bass.

Berry, J. W. (1995). The descendants of a model. *Culture and Psychology, 1,* 311–318.

Berry, J. W. (1996). On the unity of the field. *Interamerican Journal of Psychology, 30,* 89–98.

Berry, J. W. (1997a). Individual and group relations in plural societies. In C. Granrose & S. Oskamp (Eds.), *Cross-cultural work groups* (pp. 17–35). Thousand Oaks, CA: Sage.

Berry, J. W. (1997b). Immigration, acculturation and adaptation. *Applied Psychology: An International Review, 46*(1), 1–30.

Berry, J. W., & Annis, R. C. (Eds.). (1988). *Ethnic psychology.* Lisse, The Netherlands: Swets & Zeitlinger.

Berry, J. W., & Dasen, P. R. (Eds.). (1974). *Culture and cognition.* London: Methuen.

Berry, J. W., & Kim, U. (1993). The way ahead: From indigenous psychologies to a universal psychology. In U. Kim & J. W. Berry (Eds.), *Indigenous psychologies: Research and experience in cultural context* (pp. 277–280). Thousand Oaks, CA: Sage.

Berry, J. W., Kim, U., Minde, T., & Mok, D. (1987). Comparative studies of acculturative stress. *International Migration Review, 21,* 491–511.

Berry, J. W., Poortinga, Y. H., Segall, M. H., & Dasen, P. R. (1992). *Cross-cultural psychology: Research and applications.* New York: Cambridge University Press.

Berry, J. W., & Sam, D. (1997). Acculturation and adaptation. In J. W. Berry, M. H. Segall, & C. Kagitcibasi (Eds.), *Handbook of cross-cultural psychology: Vol. 3. Social behavior and applications* (rev. ed., pp. 291–326). Needham Heights, MA: Allyn & Bacon.

Boesch, E. (1991). *Symbolic action theory and cultural psychology.* New York: Springer.

Brown, B., Werner, C., & Altman, I. (1997). Human ecology and environmental psychology. In J. W. Berry, M. H. Segall, & C. Kagitcibasi (Eds.), *Handbook of cross-cultural psychology: Vol. 3. Social behavior and applications* (rev. ed., pp. 255–290). Needham Heights, MA: Allyn & Bacon.

Clanet, C. (1990). *L'interculturel.* Toulouse: Presses Universitaires du Mirail.

Díaz-Guerrero, R. (1975). *Psychology of the Mexican.* Austin: University of Texas Press.

Enriquez, V. (1990). *Indigenous psychologies.* Quezon City, Philippines: Psychology Research and Training House.

Enriquez, V. (1993). Developing a Filipino psychology. In U. Kim & J. W. Berry (Eds.), *Indigenous psychologies* (pp. 152–169). Thousand Oaks, CA: Sage.

Feldman, D. (1975). The history of the relationship between environment and culture in ethnological thought. *Journal of the History of the Behavioural Sciences, 11,* 67–81.

Frijda, N., & Jahoda, G. (1966). On the scope and methods of cross-cultural research. *International Journal of Psychology, 1,* 109–127.

Georgas, J., & Berry, J. W. (1995). An ecocultural taxonomy for cross-cultural psychology. *Cross-Cultural Research, 29*(2), 121–157.

Greenfield, P. (1996). Culture as process: Empirical methodology for cultural psychology. In J. W. Berry, Y. H. Poortinga, & J. Pandey (Eds.), *Handbook of cross-cultural psychology: Vol. 1. Theory and method* (rev. ed., pp. 301–346). Needham Heights, MA: Allyn & Bacon.

Gudykunst, W. B., & Bond, M. H. (1997). Intergroup relations. In J. W. Berry, M. H. Segall, & C. Kagitcibasi (Eds.), *Handbook of cross-cultural psychology: Vol. 3. Social behavior and applications* (rev. ed., pp. 119–162). Needham Heights, MA: Allyn & Bacon.

Horner, J. (1720). *A strategy for searching and interpreting plums.* London: Mother Goose Press.

Hui, H., & Luk, C. L. (1997). Management and organizational behavior. In J. W. Berry, M. H. Segall, & C. Kagitcibasi (Eds.), *Handbook of cross-cultural psychology: Vol. 3. Social behavior and applications* (rev. ed., pp. 371–412). Needham Heights, MA: Allyn & Bacon.

Kim, U., & Berry, J. W. (Eds.). (1993). *Indigenous psychologies: Research and experience in cultural context.* Thousand Oaks, CA: Sage.

Lonner, W. J., & Berry, J. W. (1986). Sampling and surveying. In W. J. Lonner & J. W. Berry (Eds.), *Field methods in cross-cultural research* (pp. 85–110). Thousand Oaks, CA: Sage.

Misra, G., & Gergen, K. J. (1993). On the place of culture in the psychological sciences. *International Journal of Psychology, 28,* 225–243.

Poortinga, Y. H., & Malpass, R. (1986). Making inferences from cross-cultural data. In W. J. Lonner & J. W. Berry (Eds.), *Field methods in cross-cultural research* (pp. 17–46). Thousand Oaks, CA: Sage.

Retschitzky, J., Bossel-Lagos, M., & Dasen, P. R. (Eds.). (1989). *La recherche interculturelle.* Paris: L'Harmattan.

Serpell, R., & Hatano, G. (1997). Education, schooling and literacy. In J. W. Berry, P. R. Dasen, & T. S. Saraswathi (Eds.). *Handbook of cross-cultural psychology: Vol. 3. Basic processes and human development* (pp. 345–382). Boston: Allyn & Bacon.

Shweder, R. A., & Sullivan, M. A. (1993). Cultural psychology: Who needs it? *Annual Review of Psychology, 44,* 497–523.

Taft, R. (1977). Coping with unfamiliar cultures. In N. Warren (Ed.), *Studies in cross-cultural psychology* (pp. 121–151). Orlando: Academic Press.

Van de Vijver, F.J.R., & Leung, K. (1996). Methods and data analysis of comparative research. In J. W. Berry, Y. H. Poortinga, & J. Pandey (Eds.), *Handbook of cross-cultural psychology: Vol. 1. Theory and method* (rev. ed., pp. 257–300). Needham Heights, MA: Allyn & Bacon.

CHAPTER 6

Operationalizing Cultural Values as the Mean of Individual Values
Problems and Suggestions for Research

Douglas J. Sego
Chun Hui
Kenneth S. Law

Cultural values are the primary constructs used in cross-cultural research. They are commonly conceptualized as the shared values of individual members in a given culture or collective (for example, Guba & Lincoln, 1994; Hofstede, 1980).[1] A well-accepted approach to indexing these shared individual values relies on the use of the mean value of the individuals in the collective (for example, Hofstede & Bond, 1988; Earley, 1989, 1993, 1994; Hui, 1988; Leung, 1987; Triandis, Bontempo, Villareal, Masaaki, & Lucca, 1988). Hofstede (1980) conducted a study in which he sampled IBM workers throughout the world on their personal attitudes. In an ecological factor analysis of these data, Hofstede found four common factors that he presents as collective cultural values. A nation was labeled as having a stronger collective cultural value relative to another when that nation had a higher mean of individual attitudes score than the other. Although Hofstede's analysis was based on an attitude survey and the analysis was at the country level, it is described here for its historical significance. A majority of all cultural values research is somehow related to the work first done by Hofstede.

Recent research in cross-cultural management has continued to use the mean of individual values as a measure of collective cultural values, even as changes in research methodology are being suggested. Brett, Tinsley, Janssens, Barsness, and Lytle in Chapter Four, and Lytle, Brett, Barsness, Tinsley, and Janssens (1995) propose an interesting new research paradigm for studying cross-cultural management issues. They identify *sharedness* as an underlying component of culture and theorize culture as a collage of dimensions. One way researchers can operationalize shared dimensions is by examining the patterns of shared individual values. They further propose that causal structural equation modeling techniques could be adopted in analyzing cross-cultural data. Brett and her colleagues highlight important theoretical as well as methodological issues to be considered when conducting cross-cultural management research. Their paradigm, however, continues to use the mean of individual values as the measure of collective cultural values.

The primary purpose of this chapter is to underscore three potential problems of using the mean of individual values as a measure of collective cultural values. Specifically, we identify and discuss problems with the sharedness of individual values, the changing of values over time, and the possible difference between collective and individual values. Then we examine theoretical issues relating to the relationship between cultural values and individual behaviors. Finally we offer two suggestions for alternative methods of measuring collective cultural value data. Although we will not offer an alternative model of cultural values at this time, we hope that the points we raise will stimulate thinking and debate on these issues.

Sharedness of Individual Values

An important issue related to the sharedness of values appears in the aggregation (for example, Lang, Dollinger, & Marino, 1987; Robinson, 1950). To the extent that there is variance in individual values within groups, researchers must consider aggregation biases when aggregating individual values to collective-level values. Measuring collective cultural values by using the mean of individual values is a classic case of aggregation. The principal problem in aggregation we point out here is that aggregation may lead researchers to draw erroneous conclusions. In other words, collective cultural values based on the aggregation of individual values may lead to erroneous conclusions about the relationship between collective cultural values and individual behavior.

In the extreme case, if there is complete sharedness, then there will be no aggregation bias. In this case the collective cultural value, that is, the group mean, is identical to each individual's values. However, such ideal situations do not exist. When there is variance in individual values, then one must address the relationship between these individual values and the outcome variable of interest. Take the example of a research interest in the relationship between the belief in equality and the intention to hire a member of a minority group. The individual-level relationship between belief in equality and intention to hire may be weak. The aggregate-, or cultural-, level relationship may be strong, however. This can happen when the differences in rank order of the individuals' beliefs in equality are masked in the aggregate. Table 6.1 will help illustrate this point.

The correlation between case 1 of individual equality belief and hiring intention is .90, but it is only .10 between case 2 of individual equality belief and hiring intention. Yet in both cases, the relationship between cultural-level equality belief and hiring intention is identical. The example in Table 6.1 illustrates the fact that one cannot use the mean of individual values to replace actual individual values when one is interested in predicting individual behaviors. We would argue that unless collective cultural values are strongly shared by the members of the collective, individual values are more appropriate predictors of individual behaviors than are collective cultural values. It would, however, be insightful to investigate the effect of collective cultural values on individual behaviors in addition to the effect of individual values. Even in this case, however, we would still argue that the mean of individual values is not an appropriate measure of collective cultural values, because when collective cultural values are estimated by the mean of individual values, both individual values and their mean would be used in the same prediction equation. Values at the individual and collective cultural level would be therefore mixed and contaminated in the measurement process. Researchers should try their best to come up with measures of collective cultural values that are independent of individual values.

Table 6.1. Illustration of Aggregation Bias.

Culture	Individual Equality: Case 1	Individual Equality: Case 2	Cultural Equality	Hiring Intention
A	1	5	3	1
A	2	4	3	2
A	3	3	3	3
A	4	2	3	4
A	5	1	3	5
B	3	7	5	6
B	4	6	5	7
B	5	5	5	8
B	6	4	5	9
B	7	3	5	10

Values Changing Over Time

Another problem of using mean individual values as measures of collective cultural values is that it renders the study of changes in collective cultural values difficult. When defined this way, the collective- and individual-level values will always vary at the same time and in the same direction.

It may be argued that this is a moot issue if one believes that the two levels of values will change in unison. We believe, however, that whether the individuals and the collective change at the same rate, or even in the same direction, is an empirical question. We argue that the two levels of values may change at different rates. Thus defining collective cultural values as mean individual values does not provide a way to assess these changes.

The proposition that the strength with which collective cultural values and individual values are believed changes is evident when examining the value of equality. The collective cultural value of equality in the United States has changed over the last forty years, largely due to the civil rights movement of the 1960s. Segregation was practiced extensively in many areas of the United States in the late 1950s. In these areas, primarily in the South, the idea of "separate but equal" underpinned the system even though that concept lacked substance in reality. Most facilities and services available to blacks were greatly inferior to those available to whites. In time, however, the civil rights movement was successful in drawing attention to these basic inequalities and, in turn, had an impact on the quality of life for many black Americans. Since that time many of the laws that condoned segregation between the majority whites and the minority blacks have been removed and laws been written and institutions established that reflect the collective's increased belief in equality.

It can be said that over this same period of time individuals in the United States have also changed their beliefs in the value of equality. However, there are also signs, such as an increase of racial hate speech and of the feeling that the government's social safety net should be reduced, that suggest individuals have not changed as much as the collective has. It is possible that it will take a generation or two for individual values, on average, to reflect the values of the collective. Thus changes in collective cultural values may not be mirrored by the mean of individual values at any one given point of time. Measuring collective cultural values by the mean of individual values does not provide a ready answer to the question of how such differential changes in collective cultural values and individual values can be studied.

When Collective and Individual Values Are Not Equal

We believe the largest limitation in indexing collective cultural values by the mean of individual values is that individual and collective cultural values may not always be equal. If individual values are not identical to collective cultural values, then taking the mean of individual values will not present an accurate representation of cultural values and doing so becomes methodologically difficult to justify and theoretically questionable. We argue that there are times when the mean of individual values does not represent the collective cultural value. This inequality can occur when a value has different strengths at different levels.

An example will illustrate this idea. In Putnam's rendering of civic community (1993), equality among members of a society or collective is a central concept. In the Republic of South Africa during the period of Apartheid, the belief by the minority white South Africans was that the collective culture value of equality was that inequality in levels of equality was acceptable. One manifestation of this was that even though minority white South Africans were granted the right of one person one vote, majority black South Africans were not afforded the same right. During this period South African blacks often held demonstrations demanding their civil rights, and one major civil rights issue was the demand for a policy of one person one vote that applied equally to all South Africans. Because black South Africans were the numerical majority, the mean individual value of equality in South African would presumably have favored full equality.

It can be seen from this example that the mean of the individual value of equality did not represent the collective's belief. Indexing collective values as the mean of individual values would lead to the finding that the collective value of equality was close to that of the majority black South Africans' value of equality. During the period of Apartheid, however, South Africa could hardly be labeled as a collective culture that upheld the ideas of equality between all members of the collective. In this case the mean of individual values did not equal the collective's values as manifested in the national policies and behaviors.

Suggestions

We have highlighted some of the problems with defining collective cultural values as the mean of individual values. We suggest that instead of assuming that collective cultural values can be aggregated from the mean of individual values, researchers should develop theories that describe the relationship between the two levels of values, measure each value at its level of conceptualization, and then examine how both cultural and individual values affect individual behavior. We suggest that theorizing the relationship between collective and individual values and measuring them independently is a possible way to solve the problems we have raised.

The importance of developing theories of this relationship is that this step generates insights into how individual and cultural values can be related. Such theorizing can give a fuller explanation of how individuals interact to affect collective cultural values and, in turn, of how collective cultural values affect individual behavior. When collective cultural values are not equal to mean individual values, theorizing becomes extremely important for understanding the relationship between individual values and collective cultural values and how they affect individual outcomes.

Conceptualization of Collective Cultural Values

Although culture has been defined in many and varied ways (compare Kroeber & Kluckhohn, 1952), researchers have rarely argued against the notion that sharedness is a key property of culture. In other words, cultural values at the collective level are those shared among the members of the collective. We are not debating whether cultural values are shared. Indeed we agree with that notion. But we do suggest that thinking of sharedness in terms of mean individual values has limitations. It is perhaps best to consider Jahoda's advice that "when dealing with such a comprehensive construct as culture, . . . one has to be very cautious in claiming that one formulation rather than another is the 'correct one'" (1984, p. 141). We suggest that considering alternative formulations or conceptualization of cultural values may greatly enrich researchers' understandings of those values.

A clear conceptualization of collective cultural values is required to evaluate the appropriateness of the method used to operationalize those values. Simply stating that a value shared by members of the collective is a collective cultural value does not help researchers develop testable hypotheses about how collective cultural values should influence behavior. One purpose of developing theories of collective cultural values is to then be able to place individual behavior within a context. For example, individual behavior within a highly egalitarian collective culture takes place in a very different context from individual behavior within a nonegalitarian collective culture, and certain individual behaviors that would be seen as undesirable in the former case would not be seen as undesirable in the latter case.

One way to conceptualize context in cultural study is in terms of level of analysis. Indeed, we suggest that to account adequately for how collective cultural values and individual values are related and in turn relate to individual-level outcome variables, the level-of-analysis issue must be carefully addressed. It is beyond the scope of the present chapter to describe that issue in full. We shall, however, provide a preliminary discussion in hopes that future research will generate more understanding. Inferring collective cultural values from the mean of individual values requires a large inferential leap because there are various levels of analysis between individuals and their culture. Organizations make up one such level. Individuals work in organizations, and organizations intervene for the collective interests of individual members. Therefore the impact of collective culture values on the individuals may be indirect, via organizations. Dansereau and Alutto (1990) examined four levels of analysis from individuals to organizations: the person, dyad, group, and collective (for example, a department or organization). Each of these levels may have level-specific as well as cross-level issues. When one generalizes from individuals to cultures, there are these levels that come between individuals and cultures yet to be accounted for. To the extent that we lack a clear understanding of how these different levels may affect the relationship between the constructs, generalizing individual to cultural effects to explain individual-level outcome variables is likely to result in misleading conclusions.

The deduction of how collective cultural values affect individual-level outcome variables is also subject to the level-of-analysis issue. Members of a culture do not behave in social vacuums. As discussed earlier social contexts, such as perceptions and practices based on equality, affect the cultural-level variables that will have the most salient effects on individual-level variables. Thus researchers should take into account the intermediate linkages between levels of analysis when inferring effects of a cultural-level variable on an individual-level variable.

Alternative Measures of Cultural Values

Before describing alternative measures of cultural values we need to clarify one point. We make the assumption that there are situations when the mean of individual values will not accurately represent the collective cultural values and that these differences can be significant. Consequently, our alternatives are based on different measurement methods and not on attempts to account for error variance in the mean of individual differences.

We offer two alternative methods for measuring collective cultural values. First, researchers can assess collective cultural values by measuring individuals' perceptions of these values. As we have discussed there may be incongruence between cultural and individual values. Furthermore, for the collective cultural value as measured by the mean of individual values to have an impact on behavior, individuals would have to have knowledge of what the mean of individual values is. How would they know it? In fact, what they will respond to is not their knowledge of the mean of individual values but their perception of the collective cultural values. It does not matter whether they are exactly correct or widely in error; their behavior is influenced by their perception of the value.

Work by Rousseau (1985) and James (1982) has addressed this issue as it relates to examining aggregation bias when averaging individual-level perceptions of organizational culture. This work shows increased variance in individuals' perceptions of culture can bias the estimate of culture when the scores are averaged. At first, it appears that the arguments used by Rousseau and James could be applied to the problem of creating criteria for determining the amount of sharedness in individual values that would be an appropriate measure of collective cultural values. We, however, caution cross-cultural researchers that there may be important theoretical differences between averaging individual *perceptions* of a collective cultural value and averaging individual *values* in order to represent a collective cultural value. Researchers studying cross-cultural issues have lacked a rigorous discussion of this issue.

We concede that we are still aggregating individual perceptions and inferring the collective cultural values from these data. There is precedence, however, for this method in the organizational behavior research literature on organizational cultural and climate (Schneider, 1972, 1975). In addition the methodological arguments about aggregating individual-level data and creating higher-level constructs have been openly discussed (James, 1982; Roberts, Hulin, & Rousseau, 1978). One critical point is that the units on which the theory is based should dictate the units selected for observations (Roberts, Hulin, & Rousseau, 1978). In cross-cultural research the unit of theory is the collective, but the unit of observation is the individual. This is one of many issues raised in this literature.

The second way to assess collective cultural values is to measure them at the collective instead of the individual level. In Chapter Four, Brett and her colleagues suggest that anthropological area files, anthropologists' "thick descriptions," political and historical archival sources, and the like may yield independent indicators for cultural values. Brett and her colleagues highlight the importance of obtaining these types of indicators. Specifically, they suggest that the purpose of collecting these data is to confirm that cultural values indexed by mean individual values yield the same pattern of results as those indexed by independent indicators. We agree and add that obtaining indicators of cultural values that are independent of individual values will enhance researchers' understanding of how these values are related.

Conclusion

How to measure collective cultural values is obviously a complex issue and one we are only beginning to address. It is not our intent to provide all the answers to this issue in this short chapter. Instead, our intent is to highlight the problems in the commonly practiced approach of indexing collective cultural values by the mean of individual values. Cross-cultural research has benefited greatly from previous studies on collective cultural values. Now that collective cultural values have been identified, we believe it will be fruitful to construct collective-level measures for these values and validate such values at the collective level. With sound theory and empirical research on the relationship between multilevel constructs, we can move even further in this area of research.

Theorizing about how individual and cultural values are related is by no means an easy task and could be a rich area of research. We believe future research on collective cultural values warrants more effort in the direction of theorizing about and measuring collective cultural values in ways other than as the mean of individual values.

Note

1. Discussions of culture at multiple levels can become very confusing. The larger collective is often referred to as the *culture,* and individual values are often referred to as *individual cultural values.* To avoid some of this confusion, we will refer to the higher-level aggregation of cultural values as the *collective cultural value.*

References

Dansereau, F., & Alutto, J. A. (1990). Level-of-analysis issues in climate and culture research. In B. Schneider (Ed.), *Organizational climate and culture* (pp. 193–236). San Francisco: Jossey-Bass.

Earley, P. C. (1989). Social loafing and collectivism: A comparison of the United States and the People's Republic of China. *Administrative Science Quarterly, 34,* 565–581.

Earley, P. C. (1993). East meets West meets Middle East: Further explorations of collectivistic and individualistic work groups. *Academy of Management Journal, 36,* 319–348.

Earley, P. C. (1994). Self or group? Cultural effects of training on self-efficacy and performance. *Administrative Science Quarterly, 39,* 89–117.

Guba, E. G., & Lincoln, Y. S. (1994). Competing paradigms in qualitative research. In N. K. Kenzin & Y. S. Lincoln (Eds.), *Handbook of qualitative research* (pp. 105–117). Thousand Oaks, CA: Sage.

Hofstede, G. (1980). *Culture's consequences: International differences in work-related values.* Thousand Oaks, CA: Sage.

Hofstede, G., & Bond, M. H. (1988). The Confucius connection: From cultural roots to economic growth. *Organizational Dynamics, 16,* 4–21.

Hui, C. H. (1988). Measurement of individualism-collectivism. *Journal of Research in Personality, 22,* 17–36.

Jahoda, G. (1984). Do we need a concept of culture? *Journal of Cross-Cultural Psychology, 15,* 139–151.

James, L. R. (1982). Aggregation bias in estimates of perceptual agreement. *Journal of Applied Psychology, 67,* 219–229.

Kroeber, A. L., & Kluckhohn, C. (1952). *Culture: A critical review of concepts and definitions.* Cambridge, MA: Harvard University Peabody Museum of American Archeology and Ethnology.

Lang, J. R., Dollinger, M. J., & Marino, K. E. (1987). Aggregation bias in strategic decision-making research. *Journal of Management, 13,* 689–702.

Leung, K. (1987). Some determinants of reaction to procedural models for conflict resolution: A cross-national study. *Journal of Personality and Social Psychology, 53,* 898–908.

Lytle, A. L., Brett, J. M., Barsness, Z. I., Tinsley, C. H., & Janssens, M. (1995). A paradigm for confirmatory cross-cultural research in organizational behavior. In L. L. Cummings & B. M. Staw (Eds.), *Research in organizational behavior* (Vol. 17, pp. 167–214). Greenwich, CT: JAI Press.

Putnam, R. D. (1993). *Making democracy work.* Princeton, NJ: Princeton University Press.

Roberts, K. H., Hulin, C. L., & Rousseau, D. M. (1978). *Developing an interdisciplinary science of organizations.* San Francisco: Jossey-Bass.

Robinson, W. S. (1950). Ecological correlations and the behavior of individuals. *American Sociological Review, 15,* 351–357.

Rousseau, D. M. (1985). Issues of level in organizational research: Multilevel and cross-level perspectives. In L. L. Cummings & B. M. Staw (Eds.), *Research in organizational behavior* (Vol. 7, pp. 1–37). Greenwich, CT: JAI Press.

Schneider, B. (1972). Organizational climate: Individual preferences and organizational realities. *Journal of Applied Psychology, 56,* 211–217.

Schneider, B. (1975). Organizational climates: An essay. *Personnel Psychology, 28,* 447–465.

Triandis, H. C., Bontempo, R., Villareal, M. J., Masaaki, A., & Lucca, N. (1988). Individualism and collectivism: Cross-cultural perspective on self-ingroup relationships. *Journal of Personality and Social Psychology, 54,* 328–338.

CHAPTER 7

Cross-Cultural Research Alliances in Organizational Research

Cross-Cultural Partnership-Making in Action

George B. Graen
Chun Hui
Mitsuru Wakabayashi
Zhong-Ming Wang

He was in Japan with his wife and two young sons. They were going to spend the next 12 months in this strange land as guests of his Japanese mentor and his mentor's research team at Keio University.

His family followed him without question as they had followed him to his first professorship several years earlier from the only home they had ever known in Minneapolis to the strange place called Champaign. They had adapted to their new home in Illinois, but this was different. Tokyo was not Champaign. He could not speak the language or even pronounce the words in the tourist guides. Signs and written materials were useless to him. He was a functionally illiterate with a Ph.D. in Japan. Worse than this, his

Note: We would like to thank Rajan Kamath, Yong Kim, Karin Klenke, Ken Law, Amitabh Raturi, Mary Uhl-Bien, and Nenggun Wu, our cross-cultural partners on the latest development of the model, and Harry Triandis for reading a version of this chapter.

thinking habits did not work. Time after time, his American-based assumptions led to faulty conclusions. He simply could not understand how things worked. Perhaps the most embarrassing discovery was that his doing habits didn't work. He was accustomed to doing many things without thinking—simply plugging in the operating schema and letting it run off while thinking about something else.

Fortunately, he was saved from a year as an "outsider" in Japan by his Japanese mentor who brought him "inside" his research team. He was tutored intensively by his new colleagues as they taught this "creative monkey" (as they called him) the magic of developing "partnership" relationships [Graen & Wakabayashi, 1994, p. 434].

This chapter is about building cross-cultural research. We suggest that the building of the alliances required is best understood as a partnership-making process. Cross-cultural research requires knowledge of all the cultures being studied. Much like the hero in the previous story, however, most researchers begin with only minimal or stereotypic knowledge of foreign cultures. Building cross-cultural research alliances can help researchers understand the foreign cultures under study, identify meaningful research topics, and conduct sound cross-cultural research. In this chapter we shall distinguish some of the key elements in cross-cultural research and examine how the process of partnership building facilitates the identification of these elements.

Emics, Etics, and Functional Equivalence

Cross-cultural research bridges cultures and makes comparison across these cultures. But exactly what are cross-cultural researchers bridging and comparing? Apparently, cross-cultural research studies different cultures. However, not only are there a great number of cultures on this planet but there is also no clear consensus on what a *culture* is. For example, back in the 1950s, researchers had identified over 160 meanings of culture (Kroeber & Kluckhohn, 1952). If culture does not mean the same thing to everyone, then comparing things that are within and across cultures becomes increasingly difficult. The multiplicity of cultures and of conceptualizations of cultures is but one of numerous illustrations of the complexity of cross-cultural comparison (Hofstede, 1980). Satori

(1994) suggests that the key to making cross-cultural (or cross-national) comparison is to focus on the issue of *comparability*. The identification of what is comparable and what is not can be examined in terms of emics and etics (Berry, 1990). *Emics* are things that are unique to a culture, whereas *etics* are things that are universal to all cultures. Emics are by definition not comparable across cultures. One task of cross-cultural researchers, hence, is to identify emics and etics (Berry, 1990).

We can visualize emics and etics with the aid of Figure 7.1. Each set represents a culture (in this particular example, China and the United States). For these two cultures, there are three types of cultural properties and characteristics—A: those unique to the U.S. culture (emics of the U.S. culture); B: those unique to the Chinese culture (emics of the Chinese culture); and C: those common across the two cultures (etics of the Chinese and the U.S. culture). Cross-cultural comparisons will be meaningful only when we are dealing with the intersection—the etics (Headland, Pike, & Harris, 1990).

What then would qualify as these etics? What qualifies properties and characteristics as comparable across cultures? The answer to this question lies in the identification of the functionally equivalent constructs across cultures (Dogan & Pelassy, 1984). Functional equivalence means that the construct under study has the same function in different cultural structures. Here, it is important to understand that different structures in different cultures may perform the same functions, and that the same structures in dif-

Figure 7.1. Three Types of Cultural Properties and Characteristics for Two Cultures.

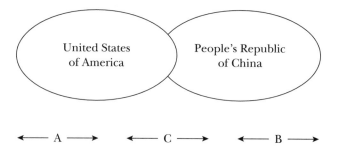

ferent cultures may perform different functions. Similarly, apparently identical constructs may mean different things in different cultures, and seemingly different constructs may mean the same thing in different cultures. Comparing seemingly identical structures with different functions and comparing constructs with different meanings across cultures can lead to very few meaningful and valid conclusions. In cross-cultural comparison, the equivalence of constructs is defined by whether they have the same function across cultures.

Identifying functionally equivalent constructs across cultures is more easily said than done. For example, suppose researchers would like to compare the construct of organizational commitment (Porter, Steers, Mowday, & Boulina, 1974) across China and the United States. Ensuring the functional equivalence of this construct necessitates examination of construct functions in both cultures. To conduct such an examination effectively, researchers must have a conceptualization and operationalization of the construct in both cultures. To attain functional equivalence as a construct, organizational commitment must perform equivalent functions in both cultures as evidenced by similar nomological networks of relationships both within and between constructs. Oftentimes cross-cultural researchers rely on translation and back-translation of the measures and factor analysis to ensure functional equivalence. However, as Hofstede (1980, p. 25) aptly stated, this is a mistake in this particular case because, "the questions are only about issues raised by the U.S. designers of the instrument which proved relevant to their test population and for which American language has words." Even worse than this is that an instrument may be meaningful only to Americans and to no one else. In this case researchers are indeed comparing the incomparable. Clearly, factor analysis in this case may produce similar but meaningless factor structures.

How, then, can we distinguish the emics from the etics, establish functional equivalence of the constructs, and conduct meaningful comparative management research across cultures? The basic requirement here is one person from China and one from the United States (that is one from each culture of interest) who together have a deep and comprehensive understanding of the cultures under study and who form a panel of experts that does the rigorous cross-cultural construct validation to establish functional equivalence. We argue that this partnership-making process will enable researchers to become *transculturals:* a special breed of people who are the most qualified for comparative management research across cultures. Forming cross-cultural research alliances entails identifying and forming partnership relationships with potential transculturals. Thus the first step in forming cross-cultural research alliances is to understand who these potential transculturals are.

Transculturals

Transculturals are people who grow beyond their own cultural socialization so that they can understand different cultures with minimal biases and make valid cross-cultural judgments. Cultures affect their members' thinking as well as their behaviors (see, for example, Hofstede, 1980, 1993; Kroeber & Kluckhohn, 1952). Cultures transfer values from one generation to the next and prescribe behavioral norms to their members. The implication is that a person raised in a particular culture perceives his or her world according to that culture's socialization. Conducting effective cross-cultural research necessitates the ability to go beyond one's particular cultural socialization (Mead, 1928). Language carries two different meanings—denotative and connotative. Denotative meaning can be learned from a book for it is dictionary meaning. In contrast, connotative meaning can only be learned through a socialization process—when one is either a child or an adult—for it is a culturally defined feeling or tone. The term "dog meat" offers an example of different connotative meanings: for Chinese the term means a gourmet delight; for Americans it means devouring a pet.

The importance of going beyond one's initial cultural socialization in order to undergo socialization in another culture can be examined in terms of *ethnocentrism*. Drever (1952) described those who regard their own culture as superior to the other cultures as ethnocentric. That definition can be expanded to describe those who judge another culture purely by the values of their own culture. The problem with ethnocentrism is that the research resulting from it cannot produce much useful information about other cultures and even less useful comparative analysis between cultures.

For example, when one can see only through a green filter but attempts to make judgment on the color red, making a valid judgment becomes a matter of chance. To compare the color green to the color red, one must first perceive the two colors without bias, then identify bases for comparisons. Ethnocentrism impedes comparison because it does not allow people to go beyond what they see though their cultural filters. All too often, people are either tempted to make ethnocentric judgments or to be biased by their own cultural values without even knowing it. For example, simply translating and back-translating a questionnaire designed and pretested in the United States and then administering it to other countries is an act of ethnocentrism (Brislin, 1970). Such research cannot add systematically to our understanding of comparative management issues across cultures (Triandis & Berry, 1980). Arrogant ethnocentrism in cross-cultural research is a waste of time and worse.

Transculturals are the people who have learned to perceive both green and red. Furthermore, transculturals can go beyond simple perception of green and red to identify bases for comparisons. It can be argued that no one can truly go beyond the socialization of his or her own culture. We suggest, however, that transculturals are better equipped to make cross-cultural comparisons than nontransculturals, because transculturals possess the affective, behavioral, and cognitive means to make cross-cultural comparisons. We argue that all three of these means are important in making valid and comprehensive cross-cultural comparisons. Nontransculturals may not possess all these means. As shown in Figure 7.2, five cumulative characteristics distinguish transculturals from nontransculturals. The transculturals are cultural adventurers, cultural sensitizers, discrepant cultural insiders, comparative culture judges, and socializing synthesizers.

Cultural Adventurer

To avoid the trap of ethnocentrism and become a transcultural, the first step is to develop an adventurer's mentality toward cultures other than one's own. Before a person can learn about another culture, he or she must first take an interest in that culture. Thus transculturals are *cultural adventurers* with an interest in other

Figure 7.2. Progressive Characteristics Distinguishing Transculturals from Nontransculturals.

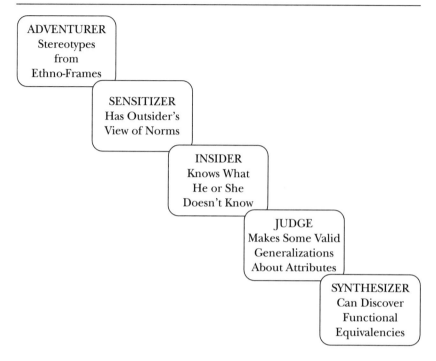

cultures and in learning about these cultures. Cultural adventurers can be likened to interested tourists. Tourists visit other cultures as leisure. They sightsee and eat at some local restaurants. However, tourists rarely get to see or experience life the way the locals live it. Consequently, they rarely possess valid knowledge of the members of the other cultures. In the absence of such knowledge, tourists oftentimes have to rely on global categorizations of members of other cultures. Thus, when trying to understand or label members of other cultures, tourists usually settle for stereotypes from their own ethnocentric frames. Similarly, cultural adventurers who have no further transcultural characteristics are limited by ethnocentric frames. In the absence of an in-depth personal experience of the other culture, cultural adventurers are limited by stereotypes.

Even though being a cultural adventurer is not enough in itself, it is still important for a researcher to start by being a cultural adventurer. The example used by Hofstede and cited earlier also clarifies the importance of being a cultural adventurer when conducting cross-cultural research. Suppose a researcher's way of conducting cross-cultural research is to translate a scale developed in the United States into a foreign language say, Chinese, and then back-translate this scale into English. The researcher administers the scale to a U.S. sample and then asks a colleague to administer it to a Chinese sample. With both an American and a Chinese sample, the researcher can now claim that the study is cross-cultural. But this research does not pass the first test of comparative research. This researcher has not even taken a real interest in the Chinese culture and people when conducting this piece of research. Without that real interest, this researcher has little chance of gathering information that is meaningful and is comparable between the Chinese and the American cultures. He or she will not find out from the back-translation whether the Chinese version of the scale is measuring a similar construct in Chinese—or even makes sense to Chinese people. To identify meaningful and comparable constructs across cultures, a researcher must at least take an interest in both cultures and understand the way of living and thinking in both cultures. Only on this basis can a researcher identify the comparable characteristics across cultures. Without the mentality of the cultural adventurer, there is little hope for fruitful cross-cultural research (Hofstede & Bond, 1988).

Cultural Sensitizer

Transculturals are also cultural sensitizers. *Cultural sensitizers* can attune their behaviors to a culture other than their own—that is, they can learn about and conform to the behavioral norms of another culture. If a person shows no knowledge of the behavioral norms of one or more other cultures, then this person's contribution to cross-cultural research will be limited. For instance, much cross-cultural comparison uses behavioral operationalization of constructs. Without researcher knowledge of behavioral norms, such operationalization will not be possible. Furthermore, if a researcher refuses to observe the behavioral norms of another culture because he or she thinks that the behavioral norms are not enforced in his or her own culture, that researcher is probably ethnocentric. Attuning behavior to the norms of the culture under study is an indication that a researcher at least accepts that there are different ways of behaving appropriately.

An example will clarify the importance to cross-cultural research of being a cultural sensitizer. Suppose the U.S. researcher described earlier who translates and back-translates scales also acquires the quality of an avid reader of literature on the Chinese culture. This researcher now has a better chance of identifying constructs that are meaningful and comparable to both the U.S. and Chinese cultures. However, without a true understanding of how people in other cultures behave, he or she may still do research that lacks validity and is safeguarded from ethnocentrism.

Discrepant Culture Insider

Taking an interest in cultures other than one's own and being sensitized to the social and behavioral norms of those cultures is necessary but not sufficient for transculturals. The shortcoming of the cultural sensitizers is that oftentimes their understanding of the norms of other cultures is restricted to that of the outsider. Although the cultural sensitizer will good naturedly attempt to understand members of other cultures in their own right and to read their behavioral and social norms, he or she lacks the critical means to go truly beyond his or her cultural biases: to become a *discrepant culture insider.*

To fully understand the values, practices, and norms of a given culture, a researcher must be a discrepant culture insider. Discrepant culture insiders have been insiders in at least two cultures that are vastly different from each other. Dogan and Pelassy (1984), when discussing how to compare nations, stated that "denied the possibility of looking beyond his or her own world, the analyst is virtually blind" (p. 5) and that "only with exposure to other cultures does one become conscious of possible occlusion" (p. 9). The best means of forming a basis for understanding one's own cultural biases is to be exposed to a completely different culture. The more discrepant the two cultures are in terms of values, behaviors, and norms, the more the transcultural will be able to understand the other culture without the bias of his or her own cultures. However, exposure to discrepant cultures means more than being just a tourist. There are many U.S. tourists to discrepant cultures such as the Japanese culture and the Chinese culture, but few of these U.S. tourists really understand why the Japanese and Chinese behave the way they do. Being an insider of a discrepant culture entails taking a true interest in the discrepant culture, being sensitized to its values and norms, and having "locals" to mentor one through the socialization process of this discrepant culture.

The importance of having the quality of a discrepant culture insider can again be demonstrated by our hypothetical cross-cultural researcher. Suppose we add now to this researcher the quality of a genuine interest in the Chinese culture. Taking our advice of becoming a cultural adventurer and a cultural sensitizer, this researcher now tours around China to observe how the Chinese people live and behave. The researcher goes to Beijing and visits the Forbidden Palace and the Great Wall, dines at local restaurants, and stays in local hotels. He or she eats with chopsticks, bows to people she or he meets, and rarely openly criticizes Chinese acquaintances. But can this researcher earn credibility as one with a true understanding of the Chinese culture? Not too many Americans will think that a Chinese can become an expert on U.S. culture by touring the Statue of Liberty, the Grand Canyon, and Hollywood and by eating with knives and forks, shaking hands with acquaintances, and being open and direct in criticism. Without the benefit of a Chinese mentor to socialize this researcher into the Chinese culture, he or she may remain an outsider. Consequently, this researcher's understanding of the Chinese culture will remain superficial and the value of his or her cross-cultural research limited. A discrepant culture insider, in contrast, has been socialized into the discrepant culture and now possesses knowledge of both cultures that is not superficial. As an insider, the researcher now has knowledge critical to the conceptualization of a meaningful and comparable research issue across two discrepant cultures.

Comparative Culture Judge

A researcher who is a cultural adventurer, cultural sensitizer, and discrepant culture insider possesses the behavioral and affective means and the knowledge base to conduct cross-cultural research. However, to become a transcultural, this researcher must also possess the cognitive means to make cross-cultural comparisons. Conducting comparative research requires, first, the ability to conceptualize differences and similarities between cultures. A discrepant culture insider has the affective and behavioral prerequisites and the knowledge base to perceive similarities and differences between cultures. Second, however, in order to make valid and meaningful comparisons, this insider also needs to conceptualize the similarities and differences among the variety of phenomena present in different cultures. As Dogan and Pelassy (1984) have stated: "comparability is not an inherent characteristic of every given series of objects. It is rather a quality which is attributed by the point of view of the observer" (p. 133). Because different people attribute different meanings to different things, much of a comparison's validity depends on the ability of the comparative culture judge to abstract relevant and useful similarities and differences for comparison.

One may well argue that the task of abstracting similarities and differences in a multitude of phenomena is not restricted to a comparative culture judge. Indeed this task is common to all scientific endeavors. However, we suggest that it is more important and difficult for the comparative culture judge than for those embarking on intracultural studies. First, as discussed above, recognizing similarities and differences across cultural boundaries requires perceivers able to perceive and judge beyond their own cultural background. Second, making judgments across cultures necessitates knowledge of all the cultures under study. Such knowledge cannot be trivial or superficial. Instead it must be insider knowledge. The stringent requirement for a comparative culture judge can hardly be relaxed if researchers are to embark upon fruitful comparisons between nations.

Socializing Synthesizer

The importance of the intercultural research alliances that are the focus of this chapter is that without them a researcher cannot be a *socializing synthesizer.* Socializing synthesizers are people who have been socialized into the cultures of interest *and* who can synthesize both the home culture and the second culture. By *synthesizing* we mean two things: first, possessing the ability to identify the emics and etics between cultures and to develop valid measures of constructs with functional equivalence (Dogan & Pelassy, 1984) and, second, possessing the ability to create or facilitate the development of a *third culture* within the alliance itself, a culture that can be understood by residents in both the home culture and its cross-cultural partner.

The distinction between socializing synthesizers and comparative culture judges is that the former can make cross-cultural comparisons at the system level whereas the latter can make such comparisons only at the attribute level. As discussed earlier, comparative culture judges can abstract similarities and differences between cultures. However, to effectively compare cultures, the researcher must be able to conceive such similarities and differences within a framework or a system. As Dogan and Pelassy (1984, p. 27) stated: "in order for an object to be accessible to analysis, it is not enough to perceive it. It is also necessary that a theory be ready to accommodate it." After abstracting the similarities and differences across cultures, the socializing synthesizer will "find the level of generalization which permits the simultaneous avoiding of sterile theory on the one hand, of useless accumulation of meaningless data on the other hand" (Dogan & Pelassy, 1984, p. 28).

An Example

An example of employing transculturals to go beyond back-translation and factor analysis is the Japanese version of the leader-member exchange (LMX) measure (Graen & Uhl-Bien, 1995). The construct was defined in 1972 as the perceived effectiveness of the working relationship between two people in a direct reporting situation. It was assessed by asking both parties to the relationship a series of questions about the effectiveness of their working relationship: for example, how would you characterize the effectiveness of your working relationship? how often do you know where you stand with the other person? how well does the other person recognize your potential? your job problems? what are the chances the other person would help you with a problem?

In working this LMX instrument back and forth between American and Japanese language and culture and between several samples, researchers found they needed additional items in the Japanese version to reduce its ambiguity. Japanese culture contains several types of relationships that needed to be clearly distinguished on the instrument. Thus questions were added about going out after work to a bar, doing career mentoring, and respect for capabilities. Once these questions were asked and validated, the expert panel of transculturals concluded that both American and Japanese versions were tapping functionally equivalent constructs in their respective cultures. In spite of the fact that the two measures asked some different content questions and contained a different number of questions, the expert panel judged that the denotations and connotations of the measures were functionally equivalent in the two target cultures. The statistical evidence showed appropriate convergence and divergence within each culture, but more important, the expert panel judged the measures not isomorphic but functionally equivalent.

Results of this Japanese version of the LMX were gratifying at the seven-, thirteen-, and twenty-two-year follow-ups. Leader-member exchange predicted the career progress of Japanese managers in terms of speed of promotion, salary level, organizational resources, job satisfaction, organization commitment, and leader-member exchange (Wakabayashi, Graen, Graen, & Graen, 1988). Clearly, the cross-cultural construct and scale development work by the panel of transcultural partners was worth the investment of the time and effort. We recommend that before any proposed cross-cultural measure is employed in research, it be reviewed by a panel of transcultural experts for its functional equivalence. Until it is judged adequate by such a panel, it should be used for developmental purposes only. Also, research journals should require that the expert panel be named (at least for the editor), to ensure that cross-cultural functional equivalence has been seriously judged by transculturals.

Facilitation of Transcultural Characteristics

Training programs have been developed to facilitate individuals' acquisition of transcultural characteristics (see, for example, the three-volume *Handbook of Intercultural Training* edited by Landis and Brislin, 1983). These programs have been directed at improving a *sojourner's* chances of successful adjustment to another culture. This successful adjustment is defined by Hawes and Kealey (1981) as manifesting (1) good personal adjustment, (2) good interpersonal relations with hosts, and (3) task effectiveness. All three criteria were deemed necessary. At times the first two criteria have been sacrificed in the short-term interests of the third. However, in the longer term, failure to meet the first two criteria may jeopardize the entire project. Clearly, if the sojourner becomes poorly adjusted or is disliked by hosts even though the tasks are effectively completed, any predecessors will likely pay the price.

Employing this three-part criterion of success with the concept of the transculturals leads to a more complex development space. Possessing only the adventurer characteristic, sojourners cannot be expected to say they are comfortable and doing well, nor can their hosts be expected to say that the sojourners pull their load and get along well with others, nor can their superiors be expected to say that they work effectively. Unless the cross-cultural project is trivial, cultural adventurers have too little competence to be successful in fulfilling these three criteria. Adventurers are so clearly incapable of even minimum performance on the criteria that most of the cross-cultural preparation work has focused on attempts to train them as, at least, cultural sensitizers. Less work has been done to move them beyond cultural sensitizers to discrepant culture insiders. In addition, to move from cultural insider to comparative culture judge requires a person to function as an insider in a nontrivial cross-cultural role. Finally, moving from culture judge to socializing synthesizer demands close and intense collaboration between two comparative culture judges.

This development space is shown in Figure 7.3. Initially, adventurers are trained to become cultural sensitizers through various cultural sensitizer training programs (Albert, 1983). This approach to developing cultural sensitizers or cultural assimilators (we prefer the former term as more descriptive) is claimed to have been researched the most and the best (Brislin, Cushner, Cherrie, & Yong, 1986). Once prospective sojourners have developed from adventurer to sensitizer they are ready to undertake insider training by an insider from the target culture who is also at least a

Figure 7.3. Training Functions for Developing the Progressive Characteristics of a Transcultural.

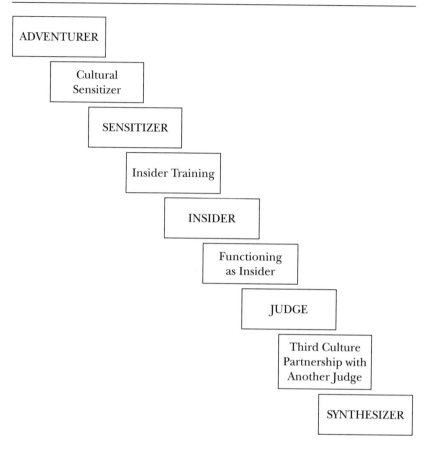

cultural insider in the sojourner's culture. This insider training is quite different from the cultural sensitizer training of adventurers in that it emphasizes seminar study and interactions between student and teacher and practical tests of adjustment to the target culture (Black, Gregersen, & Mendenhall, 1992). Once sojourners acquire insider characteristics they are ready to learn how to function in the target culture. This training is done on the job by those working with and around the sojourners, and it should be noted that simply working in a cross-cultural setting does not alone transform a person into a comparative culture judge. It takes concentrated effort by both sojourner and cross-cultural staff. Finally, a partnership with another judge, that is, the forming of a third culture, is necessary to move each judge in the partnership to the status of socializing synthesizers (Graen & Wakabayashi, 1994).

Next we turn to the life cycle of cross-cultural partnerships with transculturals, keeping in mind the three criteria of success just described.

The Life Cycle of Partnerships with Transculturals

As discussed above, only transculturals have the qualification for our cross-cultural research alliances. Without these transculturals, we would be hard pressed to achieve functional equivalence in the constructs we study. What, then, characterizes this research alliance? We propose that the research alliance with transculturals be viewed in terms of a life cycle of partnership (see Figure 7.4).

The life cycle of cross-cultural research partnership making can be conceptualized as a three-phase development similar to the leadership-making process in which leaders and members progress over time from strangers to acquaintances to sharers in a mature working relationship (Graen & Wakabayashi, 1994). Cross-cultural research partnership making progresses over time through the life cycle of an accommodation between strangers, then between acquaintances, and then between partners. We further propose that in each stage of the life cycle, the relationship can be characterized in terms of the roles of the parties, the exchange relationship, the level of cross-cultural sophistication, the collaborative maturity, and the potential contribution of the partnership.

Roles

Roles refer to the prescribed behaviors and duties for each party. Research on leader-member exchange has examined the role-making process in relationship building (Dansereau, Graen, & Haga, 1975; Fairhurst, 1993; Graen, 1976; Graen, 1989; Graen, Novak, & Sommerkamp, 1982; Graen, Orris, & Johnson, 1973; Graen & Scandura, 1987; Graen & Uhl-Bien, 1995; Graen, Wakabayashi, Graen, & Graen, 1990; Haga, 1976; Rosse & Kraut, 1983; Seers & Graen, 1984; Snyder & Bruning, 1985; Vecchio, 1982;

Figure 7.4. Life Cycle of Research Partnership Between Transculturals.

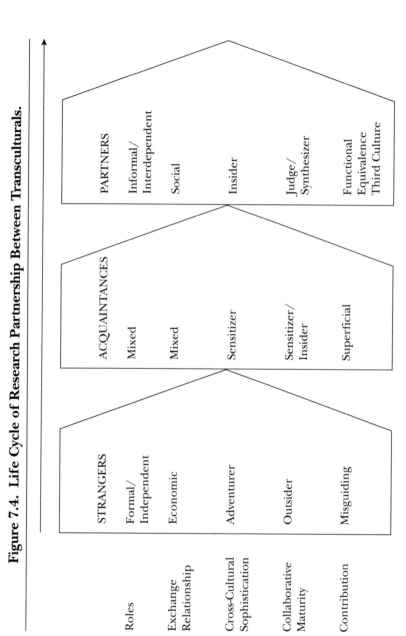

Zalesny & Graen, 1986). According to this literature, member roles are a function of the working relationship members enjoy with the leader. On the one hand roles of the *role-taking* members, that is, those with a low-quality work relationship with the leader, are more formal and prescriptive. Roles of the *role-making* members on the other hand are more informal and developmental. Similarly, in cross-cultural research partnership making, partners may have different roles as a function of the quality of the work relationship between the partners. Specifically, we suggest that the roles can be formal or informal and independent or interdependent. When the research partners are strangers to each other, roles will be formal and independent because each research partner is trying to establish the ground rules for the partnership. Because formal roles are the easiest to adapt and follow, this kind of contact or agreement will permeate stranger relationships. Similarly, as partners attempt to find their own roles and to specify the division of labor, their roles will be relatively independent until a higher-quality relationship is developed. Thus, as time progresses and the partnership matures, the partners' roles will become more informal and interdependent. Moreover, the dyadic contact becomes less influential as the working relationship matures into a real partnership with the development of respect, trust, and mutual obligation.

Exchange Relationship

Exchange relationship describes the nature of the working relationship between the partners. Exchange relationships rest on each person's discharge of obligations resulting from the rewarding services others in the relationship render to him or her (Homans, 1961). Economic exchange is typified by cash-and-carry transactions and a definite payback time span. Social exchange is typified by exchanges in kind, an indefinite payback time span, and unspecified obligations for favors furnished by others. A different exchange relationship will occur as a function of each stage of partnership making. In the early stage, that is, the stranger stage, exchanges are typically economically oriented. As partnership develops, the exchange relationship becomes more social. In the final stage, the partner stage itself, the research partners develop complete trust and respect for each other and duly honor mutual obligations even though the fulfillment of such obligation is specific neither in terms nor time.

Cross-Cultural Sophistication

Cross-cultural sophistication refers to the level of understanding the parties to the research alliance have of the cultures under study. Cross-cultural sophistication varies from cultural adventurer to cultural sensitizer to discrepant culture insider. (We believe that cultural understanding can be developed, as we described in discussing the five progressive characteristics of transculturals.) When the research alliance has been just formed, the parties to it are strangers to each other and may have a limited understanding of both each other's cultures and orientations. In this stage, research alliances may be likened to cultural adventurers who have an interest in those from other cultures but are limited in understanding. As these alliances pass into the acquaintance stage, the parties are sensitized to each other's values, needs, and cultural understanding. When alliances become partnerships, the partners can be mentors to each other on their own cultures. Cross-cultural research alliances at the partner stage have gone beyond a superficial level of communication and interaction and alliance members are now socializing each other into their own cultures so that a deep and accurate understanding of the cultures represented can be cultivated. Thus, in the partner stage, the two or more parties to the research alliances become insiders to the cultures under study.

Collaborative Maturity

Collaborative maturity is the stage that allows the alliance to perform research in greatest depth. When the parties to the research alliances are strangers to each other, their collaboration is limited to examination of outsider, or tourist type, ideas. Because the parties in the alliance are still limited in their understanding of each other's cultures, miscommunications can occur, limiting the depth of research. However, as the working collaborators' relationship becomes more mature and moves into the acquaintance stage, these research partners begin to understand the norms and values of the other cultures. This is a better background for making valid cross-cultural judgments. Because the collaborators have developed a better understanding of each other's cultures, orientations, and interests, their collaborative maturity is higher than it was at the stranger stage. However, they are still restricted to a superficial understanding of the cultures under study. Acquaintances do not invest time and energy in socializing their collaborators because it may be perceived as rude or result in loss of face. To advance to the partner stage and collaborative maturity, the researchers need insider knowledge of the cultures under study and also the ability to judge and synthesize cultural differences and similarities. Cross-cultural research partners will socialize each other into their own cultures. Thus, in the partner stage, the cross-cultural alliance can conduct research with the kind of depth afforded to cross-cultural judges and cultural synthesizers.

Contribution

Contribution refers to the potential contribution of the cross-cultural research alliance. Because both cross-cultural sophistication and collaborative maturity are low in the stranger stage, the contribution of this particular alliance will be severely limited or even misguiding. As alliance members are just starting to search for an understanding of each other's cultures and orientations, the research they generate may be hampered by miscommunications and misunderstandings. When the cross-cultural research alliance is in the acquaintance stage, its research projects will have more substance because a basic understanding between the parties has been achieved. However, as this research alliance is sensitized to the values, behaviors, and norms of the cultures represented but still lacks the in-depth understanding of the cultural insider, its contribution will remain superficial. When the alliance moves into the partner stage, it gains the ability to identify constructs with functional equivalence and make valid cross-cultural judgments. Thus meaningful and effective cross-cultural research with significant contribution can be conducted only when the cross-cultural research alliance is in the partner stage.

Furthermore, because of the partnership between members, third cultures can be created as a function of partners' in-depth interaction. The creation of this third culture (Useem, Useem, & Donghue, 1963) is particularly important for a business that seeks to create partnership with a foreign business. In cross-cultural partnership building, no one culture should be dominant. Instead, alliance members need to work together to create within their alliance a third culture that transcends the originals.

Progression Through the Life Cycle: A True Story

What we know about multinational business partnership relationship gives us a way to illustrate cross-cultural research collaborative relationships (Graen & Wakabayashi, 1994). So in this section, we turn to a consideration of the third-culture philosophy as it applies to multinational business ventures (Graen & Hui, 1994).

The Third Culture

We illustrate the *third-culture* philosophy by contrasting it with the two-cultures philosophy, the traditional form of cross-cultural business relationship, as shown in the following list of characteristics.

Two Approaches to Cross-Cultural Business Ventures

Two Cultures	*Third Culture*
CYA attitude	Trust
Disinterest	Respect
Compete	Cooperate
Confront	Accommodate
Short-term focus	Long-term focus
Legal contract	Handshake
Contract breach	Mutual obligation
Win-lose view	Win-win view

The third-culture and the two-cultures philosophies are two different approaches to business ventures across cultures. In the two cultures approach, two cross-cultural parties remain strangers to each other. They know of each other of course, and some people in the organizations may know each other personally, but they do not have a quality work relationship with each other. In two cultures relationships, dealings are characterized by mutual disinterest and a "cover-your-ass" (CYA) attitude. There is a short-term focus, which leads to competition and confrontation within the venture. The two businesses have to rely on legal contracts to define their relationship and yet suffer from a relatively high probability of contract breach. They see themselves involved in a win-lose situation in which each thinks that it can gain in the business deal only if the other loses or at least does not gain as much. Modern cross-cultural dealings are replete with this kind of venture partner–as–competitor relationship.

A third-culture approach, in contrast, is characterized by businesses that become cultural insiders rather than remaining outsiders. A cultural insider appreciates the cultural values of others and refrains from judging others' culture in terms of the insiders' own values. Instead of mutual disinterest and a CYA attitude, a third culture shows mutual respect and trust. Because now the businesses are genuine partners, they can share a long-term focus in their business dealings, leading to cooperation and accommodation. They can rely on handshakes and mutual obligation when doing business. They can look for win-win situations in which both partners can grow and make profit by collaborating with each other. It is our contention that development of a third culture is essential to the ultimate success of cross-cultural partnerships as the third-culture approach allows more flexibility in dealings because it relies on trust instead of tedious litigation, reduces inefficiencies by lessening external control mechanisms, and maximizes the efforts and the capability usage of each partner. Few multinational joint ventures in business start out with a plan to implement the two-cultures philosophy. Most begin with the plan of implementing the third-culture philosophy. However, many drift into the former approach in spite of their best efforts. As you will see in the following case, lack of a third culture can easily lead to failures in cross-cultural business ventures and the cultivation of a third culture can lead to success.

A Case of Networking Failure

A few years ago one of the top ten manufacturing companies in the world asked us to help it implement a new venture in a foreign land. The company was Japanese and the foreign land was a state in the United States. Company executives were worried that their cross-cultural partnership skills might prove inadequate to forge a successful venture in this state. The basis for their concern was a failed venture in Australia.

What had gone so wrong with their first foreign plant? The story was a sad one. The executives had done everything according to the book from an engineering perspective. They had a sound business development plan that began with low-technology screwdriver operations and slowly moved to higher value-added operations. They had built the plant in Japan and made sure it worked well. Then they broke it down, shipped it to Australia, and assembled it on site. No problems thus far.

They hired local production and human resource managers and trained them in company philosophy and procedures. However, the relationships between these two key local managers and the expatriate managers failed to mature into cross-cultural partnerships. Sure, the Australian managers were friendly and open with their Japanese colleagues, but something kept the two cultures apart. The Japanese plant manager complained that he would have long talks with his Australian reports and they would find agreement on all major projects. However, the next day the Australian managers would do things that indicated that they did not really understand. These Japanese and Australian managers never became partners. The Australian managers never developed an interest in the success of the transplant. The Japanese and the Australians never developed a third culture together.

The consequence of this failure to achieve cross-cultural partnerships was a major embarrassment for this top manufacturing company. The new plant failed to perform at the average of its industrial park and was plagued by wildcat strikes, grievances, and low quality. This last outcome was a severe blow to a company that had earned the emperor's prize for quality in Japan. Clearly, this situation required cross-cultural cooperation and failed to develop it.

Company executives would not allow this to happen again as it was a major embarrassment. For the U.S. plant, they carefully selected their managers for a high level of compatibility, a low level of ethnocentricity, and a high level of empathy; trained them in cross-cultural partnership knowledge and skills; and facilitated third-culture partnerships between Japanese and U.S. managers before they implemented their U.S. plan. The executives did not repeat their earlier mistakes because they developed third-culture networks in depth—not only among first-line managers but also second and third line. Japanese and U.S. managers developed cross-cultural partnerships that allowed them to share cultural insider hopes, fears, and solutions. They achieved real understanding and developed third-culture decision-making procedures. The new U.S. plant's performance was as outstanding as the Australian plant's was miserable. In fact, the U.S. plant outperformed the ambitious projections of the parent company. Although the company built a physical plant considered large enough to house the operations for the first two years, it was outgrown in six months. As hoped, it was a plant worthy of a top ten manufacturing parent and a source of pride for all involved.

This example illustrates the importance of cross-cultural partnerships at key interfaces where trust, respect, and mutual obligation must be exchanged. We could give similar examples of joint ventures in the People's Republic of China. We strongly believe that a firm understanding of the principles of the third-culture approach can enhance a business's ability to succeed where cross-cultural cooperation is required for effectiveness.

Certainly, Asians already network quite extensively across cultural boundaries. Their Roladexes are literally bursting with collected business cards. However, just like most people from other cultures, most Asians do not yet possess the knowledge and skills needed to identify critical linkages with key people from different cultures and successfully develop third-culture partnerships with these people. Therefore we argue that cross-cultural networking is not the same as developing third-culture partnerships with key contacts. Clearly, the latter requires much more knowledge, skill, and persistence than the former.

Third-Culture Negotiation

Joint ventures can be negotiated using the third culture, following this outline:

Moving to a Third-Culture Approach

- Find potential cross-cultural partners.
- Develop third-culture mission description.
- Select executive negotiators carefully.
- Train executive negotiators in third-culture theory and practice.
- Use third-culture partnerships of key executives to facilitate third-culture relationships among respective management teams.
- Negotiate third-culture relationships (contracts) through key executives.
- Develop third-culture partnerships in teams as they evolve on both sides.
- Administer relationships (contracts) through third-culture teams.
- Develop new third-culture partnerships as new staff are added.

First comes the development of the mission description, in which the goals and methods of the venture are detailed in third-culture terms. For example, the outcomes of the venture can be stated in terms of mutual benefit (win-win). Next the key people from each culture are selected carefully for high compatibility, low ethnocentricity, and high empathy. Key people are next trained in the theory and practice of the third culture. These key people then negotiate the overall agreement (resulting in relationships or contracts) between the two cultures. After this, staff are trained in the third-culture procedures, and new relationships are facilitated by the key people. Finally, the staff thus trained develop third-culture relationships and administer the agreement over time. As new staff come into key positions at the interfaces between cultures, they are appropriately trained and facilitated to continue the third culture.

Cross-Cultural Partnership Programs

There have been programs pioneered in Japan and the United States to facilitate business dealings across cultures. For example, the Japan-American Institute of Management Science (JAIMS) in Honolulu is a unique organization that develops cross-cultural partnerships between Japanese and Americans. Its traditional program focuses on intercultural management and on preparing participants for the task of developing third cultures through cross-cultural partnership making. Other examples are the East-West Center at the University of Hawaii and the West Lake Center for Joint-Venture Management at Hangzhou University, Hangzhou, China.

One has to wonder, given the tremendous opportunities to do business across cultures in Asia (especially in mainland China), why so few programs are available to facilitate cross-cultural business dealings in this region. More such programs need to be developed to train managers in the methods and skills of East-West partnership making.

Implications and Conclusion

At the research collaborator level, partnership-making between transculturals may require a rather intense interdependent *buddy system*. Each party must feel compelled to understand at least the set of culturally based conceptual tools of his or her partner (Swidler, 1986). To accomplish this interdependence, dyadic teams work on important parts of their research that require interacting interdependence as opposed to coacting interdependence. Moreover, appropriate training in comparative problem-solving techniques and cross-cultural partnership making should be given to such teams to enhance the development of their third cultures.

After a dyadic team has explored its cultural options (a *role-finding* process), it is ready to begin the delicate task of testing the most promising options (a *role-making* process). Clearly, team members will make mistakes, but a system should be in place to minimize any negative consequences. Finally, the promising options, those that appear to work for a dyadic team, can form the foundation for a mature leadership relationship (a *role-implementing* process). Perhaps in this way a new generation of transcultural research will emerge that can produce far better understanding of cultures through cross-cultural collaboration in the third culture.

Cross-cultural researchers need research designed to sort out those cultural variables that make a difference at the macro level (Weber [1904–1905] 1958) or the micro level (Hofstede, 1980) to cross-cultural partnership making from those that do not. A step in this direction, as we have mentioned, would be to view culture not as a system of predispositions but as a set of conceptual "tools" that may be used to solve different kinds of problems (Swidler, 1986). These tools are an essential part of what is learned by someone from another culture during a process of cross-cultural partnership making. Researchers could observe how people from different cultures learn each other's tool kits and how they integrate these tool kits into their partnership making. Two of the authors (Graen and Wakabayashi) find in retrospect that this tool-kit approach appears to explain a good deal about their own partnership making over the past twenty-plus years. Initially, they worked to understand and become comfortable with the similarities of each other's cultural tool kits. Next, they tried to integrate their two different tool kits into a new (third) set of conceptual tools. Finally, they are striving still to refine their problem-solving procedures, despite numerous examples of backsliding into old cultural habits.

Based on over twenty years of Graen's and Wakabayashi's personal cross-cultural partnership-making experience, their twenty-five years of research on Japanese and U.S. partnership making, their five years of research on cross-cultural partnership making among Japanese transplants to the United States, and their three years of research in China with Hui, we believe that the process is researchable and that joint ventures represent a unique research opportunity. Clearly, some business joint ventures have riveting needs for critical cross-cultural bridges that will allow partners to move from one cultural tool kit to another while staying on the same page of the same book, and a process for building such bridges is cross-cultural partnership making. Everything we have learned about this process leads us to expect that this third-culture building process must and will unfold in collaborative research alliances. We recommend that cross-cultural researchers engage in this unfolding process.

We recommend, furthermore, that cross-cultural researchers not simply adapt U.S. studies to foreign settings and hire some foreign research assistants. Instead, they should develop a cross-cultural partnership that can engage both sides of their constructs and their measuring instruments. Beginning by using only U.S. concepts and measures is likely to build in cultural contamination (Lynn, 1990). By developing cross-cultural research partnerships instead, researchers can sort out each other's ethnocentricities. They will build their research designs as transculturals who can develop functionally equivalent constructs and measures between two or more cultures. Clearly, not all joint ventures in business require third-culture partnerships, but we would argue that all cross-cultural research requires third-culture partnerships between collaborators.

References

Albert, R. (1983). The intercultural sensitizer or culture assimilator: A cognitive approach. In D. Landis & R. W. Brislin (Eds.), *Handbook of intercultural training* (Vol. 2, pp. 186–217). New York: Pergamon Press.

Berry, J. W. (1990). Imposed etics, emics and derived etics: Their conceptual and operational status in cross-cultural psychology. In T. N. Headland, K. L. Pike, & Y. M. Harris (Eds.), *Emics and etics: The insider/outsider debate* (pp. 84–99). Thousand Oaks, CA: Sage.

Black, J. S., Gregersen, H. B., & Mendenhall, M. E. (1992). *Global assignments: Successfully expatriating and repatriating international managers.* San Francisco: Jossey-Bass.

Brislin, R. W. (1970). Back-translation for cross-cultural research. *Journal of Cross-Cultural Psychology, 1,* 185–216.

Brislin, R. W., Cushner, K., Cherrie, C., & Yong, M. (1986). In D.W.J. Lonner & J. W. Berry (Eds.), *Intercultural interactions: A practical guide* (Vol. 9). Thousand Oaks, CA: Sage.

Dansereau, F., Graen, G. B., & Haga, W. J. (1975). A vertical dyad linkage approach to leadership in formal organizations: A longitudinal investigation of the role-making process. *Organizational Behavior and Human Performance, 13,* 46–78.

Dogan, M., & Pelassy, D. (1984). *How to compare nations.* Chatham, NJ: Chatham House.

Drever, J. (1952). *A dictionary of psychology.* New York: Penguin Books.

Fairhurst, G. T. (1993). The leader-member exchange patterns of women leaders in industry: A discourse analysis. *Communication Monograph, 60,* 321–351.

Graen, G. B. (1976). Role making processes within complex organizations. In M. D. Dunnette (Ed.), *Handbook of industrial and organizational psychology* (pp. 1201–1245). Palo Alto, CA: Consulting Psychologists Press.

Graen, G. B. (1989). *Unwritten rules for your career: 15 secrets for fast-track success.* New York: Wiley.

Graen, G. B., & Hui, C. (1994). Development of third culture partnerships for joint ventures. In M. Cumbers, P. Donohoe, & A. Pak

(Eds.), *Making Asian Managers* (pp. 14–19). Hong Kong: Hong Kong Chamber of Commerce.

Graen, G. B., Novak, M., & Sommerkamp, P. (1982). The effects of leader-member exchange and job design on productivity and satisfaction: Testing a dual attachment model. *Organizational Behavior and Human Performance, 30,* 109–131.

Graen, G. B., Orris, D., & Johnson, T. (1973). Role assimilation processes in a complex organization. *Journal of Vocational Behavior, 3,* 395–420.

Graen, G. B., & Scandura, T. (1987). Toward a psychology of dyadic organizing. In B. Staw & L. L. Cumming (Eds.), *Research in organizational behavior* (Vol. 9, pp. 175–208). Greenwich, CT: JAI Press.

Graen, G. B., & Uhl-Bien, M. (1995). Development of leader-member exchange (LMX) theory of leadership over 25 years: Applying a multi-level-multi-domain perspective. *Leadership Quarterly, 6*(2), 219–247.

Graen, G. B., & Wakabayashi, M. (1994). Cross-cultural leadership-making: Bridging American and Japanese diversity for team advantage. In H. C. Triandis, M. D. Dunnette, & L. M. Hough (Eds.), *Handbook of industrial and organizational psychology* (2nd ed., Vol. 4, pp. 415–446). Palo Alto, CA: Consulting Psychologist Press.

Graen, G. B., Wakabayashi, M., Graen, M. R., & Graen, M. G. (1990). International generalizability of American hypothesis about Japanese management progress: A strong inference investigation. *The Leadership Quarterly, 1*(1), 1–11.

Haga, W. J. (1976). Managerial professionalism and the use of organization resources. *American Journal of Economics and Sociology, 35,* 337–348.

Hawes, F., & Kealey, D. (1981). An empirical study of Canadian technical assistance: Adaptation and effectiveness an overseas assignment. *International Journal of Intercultural Relations, 5,* 239–258.

Headland, T. N., Pike, K. L., & Harris, Y. M. (1990). *Emics, and ethics: In-Out debate.* Thousand Oaks, CA: Sage.

Hofstede, G. (1980). *Culture's consequences: International differences in work-related values.* Thousand Oaks, CA: Sage.

Hofstede, G. (1993). Cultural constraints in management theories. *Academy of Management Executive, 7*(1), 81–94.

Hofstede, G., & Bond, M. H. (1988). The Confucius connection: From cultural roots to economic growth. *Organizational Dynamics, 16,* 5–21.

Homans, G. C. (1961). *Social behavior: Its elementary forms.* Orlando: Harcourt Brace.

Kroeber, A. L., & Kluckhohn, C. (1952). *Culture: A critical review of concepts and definitions.* Cambridge, MA: Harvard University Peabody Museum of American Archeology and Ethnology.

Landis, D., & Brislin, R. W. (Eds.). (1983). *Handbook of intercultural training* (3 vols.). New York: Pergamon Press.

Lynn, L. H. (1990). Technology and organizations: A cross-national analysis. In P. S. Goodman, L. S. Sproull, & Associates, *Technology and organizations* (pp. 174–199). San Francisco: Jossey-Bass.

Mead, M. (1928). *Coming of age in Samoa.* Chicago: University of Chicago Press.

Porter, L. W., Steers, R. M., Mowday, R. T., & Boulina, V. (1974). Organizational commitment, job satisfaction, and turnover among psychiatric technicians. *Journal of Applied Psychology, 5,* 603–609.

Rosse, J. G., & Kraut, A. I. (1983). Reconsidering the vertical dyad linkage model of leadership. *Journal of Occupational Psychology, 56,* 63–71.

Satori, G. (1994). Comparing, miscomparing and the comparative method. In M. Dogan & A. Kazancigil (Eds.), *Comparing nations: Concepts, strategies, substance* (pp. 14–34). Oxford, England: Blackwell.

Seers, A., & Graen, G. B. (1984). The dual attachment concept: A longitudinal investigation of the combination of task characteristics and leader-member exchange. *Organizational Behavior & Human Performance, 33,* 283–306.

Snyder, R. A., & Bruning, N. S. (1985). Quality of vertical dyad linkages: Congruence of supervisor and subordinate competence and role stress as explanatory variables. *Group & Organization Studies, 10,* 81–94.

Swidler, A. (1986). Culture in action. *American Sociological Review, 51,* 273–286.

Triandis, H. C., & Berry, J. W. (Eds.). (1980). *Handbook of cross-cultural psychology* (Vol. 2). Needham Heights, MA: Allyn & Bacon.

Useem, J., Useem, R., & Donghue, J. (1963). Men in the middle of the third culture. *Human Organization, 22*(3), 169–179.

Vecchio, R. (1982). A further test of leadership effects due to between-group and within-group variation. *Journal of Applied Psychology, 67,* 200–208.

Wakabayashi, M., Graen, G. B., Graen, M. R., & Graen, M. G. (1988). Japanese management progress: Mobility into middle management. *Journal of Applied Psychology, 73,* 217–227.

Weber, M. (1958). *The Protestant ethic and the spirit of capitalism.* New York: Scribner. (Original work published 1904–1905)

Zalesny, M. D., & Graen, G. (1986). Exchange theory in leadership research. In G. Reber (Ed.), *Encyclopedia of leadership* (pp. 714–727). Linz: Linz University Press.

CHAPTER 8

A Culture-Based Model of Work Motivation

Miriam Erez

Work motivation is shaped by the interplay between individuals and their work organizations. Organizations hire high-potential people in the expectation that they will work to the full extent of their abilities and exert all their effort and mental resources in their jobs. This expectation recognizes the existence of two important factors—a pool of potential physical and mental resources, and motivational forces that energize and regulate the allocation of those resources to work-related activities. Motivation regulates the amount of resources to be allocated, the direction or goal of those allocated resources, and the persistence of allocation and direction over time. Motivation affects choice, action, and performance.

Individuals engage in work because they expect it to satisfy their basic needs for existence, relatedness, and growth and to create opportunities for developing a sense of self-worth and well-being (Erez & Earley, 1993; Locke, 1991). However, these expectations are not always fulfilled. For several decades the Roper Organization has been polling about twelve hundred employees every few years and has found job satisfaction in the United States at its lowest level during the early 1990s. Similarly, the Hay Group, a Philadelphia consulting firm whose clients have included American Airlines, Disney, GE, Chase Manhattan, and Maytag, has surveyed 750,000 middle managers in one thousand large corporations and found that the percentage expressing favorable attitudes toward their companies dropped from 65 percent in 1987 to 55 percent in 1990 (Fisher, 1991).

Dissatisfied employees are not motivated to allocate effort and mental resources to their work, and they often show withdrawal behavior of lateness, absenteeism, and turnover, which is detrimental to productivity. Therefore motivating employees is essential for maintaining the competitive advantage of the modern workplace.

One of the challenges managers face is how to link employee motivation to organizational goals. This link occurs when employee behavior that leads to the attainment of the organizational goals also creates a sense of self-worth and well-being in the employee and leads to his or her attainment of organizational rewards and recognition as well. It is therefore important that we understand how employees seeking self-worth and well-being interpret managerial and motivational practices as either opportunities or constraints.

Employees' evaluate whether or not their self-motives have been satisfied in two ways: through personal standards guided by internal criteria and differing from one individual to another and through standards and norms that come from the social environment and are shaped by cultural values. These social standards are shared by all members of the same culture and differ across cultures. Therefore motivational practices that have positive meaning in one culture may not have the same effect in another culture. For example, working in teams may be most desirable in collectivist cultures such as Japan, Korea, and Mexico but not in individualist cultures such as the United States, Australia, and Great Britain. Organizational hierarchy may be tolerated in high power distance cultures like the Philippines, Brazil, and France but not in egalitarian cultures like Israel and Denmark. Lack of role separation between men and women may be highly regarded in societies with highly feminine values such as Sweden and Norway but not in masculine societies like Singapore and Venezuela. A high degree of formality is appreciated in societies of high uncertainty avoidance like Greece and Portugal but rejected in societies of low uncertainty avoidance like Sweden, Denmark, and Jamaica (Hofstede, 1991).

However, most theories of work motivation overlook the effect of culture on the motivation potential of various managerial and motivational approaches. Such theories focus on the individual employee and overlook the macro-level cultural, societal, and economic factors.

This chapter proposes a motivational model that incorporates cultural factors. This cognitive model of work motivation examines the differential effectiveness of different motivational techniques through the prism of culture. The discussion consists of four major parts: first, a multilevel approach to work motivation, second, cognitive models of work motivation, third, a culture-based model of work motivation, and fourth, the effectiveness of motivational techniques across cultures.

A Multilevel Approach to Work Motivation

For many decades researchers have approached work motivation mainly from an individual perspective, focusing on analyzing individual differences. However, in the last decade we have witnessed a shift toward a multilevel approach that analyzes research evidence and reframes motivational concepts on the macro level of groups, organizations, and cultures and that provides methodological tools for anchoring culture in models of work motivation.

In his 1991 annual review of organizational behavior literature, O'Reilly pointed out that authors reviewed in 1982, 1984, 1985, and 1987 called for more attention to cross-level research, studies that incorporate both individual and group- or organization-level variables. He also found that this shift is now under way: "While the micro side of OB seems to be in a dormant period, attention and interest have shifted substantially to the macro side. In 1979, 70 percent of the studies published in the *Academy of Management Journal* were on micro topics. By 1989 this figure had fallen to 38 percent" (p. 430). And O'Reilly observed that "the macro side of the field appears to generating more intellectual excitement at the present" (p. 449).

The majority of the papers O'Reilly reviewed in 1991, however, were still classified by micro–organizational behavior categories, including motivation, work attitudes, and job design. The 1993 review (by Mowday and Sutton) shows a shift toward the macro level of study with its category of "Linking Individuals and Groups to Organizational Contexts" (p. 195). Furthermore, the 1995 annual review of the literature (by Wilpert) focuses on more molar and pervasive aspects of organizational characteristics, antecedents, and consequences of practices as well as on structures and processes in and of organizations. Finally, the 1996 annual review (by Bond and

Smith) takes the field one step closer to the macro level with a category entitled "Cross Cultural Social and Organizational Psychology." Thus a significant change has occurred since Cappelli and Sherer (1991) wrote their influential chapter in which they warned that unless study of organizational behavior (OB) incorporates contextual factors to explain that behavior and unless it succeeds in bridging the micro-macro relationships "OB is likely to miss the chance to establish any independent identity" (p. 97). Their message was two fold: First, that more emphasis should be given to the macro work context and, second, that the micro and macro levels should be integrated.

Interest in multilevel analysis has led to four new developments: first, an emphasis on the meso level of analysis (Cappelli & Sherer, 1991; Rousseau & House, 1994). The meso level, that is, the organizational level, is perceived to be the bridge between micro-level individual behavior and macro-level societal, cultural, and economic factors (Cappelli & Sherer, 1991). A *meso approach* is "an integration of micro and macro theory in the study of processes specific to organizations which by their very nature are a synthesis of psychological and socioeconomic processes. Meso research occurs in an organizational context where processes of two or more levels are investigated simultaneously" (Rousseau & House, 1994, p. 15).

Second, a hierarchical approach that examines organizations within national cultures and individuals within organizations has recently been developed (Earley, 1994; Earley & Brittain, 1992; Hofstede, Bond, & Luk, 1993; Hofstede, Neuijen, Ohayv, & Sanders, 1990; Klein, Dansereau, & Hall, 1994). Models of this type examine both within- and between-group variance. The meaning of a personal attribute is determined by its deviation from the mean group. For example, social loafing can be explained by individual characteristics as well as by cultural characteristics. The individual tendency to loaf is expressed by the deviation of the individual score from the cultural mean score (Earley, 1994).

Different variables emerge on different levels of analysis. For example, cultural values differentiate between employees from different nations but not from different organizations within the same culture. In contrast, such differences are significantly explained by organizational practices (Hofstede, Neuijen, Ohayv, & Sanders, 1990; Hofstede, Bond, & Luk, 1993).

Third, micro-level concepts such as goals, self-efficacy, affect, and learning are transferred to the group, becoming organization-level group goals, group efficacy, group affect, and organizational learning (George, 1990; Crocker, Luhtanen, Blaine, & Broadnax, 1994; Erez & Katz, 1995; Senge, 1994; Weingart, 1992; Weldon, Jehn, & Pradham, 1991; Weldon & Weingart, 1993). Paralleling the effect of individual goals on individual performance, group goals were found to have a significant effect on group performance (Weingart, 1992; Weldon, Jehn, & Pradham, 1991). Collective efficacy, paralleling self-efficacy, is the belief in one's group's capabilities to mobilize the motivation, cognitive resources, and course of action needed to meet given situational demands. Collective efficacy becomes meaningful and separate from self-efficacy in groups with a high degree of interdependence among the group members. In high-interdependent tasks collective efficacy has a stronger effect on performance than self-efficacy. In contrast self-efficacy has a stronger effect on the performance of low-interdependent tasks (Erez & Katz, 1995).

Affect is also viewed as a group-level phenomenon. A study conducted on twenty-six groups of salespeople in a large department store revealed that individual affect was consistent within groups, suggesting that the affective tone of a group is a meaningful construct (George, 1990).

The concept of individual learning has been extrapolated to the macro level of organizational learning (Huber, 1991; Senge, 1994), and *Organizational Science* (Cohen & Sproull, 1991) has dedicated a special issue to the topic. Paralleling individual learning, organizational learning encompasses knowledge acquisition, information distribution, information interpretation, and organizational memory (Huber, 1991). These processes contribute to organizational changes, and they are crucial for the continual adaptation of organizations to their environments. An organization learns when any of its units acquires knowledge recognized as potentially useful to the organization. How information is framed or labeled affects its interpretation. A person's prior cognitive map (belief structure, mental representation, or frame of reference) will shape his or her interpretation of information. These cognitive maps vary not only between individuals but also between organizations and cultures. Most of the research literature on organizational learning is still on the conceptual level; empirical research is still very limited.

Fourth, new statistical methods for multilevel analysis are being developed. Within and Between Analysis (WABA) was developed to determine whether a set of data represents a significant variance between groups or individual differences only (Dansereau, Alutto, & Yammarino, 1984). Another approach to analyzing data on the group level estimates interrater reliability on judgment of a single target. Interrater reliability is the degree to which judges agree on a set of judgments (James, Demaree, & Wolf, 1984).

The multilevel approach offers new methods for comparing the different levels of analysis, but it does not offer a theoretical link between the various levels.

The only model that integrates the cultural level and the individual level of analysis in the work context is the model of cultural self-representation (Erez, 1994; Erez & Earley, 1993). This model is based on cognitive models of information processing that explains how information from the social and organizational context, as well as from internal cues, is sampled, processed, interpreted, and stored in cognitive schema and how it affects behavior. Their ability to use symbols allows people to represent external stimuli, including organizational and cultural values, in their cognitive schemata. It also allows them to develop cognitive awareness of their internal self-regulatory processes that monitor and evaluate both internal and external stimuli.

The next section reviews the existing cognitive models of work motivation that serve as the infrastructure for the model of cultural self-representation.

Cognitive Models of Work Motivation

The current dominant models of work motivation are cognitive by nature. The goal-setting model proposes that goals and intentions are the immediate regulators of human behavior (Locke, 1991); the expectancy theory postulates that people are motivated to maximize their utilities (Vroom, 1964) and that they exert effort to perform their job when they expect that effort to lead to the level of performance that attains valued outcomes. The most recent model by Kanfer and Ackerman (1989) integrates goals and expectancies into a comprehensive model of resource allocation. Therefore this model will serve as the basis for developing a culture-based model of work motivation.

Kanfer and Ackerman's model proposes that individual differences in ability and resources determine the potential total amount of resources that an individual can devote to any set of activities. However, the *actual amount of resources* allocated to the job is determined by the level of motivation. The *direction* is determined by attentional effort. *Effort* is defined as the proportion of total attention directed to the task and *persistence* as the extent to which attentional effort is maintained over time.

The model distinguishes between distal and proximal motivational processes. *Distal motivational processes* govern how much of an individual's total attention effort will be devoted to a given set of activities. Initially, this decision involves the joint operation of three cognitive mechanisms that are formulated in terms of the expectancy theory. (1) The *performance utility function* refers to the attractiveness of different extrinsic or intrinsic performance-level outcomes, such as material rewards, recognition, and feelings of competence. Dispositional factors such as achievement orientation and cultural factors such as values can also affect the relative attractiveness of these different outcomes. (2) The *effort-utility function* pertains to the anticipated costs and benefits of expending effort based on relatively stable preferences for effort. The criteria for evaluating costs and benefits are determined by personal dispositions and by cultural norms and values. (3) The *perceived effort-performance function* integrates the effort-performance and effort-utility functions. Positive motivation occurs when the effort-utility function exceeds the effort-performance function.

Distal motivational processes shape the immediate goals and intentions, which are volitional, and regulate the *proximal motivation processes.* An individual's levels of goal specificity, goal difficulty, and feedback on performance shape his or her proximal strategy of resource allocation to on-task, off-task, and self-regulatory processes during task engagement. Self-regulation subsumes three interdependent activities: *self-monitoring,* the selective attention an individual gives to specific aspects of his or her own behavior; *self-evaluation,* the individual's comparison of current performance with the desired goal; and *self-reaction,* the internal responses that occur after self-evaluation, including satisfaction and perceptions of self-efficacy (Bandura, 1986, 1991; Kanfer, 1990).

The self-regulatory process is based on the assumption that individuals have knowledge about their own cognitive processes and thus can actively influence their monitoring and appraisal processes in order to maximize perceptions of well-being. Self-regulatory processes operate in the service of the self, and they aim at developing and maintaining a positive representation of the self (Bandura, 1986; Erez & Earley, 1993). Positive representation is subject to the process of self-evaluation. The criteria for self-evaluation are determined by both personal and social factors. Personal criteria reflect individual difference characteristics, whereas social criteria reflect cultural values and are shared by all members of the same culture. Variation in cultural values leads to variation in the criteria that people of different cultures use to evaluate whether a situation is self-enhancing. Hofstede (1991) used the metaphor of culture as the software of the mind. The hardware of the mind is universal, and all people make sense of the environment and of themselves by the mechanism of self-regulatory processes (Bandura, 1986; Kanfer, 1990). In contrast, the software of the mind differs across cultures, and people interpret the same organizational cues in different ways depending on the cultural code that they use. Cultural values direct people to selective sampling, assessment, and interpretation of information. For example, individual performance appraisal will be viewed positively by members of an individualist society and negatively by members of a collectivist society. In the later case individual performance appraisal violates the concept of teamwork, where performance is the outcome of all team members' joint effort, and explicitly negative appraisal violates the high importance this culture gives to face saving.

Individuals use cultural values as they are represented in the self for evaluating how various motivational techniques will affect self-worth and well-being. The evaluation directs employees' motivation either toward or away from goal accomplishment (Erez, 1994; Erez & Earley, 1993). The model of cultural self-representation explains the causal links between culture, self, and work motivation.

A Culture-Based Approach to Work Motivation

This section discusses how a culture is represented by its values and how values affect motives, self-construal, and self-regulation. It then describes the culture-based model of work motivation.

Culture and Values

Culture is often viewed in cognitive terms: culture is "the collective programming of the mind which distinguishes the members of one group or category of people from another" (Hofstede, 1991, p. 5); it consists of patterned ways of thinking (Kluckhohn, 1954); it is a set of shared meaning systems (Shweder & LeVine, 1984); and it is a shared knowledge structure that decreases variability in individuals' interpretations of stimuli (Erez & Earley, 1993). The adoption of cultural content is selective and adaptive; therefore different ecological environments modify different cultures (Berry, 1979; Kagitçibasi & Berry, 1989).

A culture shapes the core values and norms of its members, and these values and norms are shared and transmitted from one generation to another through social learning processes of modeling and observation as well as through the effects each person experiences as a result of his or her actions (Bandura, 1986). In homogeneous societies, such as Japan and Singapore, norms and values of various in-groups are relatively homogeneous, and these societies form tight cultures. However, in heterogeneous societies, such as the United States, norms and values of various groups may be dissimilar, and consequently a loose culture is formed (Triandis, 1989, 1994). A culture's strength and degree of internal consistency are functions of the homogeneity across groups, the length of time the groups have existed, the intensity of the groups' learning experiences (Schein, 1990), and the generalizability of norms and rules of behavior across situations. Loose cultures seem to be more tolerant of variations in behavior than tight cultures.

Culture is often represented by its value system. Values can be defined as "enduring beliefs that a specific mode of conduct or end-state of existence is personally or socially preferable to an opposite or converse mode of conduct, or end-state of existence" (Rokeach, 1973, p. 5). Questions related to the importance of such various needs as good fringe benefits and the opportunity for advancement to higher-level jobs have represented work values and served for analyzing cross-cultural differences between countries (Ronen, 1994).

A comprehensive typology of value content domains should cognitively represent three universal human requirements:

individuals' biological needs, coordinated social interaction needs, and survival and welfare needs of groups (Schwartz & Bilsky, 1987). The crucial distinction among values is the type of motivational goal they express. However, the structure of the value system seems to be universal. This structure consists of ten distinct motivational types of values (derived from Rokeach's typology, 1973), organized in a circular structure in two dimensions (Schwartz, 1992). The first dimension is *openness to change* (self-direction, stimulation, hedonism) versus *conservation* (conformity, tradition, security). It represents values emphasizing each individual's independent thought and action and favoring change versus values emphasizing submissive self-restriction, preservation of traditional practices, and protection of stability. The second dimension is *self-enhancement* (achievement, power) versus *self-transcendence* (universal benevolence). It represents values emphasizing acceptance of others as equals and concern for their welfare versus values emphasizing the individual pursuit of relative success and dominance over others. Hedonism is related both to openness to change and to self-enhancement.

However, the meanings of some specific values vary across cultures. These meanings are derived from the region in which specific values are located in the typology. When a value emerges in an unexpected region it is culture specific. For example, self-respect emerges with almost equal frequency in the region of achievement and of the region of self-direction. When self-respect emerges with achievement values, an individual's sense of self-worth may be built primarily on social approval obtained when he or she succeeds according to social standards. When self-respect emerges with self-direction values, an individual's sense of self-worth may be linked more closely to living up to his or her independent self-determined standards. Self-respect emerges in the achievement region in almost all the East European samples, perhaps reflecting a socializing impact of communism, with its emphasis on grounding one's self-worth in evaluation by one's group. In the large majority of samples from strongly capitalistic countries self-respect emerged in the self-direction region (Schwartz & Sagiv, 1995).

In a Japanese study true friendship was located in the security values region, quite far from the benevolence region in which it usually appears. This may mean that for the Japanese friendship is valued more for the security it provides than for the care it expresses toward close others. Forgiving was located in universalism rather than the benevolence value region. This location means that for Japanese forgiving is motivated more by an appreciation of life's complexities than by the desire to be kind to others.

Schwartz's typology of values is context free, whereas Hofstede's typology (1980, 1991) is specifically geared toward the work context. It consists of five core values: individualism versus collectivism, power distance, intolerance of ambiguity, masculinity versus femininity, and future time orientation. Of these five values, collectivism versus individualism and high versus low power distance seem to be most relevant for evaluating the meaning of various motivational techniques. Collectivism versus individualism was found to explain most of the variance across cultures (Triandis, 1994). Collectivist values are characteristic of societies in which people from birth onward are integrated into strong, cohesive in-groups that protect them throughout their lifetimes in exchange for unquestioning loyalty. Individualist values are characteristic of societies in which the ties between individuals are loose: one is expected to look after oneself and one's immediate family (Hofstede, 1991, p. 51). These cultural characteristics are important for evaluating the effect of individual- versus team-based motivational techniques.

Power distance is defined as "the extent to which the less powerful members of institutions and organizations within a country expect and accept that power is distributed unequally" (Hofstede, 1991, p. 28). This cultural characteristic is relevant for understanding the effectiveness of participative management.

These two cultural characteristics of collectivism versus individualism and power distance create four types of culture: horizontal collectivism, vertical collectivism, horizontal individualism, and vertical individualism (see Chapter Two). Horizontal collectivism conveys a sense of oneness with members of the in-group and social cohesiveness. Vertical collectivism reflects a sense of serving the in-group, sacrificing for the benefit of the in-group, doing one's duty as expected, and behaving as expected of a good citizen. The Chinese are identified as vertical collectivists, whereas members of Israeli kibbutzim represent horizontal collectivists. Horizontal individualism is a combination of self-reliance and reluctance to be unique. Vertical individualism is shown by a combination of self-reliance and efforts to be distinguished and unique (see Chapter Two). The Swedes are horizontal individualists; middle-class Americans are vertical individualists. The two-dimensional typology is most useful for understanding cross-cultural differences in motivational practices.

Values and Motives

Values are perceived to be the cognitive representations of needs and motives (Locke, 1991). Need satisfaction in its broadest sense is an organism's survival and well-being. The motivational sequence is activated by the emergence of needs that motivate individuals to take actions toward need satisfaction. On the cognitive level needs transform into values that serve as "the cognitive representations and transformations of needs, and man is the only animal capable of such representation and transformation" (Rokeach, 1973, p. 20). Similarly, as described earlier, Schwartz and Bilsky (1987) define values in motivational terms, classifying content domains of values cognitively into three universal human requirements: individual biological needs, coordinated social interaction needs, and survival and welfare needs of groups. Although needs and motives exist on both the biological and cognitive levels, values are exclusively a product of consciousness (Locke, 1991).

Values are the cognitive representations not only of individual needs but also of societal and cultural demands (Rokeach, 1973). On the individual level values differ from needs in the sense that needs are considered to be fundamentally the same for all people, whereas values make each person a unique individual and guide his or her personal choices and actions (Locke, 1991). An extrapolation from the individual level to a higher level of aggregation suggests that members of the same culture are likely to share similar values, which they acquire in the process of socialization. These values represent the acceptable modes of conduct and end-states of existence of a particular culture. Thus values differentiate not only on the individual level but on the cultural level as well.

The correspondence between personal values of the type portrayed by Rokeach (1973) and cultural values (Hofstede, 1980) is illustrated by the following example: equality and freedom, two of the central values in Rokeach's typology, correspond with the two major cultural values of high versus low power distance, and collectivism versus individualism in Hofstede's typology. Americans as compared to Israelis, for example, rate higher on individualism and power distance, and correspondingly, they also rate higher on freedom and lower on equality (Hofstede, 1980; Rokeach, 1973).

The immediate functions of values are to give expression to human needs and to guide human action. Concern for end-states of existence, such as peace, freedom, and equality, is expressed by *terminal values,* whereas concern for modes of conduct, such as ambitious, capable, and helpful, is expressed by *instrumental values.* Values and needs correspond to each other. For example, the instrumental values independent and intellectual are highly rated by individuals who score high on need for achievement. On the other hand, the need for affiliation is highly related to the terminal values of true friendship and a world of peace (Rokeach, 1973).

Values, as the cognitive representation of needs, mediate the relationship between needs and goals and intentions in the motivation sequence. The complete motivational sequence consists of six steps: needs → values → goals and intentions → performance → rewards → satisfaction (Locke, 1991). Because goals and intentions are conscious, needs cannot be translated into goals unless they have a cognitive representation in the form of values. Thus values play a necessary role in ascribing cognitive meanings to needs and in transforming needs into goals and intentions for action. Goals can be viewed as applications of values to specific situations. Goals and intentions serve as the immediate regulators of behavior. They regulate the intensity, direction, and persistence of action.

Values have both a direct and an indirect effect on rewards and satisfaction. The indirect effect occurs through the sequence of goals → performance → rewards → satisfaction. The direct effect occurs because values determine what will be rewarding to people and what will satisfy them (Locke, 1991).

Values, the Self-Construal, and Self-Regulatory Processes

Values operate on the cognitive level, where two cognitive processes have been identified: sensory-perceptual cognitive processes and conceptual cognitive processes. The process that underlies perception is neurophysiological and nonintrospective. But at the conceptual level, the process of cognition is conscious, introspective, and based on reason. This process does not operate automatically but volitionally (Bingswanger, 1991), one chooses to use or not use one's conceptual faculty. It has been defined as "the ability to maintain and enact an action tendency the organism is committed to despite the impulsive nature of competing action tendencies" (Kuhl & Kraska, 1989, p. 344).

The causal path from values to goals and intentions is purposeful and self-regulated. The ultimate purpose of the total belief system is to maintain and enhance an individual's self-image. Positive evaluation of enhancement and efficacy is obtained through the self-regulatory processes.

The positive representation of the self is maintained by satisfying three basic motives (Gecas, 1982; Markus & Wurf, 1987): *self-enhancement*, reflected in seeking and maintaining a positive cognitive and affective state about the self; *self-efficacy*, the desire to perceive oneself as competent and efficacious; and *self-consistency*, the desire to sense and experience coherence and continuity.

The process of self-evaluation requires the individual to use a set of criteria and guidelines. One source for these criteria is the personal internal standards of the *independent self*. The independent self represents a person's view of what makes him or her unique, unlike other persons. Another source is reference groups reflecting the prevalent values in the society (Breckler & Greenwald, 1986). The collective facet of the self, or the *interdependent self*, is guided by the criteria of achieving the goals of a reference group and fulfilling one's role in that group. The interdependent self corresponds to the notion of social identity—"the part of the individual's self-concept which derives from his/her knowledge of his/her membership in a social group, together with the values and the emotional significance attached to this membership" (Tajfel, 1978, p. 63).

Individuals who live in the same cultural environment use similar criteria for evaluating the contribution of any specific behavior to the development of their sense of self-worth (Triandis, 1989). However, these criteria vary across cultures along with differences in cultural values, and they end up shaping different meanings of self-worth. Western cultures are known for their individualist values. In these cultures the self is less connected to and more differentiated from the social context. The normative imperative is to become independent from others, to be self-reliant, and to discover and express one's unique attributes. Western cultures reinforce the formation of the independent self, "whose behavior is organized and made meaningful primarily by reference to one's own internal repertoire of thoughts, feelings, and actions of others" (Markus & Kitayama, 1991, p. 226).

In contrast, the predominant values in cultures of the Far East are collectivism and group orientation, with an emphasis on harmony, conformity, obedience, and reliability. These cultures tend to be homogeneous. People in them see themselves sharing a common fate. These cultures emphasize interdependence and a sense of collectivity, mainly when in-groups are exposed to external threat and competition from out-groups (Triandis, 1989). People in collectivist cultures stress similarities with other group members that strengthen their group identity. Collectivist cultures emphasize the connectedness of human beings to each other, and they cultivate an interdependent construal of the self (Markus & Kitayama, 1991). With an interdependent self, one sees "oneself as part of an encompassing social relationship recognizing that one's behavior is determined, contingent on, and, to a large extent organized by what the actor perceives to be thoughts, feelings, and actions of others in the relationship" (Markus & Kitayama, 1991, p. 227). The focus of the interdependent self is on the relationship of one person to others.

Empirical findings demonstrate that people from Asia tend to describe themselves in terms reflecting their collectivist interdependent self more frequently than do Europeans or North Americans (Bond, Leung, & Wan, 1982; Trafimow, Triandis, & Goto, 1991). Furthermore, compared to students with an Eastern cultural background, students with a Western cultural background perceive themselves to be less similar to others. However, students with an Eastern background perceive others to be less similar to themselves than do students from Western cultures. This finding suggests that for individuals with a Western background self-knowledge is more distinctive and elaborate than knowledge about others, whereas for individuals with an Eastern background, knowledge about others is more distinctive and elaborate than knowledge about the self. Chinese, for example, who are driven by the interdependent self, have higher social needs than needs for autonomy and for personal achievement (Bond & Cheung, 1983).

The different criteria for evaluation driven by the independent and the interdependent facets of the self determine what kind of actions and situations will be perceived as satisfying the three self-derived motives—*efficacy, enhancement,* and *consistency.* Enhancement driven by the independent facet of the self motivates individuals toward personal achievement. Situations and managerial practices that provide opportunities for individual success are positively evaluated by the independent self. Conversely, enhancement driven by the interdependent facet of the self motivates individuals to contribute to the success of the group, to avoid social loafing (Earley, 1989), and to meet expectations of significant others (Markus & Kitayama, 1991).

Self-efficacy is salient for the independent self, whereas collective efficacy, which pertains to people's sense that they can solve their problems and improve their lives through concerted effort (Bandura, 1986), is salient for the interdependent self. Finally, consistency is evaluated by the independent self as it relates to the individual's own previous behavior. Consistency for the interdependent self pertains to the enduring relationship between the person and his or her reference group.

The independent and interdependent self-construals along with their self-derived motives constitute the link between culture and organizations (the macro level) and employee behavior (the micro level). Management practices are evaluated in line with cultural values as represented in the independent or interdependent self and with respect to their fulfillment of the independent and interdependent self-derived motives.

A Culture-Based Model of Work Motivation

The culture-based model of work motivation (see Figure 8.1) is derived out of the general model of cultural self-representation and has a specific focus on motivational techniques. The four structural components of the model are culture; the independent and interdependent self-construals and their derived self-motives of en-

Figure 8.1. The Culture-Based Model of Work Motivation.

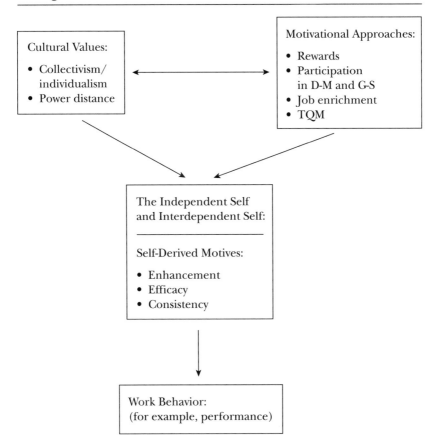

hancement, efficacy, and consistency; motivational practices; and employee behavior. The dynamic characteristic of the model is reflected in the self-regulatory processes that explain how the four components are interrelated.

The Self

According to this model self-regulatory processes operate in the service of developing and maintaining a positive representation of the self. The self regulates behavior by processing all self-relevant information, both external and internal; by evaluating this information as either contributing or not contributing to a personal sense of self-worth and well-being; and by reacting accordingly. A positive representation of the self is maintained when the three self-derived motives of enhancement, efficacy, and consistency are fulfilled. Because the experience of self-enhancement, self-efficacy, and self-consistency is affected by opportunities in the environment, these opportunities are evaluated by the self as facilitating or inhibiting the fulfillment of the self-derived motives. In the case of organizational management, opportunities for the fulfillment of the self-derived motives are created by motivational practices. Some practices (for example, differential reward systems) create opportunities for experiencing self-efficacy, whereas other practices (for example, external control and lack of feedback) inhibit opportunities to experience self-enhancement and self-efficacy.

Culture

As I discussed earlier, evaluation is guided by criteria and values shaped both by internal standards and by the cultural values of the society, particularly individualism versus collectivism and power distance. The former captures the ways members of one culture relate to each other. Collectivism, in contrast to individualism, conveys self-definition as part of the group, subordination of personal goals to group goals, concern for the integrity of the group, and emotional attachment to the in-group. Power distance describes the extent to which members of a culture accept inequality and large differentials between those having power (managers) and those having little power (subordinates).

Cultural values determine what it means to be a person in a particular society, and they are represented in the self. Therefore, different systems of values shape different self-construals. People who live in individualist cultures are socialized to be independent and self-reliant and to use internal standards of evaluation. Their cultural values reinforce the independent self. In contrast, people who live in collectivist cultures are socialized to see themselves a part of an encompassing social relationship, to stress similarities and identity with other group members, and to use the group values for evaluating situations and behaviors. These group values reinforce the interdependent self (Markus & Kitayama, 1991). Thus the dominant facet of the self varies across cultures and situations.

In more collectivist cultures the interdependent self is dominant, whereas in more individualist cultures the independent self is dominant. The value of power distance further categorizes these two self-construals into subgroups of horizontal egalitarian versus vertical hierarchical types. The horizontal type emphasizes similarities whereas the vertical type emphasizes differences. Accordingly, the independent horizontal self values opportunities for egalitarianism and independence; the independent vertical self values opportunities to experience independence and authority; the interdependent horizontal self values opportunities for egalitarian social interdependence, and the interdependent vertical self values opportunities to experience high interdependence and authority.

Motivational Practices

Motivational practices are managerial practices that aim at increasing employees' involvement and willingness to allocate physical and mental resources to their work. Four of the major motivational practices are reward allocation, participation in goal setting and decision making, job enrichment, and quality management. Individuals evaluate motivational practices as either facilitating or inhibiting opportunities for experiencing self-worth and for fulfilling the self-derived motives. The positive, neutral, or negative value assigned to the motivational practices is determined by personal and cultural values as they are represented in the self. A positive evaluation means that the motivational practices create opportunities for satisfying the self-derived motives as they are shaped by the interdependent and independent horizontal and vertical selves. Motivational practices that satisfy the horizontal independent rather than the vertical independent facet of the self are more highly valued in egalitarian and individualist cultures than in nonegalitarian individualist cultures. Practices that satisfy the horizontal interdependent rather than the vertical interdependent self are more motivating in egalitarian individualist cultures than in nonegalitarian collectivist cultures. A positive evaluation of the motivational practices results in a positive effect on employees' performance and work behavior.

Work behavior is governed by both objective and subjective criteria. Among the objective criteria are performance quantity and performance quality (which include withdrawal behavior such as absenteeism and turnover as well as extra-role behavior, that is, behavior over and above expectations). Subjective criteria involve perceptions and attribution, attitude formation, motivation, and commitment.

An Integration

Thus the causal links between culture, self, motivational practices, and performance take the following form. Cultural values of collectivism versus individualism and high versus low power distance shape the horizontal and vertical interdependent and independent facets of the self. Each person uses these values, as they are represented in the self, for evaluating the meaning of various motivational practices for his or her sense of self-worth and well-being. Positive evaluation motivates employees toward goal accomplishment, whereas negative evaluation results in poor performance.

The self-construal, as it is shaped by culture, moderates the relationship between motivational practices and employee behavior. For example, tasks performed by self-managed teams are positively evaluated by employees with a dominant horizontal interdependent self, that is, those who live in egalitarian collectivist cultures. Tasks performed by teams run by team leaders are positively evaluated by employees with a dominant vertical interdependent self, that is, those who live in cultures of high collectivism and high power distance. Enriched jobs performed by individuals are highly motivating to individuals with a horizontal independent self, that is, those who live in egalitarian and individualist cultures, whereas individual jobs performed under a hierarchy of authority are acceptable to employees with a vertical independent self, that is, those who live in cultures of high individualism and high power distance.

Managerial practices that motivate employees in one type of culture will not be highly motivating when implemented in a different culture. The following section examines the meaning of some specific motivational practices in different types of cultures.

The Differential Effectiveness of Motivational Practices Across Cultures

Managers across cultures use four major types of motivational practices: reward allocation, participation in goal setting and decision making, job and organizational design, and quality improvement like Total Quality Management. Again, two cultural values will serve for interpreting the meaning of the four motivational practices: collectivism versus individualism, which explains the preference for working individually or in teams, and power distance, which describes the degree of equality or inequality between various organizational levels.

Motivational approaches that enhance employee involvement in organizations are considered to be highly effective (Lawler, Mohrman, & Ledford, 1992). However, there are many different and sometimes opposing methods for encouraging employee involvement. It can be strengthened by allocating differential rewards or equal pay; by approaching work as the province of the individual employee or of the team; by allowing employees to actively participate in major job-related decisions; by charismatic leaders who direct their followers; and by emphasizing intrinsic motivation or external rewards for quality improvement produced by teams or individuals. The meaning of each one of these motivational practices and its effect on a person's self-worth and well-being depend upon the cultural values as they are represented in the self.

Reward Allocation

In societies with high levels of power distance, or inequality, employees pay strong respect to their superiors and avoid criticizing them. Organizations often show large discrepancies in compensation, in status symbols, and in the quality of working life between managers and nonmanagers and between different managerial levels (Hofstede, 1991; Erez & Earley, 1993). In societies with low levels of power distance, employees are not afraid to criticize their superiors and there are smaller differences in compensation, status symbols, and the quality of working life for members of different levels of the organizational hierarchy.

Reward systems across cultures are guided by three different allocation principles: the *principle of equity* (to each according to contribution), the *principle of equality* (to each equally), and the *principle of need* (to each according to need). These principles differ across cultures and are the result of preferences for either individualism or collectivism and either egalitarianism or a high power differential.

The principle of equity leads to individual incentive plans. Typically, these plans are based on individual performance evaluations that determine each employee's particular level of compensation (Gerhart & Milkovich, 1992). According to the principle of equity, two employees who have the same job can get different levels of compensation when one receives a better performance evaluation. These evaluations can be determined either objectively (for example, by number of units produced or the number of customers served) or subjectively (for example, by supervisor observation).

Theories of motivation and managerial practices developed in the United States are mainly guided by the equity rule that rewards should be differentially distributed and be contingent upon performance. The same rule is embedded in the expectancy model of motivation, in the equity model, and in models of merit-based compensation plans. This rule was first implemented by the scientific management theorists, who advocated the philosophy of performance-based compensation and the installment of individual wage incentive plans (Taylor, [1911] 1967).

Individual performance appraisals have been extensively developed and widely implemented in the United States because they are central to managerial decisions on incentives, promotions, and the like. Merit-based incentive plans are very common in U.S. corporations (Lawler, Mohrman, & Ledford, 1992), and they are consistent with the vertical individualist values of U.S. culture. However, this system leads to increasing levels of inequality in the society, and the salary gap between CEOs and nonmanagerial employees is continually widening. A report in *Business Week* (1991) shows that in 1990, even as profits declined 7 percent, the average chief executive's total pay climbed to $1,952,806. Between 1980 and 1990, employees received a 53 percent increase in pay as corporate profit increased by 78 percent and CEO compensation increased by 212 percent. A more recent report (*Business Week,* 1993) demonstrated that the gap continued to increase from 1990 to 1992. The average annual compensation was $24,411 for rank-and-file employees, $34,098 for teachers, $58,240 for engineers, and $3,842,247 for CEOs.

The acceptance of the principle of equity found in U.S. corporations may not be taken for granted in a different culture. In collectivist cultures and in cultures of low power differential the rule of equality is more congruent. For example, North European countries endorse more collectivist values than does the United States. This explains why only 19 percent of the workforce in the Netherlands and only 4 percent of the workforce in Germany receive "payment by results." The remaining employees receive equal pay (Thierry, 1987).

A comparison between the United States and Sweden revealed that the Swedes put the rule of equality first, followed by the rule of need and then the rule of equity, and that the three rules are more highly differentiated by Swedes than by Americans (Tomasson, 1970; Tornblum, Jonsson, & Foa, 1985). The equality rule was significantly stronger among Swedes; the equity rule was stronger in the United States, and the need rule was negatively viewed by Americans, whereas the Swedes were indifferent to that rule.

Similarly, the Swedish value system is oriented more toward equality than is the U.S. system (Tomasson, 1970). The Swedish education system discourages competition in favor of cooperation. Teamwork and solidarity are encouraged more than individual achievement. The high value given in Sweden to interpersonal orientation is emphasized in organizations' criteria for advancement. A positive correlation was found between persons' cooperativeness and their rate of advancement in Scandinavia and Japan but not in ten other countries, including the United States, the Netherlands, Belgium, and Germany (Rosenstein, 1985).

A comparison between the United States and India demonstrated that across situations, Indians put the principle of need first, followed by equity and equality. Americans distributed rewards on the basis of equity when positive rewards were under consideration but on the basis of need when they considered a reduction in compensation (Berman, Murphy-Berman, & Singh, 1985).

The principle of need predominates in collectivist cultures like India because people in these cultures have a high level of personal interdependence and greater sensitivity to each other's needs (Murphy-Berman, Berman, Singh, Pachauri, & Kumar, 1984). Also, the rule of need is more likely to be implemented when needs become visible, as is the case in India. Finally, Indians may be less sensitive to merit because status in their society is determined more by affiliation than achievement (Berman, Murphy-Berman, & Singh, 1985).

China and Japan are known for their collectivist values. Accordingly, Chinese used the equality rule in allocating rewards to in-group members more than did Americans, guided by individualist values (Leung & Bond, 1984; Bond, Leung, & Wan, 1982).

However, there are boundary conditions for the implementation of the rule of equality in collectivist cultures and the rule of equity in individualist cultures. Collectivists make clear distinctions between in-group and out-group members. They use the principle of equality to allocate rewards to in-group members and the principle of equity for rewards to out-group members.

In individualist cultures an interpersonal dimension attenuates the use of the equity rule and enhances the use of the rule of equality when allocation is public. Empirical findings demonstrated that Chinese and Americans both allocated more resources to themselves under private conditions, when social pressure was removed. Furthermore, high performers in both cultures allocated more rewards to themselves than did low performers; productivity was used by both cultural groups as a basis for the allocation. Chinese males used the rule of equality more than Americans both for in-group and out-group members. However, for out-group allocation they used the rule of equality when the allocation was public and the rule of equity when allocation was private (Leung & Bond, 1984).

Similarly, a comparative study of the United States and Korea demonstrated that Koreans, who are known for their collectivist values, perceived allocations using the equality rule as more socially appropriate than allocations using the equity rule but that Americans saw less distinction in social value between the two rules (Leung & Park, 1986).

Although performance appraisal is often used as the criterion for individual incentives, individual performance appraisal is not acceptable in collectivist cultures because their focus is on the group rather than the individual performance. For that reason, attempts to implement incentive plans based on individual performance appraisals are often rejected in horizontal collectivist cultures (Gluskinos, 1988). Moreover, the use of performance appraisal for predicting successful job performance by managers seems to be valid in the United States but not in a collectivist culture such as Hong Kong. A comparative study demonstrated that the following performance appraisal factors were related to the effectiveness of U.S. managers: reconciliation, persuasiveness, initiation of structure, role assumption, consideration, predictive accuracy, and superior orientation. However, none of these factors or any other factor typically found on performance appraisals was related to the effectiveness of Chinese managers in Hong Kong (Black & Porter, 1991).

The reward schemes that emerge in each country fit in with the prevailing cultural characteristics. Attempts to transfer a reward system from one culture to another can result in a mismatch and therefore be ineffective. Individually based performance pay, for example, conflicts with teamwork because it creates competition between team members and often does not provide incentives for cooperation. Thus U.S. companies that encourage teamwork have been looking for alternatives to individual incentives.

A survey of Fortune 1000 corporations revealed that 11 percent of the companies used individual incentives in 1987 compared with 20 percent in 1990; team incentives were used by 12 percent of the companies in 1990 (no data were available for 1987); use of profit-sharing plans increased slightly, from 34 percent to 37 percent; use of gain-sharing plans remained steady at 3 percent; and the use of employee stock ownership plans increased very slightly, from 48 percent to 49 percent (Lawler, Mohrman, & Ledford, 1992). Thus it seems that Fortune 1000 companies use employee stock ownership plans more than any other form of incentive over and above salary, although such ownership is divided unequally among the employees, based on organizational position and performance evaluation.

Participation in Goal Setting and Decision Making

The process of employee participation involves three psychological factors (Erez, 1993). First, it has a motivational factor that satisfies needs for influence, autonomy, and responsibility. This motivational factor is present when managers clarify performance expectations and the link between performance and outcomes, allow people personal control over their course of behavior, and enhance their self-efficacy.

Second, participation has a cognitive factor of information sharing. Such sharing is facilitated by open communication among all group participants, by upward as well as downward communication, by better use of information, and by better understanding of the job and the rationale for underlying decisions. Employees who participate in decision making learn and gain information as part of the decision-making process; therefore they make better decisions and have a better understanding of what has to be done. This point is very important in a competitive world where the ideas and contributions of every employee are needed to help companies remain competitive.

Third, it has a group participation factor, a dynamic process that puts pressure on individual members to support group decisions, especially when a decision is made publicly. Employees who are active participants in making a decision buy into the decision and perform better than employees who are not committed (Erez, 1993; Erez & Arad, 1986).

Adherence to the group is influenced by cultural values. For example, in some European countries employee participation is institutionalized by law and is anchored in a political system that advocates socialist and egalitarian values. Therefore employee participation, which occurs mainly through employee representatives, is congruent with the cultural norms. In contrast, participation is not institutionalized in the United States, which is more individualist than most European countries.

Commitment to group goals and decisions is affected by group cohesion. Therefore one might expect a higher level of commitment to group goals in a collectivist and group-oriented culture, where a priority is given to those goals and where there is a great concern for the continuity and prosperity of the group (Triandis, Bontempo, Villareal, Asai, & Lucca, 1988).

Cross-cultural differences in values may, in part, explain why participation in goal setting has had a significant effect on performance in some but not all studies. A comparative study between Israel and the United States demonstrated that Israelis' performance was significantly lower when goals were assigned than when they participated in setting the goals. In addition, their performance was lower than the Americans' in the assigned goal-setting condition, but the two groups showed no differences when goals were participatively set (Erez & Earley, 1987). These findings demonstrated the moderating effect of culture. The more collectivist and lower power distance Israelis reacted more adversely to assigned goals than did the more individualist and higher power distance Americans. Lack of participation led to a lower level of commitment among the Israelis than among the Americans, and consequently to a lower level of performance, because commitment mediates the effect of participation on performance (Erez, Earley, & Hulin, 1985; Latham, Erez, & Locke, 1988).

Differences in cultural values partially contributed to the inconsistencies in the effect of participation that my colleagues and I found (Erez & Arad, 1986; Erez, 1986; Erez & Earley, 1987), and the lack of effect in North America found by Latham and his colleagues (for a review see Latham, Erez, & Locke, 1988). Latham and his colleagues reported a high level of goal commitment across all experimental conditions in almost all their studies on North Americans. In contrast, my colleagues and I reported high variance in commitment across experimental conditions. Americans were highly committed to both participative and assigned goals, whereas Israelis were committed only to the participative goals. This difference may be explained by the higher level of power distance in the North American culture, which led Americans, unlike the Israelis, to accept their assigned goals.

Cultural differences also occur between subcultures within a larger culture. Different effects of low, moderate, and high levels of participation were found in three Israeli industrial sectors that differ in their collectivist values: the private sector holds competitive and individualist values, the public sector endorses employee participation in management, and the kibbutz sector (consisting of communes managed by all their members) is highly collectivist. Lack of participation was most effective in the private sector, participation by a representative was most effective in the public sector, and group participation was most effective in the kibbutz sector (Erez, 1986). Again, congruence between the level of participation and the cultural values led to the highest level of effectiveness.

Employees' familiarity with the practice of participation is another explanatory factor. Participation in goal setting was more effective for employees who were used to work in high-participation units, whereas assigned goals were more effective for employees used to work in low-participation units (French, Kay, & Meyer, 1966). Long-term experience with participative methods creates a work culture that facilitates the effective implementation of a particular method of participation. For example, implementation of quality circles was successful in those Israeli industrial plants where other forms of employee participation, such as labor-management councils, already existed but were unsuccessful in plants with a predominantly authoritative managerial style (Erez, Rosenstein, & Barr, 1989). When motivational techniques are inconsistent with the organizational or departmental culture, they are likely to violate employees' internal motive of self-consistency.

Perhaps the most popular example of participative management today is that practiced in Japan. Employee participation takes the forms of small-group activities, quality circles, suggestion systems, and the *ringi-sei* system, a bottom-up decision-making process. Decisions are reached by group consensus, and all employees who will be affected by the decision take part in the process. By doing so, they become committed to the decision and gain the knowledge and understanding necessary to implement it. Although the decision-making process is time-consuming, once a decision is made, its implementation is immediate and smooth. Participative management in Japan fits in with that culture's collectivist values emphasizing teamwork, group harmony, and consensus. It also fits with the strong emphasis on friendships and family relationships. Japanese individuals' sense of self-identity is shaped by their group identity. Employees' personal well-being is defined in terms of group welfare: personal competence is defined in terms of group competence, and people feel good about themselves by contributing to the group and receiving the recognition of others (Erez, 1992).

Participative management might seem to be contradictory to the value of high power distance that is also found in Japanese culture. However, hierarchy in the Japanese society is anchored in the traditional kinship relationships that are formed around the basic social unit of the father-son relationship (Kume, 1985; Erez, 1992). In work organizations power distance takes the form of *management familism,* that is, the relationship of superior and subordinate is parallel to that of father and son. Thus the meaning high power distance conveys is not that of inequality due to unequal distribution of power among social classes.

Finally, decision making and goal setting can be undertaken by individuals or teams. In low power distance cultures, like Norway or Sweden, decision making is more likely to be participative than in high power distance cultures. When a culture has a low power distance and is individualist, like the United States, individual employees have a voice and get involved in decision making. In group-centered and low power differential cultures, like China or Israel, there is more group decision making and group goal setting than in individualist cultures.

Participation has been examined hardly at all in developing countries. The dominant cultural values of most developing countries are high collectivism, high power distance, low masculinity, and high uncertainty avoidance (Kanungo & Jaeger, 1990). Given these values, participation may be an effective motivational technique in developing countries (Erez, 1995). Their high level of collectivism fits in with participative management, and although their high level of power distance acts against participation, that power distance resides in the family structure and could support a form of management familism, as in Japan. The high level of femininity coincides with social orientation and hence supports group participation. The high level of uncertainty avoidance also supports group participation because information sharing reduces levels of ambiguity. Of course, in any organization in any country effective participation requires that employees be educated and trained to become active participants. This means that they learn how to share information, analyze it, interpret it, and present it in a meaningful way. In addition, they learn to improve their interpersonal skills and to effectively interact in the group. Participation has the potential to become an effective motivational technique in developing countries, but to materialize this potential, employees in developing countries should be educated to become active participants.

Job Enrichment

The job enrichment approach to motivation calls for designing jobs to be more rewarding and satisfying and thus to facilitate effective performance. The critical psychological factors that mediate the relationship between job dimensions and work motivation consist of the experienced meaningfulness of the work (which is affected by skill variety, task identity, and task significance), autonomy (employees' experience of personal responsibility), and knowledge of results (Hackman & Oldham, 1980).

Job Enrichment for Individual Employees

Jobs can be designed to satisfy the independent and the interdependent facets of the self. The original model of job enrichment was developed in the United States. It was designed mainly for the individual employee (Hackman & Oldham, 1980), and teamwork was not recommended as a means of self-enhancement: "unless the case of self-managing workgroups is compelling, it may be more prudent in traditional organizations to opt for the less radical alternative of enriching the jobs of individual employees" (Hackman & Oldham, 1980, p. 225).

The modern approach to job design in the United States is known as *reengineering* (Hammer & Champy, 1993). It is the search for and implementation of significant changes in business practices to achieve breakthrough results. Reengineering is driven by the new managerial approach of quality improvement, which focuses on the system rather than the individual, on processes rather than outcomes, and on customer satisfaction. The following example demonstrates the difference between traditional work design and reengineering. The traditional job of GTE repair clerks was to record information from a customer, fill out a trouble ticket, and send it on to others who tested lines and switches until they found and fixed the problem. On average, only one out of two hundred repair calls could be resolved by the repair clerks themselves. Once reengineering was implemented, the repair clerks were able to handle three out of ten repairs without having to forward the problem to other personnel. The repair clerks, now called front-end technicians, were given new training that taught them how to use the testing and switching equipment, and these tools were moved to their desks. This change increased the levels of skill variety, task significance, autonomy, and responsibility and allowed immediate feedback from the customer. GTE also stopped measuring how fast these employees handled calls and instead tracked how often they cleared up a problem without passing it on (Stewart, 1993).

The job of GTE telephone operators was reengineered as well. Operators were given new software for accessing databases, and this allowed them to handle virtually any customer request. Again, the job of the operators became more meaningful, and it allowed higher levels of responsibility, autonomy, and direct customer feedback. As a result, GTE has witnessed a 20 to 30 percent increase in productivity (Stewart, 1993). From a motivational perspective, reengineering at GTE successfully matched the company's goal of improving customer service with the employees' goal of satisfying their motive of self-growth.

Job Enrichment for the Group

The approach to job enrichment developed in North European countries such as England, Sweden, and Norway (Trist, 1981; Thorsrud, 1984), where the cultures are more collectivist than U.S. culture, has usually focused on the team. In collectivist cultures, the interdependent facet of the self becomes more salient. Therefore opportunities to work in teams and to contribute to team performance are more rewarding than working independently.

Called the *sociotechnical system* or *autonomous workgroups,* this approach aims at integrating the social and technical aspects of the work system. Sociotechnical interventions almost always involve the design of jobs at the group level. At this level, the job enrichment factors are team autonomy, team responsibility, feedback on team performance, and task meaningfulness (reflected for the group as for the individual in skill variety and task identity and significance). One of the disadvantages of the sociotechnical system as viewed by U.S. experts is that it "does not adequately deal with differences among organization members in how they respond to work" (Hackman & Oldham, 1980, p. 65). This critique simply conveys U.S. culture's greater concern with differences among individuals than with groups.

The most famous sociotechnical project is that implemented in the Volvo auto plants in Kalmar and Uddevalla during the eighties. Although these plants were shut down in 1993–1994 due to poor markets and low capacity usage, they still serve as excellent examples of the benefits and limitations of autonomous work-groups (Berggren, 1994).

Volvo's major purpose in implementing autonomous work-groups was to attract a high-quality labor force and reduce absenteeism and turnover rates. Turnover rates at the plants had reached levels in excess of 20 percent, in contrast to 12 percent in U.S. auto plants and only 5 percent in Japanese car factories (Prokesch, 1991). By adopting a new form of work design Volvo hoped to "humanize" the nature of work and thus reduce turnover and increase efficiency

A sociotechnical system was substituted for the traditional assembly line in the Kalmar plant. The work was organized for teams. Each team was responsible for a particular portion of the car—electrical systems, interior, doors, and so on. Team members had the opportunity to develop task identity by assuming responsibility for a specific portion of the work. In addition, all team members developed multiple skills that allowed them to rotate jobs and substitute for each other. The multiple skill approach enhanced task meaningfulness. A sense of responsibility was developed by self-inspection of product quality. This inspection also provided immediate feedback on quality performance (that is, knowledge of results) and enhanced work motivation and performance. In the Uddevalla Volvo plant a similar approach was implemented on the departmental level by delegating to the four main departments (pressing, body work, painting, and assembly) as much autonomy as possible. Each department formed working groups to solve problems unique to that department. On the managerial level, industrial democracy took the form of work councils, consultation groups, and project groups. These groups had their own budgets to spend for the improvement of working conditions. Implementation of this sociotechnical system reduced turnover rate and improved product quality over that of the traditional assembly line. The function of management at Volvo had changed: management's task now was to create a climate where the people who mattered were able to have ideas and to try them out (Gyllenhammar, 1977).

Both plants showed a significant improvement in employee morale, turnover was reduced to 6 percent, and quality was high. In addition, Uddevalla quality surpassed that of Volvo's main assembly plant in Gothenburg, and the Volvo 940 model assembled at Uddevalla, Kalmar, and Gothenburg was ranked the best European car. The short feedback loops enhanced team learning, and productivity progress at Uddevalla was remarkable. In 1992, the number of hours spent per car at Uddevalla decreased dramatically from fifty to thirty-six, similar to the average time at the Kalmar plant and at other European car makers' assembly plants. By these standards, the autonomous workgroups in these plants were a success.

However, at this same time the number of hours spent per car was twenty-two to twenty-five in U.S. plants and seventeen in Japanese plants. These figures call into question Volvo's "success." One explanation for the lower production rate was that although the Uddevalla plant was designed for as many as forty-eight assembly teams, only thirty-five were operating, due to a dramatic decrease in sales. Further, each team could decelerate or accelerate the rate at which it received parts. Because there was no market pressure to produce more cars, the teams may not have seen any reason to accelerate their pace of work to their full capacity.

Quality Control Circles

Employee involvement in Japan has taken the form of small-group activities, or more specifically, *quality control circles.* Quality control (QC) circles are small groups whose members are all in the same workshop that voluntarily and continually undertake quality control activities, including the control and improvement of the workplace (Onglatco, 1988, p. 15). Their purpose is to enhance the companywide quality level and at the same time to contribute to employees' sense of self-worth and well-being. And indeed, QC circles in Japan have significantly contributed to the improvement of product quality, enhanced efficiency and cost reduction, and facilitated innovation. They have also been found to have a significant positive effect on employees' sense of self-worth and well-being.

The Japanese example demonstrates that motivational techniques congruent with cultural values satisfy the self-derived motives and result in high performance. In Japan the interdependent self is salient. Therefore an individual experiences enhancement, efficacy, and consistency when he or she makes a contribution to the quality circle and gets recognition for that contribution.

Teamwork in Individualist Cultures

In an attempt to compete against the Japanese, many U.S. companies also have implemented QC circles. However, these attempts have not been highly successful (Cole, 1980), owing to a lack of long-term mutual commitment between employees and their organizations; the individualist U.S. culture, which advocates individual work rather than teamwork; a lack of top-level managerial support; and short-term management strategies that contradict the long-term orientation of quality improvement (Lawler, 1994).

Research on group performance in the United States has shown that people working together do not perform as well as when working alone (Latane, Williams, & Harkins, 1979; Gabrenya, Latane, & Wang, 1983). This phenomenon of individuals exerting less effort when their efforts are combined than when they are considered individually is known as *social loafing* (Levine, Resnick, & Higgins, 1993; Shepperd, 1993). And cross-cultural research has demonstrated that social loafing is moderated by culture. Although performance loss in groups was observed in the United States, it did not occur in collectivist cultures such as China and Israel (Earley, 1989, 1993; Erez & Somech, 1996).

However, an in-depth examination of the previous research on social loafing reveals that the research conditions inhibited the development of cohesive groups. First, in almost all of the studies there were no real groups. Some studies used pseudo-groups, and subjects did not perform in the physical or social presence of others. In other studies, partitions were put between the group members so that they could not see, hear, or communicate with each other (Harkins, 1987; Harkins & Szymanski, 1989; Sanna, 1992).

Second, communication among group members, a major characteristic of interactive groups, could not occur in the pseudo-groups or when group members were separated by partitions. Yet communication has been found to be an effective method of eliminating social loafing (Shepperd, 1993; Weldon, Jehn, & Pradham, 1991) and enhancing cooperation (Chen & Komorita, 1994; Edney & Harper, 1978; Wagner, 1995). Communication and interaction among group members increased commitment and group performance (Matsui, Kakuyama, & Onglatco, 1987), and the combination of group goals and group feedback for reciprocal task interdependence led to better group performance than did a low level of interaction (Saavedra, Earley, & Van Dyne, 1993; Straus & McGrath, 1994; Mitchell & Silver, 1990). Communication between subordinates and superiors improved superiors' performance when subordinates were knowledgeable (Scully, Kirkpatrick, & Locke, 1995), and participation in goal setting and group discussion led to the highest level of commitment to personal goals and to individual performance (Erez & Arad, 1986; Latham, Erez, & Locke, 1988).

Third, only a few studies incorporated group performance goals when testing group productivity loss (Earley, 1989, 1993; Sanna, 1992; Shepperd & Wright, 1989; Weldon, Jehn, & Pradham, 1991). In most of the studies subjects did not have specific goals, and they did not receive feedback on performance (Harkins, 1987; Harkins & Szymanski, 1989; Latane, Williams, & Harkins, 1979; Weldon & Gargano, 1988; Williams, Harkins, & Latane, 1981).

It is reasonable to propose that in individualist cultures social loafing can be eliminated when the members of a group are all present, work together, communicate with each other, have specific standards and performance goals, and experience goal accomplishment reinforcement (Erez & Somech, 1996). In addition group performance loss is mitigated when the group members become personally accountable and responsible for their performance (Weldon & Gargano, 1988; Weldon, Jehn, & Pradham, 1991). All these conditions that eliminate social loafing coincide with the definition of a group as a body of people with mutual awareness and potential mutual interaction (McGrath, 1984). Thus, even in individualist cultures, teamwork is most likely to be effective when all the conditions described here are met.

Moreover, teamwork can be enhanced by creating a supportive organizational environment. One such environment is the *horizontal corporation.* Jobs that allow autonomy, responsibility, and meaningfulness are linked together in a redesign of the organization. In the horizontal corporation authority is pushed down the organizational ladder, and the level of shared responsibility is increased. "Forget the pyramid, smash hierarchy, break the company into its key processes, and create teams from different departments to run them": this is the essence of the new design (Byrne, 1993, p. 76). The horizontal corporation allows employees the autonomy to make decisions and to take responsibility for their performances.

For these reasons, horizontal organizations fit best in egalitarian cultures with low levels of power distance such as the United States, Australia, England, the Netherlands, Sweden, and Norway. In individualist cultures the horizontal organization is going to enhance personal responsibility and personal accountability. It is going to support teamwork where the team members will be personally accountable and responsible for their group performance. The horizontal organization meets the competitive demands of the twenty-first century, and it looks like more and more companies are moving in this direction (Byrne, 1993).

It is not a coincidence that individual job enrichment was developed in the United States, that autonomous workgroups were developed in North Europe, and that quality control circles were developed in Japan. Different cultures enhance the development of different motivational techniques because cultural criteria are used for evaluating these techniques. Motivational techniques that contribute to the fulfillment of the self-derived motives will presumably be congruent with cultural values. In the United States individual job enrichment satisfies the independent self, which is cultivated by the cultural value of individualism. In North Europe the sociotechnical system provides opportunities for the enhancement of the interdependent self, which is supported by collectivist cultural values, and in Japan QC circles allow fulfillment of the interdependent self, which is consonant with the collectivist values of that culture.

Quality Improvement

Quality improvement is a major factor in achieving a competitive advantage. Although the success of Total Quality Management in Japan has been widely documented, a McKinsey study in Europe and the United States found that two-thirds of the quality improvement programs have failed to show the expected results. One possible explanation is that traditional programs of quality improvement are team based and therefore fit in with the Japanese culture but not the Western cultures. Quality programs should be adapted to a country's cultures if they are to be successful.

A culture-based model of quality improvement will vary according to each culture's values of power distance and collectivism versus individualism, and the variation will be in the level of participation and teamwork. Nave, Zonenshein, and I have postulated the 3–D model of quality improvement (Nave, Erez, & Zonenshein, 1995), a general model that can be adapted to cultural variation. This model proposes that an effective program of quality improvement should be implemented on three dimensions—organizational, team, and individual. The organizational dimension includes enhancing the commitment of top management and creating the infrastructure necessary for a highly effective program. The team dimension is often where most of the activities of quality improvement (QI) take place. Yet all teams consist of individuals. Therefore allowing individuals to feel personally responsible for quality improvement and rewarding both team and individual efforts strengthens the effectiveness of the QI program. The 3–D model can be modified to fit the particular cultural characteristics of the work environment. For example, quality at the team level should be emphasized in collectivist cultures, and the quality of individual performance should be stressed in individualist cultures, where quality is perceived to be personal (Roberts & Sergeketter, 1993). Variation will also occur in top management's role. Top management may assume the major responsibility for the implementation or share that responsibility with lower managerial levels, either as individuals or as self-managed teams. In cultures with a high power differential, top management should take the ultimate responsibility, and in cultures with a low power differential, top management should share the responsibility.

The 3–D model suggests QI program implementation strategies that match the emphasis given to each dimension in the culture.

1. *The organizational dimension.* Implementation on this level is universal because it establishes the infrastructure for the companywide program, including the establishment of ISO-9000 standards, criteria and measures for quality improvement, a computerized information system (the quality database), training programs and awards, a quality bulletin, the assignment of managers to serve as quality auditors, and the restructuring of the organization as a chain of internal customers.
2. *The team dimension.* Implementation on this level involves setting up departmental and interdepartmental mission teams,

holding regular team meetings for setting quality goals, receiving feedback on team performance, solving problems in teams, and making team suggestions for quality improvement.

3. *The individual dimension.* Implementation on this level consists of training employees in appropriate skills and creating attitude change. Specific programs can be designed for training employees as certified quality auditors, self-quality inspectors, and information system operators.

The implementation of the 3–D model on all three dimensions in an Israeli vehicle repair plant was found to be very successful (Nave, Erez, & Zonenshein, 1995). At the end of sixteen months of implementation the plant's grade on the external ISO-9000 evaluation increased from 38 to 80, giving the plant its ISO-9000 accreditation. The cost of quality decreased from 22 percent to 2 percent. Inventory cost decreased by 11 percent. Savings resulting from suggestion system were four times higher than they were prior to QI implementation. The accident rate decreased by 62 percent. There was also a significant change in the organizational culture, with a growing emphasis on the values of quality, innovation, attention to details, team orientation, and supportiveness. Attitudes changed significantly toward higher levels of commitment and work satisfaction. This change toward a quality-oriented culture was highly correlated with the improvement in performance quality.

As I have discussed, the 3–D model of quality improvement can be successfully adapted to other cultures as well because it can emphasize the individual, group, or organizational level, depending on the cultural fit. QI programs in Western cultures should emphasize the individual level, and activity at the team level should allow for personal accountability and personal responsibility. Although Deming (1990), one of the founders of the QI movement, objected to individual performance appraisal, management by objectives, and individual incentives, these human resource practices should be incorporated in QI programs in Western cultures because they fit in with the cultural characteristics.

U.S. companies that have won the Baldrige Award are already known for the quality goals they set. For example, Motorola, which has already cut defects from 6,000 per million to only 40 per million in just five years, has a goal of further cutting defects by 90 percent every two years throughout the 1990s. Quality criteria are often included in Motorola's employee performance evaluations. Federal Express rates employees on both quality of work and customer service. Xerox evaluates employees individually, but contribution to the team is an important evaluation criterion.

Furthermore, all these companies offer rewards at both the individual and the team levels. At Xerox, individuals are nominated for the President's Award or the Xerox Achievement Award. Teams compete for the Excellence Award and the Excellence in Customer Satisfaction Award. Motorola sponsors the Team Quality Olympics, where teams make formal presentations of their contributions and receive gold, silver, and bronze medals accordingly. Westinghouse has implemented peer review for determining its quality achievement winners.

In addition to individual-based pay systems, some Western companies have instituted organization-based pay systems of profit sharing, gain sharing, and employee stock ownership plans (Lawler, Mohrman, & Ledford, 1992). Empowering employees to be personally accountable for quality and rewarding their contributions to quality improvement fit well with the U.S. and other Western cultures. Clearly, programs of quality improvement can be designed to fit the characteristics of different cultures.

Conclusion

The culture-based model of work motivation is a useful conceptual framework for evaluating the motivation potential of various motivational techniques across cultures. The model draws the links between culture, self, motivational practices, and employee behavior.

Individuals' system of information processing and, more specifically, their mechanism of self-regulation (including goal-setting, monitoring, evaluating, and self-reinforcing actions) are universal. The three self-derived motives of enhancement, efficacy, and consistency are universal.

What are not universal are the values and criteria individuals use to evaluate the different motivational techniques and their potential contribution to the fulfillment of the self-derived motives. The emphasis given to specific values varies across cultures. At the same time, cultural values shape the horizontal and vertical interdependent and horizontal and vertical independent facets of the self. These four different self-construals give individuals different criteria for evaluating the various motivational techniques. Therefore a motivational technique that satisfies the horizontal independent self in an egalitarian and individualist culture will not effectively satisfy the vertical independent self in a hierarchical and individualist culture or the horizontal and vertical interdependent selves in collectivist cultures. A motivational technique that pushes authority down and allows personal or team responsibility will be appreciated in cultures of low power distance but not in cultures of high power distance, where employees expect their superior to take the lead.

Table 8.1 summarizes the variations in the four motivational practices examined in this chapter and their fit with the four types of cultures: individualist and low power distance, individualist and high power distance, collectivist and low power distance, and collectivist and high power distance.

In individualist cultures of low power distance, reward allocation is guided mostly by the principle of equality, decision making is guided by the delegation of authority, effective goal setting is obtained by personal involvement, job enrichment is positively evaluated, and practices of quality improvement are geared toward individual employees.

In individualist cultures of high power distance, reward allocation is guided mostly by the principle of equity, decision making is centralized and top down, goals are assigned to the employees, jobs are designed in a hierarchy of authority, and quality improvement is centrally controlled and focuses on the individual employees.

In collectivist cultures of low power distance, reward allocation is guided mostly by the principles of equality and need, decisions are made with group participation, goals are set by the group members, jobs are designed for teams in the form of autonomous workgroups, self-managed teams, and quality circles, and practices of quality improvement are geared toward teams.

In collectivist cultures of high power distance, reward allocation is guided mostly by the principles of equity and need at the group level, decision making is centralized and top down, group goals are assigned, jobs are designed for employee and management teams that are closely controlled by top-management teams,

Table 8.1. Effective Motivational Techniques in Cultures of Collectivist Versus Individualist Values, and of High and Low Power Distance.

	Low Power Distance	High Power Distance
Individualist Rewards	*The principle of equality:* Profit sharing, gain sharing Low salary differential Welfare and fringe benefits based on demographics (for example, family size, disability)	*The principle of equity:* Individual incentives High salary differential
Decision Making	Delegation of authority Individual decision making	Top-down decision making Centralized decision making
Goal-Setting	Personal involvement in goal-setting	Assigned individual goals
Job Design	Enrichment of individual jobs	Individual jobs in a hierarchy of authority and responsibility
Quality Improvement at the level of:		
The Organization	Empowerment	Centralized control
The Team	Second to personal quality	Second to personal quality
The Individual	Individual training Individual responsibility Individual feedback Individual problem-solving Individual performance appraisal Individual rewards	Individual training Individual responsibility Individual feedback Individual problem-solving Individual performance appraisal Individual rewards

Table 8.1. Effective Motivational Techniques in Cultures of Collectivist Versus Individualist Values, and of High and Low Power Distance, Cont'd.

	Low Power Distance	High Power Distance
Collectivist Rewards	*The rule of equality or needs:* Equally distributed organization-based rewards; Equally distributed employee stock ownership plans	*The rule of equity or needs:* Group-based rewards; Unequally distributed organization-based rewards; Unequally distributed employee stock ownership plans
Decision Making	Delegation of authority; Group participation	Top-down; Centralized decision making
Goal-Setting	Group goal-setting	Assigned group goals
Job Design	Autonomous work groups; Self-managed team; Quality circles	Team work controlled by top management teams; Quality circles
Quality Improvement at the level of:		
The Organization	Self-management	Team leadership
The Team	Team training; Team responsibility; Team feedback; Team problem-solving; Team performance evaluation; Team rewards	Team training; Team responsibility; Team feedback; Team problem-solving; Team performance evaluation; Team rewards
The Individual	Second to teams	Second to teams

and quality improvement is centrally controlled and focuses on teamwork.

A culture-based approach to work motivation takes into consideration the cultural values that serve for evaluating the meaning of motivational techniques. What motivates people is influenced by culture. Reward systems, job designs, decision-making and goal-setting processes, and quality improvement programs that are shaped to accord with cultural values are most likely to motivate employees to accomplish organizational goals because they satisfy employees' motives for self-worth and well-being as those motives are conceived by the representation of cultural values in the self. Motivational practices that are incongruent with cultural values are less likely to have a positive effect on employees' performance and behavior.

References

Bandura, A. (1986). *Social foundations of thought and action: A social cognitive theory.* Upper Saddle River, NJ: Prentice Hall.

Bandura, A. (1991). Social cognitive theory of self-regulation. *Organizational Behavior and Human Decision Processes, 50,* 248–287.

Berggren, C. (1994, Winter). Nummi versus Uddevalla. *Sloan Management Review,* pp. 37–49.

Berman, J. J., Murphy-Berman, V., & Singh, P. (1985). Cross-cultural similarities and differences in perceptions of fairness. *Journal of Cross-Cultural Psychology, 16,* 55–67.

Berry, J. W. (1979). A cultural ecology of social behavior. In L. Berkowitz (Ed.), *Advances in experimental social psychology* (Vol. 12, pp. 177–206). Orlando: Academic Press.

Bingswanger, H. (1991). Volition as a cognitive self-regulation. *Organizational Behavior and Human Decision Processes, 50,* 154–178.

Black, J. S., & Porter, L. W. (1991). Managerial behaviors and job performance: A successful manager in Los Angeles may not succeed in Hong Kong. *Journal of International Business Studies, 22,* 99–113.

Bond, M. H., & Cheung, T. S. (1983). College students' spontaneous self-concept: The effect of culture among respondents in Hong Kong, Japan, and the United States. *Journal of Cross-Cultural Psychology, 14,* 153–171.

Bond, M. H., Leung, K., & Wan, K. C. (1982). How does cultural collectivism operate? The impact of task and maintenance contributions on reward allocation. *Journal of Cross-Cultural Psychology, 13,* 186–200.

Bond, M. H., & Smith, P. B. (1996). Cross-cultural social and organizational psychology: Coming of age. *Annual Review of Psychology, 47,* 205–235.

Breckler, S. J., & Greenwald, A. G. (1986). Motivational facets of the self. In R. M. Sorrentino & E. T. Higgins (Eds.), *Handbook of motivation and cognition: Foundations of social behavior* (pp. 145–164). New York: Guilford Press.

Business Week. (1991, May), pp. 52–76.

Business Week. (1993, April), pp. 38–39.

Byrne, J. (1993, December). Horizontal corporation: It's about managing across, not up and down. *Business Week,* p. 76.

Cappelli, P., & Sherer, P. D. (1991). The missing role of context in OB: The need for a meso-level approach. In B. Staw & L. L. Cummings (Eds.), *Research in organizational behavior* (Vol. 13, pp. 55–110). Greenwich, CT: JAI Press.

Chen, X.-P., & Komorita, S. S. (1994). The effect of communication and commitment in a public good social dilemma. *Organizational Behavior and Human Decision Processes, 60,* 367–386.

Cohen, M.D., & Sproull, L. S. (1991, February). Paper in honor of (and by) James G. March [Special issue on organizational learning]. *Organizational Science, 2*(1).

Cole, R. E. (1980). *Work, mobility, and participation: A comparative study of American and Japanese industry.* Berkeley: University of California Press.

Crocker, J., Luhtanen, R., Blaine, B., & Broadnax, S. (1994). Collective self-esteem and psychological well-being among White, Black, and Asian college students. *Personality and Social Psychology Bulletin, 20,* 503–513.

Dansereau, F., Alutto, J. A., & Yammarino, F. J. (1984). *Theory testing in organizational behavior: The variant approach.* Upper Saddle River, NJ: Prentice Hall.

Deming, W. E. (1990). *Out of the crisis.* Cambridge, England: Cambridge University Press.

Earley, P. C. (1989). Social loafing and collectivism: A comparison of the United States and the People's Republic of China. *Administrative Science Quarterly, 34,* 565–581.

Earley, P. C. (1993). East meets West meets Mideast. Further explorations of collectivistic and individualistic work groups. *Academy of Management Journal, 36,* 319–348.

Earley, P. C. (1994). Self or group? Cultural effects of training on self-efficacy and performance. *Administrative Science Quarterly, 39,* 89–117.

Earley, P. C., & Brittain, J. (1992). Cross-level analysis of organizations: Social resource management model. In B. Staw & L. L. Cummings

(Eds.), *Research in organizational behavior* (Vol. 15, pp. 357–408). Greenwich, CT: JAI Press.

Edney, J. J., & Harper, C. S. (1978). The common dilemma: A review of contributions from psychology. *Environmental Management, 2,* 491–507.

Erez, M. (1986). The congruence of goal-setting strategies with socio-cultural values and its effects on performance. *Journal of Management, 12,* 83–90.

Erez, M. (1992). Interpersonal communication systems in organizations and their relationships to cultural values, productivity, and innovation: The case of Japanese corporations. *Applied Psychology: An International Review, 41,* 43–64.

Erez, M. (1993). Participation in goal setting: A motivational approach. In E. Resenstein & W. M. Lafferty (Eds.), *International handbook of participation in organizations* (pp. 73–91). New York: Oxford University Press.

Erez, M. (1994). Towards a model of cross-cultural I/O psychology. In H. C. Triandis, M. D. Dunnette, & L. M. Hough (Eds.), *Handbook of industrial and organizational psychology* (2nd ed., Vol. 4, pp. 559–608). Palo Alto, CA: Consulting Psychologists Press.

Erez, M. (1995). Prospect of participative management in developing countries: The role of socio-cultural environment. In D. M. Saunders & R. N. Kanungo (Eds.), *New approaches to employee management* (Vol. 3, pp. 171–196). Greenwich, CT: JAI Press.

Erez, M., & Arad, R. (1986). Participative goal-setting: Social, motivational and cognitive factors. *Journal of Applied Psychology, 71,* 591–597.

Erez, M., & Earley, P. C. (1987). Comparative analysis of goal-setting strategies across cultures. *Journal of Applied Psychology, 72,* 658–665.

Erez, M., & Earley, P. C. (1993). *Culture, self-identity, and work.* New York: Oxford University Press.

Erez, M., Earley, P. C., & Hulin, C. L. (1985). The impact of participation on goal acceptance and performance: A two-step model. *Academy of Management Journal, 28,* 50–66.

Erez, M., & Katz, T. (1995, May). *Effects of self- and collective-efficacy on team performance of independent and interdependent tasks.* Paper presented at the tenth annual conference of the Society for Industrial and Organizational Psychology, Orlando.

Erez, M., Rosenstein, E., & Barr, S. (1989). Antecedents and supporting conditions for the success of quality circles (Research report No. 193–720). Haifa: Technion Institute of Research and Development.

Erez, M., & Somech, A. (1996). Group performance loss: The rule of the exception. *Academy of Management Journal.*

Fisher, A. B. (1991, November). Morale crisis. *Fortune,* pp. 34–42.

French, J.R.P., Kay, E., & Meyer, H. H. (1966). Participation and the appraisal system. *Human Relations, 19,* 3–20.

Gabrenya, W. K., Jr., Latane, B., & Wang, Y. (1983). Social loafing in cross-cultural perspective. *Journal of Cross-Cultural Psychology, 14,* 368–384.

Gecas, V. (1982). The self concept. *Annual Review of Psychology, 8,* 1–33.

George, J. M. (1990). Personality, affect, and behavior in groups. *Journal of Applied Psychology, 75,* 107–116.

Gerhart, B., & Milkovich, G. T. (1992). Employee compensation: Research and practice. In M. D. Dunnette & L. M. Hough (Eds.), *Handbook of industrial and organizational psychology* (2nd ed., Vol. 3, pp. 481–570). Palo Alto, CA: Consulting Psychologists Press.

Gluskinos, U. M. (1988). Cultural and political considerations in the introduction of Western technology: The Mekorot project. *Journal of Management Development, 6,* 34–46.

Gyllenhammar, P. G. (1977, July-August). How Volvo adapts work to people. *Harvard Business Review,* pp. 102–113.

Hackman, J. R., & Oldham, G. R. (1980). *Work redesign.* Reading, MA: Addison-Wesley.

Hammer, M., & Champy, J. (1993). *Reengineering the corporation: A manifesto of business revolution.* New York: Harper Business.

Harkins, S. G. (1987). Social loafing and social facilitation. *Journal of Experimental and Social Psychology, 23,* 1–18.

Harkins, S. G., & Szymanski, K. (1989). Social loafing and group evaluation. *Journal of Personality and Social Psychology, 56,* 934–941.

Hofstede, G. (1980). *Culture's consequences: International differences in work-related values.* Thousand Oaks, CA: Sage.

Hofstede, G. (1991). *Culture and organizations: Software of the mind.* London: McGraw-Hill.

Hofstede, G., Bond, M. H., & Luk, C. L. (1993). Individual perceptions of organizational cultures: A methodological treatise on levels of analysis. *Organization Studies, 14,* 483–503.

Hofstede, G., Neuijen, B., Ohayv, D. D., & Sanders, G. (1990). Measuring organizational cultures: A qualitative and quantitative study across twenty cases. *Administrative Science Quarterly, 35,* 286–316.

Huber, G. P. (1991). Organizational learning: The contributing processes and the literature. *Organizational Science, 2,* 88–115.

James, L. R., Demaree, R. G., & Wolf, G. (1984). Estimating within-group interrater reliability with and without response bias. *Journal of Applied Psychology, 69,* 85–98.

Kagitçibasi, Ç., & Berry, J. W. (1989). Cross cultural psychology: Current research and trends. *Annual Review of Psychology, 40,* 493–531.

Kanfer, R. (1990). Motivation theory and industrial and organizational psychology. In M. D. Dunnette & L. M. Hough (Eds.), *Handbook of industrial and organizational psychology* (2nd ed., Vol. 1, pp. 75–170). Palo Alto, CA: Consulting Psychologists Press.

Kanfer, R., & Ackerman, P. L. (1989). Motivation and cognitive abilities: An integrative/aptitude-treatment interaction approach to skill acquisition. *Journal of Applied Psychology, 74,* 657–690.

Kanungo, R. N., & Jaeger, A. M. (1990). Introduction: The need for indigenous management in developing countries. In A. M. Jaeger & R. N. Kanungo (Eds.), *Management in developing countries* (pp. 1–19). London: Routledge.

Klein, K. J., Dansereau, F., & Hall, R. J. (1994). Levels issues in theory development, data collection, and analysis. *Academy of Management Review, 19*(2), 195–229.

Kluckhohn, C. (1954). *Culture and behavior.* NY: Free Press.

Kuhl, J., & Kraska, K. (1989). Self-regulation and metamotivation: Computational mechanisms, development, and assessment. In R. Kanfer, P. L. Ackerman, & R. Cudeck (Eds.), *Abilities, motivation, and methodology* (pp. 343–374). Hillsdale, NJ: Erlbaum.

Kume, T. (1985). Managerial attitudes toward decision-making: North America and Japan. In W. B. Gudykunst, L. P. Stewart, & S. Ting-Toomey (Eds.), *Communication, culture and organizational processes* (pp. 231–257). Thousand Oaks, CA: Sage.

Latane, B., Williams, K. D., & Harkins, S. G. (1979). Many hands make light the work: The causes and consequences of social loafing. *Journal of Personality and Social Psychology, 37,* 822–832.

Latham, G. P., Erez, M., & Locke, E. A. (1988). Resolving scientific disputes by the joint design of crucial experiments by the antagonists: Application to the Erez-Latham dispute regarding participation in goal setting. *Journal of Applied Psychology, 73,* 553–572.

Lawler, E. E., III. (1994). Total Quality Management and employee involvement: Are they compatible? *The Academy of Management Executive, 8,* 68–76.

Lawler, E. E., III, Mohrman, S. A., & Ledford, G. E., Jr. (1992). *Employee involvement and Total Quality Management: Practices and results in Fortune 1000 companies.* San Francisco: Jossey-Bass.

Leung, K., & Bond, M. H. (1984). The impact of cultural collectivism on reward allocation. *Journal of Personality and Social Psychology, 47,* 793–804.

Leung, K., & Park, H. J. (1986). Effects of interactional goal on choice of allocation rule: A cross-national study. *Organizational Behavior and Human Decision Processes, 37,* 111–120.

Levine, J. M., Resnick, L. B., & Higgins, E. T. (1993). Social foundation of cognition. *Annual Review of Psychology, 44,* 585–612.

Locke, E. A. (1991). The motivation sequence, the motivation hub, and the motivation core. *Organizational Behavior and Human Decision Processes, 50,* 288–299.

Markus, H. R., & Kitayama, S. (1991). Culture and the self: Implications for cognition, emotion, and motivation. *Psychological Review, 98,* 224–253.

Markus, H. R., & Wurf, E. (1987). The dynamic self-concept: A social psychological perspective. *Annual Review of Psychology, 38,* 299–337.

Matsui, T., Kakuyama, T., & Onglatco, M.L.U. (1987). Effects of goals and feedback on performance in groups. *Journal of Applied Psychology, 72,* 407–415.

McGrath, J. E. (1984). *Groups: Interaction and performance.* Upper Saddle River, NJ: Prentice Hall.

Mitchell, T. R., & Silver, W. S. (1990). Individual and group goals when workers are interdependent: Effects on task strategies and performance. *Journal of Applied Psychology, 75,* 185–193.

Mowday, R. T., & Sutton, R. I. (1993). Organizational behavior: Linking individuals and groups to organizational contexts. *Annual Review of Psychology, 44,* 195–229.

Murphy-Berman, V., Berman, J. J., Singh, P., Pachauri, A., & Kumar, P. (1984). Factors affecting allocation to needy and meritorious recipients: A cross-cultural comparison. *Journal of Personality and Social Psychology, 46,* 1267–1272.

Nave, E., Erez, M., & Zonenshein, A. (1995). TQM: A three dimensional model of changing organizational culture and performance quality. In G. K. Kanji (Ed.), *Proceedings of the First World Congress of TQM* (pp. 583–586). London: Chapman & Hall.

Onglatco, M.L.U. (1988). Japanese quality control circles: Features, effects and problems. Tokyo: Asian Productivity Center.

O'Reilly, C. A., III (1991). Organizational behavior: Where we've been, where we're going. *Annual Review of Psychology, 42,* 427–458.

Prokesch, S. (1991, July 7). Edges fray on Volvo's brave new humanistic world. *New York Times,* p. V-140.

Roberts, H., & Sergeketter, B. (1993). *Quality is personal: A foundation for Total Quality Management.* NY: Free Press.

Rokeach, M. (1973). *The nature of human values.* New York: Free Press.

Ronen, S. (1994). An underlying structure of motivational need taxonomies: A cross-cultural confirmation. In H. C. Triandis, M. D. Dunnette, & L. M. Hough (Eds.), *Handbook of industrial and organizational psychology* (2nd ed., Vol. 4, pp. 241–269). Palo Alto, CA: Consulting Psychologists Press.

Rosenstein, E. (1985). Cooperativeness and advancement of managers: An international perspective. *Human Relations, 38,* 1–21.

Rousseau, D. M., & House, R. J. (1994). Meso organizational behavior: Avoiding three fundamental biases. In C. L. Cooper & D. M.

Rousseau (Eds.), *Trends in organizational behavior* (Vol. 1, pp. 15–29). New York: Wiley.

Saavedra, R., Earley, P. C., & Van Dyne, L. (1993). Complex interdependence in task-performing groups. *Journal of Applied Psychology, 78,* 61–72.

Sanna, L. J. (1992). Self-efficacy theory: Implications for social facilitation and social loafing. *Journal of Personality and Social Psychology, 62,* 774–786.

Schein, E. (1990). Organizational culture. *American Psychologist, 45,* 109–119.

Schwartz, S. H. (1992). Universals in the content and structure of values: Theoretical advances and empirical tests in 20 countries. In M. P. Zanna (Ed.), *Advances in experimental social psychology* (Vol. 25, pp. 1–65). Orlando: Academic Press.

Schwartz, S. H., & Bilsky, W. (1987). Toward a universal psychological structure of human values. *Journal of Personality and Social Psychology, 53,* 550–562.

Schwartz, S. H., & Sagiv, L. (1995). Identifying culture-specifics in the content and structure of values. *Journal of Cross-Cultural Psychology, 26,* 92–116.

Scully, J. A., Kirkpatrick, S. A., & Locke, E. A. (1995). Locus of knowledge as a determinant of the effects of participation on performance, affect, and perceptions. *Organizational Behavior and Human Decision Processes, 61,* 276–288.

Senge, P. M. (1994). *The fifth discipline.* New York: Doubleday/Currency.

Shepperd, J. A. (1993). Productivity loss in performance groups: A motivation analysis. *Psychological Bulletin, 113,* 67–81.

Shepperd, J. A., & Wright, R. A. (1989). Individual contribution to a collective effort. *Personality and Social Psychology Bulletin, 15,* 141–149.

Shweder, R. A., & LeVine, R. A. (1984). *Culture theory: Essays on mind, self and emotion.* New York: Cambridge University Press.

Stewart, A. T. (1993, August). Reengineering: The hot new managing tool. *Fortune,* pp. 33–37.

Straus, S. G., & McGrath, J. E. (1994). Does the medium matter: The interaction of task type and technology on group performance and member reactions. *Journal of Applied Psychology, 79,* 86–97.

Tajfel, H. (1978). *Differentiation between social groups: Studies in social psychology of intergroup relations.* Orlando: Academic Press.

Taylor, F. W. (1967). *Principles of scientific management.* New York: Norton. (Original work published 1911)

Thierry, H. (1987). Payment by results: A review of research 1945–1985. *Applied Psychology: An International Review, 36,* 91–108.

Tomasson, R. F. (1970). *Sweden: Prototype of modern society.* New York: Random House.

Thorsrud, E. (1984). The Scandinavian model: Strategies of organizational democratization in Norway. In B. Wilpert & A. Sorge (Eds.), *International yearbook of industrial democracy: Vol. 2. International perspectives on organizational democracy* (pp. 337–370). New York: Wiley.

Tornblom, K. Y., Jonsson, D., & Foa, U. G. (1985). National resource class, and preferences among three allocation rules: Sweden vs. USA. *International Journal of Intercultural Relations, 9,* 51–77.

Trafimow, D., Triandis, H. C., & Goto, S. G. (1991). Some tests of the distinction between the private self and the collective self. *Journal of Personality and Social Psychology, 60,* 649–655.

Triandis, H. C. (1989). The self and social behavior in differing cultural contexts. *Psychological Review, 96,* 506–520.

Triandis, H. C. (1994). Cross-cultural industrial and organizational psychology. In H. C. Triandis, M. D. Dunnette, & L. M. Hough (Eds.), *Handbook of industrial and organizational psychology* (2nd ed., Vol. 4, pp. 104–172). Palo Alto, CA: Consulting Psychologists Press.

Triandis, H. C., Bontempo, R., Villareal, M. J., Asai, M., & Lucca, N. (1988). Individualism and collectivism: Cross-cultural perspectives on self-ingroup relationships. *Journal of Personality and Social Psychology, 54,* 323–338.

Trist, E. (1981). *The evolution of a socio-technical system.* Toronto: Ontario Quality of Working Life Center.

Vroom, V. H. (1964). *Work and motivation.* New York: Wiley.

Wagner, J. A., III. (1995). Studies of individualism-collectivism: Effects on cooperation in groups. *Academy of Management Journal, 38,* 152–172.

Weingart, L. R. (1992). Impact of group goals task component complexity, effort, and planning on group performance. *Journal of Applied Psychology, 77,* 682–693.

Weldon, E., & Gargano, G. M. (1988). Cognitive loafing: The effects of accountability and shared responsibility on cognitive effort. *Personality & Social Psychology Bulletin, 14,* 159–171.

Weldon, E., Jehn, K. A., & Pradham, P. (1991). Processes that mediate the relationship between a group goal and improved group performance. *Journal of Personality and Social Psychology, 61,* 555–569.

Weldon, E., & Weingart, L. R. (1993). Group goals and group performance. *British Journal of Social Psychology, 32,* 307–334.

Williams, K., Harkins, S., & Latane, B. (1981). Identifiability as a deterrent to social loafing: Two cheering experiments. *Journal of Personality and Social Psychology, 40,* 303–311.

Wilpert, B. (1995). Organizational behavior. *Annual Review of Psychology, 46,* 59–90.

CHAPTER 9

Doing an About-Face
Social Motivation and Cross-Cultural Currents
P. Christopher Earley

Erez's analysis of work motivation (Chapter Eight) focuses on various underlying motives through which culture influences organizational behavior. According to the model Erez and I developed (Erez & Earley, 1993), an individual's self-concept is regulated by three motives—enhancement, efficacy, and consistency—and self-concept regulates the influence of culture on behavior. In Chapter Eight Erez describes a number of ways that an individual's motivation is affected by cultural and work practices. The first of the three motives underlying the self, enhancement, reflects the way that a person views him- or herself in a social context. In this chapter I extend and elaborate the self-enhancement motive described by Erez in a social and work context. Erez's discussion of the motives of the self focuses on motivation from both an intrapersonal and an interpersonal perspective, identified by the distinction Erez and I made (Erez & Earley, 1993) between the independent and interdependent selves. This chapter focuses on

Note: This chapter has been improved greatly following helpful comments made during presentations at the Chinese University of Hong Kong; Hong Kong University of Science and Technology; Manchester Business School; Nanyang Technological University; and Washington University. My hearty thanks to colleagues at these institutions whose ideas and feedback helped me refine the construct. In addition I would like to thank Larry Farh, Geert Hofstede, and Richard Whitley for their helpful comments on an earlier draft.

the self-enhancement motive as it is manifest in a social environment, or the interdependent self. In this sense my chapter should be viewed as complementary to Erez's presentation, providing an extension of her discussion.

In my commentary I will build on her approach by focusing on a person's self-presentation in a social context, or what has been referred to as *face* by a number of scholars (for example, Goffman, 1959; Hu, 1944). The concept of face has been considered a predominantly Asian construct (Hu, 1944). However, I will present a universal typology of the construct and discuss its applicability to a variety of cultural contexts, based on extensive theoretical work that I have undertaken elsewhere (Earley, in press).

A fundamental aspect of human endeavor is that we interact in a given social context for a variety of symbolic, utilitarian, and pragmatic purposes (Etzioni, 1968). Critical in this context of interaction are the way we present ourselves and how others judge our actions and self-worth. Self-worth and impression conveyed are at the heart of the concept of face. Face refers to a universal aspect of interaction and concerns how we present ourselves as well as our basis for self-definition. Within an organizational context, face regulates social exchange and individual action, and it varies systematically according to individual differences as well as societal value orientations (Redding & Ng, 1982).

Overview of Face Construct

In this section I present a preliminary description of face, describing two major categories: *lian* and *mianzi*.[1] Both the Eastern and Western origins of face are discussed, along with other relevant models. In the subsequent section the construct of face is clarified and applied to a cross-cultural organizational context.

Definition of Face

A commonly cited definition of face is "the positive social value a person effectively claims for himself by the line others assume he has taken during a particular contact. Face is an image of self delineated in terms of approved social attributes" (Goffman, 1967, p. 5). Goffman further states that "every person lives in a world of social encounters, involving him either in face-to-face or mediated contact with other participants. In each of these contacts he tends to act out what is sometimes called a *line*—that is, a pattern of verbal and nonverbal acts by which he expresses his view of the situation and through this his evaluation of the participants, especially himself. . . . [I]f he is to deal with their response to him he must take into consideration the impression they have possibly formed of him" (p. 5).

I define face similarly except that I view it as the interactive product of self- and other evaluations. More specifically, face refers to the evaluation of a person based on self- and external social judgments. Face does not lie completely within or outside the individual, and it has important implications for an individual's behavior in an organization. For example, a concern for face leads a junior executive to purchase a house in an overly expensive (and exclusive) neighborhood or to spend an exorbitant amount on private schools for his or her children. Face is not mere pride, however, in that it is a consequence of personal and social judgments. It is not enough that the junior executive knows his children are at an expensive, private school; his superiors and colleagues must know it as well for him to receive face. This example illustrates the important point that face is both given (by others) and claimed (by the self).

Seminal work on face from an Asian perspective was presented by Hu (1944) in an article entitled "The Chinese Concepts of Face." In this paper Hu distinguished between two general forms of face, *lian* and *mianzi*.[2] Briefly, Hu argued that the Chinese context recognizes two forms of face, one concerned with moral character (*lian*) and one concerned with reputation and status (*mianzi*) in the shape of "getting on in life" (p. 45). Both forms of face have numerous variations, such as individuals having no character (*bu yao lian,* "not wanting *lian*") or giving others face (*gei mianzi,* "to give face"). Other views of face include Lin's discussion (1935), which sees face as a critical aspect of Chinese social interaction, and more recently Ho's article (1976), which follows the Hu tradition with a discussion of *lian* and *mianzi* in relation to other aspects of self-concept such as standards for behavior, personality variables, honor, dignity, and prestige.

In the West, Erving Goffman's work (1959, 1967) has given the greatest attention to social exchange relevant to face and self-presentation. In brief, and at the risk of oversimplifying, Goffman's basic analogy is that people are actors in the theater of life. As the daily drama unfolds, Goffman argued, people participate in social interactions, or performances, relying on self-presentation and impression manipulation in order to regulate their self-image. Their social behavior can be divided into two categories: front-stage and backstage (Goffman, 1959, 1967, 1974). *Front-stage behavior* refers to aspects of self that others view, and *backstage behavior* refers to inner and intimate aspects of self that are private and ego threatening. *Face-work* is the "actions taken by a person to make whatever he is doing consistent with face. Face-work serves to counteract 'incidents'—that is, events whose effective symbolic implications threaten face" (1967, p. 12). Face-work refers to a social regulatory process through which individuals promote and maintain their face as well as the face of others. Two basic forms of face-work, avoidance and corrective, are used in order to regulate face. By avoidance, it is meant that a person avoids engaging in actions that would threaten the face of others or himself, and corrective refers to a proactive re-establishment of someone else's face as a result of an infraction of their face.

Characteristics of Face

Face has two general forms, *lian* (pronounced "lee-en") and *mianzi* ("me-en-ze"). Hu (1944) described *lian* as "the respect of the group for a man with a good moral character, the loss of which makes it impossible for him to function properly within the community. *Lien* is both a social sanction for enforcing moral standards and an internalized sanction" (p. 45). He referred to *mianzi* as "the kind of prestige that is emphasized in this country [China]; a reputation achieved through getting on in life, through success and ostentation. This is prestige that is accumulated by means of personal effort or clever maneuvering" (p. 45). These two forms of face differ fundamentally in as much as *lian* reflects a standard of acceptable behavior (mode of conduct) whereas *mianzi* reflects status and position based on a person's accumulation of experiences and life. Although *mianzi* functions much like a social status currency, with fortunes potentially acquired or lost as a result of key encounters, *lian* is an implicit standard for a person's behavior in relation to the society's moral standards of conduct.

A person's face has both internal and external components, which are often observable in social settings. The internal component refers to inner voice or reflection, much like the invisible observer of Adam Smith's moral sentiments (1759), and the external component refers to any attributed aspect of a person's self-presentation. For example, an employee who steals company supplies answers to both his conscience and potential observers. From Goffman's perspective, a critical external aspect of face is the symbolism of a person's actions within a given social context. Thus the employee stealing supplies may lose face in a company having high moral standards of conduct but may not lose face in a company where such actions are ignored or reinforced by peers. Face, then, captures both those aspects of self externally presented to one's peers and community and those relating to internal standards for actions as defined by important referent others.

Face in an Organization

Mianzi can be acquired through a variety of ways. First, a person gains *mianzi* as a result of the role he or she enacts in an organization. Thus a janitor has little mianzi, and a senior executive has a great deal. Status or position in an organizational hierarchy provides face directly through the prestige of a job title as well as indirectly through organizational perks such as a company car or expense account. Second, individuals gain *mianzi* through their physical attributes and characteristics. An attractive model-like man or woman has *mianzi* attributable to physical appearance. Likewise, the "dress for success" and "power dressing" phenomena are not without basis in a society (for example, the United States) in which physical appearance plays an important role. The clothes we wear, the car we drive, and our personal appearance all contribute to *mianzi*. Third, a person gains *mianzi* by acting "beautifully," as the Chinese say, as well as appearing beautiful or handsome. Someone who shows him- or herself to be generous gains *mianzi* through those beautiful actions. For instance, a person might help out a new coworker who has not learned his job, and thereby enhance his own *mianzi*.

These three personal actions enhance a person's *mianzi*, but *mianzi* is also an exchangeable social currency that can be received from others. For instance, a graduate student gains *mianzi* when a visiting scholar praises her question at a talk, and an employee gains *mianzi* when the company praises his innovative suggestion. A person also gains *mianzi* through instrumental relationships with others. A person might have a famous relative (Billy Carter, for example, gained instant notoriety much to the chagrin of his presidential brother) or important or powerful friends. Neighborhood or social competitions (for example, putting up the largest holiday display in one's front yard or giving the biggest cocktail party in one's company) can increase *mianzi*. Goffman (1967) argued that such activities are important signals of one's position within a social structure.

I have focused so far on the personal and situational aspects of accumulating *mianzi,* but *mianzi* can also be lost, and in many respects such a loss is more important than any gains a person might achieve, simply because of individuals' innate desire to safeguard their accomplishments. People are often more concerned to avoid losing face than they are to gain it, and a loss of face has a stronger impact on people's perceptions of a person. The generally poor success of the Apple Newton hurt John Scully's reputation in the computer industry in a way that was difficult to overcome despite his numerous other successes. Up to this point, the loss of *mianzi* mirrors loss of *lian*. However, two caveats are needed. First, loss and gain of *mianzi* occurs in several categories. Although Scully lost *mianzi* related to his role in the computer industry, that is not to say that this effect washes over into other areas of his work or life. To gain back the category of *mianzi* that he lost, Scully needs to prove his expertise in the computer industry. From a more general perspective, Scully still has *mianzi* attributable to various other facets of his life (for example, his personal wealth and record as key executive in other companies). Thus a person can gain *mianzi* in other facets of life even when one aspect is threatened. With this said, however, I would argue that the various sources of *mianzi* are interdependent to varying degrees, depending on the culture. In cultures like the United States, for example, a person's work role is strongly tied to her *mianzi* whereas in cultures like China *mianzi* is strongly tied to family role. Thus, loss of face in one category may wash over onto other categories.

Second, face loss is moderated by the centrality of the category to a person's self-concept (Erez & Earley, 1993). If face loss is based on a concept central to a person's self-view and social circumstance (as Scully's computer fiasco was), then it is relatively more difficult to restore equilibrium to that facet of face. If face loss is tied to a tangential aspect of self, then the loss can be more easily overcome. Face gain, however, reflects more a consistent effect, with various forms of gain adding onto one another. The relative valence of a particular gain is tied to its centrality to the self.

Lian reflects a person's moral character that is acquired as a birthright (Hu, 1944), and it refers to the respect a person derives from a society based on his or her fulfillment of societal obligations. In this sense everyone is born with *lian,* and it is through moral acts that each person reaffirms it. *Lian* is maintained as long as a person acts morally within the dictates of the society. For example, a CEO who promises his workforce that an upcoming merger will not result in the loss of jobs loses *lian* if it is later determined that he was fully aware that layoffs would occur. In this example, lying, deception, and the like reflect a violation of employees' rights, and the CEO loses *lian* as a result. However, such actions need not be public. A CEO who engages in such a deception loses *lian* even if others do not uncover the actions. It is sufficient that the person knows he has violated societal standards of moral conduct.

In a society stressing shame, the standards on which *lian* is based are heavily tied to external networks of relationships. For example, in Chinese society immoral acts are harshly judged by a person's in-group, and people avoid committing social infractions so as to avoid the judgments of others. In an internally focused culture such as the United States, people avoid committing such infractions so as to avoid the personal experience of guilt or remorse.

The general standards, or rules, that constitute a person's *lian,* or moral character, are universal. So, although some people may emphasize duty over sympathy or self-control over fairness, certain standards exist throughout the world. From the perspective of face, people's actions are judged in terms of their impact on and reflection of these moral sentiments. Thus, if we encounter someone who displays the Hobbesian tack of self-absorption and sociopathology, we judge this brute to be lacking honor, merit, and conscience. (Table 9.1. summarizes the way face is enacted in organizations.)

Using Face to Understand Organizational Behavior

What is the relative significance of each form of face to social interaction in organizations? This is a question best addressed by examining the nature of a person's interdependence in her social context. For this discussion, I adopt the forms of social ties described by Deutsch (1975), Fiske (1990), Foa and Foa (1976), and Hwang (1978)—*expressive, instrumental,* and *mixed.* An expressive tie refers to a relationship characterized by shared affection, warmth, and respect such as expected in a family context. The expressive tie is an end rather than a means. An instrumental tie refers to a relationship in which individuals concern themselves with maintaining their personal attributes and material position and possessions. These relationships are established to provide an individual with personal gain. Finally, a mixed tie refers to a relationship in which individuals seek to influence others through various means, and although some trust and mutual support exists, the individuals do not view the relationship itself as an end. In mixed tie relationships, people share common characteristics (for example, they might come from the same town or region) and some common goals, but each person views herself as the central point of the interaction. Although an expressive tie is relatively stable and long lived, a mixed tie may be somewhat short lived, and an instrumental tie can be quite short lived, a single exchange, for example, between a shopkeeper and an out-of-town visitor in need of supplies.

An example from the development of an international joint venture (IJV) illustrates the nature of face in social exchange (Olk & Earley, 1996). Three basic stages of IJV formation can be described, in accord with Gray's model (1989) of the sequence of events in creating a multiparty collaboration. The process begins with problem setting followed by setting an agreed-upon direction and concludes with the implementation of a collective course of action (Olk & Earley, 1996).

Table 9.1. Taxonomy of Face in Organizations.

	Lian	*Mianzi*
Internally enacted	Moral standard of behavior internally referenced. Example: feeling of guilt because of a personal failure such as failure to achieve a self-set goal for work.	Personal work of one's accomplishments. Example: personal status from working at a major work organization.
Externally enacted	Social evaluation of the morality or goodness of a person's actions. Example: recognition of a person's integrity and honor for engaging in extra-role work performance.	Social recognition of a person's position vis-à-vis other social actors. Example: recognition of a person's position in a company based on office location, expense account, and so forth.

Face may be an issue in all parts of this process, as shown in the following scenario. During the problem-setting phase, an initial exchange between joint venture partners occurs in order to establish the basics of the relationship. The parties involved or their representatives are introduced, and the general expectations, goals of both parties, and so on are brought forth. There is a strong emphasis on instrumental exchanges based on an equity approach. During this phase, the IJV partners emphasize their own *mianzi* and postures so as to emphasize their personal (or corporate) importance. The various parties are highly focused on maintaining *mianzi,* and threats to any party's *mianzi* signal an inexcusable inequity. For instance, it is very important that the partners' representatives have comparable organizational levels and status; otherwise one party will lose *mianzi.* Additionally, in this early stage of IJV formation people strongly anticipate reciprocity of exchange, so if one partner gives *mianzi* (for example, by making an early concession in a negotiation and thus providing another partner with extra status), the first partner will expect a reaction in kind.

In the second stage, direction setting, the partners determine their common goals and interdependent actions. These goals and organizational structures will reflect the partners' style of exchange, which in turn is determined by the congruence of their cultural propensities. For example, individualists (Parsons & Shils, 1951; Triandis, 1990) will construct elaborate structures (of transactions costs, for example) to monitor a partner's actions, whereas collectivists will prepare such structures in proportion to their belief that the partner is truly part of the in-group. Thus, when a collectivist views a partner as an out-group member, the structures will emphasize instrumental exchanges and *mianzi* will become a central concern. At this point in the IJV, partners who are out-group members can move their partnership (now heavily instrumental) forward only through proper signaling of respect for the other partner, that is through giving *mianzi*.

A difficulty partners face in some IJVs during direction setting is that their need to establish interdependent goals requires them to establish some degree of mixed or expressive ties. When one partner overrelies on *mianzi* and instrumental exchanges, the other partner may think the first partner has a short-term and myopic view of the relationship. For example, Americans dealing with Japanese are often criticized for being overly focused on the short term and material gains and not being willing to take time to establish "real" commitments (Graham & Sano, 1984; Neale & Bazerman, 1991; Ting-Toomey, 1988). This likely reflects that Americans emphasize *mianzi,* because U.S. society emphasizes equity and instrumental exchange, whereas Japanese emphasize *lian,* reflecting Japanese society's strong emphasis on equality and expressive exchange.

There is an additional complication in that the Americans and Japanese differ not only in terms of typical exchange practices but in their sources of face as well. For example, the Japanese rely on social context (that is, social networks) for assessment of face. *Lian* must be demonstrated through acts in front of in-group members. For Americans, *lian* is a predominantly private affair; a person uses internal standards to determine whether he or she has performed morally (Erez & Earley, 1993). Thus it is possible that an American

IJV partner may do something privately to reinforce *lian* and the associated expressive ties (for example, something "behind the scenes" that demonstrates loyalty and character in regard to a Japanese partner) but that the Japanese partner may not recognize the action. Meanwhile, the American partner's public behavior continues to focus on instrumental exchanges of *mianzi*, emphasizing establishment of common goals and focusing on outcomes.

The final stage, implementation, emphasizes an equality-based system in which partners exchange resources of various types in order to "equalize" themselves in their further interactions. Face concerns now focus more on *lian*, because the partners view the relationship as relatively stable and understand that trust between partners is what will make the relationship successful. The IJV partners will signal their support of their relationship to one another by showing actions of "good faith." If *lian* is lost at this stage the relationship will break down, and new partnerships will be sought out. At this point *mianzi* is no longer critical. Given that the partners now trust and endorse one another's membership in the IJV, they do not seek *mianzi* as strongly before, nor do they monitor it as a sign of commitment.

Conclusion

In this chapter I have focused on a single, but critical, facet of the self, namely, a person's face, or self-enhancement. This aspect of the self reflects the significance of self-enhancement in a social context and description of it extends Erez's discussion of motivation. The impact of culture on face is dictated by a number of influences, such as internalization versus externalization of sources, style of social exchange, and the like. Two forms of face, *lian* and *mianzi,* appear to be universal forms of self-presentation that manifest themselves in unique ways across particular cultures. In an organizational context *lian* has direct implications for the moral and ethical aspects of managers' behavior and for the expectations imposed on them by others in their organization. *Mianzi* is most apparent in the typical social exchange that occurs in an organization during mundane interchanges among employees. Actions such as praise for effective performance, promotions, and being given a larger office or a better view characterize these exchanges.

The presentation of self in an organizational environment is universal. In the West such presentation is mistakenly viewed as posturing, bravado, or ego. However, a critical role of *mianzi* is as reaffirmation of a person's position within a given organizational social context. Such confirmation is essential for individuals' proper functioning in a company.

Notes

1. In this chapter I use the pinyin spellings of the Chinese terms *lian* and *mianzi.* Also, although both terms have linguistically denotative meanings referring to a person's physical face, *lian* has the connotative meaning of shame and value, and *mianzi* refers connotatively to the individual's "outside," or external, reputation. A more specific definition and operationalization are described in the present chapter.

2. Hu used the Wade-Giles system of transliteration, and so his terms differ somewhat in spelling from mine. Thus pinyin *lian* is the same word as Hu's *lien,* and pinyin *mianzi* is the same as Hu's *mien-tzu.*

References

Deutsch, M. (1975). Equity, equality and need: What determines which value will be used as the basis of distributive justice. *Journal of Social Issues, 31,* 137–149.

Earley, P. C. (in press). *Face, harmony, and social structure: An analysis of organizational behavior across cultures.* New York: Oxford University Press.

Erez, M., & Earley, P. C. (1993). *Culture, self-identity, and work.* New York: Oxford University Press.

Etzioni, A. (1968). *The active society.* New York: Free Press.

Fiske, A. P. (1990). *Structures of social life: The four elementary forms of human relations.* New York: Free Press.

Foa, E. B., & Foa, U. G. (1976). Resource theory of social exchange. In J. W. Thibaut, T. T. Spence, & R. C. Carson (Eds.), *Contemporary topics in social psychology.* Morristown: General Learning.

Goffman, E. (1959). *The presentation of self in everyday life.* New York: Doubleday.

Goffman, E. (1967). *Interaction ritual: Essays in face-to-face behavior.* Hawthorne, NY: Aldine de Gruyter.

Goffman, E. (1974). *Frame analysis: An essay on the organization of experience.* New York: HarperCollins.

Graham, J. L., & Sano, Y. (1984). *Smart bargaining: Doing business with the Japanese.* New York: Ballinger.

Gray, B. (1989). *Collaborating: Finding common ground for multiparty problems.* San Francisco: Jossey-Bass.

Ho, D.Y.-F. (1976). On the concept of face. *American Journal of Sociology, 81,* 867–884.

Hu, H. C. (1944, January–March). The Chinese concepts of "face." *American Anthropologist, 46,* 45–64.

Hwang, K.-K. (1978). The dynamic processes of coping with interpersonal conflicts in a Chinese society. *Proceedings of the National Science Council, 2*(2), 198–208.

Lin, Y.-T. (1935). *My country and my people.* New York: Reynal & Hitchcock.

Neale, M. A., & Bazerman, M. H. (1991). *Cognition and reality in negotiation.* New York: Free Press.

Olk, P., & Earley, P. C. (1996). Rediscovering the individual in the design of international joint ventures. In S. Bacharach, P. Baumberger, & M. Erez (Eds.), *Research in the sociology of organizations* (pp. 223–261). Greenwich, CT: JAI Press.

Parsons, T., & Shils, E. A. (1951). *Toward a general theory of action.* Cambridge, MA: Harvard University Press.

Redding, S. G., & Ng, M. (1982). The role of "face" in the organizational perceptions of Chinese managers. *Organization Studies, 3*(3), 201–219.

Ting-Toomey, S. (1988). A face negotiation theory. In Y. Y. Kim & W. B. Gudykunst (Eds.), *Theory and intercultural communication* (pp. 47–92). Thousand Oaks, CA: Sage.

Triandis, H. C. (1990). Cross-cultural studies of individualism and collectivism. In J. J. Berman (Ed.), *Nebraska Symposium on Motivation, 1989* (pp. 41–133). Lincoln: University of Nebraska Press.

CHAPTER 10

Adding Value to the Cross-Cultural Study of Organizational Behavior
Reculer pour mieux sauter
Michael Harris Bond

> *There are roads which must not be followed, armies which must not be attacked, towns which must not be besieged, positions which must not be contested, commands of the sovereign which must not be obeyed.*
>
> SUN TZU, *THE ART OF WAR* (CHAP. 8, V. 3)

As I begin, a short *mise en scene* may help put my remarks into context. I was initially approached by the editors to do an introductory chapter on values. I declined because I had come to doubt the value of studies on value for cross-cultural psychology. However, valuing my association with the two editors, I agreed to do a commentary on the value chapter that someone else would write.

After two commitments made and then retracted, the editors finally found a contribution (what could be wrong with essaying this topic area, one might well begin to wonder . . .) which they sent to me for comment. This contribution appeared to me to exemplify many of the dangers in employing the values concept in

---

Note: I thank Geert Hofstede, Michael Morris, and Peter B. Smith for their constructive inputs in response to an earlier draft of this chapter.

cross-cultural psychology, and the contributors withdrew their chapter from inclusion in this volume.

At this point, I was confronted with an unusable eighteen-page commentary, two embarrassed editors, and niggling thoughts about the limits of professional candor. And more . . . was the cross-cultural study of values a seeded minefield we were all treading in hopes of attaining the promised land? Had too many scholars committed too many of their resources to study this topic in misguided good faith for them to withdraw without a pitched battle? Should I soldier on? If so, how?

I analyzed the situation in this way. First, scholars would continue to study values cross-culturally; the construct had a face validity in explaining behavior, was widely believed to hold the key to culture, and enjoyed a long history in the social sciences. Second, its cross-cultural study had been carelessly or innocently or brazenly handled by many of our luminaries; some commentary was in order to encourage improvement on our past sins. Third, many of the deficiencies in the cross-cultural study of values generalized to the cross-cultural study of *any* topic in organizational behavior; a commentary could thus be used as an object lesson by those new to this intellectual battlefield. In light of these considerations, I decided to write a new and somewhat skeptical chapter for this collection.

The Attraction of the Values Construct

If the enemy's place of encampment is of easy access, he is tendering a bait.
Sun Tzu, *The Art of War* (chap. 9, v. 20)

Popular discourse abounds with motivational explanations. Social scientists share in, and contribute, to this discourse. People are widely believed to behave well because the consequences of that behavior are attractive or will lead to attractive consequences. Expectancy-value theories (for example, Feather, 1982) are based upon this premise. As citizens and as professionals, we believe in values.

As Kluckhohn and Strodtbeck (1961) remind us, values are broad concepts with trans-situational applicability. They may be easily measured by providing respondents with lists of general words used in a given culture to justify action. Certainly, the origi-nator of the Chinese Value Survey (Chinese Culture Connection, 1987), for example, did not have to labor mightily in the produc-tion of his value survey! Such potential ease of scientific access in-creases the attraction of studying values.

Finally, and again in popular discourse, cultures' effects on be-havior are widely "unpackaged" (Whiting, 1976) by reference to values. So American individualism is used in Oriental political dis-course to explain sexual promiscuity, urban homicide, and human rights endorsement in the United States. This usage mirrors that in the social sciences, where empirical topographies of values (for example, Chinese Culture Connection, 1987; Hofstede, 1980; Schwartz, 1994; Smith, Dugan, & Trompenaars, 1996) are the most widely touted way of psychologically distinguishing cultural groups. Indeed, the cross-cultural training industry that we academics feed would suffer a serious setback had Hofstede never worked for IBM!

Early Success

It is only one who is thoroughly acquainted with the evils
of war who can thoroughly understand the profitable way
of carrying it on.
Sun Tzu, *The Art of War* (chap. 2, v. 7)

I believe that the magisterial Hofstede's mapping of values in forty countries (1980) constituted a watershed for contemporary cross-cultural research. By moving beyond the standard two-country value contrast, his work elevated our perspective on national di-versity so that we could detect reliable patterns. By validating his dimensions of national values against a host of national indicators (for example, GNP, average age of business leaders, incidence of internal political violence, and the like), Hofstede encouraged his readers to believe that the values construct was useful in "explain-ing" national differences. We are all in his debt.

The Mirror Crack'd

Without subtle ingenuity of mind, one cannot make
certain of the truth of spies' reports.
Sun Tzu, *The Art of War* (chap. 13, v. 17)

The major problem with Hofstede's findings lies in how they were misunderstood—many readers assumed that he was describing the values of people in forty nations rather than the values of forty nations. Readers committed the "ecological fallacy" that Hofstede had warned them about in his first chapter—they applied results derived from a nation-level analysis to the individual level of analysis.

Of course, the nation scores on Hofstede's thirty-two constituent values had come from surveying similar individuals in each nation and averaging responses. It was then that these thirty-two "average-value" scores were correlated across the forty nations and factor analyzed. The factor groupings that resulted in Hofstede's famed four dimensions were thus derived from these nation-level data. As Hofstede and others (for example, Hofstede, Bond, & Luk, 1993) have been at pains to point out since, the groupings of the same set of values at different levels of analysis (that is, individual, group, organization, and country) are often themselves different and hence not comparable. Nations, however defined, are not people!

Perhaps Hofstede would have preferred in 1980 to have analyzed his data at the individual level. Had he done so, there would then have been no need for subsequent psychologists to link a nation's values to the values endorsed by its citizens (see attempts by, for example, Schwartz, 1994; Triandis, 1995). We could simply have talked about the average Brazilian's score on some individual-level dimension of value, as I did (Bond, 1988) after my individual-level analysis of the value data from the Chinese Culture Connection (1987).

Perhaps Hofstede did not proceed this way in 1980 because the professional canons of cross-cultural research at the time prevented him. Before comparing individuals across nations, he would first have had to establish metric equivalences (Van de Vijver & Leung, 1996) for his value groupings in *each* of his forty national samples. As subsequent research showed (Bosland, 1985), such a happy outcome would have been impossible to attain—coefficients of congruence across individuals from different nations were simply too low. So he chose a level of analysis where the equivalence stricture did not apply.

Others (for example, Smith, Dugan, & Trompenaars, 1996) have followed Hofstede's example. And by extending his sample of nations to include the former Soviet satellites, Smith et al. have,

I believe, managed to de-conflate power distance and individualism, which Hofstede had separated only by arbitrarily prising apart his first nation-level factor. This is progress!

But it is progress in understanding variation in values at the level of nations, not at the level of individuals. And making such progress requires rare access to huge data sets, with all the problems of quality, logistics, and analysis that they entail. Very few of us (Schwartz, 1992, may be the exception) have the vision, competence, and energy to produce a data set that will take us much beyond refinements of Hofstede's 1980 *chef d'oeuvre* (for example, Chinese Culture Connection, 1987).

Moving Values into Organizations

> *Water shapes its course according to the nature of the ground over which it flows; the soldier works out his victory in relation to the foe whom he is facing.*
> Sun Tzu, *The Art of War* (chap. 6, v. 31)

There is much talk about organizational culture, both on popular (Peters & Waterman, 1982) and professional (Deal & Kennedy, 1982) circuits. Compared to the distal influence of culture, the proximal influences of the organizations where we work would seem at first blush to be more potent. Surprisingly, then, there have been few attempts to measure organizational values in a systematic manner. Again, Hofstede (Hofstede, Neuijen, Ohayv, & Sanders, 1990) established the beachhead on this front.

Organizational Values

> *Ground which can be freely traversed by both sides is called accessible.*
> Sun Tzu, *The Art of War* (chap. 10, v. 2)

Hofstede, Neuijen, Ohayv, and Sanders (1990) relied on a representative sample of organizational members to supply them, through interviews, with values (and practices) distinguishing their twenty organizational units. The researchers' reliance on participants' reports to structure their values questionnaire gives this research a phenomenological, culture-as-experienced quality. The "ground-up" survey was administered to a stratified random sample of respondents across the twenty organizations. Approximately sixty-five members of each organizational unit participated. Organizations, of course, are much smaller than cultures, so it is much more feasible to obtain comprehensive representative samples. Our confidence in the probable validity of the resulting value profile can increase accordingly.

As in Hofstede's 1980 analysis of cultural values, organizational values were defined as the average endorsement of a given value found in a particular organizational unit. The fifty-seven values were then factor analyzed using an n of 20 (organizational units). As was the case with Hofstede's earlier factor analysis, the results were quite stable despite the low cases to items ratio because the values being intercorrelated are themselves averages and hence quite stable (Hofstede, Bond, & Luk, 1993).

Three value dimensions were identified at this organizational level: need for security, work centrality, and need for authority. Each of the twenty organizations could then be located on this three-dimensional value grid and these locations associated with other characteristics of the organization. Surprisingly, however, the Hofstede team found many fewer associations between organizational values and organizational characteristics than it did between organizational practices (also measured) and organizational characteristics. The team concluded that an organization's values are determined by the demographics of its employees; these do not change after hiring (but compare O'Reilly & Chatman, 1991). Organizational practices, however, are socialized after hiring and hence show considerable variation *across* organizations and relate closely to organizational size, technology, and function (but compare Chatman & Jehn, 1994).

So the promise of values at the level of culture was not replicated at the level of organizations—dimensions of cultural values produced a rich nomological net with other culture-level variables (see also Bond & Chan, 1995), but dimensions of organizational values were not so predictive of other organization-level variables. At this lower level of analysis, it was dimensions of practice, not values, that were associated with variables of interest to organizational sociologists.

Individual Values Across Organizations

> *The end and aim of spying in all its five varieties is*
> *knowledge of the enemy, and this knowledge can only be*
> *derived . . . from the converted spy.*
> Sun Tzu, *The Art of War* (chap. 13, v. 25)

Psychologists were bypassed by the Hofstede, Neuijen, Ohayv, and Sanders analyses. None of the three dimensions of organizational values was applicable to individuals. Of course, the organizational values had been obtained by averaging the individual value endorsements of a given organization's members. And, true, the resulting three dimensions of organizational values had been given very psychological-sounding names. However, the only way to return to the individual from the organization-level analysis was to commit the ecological fallacy (Hofstede, 1980). How then to access the individual level, where psychologists were more conversant and equipped to function?

One answer was to find a method of grouping the fifty-seven values into dimensions that were common to the members of all twenty organizations. To this end a correlation matrix of the fifty-seven values was produced for *each* of the twenty organizations. Then these twenty correlation matrices were, in essence, averaged. This average correlation matrix was then factor analyzed to yield six value factors at the individual level (Hofstede, Bond, & Luk, 1993). Of course, peculiar associations between values in any particular organization were "filtered out" by this averaging process; only associations common across all units survived. But it is precisely those general associations that provided the basis for the resulting factor structures and subsequent comparisons of individuals across organizational units (see also Bond, 1988, for a parallel individual-level analysis involving cultural units).

Predictors of Values of Individuals in Organizations

> *How to make the best use of both strong and weak—that is*
> *a question involving the proper use of ground.*
> Sun Tzu, *The Art of War* (chap. 11, v. 33)

At the very least, psychologists were now campaigning in familiar territory—they had six dimensions of value with which they might go about their jobs of predicting individual behavior. The groupings of values constituting these dimensions were different from the groupings constituting the three dimensions identified by Hofstede, Neuijen, Ohayv, and Sanders (1990) at the organizational level. This lack of empirical parallelism underscores the need to treat values data in a manner appropriate to their derivation and to be vigilant against committing the fallacy of misplaced levels, to coin a phrase (see also Scheuch, 1966).

Working now at the individual level, Hofstede, Bond, and Luk (1993) gave the six value dimensions appropriate intrapsychic-sounding labels, namely, personal need for achievement, need for supportive relations, machismo, workaholism, alienation, and authoritarianism. These six dimensions were then related to the respondents' measured demographics. So, for example, women were reported as higher in need for a supportive environment, alienation, and authoritarianism but lower in machismo. Ten of Hofstede, Neuijen, Ohayv, and Sanders's original twenty organizations were from Holland and ten from Denmark. So these gender effects could be checked for generality across these two cultures in a regression equation that assesses the country by gender interaction. None was found, so the gender effects were shown to be independent of culture. Checking for generality in this way is a marked advantage of multicultural studies and can legitimately be undertaken if (and only if!) the data are analyzed at the individual level.

This data set offered another possibility. Researchers could explore the correlations between individuals' values and individuals' perceptions of their own organization's practices. Measuring perceptions of organizational practices by organizational members is *one* approach to assessing organizational culture (Bond, 1996) and may reflect nonpsychological characteristics of the organization like size, type of technology, and nationality. Of course, how an individual perceives his or her organization is also a function of psychological variables like values. Once individual-level dimensions of value have been established across organizations, such relationships can be explored. So, for example, in the Hofstede, Bond, and Luk (1993) study, the alienation value factor predicted individuals' perceptions of their own organization as less professional and as less orderly, of colleagues as less trustable and as less professional, of employees as less integrated into the organization, and of management as more distant.

In fact, all six individual-level dimensions of practice were related to the organization members' score on alienation. Interestingly, items tapping this value factor of alienation read more like those from a personality questionnaire than from a value survey and raise the intriguing question of whether Hofstede, Bond, and Luk (1993) were in fact tapping measures of personality rather than values. Personality is an important construct, which recently has been demonstrated to be measurable in metrically equivalent ways not only across cultures but also across language families (McCrae & Costa, 1995). Given the importance of personality in the study of organizational psychology (Hogan, 1992), its role in cross-cultural extensions should be more widely explored. The personality domain should also be clearly separated from the value domain in doing such work (for example, Luk & Bond, 1993).

Linking Individual Values to Individual Behavior

Now in order to kill the enemy, our men must be roused to anger; that there may be advantage from defeating the enemy, they must have their rewards.
Sun Tzu, *The Art of War* (chap. 2, v. 16)

For many of us, our driving fascination with Hofstede's national topography of values was that it psychologized culture (countries, actually). Instead of discussing cultures as congeries of ecological-economic-social-political forces (see for example, Georgas & Berry, 1995), we could now refer to them in familiar psychological terms. Of course, we often committed the ecological fallacy by translating cultural values into values characterizing people from that culture. In many cases we were lured to this psychological level by the psychological-sounding terms applied to the cultural-level constructs (masculinity, uncertainty avoidance, human-heartedness, mastery, and so forth). But many of us were simply unaware of this logical problem and its statistical consequences. Others assumed an isomorphism and dismissed the warning as pedantic. They argued that cultures differ in values; cultures differ in behaviors; the values that distinguish the cultures in question can therefore explain the differences in individuals' behavior.

A Case in Point

> *Without subtle ingenuity of mind, one cannot make*
> *certain of the truth of their reports.*
> Sun Tzu, *The Art of War* (chap. 13, v. 17)

In a sophisticated study across thirty nations, Smith and Peterson (1995) measured the degree of reliance placed by middle managers from a wide range of organizations on eight ways of managing events at work. Cultural equivalence was first established across individuals in each of the thirty national groups for the eight modes of "event management" (Smith & Peterson, 1988). Then (and this is a critical next step), country averages were computed for these eight modes. Thereafter, these country scores were correlated with the Hofstede (1980) value scores for the same countries. Among other findings, Smith and Peterson found that countries high in individualism had managers whose average scores on event management showed higher reliance on their own experience and training.

Smith and Peterson (1995) interpreted such results carefully, and so should we. The above result, for example, does *not* mean that managers high on individualism rely more on their own experience and training! Hofstede did not provide us with individual-level measures of individualism (instead try Triandis, Chan, Bhawuk, Iwao, & Sinha, 1995). Nor did Smith and Peterson use individual-level measures of event management. Instead, what we have here is a country-level relationship. The fact that Smith and Peterson used a psychological-sounding construct derived initially by Hofstede from averaging individual value responses should not mislead us into the ecological fallacy. We still do not know from the Smith and Peterson study whether the individual values of managers predict their individual strategies of event management.

Individual Values and Behavior in Cross-Cultural Context

> *For the men of Wu and the men of Yueh are enemies; yet if*
> *they are crossing a river in the same boat and are caught*
> *by a storm, they will come to each other's assistance just as*
> *the left hand helps the right.*
> Sun Tzu, *The Art of War* (chap. 11, v. 33)

The Goal

> *Make forays in fertile countries in order to supply your*
> *army with food.*
> Sun Tzu, *The Art of War* (chap. 11, v. 22)

My professional objective is to provide psychological explanations for individual behaviors that occur in organizations across a variety of cultural contexts. Values are one class of psychological variables, among others, that can be used in such an enterprise. A given behavior—absenteeism, choice of influence strategy, or *karoshi*, for example—is related to the endorsement level of a key value or value domain for subjects from each cultural group, separately. If the same value-behavior link is found in each group, a culture-general relationship has been identified (see Earley, 1989, for an example of this process). If no such relationship is found, then of course we must rethink the relevant class of psychological variable that may predict the organizational behavior of interest.

Even if found, the value-behavior link may be stronger in some cultures than in others. Certainly, beliefs about the strength of the linkage between attitudes and behavior vary across cultures (Kashima, Siegel, Tanaka, & Kashima, 1992). We then need to relate this variable strength of association across cultures to some theoretically meaningful measure of culture. So, for example, Diener and Diener (1995) found that the size of the positive correlation between self-esteem and life satisfaction varied as a function of the individualism (as measured by Hofstede, 1980) of the country from which the subjects came. They explained this variable strength of association by using their understanding of the dynamics of cultural individualism. Such theoretical elaboration will be needed when cross-cultural studies of individual organizational behavior reach such a level of outcome sophistication. That day has not yet dawned.

The Tools

> *Camp in high places facing the sun.*
> Sun Tzu, *The Art of War* (chap. 9, v. 2)

The obvious requirement in this campaign is a carefully developed individual theory of values where those values are measured by a psychometrically defensible questionnaire whose dimensions or domains are metrically equivalent across cultural groups. This tall order is met only in the exemplary project orchestrated by Shalom Schwartz (1992). Work using this theory and instrumentation has already been undertaken in such basic areas of social behavior as interpersonal cooperation, voting behavior, and out-group contact (Schwartz, 1996); it is awaiting use by organizational psychologists interested in values as explanatory constructs (see Bond, 1991, for suggestions, and Schwartz, 1996, for a preliminary foray).

The Danger

> *It is only one who is thoroughly acquainted with the evils*
> *of war that can thoroughly understand the profitable way*
> *of carrying it on.*
> Sun Tzu, *The Art of War* (chap. 2, v. 7)

Enthused by the goal described earlier, Leung, Bond, and Schwartz (1995) set out to study reward allocation, conflict resolution, and influence tactics cross-culturally, using the then eleven Schwartz value domains as predictors. On average, Hong Kong and Israeli respondents differed on four of the domains, with Israelis higher in their endorsement of hedonism and stimulation but lower in their endorsement of tradition and conformity. Israelis showed more use of ingratiation, coalition formation, and sanction (see Kipnis, Schmidt, & Wilkinson, 1980) in their influence strategies and were more supporting of threatening and arbitration in their conflict resolution (Leung, 1988).

So the stage was now set to explain the differences in individual behaviors across the two cultural groups using the value domains that distinguished those groups. Regression equations were used within each cultural group and across both cultural groups to assess whether such individual-level linkages could be established between values and behaviors. However, to quote the authors, "The results indicate that value differences failed to explain any of the observed cultural differences in specific behaviors" (Leung, Bond, & Schwartz, 1995, p. 74). Relationships at the cultural level had evaporated when subjected to an individual level of analysis.

Note that many cross-cultural studies in the past have simply documented average differences in individual behavior across cultures then related these differences through plausible but loose theorizing to previously discovered differences in values at the cultural level (for example, Bond, Wan, Leung, & Giacalone, 1985). Such speculative linking exercises helped sustain the presumption that cultural differences in values could be used to explain cultural group differences in individual behavior. No direct statistical link was forged at the individual level.

However, even the presumption that individual values direct individual behavior is subject to serious qualification. As Feather (1990) wrote, "Whether a person has a tendency to act in a particular direction will depend on that person's expectation about whether he or she can perform the action to the required standard, on a further set of expectations about the potential consequences of the action, and on the valences (or subjective values) associated with the activity and with the anticipated action outcome. Those actions will be preferred that can be coordinated to the dominant motivational or action tendencies that relate to a combination of these expectations and valences" (p. 163).

Obviously, other constructs, such as valences, will have to be measured to piece together the linkage of values to behavior. In fact, Leung, Bond, and Schwartz (1995) found that values exerted their effects on behavior *indirectly,* through the agency of valences. Reconnection of individual values to individual behaviors across cultural groups is likely to be a labyrinthine journey!

New Approaches to Studying Individual Behavior Across Cultures

> *Therefore, just as water retains no constant shape, so in warfare there are no constant conditions. The five elements: water, fire, wood, metal, earth, are not always predominant; the four seasons make way for each other in turn. There are short days and long; the moon has its period of waning and waxing.*
> Sun Tzu, *The Art of War* (chap. 6, v. 32)

Leung, Bond, and Schwartz (1995) discovered that in three of five cases, cultural differences they found in Hong Konger and Israeli behavior could be explained using expectancies (that is, beliefs that the behavior would lead to a given outcome). It was these belief endorsements that varied across cultural groups and that then could be related at the individual level to the three behaviors of coalition formation, sanctioning, and arbitration. Valences explained one of the remaining five cross-cultural differences, but overall, expectancies were a far more powerful construct than either valences or, especially, values in predicting individual behavior. A recent meta-analysis of expectancy-value studies by Von Erde (1996) supports the conclusion that expectancies may render values redundant as explanatory variables for behavior, cross-culturally or otherwise.

In light of these findings, we might well begin to wonder: would the development of a cross-cultural survey on psychological beliefs (general expectancies about the material, personal, social, political, and spiritual world) provide us with a more powerful tool for constructing a cross-cultural theory of individual behavior? Internal-external locus of control beliefs, for example, is already widely studied cross-culturally (see Hui, 1982). Control beliefs may, however, simply be one component of a broader belief dimension that could be used to distinguish cultural groups and explain differences in individual behavior both within and across cultures (see Leung & Bond, 1993).

And more. One of the Hong Konger–Israeli differences in behavior found by Leung, Bond, and Schwartz (1995), the use of threatening behavior to resolve conflicts, could not be explained by values, valences, or expectancies. It was impervious to cultural unpackaging, at least in terms of the psychological variables used in that study. Ip and Bond (1995) were similarly frustrated when trying to use values to explain a host of cultural differences in the individual use of self-concept categories.

One possible reason for such "failures" is that we are not using the right psychological constructs to unpackage culture. Dimensions of personality (McCrae & Costa, 1995), types of self-constructs (Gudykunst et al., 1994), vertical versus horizontal collectivism (Singelis, Triandis, Bhawuk, & Gelfand, 1995), acculturative attitudes (Berry, Kim, Power, Young, & Bujaki, 1989), and ethnic identification (Weinreich, 1986) are all emerging contenders, depending on the explicandum in question. In light of these recent developments, it may be judicious for us to escape the thrall of values in cross-cultural work and augment our conceptual tool kit (Bond & Smith, 1996; Markus & Kitayama, 1991; Triandis, 1995).

A less obvious reason for the "failures" is that no psychological construct is ever going to succeed in completely unpackaging or explaining a cross-cultural difference in behavior, be it organizational or otherwise. Cultural and ethnic differences are the contemporary consequences of ecological, linguistic, religious, social, and political sedimentation laid down by history. Especially in the more closed cultures, we are likely to find more standardization of behavior and a decoupling of behaviors from psychological constructs. At this point psychologists may be pushed in interdisciplinary directions to forage for the intellectual materials required to explain behavior independently of psychological constructs. This is a disturbing intellectual challenge for many of us. However, doing cross-cultural behavioral science is no trade for the faint-of-mind (Gabrenya, 1988) and the need for more interdisciplinary exploration has never been greater (Featherman, 1993).

Conclusion

> Now the general who wins a battle makes many
> calculations in his temple ere the battle is fought. The
> general who loses a battle makes but few calculations
> beforehand. Thus do many calculations lead to victory,
> and few calculations to defeat: how much more no
> calculation at all! It is by attention to this point that I can
> foresee who is likely to win or lose.
> Sun Tzu, *The Art of War* (chap. 1, v. 26)

Just as all individuals are creatures of their original cultures, we social psychologists are also creatures of our disciplinary legacies. As our planetary future pulls us ever more strongly to address and accommodate diversity, we will use our disciplinary supports already in place to help us structure the novelty and complexity of our task. To date, the values construct has been our major support.

Many of us have embraced it enthusiastically. Its face validity as a psychological construct combined with Hofstede's mapping of cultural values gave us confidence in foreign territory. Our enthusiasm frequently outstripped our caution, however. The pressing need to build an explanatory framework led to overextensions of culture-level findings to the individual level. Many fundamental canons of cross-cultural procedure were ignored; many cautionary studies within mainstream psychology were ignored; alternative psychological constructs of possible use were ignored.

These concerns have informed this chapter. Let us stand back (reculer) to learn from our past mistakes and then spring forward (sauter) with deliberate speed to achieve the greatest possible yield from research in cross-cultural organizational behavior.

> *Thus, though we have heard of stupid haste in war,*
> *cleverness has never been associated with long delays.*
> Sun Tzu, *The Art of War* (chap. 2, v. 5)

References

Berry, J. W., Kim, U., Power, S., Young, M., & Bujaki, M. (1989). Acculturation attitudes in plural societies. *Applied Psychology, 38,* 185–206.

Bond, M. H. (1988). Finding universal dimensions of individual variation in multi-cultural studies of values: The Rokeach and Chinese value surveys. *Journal of Personality and Social Psychology, 55,* 1009–1015.

Bond, M. H. (1991). Cultural influences on modes of impression management: Implications for the culturally diverse organization. In R. A. Giacalone & P. Rosenfeld (Eds.), *Applied impression management* (pp. 195–215). Thousand Oaks, CA: Sage.

Bond, M. H. (1996, February). *Surveying the foundations: Approaches to measuring group, organizational, and national variation.* Paper presented at the Conference on Work Motivation, Kibbutz Ein-Gedi, Israel.

Bond, M. H., & Chan, S.C.N. (1995). *Country values and country health.* Paper presented at the 7th European Congress of Psychology, Athens.

Bond, M. H., & Smith, P. B. (1996). Cross-cultural social and organizational psychology. *Annual Review of Psychology, 47,* 205–235.

Bond, M. H., Wan, K. C., Leung, K., & Giacalone, R. A. (1985). How are responses to verbal insult related to cultural collectivism and power distance? *Journal of Cross-Cultural Psychology, 16,* 111–127.

Bosland, N. (1985). *The (ab-)use of the values survey module as a test of individual personality* (Working paper 85–1). Arnhem, Netherlands: Institute for Research on Intercultural Cooperation.

Chatman, J. A., & Jehn, K. A. (1994). Assessing the relationship between industry characteristics and organizational culture: How different can you be? *Academy of Management Journal, 37,* 522–553.

Chinese Culture Connection. (1987). Chinese values and the search for culture-free dimensions of culture. *Journal of Cross-Cultural Psychology, 18,* 143–164.

Deal, T. E., & Kennedy, A. A. (1982). *Corporate cultures: The rites and rituals of corporate life.* Reading, MA: Addison-Wesley.

Diener, E., & Diener, M. (1995). Cross-cultural correlates of life satisfaction and self-esteem. *Journal of Personality and Social Psychology, 68*(4), 653–663.

Earley, P. C. (1989). Social loafing and collectivism: A comparison of the United States and the People's Republic of China. *Administrative Science Quarterly, 34,* 565–581.

Feather, N. T. (1982). *Expectations and actions: Expectancy-value models in psychology.* Hillsdale, NJ: Erlbaum.

Feather, N. T. (1990). Bridging the gap between values and actions: Recent applications of the expectancy-value model. In E. T. Higgins & R. M. Sorrentino (Eds.), *Handbook of motivation and cognition: Foundations of social behavior* (Vol. 2, pp. 151–192). New York: Guilford Press.

Featherman, D. L. (1993). What does society need from higher education? *Items, 47*(2–3), 38–43.

Gabrenya, W. K., Jr. (1988). Social science and social psychology: The cross-cultural link. In M. H. Bond (Ed.), *The cross-cultural challenge to social psychology* (pp. 48–66). Thousand Oaks, CA: Sage.

Georgas, J., & Berry, J. W. (1995). An ecocultural taxonomy for cross-cultural psychology. *Cross-Cultural Research, 29*(2), 121–157.

Gudykunst, W. B., Matsumoto, Y., Ting-Toomey, S., Nishida, T., Kim, K. S., & Heyman, S. (1994, July). *Measuring self-construals across cultures.* Paper presented at the meeting of the International Communication Association, Sydney.

Hofstede, G. (1980). *Culture's consequences: International differences in work-related values.* Thousand Oaks, CA: Sage.

Hofstede, G., Bond, M. H., & Luk, C. L. (1993). Individual perceptions of organizational cultures: A methodological treatise on levels of analysis. *Organization Studies, 14,* 483–503.

Hofstede, G., Neuijen, B., Ohayv, D. D., & Sanders, G. (1990). Measuring organizational cultures: A qualitative and quantitative study across twenty cases. *Administrative Science Quarterly, 35,* 286–316.

Hogan, R. (1992). Personality and personality measurement. In M. D. Dunnette & L. M. Hough (Eds.), *Handbook of industrial and organizational psychology* (2nd ed., Vol. 3, pp. 1–47). Palo Alto, CA: Consulting Psychologists Press.

Hui, C.C.H. (1982). Locus of control: A review of cross-cultural research. *International Journal of Inter-cultural Relations, 6,* 301–323.

Ip, G.W.M., & Bond, M. H. (1995). Culture, values, and the spontaneous self-concept. *Asian Journal of Psychology, 1,* 30–36.

Kashima, Y., Siegel, M., Tanaka, K., & Kashima, E. S. (1992). Do people believe behaviors are consistent with attitudes? Toward a cultural psychology of attribution processes. *British Journal of Social Psychology, 331,* 111–124.

Kipnis, D., Schmidt, S. M., & Wilkinson, I. (1980). Intraorganizational influence tactics: Exploration in getting one's way. *Journal of Applied Psychology, 65,* 440–452.

Kluckhohn, F. R., & Strodtbeck, F. L. (1961). *Variations in value orientations.* New York: HarperCollins.

Leung, K. (1988). Theoretical advances in justice behavior: Some cross-cultural inputs. In M. H. Bond (Ed.), *The cross-cultural challenge to social psychology* (pp. 218–229). Thousand Oaks, CA: Sage.

Leung, K., & Bond, M. H. (1993). *Invitation to participate in a multi-cultural study of social axioms.* Unpublished manuscript, Chinese University of Hong Kong.

Leung, K., Bond, M. H., & Schwartz, S. H. (1995). How to explain cross-cultural differences: Values, valences, and expectancies? *Asian Journal of Psychology, 1,* 70–75.

Luk, C. L., & Bond, M. H. (1993). Personality variation and values endorsement in Chinese university students. *Personality and Individual Differences, 14,* 429–437.

Markus, H. R., & Kitayama, S. (1991). Culture and the self: Implications for cognition, emotion, and motivation. *Psychological Review, 98,* 224–253.

McCrae, R. R., & Costa, P. T. (1995). *Personality trait structure as a human universal.* Unpublished manuscript, Gerontology Research Center, National Institute on Aging, National Institutes of Health, Baltimore.

O'Reilly, C. A., & Chatman, J. A. (1991). People and organizational culture: A profile comparison approach to assessing person-organization fit. *Academy of Management Journal, 34,* 487–516.

Peters, T. J., & Waterman, R. H., Jr. (1982). *In search of excellence: Lessons from America's best-run companies.* New York: HarperCollins.

Scheuch, E. K. (1966). Cross-national comparisons using aggregate data: Some substantive and methodological problems. In R. L. Merritt & S. Rokkan (Eds.), *Comparing nations.* New Haven, CT: Yale University Press.

Schwartz, S. H. (1992). Universals in the content and structure of values: Theoretical advances and empirical tests in 20 countries. In M. P. Zanna (Ed.), *Advances in experimental social psychology* (Vol. 25, pp. 1–65). Orlando: Academic Press.

Schwartz, S. H. (1994). Beyond individualism and collectivism: New cultural dimensions of values. In U. Kim, H. C. Triandis, C. Kagitcibasi, S.-C. Choi, & G. Yoon (Eds.), *Individualism and collectivism: Theory, method, and applications* (pp. 85–119). Thousand Oaks, CA: Sage.

Schwartz, S. H. (1996). *A theory of cultural values and some implications for work.* Unpublished manuscript, Hebrew University of Jerusalem.

Schwartz, S. H. (1996). Value priorities and behavior: Applying a theory of integrated value systems. In C. Seligman, J. M. Olsen, & M. P. Zanna (Eds.), *The Psychology of Values: The Ontario Symposium* (Vol. 8, pp. 1–24). Hillsdale, NJ: Erlbaum.

Singelis, T. M., Triandis, H. C., Bhawuk, D.S.P., & Gelfand, M. (1995). Horizontal and vertical dimensions of individualism and collectivism: A theoretical and measurement refinement. *Cross-Cultural Research, 29,* 240–275.

Smith, P. B., Dugan, S., & Trompenaars, F. (1996). National culture and the values of organizational employees: A 43 nation study. *Journal of Cross-Cultural Psychology, 27,* 231–264.

Smith, P. B., & Peterson, M. F. (1988). *Leadership, organizations and culture: An event management model.* Thousand Oaks, CA: Sage.

Smith, P. B., & Peterson, M. F. (1995, August). Beyond value comparisons: Sources used to give meaning to management work events in 30 countries. In P. B. Smith (Chair), *International comparisons of work meanings and values.* Symposium conducted at the meeting of the Academy of Management, Vancouver.

Smith, P. B., Peterson, M. F., Akande, D., Callan, V., Cho, N. G., Jesuino, J., D'Amorim, M. A., Koopman, P., Leung, K., Mortazawi, S., Munene, J., Radford, M., Ropo, A., Savage, G., & Viedge, C. (1994). Organizational event management in 14 countries: A comparison with Hofstede's dimensions. In A.-M. Bouvy, F.J.R. Van de Vijver, P. Schmitz, & P. Boski (Eds.), *Journeys into cross-cultural psychology* (pp. 364–373). Lisse, Netherlands: Swets & Zeitlinger.

Sun, T. (1981). *The art of war* (L. Giles, Trans.). London: Hodder & Stoughton. (Original work published 1910)

Triandis, H. C. (1995). *Individualism-collectivism.* Boulder, CO: Westview Press.

Triandis, H. C., Chan, D.-K., Bhawuk, D.P.S., Iwao, S., & Sinha, J.B.P. (1995). Multimethod probes of allocentrism and idiocentrism. *International Journal of Psychology, 30,* 461–480.

Van de Vijver, F.J.R., & Leung, K. (1996). Methods and data analysis of comparative research. In J. W. Berry, Y. H. Poortinga, & J. Pandey (Eds.), *Handbook of cross-cultural psychology: Vol. 1. Theory and method* (rev. ed., pp. 257–300). Needham Heights, MA: Allyn & Bacon.

Von Erde, M. (1996, February 23–24). *A meta-analysis of expectancy—Value studies in organizational psychology.* Paper presented at the Conference on Work Motivation, Kibbutz Ein-Gedi, Israel.

Weinreich, P. (1986). The operationalization of identity theory in racial and ethnic relations. In J. Rex and D. Mason (Eds.), *Theories of race and ethnic relations* (pp. 299–324). Cambridge: Cambridge University Press.

Whiting, B. B. (1976). The problem of the packaged variable. In K. F. Reigel and J. A. Meacham (Eds.), *The developing individual in a changing world* (pp. 303–309). The Hague: Mouton.

CHAPTER 11

The Emerging Role of Diversity and Work-Family Values in a Global Context

Shinichiro Watanabe
Kiyoshi Takahashi
Takao Minami

Over the years, work-family relations have been the subject of much sociological research. A fundamental reason this topic has attracted researchers' attention is that work and family are two important domains of most people's lives. Although people have to work to earn their living, they do not live to the exclusion of their families. Changing gender-role structure also has propelled this large body of research. Specifically, recent sociotechnical modernization of the economy has created labor markets that call for women's participation on a larger scale than before. The increase of women's workforce participation has rendered the traditional male provider–female homemaker construction of gender roles obsolete or anachronistic (Hood, 1986; LaRossa, 1988; Haas, 1993; Willinger, 1993).

The most common themes discussed in the work-family literature are (1) the balancing of work and family roles—that is, the incursion of work demands on family and vice versa (see Pleck, 1977; Gilligan, 1982; Haas, 1986; Lewis, 1992; Richter, 1992; Ishii-Kuntz,

Note: We thank Miriam Erez and James McCauley for helpful comments during the preparation of this chapter.

1993); (2) the patterns of causality affecting the work-family relationship—that is, the impact of one set of roles on the other (see Staines, 1980; Mortimer, Lorence, & Kumka, 1986; Evans & Bartolomé, 1984; Zedeck, 1992); and (3) the joint effects of work and family attitudes on life satisfaction or other variables (see Howard, 1992; Richter, 1992; Judge, Boudreau, & Bretz, 1994). Our purposes in this chapter are to provide a brief review of the extant sociological research on each of these widely discussed themes, to add psychological and cross-cultural perspectives to that sociological research, and to explore promising areas of future research that may add an orthogonal element to the contemporary understanding of the work-family relationship.

The chapter consists of four sections. The first section focuses on work-family balancing. We make cross-cultural comparisons of work-family gender role norms, discuss whether there exists a unique *national* model gender-role ideology, and examine the factors influencing men's and women's interrole balancing behaviors. The second section discusses work-family patterns of causality. Past research has produced a controversy over which model of the work-family relationship (spillover, compensation, opposition, or segmentation) is correct. Rather than confirm or disconfirm these specific models, we speculate whether the form of the work-family relationship varies by individual and by socioeconomic and cultural conditions. The third section examines the consequences of various attitudes toward work and family. Past research focused on the interrelationships among such general attitudes as overall work, family, and life satisfaction. We consider how specific facets of work and family attitudes are linked to specific outcomes such as job performance, work and family withdrawal behaviors, and so on. We also consider individual differences and situational factors that may moderate links between specific attitudes and the outcomes. The final section is devoted to a general discussion of the ideas presented in the chapter.

Balancing of Work and Family Roles

Here we first describe characteristic features of Japanese work lives and examine how work and family roles are *gendered* (that is, divided by gender) in Japan. Next we compare the situation in Japan with the situations in Britain, Israel, the United States, and Sweden.

Such comparisons reveal both the specificity and generality of work-family gender-role systems in these national contexts. Finally, we discuss what determines men's and women's involvement in work and family roles and present some interesting problems to be addressed in the future. We particularly attend to the effects of individual difference variables and structural and contextual factors.

Japanese Work Life

Characteristic features of Japanese work life have been frequently studied (see Clark, 1979; Cole, 1971; Dore, 1973; Dunphy, 1987; Keys & Miller, 1984; Lincoln & Kalleberg, 1985; Nonaka & Johansson, 1985; Smith, 1984). Researchers have devoted much effort to investigating the reasons why the Japanese work so hard, the strength of their commitment to their companies, and the situational opportunities and constraints that guide them to positive work behaviors, along with similar concerns. However, there has been little research or discussion about their family lives, let alone their work-family relationship. Because values and work ethics in Japan appear to be very different from those in Western culture, a comparison may yield some important implications for the study of the work-family relationship.

It is known that employment relationships in Japan are characterized by lifetime employment and seniority systems, and these have been regarded as central to Japanese management. Differences between Japanese and Western management stem from certain unique characteristics of Japanese society and Japanese organizations (Redding, Norman, & Schlander, 1994). Japanese society and organizations tend to value and cherish deference to seniors (or superiors), a vertical model of the senior-junior (or superior-subordinate) interpersonal and working relationship, affiliation with workgroups, a work ethic based on frugality and hard work, and a management philosophy of job security. Simply stated, Japanese workers tend to accept the seniority-based hierarchical structure in which juniors obey seniors. Workers once accepted as company "insiders" are less likely than others to be laid off or terminated before retirement. To increase their career success, workers need not only to perform well but also to show their loyalty and commitment to their workgroups and companies. Moreover, they are generally expected to give up their right to seek other employment, and they tend to accept, whether willingly or unwillingly, assignments, demands, and requirements from their organizational seniors. Some workers become so involved in their work that their health suffers.

However, this occupational life typically applies only to male full-time workers. Employment conditions for women are considerably inferior. For instance, compared to men, Japanese women have fewer chances for promotion to managerial posts and fewer opportunities for training. They tend to be paid less than men and are the first to be laid off when companies adjust employment levels (Bando, 1986). The most common job path for female workers is work before marriage, job termination following marriage or the birth of their first child, and a return to work after an extended period of homemaking. This pattern further increases Japanese companies' reluctance to treat male and female employees fairly. This unfair treatment seems to come from Japan's long-standing strict division of gender roles. Fatherhood or husbandhood in Japan can be fairly well characterized by the image of provider or breadwinner, and motherhood or wifehood can be characterized by the image of homemaker or dependent.

Work-Family Relationship in Japan

Postwar Japanese families are frequently characterized as "fatherless" (Doi, 1973; Vogel, 1979; Reischauer, 1981). Japanese fathers spend significantly more time at work and less time with their families than their Western counterparts, a pattern that has been the major contributor to Japan's "economic miracle" (Vogel, 1979). One international survey found that more than 71.2 percent of Japanese fathers spend less than thirty minutes on weekdays interacting with their children, compared to 59.7 percent and 61.3 percent of American and German fathers, respectively (Management and Coordination Agency, 1986). Ishii-Kuntz (1993) reported that Japanese fathers spend approximately fifty-four hours at work on weekdays. In contrast, U.S. fathers spend an average of forty-two hours a week in paid employment (Sweet, Bumpass, & Call, 1988).

Japanese fathers' heavy involvement at work and superficial involvement at home, however, does not mean they are marginal in their families or isolated from them. The 1986 Management and Coordination Agency survey also found that as many as 62.4 percent of Japanese children regarded their fathers as the center of the family; only 22.8 percent and 12.9 percent of U.S. and German children, respectively, had the same opinion. Moreover, 34.7 percent of Japanese children considered their fathers to be the most reliable figures at home, compared to 12 percent and 7.7 percent in the U.S. and German samples, respectively. Similarly, 45 percent of Japanese children considered their fathers to be the final authorities at home, compared to 35.1 percent and 23.4 percent in the U.S. and German samples, respectively. These findings suggest that although physically absent, Japanese fathers are psychologically present at home, in the form of a symbol of authority.

Ishii-Kuntz (1993) documented that Japanese fathers' images as authority figures and dedicated workers have been created and maintained by Japanese mothers. In her in-depth interviews and observations in Japanese families, she found Japanese mothers to be transmitters of the fathers' values and authority to children. Here, for example, are two comments made by Japanese parents. The first sketches a thirty-three-year-old homemaker's interactional style with her ten-year-old daughter and five-year-old son, and the second illustrates her thirty-five-year-old husband's interactional style with the whole family:

> When my husband returns home late, which is just about every day, he is most likely to have been at the bar with his colleagues. But I *never ever* tell that to my children. (Maybe they suspect something, but I don't want them to know that their father is goofing around at the bar.) So I tell them that their father is working late at night or attending important meetings, and he does this just to support us [Ishii-Kuntz, 1993, pp. 58–59].

> I am responsible for supporting my family. I leave home early in the morning and usually don't return until my kids are asleep. There is just no time for me to be with my kids. My only free time is on Sundays, but even then I may go play golf with my clients or colleagues. But you know, I don't do this for my own pleasure, but for my family. I think they [my wife and children] are grateful for the

kind of life I am providing. Although I spend little time with my kids, I basically trust my wife when it comes to raising and educating them [Ishii-Kuntz, 1993, p. 55].

What these comments show is that Japanese families still retain a traditional gender-segregated ideology, with the father–distant breadwinner image on the one hand, and the mother-homemaker image on the other. Most Japanese children are raised and socialized learning the importance of traditional gender roles.

Nevertheless, due to some societal demands and demographic changes, this long-continuing and still prevalent gender inequality is currently undergoing a transition. First, the current sex ratio among younger Japanese is highly imbalanced, with a surplus of 2 million men, who are competing with each other for marriageable women (Itoi & Powell, 1992). This gives today's Japanese women a legitimate reason for challenging men's traditional values. Younger Japanese women tend to demand more from men, including sharing housework and child care.

Second, Japanese local and national governments have become increasingly concerned that the Japanese "fatherless" families are the cause of Japanese youths' increasing truancy and suicide rates. Also, an increasing number of Japanese fathers have come to realize the importance of their presence at home and their role in parenting (Ishii-Kuntz, 1989). As a result, family-friendly policies are emerging in both the public and private sectors. For example, Takashimaya (a large department store chain) has granted employees of both sexes two four-day work weeks per month ("Paternity Leave Granted," 1991); the offices of education in Tokyo and Osaka allow male elementary to high school teachers to take paid leave of ninety minutes per day for fifteen months after the birth of a child ("Child Care Leave," 1994). In fact, since the Parental Leave Act was passed in 1992, the majority of Japanese companies have granted their employees one year of parental leave with partial pay (equal to the amount of the employee's social insurance premiums) following birth of a child ("Parental Leave Implemented," 1994). Educational programs addressing the importance of fathers' parenting roles have also been implemented in many cities.

Finally, the recent increase in dual-career families has contributed to changing the roles of fathers and husbands in Japan.

Recent labor statistics show that the percentage of working mothers was 48.2 percent in 1979 and had risen to 56.9 percent by 1989 (Ministry of Finance, 1990). The percentage of working wives with no children also increased, from 47 percent in 1982 to 56.9 percent in 1992 (Management and Coordination Agency, 1982, 1992). As mothers' and wives' labor force participation rates have increased, more people have suggested that fathers and husbands take greater housework and child-care responsibility at home. Japanese couples have become more concerned with balancing paid and unpaid work. So it is now inaccurate to assume that the Japanese gender-based dichotomy in individuals' roles is timeless, natural, or impervious to change.

Because of these societal and demographic changes, Japanese men are moving away from the distant breadwinner role and toward the nurturant father role. It would be unrealistic, however, to say that these changes are dramatic and will soon produce a gender-neutral environment in Japanese homes. Our everyday observations of working men and women in Japan suggest that despite working parents' changing needs, males continue to strongly resist changing gender roles. It is closer to the truth to say that some Japanese men and women have just recently begun taking small steps away from the strict separation of male and female roles that the majority of Japanese have long seen as essential to the survival of the family.

One event that simultaneously reflects both the gender-role transition and the continued dominance of sex-role differentiation was the 1986 passage of equal employment opportunity legislation. To meet the mandates in this legislation, private companies have set two career tracks for female workers, in a system known as course-based administration. In the "general jobs" (*sogo shoku*) career track, female workers take charge of a primary operation requiring unlimited knowledge, skills, and ability and offering career opportunities for advancement to managerial positions and possible relocation. In the "standard jobs" (*ippan shoku*) career track, females perform supporting jobs requiring limited skills, efforts, and responsibilities and offering restricted career opportunity, lower pay, and no relocation opportunities. Thus, although the legislation was aimed at advancing the status of working women, its effects are still colored by traditional gender-role differentiations. Working men and women are not truly equal yet; female workers are assigned either to *sogo shoku* or to *ippan shoku* depending on their levels of education and career expectations, but with very little exception male workers are assigned to general jobs. Moreover, management positions in Japanese companies are still dominated by males, a clear indication that gender inequality still exists in Japanese human resource management practices. And the majority of Japanese men continue to regard the home as women's responsibility. Therefore they are relatively reluctant to accept any gender-role transition that would reduce women's services to the household, and they tend to maintain their power base as sole, or at least main, family provider.

To summarize, in response to societal and demographic changes, the Japanese have exhibited an increasing interest in moving from a gender-segregated ideology of male providers and female homemakers toward a more egalitarian society. However, the picture that emerges is of partial transition and a tendency for Japanese men to see gender-role change as demeaning to their masculine or authoritarian identity and to believe that they have much to lose and little to gain from it. Moreover, Japanese employment conditions continue to be inferior for women. Thus men are encouraged to retain their traditional roles because these remain the culturally exalted roles.

Work-Family Relationship in Other Industrial Countries

Nearly twenty years ago Pleck (1977) argued that work-home boundaries are "asymmetrically permeable," buffering men's provider role from their family obligations but allowing women's family commitments to intrude upon their work. Pleck's comments can apply as well to Japan as to other industrial countries. Nevertheless, there are variations in practice to be observed. In the next sections, brief examinations of gender-role structures in Britain, Israel, the United States, and Sweden are followed by a discussion of both cross-cultural variations and universals in work-family balancing behaviors.

Britain

Recent studies suggest that traditional norms and values still prevail in Britain in the division of gender roles. For example, the majority of British men and women strongly believe in the importance of full-time motherhood for children's healthy development and disapprove of mothers of small children working outside the home (Lewis & Cooper, 1989; Lewis, 1992; Alwin, Brown, & Scott, 1992). About 33 percent of British fathers work over fifty hours per week (Franks, 1990), which inevitably curtails their wives' participation in the labor market. Working British women are overrepresented in lower-status and lower-paid jobs (Hansard Society, 1990). Both a reason for and a consequence of women's inferior employment conditions is that women retain the major burden of family responsibilities (Henwood, Rimmer, & Wicks, 1987). Moreover, the traditional gender role ideology influences governmental thinking and public provision of child-care and work-family benefits is poor. For instance, although they favor the introduction of paternity leave, the majority of British fathers, unlike most of their counterparts in the European Economic Community, are still not entitled to such leave (Bell, McKee, & Priestly, 1983). In addition, they have exerted little pressure to obtain the right to paternity leave (Lewis, 1992).

Brannen (1992) and Lewis (1992) argue that there is a general lack of social policies that would provide support for working mothers. For instance, in 1989, only 3 percent of British employers were providing assistance with child care. Paid maternity leave, introduced in the Employment Protection (Consolidation) Act of 1978, lasts only eighteen weeks and is available only to women who have worked full- or part-time for the same employer for at least two years. These restrictive requirements disqualify many new mothers. And because the penalty for noncompliance is not severe, some employers still refuse to provide women's full leave entitlement. These inferior employment conditions function as contextual forces, driving women away from the workplace and confining them in traditional female roles. Once British women do join the labor force, they have few chances to perform to their full capabilities. The general lack of career-friendly policies for British women can be viewed as a reflection of stereotypic beliefs regarding the gender-based division of work and family responsibilities, with work being the domain of men on the one hand and family being the domain of women on the other.

Things may be changing, however. The recent increase in British women's labor force participation, from 36.3 percent in

1970 to 46.1 percent in 1993 (International Labor Office, 1993), has resulted in some company-based initiatives to enable employees to cope with the conflicts between work and family roles (Lewis & Cooper, 1989; Hansard Society, 1990). Berry-Lound (1990) reported that the number of British employers providing assistance with child care is increasing; for example, a major bank opened a chain of workplace nurseries throughout Britain. A number of companies are now aware of the limitations of maternity leave rights and have taken steps to accommodate a longer career break (Lewis, 1992). In addition, the treatment of men's and women's wages under the British taxation system has recently changed (Lewis, 1992). Until 1990, a woman's wage was considered pin money for buying luxuries, and the man's wage was considered money essential for maintaining the family. Therefore, married men received a larger tax allowance than did married women, meaning that a smaller portion of married men's wages were subject to tax. In 1990, the married man's tax allowance was changed to the married couple's tax allowance. Viewing these changes together, it may not be too much to say that British society has recently begun taking small steps toward gender equality, a progression that compares favorably with the situation in Japan.

United States

In the United States increasing attention is being paid to the changing roles of men and women. Robinson (1975) conducted a time-use study to compare U.S. fathers' 1965 and 1975 interactional styles with their children. The results showed that on average U.S. fathers interacted with their children about two minutes per day in 1965; by 1975, that time was seventeen minutes. These data can be interpreted in several ways. First, U.S. fathers show more active involvement in their family than their Japanese counterparts. Second, U.S. fathers' more active family involvement is a recent phenomenon. At the same time, however, the data also tell us that U.S. men are less active in child care than is popularly believed (LaRossa, 1988).

More recently, Willinger (1993) used time-series data to trace college men's work and family orientations in 1980, 1985, and 1990. She found a statistically significant change in their attitudes toward gender equality in the 1980s. For example, when presented with a situation in which a couple decides to have a child but neither parent wants to quit work to care for it, 57.8 percent of college men in 1980 decided not to have the child; the ratio dropped to 50 percent in 1985 and 39.2 percent in 1990. Moreover, from 1980 to 1990 an increasing percentage of the men considered the wife's decision to work to be her own (35.8 percent in 1980, 47 percent in 1985, and 51.8 percent in 1990). Willinger also found, however, that the men still had strong resistance to the gender-role restructuring. For instance, few of the men (less than 1 percent in all survey periods) considered staying home to raise a child as desirable, and they still tended to stress the importance of the work role for men and the maternal role for women. Willinger states that despite these men's recent shift in favor of gender equality, they are still not ready to support a symmetrical relationship in which men and women share equally in both work and family responsibilities; traditional gender roles have yet to undergo the change necessary for complete gender equality to emerge.

The foregoing descriptions suggest that employed U.S. women have to spend a much longer time on family roles than do men (Walker & Woods, 1976; Nickols & Metzen, 1978; Beckman & Houser, 1979). Working wives tend to cope with their work and family roles in parallel or in a way that allows family responsibilities to intrude upon work, whereas men tend to meet work demands first and then family responsibilities (Gilligan, 1982). The dual roles of working women can be a source of role overload. It has been shown that in terms of physical and mental health, working wives are no better off than homemaking wives (Booth, 1977; Wright, 1978). Thus work-family balancing is an issue among U.S. working women.

Israel

Gender roles in Israel seem to be less traditional than those in Japan, Britain, and the United States. In 1988, Israel passed one of the world's most advanced laws concerning the employment of women, the Equal Opportunities in Employment Act. This law prohibits an employer from discriminating against employees or job applicants on the grounds of sex, marriage, or parenthood in the areas of hiring, working conditions, promotion, vocational training, dismissal, and dismissal compensation. The law also equates parental rights, so that both fathers and mothers are entitled to receive paid parental leave after the birth of a baby, to resign from work without losing their compensation rights in order to raise a newborn child, and to be absent from work to tend to a child's illness (Richter, 1992).

Yet problems remain. These gender-equal policies have not been fully implemented in practice. Richter (1992) states that compared to their male counterparts the majority of women earn less and have fewer chances to be promoted to managerial posts. She argues that this situation is not due solely to insufficient governmental efforts to ensure implementation; it also reflects traditional beliefs about gender roles that are deeply rooted in Israeli society. These prevailing norms have kept men away from the everyday business of running a household; consequently, working Israeli women, in addition to their work outside the home, have the responsibility for child care and most household chores (Peters & Katz, 1984). Thus balancing work and family responsibilities has been a major concern for working women in Israel, particularly among working mothers.

Sweden

Haas (1993, 1995) provides recent analyses of gender equality and work-family balancing in Sweden. For over twenty-five years, Sweden has officially promoted gender equality, calling for the sexes' equal involvement in work and family roles. The Swedish government has been active in providing such family-friendly policies as public child care, one year of paternal leave at 90 percent pay, sixty days off with 80 percent pay to care for sick children, and the right to reduce the workday to six hours or the work week to four days for child caring. Swedish men and women have equal access to educational opportunities and job training, and many secure job opportunities are available to women. The gender pay gap is the lowest of all industrial societies; in 1990, women's hourly wages averaged 89 percent of men's. Having young children has little effect on women's paid employment; in 1988, 86 percent of women with children under seven years of age were in the labor force (Haas, 1993). These employment conditions have resulted in high levels of female participation in the labor force. The ratio of the female workforce to the total workforce is the highest of all industrial societies except for former state socialist societies; in 1993, it was 48.9

percent, compared to 40.5 percent, 42.8 percent, 41 percent, 42.8 percent, and 45.8 percent in Japan, Britain, Israel, Germany, and the United States, respectively (International Labor Office, 1993). It is predicted that by the year 2000, men and women in Sweden will be employed to an equal extent (Persson, 1990).

The unparalleled efforts of the Swedish government to eliminate gender inequality and Sweden's uniquely high rate of women's labor force participation suggest that men and women in Sweden are equally involved in their work and family roles. Research shows, however, that Swedes do not yet live up to their egalitarian ideals. For example, mothers in dual-earner families with preschoolers work on the average 29.2 hours per week, compared to fathers' average of 42.5 hours; and most of the mothers' jobs are part-time (Haas, 1993). Gender differences can be found in attitudes toward work as well. Seventy-five percent of fathers prefer to work full-time, compared to only 6 percent of mothers (Haas, 1986). Forty-two percent of fathers consider work to be the main interest in their lives, in contrast to 19 percent of mothers (Haas, 1993). Fathers have taken less advantage than mothers of support services and programs for working parents; for instance, in 1991, only about half as many fathers as mothers took leave following the birth of child, and they generally took only a small portion, one and one-half months, of the full year to which they were entitled (Haas, 1995). These studies clearly indicate that Sweden still shows substantial gender differences in work hours, work preference, and work commitment.

Analyzing participation in child care, Haas (1993) found that Swedish men in dual-earner couples spent an average of 36.1 hours per week with their children, which was 43 percent of the total time that parents spent with their children on nonworkdays. However, by itself, time spent with children is not sufficient evidence of nongendered child-rearing practices, and Haas found a clear division of labor in how Swedish men and women spent their time with children. Fathers were more likely to participate in emotional caregiving tasks (for example, playing, teaching, and reading) than in physical caretaking (for example, feeding, diapering, and taking to the doctor); also, mothers were most likely to be responsible for the noninteractive domestic work associated with child care, such as laundry, shopping, and cooking. Although their emotional involvement may have considerable impact on children and their contribution to child care may well be unparalleled in the world, Swedish men are still not equal partners of women in the home (Haas, 1993, 1995).

Discussion

Thus far we have looked at the work-family structure in Japan, Britain, Israel, the United States, and Sweden. Viewed in the aggregate, the data seem to point to both cultural variations and cultural universals. The remainder of this section on balancing work and family is devoted to discussion of these cultural phenomena and future directions for work-family balancing research.

Cultural Variations

Reviewing the literature from a perspective of cultural relativism, we notice that there are cultural variations across nations. Japan, Britain, Israel, the United States, and Sweden each seem to approach the work-family relationship somewhat differently. Japan and Britain are characterized by traditional gender-role norms that are deeply rooted in their societies. In these two countries, the work demands put on men seem to be the kind that can be best fulfilled by someone who has a homemaker at home; working mothers and wives in dual-career families tend to find their careers foundering if they cannot successfully juggle the twin demands of career and family. Gender roles in the United States are less traditional. U.S. fathers typically spend significantly more time on family roles than do fathers in Japan and Britain. The situation in Israel is even less traditional. Israel's social policies that prohibit gender segregation at work and equate parental rights have served as a force to weaken the notion of home as women's responsibility. Some Israeli mothers who have experienced working in both Israel and the United States say that the United States is a difficult place to simultaneously raise a family and have a career (Baringa, 1994). Sweden has been more successful at altering traditional gender-role divisions, and its unparalleled family-friendly social policies have given it the highest rate among industrial societies of women's labor force participation.

Why are some societies more egalitarian and some more traditional than others? This question leads to much speculation about the variations of societal culture across nations. For example, one might argue that Japan's clear division of gender roles stems from the Confucian philosophy that boys should be *diligent providers* and that girls should be *happy homemakers*. This argument, however, does not explain why a similar and equally traditional division of labor prevails in British society, where Confucianism is not deeply ingrained.

Berry, Poortinga, Segall, and Dasen (1992) argue that individualist societies, in which the interests of the individual prevail over the interests of the group, are generally more egalitarian than collectivist societies, in which the reverse is true. Our cross-cultural review, however, does not provide strong support for their position. In Hofstede's massive studies (1980, 1991) on social values in forty and fifty-three countries, respectively, the United States is ranked as the most individualist nation; the rankings for Britain, Sweden, Israel, and Japan are third, tenth, nineteenth, and twenty-second, respectively. These nation's rankings, when compared with their rankings on the traditional-egalitarian continuum of work-family balancing, suggest a weak association between individualism and gender culture. Thus we believe that the individualism-collectivism dimension likewise does not explain much of the cultural variations in sex-role ideology.

One aspect of culture that seems to account for the cross-cultural differences is Hofstede's masculinity versus femininity dimension of social values. According to Hofstede (1980, 1991), masculinity refers to societies in which gender roles are clearly distinct (specifically, men are supposed to take assertive, dominant, and competitive social roles, and women are supposed to take more modest, tender, and caring social roles). Femininity refers to societies in which gender roles overlap (specifically, both men and women are supposed to be modest, tender, and caring). This suggests that the more traditional societies can be characterized by higher ratings on masculinity and the more egalitarian societies by lower ratings. More specifically, it is a reasonable prediction that of the five countries we have examined, the higher masculinity scores should be obtained in Japan and Britain, where the relationship between work and family roles is traditional; the scores should become lower in the United States, still lower in Israel, and lowest in Sweden. Hofstede's cross-cultural comparison (1991), in fact, confirms this prediction; Japan is ranked first, the champion of masculinity, among fifty-three different countries, followed by Britain (ninth), the United States (fifteenth), Israel (twenty-ninth), and Sweden (fifty-third). Thus we claim, and we think Hofstede would agree, that the prevailing role distribution between men and women in a society is reflected in the society's position on the masculinity-femininity dimension. However, before this conclusion is generally accepted, researchers must further examine the association between masculinity and gender culture, using a wider range of cross-cultural investigation.

Cultural Universals

We also argue that some transculturally generalizable themes run through the gender-role structures in the countries discussed here. One such theme is gender inequality in work-family balancing. Sex-role ideology, which we have just suggested is different from society to society, can also be conceived as a cultural universal. Recall that none of the countries reviewed has completely eliminated the division of labor that puts men primarily in the workplace and women primarily in the home. Every society seems to think that some behaviors are more suitable for males and others are more suitable for females. However, it is a justifiable argument that each country is different from other countries in just how far it has achieved the gender-role transition; different nations take different positions on the traditional-egalitarian continuum. Thus future cross-cultural examinations of the work-family relationship may be able to forecast a particular country's gender-role structure rather than merely discover cultural differences. For example, Ishii-Kuntz (1993) found that the amount of time Japanese fathers spent on family responsibilities in recent years is similar to the amount of time U.S. fathers spent in the 1960s and 1970s. This finding can be interpreted to mean that it will still take many years for Japan to eliminate its gender gap.

Other culturally universal phenomena are the increasing labor force participation of wives and mothers and the accompanying changes in gender-role norms. The changing composition of the workforce has changed workers' needs. An increasing number of today's women are demanding a gender-neutral society where men and women are equally involved in the work and family domains. In response to women's demands, gender-role change, albeit with varying degrees of progress, is now emerging worldwide. An increasing percentage of husbands and fathers are spending more time involved with their families. Governments and companies are creating programs to help workers to balance work and family.

This ongoing gender-role transition has resulted in much speculation and concern about the factors that influence men's and women's interrole balancing behaviors. Most studies to date have placed considerable emphasis on such situational factors as business policies and practices and governmental legislation. Their major assumption is that structural or contextual factors reflect, and in turn influence, men's and women's opportunities to be involved in work and family roles. These chains of causes and effects have been the heart of this line of research. From this emphasis on situational factors has emerged a mounting body of research positing that gender inequality can be eliminated by governmental legislation (see Lewis, 1992; Richter, 1992; Haas, 1993; Ishii-Kuntz, 1993), by changes in business policies and practices (see Maklan, 1977; Lee, 1983; Lamb et al., 1988; Kingston, 1989), and by changes in the social or historical contexts in which a person is born and raised (see Mason & Lu, 1988; Davis & Robinson, 1991; Willinger, 1993; Dennehy & Mortimer, 1993).

Some studies have recently looked at social demographic variables in relation to the division of sex roles (see Pascarella & Terenzini, 1991; Willinger, 1993). For example, the Willinger (1993) study found a significant association between men's gender-role attitudes and their age, race, religion, education, income, and so on. Specifically, she found a greater probability that older men, nonwhite males, Catholic men, and men with higher education and income would retain traditional attitudes about men's work role and women's child-care role. The experience of marriage tended to relax men's traditional attitudes until they became fathers; the birth of one or more children, however, was likely to bring a reversion toward accepting the sex-role division. This examination explains at least partly why, in what appear to be the same situations, some people hold more traditional beliefs than others.

Generally ignored in the research on work-family balancing to date are psychological individual difference variables, which may provide more information about the psychology of the interrole balancing than will social demographic variables. Some men may be more willing than others to involve themselves in household chores and child care because they value the care of loved ones over attainment of the highest standard of excellence at work. Some women may be more likely than other women to prefer traditional female roles because they are dispositionally suited to a domestic environment and have reservations about equally sharing work and family responsibilities with men. For instance, in their study on life-course consequences of shyness, Caspi, Elder, and Bem (1988) showed that women with a history of childhood shyness continued to be shy as adults and were more likely than other women to follow a conventional pattern of marriage, childbearing, and home-making, rather than venturing into employment outside the home. Individuals may be predisposed to respond to the environment in a personality-based manner, and this may be reflected in their interactional styles with their work and families. More research is needed to examine the psychology of work-family balancing.

A promising area for future research will be to explore dynamic interactions between person variables and contextual variables in relation to the men's and women's interrole balancing. A person, guided by his or her individual characteristics, not only interprets and reacts to a situation but also selects or shapes it; the selected or shaped situation in turn affects future behavior, which may then change or modify the situation again (Magnusson & Endler, 1977; Terborg, 1981; Caspi, Elder, & Bem, 1987, 1988; Caspi, Bem, & Elder, 1989; Caspi & Bem, 1990; Watanabe, 1994). Consider, for example, a father who equally values his family and work roles. His strong needs for behaving in this "feminine" way cause him to select a workplace that, he subjectively perceives, has family-friendly business policies and practices (choice of situation). This father, through strong involvement in family roles, also successfully creates a gender-neutral family structure (shaping of situation). He subjectively perceives the workplace as satisfactory and reacts to it positively, behavior that in turn reinforces the gender-role structure of the workplace (shaping of situation). The examination of such dynamic person-situation interactions will make a unique contribution to contemporary understanding of interrole balancing.

Forms of Work-Family Relationship

The form of the relationship between work and family attitudes has long been of interest to researchers (see, for example, Hardesty & Betz, 1980; Mortimer, Lorence, & Kumka, 1986; Ladewig & McGee, 1986; Crouter, Perry-Jenkins, Huston, & Crawford, 1989; Marshall, Chadwick, & Marshall, 1992). The literature in this domain can be characterized by four major competing models: spillover model, compensation model, opposition model, and segmentation model (for a review see Voydanoff, 1989; Zedeck, 1992).

Four Major Models

Spillover model. This model posits that satisfaction at work spills over into satisfaction at home (Champoux, 1978; Staines, 1980; Crouter, Perry-Jenkins, Huston, & Crawford, 1989; Marshall, Chadwick, & Marshall, 1992). Stated differently, it maintains that work variables are positively associated with family variables. For instance, those who show high job involvement, job satisfaction, and career progress tend to have meaningful and enjoyable interaction with family members and show high satisfaction with life at home. Negative spillover also occurs. Research shows that negative work experiences such as job stress and low job satisfaction reduce commitment to family activities and increase negative interaction at home (Crouter, Perry-Jenkins, Huston, & Crawford, 1989) and that interpersonal conflicts in the workplace raise the likelihood of subsequent spousal arguments at home (Bolger, DeLongis, Kessler, & Wethington, 1989). Those who are frustrated at work may bring bad feelings home, showing rough behaviors and inappropriate attitudes; alternatively, they may withdraw into themselves, avoiding an interactive relationship with family members. The spillover model thus suggests a positive relationship between work and family variables.

Compensation model. This model, conversely, posits that workers with dissatisfying jobs seek out more pleasurable experiences at home and vice versa, suggesting an inverse relationship between work and family variables (Dubin, 1956; Aldous, 1969; Young & Willmott, 1973; Champoux, 1978; Staines, 1980; Evans & Bartolomé, 1984). Undesirable work experiences or job dissatisfaction are redressed in family settings; alternatively, desirable experiences and positive psychological states that are insufficiently present at home are pursued in work settings. Pursuit of family leisure activities to compensate for stressful experiences at work is an example of this model. For instance, people may seek enjoyable leisure activities that enable them to forget about mistakes that they made on the job.

Opposition model. This model postulates that work and family activities conflict with each other; engaging in activities in one domain can negatively affect activities in the other (Evans & Bartolomé, 1984; Greenhaus & Beutell, 1985; Voydanoff, 1989). Conflict occurs, for instance, when a father takes his child to the movies the day before an important business meeting. For the sake of his family role, the father must sacrifice some of his preparation time for the meeting. Underlying this theory is the assumption that because the work and family domains have distinct norms and requirements, success or satisfaction in one domain entails sacrifices in the other. Thus, like the compensation model, this model also maintains that work and family variables are inversely related.

Segmentation model. This model posits that work and family are two independent domains of life, suggesting that there is no meaningful association between work and family variables (Payton-Miyazaki & Brayfield, 1976; Evans & Bartolomé, 1984). According to the segmentation view, positive experiences, behaviors, and attitudes in one domain have nothing to do with those in the other domain. Individuals who are happy at home may or may not be happy at work; workers who have dissatisfying work experiences may or may not seek out satisfaction at home, and work and family roles may or may not be compatible with each other. The segmentation model thus constitutes the null hypothesis among theories about work and family linkages (Zedeck, 1992).

Three more models exist that seem to overlap somewhat with the spillover model of work-family relationship. First, the *instrumental model* postulates that experiences and attitudes in one domain function as means by which things are obtained in the other domain. Without job security or vocational stability, for instance, it would be difficult for workers to bring some of the pleasures of life to the family (Evans & Bartolomé, 1984; Payton-Miyazaki & Brayfield, 1976). Second, the *integrative model* maintains that work and family are related too closely to consider separately (Morf, 1989). Finally, the *congruence model* holds that some third factor (for example, a personality variable) mediates the work-family relationship and that this factor causes people to elicit similar responses in both domains (Morf, 1989).

To summarize, despite considerable efforts to confirm or disconfirm specific patterns of causality in the work-family relationship, the research to date has produced competing models and no indication of which models are correct. In the next section, we briefly discuss limitations of the past research and directions for future investigation.

Discussion

As we have noted, there is little coherence in the work-family relationship literature. Although past research has provided considerable evidence showing both positive and negative relationships between work and family (Voydanoff, 1989), much remains unknown. In particular, very little research has investigated how individual, or personal, characteristics and situational conditions affect the functional form of the relationship between work and family variables (for some exceptions, see Barling, 1990; Judge & Watanabe, 1994) and whether the form of the work-family relationship is stable over time. Different models of the work-family relationship might be true for different individuals and in different situations and at different points in time for the same individual. This may explain why the research to date is inconclusive. Here are some further thoughts on the promising issues to be explored.

Individual Differences
It is worth exploring whether different forms of the relationship between work and family are possible for different individuals. An attempt to translate this line of thinking into empirical research has been recently made in the job-life satisfaction literature. Logically extending the techniques of Ghiselli (1960) and Zedeck (1971) for differentiating individuals by the degree to which their scores on two variables are related or unrelated, Judge and Watan-

abe (1994) proposed a technique for extracting three groups of individuals with three different forms of job satisfaction–life satisfaction relationship: positively related, negatively related, and unrelated. For their study, they used data from Quinn and Stainer's Quality of Employment Surveys (1979) ($n = 804$). They found that for about 67.7 percent of the sample ($n = 544$), job and life satisfaction were significantly positively related ($r = .77$, $p < .01$); for about 11.9 percent ($n = 96$), the relationship was significantly negative ($r = -.77$, $p < .01$); and for the remaining 20.4 percent, nonsignificant correlation was obtained ($r = -.01$, n.s.). The implication was that each form of the job-life satisfaction relationship could be true for different individuals. Judge and Watanabe argued that more research attention should be directed to the identification of individual difference factors that sort heterogeneous aggregates of individuals into homogeneous subgroups, each with a similar form of job-life satisfaction relationship. Although Judge and Watanabe's study specifically concerned forms of relationship between job and life satisfaction, its implications can be applied to the study of the work-family relationship. Thus we urge abandonment of efforts to confirm or disconfirm specific forms of work-family linking and instead encourage the identification of individual difference variables that will explain the relevance of different models to different individuals.

The individual difference variables fall into two major classes: demographic and psychological. It is important to draw a clear distinction between these classes because individual demographic variables, theoretically, can affect the form of the work-family relationship only through their influence on situational variables and on psychological individual difference variables. For example, it is frequently found that husbands' attitudes toward work are positively associated with the quality of their interaction with family members (Marshall, Chadwick, & Marshall, 1992). However, a negative association has been found for wives (Hardesty & Betz, 1980; Ladewig & McGee, 1986). Another line of research shows that being married and having children are negatively associated with absenteeism, tardiness, and turnover among husbands (Burden & Googins, 1986). However, this is not true for wives. Family-related reasons (for example, child care, household responsibilities) cause women to be absent from, arrive late at, and leave early from the workplace more often than men (Crouter, 1984; Emlen & Koren, 1984). The point here is that it is unclear whether the still-prevalent traditional gender-role system keeps women from having positive work experiences spill over to family (a situational influence) or whether women tend to value family security or taking care of loved ones over a sense of accomplishment at work (a psychological influence). Either or both of these influences could underlie the negative work-family association for women. Thus we propose that future research treat demographic variables as exogenous factors and identify psychological individual difference variables to sort heterogeneous aggregates of individuals into homogeneous subgroups, each with a similar form of work-family relationship. Much remains to be learned about the psychology of individual differences.

Situational Differences

As discussed earlier, situational, or contextual, factors affect men's and women's involvement in work and family roles and, we believe, influence the form of the work-family relationship. There are at least four kinds of situational factors to examine: employment conditions, family conditions, societal conditions (culture), and sociohistorical conditions. For example, if business policies and practices reflecting an organization's level of gender equality or family supportiveness (pay system, parental leave, and so on) were associated with people who have similar forms of the work-family relationship and not with any other people, that would be evidence that those employment conditions affect the nature of the work-family relationship.

Family conditions should also be relevant influences on the link between the work and family lives. For example, Willinger's finding (1993) that married men relax their traditional attitudes until they become fathers and then regress implies that mothers tend to be more responsible for home child care than fathers; women's household responsibilities in turn would lower their work performance. Logic suggests it would be relatively difficult for working mothers to have positive work experiences or to have such experiences spill over to family. Variables such as each spouse's financial role as main or secondary provider in the household economy and each spouse's willingness to accept untraditional lifestyles may also be important family conditions that affect the form of the work-family relationship.

Societal culture is also worth examining as an explanatory factor for the form of the work-family links. It is possible that in a strongly masculine society, a model of positive work-family relationship may prevail for working fathers and a work-family conflict model for working mothers. Recall that Japanese homemaker mothers tend to create positive images of the father who is at work most of the day; Japanese working mothers and wives tend to be in a double bind, damned by society if they do not devote the majority of their time to their families and damned by their employers if they do not devote the majority of their time to their work. In a highly egalitarian society where both sexes can combine parenthood and employment, thereby eliminating the division between private and public spheres of social life, the work-family conflict may be alleviated. Moreover, in individualist cultures, where everyone is expected to look after himself or herself, working men and women do not get sufficient family support to enable them to experience the highest satisfaction at work; therefore, work-family conflict may tend to ensue in that situation. Furthermore, in collectivist cultures, where family members form strong cohesive ingroups that protect them throughout their lifetime in exchange for unquestioning loyalty, the spillover model of the work-family relationship may be more prevalent. Research that examines whether a dominant form of work-family linkage varies with cultural settings or transcends all cultures would be a valuable addition to the literature.

Rapidly changing sociohistorical conditions also operate on the work-family relationship. In recent decades, an increasing number of women have pursued higher levels of education, delaying their marriage, participating in the labor force, and remaining employed after marriage and following the birth of children (McLaughlin, Melber, Billy, Zimmerle, Wingers, & Johnson, 1988). From the changing composition of the workforce is emerging a new ideal of gender-neutral parenthood (Bronstein, 1988; Pleck, 1987), family-supportive legislation (Lewis, 1992; Richter, 1992; Haas, 1993; Ishii-Kuntz, 1993), and business policies and practices (Maklan, 1977; Lee, 1983; Lamb et al., 1988; Kingston, 1989). The gender-role change, albeit slow, is global. Due to the recent ideological commitment to and public support for equality in the home and the workplace, the traditional work and family structure that was still dominant in the 1950s is becoming increasingly anachronistic, and work and family are becoming more and more inseparable spheres of life. According to Barling (1990), the two spheres were interdependent during the 1950s, intertwined by the early 1970s, and overlap each other today. We see in Barling's historical perspective an implication that the strength of a person's work-family relationship is partly a reflection of the social and historical contexts in which that person is born and raised.

Generality over Time

Much of the research on the work-family interface has drawn on conventional cross-sectional methodologies, based on an assumption that the form of the relationship between the work and family domains is stable over time. This is a weak assumption unless it can be proven in studies that deal with time-structured data. Thus it seems fair to test it. Research is needed to examine and assess the long-term stability or continuity of the work-family linkage.

One way to answer this continuity question is to apply Judge and Watanabe's methodological invention (1994) and identify groups of people at one point in time for whom the work-family relationship is positively related, negatively related, or unrelated. Applying the same methodology to the same sample at a different point or points in time will allow researchers to examine whether people who belonged in a certain group in the past continue to belong in the same group in the future. A computation of a ϕ coefficient for the data at two different points in time will accomplish this purpose. If the coefficient fails to reach statistical significance, that would be evidence that the nature of work-family linking is not consistent over time. Also, the successive waves of data, if obtained during relatively short-term measurement windows, will help researchers investigate how long it takes for the nature of the work-family relationship to change, a question that has never been addressed and therefore remains untested.

Thus far we have summarized past research on the work-family relationship and have presented some interesting issues to be explored in future research. The past research is right in that it has discovered different forms of the work-family relationship, but it is limited in that it has not successfully explained why the results are inconsistent. We have not attempted to determine which of the four major competing models is correct because we think the incoherence of the work-family relationship literature may be a reflection of the reality. We propose that future research examine both individual difference variables and situational difference variables that may account for the inconsistency of the past research.

A man who equally values his work and family lives and who has a homemaking wife and dependent children may carry his work experiences over into his home life and may also carry his family experiences over into his work life. However, this man's orientation to the values of work and family may change as his children become more independent, as societal gender-role norms change, and as his wife joins the workforce. In that case, the two spheres of work life and family life may exist side by side for him and yet be separated from each other. What this scenario suggests is that if a person's characteristics (needs, value orientation, and so on) and situational conditions (the gender culture and social policies that affect him, his number of preschoolers, and so on) change, the form of his work-family relationship might also change. A longitudinal research design is needed to investigate how individual and situational characteristics change over time and how they interact with each other over time to affect the form of the work-family relationship.

Joint Effects of Work and Family Attitudes

Work and family are two important parts of a whole life. This is an assumption with which most people would not disagree. And it has generated much speculation about the *joint effects* of work and family attitudes on life satisfaction. For example, Smith (1992) has recently conceptualized a system of interrelated satisfaction as analogous to a river that is fed by tributaries of various facets of work- and family-related satisfaction and that empties into a sea of life satisfaction. A line of research that follows this conceptualization would add important insights to the work-family literature.

An Example of Attitudes Research

Howard's study (1992) of white male managers in Bell System telephone companies represents an example of such research. She developed a comprehensive model investigating the causal rela-tionships among psychological individual difference variables (for example, religiosity, needs for growth and security, cognitive abil-ities, administrative and interpersonal abilities); work and family involvement; work, family, and life satisfaction, and so forth. Here we focus only on her findings about the relationships among the three satisfaction constructs.

To measure the male managers' work satisfaction, Howard used the Management Questionnaire, an attitude survey widely used in the Bell System. Each subject rated his attitudes toward various facets of work such as salary, supervision, personal satisfaction, job satisfaction, pride, impersonal communications, personal com-munications, identification with management, and confidence in higher management. Howard formed a composite scale to repre-sent the subject's general work satisfaction measure. Family satis-faction was assessed through the Thematic Apperception Test (TAT) and the Adult Development Incomplete Sentence Test. These projective techniques were used to record each subject's lev-els of satisfaction and harmony with respect to his marriage (for example, feeling loved, seeing his wife as a source of help, feeling closeness and intimacy, expressing good fortune to have his wife) and with respect to his children and his role of father (for exam-ple, regarding his children as a source of comfort and pride, enjoying the role of father, and enjoying interactions with his chil-dren). Life satisfaction was measured by assessing the subject's per-ceived happiness (the extent to which he indicated feelings of great pleasure and contentment with his life) and adjustment (the extent to which he adapted himself to his life situation in an emo-tionally healthy way).

Howard used LISREL to investigate the effects of work and family satisfaction on life satisfaction. The variables included in the structural model are boss support, job challenge, boss fairness, job problems, occupational involvement, number of children, fam-ily problems, and marital-familial involvement. The work- and family-related variables were modeled as precursors to work satisfaction and family satisfaction, respectively. The standardized parameter estimates were generated by the maximum likelihood method within the LISREL program ($n = 237$; $\chi^2 = .324$, $p = .324$, $df = 37$). With regard to the reciprocity between work and family satisfaction, Howard found that increases in work satisfaction caused increases in family satisfaction ($\beta = .286$) more than the reverse situation ($\beta = -.026$). These results are consistent with earlier literature that specified more influence of work on the family than vice versa (see, for example, Evans & Bartolomé, 1984; Staines, 1980). As for the assumption that work and family are parts of a whole life, Howard found positive and significant links from work satisfaction to life satisfaction ($\beta = .259$) and from family satisfaction to life satisfaction ($\beta = .676$). The reciprocal relationships between life satisfaction and satisfaction with work and family were not significant, supporting the validity of the part-whole assumption.

Discussion

Rather than extensively review the relevant literatures, we focused on Howard's comprehensive study (1992), which, we believe, will inspire future investigation of the combined effects of work and family satisfaction. In what follows, we discuss the meanings of her findings and the issues that need to be addressed in future research.

Whereas most of the past research has focused on the relationships between work and family satisfaction or between work and life satisfaction, Howard offered a triangular model of work, family, and life satisfaction, where satisfaction in the work and family domains are seen as determinants of life satisfaction. This model has made an important contribution to the work-family literature in that it shows that attitudes in the work and family domains can be significant sources of life satisfaction. Future research using a more heterogeneous sample with respect to race, gender, job level, geographical location, and societal cultures would provide a useful extension of these findings.

It should be noted that Howard looked at the interrelationships among *general* attitudes. Work satisfaction defined as a collection of numerous attitudes toward various job facets represents a very general attitude. Likewise, multifaceted measures of family and life attitudes positively covary and form constructs of overall family and life satisfaction, respectively. Howard's model is based on a widely believed assumption that general attitudes best predict general classes of behaviors. The next logical step in the study of the joint effects of work and family attitudes would be to link specific facets of satisfaction in the two domains to a specific outcome such as job performance, work withdrawal behaviors (for example, turnover, absenteeism, and lateness), family withdrawal behaviors (for example, divorce and separation), spouse abuse, and so on. It has been suggested that specific behaviors are most strongly related to specific attitudes.

With regard to the combined effects of satisfaction in the work and family situations, the greatest understanding would probably come from examining specific attitudes related to specific behaviors along with psychological individual difference variables that moderate the links between the specific attitudes and the behaviors. Classifications are needed of work and family situations and individual characteristics with regard to behaviors they elicit. Therefore we next identify a suitable methodology that addresses this point.

A three-dimensional data matrix is required to develop such taxonomies, the three dimensions representing individuals, behaviors, and stimulus situations. Thus we do not propose the use of two-way factor analysis, which would search for relationships in data that have been classified by individuals × work attitudes or by individuals × family attitudes. Instead of assigning stimulus situations on the basis of their mutual possession of various attitudes, it is possible to group these situations on the basis of their tendency to elicit similar behaviors (Frederiksen, 1972). The methodology available to develop such taxonomies is three-mode factor analysis, developed by L. R. Tucker (see Tucker, 1963, 1964, 1966; Frederiksen, 1972; Frederiksen, Jensen, Beaton, & Bloxom, 1972). Three-mode factor analysis, which is applicable when three-way cross-classifications of data are used, seems to be especially appropriate when the researcher's ultimate purpose is the investigation of person-situation interactions in predicting behavior. Tucker's invention, if applied to the work-family relationship literature, will reveal some of the more complex interrelationships of individual characteristics, situations, and behavior.

Figure 11.1 is a pictorial representation of the three-dimensional data matrix. To illustrate how it would work, assume that we are exploring a model predicting the performance of 200 male and female executives based on their attitudes toward various facets of work and family situations. Also suppose we have data containing a large number of items descriptive of the subjects' performance and satisfaction in the work and family arenas. Such items can be obtained from job descriptions of the executives and literature on work and family (for a review see Rice, Near, & Hunt, 1980; Zedeck, 1992). Regarding performance assessment, for example, we have items related to supervision of work; business control; long-range planning; technical expertise in markets and products; exercise of power and authority; human, community and social affairs; and so on. On the family side of situational satisfaction, we have variables measuring attitudes toward marriage, spouse, and children; family activities; leisure; role sharing and bargaining; and so on. On the work side, there are variables measuring attitudes toward pay, promotion, coworkers, physical conditions, job comfort, challenge, job security, work schedules and contents, and so on.

Figure 11.1. Three-Dimensional Matrix Representing Individuals, Situations, and Behaviors.

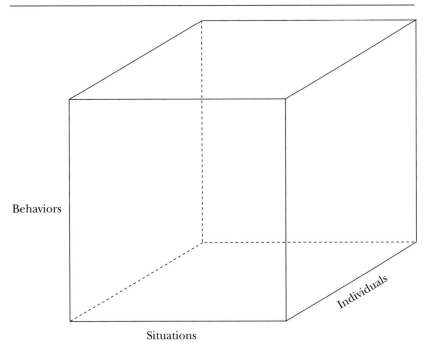

Behaviors

Individuals

Situations

At this point, we have variables that encompass the domains of performance, work, and family. Pooling all the variables of the work and family arenas, we have the data to form a three-dimensional data matrix, the three dimensions representing subjects, behaviors, and situations (see Figure 11.1). Given such a data matrix, our first step would be to collapse the data across situations to obtain a subject × behavior matrix and to factor the intercorrelations of the behaviors, thereby identifying a classification of behaviors. If the data are collapsed across subjects, we have a behavior × situation matrix, and factors in the domain of situations may be identified, each factor representing a cluster of situations that resemble one another with regard to the kinds of behaviors they elicit.

The steps described so far are preliminary to the three-mode factor analysis. Once factors in the domain of behaviors and in the domain of situations are obtained, the researcher can go on to the computation of factors in the domain of subjects. This can be performed by inverting the subject × behavior matrix and computing and factoring the correlations between all pairs of *individuals*. A high correlation between members of a given pair means that two persons behave similarly. A factor then represents a group of persons who are alike with respect to their behavioral pattern, or tendency; such person factors, if found, can be a basis for a typology of individuals as well as a demonstration of the existence of a person-situation interaction (Frederiksen, 1972).

The final step in the procedure is to produce a reduced three-mode matrix representing relationships between behavior factors, situation factors, and person factors. The reduced matrix, which Tucker calls the central or core matrix, involves only the derived factors of the behaviors, situations, and individuals. This matrix, like the original data matrix, is three-dimensional but has fewer behavioral items, fewer situational variables, and fewer types of subjects.

To illustrate how this procedure would work in the present context, assume that we obtained four person factors, three performance factors (control of subordinates, business planning, and extra-role behaviors), and four situation factors (job challenge, identification with management, spousal satisfaction, and harmony with children). The person factors can be interpreted on the basis of the relationships between the performance factors and the situation factors that characterize each person factor. Thus a separate table can be presented for each of the person factors; the entries (loadings) in that table will show that particular kinds of performance are associated with particular kinds of situations for subjects who represent that particular factor.

For example, if high loadings for person factor *I* are found in the cells corresponding to situation factor *II* (identification with management) and each of the performance factors (control of subordinates, business planning, extra-role behaviors), then the typical person in person factor *I* is likely to perform well when the managerial policies and practices are consonant with his or her personal values or characteristics. If the table for person factor *II* reveals high levels of association of the performance factors with situation factor *I* (job challenge), it would be evidence that people in person factor *II* tend to be motivated to work hard by their desire to attain high standards of excellence in their jobs. Moreover, if the loadings for the performance factors and situation factors *III* (spousal satisfaction) and *IV* (harmony with children) are high for members of person factor *III*, it would be evidence that family attitudes affect work. It would also demonstrate that for some people, such values as mature love (sexual and spiritual intimacy with spouse) and family security (taking care of loved ones) function as guiding principles in work life. We may also find strong associations between all the performance factors and all the situation factors for members in person factor *IV*, suggesting that overall, work satisfaction and family satisfaction operate as equally important motivators for performing various tasks. What these hypothetical scenarios suggest is a plausible assumption that there exist person × situation interactions that determine behavior.

Some additional remarks are in order that concern the exploration of the person × situation interaction effects on performance. First, it is possible that for each person factor, there are many association patterns of performance factors with work-family situation factors. High loadings may be found in one or more cells corresponding to one or more situation factors and one or more performance factors. It is also possible that some family variables and some work variables will combine to form one situation factor that is associated with a particular type of performance. We can find no reason for denying this possibility when investigating joint effects of work and family variables.

Second, a considerable amount of additional information is needed to provide meaningful interpretations of person factors. One way to obtain such information would be to compute correlations of the person-factor scores with psychological individual difference variables (see Frederiksen, 1972). To explore this avenue, person descriptors are needed that are sufficiently general to cover a wide variety of people, a criterion for investigating person-situation relations suggested by Bem and Funder (1978). Examples of some promising descriptors can be found in Norman's "big five" personality traits (1963) (openness to experience, conscientiousness, extroversion, agreeableness, and neuroticism) and Rokeach's "human values" descriptors (1973) (a comfortable life, an exciting life, a sense of accomplishment, a world at peace, a world of beauty, equality, family security, freedom, happiness, inner harmony, mature love, national security, pleasure, salvation, self-respect, social recognition, true friendship, and wisdom). The correlations between the person-factor scores and these person descriptors will, we can hope, aid in the interpretation of the person factors.

Third, this avenue of research in which interactions of specific facets of work and family situations and specific person characteristics are modeled as predictors of specific behaviors, will place more specific issues in sharper relief and will produce more practical implications for management than would any attempt to study or explain the interrelationships among such general attitudes as work, family, and life satisfaction. Specifically, if research in a company were to reveal significant positive effects of job challenge and family security on task performance for a large group of employees who value their work and family lives equally, it would suggest that management should focus both on enriching jobs (for example, increasing job requirements for personal competencies and autonomy) and on creating family-friendly business policies and practices (for example, a policy that entitles parents to paid leave when absent from work to be with an ill child).

Fourth, to be validated such results need to be checked across different samples and different sites. As noted, the three-mode factor analysis is a useful *exploratory* tool for studying person-situation interactions that might determine behavior. Cross-cultural investigations could also be meaningful validation efforts. It is possible that in an egalitarian society where work is organized so that both sexes can combine parenthood and employment and the work-family split is alleviated, work and family variables combine to form joint situation factors affecting particular behaviors. Alternatively, in a traditional society where work and family roles tend to conflict, the possibility of forming such joint factors may be less. Massive data based on a wide range of work in many different contexts are needed for a good understanding of how the work and family spheres of life determine behavior.

Finally, temporal generalizability of the results also needs to be examined. As pointed out earlier, it is a weak assumption that predictor-criterion relationships are stable over time. Longitudinal studies are needed that examine the long-term stability of the effects of person-situation relations on behavior. Longitudinal research takes a long time to complete and requires the researcher to have a high tolerance for delayed gratification, but we believe that researchers will achieve the most meaningful understanding of work-family joint effects when they undertake and complete these studies designed to trace, at multiple points in time, the effects of work and family variables on behavior, along with various life events that occur in those two domains.

Summary and Conclusion

This chapter provided an overview of the work-family literature and presented avenues of research to be addressed in future investigations. We first examined the balancing of men's and women's work and family roles. To see whether there are *national* models of work-family balancing behaviors, we made comparisons among Japan, Britain, Israel, the United States, and Sweden. The data suggested that these countries approached the issue of work-family balancing somewhat differently. Japan and Britain seem to retain the most traditional sex-role ideology; deeply internalized for both men and women is the notion that a clear separation of men's work roles and women's family roles is essential to the survival of the family as a social institution. Sweden has achieved the most egalitarian society; the benevolence of the Swedish welfare system helps both sexes combine parenthood and employment. Israel and the United States fall in the middle, although Israel is more egalitarian than the United States. In order to explain these variations in work-family balancing behaviors from a perspective of cultural relativism, we examined how each society's characteristic style of interrole juggling is associated with such social values as Confucianism, individualism, and masculinity. Consequently, we found that the variations can be explained fairly well by the society's position on the masculinity-femininity dimension. To check the validity of the finding, we suggested further examination using a wider range of cross-cultural data.

The data also pointed to two transculturally generalizable phenomena. One is gender inequality. Specifically, there is a general tendency across the nations that family roles are allowed to intrude upon women's work, whereas men's work roles can intrude upon family. The differences among the nations, therefore, can be portrayed in terms of quantitative variations in their levels of gender-based traditional role structure.

The second cultural universal we identified is the gender-role transition away from role separation and toward a gender-neutral society. This ongoing transition has resulted in much speculation about factors beyond societal culture that might influence men's and women's changing behaviors. Most studies to date have emphasized situational factors and generally ignored psychological individual differences as factors. The reason for this probably lies in the fact that much of the research has been conducted by researchers, family sociologists, and occupational sociologists whose normal focus is situational (see Zedeck, 1992). We believe that future research should consider interactions between situational conditions and psychological individual difference variables in determining interrole balancing. A psychology of work-family juggling will be a unique contribution to the existing sociological investigation.

Second, we reviewed the literature on causal links within the work-family relationship. We argued that each of the four primary competing models produced by past research was possible for different individuals, in different situations, and at different points in time for the same individual. It is possible that the model of work-family conflict is dominant for working mothers in dual-career families in a traditional gender-segregated society. However, it is also possible that as the rate of women's labor force participation increases, the mothers will demand more from their husbands, including sharing of housework and child care, and the societal culture will undergo a transition, with both sexes moving away from role separation and toward gender equality and the emergence of family-friendly social policies, which in turn will reduce the work-family conflict. This scenario suggests that if a person's individual characteristics and situational conditions change, the form of the work-family relationship might also change. Thus we propose that future research adopt a framework in which to trace the effects of person-situation interactions on the work-family relationship over time.

Finally, we looked at the joint effects of work and family satisfaction on life satisfaction. Past research shows that general attitudes in the work and family domains converge into people's general attitudes about their lives. One limitation of this line of research is that psychological individual differences are not considered in explaining the interrelationships among the three constructs. Also, although it is of considerable importance in its own right, focusing on general attitudes masks potential differential effects of facets of work and family satisfaction on specific attitudes or behaviors. For organizations, predicting specific attitudes toward work is a more important (or practical) concern than predicting such general attitudes as overall life satisfaction. Research is needed to explore the links between specific facets of work and family satisfaction with specific outcomes. Examination across various samples and sites in many different cultures will be a unique contribution to the literature.

A final word: the recent increase of women's labor force participation has resulted in and will continue to stimulate much speculation and concern about the functioning and flexibility of the work-family relationship. A large body of research has investigated the changing work-family dynamics, but as we have shown there are still many interesting problems in this domain of research that remain to be addressed. We hope that the examination of those problems will be a valuable addition to the work-family literature.

References

Aldous, J. (1969). Occupational characteristics and males' role performance in the family. *Journal of Marriage and the Family, 31,* 707–712.

Alwin, D., Brown, M., & Scott, J. (1992). The separation of work and family: Attitudes toward women's labor force participation in Germany, Great Britain and the United States. *European Sociological Review, 8,* 13–36.

Bando, M. S. (1986). *Japanese women yesterday and today.* Tokyo: Foreign Press Center.

Baringa, M. (1994, March). Overview: Surprises across the cultural divide. *Science, 263*(11), 1468–1472.

Barling, J. (1990). *Employment, stress and family functioning.* New York: Wiley.

Beckman, L. J., & Houser, B. B. (1979). The more you have, the more you do: The relationship between wife's employment, sex role attitudes, and household behavior. *Psychology of Women Quarterly, 4,* 160–274.

Bell, C., McKee, L., & Priestly, K. (1983). *Fathers, childbirth and work.* Manchester, England: Equal Opportunity Commission.

Bem, D. J., & Funder, D. C. (1978). Predicting more of the people more of the time: Assessing the personality of situations. *Psychological Review, 85,* 485–501.

Berry, J. W., Poortinga, Y. H., Segall, M. H., & Dasen, P. R. (1992). *Cross-cultural psychology: Research and applications.* New York: Cambridge University Press.

Berry-Lound, B. (1990). *Work and the family: Career friendly employment practices.* London: Institute of Personnel Management.

Bolger, N., DeLongis, A., Kessler, R. C., & Wethington, E. (1989). The contagion of stress across multiple roles. *Journal of Marriage and the Family, 51,* 175–183.

Booth, A. (1977). Wife's employment and husband's stress: A replication and refutation. *Journal of Marriage and the Family, 39,* 645–650.

Brannen, J. (1992). Money, marriage and motherhood: Dual earner households after maternity leave. In S. Arber & N. Gilbert (Eds.), *Women and working lives* (pp. 54–70). London: Macmillan.

Bronstein, P. (1988). Father-child interaction: Implications for gender role socialization. In P. Bronstein & C. P. Cowman (Eds.), *Fatherhood today: Men's changing role in the family* (pp. 107–124). New York: Wiley.

Burden, D., & Googins, B. (1986). *Boston University balancing job and home-life study: Managing work and family stress in corporations.* Boston: Boston University, School of Social Work.

Caspi, A., & Bem, D. J. (1990). Personality continuity and change across the life course. In L. A. Pervin (Ed.), *Handbook of personality: Theory and research* (pp. 549–575). New York: Guilford Press.

Caspi, A., Bem, D. J., & Elder, G. H., Jr. (1989). Continuity and consequences of interactional styles across the life course. *Journal of Personality, 57,* 375–406.

Caspi, A., Elder, G. H., Jr., & Bem, D. J. (1987). Moving against the world: Life-course patterns of explosive children. *Developmental Psychology, 23,* 308–313.

Caspi, A., Elder, G. H., Jr., & Bem, D. J. (1988). Moving away from the world: Life-course patterns of shy children. *Developmental Psychology, 24,* 824–831.

Champoux, J. E. (1978). Perceptions of work and nonwork: A reexamination of the compensatory and spillover models. *Sociology of Work and Occupations, 5,* 402–422.

[Child care leave for male teachers]. (1994, January 12). *Asahi Shinbun,* p. 10.

Clark, R. C. (1979). *The Japanese company.* New Haven, CT: Yale University Press.

Cole, R. E. (1971). The theory of institutionalization: Permanent employment and tradition in Japan. *Economic Development and Cultural Change, 20,* 47–70.

Crouter, A. C. (1984). Spillover from family to work: The neglected side of the work-family interface. *Human Relations, 37,* 425–442.

Crouter, A. C., Perry-Jenkins, M., Huston, T. L., & Crawford, D. W. (1989). The influence of work-induced psychological states on behavior at home. *Basic and Applied Social Psychology, 10,* 273–292.

Davis, N. J., & Robinson, R. V. (1991). Men's and women's consciousness of gender quality: Australia, West Germany, Great Britain, and the United States. *American Sociological Review, 56,* 72–84.

Dennehy, K., & Mortimer, J. T. (1993). Work and family orientations of contemporary adolescent boys and girls. In J. C. Hood (Ed.), *Men, work, and family* (pp. 87–107). Thousand Oaks, CA: Sage.

Doi, T. (1973). *The anatomy of dependence.* Tokyo: Kodansha International.

Dore, R. P. (1973). *British factory, Japanese factory: The origins of national diversity in industrial relations.* Berkeley: University of California Press.

Dubin, R. (1956). Industrial workers' worlds. *Social Problems, 3,* 131–142.

Dunphy, D. C. (1987). Convergence/divergence: A temporal view of the Japanese enterprise and its management. *Academy of Management Review, 12,* 445–459.

Emlen, A. C., & Koren, P. E. (1984). *Hard to find and difficult to manage: The effects of child care on the workplace.* Portland, OR: Portland State University.

Evans, P., & Bartolomé, F. (1984). The changing picture of the relationship between career and family. *Journal of Occupational Behavior, 5,* 9–21.

Franks, A. (1990, April 9). Does the workadaddy deserve a break? *Times* (London), p. 17.

Frederiksen, N. (1972). Toward a taxonomy of situations. *American Psychologist, 27,* 114–123.

Frederiksen, N., Jensen, O., Beaton, A. E., & Bloxom, B. (1972). *Prediction of organizational behavior.* New York: Pergamon Press.

Ghiselli, E. E. (1960). The prediction of predictability. *Educational and Psychological Measurement, 20,* 3–8.

Gilligan, C. (1982). *In a different voice: Psychological theory and women's development.* Cambridge, MA: Harvard University Press.

Greenhaus, J. H., & Beutell, N. J. (1985). Sources of conflict between work and family roles. *Academy of Management Review, 10,* 79–88.

Haas, L. (1986). Wives' orientation toward breadwinning: Sweden and the United States. *Journal of Family Issues, 7,* 358–381.

Haas, L. (1993). Nurturing fathers and working mothers: Changing gender roles in Sweden. In J. C. Hood (Ed.), *Men, work, and family* (pp. 238–261). Thousand Oaks, CA: Sage.

Haas, L. (1995). Household division of labor in industrial societies. In B. B. Ingoldsby & S. Smith (Eds.), *Families in multicultural perspective* (pp. 268–296). New York: Guilford Press.

Hansard Society. (1990). *The report of the Hansard Society Commission on women at the top.* London: Author.

Hardesty, S. A., & Betz, N. E. (1980). The relationships of career salience, attitudes toward women, and demographic and family characteristics to marital adjustment in dual-career couples. *Journal of Vocational Behavior, 17,* 242–250.

Henwood, M., Rimmer, L., & Wicks, M. (1987). *Inside the family: Changing roles of men and women.* London: Family Policies Study Center.

Hofstede, G. (1980). *Culture's consequences: International differences in work-related values.* Thousand Oaks, CA: Sage.

Hofstede, G. (1991). *Cultures and organizations. Software of the Mind.* London: McGraw-Hill.

Hood, J. C. (1986). The provider role: Its meaning and measurement. *Journal of Marriage and the Family, 48,* 349–359.

Hood, J. C. (Ed.). (1993). *Men, work, and family.* Thousand Oaks, CA: Sage.

Howard, A. (1992). Work and family crossroads spanning the career. In S. Zedeck (Ed.), *Work, families, and organizations* (pp. 70–137). San Francisco: Jossey-Bass.

International Labor Office. (1993). *Yearbook of labor statistics* [Rodo tokei chosa nenpo]. Tokyo: Author.

Ishii-Kuntz, M. (1989). Collectivism or individualism? Changing patterns of Japanese attitudes. *Sociology and Social Research, 73,* 174–179.

Ishii-Kuntz, M. (1993). Japanese fathers: Work demands and family roles. In J. C. Hood (Ed.), *Men, work, and family* (pp. 45–67). Thousand Oaks, CA: Sage.

Itoi, K., & Powell, B. (1992, August 10). Take a hike, Hiroshi. *Newsweek,* pp. 22–23.

Johnson, T. R. (1988). *The changing lives of American women.* Chapel Hill: University of North Carolina Press.

Judge, T. A., Boudreau, J. W., & Bretz, R. D. (1994). Job and life attitudes of male executives. *Journal of Applied Psychology, 79*(5), 767–782.

Judge, T. A., & Watanabe, S. (1994). Individual differences in the nature of the relationship between job and life satisfaction. *Journal of Occupational and Organizational Psychology, 7,* 101–107.

Keys, J. B., & Miller, T. R. (1984). The Japanese management theory jungle. *Academy of Management Review, 9,* 342–353.

Kingston, P. (1989). Studying the work-family connection. In E. B. Goldsmith (Ed.), *Work and family: Theory, research, and applications* (pp. 55–60). Thousand Oaks, CA: Sage.

Ladewig, B., & McGee, G. W. (1986). Occupational commitment, a supportive family environment, and marital adjustment: Development and estimation of a model. *Journal of Marriage and the Family, 48,* 821–829.

Lamb, M. E., Hwang, P., Broberg, A., Bookstein, F., Hult, G., & Frodi, M. (1988). The determinants of parental involvement in a representative sample of primiparous Swedish families. *International Journal of Behavior and Development, 11,* 433–449.

LaRossa, R. (1988). Fatherhood and social change. *Family relations, 37,* 451–457.

Lee, R. A. (1983). Flextime and conjugal roles. *Journal of Occupational Behavior, 4,* 297–315.

Lewis, S. (1992). Work and families in the United Kingdom. In S. Zedeck (Ed.), *Work, families, and organizations* (pp. 395–431). San Francisco: Jossey-Bass.

Lewis, S., & Cooper, C. (1989). *Career couples.* London: Unwin Hyman.

Lincoln, J. R., & Kalleberg, A. L. (1985). Work organizations and work force commitment: A study of plants and employees in the U.S. and Japan. *American Sociological Review, 50,* 738–760.

Magnusson, D., & Endler, N. S. (Eds.). (1977). *Personality at the crossroads: Current issues in interactional psychology.* Hillsdale, NJ: Erlbaum.

Maklan, D. (1977). *The four-day work week.* New York: Praeger.

Management and Coordination Agency. (1982). *Shugyo kozo kihon chosa hokoku—zenkoku hen* [Employment status survey—Whole Japan]. Tokyo: Author.

Management and Coordination Agency. (1986). *Kodomo to chichioya ni kansuru kokusai hikaku chosa* [International comparative survey on children and fathers]. Tokyo: Author.

Management and Coordination Agency. (1992). *Shugyo kozo kihon chosa hokoku—zenkoku hen* [Employment status survey—Whole Japan]. Tokyo: Author.

Marshall, C. M., Chadwick, B. A., & Marshall, B. C. (1992). The influence of employment on family interaction, well-being, and happiness. In S. J. Bahr (Ed.), *Family research: A sixty-year review, 1930–1990* (Vol. 2, pp. 167–229). San Francisco: The New Lexington Press.

Mason, K., & Lu, Y. (1988). Attitudes toward women's family roles: Changes in the United States, 1977–1985. *Gender and Society, 2,* 39–57.

McLaughlin, S. D., Melber, B. D., Billy, J., Zimmerle, D. M., Wingers, L. D., & Johnson, T. R. (1988). *The changing lives of American women.* Chapel Hill: University of North Carolina Press.

Ministry of Finance. (1990). *Fujin rodo hakusho* [White Reports on women's labor]. Tokyo: Author.

Morf, M. (1989). *The work/family dichotomy.* Westport, CT: Quorum/Greenwood.

Mortimer, J. T., Lorence, J., & Kumka, D. S. (1986). *Work, family and personality: Transition to adulthood.* Norwood, NJ: Ablex.

Nickols, S. Y., & Metzen, E. J. (1978). Housework time of husband and wife. *Home Economics Research Journal, 7,* 85–97.

Nonaka, I., & Johansson, J. K. (1985). Japanese management: What about the "hard" skills. *Academy of Management Review, 10,* 181–191.

Norman, W. T. (1963). Toward an adequate taxonomy of personality attributes: Replicated factor structure. *Journal of Abnormal and Social Psychology, 66,* 574–583.

[Parental leave implemented by the majority of companies]. (1994, January 26). *Nikkei Shinbun,* p. 34.

Pascarella, E. T., & Terenzini, P. T. (1991). *How college affects students: Findings and insights from twenty years of research.* San Francisco: Jossey-Bass.

[Paternity leave granted to male employees]. (1991, January 11). *Nikkei Shinbun,* p. 11.

Payton-Miyazaki, M., & Brayfield, A. H. (1976). The good job and the good life: Relation of characteristics of employment to general well-being. In A. D. Biderman & T. F. Drury (Eds.), *Measuring work quality for social reporting* (pp. 125–150). Thousand Oaks, CA: Sage.

Persson, I. (1990). The third dimension: Equal status between Swedish women and men. In I. Persson (Ed.), *Generating equality in the welfare state: The Swedish experience* (pp. 223–244). Oslo: Norwegian University Press.

Peters, Y., & Katz, R. (1984). *The working mother and family.* Report submitted to the Israeli Ministry of Work and Social Welfare.

Pleck, J. H. (1977). The work-family role system. *Social Problems, 24,* 417–427.

Pleck, J. H. (1987). American fathering in historical perspective. In M. S. Kimmel (Ed.), *Changing men* (pp. 83–97). Thousand Oaks, CA: Sage.

Quinn, R. P., & Stainer, G. (1979). *Quality of Employment Survey, 1973–1979: Panel.* Ann Arbor, MI: Interuniversity Consortium for Political and Social Research.

Redding, S. G., Norman, A., & Schlander, A. (1994). The nature of individual attachment to the organization: A review of East Asian variations. In H. C. Triandis, M. D. Dunnette, & L. M. Hough (Eds.), *Handbook of industrial and organizational psychology* (2nd ed., Vol. 4, pp. 647–688). Palo Alto, CA: Consulting Psychologists Press.

Reischauer, E. O. (1981). *The Japanese.* Cambridge, MA: Harvard University Press.

Rice, R. W., Near, J. P., & Hunt, R. G. (1980). The job satisfaction/life satisfaction relationship: A review of empirical research. *Basic and Applied Social Psychology, 1,* 37–64.

Richter, J. (1992). Balancing work and family in Israel. In S. Zedeck (Ed.), *Work, families, and organizations* (pp. 362–394). San Francisco: Jossey-Bass.

Robinson, J. P. (1975). *American's use of time project.* Ann Arbor: University of Michigan, Survey Research Center.

Rokeach, M. (1973). *The nature of human values.* New York: Free Press.

Smith, P. B. (1984). The effectiveness of Japanese styles of management: A review and critique. *Journal of Occupational Psychology, 57,* 121–136.

Smith, P. C. (1992). In pursuit of happiness: Why study general job satisfaction? In C. J. Cranny, P. C. Smith, & E. F. Stone (Eds.), *Job Satisfaction* (pp. 5–19). San Francisco: The New Lexington Press.

Staines, G. L. (1980). Spillover versus compensation: A review of the literature on the relationship between work and nonwork. *Human Relations, 33,* 111–129.

Sweet, J., Bumpass, L., & Call, V. (1988). *National survey of families and households.* Madison: University of Wisconsin, Center for Demography and Ecology.

Terborg, J. R. (1981). Interactional psychology and research on human behavior in organizations. *Academy of Management Review, 6,* 569–576.

Tucker, L. R. (1963). Implications of factor analysis of three-way matrices for measurement change. In C. W. Harris (Ed.), *Problems in measuring change* (pp. 109–127). Madison: University of Wisconsin Press.

Tucker, L. R. (1964). The extension of factor analysis to three-dimensional matrices. In N. Frederiksen & H. Gulliksen (Eds.), *Contributions to mathematical psychology* (pp. 109–127). Austin, TX: Holt, Rinehart and Winston.

Tucker, L. R. (1966). Some mathematical notes on three-mode factor analysis. *Psychometrika, 31,* 279–311.

Vogel, E. E. (1979). *Japan as number one: Lessons for America.* Cambridge, MA: Harvard University Press.

Voydanoff, P. (1989). Work and family: A review and expanded conceptualization. In E. B. Goldsmith (Ed.), *Work and family: Theory, research, and application* (pp. 1–22). Thousand Oaks, CA: Sage.

Walker, K. E., & Woods, M. E. (1976). *Time use: A measure of household production of family goods and services.* Washington, DC: Center for the Family of the American Home Economic Association.

Watanabe, S. (1994). The distinction between latent and manifest person-situation relations: Mechanism of the mode transformation and links to situational satisfaction and attachment. *Dissertation Abstracts International, 55*(07), 3053B–3054B. (University Microfilms No. 9501297)

Willinger, B. (1993). Resistance and change: College men's attitudes toward family and work in the 1980s. In J. C. Hood (Ed.), *Men, work, and family* (pp. 108–130). Thousand Oaks, CA: Sage.

Wright, J. D. (1978). Are working women really more satisfied? Evidence from several national surveys. *Journal of Marriage and the Family, 40,* 301–313.

Young, M., & Willmott, P. (1973). *The symmetrical family.* New York: Pantheon.

Zedeck, S. (1971). Problems with the use of "moderator" variables. *Psychological Bulletin, 76,* 295–310.

Zedeck, S. (1992). Introduction: Exploring the domain of work and family concerns. In S. Zedeck (Ed.), *Work, families, and organizations* (pp. 1–32). San Francisco: Jossey-Bass.

CHAPTER 12

Commentary on Diversity and Work-Family Values
Sheldon Zedeck

The preceding chapter, by Watanabe, Takahashi, and Minami, focuses on three aspects of the work-family relationship: efforts to balance work and family, causal links in the work-family relationship, and the joint effects of attitudes and behavior on work and family domains. This commentary, first, will briefly review the chapter and, second, present a framework for studying work and family relationships within a cross-cultural perspective.

Review of Chapter Eleven

Chapter Eleven provides an interesting discussion of work and family relationships from a cross-cultural perspective. The fact that it pursues balance, causal linkages, and antecedents and consequences may make it appear to be a traditional work-family chapter, for which there is an increasing body of literature (Zedeck, 1992). But in keeping with the theme of this volume, Watanabe, Takahashi, and Minami broaden their discussion to provide cross-national comparisons, particularly with respect to work-family balancing. In their discussion of balancing work and family the major departure from the traditional literature is their drawing upon data and results from Japan, Britain, the United States, Israel, and Sweden. Of particular interest is the focus on gender-role differences. The authors reach the conclusion that there are cultural variations and cultural universals. The variations relate to traditional versus more modern gender-role norms (for example, the egalitarian view) and to differences in social values that can be described along a masculinity-femininity dimension. The cultural universals also arise from gender inequality, in that Watanabe, Takahashi, and Minami indicate that every society seems to think that some behaviors are more suitable for males and others are more suitable for females. Other culturally universal findings pertain to the increasing labor force participation of females and changing gender-role norms within each country explored. From my perspective the focus in the work-family balancing discussion is on macro variables that have resulted from enactment of legislation and social policies supporting female participation in the work force, structural variables such as time spent in organizations versus the home, and attitudinal variables such as perceptions of equality. Missing from the analysis, however, is the concern for what Watanabe, Takahashi, and Minami describe as "psychological individual differences." Watanabe, Takahashi, and Minami call for increased research on the dynamic interactions between person variables and situation variables in determining the work-family balance dynamics. They argue that individual differences affect how people interpret, react to, and shape a situation, and that the shaped situation affects future behavior. I agree with this premise and expand upon it later.

Very little of the discussion on the chapter's second focus—on the various causal models of work-family relationships (spillover, compensation, opposition, and segmentation)—relates to a cross-cultural perspective. In general the emphasis is on the need to understand the models and on how individual variables and context affect the functional form of the work-family relationship. The exception is the discussion of societal culture as a situational variable that influences causal linkages.

The authors also make the point that different models of the work-family relationship might be true for different individuals, in different situations, and at different points in time for the same individual. They encourage future research on individual difference variables that will explain the relevance of different models to different individuals, and they argue such research may explain why the literature has found inconsistent results when proposing causal models.

I agree with their different model–different individual premise, and will expand it later also. In particular I will argue that different models will be true for the same individual at the same time but that the appropriateness of the model will be dependent on the nature of the work dimension being studied, regardless of whether the dimension pertains to personal characteristics or contextual factors.

The authors' third focus is on the joint effects of work and family attitudes on life satisfaction. This section stresses that future research should attempt to study these joint effects and to link such variables to outcomes such as job performance, work withdrawal behaviors, family withdrawal behaviors, and the like. Watanabe, Takahashi, and Minami develop their premise by suggesting three-way analyses: individual × behavioral × situational dimensions. Here, again, I agree, but I would argue for stronger concern for studying the influence of culture in the model. The authors state that cross-cultural investigations would be meaningful for the validation efforts of their model; my view is that the three-way interaction takes place within a cultural context.

In what follows, with Chapter Eleven as a point of departure, I briefly explore the connection between cross-cultural research and work-family linkages and also propose a framework for studying such linkages.

The Cross-Cultural Study of Work-Family Relationships

Review of articles and books by those who have written or conducted research on cross-cultural psychology (for example, Berry, Poortinga, Segall, & Dasen, 1992; Bond & Smith, 1996; Erez, 1994; Kagitçibasi & Berry, 1989) from an industrial and organizational psychology (as well as organizational behavior) perspective leads me to the following working definition:

> Cross-cultural psychology is the study of similarities and differences in individual functioning in various cultures. Cross-cultural psychology attempts to discover systematic relationships between psychological variables at the individual level and cultural, ethnic, situational, contextual, legal, political, and economic variables at the "group" level.

This definition, or perspective, guides my framework for studying work-family issues within a cross-cultural context. In essence, an individual, who is employed by an organization or who functions as a family member, has values, needs, interests, personality, abilities, and so forth—all of these are psychological individual difference variables. The employing organization is a situation, or context, with its own structure, reward systems, demands, and the like. The same is true for a family organization, which has its own configuration, systems, and so forth. In essence we have individuals behaving in two types of situations—the employing organization and the family organization. The interaction of the individual's characteristics within his or her organization, however, takes place within a larger situation, or context, which is society. Societal factors such as policy, legislation, entitlements, and privileges influence how the individual functions within the employing organization and the family organization. (Naturally, the organizational roles have a reciprocal impact and influence, for example, the type of legislation enacted.)

As we explore individual × behavioral × situational interactions *across* countries or nations, we gain a cross-cultural perspective that allows us to identify cultural universals or variations. In general, research in industrial and organizational psychology has looked at psychological phenomena at the individual level as being the same across cultures (Erez, 1994), but this needs to be challenged. Figure 12.1 depicts the model, the network of variables, to be studied. Central to the model are the psychological individual difference variables mentioned by Watanabe, Takahashi, and Minami, which would be included in the model's individual dimension. As I elaborate on each of the dimensions identified in the model, I will focus on a psychological individual difference variable that has much promise as a subject of cross-cultural research: the *meaning of work*.

Framework for Cross-Cultural Study of Work-Family Relationships

The study of work-family relationships requires definition of the three following relevant variables (Zedeck, 1992; Zedeck & Mosier, 1990):

**Figure 12.1. Representation of Work-Family
Model to Be Studied.**

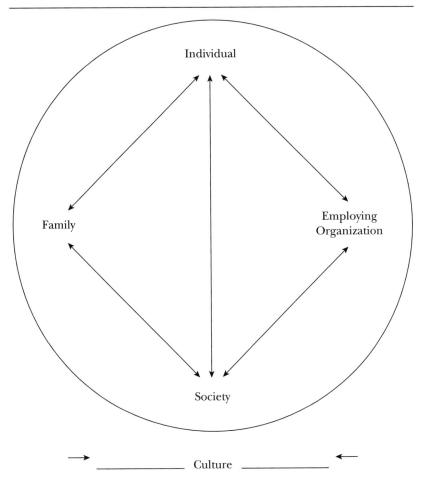

1. *Work.* Though many define work simply as activities for which a person is paid, the definition has also been extended to include nonmarket and volunteer work (Kanter, 1977). For others work is a set of prescribed activities that an individual performs while occupying a position in an organization (Kabanoff, 1980). For still others work is any physical or mental activity performed with the intention of meeting some job, work, or organizational objective of providing goods and services (Kanungo & Misra,

1984). Given some of the constraints posed in these definitions, I treat work as a set of tasks performed with an objective or goal in mind. This definition poses no restrictions on where the work is performed.

2. *Organization.* In the world of work, organization has been defined as a purposeful open, dynamic system characterized by a continuing process of input, transformation, and output (Katz & Kahn, 1978). More simply, an organization exists when two or more people get together with the purpose in mind to obtain some goal (Zedeck & Blood, 1974).

3. *Family.* This has been defined as two or more people interacting, responding to each other, or having the capacity to influence one another for the purpose of accomplishing some goal and with a sense of shared identity (Burke & Bradshaw, 1981). In some family literature a family is considered a small group, continuous in time, composed of interdependent roles and people who interact according to implicit rules of psychological and social interactions (Piotrkowski, 1978). In general, cross-cultural research on the family is sparse (Kagitçibasi & Berry, 1989).

It can be assumed, given these definitions of organization and family, that there may be little or extreme difference between the two with respect to how work is defined. Family may deal with the realm of affectivity, intimacy, and significant ascribed relations whereas the realm of the employing organization may be more competitive and characterized by the instrumental rather than the expressive (Piotrkowski, 1978). Work, however, takes place in *both* the family and the employing organization.

Thus a basic assumption in my framework is that family and employing organizations are both organizations; they are two spheres in which people exist and function. A second assumption is that work is a set of tasks or activities that can be performed in *any* type of organization. Given these two assumptions, the fundamental building block for understanding work-family balances, linkages, and universalities is the *meaning of work* for the individuals studied. The psychological impact of day-to-day work experiences is tied not to a specific task or activity but to the nature of the work process and the conditions under which the work is performed. Thus work of substantively different content can have similar meanings, and work of the same content can take on different meanings for different people (Schooler, Miller, Miller, & Richtand, 1984). Within both the employing and family organizations, work can be discussed in terms of similar dimensions, such as interpersonal relationships, altruism, division of labor, hierarchical position, and other similar concepts that we have typically confined to activities in employing organizations. In essence I am arguing that we should study the meaning of work in both family *and* employing organization spheres as processes and not structures. An individual brings his or her values, needs, interests, personality, abilities, skills, and other personal characteristics to both the employing organization and the family organization. In order to understand how and why the individual functions in either environment, it is necessary to study the meaning of work for that individual in both environments.

To study the meaning of work, I draw from two particular research programs that have studied work from a cross-cultural perspective: the Meaning of Working project (MOW, 1987) and the Work Importance Study (Super & Sverko, 1995). The MOW project assessed the meaning of working in eight countries: Belgium, Britain, Germany, Israel, Japan, Netherlands, the United States, and Yugoslavia. The purpose of the research project, in part, was to obtain information about working in different cultures and to test for general laws of behavioral science. The focus on the meaning of work is premised on the researchers' belief that it is related to the meaning of life in modern society.

The second project, the Work Importance Study (WIS) (Super & Sverko, 1995), studied the meaning of work in eleven countries: Australia, Belgium, Canada, Croatia, Israel, Italy, Japan, Poland, Portugal, South Africa, and the United States. In particular, these researchers examined work in the context of other specific life roles such as home and family, community, and leisure.

These projects are exemplars of the study of work from a cross-cultural perspective. They focus on the types of psychological individual difference variables that Watanabe, Takahashi, and Minami call for in their suggestions for future research. These two research programs serve as a point for departure for my framework.

The meaning of work is the central component in the MOW study (1987). The researchers' premise is that people not only develop work meanings as a result of their experiences with work and work conditions but that they also use work meanings in social structures, which I extrapolate to family organizations. Once people have developed work meanings, they will, in turn, influence organizations (work and family), societies, and cultures on a number of behavioral and performance variables. These influences, which are bidirectional, are the essence of the three-way interactions suggested by Watanabe, Takahashi, and Minami.

The MOW team developed a heuristic model that identified conditional variables (antecedents), central variables (meaning of work), and consequences. The major components of the meaning of work are as follows:

1. *Work centrality*, or the general belief about the value of working in one's life. This measure focused on a value orientation toward working as a life role and, in addition, involved a decision orientation about preferred life spheres for an individual's behavior. The two major properties of this component are identification with work and involvement or commitment to working.
2. *Societal norms*, a focus on obligations, personal responsibility or internalized norms of duty, and social commitment.
3. *Valued outcomes and goals* that an individual can expect.
4. *Importance* of the goals and outcomes.

The underlying notion for the definition of work stemmed from three sources: broad rationales or reasons for doing work, personal outcomes or states that result from performing or engaging in working activities, and constraints or controls related to the context in which working activities are performed (England & Harpaz, 1990).

The second exemplar, the Work Importance Study, viewed the meaning of work as a general set of beliefs about work held by an individual (Sverko & Vizek-Vidovi, 1995). In this project, the meaning of work focuses on work values or goals that an individual tries to attain through his or her work or the importance of work in a person's life. Work has an important psychological function in terms of its intrinsic meaning and how it relates to a person's self-concept, self-esteem, and self-fulfillment. The underlying notion of the WIS project was that there are great differences in the meaning of work across different societies and cultures.

Within the WIS, work values are organized sets of general beliefs, opinions, and attitudes about what is preferable, right, or simply good in life (Sverko & Vizek-Vidovi, 1995); they are the goals that people try to reach through work. Sverko and Vizek-Vidovi view values as the qualitative aspect of the meaning of work; they view work importance and work salience as the quantitative aspect of meaning of work.

The central concept of the WIS project is work values (Sverko & Vizek-Vidovi, 1995). A *value* is defined as "an objective, either a psychological state, a relationship, or a material condition, that one seeks to attain or achieve" (Ferreira-Marques & Miranda, 1995, pp. 63–64). Work values influence the importance of work in the life of the individual, but the relationship is moderated by the perceptions one has for the attainment of the goals through work. How are work values established? Sverko and Vizek-Vidovi argue that work values are primarily determined by the process of socialization, which influences the degree of their importance as well as influencing the perceptions; the latter also are influenced by a person's experience in the world of work. In short, work values relate to perceptions, expectancies, experiences, importance, and salience.

In addition to values, the WIS focused on needs and interests, two other variables that contribute to meaning of work. *Needs* were defined as wants, manifestations of physiological conditions (Super, 1995). They are the result of interaction between the individual and the environment. Super (1995) defined *interests* as the activities within which people expect to attain their values and thus satisfy their needs. Values differ not only within a culture but also across cultures. Values that were measured in the WIS include, from a set of twenty, ability utilization, advancement, authority, autonomy, creativity, prestige, responsibility, risk, and variety.

The variables studied in both the MOW and WIS projects overlap. My proposal is to adapt the MOW and WIS definitions of values and construct a research paradigm that fits the representation in Figure 12.1. The focus on work values and similar concepts reflects a focus on the individual. Though the MOW and WIS projects studied work values and other constructs from the perspective of the employing organization, I extend the study of such variables (for example, the meaning of work) to the family organization. The question for researchers, then, is to explore what beliefs and values exist with respect to a person's functioning in an employing organization *as well as* in a family organization. It is the premise of this commentary that work salience, work values, work importance, work centrality, interests, needs, goals, and other such psychological individual difference variables should be incorporated into a study of the meaning of work in both environments. Furthermore, these variables can be studied from a common base in *all* environments. That is, a questionnaire should be developed that elicits information on values, centrality, and the like, but the questions should be written in as generic a manner as possible to allow them to be used in any environment. The notion of looking at common denominators is not without example: Yogev and Brett (1985) studied the concept of *involvement* in an employing organization *and* in family. They studied the identification with the job *and* with the family and the importance of job *and* family roles to self-image and self-concept.

Once we understand the meaning of work for individuals in both environments, it will be possible to study the linkage models mentioned by Watanabe, Takahashi, and Minami, such as the spillover, compensation, segmentation, and opposition models. If a work value such as autonomy is "meaningful" for an individual in the employing organization environment, is it also meaningful for that individual in the family environment (spillover)? Or if creativity is a meaningful and fulfilled value in the employing organization, does the individual seek other values in the family environment (segmentation)? As mentioned previously, the authors of Chapter Eleven stated that different models of the work-family relationship might be true for different individuals, in different situations, and at different points in time for the same individual. My view is that different models might be true for the same individual at the same point in time; that is, an individual can be looking for spillover with respect to autonomy but segmentation with respect to creativity. This multiple focus can exist because the meaning of work is complex, composed of many different values, many of which are equally important and desired but differing in the degree to which they are fulfilled in the different environments. Furthermore, once the meaning of work dimensions are identified, it will be feasible to study the joint effects of work meaning on work and family behavior (for example, performance and withdrawal) and attitudes (for example, job, marital, and life satisfaction).

Another perspective would be to adopt the transactional model proposed by Lazarus and Folkman (1984). This model views a person and the environment in a *conjoint* relationship in which independent identities are lost in favor of a new condition, or state. The person in the family environment, with values, interests, goals, and so forth, and that same person in the employing organization, with values, interests, goals, and so forth in that environment are in a dynamic, mutually reciprocal, bidirectional relationship. What happens in one environment can be a consequence of or antecedent to what happens in the other environment. Use of *transaction* implies a newly created level of abstraction in which the two environments are joined together to form a new relational meaning. Rather than being concerned with how one environment affects another, we could be studying how the conjoined situation (that is, one's place in both the family *and* employing organization) affects other variables such as performance, decisions, or choice of behavior in the individual environments. The focus should be on the transaction or relationship as a unit of analysis (Zedeck, 1992). The basis for the transaction would be the common meaning sought and fulfilled in the environments.

The next step in the framework (see Figure 12.1) would be to study the interaction of the psychological individual difference variables with employing organization and family dimensions. On the employing organization side, these factors might include organizational structure, organizational climate, and organizational process (for example, decision-making modes, leadership styles, communication patterns), as well as more specific determinants that influence work values such as lifetime security and "glass ceiling" conditions. On the family side, configurations such as single parents, working mothers, dual-career couples, and the like will influence work values and behavior in the family; also, the degree to which the family (or family member) has support from others, the need to care for the elderly, conflicting role demands, and other such variables are relevant as we examine balancing and linkages from a family perspective.

This recommendation to focus on interactions is consistent with the future research suggestion offered by Watanabe, Takahashi, and Minami. They suggest studying heterogeneous groups to isolate common work-family linkages for homogeneous clusters. They also suggest three-mode factor analysis to study person-situation interactions. Regardless of which approach or method is used, any moderated regression strategy (Zedeck, 1971) would be valuable for exploring the interaction among psychological individual difference variables and employing organization and family organization dimensions.

The society dimension in Figure 12.1 represents, in part, the socialization process; it represents factors local to the situation, such as norms and obligations imposed by coworkers, neighbors, families, communities, and the like. Requisite behaviors, values, and beliefs that exist outside of the immediate employing or family organization influence the individual being studied. These bidirectional influences take place within the larger context of the society, the nation. Here, a number of additional factors are relevant. Governmental regulations (such as laws on gender discrimination or fair labor standards for employment conditions) and "socialized" systems for child care, welfare, and insurance coverage have reciprocal influence on values and perceptions. Likewise, movements within society, such as the feminist movement for more opportunity in the workplace, influence values and behavior in employing and family organizations.

Finally, examination of this individual × behavior × situation interaction *across* nations would provide information on the universality of the relationships identified within specific nations. The variables depicted within Figure 12.1 are possibilities for differentiating countries as well as for examining the universals. If universals exist, they most likely do so in the form of moderated relationships. Cross-cultural research is needed to identify the extent of the influence of the processes and interactions that go beyond an individual's immediate environment. This is consistent with the suggestion by Watanabe, Takahashi, and Minami to study individual × behavior × stimulus situation interactions.

Hofstede (1980)—whose research figures prominently in many chapters in this volume—has described culture along four dimensions—power distance, uncertainty avoidance, individualism-collectivism, and masculinity-femininity. These are higher-level values than the psychological individual difference variables that I am proposing, but they can be used to study, define, and differentiate societies.

Conclusion

In Chapter Eleven, Watanabe, Takahashi, and Minami discussed work-family balance, linkages, and joint effects with an emphasis on psychological individual difference variables and from a cross-cultural perspective. This commentary has attempted to expand upon their premises and has suggested that the individual × behavior × situation interaction that they propose should focus on the meaning of work as the primary psychological individual difference variable. Focus on such a variable will facilitate identification of universals and variations within and between societies and cultures.

References

Berry, J. W., Poortinga, Y. H., Segall, M. H., & Dasen, P. R. (1992). *Cross-cultural psychology: Research and applications*. New York: Cambridge University Press.

Bond, M. H., & Smith, P. B. (1996). Cross-cultural social and organizational psychology. *Annual Review of Psychology, 47*, 205–235.

Burke, R. J., & Bradshaw, P. (1981). Occupational and life stressors and the family. *Small Group Behavior, 12*, 329–375.

England, G. W., & Harpaz, I. (1990). How working is defined: National contexts and demographic and organizational role influences. *Journal of Organizational Behavior, 11*, 253–266.

Erez, M. (1994). Toward a model of cross-cultural industrial and organizational psychology. In H. C. Triandis, M. D. Dunnette, & L. M. Hough, (Eds.), *Handbook of industrial and organizational psychology* (2nd ed., Vol 4., pp. 559–607). Palo Alto: Consulting Psychologists Press.

Ferreira-Marques, J., & Miranda, M. J. (1995). Developing the work importance study. In D. E. Super & B. Sverko (Eds.), *Life roles, values, and careers: International findings of the work importance study* (pp. 62–74). San Francisco: Jossey-Bass.

Hofstede, G. (1980). *Culture's consequences: International differences in work-related values*. Thousand Oaks, CA: Sage.

Kabanoff, B. (1980). Work and nonwork: A review of models, methods, and findings. *Psychological Bulletin, 88*, 60–77.

Kagitçibasi, Ç., & Berry, J. W. (1989). Cross-cultural psychology: Current research and trends. *Annual Review of Psychology, 40*, 493–531.

Kanter, R. M. (1977). *Work and family in the United States: A critical review and agenda for research and policy.* New York: Russell Sage Foundation.

Kanungo, R. N., & Misra, S. (1984). An uneasy look at work, nonwork, and leisure. In M. D. Lee & R. N. Kanungo (Eds.), *Management of work and personal life* (pp. 143–165). New York: Praeger.

Katz, D., & Kahn, R. L. (1978). *The social psychology of organizations* (2nd ed.). New York: Wiley.

Lazarus, R. S., & Folkman, S. (1984). *Stress, appraisal, and coping.* New York: Springer.

MOW [Meaning of Working] International Research Team. (1987). *The meaning of working.* Orlando: Academic Press.

Piotrkowski, C. S. (1978). *Work and the family system: A naturalistic study of working-class and lower-middle-class families.* New York: Free Press.

Schooler, C., Miller, J., Miller, K. A., & Richtand, C. N. (1984). Work for the household: Its nature and consequences for husbands and wives. *American Journal of Sociology, 90,* 97–124.

Super, D. E. (1995). Values: Their nature, assessment, and practical use. In D. E. Super & B. Sverko (Eds.), *Life roles, values, and careers: International findings of the work importance study* (pp. 54–61). San Francisco: Jossey-Bass.

Super, D. E., & Sverko, B. (1995). *Life roles, values, and careers: International findings of the work importance study.* San Francisco: Jossey-Bass.

Sverko, B., & Vizek-Vidovi, V. (1995). Studies of the meaning of work: Approaches, models, and some of the findings. In D. E. Super & B. Sverko (Eds.), *Life roles, values, and careers: International findings of the work importance study* (pp. 3–21). San Francisco: Jossey-Bass.

Yogev, S., & Brett, J. (1985). Patterns of work and family involvement among single- and dual-earner couples. *Journal of Applied Psychology, 70,* 754–768.

Zedeck, S. (1971). Problems with the use of "moderator" variables. *Psychological Bulletin, 76,* 295–310.

Zedeck, S. (1992). Introduction: Exploring the domain of work and family concerns. In S. Zedeck (Ed.), *Work, families, and organizations* (pp. 1–32). San Francisco: Jossey-Bass.

Zedeck, S., & Blood, M. R. (1974). *Foundations of behavioral science research in organizations.* Pacific Grove, CA: Brooks/Cole.

Zedeck, S., & Mosier, K. L. (1990). Work in the family and employing organization. *American Psychologist, 45,* 240–251.

PART 3

Working Across Cultural Borders

Intercultural Communication

Social Motives and the Design of Work Teams Across Cultural Boundaries

Relationships in Context

New Developments in International/Intercultural Human Resource Management

CHAPTER 13

Do You Hear What I Hear?

A Framework for Reconciling Intercultural Communication Difficulties Arising from Cognitive Styles and Cultural Values

Cristina B. Gibson

This chapter seeks to accomplish four objectives. The first objective is to review traditional thinking on the communication process, highlighting specific features of communication that are expected to differ across cultures. The second objective is to outline specific propositions about the manner in which cognitive styles and cultural values influence these common features of communication. The third objective is to illustrate intercultural differences in communication that result from particular configurations of cognitive styles and cultural values. And finally, the fourth objective is to demonstrate a process for reconciling these intercultural differences in order to draw upon the strengths of each culture represented in a multicultural workgroup.

The Process of Communication

Communication is the process of transferring information, meaning, and understanding from sender to receiver. This process includes five phases. During the first phase, often labeled the *encoding* phase, the sender constructs the message to be sent. During the second phase, sometimes referred to as the *sending* phase, the sender transmits the message. In the third phase, referred to as the *receiving* phase, the receiver acquires the message. During the fourth phase, often labeled the *decoding* phase, the receiver interprets the message. And finally, during the fifth phase, often called the *feedback* phase, the receiver responds to the interpreted message.

It has been suggested that these five phases of the communication process are universal; that is, they exist whenever communication takes place, regardless of the specific culture or organization in which it takes place. It is also commonly accepted that similarity in culture between a sender and a receiver facilitates successful communication at each phase of the process. Stated another way, research suggests that the greater the cultural differences between sender and receiver, the greater the expected difficulty in communicating. Although researchers have gathered ample evidence that certain features of the communication process differ across cultures, the mechanisms through which the cultural influence occurs are still unclear. Previously developed frameworks have failed to propose a process by which these intercultural differences can be reconciled.

It is proposed here that intercultural differences in communication are most evident during the first two phases of the communication process, during which messages are *constructed* and *transmitted*. When such differences are prevalent, as is often the case when a workgroup is composed of members from diverse cultures or when workgroups from different cultures must communicate, we might expect a disruption in the work flow and errors in work performance. Such difficulties may indeed occur; however, it will be suggested here that the intercultural differences evident in the first two phases of the process can be reconciled during the third, fourth, and fifth phases of the process, during which receivers acquire, interpret, and respond to messages. Furthermore, it is expected that the most successful multicultural and intercultural workgroups will be those able to focus on these latter stages of the communication process and hone the skills necessary to overcome the difficulties associated with the intercultural differences apparent in the earlier phases of the process.

This point will be elaborated in the next two sections. I first address cultural differences often exhibited during the early phases of the communication process. Features expected to differ across cultures during the early phases are depicted in the first panel of Figure 13.1. As each feature is discussed, several propositions about the specific nature of cultural differences are outlined. The discussion of differences is then followed by an exploration of how potential difficulties in communication can be reconciled during the latter phases of the communication process. Several techniques for reconciliation are proposed. These techniques for the latter phases of the communication process are depicted in the second panel of Figure 13.1.

The existing research suggests that intercultural differences in communication occur due to differences in cognitive styles and cultural values (Glenn & Glenn, 1981; Gudykunst & Kim, 1984; Gudykunst, Ting-Toomey, & Chua, 1988; Dodd, 1987; Triandis & Albert, 1987). *Cognitive styles* reflect methods of information processing. Research suggests that certain characteristics of cognition, including the level of differentiation and the potency of the context, are developed through patterns of socialization that vary across cultures (Witkin & Berry, 1975; Carli, Lancia, & Paniccia, 1986; Oltman, 1986).

Cultural values are preferences for certain modes of behavior or particular end states (Rokeach, 1973). Values ascribe meaning to information and capture a major portion of cultural variation (Erez & Earley, 1993). The empirical research conducted by Hofstede (1980) suggests that cultures differ from one another on several key dimensions of values. It is proposed here that three of these, masculinity-femininity, individualism-collectivism, and power distance are related to certain features of the communication process.

Differences in cognition and values across cultures will be elaborated later. Key cognitive styles and cultural values that influence features of the communication process are outlined as each phase of the process is discussed.

Cultural Differences During Encoding

During the encoding phase, the features of the communication process expected to differ across cultures include (1) the source of information used in constructing the message, (2) the content

Figure 13.1. Features and Techniques of Effective Intercultural Communication.

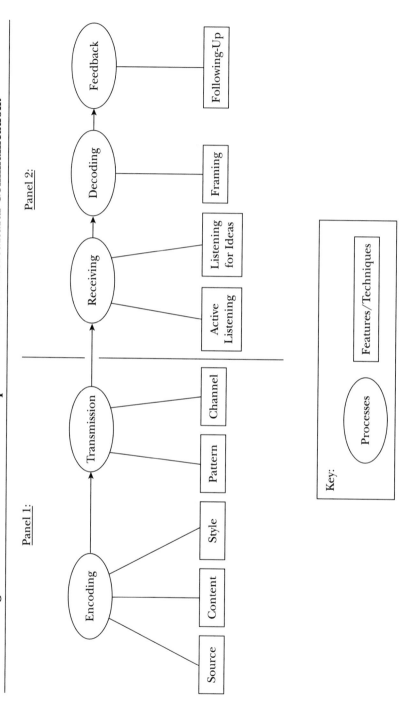

Panel 1:

Panel 2:

Key:

of the message, and (3) the style of the message. Because the aim here is to provide a comprehensive overview of the entire communication process, each feature of communication is discussed in terms of a single continuum (for example, message sources are described as ranging from internal to external; content is described as ranging from rational to emotional, and style is described as ranging from implicit to explicit). It should be noted, however, that in-depth analysis of a given feature could conceivably reveal cultural differences across multiple dimensions or independent dimensions for each end of the proposed continua (for example, message content could perhaps be described in terms of a rational dimension and an emotional dimension rather than a single continuum). With that in mind, the discussion now turns to an examination of how and why source, content, and style are expected to differ across cultures during the encoding phase of the communication process.

Message Source

The source of the information used by the communicator during message construction can range from external to internal. External sources include any person or information medium located in the external social surroundings. External cues are often gathered from feedback provided by other members of the communicator's workgroup, for example. External cues may also take the form of symbols or signs within the organizational context, such as indicators of status or reputation. These cues are often embedded within the larger context and can be detected only when the sender uses a specific cognitive style.

Alternatively, a sender may also gather information from internal sources. Internal information consists of knowledge stored in the communicator's cognitive schema. Wyer and Srull (1980) suggest that there are four general categories of schema: goal schema (for example, a profit margin), person schema (for example, "leaders"), semantic schema (for example, "high performance" versus "low performance"), and event schema (for example, performance appraisals). Other models (Markus, 1977; Taylor & Crockner, 1981; Cantor, Mischel, & Schwartz, 1982; Lord & Foti, 1985) have suggested that a fifth type of schema, the self-schema, should be added to the Wyer and Srull model. Self-schema contain information about an individual's own personality, appearance, and behavior (Markus, 1977) (for example, information such as "I am independent").

It is suggested here that the sender's use of internal or external sources is dependent upon his or her level of cognitive differentiation. Cognitive differentiation is nurtured through cultural socialization practices. A large body of evidence has demonstrated that people raised in societies that emphasize responsibility and obedience and in which there is strong pressure to conform to a societal norm of conduct tend to have an interpersonal orientation, are more attentive to social stimuli, and are emotionally open (for a review see Carli, Lancia, & Paniccia, 1986). This cognitive style is commonly referred to as *low differentiation* because individuals who possess it make only a slight distinction between the self and others. In general, when they need information, those low in differentiation tend to look to other people in the external social surroundings rather than within themselves (Oltman, 1986); thus they are expected to use external sources of information more often than internal sources when constructing messages. Research indicates that among others, members of societies located in Japan, China, Indonesia, Mexico, and India tend to be low in differentiation (Witkin & Berry, 1975; Hall & Hall, 1987; Gudykunst, Ting-Toomey, & Chua, 1988).

However, people raised in societies that emphasize independence and self-reliance and that exert fewer pressures to conform tend to function more autonomously of others in social-interpersonal situations, tend to be less attentive to social stimuli, and tend to have an impersonal orientation, particularly under conditions of ambiguity (Shulman, 1976; Sloar, Davenport, & Bruehl, 1969; Weinberg, 1970; Witkin & Goodenough, 1977; Witkin, Goodenough, & Oltman, 1979). This cognitive style is often referred to as *high differentiation* due to the relatively strong distinction made between self and others. In general, when seeking information, those high in differentiation look within themselves to internal categories of cognitive schema (Oltman, 1986); thus they are expected to use internal sources of information more often than external sources when constructing messages. Research suggests that the Swiss, Germans, Australians, and Americans tend to be high in differentiation (Witkin & Berry, 1975; Hall & Hall, 1987; Gudykunst, Ting-Toomey, & Chua, 1988).

Two propositions summarize expectations regarding intercultural differences in sources used during the encoding phase:

PROPOSITION 1a: Communicators low in differentiation will use external sources of information more often than internal sources when constructing messages.

PROPOSITION 1b: Communicators high in differentiation will use internal sources of information more often than external sources when constructing messages.

Message Content

A second important feature of the communication process during the encoding phase is the content of the message being constructed. *Content* refers to what is actually being said or communicated. It is the subject matter of the message. There are many potential ways of characterizing this content. For example, messages with "abstractive" content (describing cause-and-effect relationships, for example) can be contrasted with messages having associative content (describing similarity and frequency, for example) (Glenn & Glenn, 1981). Message content can also be examined in terms of temporal focus. Some messages focus on the past, others on the present, and still others on the future (Kluckhohn & Strodtbeck, 1961).

Research suggests, however, that one of the most important characteristics of content is the degree to which messages contain highly emotional material based on intuition and personal perspective versus rational material based on facts (Glenn, Witmeyer, & Stevenson, 1977). It is proposed here that the degree to which messages will have emotional content versus rational content will be dependent on the degree to which a culture emphasizes values associated with femininity versus masculinity. These are terms used in Hofstede's research (1980) to characterize one value dimension of culture. However, several social psychologists have subsequently suggested replacing the terms femininity and masculinity with, respectively, the relatively gender-neutral terms *communal values* and *agentic values* (Eagly, 1987),[1] and those are the terms I will use here.

The communal value orientation is characterized by nurturance, affection, achievement through the devotion of self to others, sympathy, awareness of the feelings of others, emotional expressiveness, and a concern for the welfare of other people (Werner & LaRuss, 1985; Deaux & Lewis, 1983; Ruble, 1983; Spence & Helmreich, 1978; Bem, 1974; Broverman, Vogel, Broverman, Clarkson, & Rosenkrantz, 1972). Members of societies in Indonesia, China, Israel, Taiwan, Thailand, and Chile tend to be characterized by communal values (Hofstede, 1980). It is expected that communicators from these cultures will tend to construct messages that have more emotional than rational content in interpersonal communication.

At the opposite end of the continuum, an agentic value orientation is characterized by an emphasis on aggressiveness, ambition, dominance, independence, achievement through self-reliance and self-sufficiency, directness, and decisiveness (Werner & LaRuss, 1985; Spence & Helmreich, 1978; Bem, 1974). Members of societies in Switzerland, Great Britain, Germany, and the United States tend to be characterized by agentic values (Hofstede, 1980). Based on prior research (Glenn, Witmeyer, & Stevenson, 1977), it is expected that members of cultures that emphasize agentic values will tend to construct messages with more rational than emotional content in interpersonal communication.

Expectations for intercultural differences in communication content during the encoding phase are summarized in the two following propositions:

PROPOSITION 2a: Communicators who emphasize communal values will construct messages with more emotional content than rational content.

PROPOSITION 2b: Communicators who emphasize agentic values will construct messages with more rational content than emotional content.

Message Style

A third important feature of communication during the encoding phase is the style of the language used in constructing the message. Research conducted by Rosch and Segler (1987) contrasts implicit language with explicit language. Implicit language carefully imbues messages with a positive tone in order to decrease the chances of unpleasant encounters, direct confrontations, and disagreements. Conversely, explicit language communicates exactly what is meant in a much more direct manner, even if the resulting message is negative or somewhat harsh.

It is proposed here that whether a sender will use an implicit or explicit style will be dependent upon the extent to which the sender's culture emphasizes a collectivistic versus individualistic value orientation. Collectivism is characterized by subordination of individual goals to group goals and a strong need to preserve group harmony (Triandis, 1989). Members of societies in Indonesia, China, Japan, Thailand, Chile, Brazil, and Pakistan tend to emphasize collectivistic values (Hofstede, 1980). It is expected that communicators from these cultures will tend to adopt an implicit style of communication.[2] Research suggests, for instance, that Chinese, Japanese, Koreans, and Indonesians make frequent use of qualifiers and ambiguous words such as "maybe," "perhaps," and "somewhat" in order to avoid confrontation (Adler, Brahm, & Graham, 1992; Okabe, 1983; Ueda, 1974; Van Zandt, 1970; Nakane, 1970). Similarly, members of these cultures tend to avoid negative responses when communicating with members of their own workgroup, in order to preserve a sense of group harmony (Sutiyono, 1994; Bayerl, 1994; Adler, Brahm, & Graham, 1992; Park, 1979).

In contrast, individualism implies a social framework in which people are supposed to subordinate group goals to individual goals and take care of themselves (Triandis, 1989). Members of societies in the United States, Canada, Great Britain, Australia, and Germany tend to emphasize individualistic values (Hofstede, 1980). In such cultures there is relatively little concern for preserving group harmony and a much more direct style of interpersonal interaction. It is expected that communicators from these cultures will tend to use explicit communication more often than implicit communication. Indeed, research suggests that Canadian and American communicators tend to use words such as "absolutely," "certainly," and "positively" more often than do the Japanese in constructing messages (Adler, Brahm, & Graham, 1992; Okabe, 1983).

The following two propositions summarize the expectations for communication style during the encoding phase:

Proposition 3a: Communicators with collectivistic values will use an implicit style of communication more often than an explicit style.

Proposition 3b: Communicators with individualistic values will use an explicit style of communication more often than an implicit style.

Cultural Differences During Transmission

During the second phase of communication, cultural differences are expected to be evident in two important features of communication: the patterns of messages and the channels through which the messages are sent.

Communication Patterns

In transmitting messages, communicators repeatedly use identifiable patterns of communication. Put another way, communication patterns are systems of interconnections that involve a series of linkages between particular senders and receivers. These patterns are also sometimes referred to as networks. A growing body of research has investigated numerous characteristics of communication patterns. One characteristic that appears to be of critical importance in examining intercultural communication is the number of patterns used and their corresponding specificity. When a communicator uses a large variety of patterns for transmission, the patterns tend to be very context specific and concrete. Each message tends to be associated with a specific real-life context from which the sender derives meaning (Cousins, 1989). Conversely, when communicators use only a small number of patterns, the patterns tend to be generalized and abstract. Communicators using these abstract patterns mentally isolate objects from their attributes and generalize across contexts on the basis of conceptual similarities.

It is proposed here that the extent to which a communicator uses either numerous concrete patterns or a few generalized and abstract patterns will correspond to the potency of the cognitive context. Attention to cognitive context is encouraged or discouraged through socialization practices. A *high-context* cognitive style is characterized by a perceptual tendency to focus on the context in which any event, object, or experience is embedded. Societies that encourage social conformity and sociocultural stratification also tend to nurture a high-context cognitive style (Hall & Hall, 1987; Witkin & Berry, 1975). This tendency is often exhibited by Indonesians, Japanese, Chinese, and Arabs (Hall, 1976; Gudykunst, Ting-Toomey, & Chua, 1988). It is expected that communicators from these cultures will use numerous patterns of communication in which the message is concrete and context specific. In other words, when the communicator uses a high-context cognitive style, he or she will select specific communication patterns that vary depending on his or her experience with the subject being communicated (Glenn & Glenn, 1981; Gudykunst & Kim, 1984; Ting-Toomey, 1985). Because the context continually changes, communicators in high-context cultures continually change patterns of communication, based on their experiences in each specific context. Japan, for example, is a high-context culture that has three distinct levels of language that a communicator must use depending on his or her status compared to that of the receiver. Thus there are five different words for "you" in Japanese, used in accord with relative rank and status.

At the opposite end of the continuum, a *low-context* cognitive style is characterized by the tendency to organize a perceptual field into discrete parts and to then abstract those parts from context so as to generalize across settings. Societies that encourage self-reliance and self-control in children (Hall & Hall, 1987; Witkin & Berry, 1975) also tend to nurture a low-context cognitive style. This tendency is often exhibited by the Swiss, Germans, Americans, and British (Hall, 1976; Gudykunst, Ting-Toomey, & Chua, 1988). It is expected that communicators from these cultures will tend to use a small number of general abstract patterns to convey their messages. In other words, in low-context cultures, the way something is stated will vary little in relation to situational nuances. In fact, research suggests that members of low-context cultures often interpret a person's dramatically different uses of language as a negative personal characteristic. They often use such labels as "two-faced," "insincere," or "hypocritical" to describe someone who changes the way in which he or she communicates depending on the situation.

The following propositions summarize expectations for patterns of communication during the transmitting phase:

PROPOSITION 4a: Communicators who exhibit a high-context cognitive style will use a larger number of communication patterns, and these patterns will be more specific and concrete than those used by low-context communicators.

PROPOSITION 4b: Communicators who exhibit a low-context cognitive style will use a smaller number of communication patterns, and these patterns will be more general and abstract than those used by communicators who exhibit a high-context cognitive style.

Communication Channels

A final important feature of communication during the transmission phase of the communication process is the channel through which messages are communicated. The channel of communication is the route that a message usually follows when being transmitted. There are two fundamental types of channels: formal and informal. Formal communication channels are authorized, planned, and regulated by the organization and are directly connected to its official structure. Formal communication channels create expectations among group members about who is responsible for making sure that they receive appropriate messages relating to their work from the levels above and below them and from adjacent units. Conversely, informal communication channels are routes that are not prespecified but that develop through the typical and customary interpersonal activities of people at work. Informal channels can come into existence and then rapidly change or disappear depending on the circumstances. They tend to operate laterally (among members with relatively equal status) rather than vertically precisely because they consist of routes not designated by the organization and its top officials.

It is proposed here that choice of either formal or informal channels of communication depends upon the level of power distance existing within the communicator's culture. Power distance is a cultural value that reflects the extent to which a society accepts an unequal distribution of power in organizations; power distance may also explain differences in the perception of legitimate authority (Hofstede, 1980). Members of cultures such as those found in Indonesia, China, Japan, South America, India, and Pakistan tend to exhibit high power distance (Hofstede, 1980). Research suggests that communicators in these high power distance cultures will be more likely to use the formal channels of communication rather than the informal channels of communication (Negandhi & Prasad, 1971; Graves, 1972).

It should be noted, however, that though the majority of decisions and most information will be passed on through the formal hierarchy in high power distance cultures, this is not to say that informal channels will never be used. Most Japanese organizations, for example, have a complex formal communication system, but it is complemented by horizontal communication among peers. Japanese leaders encourage employees who work together to meet socially after work because these informal meetings contribute to a smooth flow of information, shared meaning, and mutual support in decision making at work (Erez, 1992).

In contrast to members of high power distance cultures, members of societies in the United States, Canada, Great Britain, Germany, and Australia tend to view unequal power distributions as unacceptable (Hofstede, 1980). Communicators in these low power distance cultures are expected to depend more often on informal channels of communication than on formal channels of communication. In Australia, for example, informal channels carry the most critical and valued information, and formal channels are less well developed (Limmerick, 1990).

The following propositions summarize this notion:

PROPOSITION 5a: Communicators from high power distance cultures will use formal channels of communication more often than informal channels.

PROPOSITION 5b: Communicators from low power distance cultures will use informal channels of communication more often than formal channels.

Clusters of Communication Features

Empirical research suggests that certain combinations of cultural characteristics are more likely to occur than others (Hofstede, 1980), and at least two distinct clusters of cultural characteristics can be identified (see Table 13.1). For example, cultures low in cognitive differentiation and high in cognitive context also tend to emphasize communal and collectivistic values and exhibit high power distance (Cluster A). The research reviewed previously suggests that communicators from Indonesia, Japan, China, Thailand, Brazil, Chile, Israel, and Pakistan tend to demonstrate Cluster A cultural characteristics.

On the other hand, cultures high in cognitive differentiation and low in cognitive context often exhibit agentic and individualistic values and low power distance (Cluster B). Research suggests that communicators from the United States, Canada, Australia, Great Britain, Germany, and Switzerland tend to demonstrate Cluster B cultural characteristics.

Table 13.1. Cultural Clusters and Corresponding
Features of Communication.

| | Cultural Cluster | |
| | A | B |
Feature of Communication	Low Cognitive Differentiation Communal Values Collectivistic Values High Cognitive Content High Power Distance	High Cognitive Differentiation Agentic Values Individualistic Values Low Cognitive Content Low Power Distance
I. Source	External	Internal
II. Content	Emotional	Rational
III. Style	Implicit	Explicit
IV. Pattern	Specific	Generalized
V. Channel	Formal	Informal

Note that certain combinations of communication features are also more likely to occur than others (Erez & Earley, 1993). Communicators who exhibit Cluster A cultural characteristics tend to draw upon external social information sources, tend to construct messages with emotional content, and tend to use an implicit style. They are also more likely to use numerous context-specific patterns of communication and formal communication channels. Communicators who exhibit Cluster B cultural characteristics tend to rely on sources of information internal to the self, tend to construct messages with rational content, and tend to use an explicit style. They are also likely to favor only a few generalized patterns of communication and tend to use informal communication channels.

Intercultural Communication: An Extended Example

An extended example will illustrate Cluster A and B communication. The example is based on an encounter I observed while conducting research in matched Indonesian and U.S. organizations. Communicators from Indonesia tend to emphasize cultural characteristics and communication features associated with Cluster A. They tend to be low in cognitive differentiation and high in cognitive context. Indonesians also emphasize communal and collectivistic values and are high in power distance.

Although variation occurs within U.S. subcultures, communicators from the United States tend to emphasize cultural characteristics and communication features associated with Cluster B. They tend to be higher in cognitive differentiation and lower in cognitive context than Indonesians. Americans also tend to place greater emphasis on agentic and individualistic values and tend to be lower in power distance than Indonesians.

In both the Indonesian and American organization, the communication sequence in question concerned the topic of uniforms. The team leader in a small team of employees in each organization needed to communicate a request for work uniforms to the organization's administrative staff. In both organizations the key members of administration included an administrative assistant who would be responsible for processing the request, an administrative director who would need to approve the request, and a supply clerk who would be responsible for actually obtaining the uniforms. Although the topic and the participants were similar, two very different communication sequences took place. The encoding and transmitting of the message differed dramatically in the two organizations, based on intercultural differences in cognitive styles and cultural values.

In the Indonesian organization, Sri serves as team leader for a workgroup consisting of three employees whom I shall call Ida, Murli, and Agus.[3] Murli has approached Sri several times with complaints about the fact that nearly every other department in the organization has been given uniforms. After checking with team leaders in several other departments, Sri confirmed that this was indeed true. Over the previous month, six out of the eight departments in the organization had been assigned uniforms for daily use. Based on this observation, Sri included uniforms on the agenda for the next team meeting. At this meeting, Sri noticed that Ida, Murli, and Agus seemed less enthusiastic and dedicated than was normally the case; however, all the team members seemed to agree that uniforms would make them feel much more a part of the organization. Following this meeting, Sri concluded that uniforms would contribute to the general morale of her team.

Because uniforms are a type of supply, Sri followed the specific organizational procedure for requesting supplies. She first notified her team members that she would be making the request. She then obtained and completed a written request form and submitted it to Arli, the organization's administrative assistant. Next she scheduled a meeting with the administrative director in order to plead her case. During this meeting Sri made a statement along these lines: "Mr. Widya, I have been your loyal employee for twenty-five years now. The members of my team have also been with this organization for many years. Our team is an important part of this organization, but in order to feel as though we are truly a part of the collective efforts we must also share in the privilege of wearing the corporate uniform. In representing the best interests of my team members, I would like to suggest that my team can best serve the organization if we are granted our request for uniforms."

In accordance with Cluster A communication features, Sri used external social sources of information (for example, her team members) in constructing her message. The message contained emotional content, including phrases such as "loyal employee" and "to feel a part of collective efforts." Furthermore, Sri used an implicit style; the request was framed in a positive light so as to decrease the chances of an unpleasant confrontation with the administrative director. And finally, Sri used the special pattern of communication designated for requesting supplies. This pattern included formal channels of communication that adhered to the organization's chain of command.

In the American organization, Deborah serves as the team leader for a team consisting of Susan, Beverly, and John. In making her rounds, Deborah noticed that her team appeared to be the only one in the organization without uniforms. Because her team is one of the organization's highest-performing teams and in fact performs some of the most physically demanding work, it did not seem logical or fair for her team to lack uniforms. In addition, Deborah had noticed that clients often had difficulty identifying who was actually an employee. This sometimes resulted in confusion when a client needed urgent assistance. All things considered, Deborah deduced that the need for uniforms in her department was justified.

Although the formal procedure suggested that Deborah should request supplies by filling out and submitting certain forms to Nancy, the administrative assistant, Deborah used the same tried-and-true method she used whenever she had a complaint: she went straight to the administrative director's office and talked with him directly. During this conversation, Deborah made a statement along these lines: "Jack, this organization seeks to encourage fair and equal treatment among all departments. Furthermore, our guiding principles of operation suggest that customer service is our number one concern. In order to meet these objectives, our team must have uniforms."

In accordance with the communication features in Cluster B, Deborah relied mainly on sources of information internal to herself (for example, her private observations and powers of deduction) in constructing her message. The content of her message was rational and factual rather than emotional. Furthermore, the style of her message was explicit. She stated directly what she wanted without trying to "soften the blow." Deborah also used the generalized pattern of communication that she routinely applied regardless of specific context. For example, she appealed to the abstract principles stated in the corporate mission statement rather than describing the specific needs that had arisen in her team's situation. Finally, in bypassing the administrative assistant and speaking directly to the administrative director, Deborah used informal channels of communication as opposed to the formal chain of command.

The point here is not that one cluster of communication features and cultural characteristics is more effective than the other. As many intercultural researchers have been quick to point out, neither end of any cultural continuum is necessarily "better" (Witkin & Berry, 1975; Hofstede, 1980; Erez & Earley, 1993). Each has its own strengths. Indeed, in each of these scenarios, the request for uniforms was quickly granted. This suggests that within each culture, communication features that have survived the test of time will be those most effective for that culture.

Difficulties may arise, however, when we bring together employees with different cultural backgrounds. When the cultures share the same cluster (as Australia and the United States do, for example), fewer communication problems are likely to occur than when the cultures come from different clusters. However, when employees' cultures are quite distinct (as is the case with Indonesia and the United States, for example), are there certain steps that can be taken to reduce miscommunication?

Reconciliation of Cultural Differences in Communication: Acquiring, Interpreting, and Responding to Messages

Several researchers have suggested that the sharing of cultural beliefs is not always essential to successful communication (Donnellon, Gray, & Bougon, 1986; Erez & Earley, 1993). In accordance with the theory of "equifinality" proposed by Weick (1979), communication sequences with different content can still have similar behavioral implications. These researchers suggest that what must be shared are expectations about what will be exchanged and a *code* for the production of action. This shared code describes a repertoire of behavioral options that members of a group recognize, respond to, and use to interact with one another regardless of their cultural backgrounds and the meanings they ascribe to the message being communicated (Donnellon, Gray, & Bougon, 1986).

Donnellon, Gray, and Bougon provide empirical support for their argument by using a case study in which group leaders in a production department learned of an impending layoff. In reaction, the group leaders discussed the possibility of going on strike. Two rationales for going on strike were communicated: "striking is getting revenge" and "striking is principled behavior." The strike was actively opposed by several group members who disagreed with the first rationale. However, when the second rationale was introduced into the discussion, they unanimously agreed to go on strike. Action therefore did not result from a shared meaning among group members but rather from a shared knowledge that the exchange process would continue. The use of multiple arguments was found to be effective for creating equifinal meaning leading to joint action. Donnellon, Gray, and Bougon concluded that it is possible for group members to "agree to disagree" within a continual flow of organized action. It is only when group members say flat out, "we disagree," that the continual flow of communication and organized action comes to a halt.

In summary, the point here is that elements of organized action can be formed, even in the absence of shared meaning, as long as group members agree to continue the communication process and as long as they share similar codes for decoding information. In other words, reconciliation of key cultural differences can most readily occur after the message has been sent, during the receiving, decoding, and feedback phases of the communication process.

As each of these phases is elaborated upon below, processes expected to occur at each phase within a multicultural workgroup are discussed. For illustrative purposes, this hypothetical workgroup will consist of some of the employees described in the example of Cluster A and Cluster B communication: Jack, the American administrative director; Arli, the Indonesian administrative assistant; Sri, the Indonesian team leader; Deborah, an American team member; and Agus, an Indonesian team member. For each of the last three phases of the communication process, I review potential tactics for reconciling the intercultural communication difficulties in this multicultural workgroup.

Receiving

During the third phase of the communication process, the receiver acquires the message being sent. Whether the message is sent in an oral, written, or visual format, the receiver must listen to it carefully. Effective listening is one technique through which intercultural differences can be reconciled. Indeed, in one study of patterns of success and failure in cross-cultural adjustment, listening skills were found to be closely related to interactional effectiveness (Nishida, 1985). Research suggests at least two effective listening techniques that apply regardless of the cultural backgrounds of the sender and receiver: *active listening* and *listening for ideas* (Okum, 1975; Ruben, 1976; Hawes & Kealey, 1979, 1981; Rowe & Baker, 1984; Spitzberg & Cupach, 1984; Morgan & Baker, 1985).

The first key to reconciling differences during the receiving phase is that the receiver should be an active listener (Morgan & Baker, 1985). This skill has also been referred to as interaction management, degree of involvement in the conversation, and expressiveness (Ruben, 1976; Spitzberg & Cupach, 1984). Basically, active listeners request elaboration or clarification whenever the message being sent is not clear. Active listening is important because it can avert potential misunderstandings arising from the differences between low and high cognitive differentiation. Recall that those low in cognitive differentiation tend to prefer external sources of information when constructing messages, and those high in cognitive differentiation tend to prefer internal sources. Here is an example of reconciling this intercultural difference with the active listening technique. Suppose that Sri (a receiver from a low-differentiation culture with a natural tendency to use external sources of information) receives a message from Deborah (a communicator from a high-differentiation culture with a natural tendency to use internal sources of information). Sri may initially be uncomfortable with the lack of external social referents in Deborah's message. Ordinarily, Sri might then discount the message. However, if she is aware of the cultural differences and practices active listening, she can request additional clarification by asking Deborah to verify her internally deduced information with external sources of information. Sri might ask Deborah, for instance, whether other team members have similar information, opinions, or experiences. Such additional clarification is expected to help Sri overcome her initial frustration.

The second key to reconciling differences during the receiving phase is that the receiver should listen for ideas (Hawes & Kealey, 1979, 1981; Morgan & Baker, 1985). Listening for ideas can help people overcome difficulties attributable to differences between collectivistic and individualistic cultural value orientations. Recall that collectivistic communicators tend to use an implicit style of communication, and individualistic communicators tend to use an explicit style. For example, imagine that Jack (an individualistic receiver accustomed to explicit communication) is sent an implicit message from Sri (a collectivistic communicator). He may at first have difficulty finding the gist of the message. However, if he is aware of the intercultural differences, he can listen carefully and extract the ideas Sri has framed within her implicit message.

Expectations for reconciling intercultural differences during the receiving phase of the communication process are summarized in this proposition:

PROPOSITION 6: Receivers' frequent use of *active listening* and *listening for ideas* techniques will be associated with fewer intercultural communication difficulties in multicultural workgroups.

Decoding

During the fourth phase of the communication process, the message sent by the communicator is decoded. Decoding is the process by which a receiver interprets a message to derive meaning from it. Research suggests that a receiver interpreting a message can avoid intercultural miscommunication by using the *framing* technique. Framing has also been referred to as the ability to empathize with the communicator (Allen & Brown, 1976; Ruben, 1976; Larson, Backlund, Redmond, & Barbour, 1978; Wieman & Backlund, 1980; Gudykunst & Kim, 1984; Dodd, 1987; Hammer, 1989). Basically, framing involves taking the other person's frame of reference (Flavel, Botkin, Fry, Wright, & Jarvis, 1968; Hale & Delia, 1976; Hammer, 1989).

Framing can help reconcile intercultural communication difficulties attributable to the differences between communal and agentic values. As discussed earlier, it is expected that these values will be associated with differing degrees of emphasis on emotional and rational content. In our multicultural workgroup, for example, it is quite probable that Sri will construct messages with emotional content (due to the Indonesian tendency to emphasize communal values). Because Jack's natural tendency is to construct messages with rational content (attributable to the American emphasis on agentic values), Jack may initially feel uncomfortable when receiving Sri's messages. However, by using the framing technique, that is, empathizing with Sri and attempting to adopt her communal frame of reference, Jack may benefit from the communication sequence. After several such encounters, he will have expanded his level of adaptability to cultural context, a skill repeatedly shown to be important in intercultural interaction (Kim, 1991).

The following proposition summarizes the expectations for reconciling intercultural differences during the decoding phase of the communication process:

PROPOSITION 7: Receivers' frequent use of the *framing* technique will be associated with fewer intercultural communication difficulties in multicultural workgroups.

Feedback

During the final phase of the communication process, the receiver responds to the sender's message. Recent research has begun to investigate differences in responses to performance feedback across cultures (Earley, Gibson, & Chen, 1995); however, very few studies have evaluated cultural differences in responses to interpersonal communication. What little research has been conducted indicates that a technique often referred to as *following-up* is associated with intercultural communication competence (Hawes & Kealey, 1979, 1981). Following-up involves accurately repeating the communicator's message. Doing so quickly and without obvious nervous discomfort appears to be especially effective (Dodd, 1987; Gudykunst & Kim, 1984; Nishida, 1985; Hammer, 1989).

In the feedback phase, following-up may reconcile intercultural differences attributable to cognitive context and power distance. As discussed earlier, such differences are associated with communication pattern and channel preferences. For example, in our multicultural workgroup, Deborah may prefer using a general pattern of abstract communication, regardless of the specific topic, and may often bypass the formal chain of command, tendencies probably attributable to the low cognitive context and low power distance characteristic of American culture. Such patterns and channels of communication may result in a great deal of psychological stress and discomfort when Deborah communicates with Sri, who is more likely to use concrete, context-specific patterns of communication and to follow the formal chain of command. Sri may be able to clear up any miscommunications, however, by following up on all communications from Deborah. Using this technique, Sri might repeat the message received, paraphrasing it in language that is slightly more specific and concrete. Furthermore, Sri and Deborah may have to go through the statement-paraphrase cycle more than once before the message is entirely clear. If Deborah and Sri both become fluent in the use of formal *and* informal channels, then the stress associated with using unfamiliar channels of communication should eventually subside and both communicators will enhance their communication skills.

A final proposition summarizes the expectations for reconciling intercultural differences during the feedback phase:

PROPOSITION 8: Receivers' frequent use of the *following-up* technique will be associated with fewer intercultural communication difficulties in multicultural workgroups.

Conclusion

This chapter outlined the five phases of the communication process. It presented propositions that summed up the intercultural differences evident in the first two stages (encoding and transmitting) and reconciled them with propositions summing up techniques for addressing these differences in the last three stages of the process (receiving, decoding, and feedback).

The first and perhaps most important step in reconciling intercultural communication differences is developing an awareness of the communication features that differ across cultures and an understanding of the cultural characteristics that drive these differences. Beyond this initial step, people must then work to develop their skills as effective listeners, interpreters, and responders to intercultural messages. Researchers such as Kim (1991) suggest that intercultural communication competence should not necessarily be considered competence in dealing with a specific culture but rather as the holistic cognitive, affective, and operational ability of an individual's internal system across all intercultural communication contexts. This would suggest that as people fully develop their skills as effective communicators within their own cultures, these skills can carry over into their intercultural interactions. Perhaps then they can truly hear the messages being communicated by their multicultural coworkers.

Notes

1. These new terms capture the essence of value differences across cultures and at the same time allow for the fact that any given male or female may exhibit a tendency toward either end of the value continuum.

2. Israeli communicators may exhibit a notable exception to this tendency. The Israeli culture is often described as collectivistic (Hofstede, 1980), but Israeli members of collective groups such as the kibbutzim are known for their frank speech. This explicit style is based on the Israeli belief that frankness is conducive to group longevity (Erez & Earley, 1993).

3. Names of the participants in the communication sequences have been changed to protect confidentiality. The conversations reported here are based on actual observations but have been altered slightly to illustrate the key points. Syntax and word choice are not extracted from recorded interview transcripts.

References

Adler, N. J., Brahm, R., & Graham, J. L. (1992). Strategy implementation: A comparison of face-to-face negotiations in the People's Republic of China and the United States. *Strategic Management Journal, 13,* 449–466.

Allen, R. R., & Brown, K. L. (1976). *Developing communication competence.* Lincolnwood, IL: National Textbook Company.

Bayerl, A. (1994, July). *Human resource management in Indonesian companies: The high significance of personal relationships: A blessing in disguise.* Paper presented at the 4th annual International Human Resource Management Conference, Gold Coast, Australia.

Bem, S. L. (1974). The measurement of psychological androgyny. *Journal of Consulting and Clinical Psychology, 42,* 155–162.

Broverman, I. K., Vogel, S. R., Broverman, S. M., Clarkson, F. E., & Rosenkrantz, P. S. (1972). Sex stereotypes: A current appraisal. *Journal of Social Issues, 28,* 59–78.

Cantor, N., Mischel, W., & Schwartz, J. (1982). Social knowledge: Structure, content, use, and abuse. In A. Hastrof & A. Isen (Eds.), *Cognitive social psychology.* Hillsdale, NJ: Erlbaum.

Carli, R., Lancia, F., & Paniccia, R. (1986). Implications of field dependence for social psychology. In M. Bertini, L. Pizzamiglio, & S. Wapner (Eds.), *Field dependence in psychological theory, research and application* (pp. 63–91). Hillsdale, NJ: Erlbaum.

Cousins, S. D. (1989). Culture and self-perception in Japan and the United States. *Journal of Personality and Social Psychology, 56,* 124–131.

Deaux, K., & Lewis, L. L. (1983). Components of gender stereotypes (Ms. No. 2583) [Special issue]. *Psychological Documents, 13*(25).

Dodd, C. H. (1987). *Dynamics of intercultural communication.* Dubuque, IA: William C. Brown.

Donnellon, A., Gray, B., & Bougon, M. G. (1986). Communication, meaning, and organized action. *Administrative Science Quarterly, 31,* 43–45.

Eagly, A. H. (1987). *Sex differences in social behavior: A social-role interpretation.* Hillsdale, NJ: Erlbaum.

Earley, P. C., Gibson, C. B., & Chen, C. C. (1995). *How did I do versus how did we do? Intercultural contrasts of performance feedback search and self-efficacy in China, Czechoslovakia, and the United States* (Working paper). Irvine: University of California.

Erez, M. (1992). Interpersonal communication systems in organizations and their relationships to cultural values, productivity, and innovation: The case of Japanese corporations. *Applied psychology: An international review, 41,* 43–64.

Erez, M., & Earley, P. C. (1993). *Culture, self-identity, and work.* New York: Oxford University Press.

Flavel, J. H., Botkin, P. T., Fry, C. L., Wright, J. W., & Jarvis, P. E. (1968). *The development of role taking and communication skills in children.* New York: Wiley.

Glenn, E. S., & Glenn, C. G. (1981). *Man and mankind: Conflicts and communications between cultures.* Norwood, NJ: Ablex.

Glenn, E. S., Witmeyer, D., & Stevenson, K. (1977). Cultural styles of persuasion. *International Journal of Intercultural Relations, 1,* 52–66.

Graves, D. (1972). Cultural determinism and management behavior. *Organizational Dynamics, 1,* 46–59.

Gudykunst, W. B., & Kim, Y. Y. (1984). *Communicating with strangers: An approach to intercultural communication.* New York: Random House.

Gudykunst, W. B., Ting-Toomey, S., & Chua, E. (1988). *Culture and interpersonal communication.* Thousand Oaks, CA: Sage.

Hall, E. T. (1976). *Beyond culture.* New York: Doubleday.

Hall, E. T., & Hall, M. R. (1987). *Hidden differences: Doing business with the Japanese.* New York: Doubleday.

Hale, C. L., & Delia, J. C. (1976). Cognitive complexity and social perspective-taking. *Communication Monographs, 47,* 304–311.

Hammer, M. R. (1989). Intercultural communication competence. In M. K. Asante & W. B. Gudykunst (Eds.), *Handbook of international and intercultural communication* (pp. 247–260). Thousand Oaks, CA: Sage.

Hawes, F., & Kealey, D. J. (1979). *Canadians in development: An empirical study of adaptation and effectiveness on overseas assignments.* Ottawa: Canadian International Development Agency, Communication Branch Briefing Center.

Hawes, F., & Kealey, D. J. (1981). An empirical study of Canadian technical assistance: Adaptation and effectiveness on an overseas assignment. *International Journal of Intercultural Relations, 5,* 239–258.

Hofstede, G. (1980). *Culture's consequences: International differences in work-related values.* Thousand Oaks, CA: Sage.

Kim, Y. Y. (1991). Intercultural communication competence: A systems-theoretic view. In S. Ting-Toomey & F. Korzenny (Eds.), *International and intercultural communication annual* (Vol. 15, pp. 259–275). Thousand Oaks, CA: Sage.

Kluckhohn, F. R., & Strodtbeck, F. L. (1961). *Variations in value orientations.* New York: HarperCollins.

Larson, C., Backlund, P., Redmond, M., & Barbour, A. (1978). *Assessing functional communication.* Falls Church, VA: Speech Communication Association.

Limmerick, D. C. (1990). Managers of meaning: From Bob Geldof's Band Aid to Australian CEOs. *Organization Dynamics, 18*(4), 22–33.

Lord, R. G., & Foti, R. J. (1985). Schema theories, information processing, and organizational behavior. In H. P. Sims, D. A. Gioia, & Associates, *The thinking organization: Dynamics of organizational social cognition* (pp. 21–48). San Francisco: Jossey-Bass.

Markus, H. R. (1977). Self-schemata and processing information about the self. *Journal of Personality and Social Psychology, 35,* 63–78.

Morgan, P., & Baker, H. K. (1985). Building a professional image: Improving listening behavior. *Supervisory Management, 30*(11), 34–38.

Nakane, C. (1970). *Japanese society.* Berkeley: University of California Press.

Negandhi, A. R., & Prasad S. B. (1971). *Comparative management.* Englewood Cliffs, NJ: Appleton-Century-Crofts.

Nishida, H. (1985). Japanese intercultural communication competence and cross-cultural adjustment. *International Journal of Intercultural Relations, 9*(3), 247–269.

Okabe, R. (1983). Cultural assumptions of East and West: Japan and the United States. In W. B. Gudykunst (Ed.), *Intercultural communication theory* (pp. 123–145). Thousand Oaks, CA: Sage.

Okum, S. K. (1975, August). How to be a better listener. *Nation's Business,* pp. 62–63.

Oltman, P. K. (1986). Psychological differentiation theory in social and cross-cultural psychology. In M. Bertini, L. Pizzamiglio, & S. Wapner (Eds.), *Field dependence in psychological theory, applications and research* (pp. 85–91). Hillsdale, NJ: Erlbaum.

Park, M. (1979). *Communication styles in two different cultures: Korean and American.* Seoul: Han Shin.

Rokeach, M. (1973). *The nature of human values.* New York: Free Press.

Rosch, M., & Segler, K. G. (1987). Communication with the Japanese. *Management International Review, 27*(4), 56–67.

Rowe, M. P., & Baker, M. (1984). Are you hearing enough employee concerns? *Harvard Business Review, 62,* 127–135.

Ruben, B. (1976). Assessing communication competency for intercultural adaptation. *Group and Organization Studies, 1,* 334–354.

Ruble, T. L. (1983). Sex stereotypes: Issues of change in the 1970s. *Sex Roles, 9,* 397–402.

Shulman, E. (1976). Conformity in a modified Asch-type situation (Doctoral dissertation, City University of New York, 1976). *Dissertation Abstracts International, 36,* 6455B.

Sloar, D., Davenport, G., & Bruehl, D. (1969). Social compliance as a function of field dependence. *Perceptual and Motor Skills, 29,* 299–306.

Spence, J. T., & Helmreich, R. L. (1978). *Masculinity & femininity: Their psychological dimensions, correlates, & antecedents.* Austin: University of Texas Press.

Spitzberg, B. H., & Cupach, W. R. (1984). *Interpersonal communication competence.* Thousand Oaks, CA: Sage.

Sutiyono, W. (1994, July). *Practices and trends of human resource management in Indonesia.* Paper presented at the 4th International Human Resource Management Conference, Gold Coast, Australia, 1994.

Taylor, S. E., & Crockner, J. (1981). Schematic bases of social information processing. In E. T. Higgins, C. P. Herman, & M. P. Zanna (Eds.), *Social cognition: The Ontario symposium* (Vol. 1). Hillsdale, NJ: Erlbaum.

Ting-Toomey, S. (1985). Toward a theory of conflict and culture. In W. B. Gudykunst, L. P. Stewart, & S. Ting-Toomey (Eds.), *Communication, culture, and organizational processes* (pp. 71–86). Thousand Oaks, CA: Sage.

Triandis, H. C. (1989). The self and social behavior in differing cultural contexts. *Psychological Review, 96,* 506–520.

Triandis, H. C., & Albert, R. D. (1987). Cross-cultural perspectives. In F. M. Jablin, L. L. Putnam, K. H. Roberts, & L. W. Porter (Eds.), *Handbook of organizational communication: An interdisciplinary perspective* (pp. 264–295). Thousand Oaks, CA: Sage.

Ueda, K. (1974). Sixteen ways to avoid saying "no" in Japan. In J. C. Condon & M. Saito (Eds.), *Intercultural encounters with Japan* (pp. 185–192). Tokyo: Simul Press.

Van Zandt, H. F. (1970, November-December). How to negotiate in Japan. *Harvard Business Review,* pp. 45–56.

Weick, K. E. (1979). *The social psychology of organizing* (2nd ed.). Reading, MA: Addison-Wesley.

Weinberg, H. J. (1970). Changing perceptions on the RFT by conditioning subjects to relieve dissonance and/or escape from the anxiety in a new manner (Doctoral dissertation, University of Nebraska, 1970). *Dissertation Abstracts International, 31,* 1637A.

Werner, P. D., & LaRuss, G. W. (1985). Persistence and change in sex-role stereotypes. *Sex Roles, 12,* 1089–1110.

Wieman, J. M., & Backlund, P. (1980). Current theory and research in communicative competence. *Review of Educational Research, 50,* 185–199.

Witkin, H. A., & Berry, J. W. (1975). Psychological differentiation in cross-cultural perspective. *Journal of Cross-Cultural Psychology, 6,* 4–87.

Witkin, H. A., & Goodenough, D. R. (1977). Field dependence and interpersonal behavior. *Psychological Bulletin, 84*(4), 661–689.

Witkin, H. A., Goodenough, D. R., & Oltman, P. K. (1979). Psychological differentiation: Current status. *Journal of Personality and Social Psychology, 37,* 1127–1145.

Wyer, R. S., Jr., & Srull, T. K. (1980). The processing of social stimulus information: A conceptual integration. In R. Hastie, T. M. Ostrom, E. B. Ebbesen, R. S. Wyer, Jr., D. L. Hamilton, & E. E. Carlston (Eds.), *Person memory: The cognitive basis of social perception* (pp. 227–300). Hillsdale, NJ: Erlbaum.

CHAPTER 14

Ambiguity with a Purpose
The Shadow of Power in Communication
Zhiang Lin

Chapter Thirteen, by Cristina Gibson, has neatly outlined a list of cultural differences in each phase of intercultural communication. Gibson notices, for example, that when encoding messages, people from certain cultures may choose comparatively ambiguous expressions and people from other cultures may use comparatively definite words. She also proposes processes for reconciling these intercultural differences in multicultural workgroups, processes I believe are very important in today's globalized environment. One issue I find particularly worth further exploration is the phenomenon of ambiguity in communication. Gibson has suggested that communication ambiguity, while occurring most among people from different cultural groups, can be easily eliminated among people from the same cultural group and that ambiguity occurs mostly when messages are constructed and transmitted. I would argue that ambiguity occurs in each phase of the communication and in both sociocultural and organizational settings. I further propose that ambiguity in communication results from power influence. In this chapter I first propose a new perspective for understanding communication ambiguity. Then I explore the relationship between power and ambiguity in communication in

Note: My thanks to Martha Dahlen and Catie Lott for their editing help on earlier versions of this chapter and to the editors of this volume for their constructive comments.

both a sociocultural setting and an organizational setting. Finally, I provide a general framework for a broader view of communication ambiguity.

A New Perspective on Communication Ambiguity

Communication starts when one party wants to tell another party something. In the process messages are encoded, transmitted, and decoded and feedback is returned. Differences in encoding and decoding cause ambiguity, that is, multiple or incorrect interpretations occur. Although communication technologies like electronic mail and teleconferencing now offer additional and sometimes more efficient means of transmitting messages, there is no evidence that ambiguity necessarily decreases in these formats. The limited ability of information technology to control communication ambiguity and the fact that such ambiguity persists despite numerous efforts by researchers and practitioners to eliminate it highlights the need to search for deeper and broader explanations.

Not surprisingly, we find that no matter how sophisticated information technology may be, it is still human beings who determine what messages to send and receive and how to encode and decode these messages. Human beings not only live in particular sociocultural environments, they are also bounded by their organizations. Communication ambiguity becomes a reflection of their environments, both sociocultural and organizational, because these environments are a source of information, as Gibson describes. Studies have largely regarded communication ambiguity as dysfunctional and something to be eliminated. One aspect of communication that has often been overlooked in various studies is the role of power. Power is the ability to influence people to do things that they would not otherwise do. Contrary to the common assumptions that individuals and organizations always strive to improve communication and that communication can always become more clear and effective by employing more sophisticated information technology, people seem to neglect the fact that it is often in the sender's and/or receiver's best interest to keep communication ambiguous (Kursh, 1971).

Power is so pervasive that nothing escapes its influence. Human communication is no exception. With or without our consciousness, our communication reflects the influence of power. The role of power in communication, however, is rooted in a variety of settings, including societies and organizations. To understand how communication ambiguity is influenced by power, therefore, we must examine these settings and their influence on how people communicate.

Sociocultural Setting

Power is deeply rooted in every society's history and culture. In this chapter, as an example of how power operates in a sociocultural setting and affects individuals' behavior and their way of communication, I focus on the role of power in communication in Chinese society, with some comparisons with Western societies (Europe and North America), as the Eastern and Western types of societies have frequently been shown to have distinct characteristics.

Ambiguous Communication with Cultural Characteristics

Observations and studies have frequently shown that there are distinct communication differences between Oriental people and Western people (for example, Gimpl, 1986). Westerners are found to have a low tolerance for ambiguity in communication while Orientals have a much higher tolerance. For example, an American might consider ambiguous communication as something to be avoided because it causes inefficiency, but a Chinese might consider ambiguous communication as something helpful for showing politeness to the other party. Such differences have puzzled both Orientals and Westerners in their exchanges.

So how do the Chinese communicate? Almost all Chinese have read or seen plays based on the classical book *The Legend of Three Kingdoms,* which details the strategy and tactics involved in the long battles among three warlords during the post-Han dynasty in China (220–280 A.D.). A sample episode from this book makes a useful example. Early in his career, warlord Liu Bei had little power compared with other more prominent forces. In order to expand his territory and further realize his dream of becoming the sole ruler of all China, he needed help. He found Zhuge Liang, who at that time was a great and ambitious strategist in China. Not serving any warlord, Zhuge had been relaxing at home and reading books, wishing one day to be able to work for some warlord to achieve his lifetime ambition. Liu went to Zhuge's home and sincerely invited Mr. Zhuge to help him. Liu could not get a definite answer. Liu traveled to Zhuge's home a second time and again got a similar treatment. Liu went to Zhuge's home the third time and finally after repeated requests (the recounting of which would cover a whole chapter in the book), Zhuge agreed to work for Liu. After that, of course, things became much brighter for warlord Liu.

A Westerner might feel puzzled by the communication processes Liu and Zhuge go through and wonder what was really going on in them. After learning that during the whole time he was saying no to Liu, Zhuge was actually very eager to work for a warlord and thus become famous, the Westerner might even think Zhuge a hypocrite. Indeed, it is often taken for granted in the Western culture that a person who says no means no. Thus, if someone says he is not qualified for the job, he usually will not get the job. Such clear and direct communication, however, would not be too welcomed by most Chinese. For example, the author of *The Legend of Three Kingdoms* regards Zhang Fei, one of Liu's honorary brothers, as rude and uneducated because he took what Zhuge said to mean exactly what Zhuge meant and suggested that Liu find someone else.

Similar incidents appear frequently in other Chinese books, legends, and dramas, reflecting just how the Chinese can be experts in ambiguous communication. However, sometimes ambiguous communication also frustrates the Chinese. This is echoed in the book *The Ugly Chinese*, when the infamous Taiwanese Chinese writer Bo Yang says, "Many Westerners told me that 'when dealing with a Chinese, you can spend half a day or so but still don't know what he really thinks about.' I said: 'That's not strange. It not just happens to you foreigners; even when a Chinese talks with another Chinese, neither side knows what's really in the other's mind'" (Bo, 1993, p. 29). And Bo adds: "A Westerner will say, 'I am a good choice for this position. Please elect me.' A Chinese, on the other hand, is more hypocritical: no matter how hard other people try to persuade him to take the position, he will say, 'I am really not qualified to take that position.' . . . However, if you finally give him up and let someone else take that position, he would hate you for life" (p. 30).

Bo not only shows his frustration with the way Chinese communicate but also points out many absurd phenomena within the Chinese society. To his mind, the 5,000-year-old traditions of the Chinese culture may actually hinder the modern development of the Chinese society as a whole. Though his observations are mainly based on the Chinese in Taiwan, many of his findings may be extended to mainland China. The fact that he was jailed by the government in Taiwan for over ten years for being too direct in expressing his critical views and that his book was later banned by the mainland China government for the similar reason seems to suggest that regardless of differences in political systems, the Chinese really have something in common: they do not tolerate clear and direct communication.

The Influence of Power on Ambiguous Communication

Although ambiguous communication certainly happens in Western societies, it seems to occur significantly more in Chinese culture. Or at least, in Western cultures a preference for communication ambiguity is not regarded as a value to be proud of. What then causes the Chinese to "like" ambiguity in communication?

Numerous explanations have been offered for differences in ambiguity tolerance across people from different sociocultural environments. Although I agree that many factors may have contributed to some degree to the phenomenon of ambiguous communication, I argue that one fundamental factor is the real force behind it. I call this factor the *shadow of power* in the Chinese society. It is power that influences people to be ambiguous in communications.

First of all, in a society like China, being ambiguous in communication can often save an individual from much trouble, sometimes even death. In the long history of China, personal power has been strictly hierarchically distributed. Chinese society has traditionally been run by persons, not by laws. The emperor and his officials had the power to punish or kill anyone they disliked. They were also notorious for their intolerance toward anything and anyone that might make them look stupid. Imagine trying to point out to such an official that he might not be correct in his handling of a certain issue. Would you dare to say that unequivocally to his face? The Chinese people learned that one way to communicate in these cases was to be ambiguous in order to appear respectful. Gradually, ambiguous communication became a standard and acceptable way of conveying information and even a sign of politeness. This value is also reflected in the Confucian philosophy of the Chinese society—always take the middle way—which in communication becomes—always say half of what is really on your mind.

Confucian philosophy has dominated the long history of China and has often been raised to an almost religious level by many Chinese rulers, a practice that does not seem out of place once we understand that the essence of the Confucian philosophy actually advocates the hierarchy of power. It requires people to obey the leader and let the leader do the thinking, talking, and disciplining. For example, during the long tradition of Chinese education all children have been required to memorize "The Three-Word Classic Poem," a work based on Confucian philosophy and centered around obedience to authority and the elderly. Gradually, under the authority of this philosophy, not only did the Chinese become less willing to talk clearly; given the often severe consequence of such talk, they also actually lost the ability to express their views unambiguously. This is also reflected in the popular advice for people who want to succeed in the Chinese society: "More kowtow, less talk." Moreover, people at higher hierarchical levels have had no incentive to express what is on their mind to people at lower hierarchical levels. Oftentimes, they would regard it a challenge to their power if people at lower levels knew too much. Under the influence of Confucian philosophy, it is no wonder ambiguous communication has become so popular at all levels of the Chinese society.

In contrast to Chinese history, which has been filled with the obsession for hierarchy of power, for quite some time the history of many Western societies has been one of building democratic and power-sharing systems like parliaments or congresses, activity that assumes a much less hierarchical structure of power distribution. While there is no conclusive evidence that a democratic system will always be better in every aspect, one thing we can say is that a democratic society that assumes that people are created equal will tend to allow people to express opinions more freely and with less severe consequences. As a result, people feel less social pressure to disguise what they really have on their minds and are thus less ambiguous in their communication. Viewed in that light, it is not too difficult to understand why the Americans, for example, usually talk more straightforwardly than the Chinese. One reason is that the consequences of being rude or of disagreeing are much less severe.

Some people might say that the Chinese use more ambiguous communication because of Chinese syntax: for example, Chinese speakers do not have to choose between masculine and feminine pronouns when referring to a person. If linguistic syntax is a reason for Chinese ambiguity, then what caused such syntax and just how important is it to ambiguous communication? English also has many phrases that allow ambiguous communication, but Westerners seem to choose to avoid them as much as possible. Do the Chinese do that? Not really. They create more ambiguity than necessary by their choice of syntax and vocabulary. Fundamentally, I argue that the Chinese choice of ambiguous expression in languages is the consequence of historical evolution and reflects the shadow of power.

So what would happen to the way the Chinese communicate if this shadow of power had a minimal influence? Would people in China have a much lower preference for ambiguous communication? I believe they would. Support for this belief may be found in the Chinese people's love for the story of Judge Bao, an official in the Sung dynasty of China (960–1127 A.D.). He was famous for his frankness and righteousness when he talked to superiors and even the emperor. Movies and television series depicting stories about him are extremely popular in Chinese cultures including Hong Kong, Taiwan, and mainland China. In fact, television stations in Hong Kong have lengthened the Judge Bao series several times due to the overwhelming reception by the audience. Thus on the one hand Chinese people use ambiguous communication, but on the other hand they respect people who are not afraid to use unequivocal language in dealing with powerful people. Is this an inconsistency? I would say no, because it exactly reflects the wish of Chinese people to be rid of the shadow of power.

Based on Chinese history, I argue that it is fear of power that causes ambiguity to arise in communication. The fact that even today many Chinese people in different regions use ambiguous communication may reflect exactly another fact—that Chinese society is still largely ruled by a few people with much power. This may suggest that we could use power distance as a predictor of degree of ambiguity in communication across different cultures.

Finally, how might the influence of power change in Chinese society? Economic and political developments can change the Chinese attitude toward ambiguous communication. As economic and political systems drift toward more Western models and with the dispersion of authority into the hands of more people, the shadow of power may gradually fade away. The Chinese, as a result, will adopt a more unequivocal communication style and show less tolerance of ambiguous communication. The televised scenes of Taiwanese parliament members, both male and female, shouting at one another and even breaking into physical fights, as millions look on, may give us some indication of just how radically the Chinese may change from their traditionally modest and not-so-direct manner of speaking.

Organizational Setting

Ambiguity also exists in organizational communication, which is the core of organizational operation, both Western and Oriental. In Chapter Thirteen Gibson concludes that there should be fewer communication problems when people are from the same cultural groups. This may or may not be so. The fact that people resort to ambiguous communication in Western organizations too suggests that perhaps, in addition to the cultural and social factors, individual people and organizations play strong roles in controlling ambiguity. The common factor is, again, the influence of power. Power appears as a term in many studies on Western organizations. The word has also existed in the Chinese vocabulary for a long time and the actions it encompasses have been practiced to perfection in many Chinese organizations. Most previous studies on communication from an organizational perspective have focused mainly on how to improve communication, for example, how to make it more efficient and reliable by employing information technology. Exploration into the role of power in organizational communication has been lacking. The remainder of this chapter examines how organizational factors influence communication ambiguity.

Ambiguous Communication in Organizations

Ambiguous communication does have reason to exist in organizations, despite efforts by organizational researchers and practitioners to eliminate it. Contrary to popular belief, for example, keeping communication fuzzy can actually be an advantage for some members of the organization, even though the organization as whole may not benefit from it.

Ambiguous communication occurs at all levels in organizations. On the one hand a large part of managerial work is to manipulate communication through myths, images, symbols, labels, and so forth (Weick, 1979). Because information is the key to power and control in an organization, managers frequently withhold information, even when that action may inhibit employees' productivity. Managers can also use ambiguous communication to cut down on objections and to preserve the freedom to change their minds without breaking promises or losing face, thus increasing their efficiency (Eisenberg & Witten, 1987).

On the other hand people with less power also tend to hold onto whatever knowledge they have and resist sharing with other people or even their bosses. Fear of those who are more powerful also causes ambiguity in communication. Showing that you know more than your boss often does not result in positive feedback. It can be even more risky if your words are interpreted by your boss as criticisms or challenges.

While managers or others in the higher power positions tend to force those in the lower power positions to receive ambiguous information by only allowing them to see or hear a partial and discontinuous picture of what those in power know, those in the lower positions tend to form informal networks to counter this ambiguity. Through these informal networks, people in lower positions effectively transfer and share information among themselves, thus ensuring each has a more complete picture (Krackhardt, 1990).

Managers, not surprisingly, are usually not included in these friend-ship networks.

Ambiguous communication often occurs in the form of ma-nipulated information. Information is largely regarded as the most important resource in an organization. Power often comes from the control of information. By making communication ambiguous, a person can manipulate power in an organization. There is an old saying that knowledge is power, and it certainly is true in organi-zations. For example, an ambiguous message can cause uncertainty for the receiver, thus making the sender more powerful (Sitkin, 1987). Quite often an employee is kept from knowing what to ex-pect from his or her boss. Holding back information, being am-biguous in delivering information, and being selective in transmitting information are all forms of control.

Studies have shown that it is not only a person's position that makes him or her powerful but also the information he or she controls (Krackhardt, 1990). This information is not only tech-nical knowledge about the work process itself but also knowl-edge of the firm's social system (Pfeffer, 1992). Access to informa-tion depends upon one's position in the network of communication and social interaction, and reluctance to share such information, and thus power, is often expressed in the form of ambiguous communication.

Organizational Design and Communication Ambiguity

Organizations fear uncertainty and the loss of power. Managers in organizations worry that they are receiving ambiguous information and are therefore keen to design structures that they hope will en-sure their control of ambiguous communication. Organizational structure decides who reports to whom and how he or she will report. Organizational structure is often designed so that only the person at the highest level can have a clear understanding of orga-nizational information. Those in the upper positions use organi-zational structure to make sure they know all their subordinates' activities, requiring subordinates to report frequently and clearly. At the same time, this structure allows them to be ambiguous with the subordinates. Organizational structure is never symmetri-cal or reciprocal. The imbalance of power affects communication between levels of hierarchy. Ambiguity as a result of power influence becomes a way of manipulating communication. Under the influence of power, almost every organization in the world has a hierarchical structure, which strongly favors strict allocation of power. Organizational structure, in turn, becomes a synonym for power distribution.

The belief that organizations implement information technologies to reduce communication ambiguity overlooks two important factors: the nature of the organizational design that will implement the information technology and the people who will use the information technology. System design and system users can make information technology a source of ambiguity. In addition the technology itself can create ambiguity because it forces people to transfer information through media different from more familiar or natural ways of communication as talking face to face. Communication has both verbal and nonverbal aspects. Information technology that limits the use of such nonverbal communication as facial expression and vocal inflection can increase the chance of misunderstanding.

There is no doubt that ambiguous communication can sometimes be very dysfunctional for an organization and that sometimes some organizational members do wish to limit ambiguity. And there are ways for organizations to move beyond the obsession with power and its corollary, ambiguous communication. One way of reducing ambiguous communication and getting things done in a more open spirit may be to develop a strongly shared vision or organizational culture (Pfeffer, 1992). A more open and democratic organizational culture increases the trust between people and decreases communication ambiguity. For example, organizations can adopt participative management and team structure, thus reducing employees' reliance on information controlled by managers. There is always a threshold, however, for how far management is willing to give up power.

Though organizations may strive to design structures to control communication ambiguity, such designs may not work if they do not match the sociocultural environment they face. This result may be reflected in the difficulty U.S. companies have in implementing team structures invented in Japan. The U.S. cultural tradition favors individual responsibility and clear information flow, but team structures may reduce U.S. managers' power by reducing chances for information manipulation through ambiguous communication. Instead, mass production, which emphasizes clearly specified individual duty and strong managerial control, has become the model in the United States.

Researchers have found that organizational structure is also influenced by sociocultural factors (Gibson, 1994; Lincoln, Olsen, & Hanada, 1978), and through that influence these factors affect organizational communication style.

Thus international joint venture organizations provide a special setting for ambiguous communication. In joint ventures all the factors of ambiguous communication are often entangled: sociocultural, organizational, individual, and so on. An understanding of communication ambiguity and the influence of power in such settings requires a broad perspective.

A Framework for Understanding Communication Ambiguity

Whether communication ambiguity is intentional or unintentional, its sources can largely be found in the influence of power that is deeply rooted in a society's sociocultural system as it is characterized by factors such as valuing social order or valuing democracy. In addition communication ambiguity is influenced by power within the organization itself, reflecting such factors such as organizational authority structure and organizational culture.

To understand communication ambiguity from a more comprehensive perspective, we need a framework broad enough to encompass the factors and influences discussed in this chapter. Figure 14.1 depicts such a framework. It summarizes this chapter's attempt to better understand communication ambiguity. Using this framework, we may be able to test empirically the relationships between power and ambiguity in communication by examining societies and organizations with a focus on some important dimensions.

Conclusion

In this commentary I have suggested ways to explore the effect of power on communication ambiguity from both a cross-cultural and

Figure 14.1. A Framework for Understanding Communication Ambiguity.

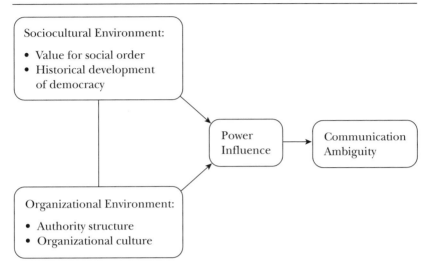

an organizational perspective. The issue of communication ambiguity is especially worth looking into when organizations are international (for example, joint ventures), owing to their mixture of sociocultural and organizational factors. Gibson's processes of reconciling intercultural differences will surely be of great value in this setting. The expanded view of communication ambiguity illustrated in the framework I have proposed is also of potential value because it allows a systematic exploration into influences on communication and relates them to the fundamental issue of power influence, thus providing a means for better understanding communication ambiguity in both societies and organizations.

References

Bo, Y. (1993). [*The ugly Chinese*]. Kowloon, Hong Kong: Yiwen. (Translations in this chapter supplied by the chapter author)

Eisenberg, E. M., & Witten, M. G. (1987, July). Reconsidering openness in organizational communication. *Academy of Management Review,* pp. 418–426.

Gibson, C. B. (1994). The implications of national culture for organization structure: An investigation of three perspectives. *Advances in International Comparative Management, 9,* 3–38.

Gimpl, M. L. (1986). Decision making under ambiguity: Western vs. Japanese managers. *Journal of Business Forecasting, 5*(2), 9–10.

Krackhardt, D. (1990). Assessing the political landscape: Structure, cognition, and power in organizations. *Administrative Science Quarterly, 35,* 342–369.

Kursh, C. O. (1971, Summer-Fall). The benefits of poor communication. *The Psychoanalytic Review,* pp. 189–208.

Lincoln, J. R., Olsen, J., & Hanada, M. (1978). Cultural effects on organizational structure: The case of Japanese firms in the United States. *American Sociological Review, 43,* 829–847.

Pfeffer, J. (1992). *Managing with power: Politics and influence in organizations.* Boston: Harvard Business School Press.

Sitkin, S. (1987). *Secrecy in organizations: The limits of legitimate information control* (Working paper). Austin: University of Texas.

Weick, K. E. (1979). Cognitive processes in organizations. In B. M. Staw (Ed.), *Research in organizational behavior* (Vol. 1, pp. 41–74). Greenwich, CT: JAI Press.

CHAPTER 15

Effective Decision Making in Multinational Teams

Daniel R. Ilgen
Jeffrey A. LePine
John R. Hollenbeck

Improved information technology, economic integration of international communities, increased dependence on technological transfer, complex distribution networks, and a desire to spread costs and risks have led to a rapid increase in the internalization of business organizations (Humes, 1993). A recent *Business Week* article described this internationalization of business as creating a need for the "most fundamental reorganization since the multidivision corporation became the standard in the 1950s" (Dwyer, Engardio, Schiller, & Reed, 1994, p. 81). This reorganization is resulting in and in part is driven by a workforce diverse in culture, expectations, roles, and many other critical variables (Maznevski, 1994).

Almost without exception, reorganization to meet the needs of internationalization results in the creation of multinational teams. Such teams share the common characteristics of teams in general. Specifically, they are composed of two or more members who interact with each other, are interdependent, and share some common goals or objectives (Morgan, Glickman, Woodward, Blaiwes, & Salas, 1986). However, members of international teams do not share the same primary national identification.

It is argued at Ford and Citicorp that competing in a global economy requires a company to establish multinational teams in order to decrease redundant operations across countries (Dwyer, Engardio, Schiller, & Reed, 1994). Instead of having Europeans at work in Europe designing a product for Europe and Americans at work in North America designing a product for North Americans, Ford is now using multinational teams to design and market global products, thus leveraging economies of scale. These multinational teams are typically composed of individuals from the host country, the organization's parent country, and countries where the product will be marketed. Attention is also being paid to giving team representation to countries where raw materials are sourced or critical technology is located.

Multinational teams are also increasing rapidly owing to the current geopolitical environment. The post–Cold War era has seen a dramatic increase in the use of multinational teams for addressing world problems. Multinational United Nations forces are often replacing unilateral military actions as the first line of response to political upheavals. The success of these forces requires people from different nations to cooperate, to work together as a team to solve complex problems.

In spite of the increased use and importance of teams composed of members from different nations, research on such teams is sparse and tends to take the form of case study narratives, describing one or more teams whose members typically come from no more than two nations. General theories about behavior in international teams do not exist, and little systematic structure exists for thinking about issues of behavior in these teams. In the pages that follow we attempt to provide some structure for multinational decision-making teams and to suggest which research pursuits are likely and unlikely to be fruitful if future research is to contribute to understanding behavior in multinational teams.

Why Create Multinational Teams?

People with heterogeneous national backgrounds are frequently assigned to a team under the assumption that a multinational team will have available a wider variety of skills, beliefs, values, experiences, and other resources than could be expected if its members shared a common national background. Heterogeneity among team members on such dimensions as personality, attitudes, and gender has been shown to improve a team's quality of decision making and problem solving (Jackson, May, & Whitney, 1995). Similarly, heterogeneity on critical abilities affects performance, in ways that depend on the nature of the task (Laughlin, 1980; Steiner, 1972).

Another assumption implicit in the selection of team members from differing national backgrounds is that there are systematic differences among people according to national background. To many, this assumption seems so obvious that it needs no further comment. Yet whether national differences do in fact represent differences that are sufficiently large or unique to expand the pool of resources critical for team performance is not clear. At the very least, before the use of international teams to expand the resource pool can be advocated, reliable differences among nations on valued dimensions must be shown to exist.

In addition to expanding the pool of team resources, multinational teams may be constituted for political reasons. Often it is desirable to ensure representation of key national groups on teams. On international governing bodies, commissions, and the like, representation of key nations may be a necessary condition for those nations to accept any recommendations from these units. Similarly, in multinational firms often the critical issue is not whether teams with the "proper" nationality mix will perform better, but rather whether consituent groups are satisfied with their representation on decision-making teams.

We accept both organizational and political reasons for multinational team composition as legitimate and important. But there is little we can add regarding the political issues of team composition. Numerous issues, many of them specific to each individual team and to the technical, social, and organizational setting in which it is embedded, influence political activity and its outcome. These issues are too idiosyncratic to generate general principles of interest across broad classes of behaviors within teams. For the most part, then, we shall ignore political reasons for forming multinational teams.

Multinational Teams and Decision Making: Defining Characteristics

Not every team composed of multinationals fits our conception of a functional multinational team. Multinational teams that can perform the work expected of them will have certain characteristics and will perform certain tasks.

Multinational Teams

Some of the critical features of multinational decision-making teams stem from their international heterogeneity; others do not. We shall be considering teams that we assume to have the following features that do not relate to heterogeneity. The teams are (1) composed of two or more members. These persons (2) interact with each other, (3) are interdependent, and (4) share some common goals or objectives. Furthermore, it will be assumed that the team members (5) are not necessarily of equal status and (6) do not all share the same task-relevant knowledge. Finally, we shall assume that the team's goals or objectives (7) are relatively unstructured, with a level of unprogrammed discretion that necessitates some team decision making. With the exception of numbers five and six, these seven characteristics are consistent with most definitions of what Guzzo and Shea (1992) described as "*real* groups with a *task* to perform in an *organization*" (p. 292).

To these seven characteristics, we add an eighth that defines a *multinational decision-making* team. On a multinational team, team members (8) are drawn from two or more different nations. Although we recognize that determining who is or is not representative of a particular nation may sometimes not be clear, we limit ourselves to the large proportion of cases where it can be done.

Team Tasks of Decision Making and Problem Solving

Decision-making teams in organizations are involved in all phases of problem solving, as outlined in the classic works of Newall and Simon (1972). Problem solving begins by identifying the problem. This is followed by generating alternatives for addressing the problem, evaluating these alternatives, and taking some action based on the evaluations. This widely accepted model for problem solving is rationally driven and follows linearly from start to finish. Actual practice degrades both the rationality and the linearity. Problem solving in real-world teams is far more irrational and chaotic, with various phases of the process occurring simultaneously, recycling back through the subtasks, and being reevaluated and modified (Gersick, 1988). Nevertheless, the basic subtasks of the problem-solving model reasonably capture the primary activities of strategic, production, and other types of multinational teams, even if the execution is less clear-cut than the model suggests. In this chapter we use *decision making* to describe both teams involved in the broader process of problem solving and those for whom the decision-making task is restricted to choosing among a limited set of alternatives. Although the technical literature on decision making often attempts to keep these two types of decision making separate, the way in which organizations talk about decision making does not. Furthermore, real-life teams, because they exist over time, are involved in both decision making and problem solving in such a way that isolating the two processes seems to have had little or no practical or theoretical value. Therefore, we use decision making to include both problem solving and decision making, as is consistent with the way decision making is commonly understood.

Cultural Differences

For decision making in multinational teams to differ from decision making in nationally homogeneous teams, systematic differences in national cultures must exist and must be likely to affect team decision-making processes. This section considers the way some have described relevant differences.

Content of Culture

That national cultures differ in many ways is well documented. Researchers never cease to delight in drawing convenience samples whose members represent two or more nations. They then describe the differences and ascribe them to culture. Yet unless supported by some systematic approach to the study of culture, idiosyncratic differences observed in small samples at one point in time provide little insight into broader cultural issues (Triandis, 1994). Even substantial differences are often quickly bounded within narrow temporal periods, becoming dated as attitudes, values, knowledge, and experiences within cultures shift over time.

One solution to providing structure to cultural differences is empirical. Data have been collected on many diverse characteristics across several cultures, with or without a focus on a particular issue. The works of Cattell and his colleagues (Cattell, 1949, 1950; Cattell, Breul, & Hartman, 1952; Cattell & Gorsuch, 1965; Cattell, Graham, & Wolvier, 1979; Wolvier & Cattell, 1981) and Rummel (1972) represent this approach. When Wolvier and Cattell (1981) summarized the previous thirty years of cultural difference research in the factor analytic tradition, they concluded that eight factors formed the basic dimensions of national profiles and that these dimensions describe a national culture much as personality dimensions describe individuals. Their eight-dimensional typology consisted of vigorous adapted development versus underdeveloped resources; intelligent affluence; a simple life morality versus anomie; size (number of persons and land mass); cultural pressure, expressed in intolerance of burden; efficient use of large resources versus high population density; cultural pressure with sublimation; and Mohammedan Mid-Eastern.

Although empirical clustering of large numbers of diverse items may form a multidimensional space in which national cultures can be located with some degree of reliability, this approach often challenges the limits of inductive reasoning when attempts are made to create a coherent theory of culture that fits the population of cultures represented by the data. Furthermore, the usefulness of such descriptive models for understanding particular cross-cultural problems (such as the effectiveness of multidimensional teams) is limited at best. These limits are clear from the list of national dimensions just described.

A second approach is to develop theories of cultural differences within a limited problem domain and then conduct empirical research that is guided by the theory. Triandis (1994) laments that very little cross-cultural work has proceeded in this fashion and adds that without theoretical structure, cross-cultural research will be of limited value. We agree. Triandis's own work on individualism and collectivism (1990, 1992) (discussed later) is an effort to address this concern. The research of Hofstede (1980a) on values and the work that has followed has also been more theoretically guided and, thus, has had a greater impact on the way cultures are perceived.

Working with an extensive worldwide sample of IBM employees (Hofstede, 1980a, 1980b, 1991), Hofstede (1980a) defined culture as collective mental programming of individuals within environmental boundaries. Culture results when a group of people are conditioned by the same education, institutions, and experiences. An individual's *cultural characteristics* are relatively stable psychological tendencies resulting from significant environmental influences, according to Hofstede. They are not immutable traits.

Hofstede (1980a) identified four dimensions on which national cultures differ: power distance, uncertainty avoidance, masculinity, and individualism. *Power distance* refers to the extent to which individuals in a society tend to accept unequally distributed power. Individuals from societies high in *uncertainty avoidance* feel threatened by uncertainty and ambiguity according to Hofstede. Individuals in low uncertainty avoidance societies are more likely to take risks and accept dissent. *Masculinity,* the third dimension, refers to the extent to which values such as aggressiveness, assertiveness, independence, and ambition prevail over values such as nurturing, sympathizing, calmness, and equality. Finally, variations in *individualism* are seen as affecting the extent to which people within a society are psychologically tied to social frameworks.

Others treat individualism as a continuum running from individualism at one end to collectivism at the other (individualism-collectivism). This continuum has received considerable attention and has been applied to groups and organizations existing both within and across national boundaries (Wagner, 1995; Wagner & Moch, 1986). In collectivist societies, individuals are seen as tied to a few close social networks (in-groups) where they "look out for each other" and exchange a great deal of loyalty. An in-group can be thought of simply as a stable set of individuals with whom a person works or identifies. Triandis, Leung, Villareal, and Clack (1985) point out that individuals in a collectivist society will sacrifice their personal goals for the goals of their group. Individuals in a collectivist society also stress group harmony and safety over group competition and risk, according to these authors. In individualist societies, individuals look out for themselves and immediate family. They tend to belong to more in-groups than do individuals in collectivist societies, but that membership tends to be for instrumental purposes (that is, achieving individual goals). Thus in-groups in an individualist society tend to have less stable membership than they do in a collectivist society. Individuals in an individualist society tend to stress individual goals, self-sufficiency, and competition over group goals, interdependence, and collaboration.

Two recent cross-cultural studies demonstrate that the effects of culture differences are indirect and operate through mediating culturally specific psychological tendencies. Although both studies examined the effect of individualism and collectivism on individual-level outcomes, their findings are applicable here.

Earley (1989) examined the role of individualism-collectivism on the social-loafing tendencies of managerial trainees in the United States and the People's Republic of China. As expected, collectivism was significantly higher among managerial trainees in the People's Republic of China. A more interesting finding was that collectivists given shared responsibility performed better than collectivists given individual responsibility, regardless of the amount of personal accountability. Conversely, individualists performed better in the individual responsibility condition; however, this effect was reduced somewhat under conditions of high personal accountability.

In a later study, Earley (1994) addressed how individualism-collectivism affects the relationship between training method and individual self-efficacy and performance. Like social loafing, training and self-efficacy are not constructs of concern in this chapter; however, the implications of the study are directly relevant. The theme was that a person's cultural orientation (individualism-collectivism) determines whether his or her level of self-efficacy is affected by different forms of training information. Self-efficacy is a person's estimate concerning his or her capability to perform a specific task and is important because it is believed to be related to a person's motivation to perform that task (Bandura, 1986). Earley proposed that training on a task influences a person's estimate of future performance on that task because people make normative comparisons as an initial estimate of capability. Earley found support for his hypothesis that collectivists' efficacy beliefs were more affected by group-focused training, because collectivists focus their attention on group-level normative cues. Individualists' efficacy beliefs were more affected by individual-focused training, because they focused their attention on individual-level normative cues.

Distribution of Cultural Differences

The literature just cited supports the conclusion that cultural differences exist across nations. However, to conclude that knowledge of team members' national origin is *sufficient* to draw inferences about their cultural differences is not legitimate, given the nature of the published data. Clearly, some nations are more culturally homogeneous than others (consider, for example, Japan as compared to the United States). In addition the size of the differences between nations on any one cultural dimension may be small. All that can be concluded is that national origin is a very loose marker, or cultural indicator, for drawing conclusions about national effects on behaviors in multinational teams.

Impact of Culture: Three Key Problems

If multinationality is to contribute to decision-making teams' effectiveness, two conditions must hold. Reliable differences attributable to nationality must exist among team members, and those same differences must contribute positively to the team's product or output. The literature on cultural difference supports the first of these two necessary conditions. The second necessary condition has two primary components, one specific and one general. At the specific level, the issue is the content of nationality differences. Whether heterogeneity on any particular content dimension has the potential to contribute to team effectiveness will depend on whether that dimension is relevant to the team's decision task. If, for example, the team's work is to develop an economic development plan for a Third World country, national diversity that increases the knowledge and experience pool to include not only knowledge about economic factors but also in-depth knowledge about the indigenous people who must carry out the plan, then national heterogeneity is of value. Heterogeneity along the same lines of expertise may contribute little if the decision task is that of playing fantasy football.

A second, more general, and more complex way in which multinationality influences team effectiveness is through its effect on team process. The members of decision-making teams must work together *by design* to accomplish the team's task. To solve problems, they must coordinate and cooperate in all the components of problem solving, from defining the problem, through generating and evaluating alternatives, to selecting a course of action and taking action. Unfortunately, the very advantage gained from the diversity in nationality—bringing a bigger pool of ideas, values, and perspectives to bear on the problem—may exacerbate team members' ability to coordinate, cooperate, and reach consensus as they work through the problem. Argote and McGrath (1993) refer to this problem as the classical "diversity/consensus dilemma." It occurs when teams need diverse personnel with a wide range of talents, skills, personal experiences, and different perspectives and also need people who can form a common perspective and work together, resolve conflicting viewpoints, and agree upon and carry out a common plan of action. Needs for both diversity and consensus create a true dilemma because the advantages of diversity are almost always purchased at the cost of consensus, and vice versa.

Although few data exist on the effects of multinationality on team process, a great deal of work exists on the effects of team composition on processes critical to problem-solving teams. From this work, three potential problems appear to be particularly relevant in multinational teams. These are reaching a common understanding of the nature of the team problem (problem definition), sharing relevant information in the team, and resolving interpersonal conflict.

Defining the Problem

The impact of national diversity among members of decision-making teams begins with the initial definition of the problem to be addressed. Examples abound where outsiders unfamiliar with local conditions have failed to recognize problems or have interpreted conditions as if they were one kind of problem when indeed they were another. From the organization's perspective, it is hoped that internationally diverse teams will be better able to identify problems correctly as well as generate solutions to them.

Whether this potential will be realized, however, is less clear. Again, to our knowledge, no research has looked at the nature of problem definition in internationally diverse teams. On the one hand, work on diversity among team members has found that teams with members heterogeneous in personality (Hoffman & Maier, 1961) and attitudes (Triandis, Hall, & Ewen, 1965) have produced higher quality decisions. However, it is not possible to isolate whether this effect was due to superior problem definition or other factors.

On the other hand, Maznevski (1994) argued that cultural diversity creates barriers to effective interaction that are likely to decrease the performance of problem-solving teams. Recent work on team mental models (Klimoski & Mohammed, 1994; Orasanu, 1990; Orasanu & Salas, 1993) provides further reason for caution. A *mental model* is a construct used in cognitive psychology to describe the way in which an individual construes a problem or situation. Team mental models are the common views of the task and problems held by all members of the team. It has been found that teams function best when they possess a shared view of the problem and ways to respond to it (Klimoski & Mohammed, 1994; Orasanu, 1990). This is counter to the rationale behind constituting multinational teams. Therefore research is needed that explores multinational teams' ability to realize their assumed potential for generating broad problem definitions.

Sharing Information

A necessary but not sufficient condition for effectively using diverse team members' knowledge, skills, abilities, and values is that team members share information. Larson and Christensen (1993), framing team decision making in cognitive terms, refer to this sharing as the "information retrieval function" of teams. The members represent, in a sense, a memory bank, and team process must pull out of that bank information that the team can use to inform the decision. In behavioral terms this information retrieval occurs when information possessed by individual team members is shared with others in the team.

Research with nationally homogeneous decision-making teams has shown that often critical information is not shared. Stasser and Titus (1985) found that teams composed of members who possessed some information in common and other information unique to each individual overrepresented the common information in their discussions. Unique information, even when just as valid and important with respect to the decision outcome as common information, was mentioned much less than expected given its base rate. Subsequent research has found this effect to be very robust (Stasser & Stewart, 1992; Stasser, Taylor, & Hanna, 1989; Stasser & Titus, 1987). When specific instructions were given to teams in an attempt to overcome this effect, not only did the instructions not work (Stasser, Taylor, & Hanna, 1989) but the effect was even stronger.

Groupthink is another team-level phenomenon that militates against the sharing of multiple points of view. *Groupthink* occurs when members of the team converge on a decision alternative by collectively bolstering each others' beliefs and creating an inflated impression of the level of their agreement (Taylor, 1992). Janis's classic analysis (1972) of the decision of President Kennedy and his advisers to undertake the Bay of Pigs invasion of Cuba epitomizes the phenomenon. Subsequent case study analyses of other decisions were consistent with those groupthink findings (Janis, 1982; Janis & Mann, 1977). Team members interviewed some time after the decisions were made revealed that as the alternative courses of action were discussed, support for the preferred alternative grew, and members with reservations about the decision became reluctant to go against the building momentum in its favor. They either refrained from expressing opposition or did so very tentatively.

To our knowledge, none of the literature on sharing information has addressed the groupthink effect in international teams. Yet from what we know about cultural diversity, it seems likely that national heterogeneity may heighten the tendency to overrepresent common information.

Heterogeneity in comparison to homogeneity along any dimension is likely to increase the difficulty of communication. Studies of communication patterns in workgroups have shown that ethnic diversity leads to lower amounts of communication among coworkers (Jackson, May, & Whitney, 1995). Because information held in common tends to form the pool of topics on which conversation can occur most easily, it is likely that nationally heterogeneous teams will be even more likely than homogeneous ones to dwell on topics and issues about which team members agree.

Groupthink, however, may be less of a problem for culturally diverse teams than homogeneous ones. According to Janis (1972), three classes of conditions enhanced the likelihood of groupthink. The first of these was strong group cohesion; team members were less likely to want to disagree with those with whom they were closely aligned. Nationally heterogeneous teams by their very makeup are, at least when first constituted, less likely to be cohesive. They are created to represent different points of view, so by definition they lack cohesion.

The second condition likely to facilitate the occurrence of groupthink was structural faults. Excessive homogeneity, insulation from the outside world, and lack of an impartial leader are some examples of these faults. Internationally diverse teams will not suffer from the first two faults and are no more or less likely to have impartial leaders than any other teams. Although teams consisting of members from cultures that tend to accept power differences among persons (that is, high on Hofstede's power distance dimension) should be more likely to be affected by leaders who are less impartial. Finally, Janis suggested that provocative contexts, where threat or stress was high, were more likely than less provocative ones to lead to groupthink. Here nationally heterogeneous teams are likely to be somewhat more likely to experience provocative contexts than homogeneous ones. We would expect that the strength of the context effect would depend on the interaction between the context and the cultural characteristics represented on the team. Whether cultural values would increase the tendency for groupthink would depend upon the extent to which they overrode the effects of low cohesion.

In sum, we would predict that the sharing of information in internationally heterogeneous teams is likely to be as much or more of a problem than it is in homogeneous teams. Groupthink is not likely to be the reason behind this, for the reasons just given. Furthermore, groupthink may not be a problem, as the effect has only been observed using retrospective case studies (Aldag & Fuller, 1993). The tendency to oversample from a shared pool of information is the more likely problem to be faced. Given the fact that training was not successful at reducing this effect in homogeneous teams (Stasser, Taylor, & Hanna, 1989), we would expect it to be difficult to overcome, in spite of the fact that it is precisely the desire to access a broader pool of information, values, and perspectives that often leads to advocating the use of multinational teams.

Intrateam Conflict

The very nature of team problem solving and decision making demands that the team members share, integrate, and combine information (Larson & Christensen, 1993). Such interactions are very likely to lead to disagreements. Disagreements, no matter how small, are a subtle form of conflict.

Intrateam conflict when solving problems and making decisions is both cognitive and social. Cognitive conflict occurs when members share a goal but disagree on the best way of accomplishing the goal (Brehmer, 1976). It also exists when members disagree about the interpretation of shared events, conditions, or experiences (Cosier & Rose, 1977). The latter disagreement may arise out of fundamental differences in interpretation between team members. A similar scenario may result when members do not disagree but are unable to express their positions in ways that allow them to recognize their agreement (Brehmer, 1976).

Social conflict involves some agitation, annoyance, or interpersonal hostility among team members and is the more familiar interpersonal conflict (Katz & Kahn, 1978). It often results in the psychological withdrawal of one or more team members and inhibits communication in the team (Levine & Moreland, 1990; Bettenhausen, 1991). Social conflict may also result from the presence of cognitive conflict (Brehmer, 1976).

Once again, we located no research on national heterogeneity in problem-solving groups related to conflict, but diversity on dimensions other than nationality has been found to obstruct communication, to lead to overt acts to inhibit the participation of some team members, and to lower cohesion (Jackson, 1992). Also ethnocentricity, people's tendency to place higher value on the inputs of people similar to themselves, has been observed (Cox, 1994; Ziller, 1973).

When diversity of gender within teams has been investigated, sex effects and sex-role stereotypes have tended to interact with tasks (Eagly, 1987). Although gender diversity is much different from multinational diversity, looking for interactions between tasks, roles, and cultural factors related to nationality may be fruitful. Consider for a moment, the four dimensions on which Hofstede (1980a, 1980b, 1991) found cultures to vary—power distance, uncertainty avoidance, masculinity, and individualism. The extent to which these factors are likely to affect conflict and communications in teams is likely to be as much a factor of the interaction among team members' values, the nature of role definitions within teams, and the decision task as it is a factor of the mix of team members on the dimensions themselves. Power distance values are as likely as masculinity values to interact with the authority structure of team roles. Uncertainty avoidance would appear to be closely related to the types of decision tasks assigned to a team, and individualism-collectivism should interact with the level and structure of participation expected of team members.

Multinational Composition and Team Decision-Making Effectiveness

It is our position that the effectiveness of multinational decision-making teams lies in their ability to manage the diversity-consensus dilemma (Argote & McGrath, 1993). The advantages offered by an expanded pool of skills, values, perspectives, and the other inputs persons of multiple cultures bring to the task must outweigh the team process costs that result when people from different backgrounds must work together. In decision-making teams heterogeneity among members most likely manifests in problems with defining the decision problem, sharing information, and interpersonal conflict.

The diversity-consensus dilemma is just that, a dilemma, not something that can be resolved in a singular way. As with any dilemma, there are trade-offs. The best that can be done is to understand where the trade-offs lie, then estimate the gains and losses associated with choices.

Because the level of diversity in multinational teams is assumed to be directly related to the differences among cultures represented by the team members, one way to address the diversity-consensus dilemma directly is to influence the amount of diversity represented in the team. Some mixes of national cultures will create higher levels of heterogeneity than others. Thus, depending on the severity of the problems created by diversity, one could give up some gains in differing points of view and get in return some reductions in problems caused by high levels of heterogeneity. Although manipulating diversity through team composition and other means can affect diversity, control along the homogeneity-heterogeneity dimension may be limited by practical constraints. Nevertheless, composition does represent a, if not the, major dimension to be considered when thinking about trade-offs.

A second way to influence multinational diversity effects is through influencing the nature of the decision-making situation, or task. In a manner similar to that demonstrated for individual personality variable effects on performance, the strength of the decision-making situation is likely to moderate the impact of member heterogeneity on team decision-making effectiveness. Weiss and Adler (1984) argue that certain situational characteristics are widely recognized and accepted as rules of conduct that constrain and direct the behaviors of individuals in those situations. When the situational demands are strong, personality variables have little impact on observed behavior; when they are weak, individuals' personality characteristics come into play. Mischel (1977) described strong situations as ones that most people construe the same way, sharing the same view of the most appropriate course of action. In addition strong situations possessed strong incentives encouraging the choice of the most appropriate alternative, and required skills that everyone possessed. In contrast, weak situations did not lead people to define them in the same way, led persons to perceive multiple ways to reach a solution, offered little or no incentives for performance, and were not structured so that people could easily learn what successful behavior might be. Using the strong-weak distinction in a team setting, Meier (1970) found a gender effect for discussion team leaders (women outperformed men) when the task was unstructured. Under very structured conditions, there were no gender differences. Meier argued that the press of the strong situation suppressed the opportunity for gender-related differences in style to come into play.

Team decision-making tasks also vary in strength. Strong situations are ones in which the task demands are clear and inflexible. There are well-recognized standard operating procedures for reaching decisions, and these procedures are known and understood by team members. Weak situations are ones in which there is far less agreement about how the task should be done.

Figure 15.1 illustrates a two-dimensional framework that incorporates team member heterogeneity and the strength of the decision task situation. Multinational decision-making teams typically fall in the lower half of the figure, and we will argue that effective performance in those teams depends upon the strength of the tasks assigned and the mix of task and interpersonal behaviors that emerge as the team responds to the task situations. That is, team effectiveness depends upon the way in which the diversity-consensus dilemma is managed. In strong situations the lower potential for disagreement on task demands and high consensus on the cohesive nature of responses to them should reduce the likelihood for disagreement on task-related issues across cultures and make it easier for cross-cultural teams to function. The rapid increase in sharing of information and technology across national boundaries, the extent to which higher education in the United States has been the training ground for persons from very diverse cultures, and the pressure of similar trends should tend to drive task situations toward the strong task cell in the framework shown in Figure 15.1 and ease some of the potential for conflict within multinational teams. Whether the same is true in the interpersonal domain is less clear, but public opinion tends to support movement toward cultural homogenization. Attempts to create trade barriers in European and other markets against U.S. television and movies are evidence of fears of cultural homogenization. However, regardless of the pressures pushing multinational decision-making teams toward the upper-right-hand cell, sufficient cases map into the lower-right-hand cell to be worth attention.

Interventions in Multinational Teams

Our discussion of team processes to this point has been descriptive. In Figure 15.1, we illustrated a taxonomic heuristic in which to locate multinational teams charged with making decisions. We described cultural characteristics interacting with the task and team processes from the standpoint of what may go on in such teams. As we have shown, there is good reason to believe that multinational

Figure 15.1. Heuristic for Managing Multicultural Decision-Making Teams.

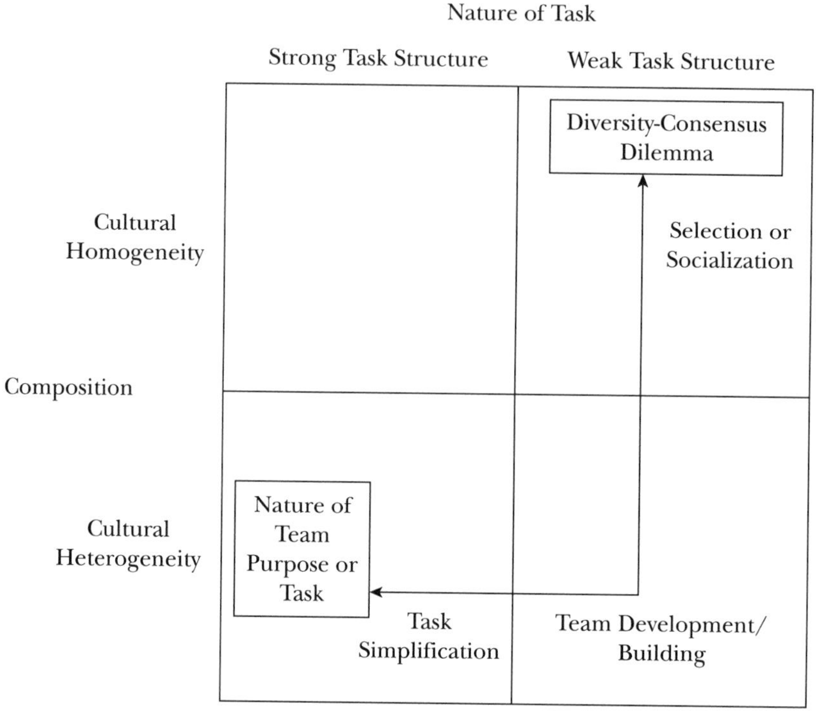

teams' diversity may be as likely to inhibit decision-making quality as to enhance it.

From a prescriptive perspective, it would be desirable to intervene in a way that would enhance the effectiveness of multinational teams. Three sets of interventions are suggested and discussed within the two-dimensional framework of Figure 15.1. Interventions in the first set try to facilitate team process while maintaining team heterogeneity and an unstructured decision task. The second set restructures the task so as to reduce likely disagreements among members. And the third set attempts to influence the cultural values and expectations that the members bring to their teams.

Team Building

The most common approach to addressing a wide range of problems occurring in multinational teams located in the lower-right-hand quadrant of Figure 15.1 has been to engage in organizational development interventions such as team building or team development (Beckhard, 1983; Dyer, 1977). The basic idea behind such interventions is that interpersonal skills, trust, and understanding are necessary if people are to effectively communicate. Through this effective communication and constructive conflict, common purposes can be achieved. Most team-building interventions require a facilitator, or consultant, who (ideally with the full support of top management) gathers data, diagnoses problems, plans an intervention, implements the intervention, and finally, evaluates the intervention (Dyer). Some team-building approaches such as Herman's gestalt orientation (1972) encourage deep and strong interactions wherein participants engage in dramatic and exaggerated behavior until they understand each other's positions.

Sundstrom, DeMeuse, and Futrell (1990) examined the research on team development interventions and found some limited support for their effectiveness, although they point out that unsuccessful interventions are not likely to be published. Besides the lack of convincing empirical support for team-building interventions, there are three problems particular to multicultural teams that may arise in using such interventions. First, interventions acceptable in one culture may not be so in another. Different cultural orientations on masculinity, power distance, uncertainty, and individualism are likely to interact differentially with team-building methods, making it difficult for a single intervention to be equally well received by all team members. Second, although the strategy of team building may have essentially the same goals of increasing communication and constructive conflict, team building relies on the assumption that if team members appreciate each other's differences they will be able to work through these differences. This assumption may be defensible where team members do not recognize major differences in perspectives, for instance, in culturally homogeneous teams. However, in multinational settings, differences in perspectives are likely to be fairly apparent prior to team building. Even when members do learn to appreciate each other's perspectives, the perspectives themselves will of course persist, which could create the impression that little has been learned from the team building. Finally, team development interventions require top-management support and an appropriate corporate culture. Moreover, Wright and Brauchle (1994) point out that these interventions can take three to five years. Such an extended time period may be unacceptable in organizations that need to create effective multinational teams for relatively specific and short-term tasks.

Shifting the Team Toward Homogeneity

Team building as an intervention accepts multinational teams as composed of individuals with dissimilar value systems existing in weak situations. We suggest that other interventions, targeted on reducing process losses associated with team diversity, could attempt to change the team members or situations so as to shift teams from the lower-right-hand cell shown in Figure 15.1. These interventions are familiar human resource management practices applied in a new (multinational team) setting. The choice of any of these proposed alternatives depends on the nature of the team's purpose. This last point will become clearer as these alternatives are presented.

The first intervention would be to shift members of multinational decision-making teams toward homogeneity in beliefs and values (moving the team toward the upper-right-hand block of Figure 15.1). Such a shift would be consistent with helping team members acquire a more common mental model, a team mental model. Although there is much conceptual work to be done before team mental models become useful as a construct in organizational behavior (Klimoski & Mohammed, 1994), many researchers (for example, Bettenhausen, 1991; Bettenhausen & Murnighan, 1985; Cannon-Bowers, Salas, & Converse, 1990) have noted that shared understandings among team members are critical for effective team functioning. Bettenhausen and Murnighan found that members of new groups interpret their surroundings based on norms they hold in other groups in similar situations. When people's national backgrounds mean they have few common experiences, misunderstandings and conflict are likely.

Increased value homogeneity can be accomplished in several ways. Two methods that are used to a greater or lesser extent in nearly all organizations are discussed here: *selection* of team members who are from different cultures but who are similar to each other in values, and *socialization* of team members with the intent of fostering a convergence of values thought to be important to the organization.

Selection as the Homogenizer

Researchers interested in cultural differences have long acknowledged that although there is between-culture (actually, between-nation) variance in values, there is also a great deal of within-culture variance (Triandis, 1989). Because of this within-culture variance, it should be possible to compose a team of people who are heterogeneous in terms of culture or national origin but who share some common values. For instance, Earley (1989, 1994) found mean differences between Chinese and U.S. managers on the individualism versus collectivism dimension, but he also found overlap between distributions of the variable in the two cultures, meaning it may have been possible to compose multinational teams whose members differ less from each other in values on that dimension than one would expect, given the mean differences.

Three caveats are in order, however. First, selection does nothing to help an existing intact decision-making team. Thus selection is not a viable alternative unless the team is starting fresh or there is member turnover. Second, technical knowledge and systems converging across cultures may create the illusion that people have more between-culture similarity than actually exists. Finally, as stated previously, some fundamental cultural differences are more lasting, widespread, and obvious than others. For example, in U.S. organizations individualism traditionally has been a necessary key ingredient for upper-level managers. In collectivist societies, however, the situation is reversed (Earley, 1994). Thus, to compose a team of upper-level managers from individualist and collectivist cultures and do it so those members are neutral in terms of individualism versus collectivism may be extremely difficult. Selection earlier in their careers may have selected out managers with the desired orientation.

Socialization as the Homogenizer

Socialization is a second method of increasing value homogeneity in multinational teams. Through socialization organizational members develop common perspectives that allow them to share interpretations and understandings of their experiences within a given setting so they will operate within the ground rules of that setting (Van Maanen & Schein, 1979). Although not synonymous with making team members' values and beliefs homogeneous, increasing the similarities among members' perspectives should reduce potential misunderstandings among those members.

One popular model of socialization describes three dimensions in which individuals experience socialization (Van Maanen & Schein, 1979). The *functional* dimension encompasses the type of job or tasks an individual performs. The *hierarchical* dimension is the authority structure within the organization. In other words who is responsible for whom. Finally, the *inclusionary* dimension is the "interactional dimension," the extent to which an individual is included as an important or central figure in an organization as opposed to being on the periphery.

In this chapter the inclusionary dimension is the one with which we are most concerned. Multinational team members come to a team with their functional expertise and hierarchical positions to a greater or lesser extent already established. The inclusionary dimension, however, is much more a function of the dynamics of the team itself. "To move along this dimension is to become accepted by others as a central and working member of the particular organizational segment and this can normally not be accomplished unless the member-in-transition demonstrates that he or she too shares the same assumptions as others in the setting as to what is organizationally important and what is not" (Van Maanen & Schein, 1979, p. 222). In a multinational decision-making team where the level to which values, beliefs, or perspectives are shared is likely to be low, without explicit action team members stay on the periphery of the inclusionary dimension.

In order for socialization to be an effective tool for increasing multinational decision-making team effectiveness, however, the issue of what behaviors should be developed as common ones needs to be addressed. Again, there are few guidelines from past work. As a starting point for socialization, Chao, O'Leary-Kelly, Wolf, Klein, and Gardner (1994) suggest six content areas: performance proficiency, people, politics, language, organizational goals and values, and history. We argue next that socialization in each of these different content areas differentially affects the shared understanding of task-specific knowledge among team members and the shared beliefs or values that affect members' ability to influence each other.

Socialization in *performance proficiency* refers simply to learning the specific tasks that compose the job. Socialization in this area focuses on task-specific knowledge. Socialization with respect to *people* refers to establishing successful and satisfying work relationships with others in the team (Chao, O'Leary-Kelly, Wolf, Klein, and Gardner, 1994). Because socialization in this area will affect how well team members accept each other, team members' communication and thus their ability to influence each other should increase. *Political* socialization refers to gaining information about formal and informal work relationships and power structures (Chao et al.). This dimension may be important in gaining influence; however, in teams with only a few members, power structures, both formal and informal, may be obvious. This may lessen people's need for socialization on this dimension.

Language socialization refers to learning task-specific as well as organizationally relevant jargon. We are not as concerned with the task-specific component of jargon as with jargon that meets team members' need to communicate with each other in order to share knowledge and obtain influence. Where different nationalities are concerned, it is expected that language socialization will be particularly critical. Socialization in *goals and values* again focuses on both task-specific and interpersonal influence components. Obviously, organizations have explicit goals concerning task-specific performance outcomes; however, there are also informal goals and values that allow individuals to understand unspoken rules, norms, and informal networks (Chao, O'Leary-Kelly, Wolf, Klein, and

Gardner, 1994). Adherence to these unspoken rules and norms would seem to be important to multinational team members' ability to gain influence. Finally, socialization in *history* is the passing down of stories, myths, and rituals so that the organization can perpetuate its culture. History may be important in helping team members gain influence because it transmits information about what has been considered appropriate and inappropriate behavior in the past. In summary, we are proposing that increasing the use of socialization focused on content dimensions such as people, language, goals and values, and history, will facilitate increased homogeneity in terms of values and beliefs, and through this increased homogeneity, team members should be better able to integrate their unique knowledge and expertise.

A proposal that multicultural teams become more homogeneous may lead to improved team functioning but may also reduce the differences that were the very basis for the teams' formation. Here we are again speaking about the diversity-consensus dilemma, which in essence refers to the fact that teams need both "(i) to solve technical problems involved in their task performances; and (ii) to resolve conflicting viewpoints among members and groups regarding goals, strategies, and plans of action. To do the former (that is, solve technical problems) they need a diversity of personnel with a wide range of talents, information, skills, and knowledge. To do the latter (that is, resolve conflicting viewpoints) they need a set of personnel who are homogeneous in values, beliefs, and cultural styles" (Argote & McGrath, 1993, p. 336). As we described earlier, this dilemma is extremely applicable to multinational teams because one reason for their very existence is to take advantage of their diversity. Yet without some common ground for resolving conflicting viewpoints, the team will not function well. Thus organizations attempting to increase value heterogeneity should be cautious about pushing too far up into the upper-right-hand cell of Figure 15.1. Clearly, there is a trade-off here that cannot be resolved in the abstract but must be recognized and addressed case by case.

Shifting the Task Toward Structure

A second strategy for managing multinational team performance is to change the nature of the team's task. We commented earlier on our assumption that the nature of a decision-making team's task varies on the degree of strength of the task situation. Strong tasks are relatively straightforward in terms of structure, require few assumptions, and have unambiguous performance criteria. Weak ones are unstructured, ambiguous, and complex, and performance criteria are less clear. Strong situations have more standardized interpersonal interaction requirements and typically communicate these to team members. As the strength of the situation increases, so should the shared understanding concerning task requirements. That is, as the situation provides more cues and clearer criteria, it should be easier for people to converge on a common view of the problem.

Often the nature of the task is defined by the problem, and team members may not be able to manipulate it much. Yet even when the problem is complex, it is often possible to subdivide the task and create subtasks with more structure. Therefore even with complex problems we suggest that teams could look for ways to make the task more concrete and thus increase the possibility that diverse team members will come to a more common understanding. A more likely time for shifting a task toward more structure occurs when a primary purpose for establishing the multinational team is political. Here the nature of the task and the complexity of the decision may be less important than the involvement of critical national constituencies on the team. Therefore selecting the team's task so as to increase its clarity may accomplish the political goals while reducing potential intrateam process problems.

A Case Example of Considering Variables in Multinational Teams

In this chapter we have proposed that multicultural teams be considered in a two-dimensional space, one side of which is the level of heterogeneity with respect to culture and the other side the objectivity of the decision task. Superimposed on this framework is Hofstede's four-dimensional space (1980a, 1980b, 1991) in which national cultures have been located. We suggest that with a careful consideration of that task-by-culture space, theory-guided research could address trade-offs between the effects of diversity that facilitate and those that inhibit the ability of multinational teams to reach good decisions. An example of how organizations might use such a framework is offered next. We recognize that this discussion is very speculative. Yet we provide it as an example of how one might use the framework presented to think about the effect of multinationalism on decision-making teams.

Hollenbeck et al. (1995) recently published the description of a theory along with two empirical studies of decision making in teams with leaders and with members who possess different areas of expertise. According to their theory, three core variables mediate the relationship between team member characteristics and team effectiveness. The first mediating variable is *team informity* and refers to the extent to which a team shares information relevant to the task and gets that information to the persons who need it in order to make well-informed decisions. The second mediator is *staff validity,* the quality of the decisions made by individual team members. Finally, *hierarchical sensitivity* is the extent to which team leaders are able to learn which team members make good decisions related to the task and then to weight team member judgments according to their validities. That is, hierarchical sensitivity is the extent to which the leaders pay attention to a team's good decision makers and are not influenced by the ones whose decisions are not very good.

Although this model did not describe multinational team decision making, one could ask how various multinational team members measure up against the core variables of the theory and what might be done to enhance the positive benefits of diverse information while decreasing the impact of diversity on team process. Beginning with informity, it is likely that within-team heterogeneity on power distance and tolerance for uncertainty will affect the ability of team members to generate ideas and share information in ways that foster good decisions. On the one hand organizations could consider responses that structure the decision task so as to reduce resistance to sharing information due to power distance and uncertainty. On the other hand any effort to compose a more homogeneous team would also have to consider the potential reductions in the team's pool of expertise.

Because the second variable, staff validity, looks at individual members' personal ability, it is unlikely to be very much affected by cultural diversity. Thus we would expect that the research that has been done within nationality would generalize to multinational teams with respect to this variable.

Finally, hierarchical sensitivity—the extent to which leaders are able to accurately assess subordinates' performance and weight subordinates' opinions according to quality—is the most interpersonally sensitive of the three variables and the most likely to be affected by team heterogeneity. Culturally derived power distance values are likely to affect leaders as they interact with subordinates and subordinates as they interact with leaders. Subordinates who accept high power distance, for example, may be unwilling to share their informal as well as formal opinions with leaders, making it difficult to judge the quality of their decisions. Individualism is also likely to affect superior-subordinate roles and thus the ability of superiors to get to know subordinates' ability. Cultural differences on masculinity may also affect the frequency and nature of the superior-subordinate interaction. Finally, uncertainty avoidance may influence the willingness and timing with which subordinates disclose their decisions. All these issues would need to be considered, and organizations could react to them by structuring the decision task, carefully selecting team members to minimize conflicting cultural perspectives, socializing all team members, or trying some combination of these three. As will always be the case, the organization will be trading off the benefits of a diverse information and expertise pool against the reduction of anticipated team process tensions.

Conclusion

The number of multinational decision-making teams is on the rise and is likely to continue to increase in the foreseeable future. The rapid increase in multinational corporations, the changing geopolitical conditions, and the technological advances in communications systems that sharply reduce the influence of time and distance on access to information can only increase the demand for teams composed of persons from more than one nation.

We argued that multinational teams are created for one of two sets of functional purposes: political purposes, which were not addressed here, and purposes of creating a more diverse pool of knowledge, skills, values, and experiences that can be brought to bear on the team's task.

Whether teams with the second set of purposes will reap the benefits of their members' diversity of expertise is uncertain, for such teams, by their very nature, confront the diversity-consensus dilemma. That is, the complex problems given to these teams demand diversity in expertise and points of view, yet that same diversity is likely to create difficulties in team process, making it less likely that the team can reach consensus. We have argued here that this dilemma is present from the very beginning, when team members attempt to define the problem and share information, through the point of reaching a decision. The dilemma is inherent in the process of mixing diverse cultures within groups, and it will not go away. We also concur with Triandis (1994) that those working with multinational teams will not be well served by simple descriptions of convenience samples of teams with members from two or more nations. In our opinion advances will be made only when the diversity-consensus dilemma is faced and responses to it are derived from working through a theoretically driven program of research.

Our discussion has focused entirely on the inner processes of the multinational team. That is, we have addressed issues of team composition and team task from the team's perspective and independently of the team's external environment. Obviously, teams rarely exist as independent units. Most are nested within some broader organizational structure and cannot be fully understood outside of that context (Guzzo & Shea, 1992; Hackman, 1989; Ilgen, Major, Hollenbeck, & Sego, 1993; McGrath, 1991). Multinational decision-making teams are no exception. Yet one environmental characteristic is likely more complex for multinational than for other teams. Teams in multinational organizations will operate either within the national boundaries of the dominant member of the business partnership or in a nation outside those boundaries, and where they operate will affect the mix of cultural influences coming from within and without the organization and affecting team interactions. Similarly, the fact that some team members will likely be working and living in the nation that is "home" to them while others will be working and living in a nation that is "foreign" to them cannot help but affect team member behavior. For example, we expect that the relationship between a team leader from Culture A and team members from Culture B will vary depending on whether the team is set in the home nation of the leader or of the team members. We know of no work on multinational teams that is systematically addressing the congruence between team member culture and the culture in which the team is set. This is just one more example of how we must begin to construct theories that get beyond simplistic cultural comparisons and gross generalizations about different nations' cultural characteristics if we want to make serious attempts to understand multinational teams. At present the need for understanding is growing rapidly with the increasing appearance of multinational teams in business and government, but theory and research lag far behind.

References

Aldag, R. J., & Fuller, S. R. (1993). Beyond fiasco: A reappraisal of the groupthink phenomenon and a new model of group decision processes. *Psychological Bulletin, 113,* 533–552.

Argote, L., & McGrath, J. E. (1993). Group processes in organizations: Continuity and change. In C. L. Cooper & I. T. Robertson (Eds.), *International review of industrial and organizational psychology* (pp. 333–389). New York: Wiley.

Bandura, A. (1986). *Social foundations of thought and action: A social cognitive theory.* Upper Saddle River, NJ: Prentice Hall.

Beckhard, R. (1983). Optimizing team building efforts. In W. L. French, C. H. Bell, Jr., & R. A. Zawacki (Eds.), *Organizational development: Theory practice and research* (pp. 182–189). Plano, TX: Business Publications.

Bettenhausen, K. L. (1991). Five years of group research: What we have learned and what needs to be addressed. *Journal of Management, 17,* 345–381.

Bettenhausen, K. L., & Murnighan, J. K. (1985). The emergence of norms in competitive decision-making groups. *Administrative Science Quarterly, 30,* 350–372.

Brehmer, B. (1976). Social judgment theory and the analysis of interpersonal conflict. *Psychological Bulletin, 83,* 985–1003.

Cannon-Bowers, J. A., Salas, E., & Converse, S. A. (1990). Cognitive psychology and team training: Shared mental models in complex systems. *Human Factors Bulletin, 33,* 1–4.

Cattell, R. B. (1949). The dimensions of culture patterns by factorization of national characters. *Journal of Abnormal and Social Psychology, 44,* 443–469.

Cattell, R. B. (1950). The principal culture patterns discoverable in the syntal dimensions of existing nations. *The Journal of Social Psychology, 32,* 215–253.

Cattell, R. B., Breul, H., & Hartman, H. P. (1952). An attempt at a more refined definition of the cultural dimension of syntality in modern nations. *Sociological Review, 17,* 404–421.

Cattell, R. B., & Gorsuch, R. L. (1965). The definition and measurement of national morale and morality. *Journal of Social Psychology, 67,* 77–95.

Cattell, R. B., Graham, R. K., & Wolvier, R. E. (1979). A reassessment of factorial dimensions of modern nations. *The Journal of Social Psychology, 108,* 241–258.

Chao, G. T., O'Leary-Kelly, A. M., Wolf, S., Klein, H. J., & Gardner, P. B. (1994). Organizational socialization: Its content and consequences. *Journal of Applied Psychology, 79,* 730–743.

Cosier, R. A., & Rose, G. L. (1977). Cognitive conflict and goal conflict effects on task performance. *Organizational Behavior and Human Decision Performance, 19,* 378–391.

Cox, T. H. (1994). *Cultural diversity in organizations.* San Francisco: Berrett-Koehler.

Dwyer, P., Engardio, P., Schiller, S., & Reed, S. (1994, November 18). The new model: Tearing up today's organization chart. *Business Week,* pp. 80–90.

Dyer, W. G. (1977). *Team building: Issues and alternatives.* Reading, MA: Addison-Wesley.

Eagly, A. H. (1987). Reporting sex differences. *American Psychologist, 42,* 755–756.

Earley, P. C. (1989). Social loafing and collectivism: A comparison of the United States and the People's Republic of China. *Administration Science Quarterly, 34,* 565–581.

Earley, P. C. (1994). Self or group? Cultural effects of training on self-efficacy and performance. *Administrative Science Quarterly, 39,* 89–117.

Gersick, C.J.G. (1988). Time and transition in work teams: Toward a new model of group development. *Academy of Management Journal, 31,* 9–41.

Guzzo, R. A., & Shea, G. P. (1992). Group performance and intergroup relations in organizations. In M. D. Dunnette & L. M. Hough (Eds.), *Handbook of industrial and organizational psychology* (2nd ed., Vol. 3, pp. 269–313). Palo Alto, CA: Consulting Psychologists Press.

Hackman, J. R. (Ed.). (1989). *Groups that work (and those that don't): Creating conditions for effective teamwork.* San Francisco: Jossey-Bass.

Herman, S. M. (1972). A gestalt orientation to organizational development. In W. W. Burke (Ed.), *Contemporary organizational development: Conceptual orientations and interventions* (pp. 69–89). Arlington, VA: National Training Laboratories Institute.

Hoffman, L. R., & Maier, N.R.F. (1961). Quality and acceptance of problem solutions by members of homogeneous and heterogeneous groups. *Journal of Abnormal and Social Psychology, 62,* 401–407.

Hofstede, G. (1980a). *Culture's consequences: International differences in work-related values.* Thousand Oaks, CA: Sage.

Hofstede, G. (1980b). Motivation, leadership and organization: Do American theories apply abroad? *Organizational Dynamics,* pp. 42–63.

Hofstede, G. (1991). *Cultures and organizations. Software of the Mind.* London: McGraw-Hill.

Hollenbeck, J. R., Ilgen, D. R., Sego, D. J., Hedlund, J., Major, D. A., & Phillips, J. (1995). Multilevel theory of team decision making: Decision performance in teams incorporating distributed expertise. *Journal of Applied Psychology, 80,* 292–316.

Humes, S. (1993). *Managing the multinational: Confronting the global-local dilemma.* Upper Saddle River, NJ: Prentice Hall.

Ilgen, D. R., Major, D. A., Hollenbeck, J. R., & Sego, D. J. (1993). Team research in the 1990s. In M. M. Chemers & R. Ayman (Eds.), *Leadership theory and research* (pp. 245–270). Orlando: Academic Press.

Jackson, S. E. (1992). Team composition in organizational settings: Issues in managing a diverse workforce. In S. Worchel, W. Wood, & J. Simpson (Eds.), *Group process and productivity* (pp. 138–173). Thousand Oaks, CA: Sage.

Jackson, S. E., May, K. E., & Whitney, K. (1995). Understanding the dynamics of diversity in decision-making teams. In R. A. Guzzo, E. Salas, & Associates, *Team effectiveness and decision making in organizations* (pp. 204–261). San Francisco: Jossey-Bass.

Janis, I. L. (1972). *Victims of groupthink: A psychological study of foreign policy decisions and fiascos.* Boston: Houghton Mifflin.

Janis, I. L. (1982). *Groupthink: Psychological studies of policy decisions and fiascos.* Boston: Houghton Mifflin.

Janis, I. L., & Mann, L. (1977). *Decision making: A psychological analysis of conflict, choice and commitment.* New York: Free Press.

Katz, D., & Kahn, R. L. (1978). *The social psychology of organizations* (2nd ed.). New York: Wiley.

Klimoski, R. J., & Mohammed, S. (1994). Team mental model: Construct or metaphor. *Journal of Management, 20,* 403–437.

Larson, J. R., Jr., & Christensen, C. (1993). Groups as problem solving units: Towards a new meaning of social cognition. *British Journal of Social Psychology, 32,* 5–30.

Laughlin, P. R. (1980). Social combination processes of cooperative problem-solving groups on verbal intellective tasks. In M. Fishbein (Ed.), *Progress in social psychology* (Vol. 1). Hillsdale, NJ: Erlbaum.

Levine, J. M., & Moreland, R. L. (1990). Progress in small group research. *Annual Review of Psychology, 41,* 585–634.

Maznevski, M. L. (1994). Understanding our differences: Performance in decision making groups with diverse members. *Human Relations, 47,* 531–552.

McGrath, J. E. (1991). Time, interaction, and performance (TIP): A theory of groups. *Small Group Research, 22,* 147–174.

Meier, N.R.F. (1970). Male vs. female discussion leaders. *Personnel Psychology, 23,* 455–461.

Mischel, W. (1977). On the future of personality measurement. *American Psychologist, 32,* 246–254.

Morgan, B. B., Glickman, A. S., Woodward, E. A., Blaiwes, A. S., & Salas, E. (1986). *Measurement of team behaviors in a Navy environment* (Technical report NTSC TR-86–014). Orlando: Naval Training Systems Center.

Newall, A., & Simon, H. S. (1972). *Human problem solving.* Upper Saddle River, NJ: Prentice Hall.

Orasanu, J. (1990). *Shared mental models and crew performance.* Paper presented at the annual meeting of the Human Factors Society, Orlando.

Orasanu, J., & Salas, E. (1993). Team decision making in complex environments. In G. Klein, J. Orasanu, R. Calderwood, & C. E. Zsambok (Eds.), *Decision making in action: Models and methods* (pp. 327–346). Norwood, NJ: Ablex.

Rummel, R. H. (1972). *The dimensions of nations.* Thousand Oaks, CA: Sage.

Stasser, G., & Stewart, D. (1992). Discovery of hidden profiles by decision making groups: Solving a problem versus making a judgment. *Journal of Personality and Social Psychology, 63,* 426–434.

Stasser, G., Taylor, L. A., & Hanna, C. (1989). Information sampling in structured discussions of three- and six-person groups. *Journal of Personality and Social Psychology, 57,* 67–78.

Stasser, G., & Titus, W. (1985). Polling of unshared information in group decision making: Biased information sampling during discussion. *Journal of Personality and Social Psychology, 48,* 1467–1478.

Stasser, G., & Titus, W. (1987). Effects of information load and percentage of shared information on the dissemination of unshared information during group discussion. *Journal of Personality and Social Psychology, 53,* 81–93.

Steiner, I. D. (1972). *Group process and productivity.* Orlando: Academic Press.

Sundstrom, E., DeMeuse, K. P., & Futrell, D. (1990). Work teams: Applications and effectiveness. *American Psychologist, 45,* 120–133.

Taylor, R. N. (1992). Strategic decision making. In M. D. Dunnette & L. M. Hough (Eds.), *Handbook of industrial and organizational psychology* (2nd ed., Vol. 3, pp. 961–1007). Palo Alto, CA: Consulting Psychologists Press.

Triandis, H. C. (1989). The self and social behavior in differing contexts. *Psychological Review, 96,* 506–520.

Triandis, H. C. (1990). Cross-cultural studies of individualism and collectivism. In J. Berman (Ed.), *Nebraska Symposium on Motivation: 1989* (pp. 41–133). Lincoln: University of Nebraska Press.

Triandis, H. C. (1992). Cross-cultural research in social psychology. In D. Granberg & G. Sarup (Eds.), *Social judgment and intergroup relations: Essays in honor of Muzafer Seriff* (pp. 229–244). New York: Springer.

Triandis, H. C. (1994). Cross-cultural industrial and organizational psychology. In H. C. Triandis, M. D. Dunnette, & L. M. Hough (Eds.), *Handbook of industrial and organizational psychology* (2nd ed., Vol. 4, pp. 103–172). Palo Alto, CA: Consulting Psychologists Press.

Triandis, H. C., Hall, E. R., & Ewen, R. B. (1965). Member heterogeneity and dyadic creativity. *Human Relations, 18,* 33–55.

Triandis, H. C., Leung, K., Villareal, M., & Clack, F. (1985). Allocentric vs. idiocentric tendencies: Convergent and discriminant validation. *Journal of Research in Personality, 19,* 395–415.

Van Maanen, J., & Schein, E. H. (1979). Toward a theory of organizational socialization. *Research in Organizational Behavior, 1,* 209–264.

Wagner, J. A., III. (1995). Studies of individualism-collectivism: Effects on cooperation in groups. *Academy of Management Journal, 38,* 152–172.

Wagner, J. A., III, & Moch, M. K. (1986). Individualism-collectivism: Concept and measurement. *Group and Organization Studies, 11,* 280–304.

Weiss, H. M., & Adler, S. (1984). Personality and organizational behavior. In L. L. Cummings & B. M. Staw (Eds.), *Research in organizational behavior* (Vol. 6, pp. 1–50). Greenwich, CT: JAI Press.

Wolvier, R. E., & Cattell, R. B. (1981). Reoccurring national patterns for 30 years of multivariate cross-cultural studies. *International Journal of Psychology, 16,* 171–198.

Wright, D. W., & Brauchle, P. E. (1994, September). Teaming up for quality. *Training and Development,* pp. 67–73.

Ziller, R. C. (1973). *The social self.* New York: Pergamon Press.

CHAPTER 16

Those Things Yonder Are No Giants, but Decision Makers in International Teams

José M. Prieto
Rosario Martinez Arias

> *Pray look better, Sir, . . . those things yonder are no giants,*
> *but windmills.*
> MIGUEL DE CERVANTES, *DON QUIXOTE*, (1605)
> (SANCHO PANZA SPEAKING TO DON QUIXOTE)

The main focus of this chapter is not giants, but decision makers in teams whose members come from different countries and different cultural backgrounds and who have both national and cosmopolitan customs and manners.

People, organizations, and cultures look at windmills but see giants (that is, look at reality but see illusions) after they have made an investment in one or several propositions. Like any other moving bodies, individuals, organizations, and cultures follow the path of least resistance. For instance, Barbara Tuchman (1982, p. 171) observed that "in April 1917 the illusion of isolation was destroyed, America came to the end of innocence, and of the exuberant freedom of bachelor independence. That the responsibilities of world power have not made us happier is no surprise. To help ourselves manage them, we have replaced the illusion of *isolation* with a new illusion of *omnipotence.*" The consequence of this particular illusion has been that, little by little, many U.S. agencies, firms, and citizens started to feel quite at home in the international arena during the twentieth century. These organizations' executive committees and boards have a background of only eight decades of experience in the role of decision makers in international affairs! Few people in other parts of the world take this fact into account. The United States became international during the years of World War I! Until 1917, the U.S. motto was "Thus far shalt thou go and no further." The Monroe Doctrine, enunciated in 1823, stated a nationalistic determination to remain aloof from non-American conflicts. The U.S. area of interest and influence was solely "the American continents."

Windmills are facts, not perceptual errors in themselves; but judgments about facts can be highly erroneous. Today, countries are becoming set in their ways and set in their judgments, slowly embalming themselves beneath the wrappings of their geographical borders. However, the geographical frontiers of many nation states have not remained frozen during the last century. For instance, during the 1920s, 1940s, and 1990s, several new borders have emerged out of the shadows in Eastern Europe as a consequence of the decline of three subsequent empires. The cognitive map behind the idea of "my country" was changed abruptly by decisions made by winners somewhere else. For many people, frontiers have been just giants.

It is common for people to judge that a firm is American because the founding stockholder was born in the United States or Spanish because the headquarters are in Spain and so on. In contrast, people do not consider the distribution of nationalities at the shareholders' meeting or on the board of trustees or directors the basic criterion by which to fix the nationality of an multinational company. And it is considered surrealistic to attribute a given nationality to stock-market quotations, exchange turnovers, inflows and outflows, runs on a currency, and so on. They are part of a global and digital economy.

Quite often the nationalities of the principal shareholder and the chief executive officer (CEO) in an international firm do not coincide. Those nationalities are of no importance when determining the nationality of that firm, although is of vital importance to keep track of the quality and the consequences of the decisions these individuals make. These decisions do not need or show a passport, but they influence many lives and regions across borders. However, in many countries and regions, natives continue to believe that it is sound to judge the quality of a decision by the hometown of the decision maker, because the accent of non-native decision makers remains in their minds and in their hearts as in their speech. Apparently, decision makers bear vernacular beliefs as windmills bear sails!

Two Belief Systems: Nationalist and Cosmopolitan

The history of Europe shows periodic pendulum swings from an all-embracing cosmopolitan view of events and leaders to a rather restrictive nationalist view (Duroselle, 1990). For instance, the Mycenaean civilization, the period of the Phoenician traders, the civilization of imperial Rome, the Byzantine empire, the period of nomadic invaders, the expansion of Christianity, the period of Gothic cathedrals, the Renaissance, and the Enlightenment are landmarks emphasizing universal and munificent standpoints. The place of birth of leading figures and decision makers was considered irrelevant. Great masters, savants, and artists, born here and there, congregated around the pavilions of Caesars and rulers, periodically straying away from one cultural or political center to move on to another.

At other periods during the last millennium, however, a person's place of birth became the main guarantee of his suitability for leading positions in many countries (Fernández-Armesto, 1995). During these periods, the homeland gained importance and was emphasized by leaders who stirred up national pride: "Men are free when they are in a living homeland" (Lawrence, 1923, p. 6) Masters, savants, or artists received public recognition only when they were autochthonous and only from fellow countrymen or -women. A unitarian relationship between the territory and the identity of citizens or subjects was regarded as singular and sacred. Biological and psychological attributes were attached to people of the nation through pointing out developmental profiles in the analysis of past and present historical events. National boundaries were revered; some would say that the idea of nation was worshiped.

In certain countries the assumption of some common ancestors supports the idea of a national identity (for instance, among Japanese Shintoists). In some nations, people showing evidence of pertinent genealogical relationships through the father (for instance, in the Roman tradition) or through the mother (for instance, in the Jewish tradition) have the right to be accepted as full members of the nation and to obtain the appropriate citizenship or passport when they decide to migrate. However, the analysis of blood groups and genetic markers or diseases among characteristic families shows that genetic distance is larger than idiosyncratic distance (Ramon, Picornell, & Castro, 1995). The idea of a biological and common stock underlying a nation is a product of value judgments about mythical figures and not of judgments from proven facts about the track of DNA profiles. The analysis of the genetic variations in different chromosomes or the follow-up of hereditary diseases shows that more base pairs bands and more diseases match with those found among families living for centuries in the immediate neighborhood than with those laid down among families considering themselves members of a given ethnic group but residing for centuries in quite distant geographical areas.

Views on the nationalist-cosmopolitan dimension are based on a more or less organized set of beliefs that affects daily behavior, interpersonal relationships, and attitudes toward life (de Ventós, 1994). Jastrow (1935) took the lead showing that the mind is a belief-seeking rather than a fact-seeking apparatus. And when there are many different ideological layers arguing against each other, empirical, scientific, or technological findings are used only as assault weapons or are swept away as soon as they spring into existence.

Table 16.1 summarizes the set of descriptive opinions, informed guesses, and convictions many persons use when interfacing with their political environment. Again, the nationalist and the cosmopolitan profiles are highlighted. Each set shapes a belief system that specifies what takes precedence over every other consideration. Each set spotlights shared images that summarize "decision maker's knowledge about what must be accomplished and why, about how it is to be done, and about the results of efforts to do it" (Beach, 1990, p. 6). Thus each column in Table 16.1 points to the normative beliefs and value images held by individuals about what they

Table 16.1. Nationalist Versus Cosmopolitan Profiles and Belief Systems.

Critical Aspects	Nationalist Profile	Cosmopolitan Profile
What is the basic structured reality?	The world is built and structured by nations.	The world may survive better without nations.
What is the suitable cultural background?	Each nation has cultural and language features specific to that geographical territory.	Cultural and physical features breach national or regional borders.
Where do you belong?	A nationality is essential for every human being.	Nationality is a circumstance in a person's lifestyle.
What is your nationality?	I am a citizen of a state.	I am a citizen of an age.
Do you have any means of identification?	Each person is identified by a national identity card.	Each person is identified by a name and a biography.
Are you ready to fight for . . . ?	Solidarity with the country's interests.	Solidarity with mankind and the ecosystem.
What is a safe place?	The homeland.	Here and everywhere.
Show me your personal preferences?	Homegrown products are the best.	I am always open to suggestions.
Power emerges from . . . ?	The nation.	The common people.
Do you know your rights?	Constitutional rights.	Human rights.
Above all, loyalty to . . . ?	The national cause.	A humanitarian cause.

consider natural, what they view as essential in their cultural background, where they belong with affection and pride, their sense of identity, their gestures of solidarity, what surroundings constitute a safe bet, their personal tastes and preferences, the source of power, the basis of their civil and social rights, and the premise of their loyalties and duties.

People who find the nationality of leading figures or decision makers highly meaningful consider the nation as the basic unit of analysis; it is the nation that is seen to structure and introduce rationality in a geographical space. The nation backs up an essential framework that sanctions an understanding that past and contemporary events in the history of its inhabitants have naturally catapulted it to prominence and prestige among affluent societies. The native language is contemplated as a unique and genuine homegrown product of the national spirit. Nationality is an imperative that introduces and identifies a person; each citizen has the nationality of a given state, and persons with a double nationality cannot be trusted. Solidarity starts at home because in cases of extreme difficulties compatriots pluck up their courage and keep going. People are proud to introduce measures to encourage national craftsmanship, products, and services; every right-thinking person favors provisions calling for protectionism. The people who live in a nation are often themselves referred to as the nation, and as the nation they are the main source of power for leaders and decision makers in that territory. Constitutional rights are the fundamental principles on which the recognition of individual dignity is based. All members of a nation must put their shoulders to the wheel, and their conviction is no laughing matter.

People who have a cosmopolitan view consider the world to be the molar unit of analysis, a unit that survives in spite of the existence of nations, which always show an ephemeral profile in any given geographical space. Past events are only historical antecedents, and contemporary dwellers must proceed with great caution because they all have vested interests. There is always a lingua franca that influences and shapes real communication; the native language is merely an evolutionary and temporal by-product of a melting pot of dead and living languages and cultures. Nationality is a situational nuance in a biography; a person is a citizen of his or her age and time. Passports can be changed as a consequence of personal circumstances and dilemmas. In decisive moments and events each individual depends on the kindness or rudeness of acquaintances and strangers. It makes sense to make room for persons, products, and services from all around the world; humankind's progress cannot be understood apart from the history of migrations and the exchange of ideas, services, and goods. Nothing human is strange for right-minded persons who feel protective towards the needy. The Universal Declaration of Human Rights reasserts and supports the notion of personal dignity and worth. The consequence is that national borders must remain open for migrant workers looking for a place to live and a way to increase the quality of their lives. Humanitarian causes are worthwhile for leaders and decision makers.

It is clear that different *cognitive* processes (including perception, learning, and thinking) and *conative* processes (including drives, desires, instincts, and motives) are involved in both sets of belief systems and shared images. Followers of each set of beliefs evaluate the consequences of each set positively or negatively as faits accomplis that cannot be reviewed. Behavioral patterns observed among pacesetters (in a country or organization) are emulated, becoming a referent to strive for. Followers endeavor to obey guidelines advanced by dominating rulers insofar as they are viewed as referents to imitate. Both nationalist and cosmopolitan leaders fix the standard in the subjective norm accepted by followers as a reliable information basis. Each set of beliefs sustains a specific set of intentions and actions (Fishbein & Azjen, 1975).

Societies and institutions throughout history have had a profound embarrassment and ambivalence about the disruptive effects of pendulum swings between the national and cosmopolitan sets of belief systems (Unzueta, 1988). There is great upheaval and struggle when, for instance, a cosmopolitan view leads to a new distribution of power and wealth that undermines the wealth and power of an existing nationalist elite. Upheaval and struggle also occur in the reverse situation. Of course few of the partisans in such confrontations stop to acknowledge that what constitutes beneficial or detrimental is entirely in the mind of the beholder. The choice is between courses that are convenient or inadequate according to official sources.

Examples of Nations and Rulers

We offer two cases here from European and Mediterranean history that illustrate, first, the cosmopolitan view and, second, the nationalist view among leaders. Both types of leader have been promoters and protectors of a system of values and goals.

The Cosmopolitan View in History

The Roman, Christian, and Arab empires were led by rulers who cherished a new and enlightened "world brotherhood of all men." Public knowledge of their place of birth was considered inappropriate; it was information that necessarily belonged to a misty part of the past. Many of them adopted manners, languages, and cults originating in other areas to bring the rulers closer together. At the individual level, the case of Charles V is a striking example. In many textbooks he is mentioned as a famous Spanish monarch. In fact he was born and brought up in Ghent under the tutelage of his aunt, Princess Margaret. His mother tongue was the local vernacular: Dutch. He had a good command of German and Latin. He went to Spain in 1517 and learned Spanish when he was a young adult. As Holy Roman Emperor Charles V, he ruled the Habsburgs' domains and overseas empire with the assistance and support of a large number of noblemen, commanders, cardinals, gentlemen, and scholars from Austria, Germany, Italy, the Netherlands, and Spain. He was rather enthusiastic about his international entourage of experts, artists, and great savants. Many of them worked together to solve complex problems and produce think-tank reports at the court. Only after his mother's death in 1555 did he become Charles I of Spain, that is, King of Castile and Aragon.[1] He died one year later as an aged and decrepit man. He was fifty-five years old. His cosmopolitan view illuminated his projects, and he used decentralized organizational systems. Regularly, national leaders from Italy, the Netherlands, and Spain confronted him and his entourage, making it clear that commitment and loyalty to regional interests should constitute their priorities in actions, plans, and decisions enacted in the court. Charles V used to react by making it clear that in the light of history, progress has resulted from monarchs who took unpopular positions, adjusting decisions to new facts and challenges (Fernández-Alvarez, 1995; Hendricks, 1976). That is, the mind of a monarch cannot go blank in the decision-making process when dealing with unpopular measures. Quite often, however, the mind of a person-oriented leader goes blank in similar circumstances.

The Nationalist View in History

In contrast a number of charismatic leaders (such as Bismarck, de Gaulle, Franco, Gadhafi, Garibaldi, Khomeini, and Stalin) have had enormous influence on their countries and have accentuated nationalist policies to gain more power and longer continuance. Each showed and favored strong feelings of pride and loyalty for his nation. Each was surrounded and assisted in decision-making processes exclusively by persons born in that country. The consequence has been a lack of awareness of the rich variety of regional cultures and languages. Another consequence has been permanent and direct confrontation with plans and actions launched by international organizations that stress that societal problems and dilemmas are the same throughout the world (with minor nuances in each community) and require universal and coordinated plans, actions, and efforts (Hobsbawm, 1995).

Examples of Organizations

Nationalist and cosmopolitan schemata are also present in contemporary organizations, influencing organizational members' thinking when they must figure out who their best representatives will be on a committee or task force. Here are two domain-specific examples.

The International (Cosmopolitan) Organization

For centuries the Jesuits have been well organized and established throughout the world. Probably this is one of the oldest private societies still surviving even though it has been under continual attack (Bertrand, 1985; Martin, 1987). The homelands of this organization's leaders and decision makers have been considered irrelevant to making a success of strategic projects and actions. Rarely do the Jesuits identify themselves (and rarely are they identified by others) as members of an international organization, though that is what they are, operating on home ground in many different surroundings, fitting into the society where they find themselves. What does this mean? They are invited to distance themselves from their hometown. Many of them also get used to doing without their native language in daily affairs. They learn and use fluently the language and the culture of the region where they stay and develop a project. Few persons know where this society was first established, the nationality of its founder or of the present CEO, the site of its headquarters, and so on. Other well-known organizations following quite similar schemes are the Red Cross, Greenpeace, and Doctors Without Frontiers, present in almost every country, whose projects and plans obtain the financial support of many people. Their leading figures and decision makers come from different nations, but their contributions and representativeness are not highlighted or filtered by their nationality. The decision-making teams that lead each of these organizations have a cosmopolitan background.

The Multinational (Nationalist) Organization

In contrast, many contemporary corporations identify themselves (and are currently identified by others) as *multinational.* The composition of a multinational's executive committee is usually predictable: the nationality of the large majority of top officers and managers coincides with the country where the company was first established. There is also a correspondence between nationalities in a minority among decision makers and the countries where the company maintains branch offices or factories. Quite often the official language of the corporation is the native language of the founder or of the CEO. When the CEO chairs public events taking place in branch offices, he or she addresses the audience using the official language in the headquarters, not the vernacular language of the audience. The prevalent culture in the corporation is a consistent development of the dominant customs and conventions in the primeval firm. These corporations accept local cultures or regional languages merely as a part of marketing or industrial relations strategy. Managers appointed to foreign branches rarely learn to speak fluently the language of the people with whom they will work and rarely feel on home ground within the community where they take up residence. This is typically the case when the decision-making teams that lead a company have a nationalist background.

More Multinational-International Differences

Insofar as the idea of multinationality is present in the distinguishing marks of a corporation, that organization will show signs of a nationalist view in the way things are understood and organized. In fact multinational seems to mean that the organization is a network of national branches. In the cosmopolitan view, however, what matters is that decisions are backed by an international floor of shareholders and that projects and actions rely on the expertise of leaders and decision makers recruited in many countries. In this way an organization becomes an *internationally* based organization, open and accommodating to the diversity of languages and cultures of each branch where business is done and cultivated.

A critical aspect here is that primary and high school educational systems established throughout the world favor mainly nationalist approaches and views. It is enough to look at textbooks and newspapers to confirm this emphasis on national interests and priorities. However, scholars and researchers—university graduates—are educated in a very subtle way to consider that their reference group is the international community of scientists and technologists. Yet a large majority of their jobs and research projects are sponsored by national funds, institutes, and agencies. During the initial phases of an academic career, the campus becomes the scholar's hometown, and national journals and publications constitute the scholar's setting, which fosters a rather nationalistic or local view. As the scholar becomes more successful, his or her personal prestige may grow stronger with publication in international journals, leading to invitations to lecture abroad and recognition through foreign awards. Success brings with it a more uncompromising, tougher, more cosmopolitan view.

To sum up, international teams address an old dilemma, insights and prejudices are made of the same stuff. Both the presence and absence of a framework interpret the idea of representativeness, the determination of the "right" member to be appointed to a team. Multinational views pay attention to persons standing or acting on behalf of national groups and interests during the decision-making process. Cosmopolitan (international) views introduce a deconstructive framing in an attempt to eliminate any notion of indigenous essence within national boundaries: claimed fixed identities break out of their boundaries during the decision-making process.

National Culture Versus Occupational Mentalities

In their daily language, speakers of English use the term *mentality*, which is rather absent in psychosocial research based on behaviorism. Mentality has to do with the set of one's mind, one's rather stable mental attitude about an aspect of one's life and one's personal prospects in it. Mentalities differ in many ways because the intended end points of human actions differ. Mentalities vary not only across the population, but a single person can switch tactically to different mentalities in order to deal successfully with different interlocutors or circumstances in his or her life. It is possible to distinguish between individual and collective mentalities, but there is an important overlap between the concept of *mentality* and the concept of *culture*.

Both occupational mentalities and regional cultures suggest a particular form of civilization; they suggest an agenda of goals, and the temporal aspects of that agenda then decide subsequent choices. Both mentalities and cultures have to do with the idea of quality in a society, with concern for what is regarded as excellent in a certain period or stage in the development of a community. Both point to the degree of improvement of the mind achieved by education or training. Both allude to the set of behaviors and beliefs characteristic of particular social, ethnic, or age groups. Both call upon the sum total of lifestyles and wishful thinking built up by a group of human beings and transmitted from one generation to another. Mentalities and cultures are the product of growth resulting from a more or less controlled and defined medium.

For a period of five years the first author of this chapter carried out a qualitative analysis in the Spanish banking sector.[2] A minimum of four branch offices were visited every month to analyze the kind of relationships maintained by their managers and directors when dealing with clients and personnel, when reporting to headquarters, and when dealing with local authorities and civil servants. These issues were approached in the context of a protocol on job analysis and work performance of middle managers and their subordinates when dealing with bank customers. The total number of branches visited was 130, and in each office a minimum of three persons were interviewed, using semistructured scripts.

The purpose of this qualitative analysis was to find out and then follow up on the strategic images and frameworks used by successful managers when dealing with delicate matters related to complaints or requests submitted by permanent employees and distinguished customers. Another focus of analysis in each interview with branch office managers and senior subordinates was to identify problem-solving strategies used by the decision-making committees that met every week. From the very beginning, diversity antecedents and causal patterns were on the agenda. Initially, regional stereotypes were considered for producing a coherent classification system, but the outcome was a mess. In the second phase the classification focus changed to the type of industrial and productive activity characteristic of the region or the city where the branch office was established. The analysis identified a minimum of six mentalities (outlined in Table 16.2); the seventh mentality (wiring) has been reviewed and added for this chapter.

In each region served by the bank one or two occupational profiles prevailed. Branch managers (middle managers) and senior subordinates were invited to share their cherished memories about adequate procedures to follow when deciding who was a reliable bank customer. In addition, examples of their behavioral patterns were observed during a normal meeting of the decision-making committees. (The psychologist was present as an observer from the human resource department.) Two sets of findings are underlined here: critical aspects branch managers and senior subordinates considered when studying the origin of a customer's income and critical aspects they considered when closing a deal.

Farming

In regions where farming was the main activity, it was clear that documents supplied by the notary public office and the mortgage registry and also registered cattle pedigrees were quite important in the decision-making process. Entrepreneurs or clients were important when their plots of land, animals, and farming implements

Table 16.2. Mentalities Identified by Analyzing Frames of Reference That Middle Managers in Branch Offices of Spanish Banks Use When Making Decisions.

Kind of Mentality	You Are Rich If . . .	What Is Important as an Output in Decision Making Is . . .
Farming	Pieces of land and animals are registered in your name.	Written agreements and statements
Fishing	Nobody knows where your shoal of fish is.	A touch of secrecy and discretion
Mining	The firedamp does not play a dirty trick on someone.	Social cohesion and solidarity
Trading	Merchandise turnover is the norm, not the exception.	Oral agreements and open-and-shut sales
Worshiping	The gods or destiny give you a good day.	To push one's luck
Lobbying	You know in advance confidential and reliable information.	Access to classified material
Wiring	You reach or forward bits that are just a click away.	Instant transportation to the on-line world

were registered. In negotiations written statements were considered the critical piece of evidence for future reference. Quite often several versions were written and revised by each party to fix an agreement. In a similar manner written instructions and guidelines circulated among employees and were considered internal bylaws. The decision-making process existed during the writing of the statements and ended as soon as the final commitment or a formal covenant was written.

Sea Fishing

In regions where sea fishing was the main activity, it was clear that skippers and crews followed measures to ensure that nobody in the village learned where they located shoals of fish. Conventionally they considered it tactically wise for ships to sail a course that changed at night to shake off neighboring competitors. Secrecy and discretion were the norm in the conversation. Thus the middle managers accepted as valid implicit and very vague explanations about the origin of sea fishers incomes. Crews explained very vaguely standard labor rates, compensation for injuries at work, labor troubles, voluntary redundancies, and layoffs. It was very difficult to reconstruct the decision-making process from the minutes of the meeting and the comments made by participants. Subtle and quick nuances predominate in the conversation.

Mining

In regions where mining was the main activity, people feared the perils of digging and tunneling; mining is a chancy business. In the past many men were buried when there was an accident at the mine, and miners and colliers have learned various measures and rules intended to prevent accidents at the workings. In their daily lives they considered themselves fortunate as long as everything remained under control in the colliery or they escaped unharmed in the case of a mishap. Social cohesion and solidarity (showing support for each other at delicate moments) were considered essential strategies for success, as were preventive actions to stop damage and loss of life. The consequence was that during the decision-making process the middle managers had to gauge the sense of common purpose and social attachment among groups of miners applying, for instance, for a credit or for a delay in a deadline. Quite often the groups of miners endorsed each other. This reduced the room for maneuver of miners employed in small mines where an individualist climate prevailed. More guarantees were requested from these latter customers as soon as it was clear that they were used to doing things by themselves and in their own way.

Trading

In regions where trading is the prevailing occupation, people were used to negotiating directly with any of the parties involved in a potential agreement and to shake hands on the bargain. Good profits were to be made if traders showed a daily replacement of shop-soiled goods. A merchant took a loss each day a product remained in the stockroom. It was a strategic mistake to keep a large supply on the shelves because that inventory had to be paid for. Products that were purchased, that were in the shop window during the day but somewhere else by night, were the main source of income. The consequence was that oral agreements and a horse-trading style were enough for handling daily affairs. Verbal contracts and agreements were accepted and considered essential ingredients in the decision-making process between parties. Merchants were always open to reach an agreement on specific issues and to sit down at the negotiating table if there were sufficient grounds for it.

Worshiping

In regions where worshiping maintained a climate of reverence it was common sense to stress that destiny sends us heralds, and as a consequence, the course of business must remain under the influence of a large series of superstitious and ceremonious prescriptions. That is, fatalism. A provident deity, ineffable forces, or bad omens were considered the masters of the destiny of business affairs. Decision makers were invited to use rituals, astrology, or the reading of palms to guide them in the right direction. A wrong decision was viewed as a settlement with a jinx on it. Success and fortune were the outcome of decision makers' ability to push their luck in the right place and at the right moment. Decision making and destiny were subtly interconnected. It was considered irreverent and risky to make decisions without consulting the fortune tellers. The middle managers did not trust anyone regarding good luck as another name for tenacity of purpose.

Lobbying

Cities where the court or capital of a country has been established for centuries have long traditions of people getting things done through knowing and influencing courtiers and favorites; it is critical to know twenty-four hours in advance delicate matters to be made public just the next day. Similarly in this study, in areas where lobbying of some kind was important, bank middle managers considered as a source of success in business affairs to be information-gathering strategies developed and maintained by decision makers who were aware in advance of plans and projects sponsored or supported by resource allocators. The purpose of these strategies was to monitor ephemeral but reliable news that arrived in oral form and just in time by virtue of personal contacts. Decisions emerged as a series of small actions and speculations sequenced over time after learning classified information about hidden moves before they were implemented in the market. An agile decision maker also seemed to be considered a skillful wizard who knew how to deal with wealthy or powerful lobbies to prevent, promote, or advance legislative changes.

Wiring

There is a new region on the contemporary scene, where almost everything is digital (Negroponte, 1995). This region has been formed by bringing many computers and networks together to create an ultimate information resource, a computerized communications network that enables, for instance, both electronic mail exchange and on-line group discussion among decision makers. We find that this new region, like the others described here, has its own occupational mentality. The criteria for success established by this new occupational mentality emerging from the domain of information technologies and highways are knowledge of how to reach the right sites or find the right information on the net and the ability to let others know the kinds of information and databases available at a given net address. Using their desktop computers as high-speed links to places where useful information is available, wired decision makers are ready to map out a broad repertoire of multiple modes of representation, gaining further control over daily problems by rapidly producing and exchanging relevant questions and knowledge. Wired people know that geographical distance no longer matters for countries, cities, and organizations belonging to the same telecommunication network; a click of the mouse is all that lies in between points in cyberspace. Decision makers interconnected on the net know that in this surrounding they can conduct business, follow the stock market, collaborate with distant interlocutors, open new markets, and make new contacts. In this new occupational mentality, information bits are riches and rapid action is an important output.

Occupational Mentalities Are Not Nationalist Mentalities

None of the mentalities described here can be confined within a single regional border. Although each mentality was linked mainly to a professional profile that currently predominates in a region, each of these occupations is also found in many other regions of Spain and of all other countries. Each mentality points to the *personal* surroundings where individuals grew in understanding, where they learned what they should consider adequate and feasible. Each mentality points to goals adopted by individual incumbents of occupations.

In fact the idea that series of occupational mentalities exist is not compatible with the idea that unique national or regional cultures exist. An occupation is a biographical territory, with its own practices of sovereignty and with its own politics of identity. Nations and regions exist somewhere else, in the bidimensional space of road maps.

In summary, we point out that the idea of occupational backgrounds opens up a quite specific territory for thought when managers and entrepreneurs make difficult decisions to survive in business. For example, the information summarized in Table 16.2

was used to train selected middle managers to improve the set of strategies they used when approaching distinguished customers and to accommodate during the decision-making process standards that dealt with specificities in bank transactions.

For centuries, as sovereigns, flags, and borders have come and gone as a consequence of royal legacies, gifts, and wars, the common people have survived because they had learned a trade. The idea that they owe their mentalities mostly to a unique national culture that somehow emerges from the mists of time seems to be off the point. Instead, the prevailing occupational profiles in their near surroundings are the ones germane to behavioral patterns observed among employers in decisions concerning customers and employees. Occupational activities and successful occupational strategies, and not the geographical space, generate the cognitive schemata and scenarios that their incumbents apply to forecasting complex chains of events and to problem solving in specific settings.

Puzzling Aspects of Decision Making in International Teams

As the business environment becomes more complex and competitive, high-quality decision making in management teams becomes more essential. The internalization of business has also led to an increase in the use of international teams; typical marketing, finance, political, and human resource decisions now require both specialized skills and international experts. Few individuals possess all of the needed skills, making a group of experts unavoidable. Differences in national markets, labor force, regulations, and so on also make the international team unavoidable. Similarly, sociopolitical decisions require the expertise of more than one nationality.

At this point, we want to introduce some important concepts for the descriptive (not prescriptive) analysis of international groups, based on the theoretical and experimental work with national groups in social and industrial psychology. Then we will analyze the few specific problems that affect the international team. We assume that this team is a group of individuals from different nations, concerned with identifying a problem, generating alternatives and choosing among them. The decision problem might be one of choice or judgment.

Our overriding point in this section is to illustrate that international teams can respond to the same group-management techniques as any other decision-making teams. Moreover, the phases of group decision making are similar to those typical of the decision-making process at the individual level: problem finding and representation, problem analysis, evaluation and choice of different options, and implementation and legitimation of the solution.

Because individual and group decision making have much in common, groups can be studied from the perspective of the information-processing values, beliefs, and limitations of their individual members. However, groups also have some specific characteristics that establish some important features special to team decision making. The interaction of individual characteristics and group processes is illustrated in Figure 16.1.

As can be seen in Figure 16.1, the performance of a group in a task depends on many interacting factors analyzed in depth by Steiner (1972). First, the group performance is a function of the task characteristics and is also influenced by aspects of the particular situation, especially by both the resources available to the group (data, computers, and the like) and the strategies the group uses in employing these resources. Second, some procedural features of the group process influence the final output; for instance, the agenda the group follows, the behavior of the group leader, the time pressure and the incentive structure under which the group operates. Third, the group is composed of individual members who normally manifest heterogeneity in their knowledge, beliefs, values, and so on. Furthermore, the individual decision-making process is affected by information-processing limitations, heuristics and biases, that can reduce the quality of decisions (see Hogarth, 1987; Kleindorfer, Kunreuther, & Schoemaker, 1993). Fourth, groups also have integrative existential characteristics, such as trust and cohesion, that go beyond simple extrapolations of the knowledge, values, and beliefs of individual members. The group process itself is also central in predicting performance. Aspects such as communication, goal setting, and group procedures in general are crucial in generating a good solution. Finally, group performance is an outcome of all of these interacting factors.

Figure 16.1. Factors Influencing Group Performance.

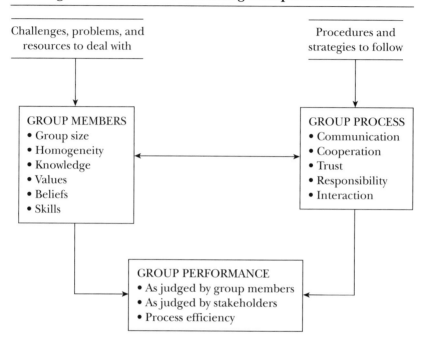

The indicators of group performance also need to be identified. A primary measure of a group's decision performance is the quality of the group's final solution, as judged by both group members and people external to the team. Other measures, such as the number of solutions considered and the number of voting rounds required to reach a group consensus, can enhance understanding of how a particular environment influences the group process.

Team Decision Making in General

Some issues relating to the quality of team decision making and to the phenomenon of groupthink are found across decision-making teams in general.

Decision Quality

One of the potential benefits of group decision making is that it allows the sharing of unique information. Another potential advantage is that if each person is considered to possess a finite number of answers to the problem, then the fact that the group context increases the number of knowledgeable people involved in the decision making also increases the chances that at least one of these people will have a high-quality answer. Indeed, previous research has indicated that the collective decision reached usually does not surpass in quality the initial pre-meeting work of one or two individual participants (Forsyth, 1990). Moreover, the study of group judgment has suggested that interacting groups working on bias-evoking tasks do not reach the level of accuracy of their most capable members for at least two reasons: process losses caused by the *interpersonal* or *interactional* problems that groups face (Hackman, 1989) and cognitive processing problems related to task complexities (problems examined primarily in research pertinent to behavioral decision theory, Hogarth, 1987, and decision analysis, Von Winterfeldt & Edwards, 1986). In fact key features of individual decision making continue to manifest themselves at the group level. Information-processing limitations afflict groups as well as individuals (Miller & Simons, 1974). Groups are subject to *framing effects* and *probability assessment biases* (Hogarth, 1987) as well as to biases and characteristics of their own.

Groupthink

Janis and Mann (1977) did a comprehensive revision of the research in group decision making. They showed the effects of social pressures on the decision that an individual in a group makes. Two such pressures are anticipatory regret and the tendency for the individual to worry about how disappointed he or she and the others might feel after the event if they make the wrong decision. Sometimes, groups composed of excellent and expert individuals have arrived at a poor solution and spent their energies warding off challenges to the group consensus. Janis (1972) termed this phenomenon *groupthink*. There are numerous political, business, and military examples of group decisions that exhibit this phenomenon (see Kleindorfer, Kunreuther, & Schoemaker, 1993, for examples).

Upon analyzing the circumstances under which these groups functioned, researchers discovered some common elements. Often, the groups were highly cohesive; their members knew each other well and liked each other. Insulation of the group due to a need for secrecy also seemed to be a common factor. Strong directive leadership seemed to be present. Finally, high stress, the importance of the decision, and task complexity all seemed to be contributing factors to the groupthink that occurred.

Groupthink presents distinct symptoms such as the illusion of invulnerability, stereotyping of people outside the group, and pressuring people who disagree with the majority opinion to remain silent. People practice self-censorship for fear of ridicule or from the desire to maintain harmony. The end result of the groupthink is that too few alternatives are examined and too few objectives taken into account. The information search is usually poor, with few counter-arguments offered to the preferred alternative being discussed.

There are some useful remedies for groupthink: delaying consensus, spreading power, seeking additional inputs, and encouraging conflict among ideas. Inviting external experts into the group is a good way to introduce new considerations. Finally, asking team members to role-play adversaries and other stakeholders is an excellent technique for ensuring a multiplicity of viewpoints. The key is to encourage diversity and to challenge assumptions before a convergence and choice are attempted (Nutt, 1989).

Polarization Effect

Social influence in groups is also manifested in a phenomenon called the *polarization effect* (Stoner, 1968). The groups studied often ended up being more likely to take risks than the individual opinions prior to the group meeting would have predicted. This effect may be due to framing factors.

Mutual Reinforcers

Other interpersonal issues in the groups are trust, communication, cooperation, and learning effects. A central result of experimental social psychology is that trust, communication, and cooperation are mutual reinforcers (Golembiewski & McConkie, 1975).

Decision Making in International Teams

Little research exists on international teams, and there are no general theories about behavior in these teams. Chapter Fifteen describes these aspects of international teams: the team is composed of a diverse workforce, diverse in cultures, expectations, and roles and many other critical variables (see also Maznevski, 1994); some individuals are from the host country, some from the organization's parent country, and some from other countries where the product will be marketed; and heterogeneity in national backgrounds is expected to make available to the team a wider variety of skills, beliefs, values, and experiences, which could contribute to the team's task. Heterogeneity among team members on such dimensions as personality, attitudes, and gender is expected to improve the quality of decisions.

However, the overlap between members in these groups may be high, with strong homogenization revealed in technical backgrounds and prevailing organizational styles; Ilgen, LePine, and Hollenbeck (Chapter Fifteen) also emphasize the rapid increase in the information and technology shared across national boundaries and the extent to which higher education in the United States has served as a training ground for persons from diverse cultures.

Researchers and organizations may also overlook the idea of multicultural awareness in international teams. The major features of international teams are similar to features found in other teams: (1) several members (2) interact with each other, (3) show a certain degree of interdependency, and (4) share some common resources and objectives. These teams also (5) involve people of different status in the organization and (6) enhance or level differences in access to information bearing on the question.

Moreover, the presence of cultural differences cannot be assumed from the existence of different nationalities among members of an international team. The second major section of this chapter introduced a taxonomy of different occupational mentalities that are not compatible with the idea of a single and unique national culture. This taxonomy seems to be quite reliable in European and Latin American countries. The first author of this chapter obtained positive feedback from several audiences in different countries when he introduced this schema in colloquia held on the subject.

Separately, Hofstede (1980, 1991) and Triandis (1990) advocate a psychosocial framework based on cultural dimensions such as power distance, individualism, masculinity, and uncertainty avoidance. And the presence of team members from different countries and with different native languages may influence the way international teams identify and define the contours of a problem and the kind of interactions occurring in this process. Disagreements may emerge when representational skills applied to understanding the problem use different images, words, and concepts to introduce the basic logic of the case. But these disagreements may have other origins, such as differences in the availability of home ground knowledge and information technology. Team members who use a nonnative language to participate in the team must familiarize themselves with terms, conditions, implicit learning, and other information taken for granted among members using their native language. The nonnative speakers have to understand, in depth, what other team members connote when they use colloquial expressions and when they refer to leading figures or heroes. Nonnative speakers need to be able to understand what is going on in the mass media in the locality of headquarters. Because nonnative speakers' knowledge of all these things will never be quite the same as native speakers' knowledge, the simple fact that team members have different native languages may be an important factor in team processes and outcomes.

We agree with Maznevski (1994), who points out some of the barriers that accompany linguistic diversity and are likely to decrease the performance of decision-making teams. In addition to these specific linguistic barriers and differences in recognized verbal cues, there may be differences in regard to the information team members have at hand; biases in the interpretation of facts and values; framing effects; differences in behavioral and action patterns considered appropriate; differences in political contexts or traditions concerning the freedom of speech, the freedom of assembly, and the freedom of conscience in decision making; and differences in the geopolitical status of each country represented.

Again, the distinction between what a word denotes and connotes helps us understand these differences. Many linguistic components are involved. For example, expressions such as "liberal policies," "nationalistic fervor," and "charismatic leadership" have different connotations in the United States than they do in the European Union. The use of many Latin words and expressions facilitate communication and understanding between managers in

European countries and raises the tone of the conversation. However, U.S. managers in the same firm would consider the use of many Latin words in a discussion among themselves to be pompous; in the United States, idiomatic expressions are preferred. Jokes are an essential ingredient of formal business presentations in American firms but are welcomed parsimoniously in European business meetings. In Latin countries, mutual interruption during discussion is considered an occupational hazard, but in Japan, where silence follows the end of a speech, interruption is considered very impolite. In many organizational cultures, silence is avoided during business meetings.

Good reflexes and a capacity for retention, automatic memory, and fluent expression are cognitive traits reinforced among members who successfully use a second language to convey their ideas in an international decision-making group. On the positive side, however, linguistic heterogeneity reduces the likelihood that the team will experience the groupthink phenomenon already analyzed.

Group Decision Support Systems

In this section, we propose some useful strategies to reduce some of the sources of team disagreement and imbalance and to improve the overall decision-making performance of teams, including international teams. These strategies are based on new technologies and on recent advances in both group-management techniques and behavioral decision theory.

As technology evolves, more and different options become available to support group interaction. There are several mechanisms by which these technologies can affect group decision making and performance. One of the most fundamental differences technology has introduced is that between traditional face-to-face communication and advanced communication environments. Media richness favors the view that the most efficient medium should be used for the level of task ambiguity and that a group's performance on a given task may be significantly affected by the available communication environments (Daft & Lengel, 1984).

Computer-mediated group work environments, or group support systems (GSS) (see Jessup & Valacich, 1993), represent one promising technology for improving team decisions, and recent studies have demonstrated its potential benefits (Valacich, Dennis, & Connolly, 1994; Valacich & Schwenk, 1995). Huber, Valacich, and Jessup (1993) define group support systems as "computer-assisted technologies used to aid group efforts directed to identifying and addressing problems, opportunities and issues. By 'groups' in this context, we mean both face-to-face groups supported by GSS technology during a meeting and also groups whose members are physically separated but who use GSS technology to exchange information either synchronously or asynchronously" (p. 257). GSS may be used alone or combined with more traditional group decision aids.

Technologies such as electronic mail and computer conferencing are also being rapidly diffused. The benefits of these environments for group meetings have been touted to include allowing more equal group participation, allowing anonymity for member contributions, and providing process support structures (for example, making it easier to rank order a list of ideas).

The most important implication of the considerations for group decision making described earlier is that openness and learning must be actively pursued. One common obstacle to effective group decision making is bounded rationality, that is, the inability to evaluate possible compromise solutions. As a result of bounded rationality, group members may choose whichever alternative appears initially safest and begin marching down the path of groupthink to shore up their position. An obvious solution would be to use computers or other decision aids to facilitate communication and also the generation and evaluation of alternatives. Systems that aid groups in decision making are growing in number and scope; a typical one is the group decision support system (GDDS), which entails a meeting room with enough computer terminals to accommodate each individual in the group. These terminals are networked and serviced by a master workstation controlled by a facilitator. The input of each group member and summaries of the group's input and decisions are shared visually through an overhead projection controlled by the facilitator.

Past research on group member satisfaction with computer-mediated decision making has shown mixed results. Meta-analyses by McLeod (1992) and by Benbasat and Lim (1993) found face-to-face groups to have higher satisfaction levels than computer-mediated groups had. However, researchers studying field groups have typically found them to be highly satisfied by computer-mediated processes and with their solution outcomes (Dennis & Gallupe, 1993).

The electronic meeting system (EMS) has become vital to the adaptive evolution of organizations; these systems combine human communication technologies (audio, video, and computer conferencing) and link dispersed group members with computer support technologies (for reviews of this line of research, see Dennis & Gallupe, 1993).

Electronic media appear to remedy several of the dysfunctional psychological and group communication processes found in new groups (Culnan & Markus, 1987). The literature on group problem solving shows that decision performance suffers when discussion is not focused, underlying problems are not brought to the surface, alternatives are prematurely and superficially evaluated, conflicts become highly personalized, and discussion is dominated by one or two members (Hiltz, 1984). An EMS promotes a task-oriented focus, with proportionally more discussion time devoted to the problem and less social maintenance (Rice, 1984). However, the more vigorous debate that typically occurs within the depersonalized atmosphere of electronic meetings usually leaves the members of new electronic groups less cohesive and less confident and supportive of group decisions (Watson, de Sanctis, & Poole, 1988).

The effects of an EMS on group structure are a major practical consideration for team leaders and executives who are concerned that EMS may diminish hierarchy and disrupt leader control. All electronic media represent a substantial process change. They eliminate the ability to manipulate physical positioning or social distance to reinforce status. They suppress the emergence of a status hierarchy in groups. Therefore participation and influence in new electronic groups are more equal than they are in face-to-face groups, and leaders less often emerge (Dubrovsky, Kiesler, & Sethna, 1991).

A computerized system also plays a critical role by providing immediate feedback to the group about the implications of members' judgments, so that communication of individual differences is made more efficient, focused, and precise.

Group-Management and Behavioral Decision Theory

Group-management and behavioral decision theory offers another series of techniques that might be used to improve team decisions (alone or in combination with the technologies just described).

The *dialectical approach* has been advanced by several decision scientists as a means of increasing the effectiveness of group planning (Mason & Mitroff, 1973). In this approach, each side advances its arguments, and a third party tries to reconcile the conflicting viewpoints. This approach has been especially embraced in legal discussions and in many corporations when subgroups are given the task of advocating different and conflicting courses of action.

A substantial body of research has shown that conflict can improve decision making (Janis & Mann, 1977; Mason & Mitroff, 1981; Schwenk, 1988). *Devil's advocacy* and *dialectical inquiry* are two techniques for promoting structured conflict in decision making that have been applied both to individuals who disagree and within formal groups (see Schwenk, 1990, for a revision). Mason (1969) suggests that the most common decision-making approach within organizations is not conflict based but what he calls the *expert approach*. In both devil's advocacy and the expert approach, a plan is identified and discussed. This initial plan is typically advocated by an individual planner or subgroup. Next a different planner or subgroup takes the role of the devil's advocate, attempting to discover all that is wrong with the initial plan and argue why and how the plan is flawed. Finally, a structured debate is conducted in which those responsible for making the decision hear arguments in support of both the plan and the counterplan.

Group decision making frequently confuses facts and values. *Social judgment theory* proposes that decision makers separate facts and values by consciously sorting their ideas and information into four categories: scientific data, scientific judgments, value judgments, and social judgments. Hammond, McClelland, and Mumpower (1980), for example, discuss how breaking a problem down into factual judgments and value judgments identified a common fulcrum that was acceptable in the view of all parties concerned. Separation of facts and values is often a good technique in dealing with complex and emotionally charged issues.

When there is severe disagreement about facts or values in a given group, a collective opinion or consensus choice may not be possible, and the group may resort to *aggregation of opinions and probabilities*. (Indeed, a major purpose of research on group decision making is to learn to recognize both the possibilities for achieving group consensus *and* the inherent limitations involved in group choice.) The simple answer to failure to achieve consensus seems to be just to average experts' opinions. Some approaches derived from utility theory, as described by Von Winterfeldt and Edwards (1986), could be important aids to this process.

Another way to achieve agreement is through consecutive polls of individual team members; this is the essence of the *Delphi technique* (Linstone & Turoff, 1975), which completely eliminates all direct communication between individuals by eliciting opinions through a series of surveys and providing summarized feedback to group members regarding the judgments of anonymous others. It is assumed that people will progressively revise their opinions in the light of the impersonal feedback, reaching an agreement that reflects the best parts of several viewpoints. However, for certain types of problems, interaction and open dialectical processes are important if teams are to arrive at the better decisions.

Sharing task-relevant information during group discussion is another means by which groups can become more accurate. Without guidance some groups might be inclined to rely on irrelevant nonverbal cues rather than on the content of what a member contributes.

Innami (1994) presents the verbal aid of *reasoning and positional orientation* for encouraging the degree to which group members exchange facts and reasons in support of their positions. Reasoning-oriented group discussions involve knowledge-based logical arguments that substantiate group discussions by adding related facts and knowledge to material already introduced by someone and exploring the reasons for a particular judgment or inference. These discussions serve as error correction mechanisms. They also prevent groups from adopting a solution prematurely, an occurrence that has been characterized by small-group theorists as the major drawback of group problem solving (Hoffman, 1979).

Both interaction processes and cognitive processes are supported through the use of an *external facilitator*. The function of the facilitator is to ensure that all group members are able to participate fully in the process and that the group session is not dominated by a minority of group members.

And finally, interaction processes are also supported through the use of a *decision model*. Modeling improves interaction by providing a common language that participants can use regardless of their substantive backgrounds, a framework that enables participants to create a shared social reality and a set of task-relevant procedures (Phillips, 1984).

Combining Support Systems

It seems reasonable to postulate that structured conflict techniques, such as devil's advocacy and dialectical inquiry, may have different effects on group processes and outcomes when they are computer mediated and when they carried out through face-to-face communication. Computer-mediated communication provides significantly fewer social cues, and it seems to induce dehumanizing effects. It seems convenient to use a combined approach: for example, employing an asynchronous electronic mail system to surface and share solutions and face-to-face communication to select a final solution.

Conclusion

The guiding mind of international organizations is not the individual decision maker, as might appear at first glance. The guiding mind is a hierarchy of groups of experts that ensures productive capacity and fair trade through effective workgroup performance and decision making (Prieto, 1993). This hierarchy of decision-making groups constitutes the technostructure (Galbraith, 1973) that brings experts into a working relationship with other experts for clarifying relevant criteria, for building evanescent castles in the air in the meeting room, for experimenting with variations on how to attain desired ends through business planning and successful competitiveness, and ultimately for achieving the overall success or failure of the international organization. In that successful organization, participation in goal setting increases team members' feeling of control over the goal-setting process, and they can outperform assigned-goal groups (Erez, Earley, & Hulin, 1985).

A successful organization's experts take into account not only the world as it is but as it might be. Each group member playing a qualified role in the technostructure is expected to show competence in the relevant aspects of the goal agenda and its related timelines (Heller & Wilpert, 1981). People must think in terms of "science fiction," because even though the future is not yet present, it must be advanced.

The nationality of each team participant is a minor segment in the cognitive structure that gives direction or arguments to his or her efforts and in the strategic goals toward which efforts must be directed and by which success and worth are measured. The consequence is that international, cosmopolitan, national, or regional teams must all be considered *interdisciplinary teams of experts* facing similar dilemmas and resorting to a similar array of strategies for decision framing and decision deliberation.

Notes

1. In Spain, the rights of the mother prevail over the rights of the son and over the rights of the husband in cases of conflict. Wives do not change their maiden names and rarely use their husband's surname. Queen Johanna succeeded her mother Elisabeth as sovereign of the Kingdom of Castile. Johanna's spouse, Phillip, died in 1506. The couple had only one child, Charles, who was born in 1500. Johanna's father, Ferdinand, was King of Aragon and Regent of Castile because Johanna was considered mentally unsound. Before Ferdinand died in 1516, he named two Regents—one for Aragon, the other for Castile. His last will stated that Charles, his grandson, should become King of Aragon and Castile in 1520. The Regents advanced the execution of the will to 1516. However, Johanna was still alive, had not abdicated, and did not accept her father's last will. Instead, she honored her mother's last will and remained de facto Queen of Castile until her death in 1555. Her son Charles did rule as usufructuary, but not as title holder, of the Kingdom of Castile until Johanna's death.

2. He was in charge of personnel selection, promotion, and training procedures as assistant to the personnel manager. From 1972 to 1984, he was successively employed in three national banks with branches in every main Spanish city and town.

References

Beach, L. R. (1990). *Image theory: Decision making in personal and organizational contexts.* New York: Wiley.

Benbasat, I., & Lim, L. H. (1993). The effects of group, task, context, and technology variables on the usefulness of group support systems: A meta-analysis of experimental studies. *Small Group Research, 24,* 430–462.

Bertrand, D. (1985). *La politique de S. Ignace de Loyola.* Paris: Les Éditions du Cerf.

Culnan, M. J., & Markus, M. L. (1987). Information technologies. In F. M. Jablin, L. L. Putnam, K. H. Roberts, & L. W. Porter (Eds.), *Handbook of organizational communication: An interdisciplinary perspective* (pp. 420–443). Thousand Oaks, CA: Sage.

Daft, R. L., & Lengel, R. H. (1984). Information richness: A new approach to managerial behavior and organizational design. In L. L. Cummings & B. M. Staw (Eds.), *Research in Organization Behavior* (Vol. 6, pp. 191–233). Greenwich, CT: JAI Press.

Dennis, A. R., & Gallupe, R. B. (1993). A history of group support systems empirical research: Lessons learned and future directions. In L. M. Jessup & J. S. Valacich (Eds.), *Group support systems: New perspectives* (pp. 59–77). Old Tappan, NJ: Macmillan.

Dubrovsky, V. J., Kiesler, S., & Sethna, B. N. (1991). The equalization phenomenon: Status effects in computer-mediated and face-to-face decision making groups. *Human Computer Interaction, 6,* 119–146.

Duroselle, J. B. (1990). *Historia de los Europeos.* Madrid: Aguilar.

Erez, M., Earley, P. C., & Hulin, C. L. (1985). The impact of participation on goal acceptance and performance: A two-step model. *Academy of Management Journal, 28,* 50–66.

Fernández-Alvarez, M. (1995). *Power y seceded en la España del quinientos.* Madrid: Alianza.

Fernández-Armesto, F. (1995). *Millennium.* London: Transworld (in English); Barcelona: Planeta (in Spanish).

Fishbein, M., & Ajzen, J. (1975). *Belief, attitude, intention and behavior: An introduction to theory and research.* Reading, MA: Addison-Wesley.

Forsyth, D. R. (1990). *Group dynamics.* Pacific Grove, CA: Brooks/Cole.

Galbraith, J. K. (1973). *Economics and the public purpose.* Boston: Houghton Mifflin.

Golembiewski, H., & McConkie, M. (1975). The centrality of interpersonal trust in group processes. In C. L. Cooper (Ed.), *Theories of group processes* (pp. 131–186). New York: Wiley.

Hackman, J. R. (Ed.). (1989). *Groups that work (and those that don't): Creating conditions for effective teamwork.* San Francisco: Jossey-Bass.

Hammond, K. R., McClelland, G. H., & Mumpower, J. (1980). *Human judgment and decision making.* New York: Praeger.

Heller, F. A., & Wilpert, B. (1981). *Competence and power in managerial decision-making.* New York: Wiley.

Hendricks, C. (1976). *Charles V and the Cortes of Castile: Politics in the Renaissance.* Ithaca, NY: Cornell University Press.

Hiltz, S. R. (1984). *Online communities: A case study of the office of the future.* Norwood, NJ: Ablex.

Hobsbawm, E. (1995). *Historia del siglo XX.* Madrid: Crítica.

Hoffman, L. R. (1979). The group problem-solving process: Studies of a valence model. New York: Praeger.

Hofstede, G. (1980). *Culture's consequences.* Thousand Oaks, CA: Sage.

Hofstede, G. (1991). *Cultures and organizations: Software of the mind.* London: McGraw-Hill.

Hogarth, R. M. (1987). *Judgment and choice.* New York: Wiley.

Huber, G. P., Valacich, J. S., & Jessup, L. M. (1993). A theory of the effects of group support systems on an organization's nature and decisions. In L. M. Jessup & J. S. Valacich (Eds.), *Group support systems: New perspectives* (pp. 255–268). Old Tappan, NJ: Macmillan.

Innami, I. (1994). The quality of group decisions, group verbal behavior and intervention. *Organizational Behavior and Human Decision Processes, 60,* 409–430.

Janis, I. L. (1972). *Victims of groupthink: A psychological study of foreign policy decisions and fiascos.* Boston: Houghton Mifflin.

Janis, I. L., & Mann, L. (1977). *Decision making: A psychological analysis of conflict, choice and commitment.* New York: Free Press.

Jastrow, J. (1935). Wish and wisdom: episodes in the vagaries of belief. Englewood Cliffs, NJ: Appleton-Century-Crofts.

Jessup, L. M., & Valacich, J. S. (Eds.). (1993). *Group support systems: New perspectives.* Old Tappan, NJ: Macmillan.

Kleindorfer, P. R., Kunreuther, H. C., & Schoemaker, P.J.H. (1993). *Decision sciences: An integrative perspective.* New York: Cambridge University Press.

Lawrence, D. H. (1923). *Studies in classic American literature.* New York: Viking Penguin.

Linstone, H. A., & Turoff, M. (1975). *The Delphi method: Techniques and applications.* Reading, MA: Addison-Wesley.

Martin, M. (1987). *The Jesuits.* New York: Linden Press/Simon & Schuster.

Mason, R. O. (1969). A dialectical approach to strategic planning. *Management Science, 15,* 403–414.

Mason, R. O., & Mitroff, I. I. (1973). A program for research on management information systems. *Management Science, 19,* 475–487.

Mason, R. O., & Mitroff, I. I. (1981). *Challenging strategic planning assumptions.* New York: Wiley.

Maznevski, M. L. (1994). Understanding our differences: Performance in decision making groups with diverse members. *Human Relation, 47,* 531–552.

McLeod, P. L. (1992). An assessment of the experimental literature on electronic support of group work: Results of a meta-analysis. *Human-Computer Interaction, 7,* 257–280.

Miller, G. R., & Simons, H. W. (Eds.). (1974). *Perspectives on communication in social conflict.* Upper Saddle River, NJ: Prentice Hall.

Negroponte, N. (1995). *Being digital.* New York: Knopf.

Nutt, P. C. (1989). *Making tough decisions: Tactics for improving managerial decision making.* San Francisco: Jossey-Bass.

Phillips, L. D. (1984). A theory of requisite decision models. *Acta Psychologica, 56,* 29–48.

Prieto, J. M. (1993). The team perspective in selection and assessment. In H. Schuler, J. L. Farr, & M. Smith, *Personnel selection and assessment: Individual and organizational perspectives* (pp. 221–234). Hillsdale, NJ: Erlbaum.

Ramon, M., Picornell, A., & Castro, J. A. (1995). La genética de los chuetas Mallorquines. *Investigación y Ciencia* [Scientific American], (228), 42–48.

Rice, R. (1984). Mediated group communication. In R. Rice & Associates (Eds.), *The new media* (pp. 129–153). Orlando: Academic Press.

Roudchoudhury, A. K., & Nei, M. (1988). *Human polymorphic genes: World distribution.* Oxford, England: Oxford University Press.

Rubert de Ventós, X. (1994). *Nacionalismos: El laberinto de la identidad.* Madrid: Espasa.

Schwenk, C. (1988). *The essence of strategic decision making.* San Francisco: The New Lexington Press.

Schwenk, C. (1990). Effects of devil's advocacy and dialectical inquiry on decision making: A meta-analysis. *Organizational Behavior and Human Decision Processes, 41,* 161–176.

Steiner, I. D. (1972). *Group process and productivity.* Orlando: Academic Press.

Stoner, J. A. (1968). Risky and cautious shift in group decision: The influence of widely held values. *Journal of Experimental Social Psychology, 4,* 442–459.

Triandis, H. C. (1990). Cross-cultural studies of individualism and collectivism. In J. Berman (Ed.), *Nebraska Symposium on Motivation: 1989* (pp. 41–133). Lincoln: University of Nebraska Press.

Tuchman, B. (1982). How we entered World War I. In B. W. Tuchman, *Practicing history: Selected essays* (pp. 158–172). Old Tappan, NJ: Macmillan.

Unzueta, P. (1988). *Los nietos de la ira: Nacionalismo y violencia en el Pais Vasco.* Madrid: El Pais/Aguilar.

Valacich, J. S., Dennis, A. R., & Connolly, T. (1994). Idea generation in computer-based groups: A new ending to an old story. *Organizational Behavior and Human Decision Processes, 57,* 448–467.

Valacich, J. S., & Schwenk, C. (1995). Devil's advocacy and dialectical inquiry effects on face-to-face and computer-mediated group decision making. *Organizational Behavior and Human Decision Processes, 63,* 158–173.

Voltes, P. (1989). *Nueva historia de España: Superando la historia del estado, surge la historia de los pueblos de España.* Barcelona: Plaza y Janés.

Von Winterfeldt, D., & Edwards, W. (1986). *Decision analysis and behavioral research.* New York: Cambridge University Press.

Watson, R. T., de Sanctis, G., & Poole, M. S. (1988). Using a GDSS to facilitate group consensus: Some intended and unintended consequences. *MIS Quarterly,* pp. 463–480.

CHAPTER 17

Individual-Union-Organization Relationships in a Cultural Context

Tove Helland Hammer
Jean F. Hartley

The study of the relationships between employers, employees, and employee unions is the traditional domain of industrial relations. The questions of interest are how labor, management, and the government shape employment relationships to attain equity, efficiency, and quality of working life and what effects their actions have on the labor market, firm performance, union effectiveness, and workers' economic and social well-being. In the United States, industrial relations has come to mean collective bargaining and blue-collar workers. But during the last two decades union membership has declined in the United States and many other industrialized countries (Bamber & Lansbury, 1992). Presently, only 11.2 percent of the U.S. private-sector nonagricultural workforce and 35 percent of public-sector employees are union members.

Part of the decline has been caused by structural changes in employment, which has shifted from large "smokestack" manufacturing companies employing men working full-time (where union membership was traditionally based) to smaller workplaces and service industries employing women working part-time (where

---

Note: We thank Shinichiro Watanabe for his comments on an earlier draft.

the traditional allegiance of employees to trade unions cannot be assumed and the advantages of collective bargaining are not so immediately evident). In addition, in the United States, legislation protecting workers' employment rights and working conditions has taken the place of collective bargaining as a regulator of companies' employment policies.

The shift in the structure of the workforce, to more white-collar, more service, more women, and more part-time workers, has led many to question the utility of the *industrial relations* label and to suggest that a term like *employment relations* captures current research and practice much better. Indeed, some writers would argue that on theoretical grounds, industrial relations should be concerned about employees in their relations with employers regardless of whether employees are in trade unions or covered by collective bargaining (Keenoy, 1985; Hartley, 1992b). In this chapter we will use the term *employment relations* to describe the relationship between employees and employers, because we do not limit the discussion to organized labor. When we describe the entire system of relations, which includes employers, workers, unions, and the government, we will call it the *industrial relations system* (*IR system*).

Industrial relations as a field of study comprises collective bargaining, labor economics, labor history, and labor law. Social sciences such as anthropology, psychology, and sociology also contribute to understanding in this field. It has also been argued that industrial relations has an irreducibly psychological component because it is a form of social relations (Hartley & Stephenson, 1992).

The most common unit of analysis has been the organization or union on the one hand or the industrial relations system as a whole on the other, rather than the individual employee or union member. The central research questions have concerned the effects of collective bargaining on economic and labor market outcomes, such as wages and benefits, job security and employment opportunities, worker productivity, firm-level economic performance and investments, and the effects of labor law and protective legislation on the collective bargaining process and union strength. A sizable part of the research literature consists of case studies of individual unions (*institutional research*) and international comparisons of IR systems. The breadth of inquiry, especially in comparative and institutional research, often ensures (but does not guarantee) that a cultural context is provided, although culture is not necessarily a factor in formal theoretical models.

In contrast, when industrial psychologists have studied unions they have tended to keep their traditional focus on the individual as the unit of analysis, often proceeding as though there were no context of any kind for their predictions of a few favorite variables: pro-union voting, union commitment and satisfaction and, to a more limited extent, union leadership. Much psychological research on the causes and consequences of union membership has ignored the very important fact that unions are political organizations with unique histories and that this context will influence members' behaviors and attitudes. The exceptions are a few European studies of union participation and strike behavior that have emphasized the importance of the group, the organization, and the political and economic context as causes of individual action (for example, Nicholson, Ursell, & Blyton, 1981; Hartley, Kelly, & Nicholson, 1983; Klandermans, 1986, 1992; Waddington, 1987).

What do we mean when we talk about a *cultural context* in the study of employment relations? It is the particular configuration of values, beliefs, and norms held by management, labor, and others who influence the governance of the industrial relations system and the behaviors that follow from these values and beliefs. Hofstede (1991) described culture as patterns of thinking, feeling, and acting that are programmed into the mind of each member of a group, or collectivity, through learning. The cultural context for employment relations includes the beliefs of employers, managers, and employees about labor's and management's rights and obligations and the functions of trade unions. It also includes beliefs about the appropriate role of the government in regulating the actions of employers, workers, and unions and in setting economic and industrial policies that determine how private- and public-sector organizations use their resources.

In this chapter we examine how relations between employers, employees, unions, and the government have produced the employment policies and practices we find in today's workplaces, and what role the values, beliefs, and norms of the key actors have played in shaping national employment relations and industrial relations systems. Of particular interest is the question of whether dominant value systems can explain national peculiarities in managers' and workers' attitudes and behaviors toward labor unions.

Values are not frequently occurring explanatory variables in industrial relations research, however; though it is interesting to reflect that an early and influential model of industrial relations by the economist Dunlop (1958) gave a key role to the ideology, or belief system, that binds managers and employees together. The dominant models of IR systems emphasize market forces and economic factors, labor laws and legal structures, and technology. Very few studies include values, or culture, in their analyses. A notable exception is Kochan, Katz, and McKersie's study (1986) of the transformation of the U.S. industrial relations system, in which management values were incorporated in the theoretical model that described the causes of firm-level IR policies and human resource management practices.

Management and trade union ideologies, workers' values, and past history have often been used as post hoc explanations for data patterns, however, particularly in comparative international research. For example, in a study of IR policies and human resource management practices in developing countries, Kuruvilla (1995) found that national industrialization strategies—such as producing for a home market to avoid having to import goods or producing primarily for export—determined IR policies and practices in Singapore, Malaysia, the Philippines, Hong Kong, India, and South Korea because the different industrialization strategies required different IR policies to control and motivate the workforce. However, he also found considerable variation in the way each country had translated its industrial relations policy goals into personnel practices at the firm level, variation that he attributed to national values and ideologies and a country's previous industrial relations history.

Furthermore, there is a growing interest among researchers and practitioners in learning how cultural values cause, or contribute to, the survival (or demise) of specific employment and personnel practices. The question whether there is a *cultural prerequisite* for the effectiveness of specific human resource management programs and practices or whether they can be transplanted successfully from one culture to another as long as all the original structural features are retained has been asked frequently in the last decade, particularly with reference to Japanese production systems and employment relations (for example, Womack, Jones, & Roos, 1990). That question has also come up in discussions about the utility of introducing in the United States worker participation programs modeled on European industrial democracy legislation (Kochan & Osterman, 1994; Morris, 1995) and the possibility of introducing German-style works councils into British firms (Hall, Carley, Gold, Marginson, & Sisson, 1995).

But there is much work to be done, conceptually and empirically, to determine the importance of values, or culture, as a cause of IR policies and practices. What little scholarly debate there is on this topic is interesting, but it is based on very few data points and filled with conjecture. This is not surprising, given the fact that it has dealt with sociological variables and psychological constructs but that the debaters have come largely from other disciplines, with scant knowledge of psychology (see, for example, Dlugos & Weiermair, 1981).

In this chapter we bring the psychological theories of values and culture, primarily the work of Hofstede (1980, 1991), Schwartz (1992, 1994), and Triandis (1995), to bear on research findings from collective bargaining, labor economics, and labor history. We do not cover the usual psychological models of union membership because a comprehensive summary of the psychological research conducted up through 1990 is available elsewhere (Barling, Fullagar, & Kelloway, 1992; Hartley, 1992b). But we do include research that shows what effects IR policies and workplace practices have on workers' well-being, behaviors, and attitudes.

A large part of the chapter is devoted to an analysis of U.S. industrial relations because so much of the research has been conducted in, and on, this system. However, there is also a sizable literature on Canadian and European industrial relations (for example, Ferner & Hyman, 1992; Edwards, 1995) as well as a small collection of recent studies of labor relations in Asia and the Pacific Rim (Frenkel, 1993; Frenkel & Harrod, 1995) from which we draw information. Although we compare U.S. employment relations and trade unionism with their equivalents in some other countries, we cannot, given space limitations, provide comprehensive information about a number of other countries' industrial relation systems. But we do offer additional detail about one other system—the United Kingdom's—to illustrate both the contribution that a cultural context can make to an understanding of employment relations and the limitations of cultural values as an explanatory construct.

As we shall show, the development of the IR systems in the United Kingdom and United States have moved in very different directions, encouraged by both political and economic factors, even though the cultural value systems, broadly defined, are quite similar.

In the U.K., union membership, both in absolute levels and in terms of employment density (percentage of the employed labor force that is unionized), declined fairly steadily from a peak of 12.6 million (a density of 55.8 percent) in 1979 to a low of 7.7 million (a density of 31 percent) in 1992. Under the Thatcher government, British trade unions lost much of their once considerable influence at the national, organizational, and workplace levels as legislation was passed to remove freedoms that the unions had enjoyed for years to manage their internal affairs and to engage in industrial action. Despite this recent decline in union power, the social meaning of joining and participating in a trade union in the U.K. is likely to be different from the U.S. meaning. In the United States, to join a union is to become a member of a small minority within the labor force. In the U.K., to join and participate in a union was, until 1984, to act in concert with the majority of working men and women (Waddington & Whitston, 1995).

The Two Faces of Unionism

The debate about the effects of unions on workers, managers, the individual organization, and society at large has been emotionally charged since the emergence of trade unionism. European unions, in particular, have distinctive ideological orientations. They can be pure member-interest organizations that function to protect employees' positions in the labor market, vehicles for raising workers' status in society, or "schools of war" in a class-based struggle between labor and capital (Hyman, 1996).

Freeman and Medoff (1984) have proposed that unionism has two faces. One is a "monopoly face," which depicts unions as monopolies that, first, decrease the economic efficiency of firms by raising wages beyond competitive levels and imposing restrictive work rules on management; second, contribute to increasing income inequality in society between well-paid high-skilled union members and large numbers of unskilled low-paid workers; and, third, lead to corruption and undemocratic behavior in union governance and the use of coercive power tactics to gain legislation to protect union interests.

The other side is the "collective voice/institutional response face," which depicts the union as a mechanism through which workers can express their discontent over conditions of employment in an orderly fashion and get justice. In theory, in a perfect market, employees who experience inequities in the labor exchange, or believe they have been unfairly treated in other ways, can express their discontent by going to work for another employer. If enough good workers quit, leaving only those incapable of attracting better job offers, the offending employer will have to improve employment conditions or suffer the economic consequences of having an inadequate labor force. The union can act as a voice for workers, so that elected workforce representatives and the employer can discuss employment policies and practices that need change, thereby preventing such individual expressions of dissatisfaction as turnover, absenteeism, sabotage, slow-downs, and the like. In this model the union is a mechanism for labor-management communication.

Labor's voice should be collective rather than individual for two reasons. A number of issues are "public goods" such as safety and health measures, pensions, cost-of-living wage adjustments, and lay-off policies that affect all, or large groups of, employees and therefore should be addressed by representatives of the whole workforce, not by individual employees. Second, most individual workers are in a poor bargaining position vis-à-vis the employer; because of the employer's superior power, they are vulnerable to reprisals if they voice discontent. Collective bargaining can reduce power differences and protect the individual. As part of their voice-response function, unions also try to ensure that workers are not treated as a commodity, used and disposed of at the employer's discretion, but that they have certain rights, protected (in the United States, at least) by legally binding contracts. Such contracts do, of course, interfere with the employer's freedom to manage his or her resources at will, and contribute to the union's monopoly face (Freeman & Medoff, 1984).

Opposition to unions comes not only from those who believe that unions have mostly negative effects. It also comes from people who think that unions are simply unnecessary. Whether or not one sees unions serving a unique function in the workplace for which there is no adequate substitute depends on one's beliefs about the causes of, and remedies for, industrial conflict.

Models of Labor-Management Conflict

Early in the history of U.S. trade unionism, a series of violent strikes and lockouts brought the "labor problem," that is, the struggle between workers and owners over the control of production and conditions of employment, to the attention of the general public. During the 1880s and 1890s, union membership had grown rapidly, from 447,000 in 1897 to over 2 million in 1904 (Brody, 1980), and unions had become increasingly militant (Montgomery, 1979). The conflict, played out on the societal level as a political class struggle over the relative rights of capital and labor, was mirrored in the workplace by a number of practical problems. Employers faced high turnover, unproductive labor, waste, and inefficiency, and workers lived with employment insecurity, low wages, unsafe working conditions, and child labor.

One school of thought, formed in the United States during the 1920s and led by institutional labor economists, argued that this form of labor-management conflict was the inevitable result of divergent interests built into the exchange between the worker and employer of labor for wages. At worst the labor exchange was a zero-sum game in which employers tried to maximize their profits by extracting as much labor as possible from their employees while paying the lowest possible wages, and employees resisted this exploitation by withholding labor to ensure that the amount they worked did not exceed the value of their wages.

In reality, of course, the employment relationship is more complex and includes both cooperation and conflict. As the economists argued, there has to be some cooperation, or there cannot be a labor exchange to begin with. Labor and management often have conflicting goals, but the conflicts can be resolved through negotiations and adherence to rules that regulate the behavior of, and produce solutions acceptable to, both parties. With the right institutions and proper procedures, conflict will lead to compromise and collaboration.

The practical implication of this argument was that the employment relationship had to be managed by both parties coming together to bargain over its terms. But full comanagement would require power equalization, and as the individual worker was at a power disadvantage vis-à-vis the employer, workers would have to bargain collectively, through a union that could represent their interests. In the United States this view meant that employees' rights to join a union should be protected by law and an employer's obligation to bargain with the union chosen by his or her employees should be established by law. In brief, the solution to the labor problem was for the state to pass legislation that allowed workers to join unions and bargain collectively with employers over wages, benefits, and working conditions (Kaufman, 1993). The use of trade unions to solve labor-management conflict comes from a pluralist model (Fox, 1973) that is fundamental to industrial relations and to the acceptance of a third party in the employment relationship.

Other countries developed different models for channeling conflict and managing the employment relationship. For example, in the U.K. trade unionism emerged incrementally, initially among skilled workers whose value to employers gave them a strong labor market position. Employers reluctantly accepted these unions and collective bargaining, and the government, which at that time took a laissez-faire approach to the economy, let the two parties develop their own rules and practices for managing employment relations. British trade unionism was founded on this voluntarism, with a minimum of statutory rights and obligations imposed on employers and unions by the state (Flanders, 1974). Although the state began to take a much more active role in regulating employment relations under the Thatcher government, as we shall discuss later, voluntarism represents the foundation on which much industrial relations and trade union culture has been built. Thus the common commitments of the United States and the U.K. to a type of business unionism and to collective bargaining are based on opposing principles about the role of the law and the state: positive involvement in the United States and negative in the U.K.

A competing explanation for industrial conflict came from the *personnel management* branch of industrial relations (Kaufman, 1993). People of this school assumed that employees and employers (labor and management) had a common interest in maximizing productivity and firm profits because there would then be more to share for everyone. Labor-management conflict would only erupt when one party or both lost sight of the common goal and the necessity for cooperation to achieve it. Conflict was unnecessary and undesirable and would be eliminated once the parties recognized that they were a common interest group. This perspective, called the *unitarist model* (Fox, 1973), did not consider power differences between labor and management to be a problem because it assumed common-interest partners would not exploit one another for private gain. Thus there was no need for trade unions to balance management's power.

For those who took the personnel management view, the "labor problem" came from within the firm and was rooted in poor management policies and practices. Only good management, not legislation, could eliminate it. Research and practice were therefore aimed at improving the procedures managers used to recruit, select, train, reward, and otherwise motivate employees and at creating a social and psychological work environment that would enhance worker productivity and job satisfaction.

Such opposition to the use of legislation to contain labor-management conflict does not necessarily mean lack of support for trade unionism, however. In the U.K. both unions and employers have also been, until recently, deeply suspicious of any involvement with law or with employment rights.

These opposing views on the best way to manage labor conflict suggest the following questions: are unions necessary to ensure equity and efficiency in the workplace (that is, a fair labor exchange and labor-management cooperation in the productive use of capital and human resources), or are there other means available that will accomplish the same result (and at an equal or lower cost)? Would the individual worker, the organization, and society be better off with or without unions as a party in employment relations?

Different countries have reached different conclusions about the utility and role of trade unions. And countries' answers to the questions have changed over time. For example, in Scandinavia, Finland, the former West Germany, Belgium, Holland, and Austria the trade union has been for several decades a strong and well-integrated partner with the employers and the government in setting economic and social policy and an active presence at all levels in the workplace. In Japan, unions are dependent on the firm and are integrated in it as enterprise, or company, unions instead of being independent voices of labor.

In the U.K., unions have had a strong presence on the shop floor but virtually none at the upper levels in the organization, and until recently they have received some support from the Labour Party for their political and economic aspirations. Over the last decade and a half, though, British unions have met solid opposition from a Conservative government and have been displaced at both the workplace and enterprise level by employers. Because British collective bargaining has been voluntary, unions and their officials have, by common agreement, been immune from prosecution for activities otherwise illegal under civil law. These immunities, such as being able to call work stoppages without a secret membership vote and without giving the employer prior notice or engaging in industrial action against other employers but not one's own ("secondary" industrial action), have now been removed by a flurry of legislation aimed at curbing union power. The new laws have also made it more difficult for local unions to gain new members, as the *closed shop* (a requirement that the employer hire only union members—made illegal in the United States in 1947) is now forbidden (Dickens & Hall, 1995). The result of this legislation is that although the procedures of negotiation and collective bargaining are still in place, employers are not necessarily using them, leading to observations that collective bargaining in Britain has become an "empty shell" (Legge, 1988).

Before we analyze the studies that attempt to answer the question whether unions are a necessary part of today's employment relations, we give a brief description of the research on cultural values on which we will draw throughout the rest of the chapter.

The Nature of Cultural Values

Values are strongly held beliefs about desirable end states or behaviors and can be thought of as desirable goals that guide the selection and evaluation of behaviors and events. An individual's values differ from his or her attitudes by being more general, or abstract, and by having a hierarchical order of importance to that individual (Schwartz, 1992). As individual-level variables, values are produced both by the individual's unique experiences and the culture (here, the national or social culture) to which he or she belongs. It is possible therefore to make inferences about cultural-level values from the values held by the individual members of the collectivity that makes up the culture (Hofstede, 1991; Schwartz, 1994). To answer the question of how the national or societal cultural context shapes employment relations in different countries, we want to know how the common core of values—shared by all its members—influences the behaviors of the key players in the IR system.

The best-known and most frequently used model of cultural values comes from Hofstede's research to discover the dimensions of national cultures. From a study of the values of IBM employees in fifty-three countries, Hofstede (1980, 1991) identified four dimensions:

High versus low power distance, which is the extent to which members of a society accept inequality in society as legitimate.

Individualism versus collectivism, which describes the relationships between the individual and the social group as a preference either for a loosely knit social framework in which individuals take care of themselves or their immediate family or for a tightly knit social framework in which individuals can expect relatives or in-group members to take care of them in exchange for their loyalty.

Masculinity versus femininity, which refers to the existence of separate or overlapping gender roles in society. Masculinity pertains to societies with distinct gender roles (men are assertive, achievement-oriented, tough, and concerned with material success, whereas women are modest, nurturing, tender, and concerned with relationships and the quality of life), and femininity pertains to societies where both men and women share the feminine role characteristics.

High versus low certainty avoidance, which is the degree to which members of a society feel uncomfortable or threatened by ambiguous or unknown situations. In societies with high uncertainty avoidance there is a stronger tendency for rules and regulations to control behavior.

A fifth dimension, *long-term versus short-term orientation* to life, was later added to the list (Hofstede, 1991).

The individualism-collectivism dimension has been used frequently in cross-cultural studies to explain national variations in behaviors and attitudes, and it has also received attention from researchers interested in developing a better understanding of its psychological properties (for example, Schwartz, 1992, 1994; Triandis, 1995).

Schwartz (1992, 1994) identified seven dominant value types based on data collected in thirty-eight nations (a number of which were not included in Hofstede's sample). These values are conservatism, intellectual autonomy, affective autonomy, hierarchy, mastery, egalitarian commitment, and harmony. There are substantial overlaps between these and Hofstede's dimensions, but the interpretation of Schwartz's data allows a more differentiated picture of the original dimensions.

The *autonomy* values, which correspond most closely to individualism, define the culture where the individual is seen as an autonomous entity with independent rights who pursues his or her individual interests and desires and relates to others in terms of negotiated settlements. The *mastery* value, which means mastery of the social environment through self-assertion, is also related to individualism.

Conservatism describes a society where the individual is part of the social fabric and derives his or her significance from participation in and identification with the group. Some of the individual-level values subsumed under this dimension are security, social order, tradition, conformity, obedience, self-discipline, and reciprocation of favors.

A fourth value of relevance is egalitarian commitment, a voluntary commitment to promote the welfare of other people, which Schwartz (1994) argued must be an integral part of the social values and norms in individualist cultures if they are to function smoothly. In collectivist cultures there is no need to emphasize voluntary prosocial behavior because it is enacted through the close interdependence of in-group members.

Triandis (1995) provided a more detailed description of the characteristics of the individualist-collectivist dimension. In collectivist cultures people define themselves as interdependent; personal goals are closely aligned with communal or in-group goals;

much of social behavior is focused on adherence to norms, obligations, and duties; and there is an emphasis on maintaining relationships, even when they are disadvantageous. In individualist cultures people define themselves as independent; personal goals have priority over communal or group goals; social behavior is guided by attitudes, personal needs, rights, and contracts; and members make calculative analyses of the advantages and disadvantages of maintaining a relationship.

Triandis (1995) further categorized individualist and collectivist cultures into horizontal and vertical forms. In the horizontal form people are similar on most attributes, or will prefer similarity, particularly with respect to status. In the vertical form people accept inequality and respect rank. For our purpose the distinction between horizontal and vertical individualism is particularly relevant. For example, in a rank-ordering of fifty nations and three regions on the cultural dimensions, Hofstede (1991) found the United States to be the most individualist country. The Scandinavian countries were also ranked high on this dimension (Denmark and Sweden were ranked 9 and 10, respectively, and Norway was ranked 13). However, Scandinavia is characterized by horizontal individualism, the United States by vertical individualism. Danes, Swedes, and Norwegians are independent and self-reliant, but they do not want to be individually unique and conspicuous, and dislike people who stick out. No one is better and brighter than any other, at least not openly so, and there is a preference for both wage and social equality. Being "the same" is valued. Americans value and encourage public recognition of individual achievement and accept income inequality (Triandis, 1995).

A wage system that acknowledges individual differences in skill, ability, and effort contributions, as performance-contingent pay does, for example, fits well with a vertical individualist culture but would not be acceptable in a horizontal individualist society. Therefore trade unions' position that wages should be determined more by job classification and seniority than by individual performance fits better with horizontal than vertical individualism.

This view of values and culture informs the following analysis of how three key actors in the U.S. industrial relations system—employers (or their management representatives), unions, and the state—have responded to trade unionism and how cultural values may have contributed to their responses.

Emergence and Institutionalization of Business Unionism

In early scholarly analyses of U.S. industrial relations most explanations for the development of the system were economic, structural, and political. In general it was thought that the attitudes of employers and workers toward unions and employment relations were anchored in beliefs about property rights, power relations, and the role of the government as a regulator of relationships between social classes (for example, Dunlop, 1958; Shalev, 1981).

An exception was Lipset's argument (1961, 1962) that the two U.S. "core" values of achievement and equality had shaped U.S. unions, making them more conservative, less class conscious, more militant, and more bureaucratic than Northern European unions. Americans believed each person should strive to be a success and that success was open to all. As long as workers thought that they could always escape their working-class status by hard work, and were anxiously trying to do so, a political working-class consciousness would be an unlikely foundation for a trade union movement in the United States

Indeed, one of the most puzzling questions U.S. labor historians have tried to answer is why, given a considerable amount of labor conflict and the reality of a large working class, did the U.S. labor movement not become institutionalized as a political power in the form of a labor, or social-democratic, political party, as has been the case in the U.K. and several other European countries? The question is important because linkages between unions and political parties on the national level can be a source of union power to shape industrial relation policies and practices.

A number of explanations have been offered for why U.S. workplace militancy, which in the nineteenth century was as strong as any in the industrial world (Montgomery, 1979), was so rarely translated into the politics of class. One possible answer lies in the cultural heterogeneity of the U.S. working class, shaped by successive waves of immigrants from different ethnic backgrounds. New immigrants did not immediately abandon their cultural identity and melt into the existing working class, and their common status as industrial workers was not sufficient to overcome their cultural differences and create a political working-class consciousness (Dawley, 1989; Wilentz, 1989).

Another hypothesis is that capitalism's success ensured socialism's failure. Their high rates of geographical and social mobility and ability to acquire property made U.S. workers complacent and socialism irrelevant to them (Foner, 1984). Embedded in this line of thinking is the idea that the pursuit of self-interest, the importance of the free and independent individual and the equal citizen who gains mastery over a social environment—the essence of individualism—could at least partly explain why open labor-management conflict in the workplace coexisted with nonideological political parties.

In contrast, a cultural values analysis suggests that the workplace militancy and open conflict of U.S. labor relations is a behavioral implication of both masculinity and individualism, on which the United States ranks relatively high (Hofstede, 1991). The idea that conflict should be resolved with a good fight in which the best man or woman wins fits the often combative stance of U.S. unions and employers and contrasts sharply with the compromise-and-negotiation approach to labor-management conflict of the Scandinavian countries (Slomp, 1996), which are among the four lowest ranked countries on Hofstede's masculinity index. (However, we also note that masculine or individualist cultural values alone do not seem sufficient for the development of combative labor relations. For example, Japan, has very high masculinity scores but low-conflict labor relations, and it is a collectivist society. In Scandinavia feminine cultural values coexist with high individualism.)

Not only did U.S. workers eschew political socialism; U.S. union leaders also took a strong stance against a major union role in national party politics. The trade unionism that appealed to the skilled workforce in the United States was pragmatic, aimed at improving wages and working conditions. The clearest expression of this *business unionism* philosophy came from the American Federation of Labor (AFL), formed in 1886 as a federation of separate national craft unions that had organized the skilled trades in large manufacturing firms. AFL leader Samuel Gompers argued that improvement in the worker's lot would come through collective bargaining, not through party politics, and that the union's role was to fight for bread-and-butter issues (Salvatore, 1984). Despite the limited role the AFL unions defined for themselves—organizing only the crafts and not the large mass of industrial workers, bargaining only over wages and working conditions and not over managerial authority, and having no political agenda other than supporting social welfare legislation—employers were bitterly opposed to them and used a variety of strategies to stop union organizing.

Employers' and management's responses to a national union movement have shaped U.S. industrial relations as much as, if not more than, the unions have (Jacoby, 1990). Their opposition to collective bargaining was rooted in beliefs about their property rights—their rights to use plants and capital equipment as they saw fit. Unions would interfere with these rights if they bargained over conditions of employment (Cullen & Chamberlain, 1970). These beliefs also supported employers' strong desire for autonomy from government or any other institution. Their initially successful efforts to block the unions included intimidation and suppression tactics (later made illegal), progressive personnel policies and practices including pension, welfare, and profit-sharing programs (*welfare capitalism*), and attempts to encourage employees to form company-controlled unions that would be independent of the AFL. Between 1921 and 1931, union membership fell from 5.8 million to fewer than 2 million (Katz & Kochan, 1992).

The union movement rallied again, however, as a result of three interrelated events: the Great Depression, a move from craft-based to industrial unionism, and the passage of the National Labor Relations Act (NLRA). The economic and social crisis caused by the Depression, which left 13 million people—about 25 percent of the labor force—unemployed and reduced hourly wages by 60 percent, shifted the country's political views and thus political power, resulting in the 1932 election of Franklin Roosevelt as president, on a New Deal platform of social and economic reform.

The AFL's insistence on unionizing workers by craft had left the mass of unskilled manufacturing workers without union protection and had also weakened the existing unions' main source of power—the strike threat—because it proved difficult to mobilize the several different craft unions jointly in order to strike against a large employer. In 1935, the union movement split, and its more militant and politically radical elements, led by John L. Lewis, left the AFL to form the Congress of Industrial Organizations (CIO) (Cullen & Chamberlain, 1970).

The formation of the CIO revitalized the union movement, and the new union was very successful in organizing mass-production industries. However, the tremendous growth in private-sector union membership, from 3.5 million in 1934 to a peak of 17 million (35 percent of the nonagricultural labor force) in the mid-1950s, would not have happened without another event: pro-labor legislation.

The National Labor Relations Act was passed in 1935, over considerable employer opposition. It gave workers the right to unionize, specified how union elections should be run and how labor and management should behave during organizing campaigns, and if a majority of workers voted for union representation, required management to negotiate over wages, hours, and working conditions. However, the rights to make business decisions and to determine the organization of work were left with management; they were not made mandatory topics for labor-management bargaining. The NLRA also established the National Labor Relations Board (NLRB), which had the power to determine union representation and election questions and investigate and rule on charges of unfair labor practice.

The New Deal Industrial Relations System

The industrial relations system most closely associated in people's mind with U.S. unions developed between 1935 and the early 1950s and lasted until the 1980s. It had three primary components: collective bargaining at the industrial-level, management authority over firm-level strategic decision making and shop floor activity, and *job control* unionism in the workplace.

The purpose of centralized collective bargaining was to obtain a standard wage across industries to raise the standard of living for all unionized workers and take wages out of competition. Therefore, contracts between individual employers and their unions would follow a pattern set by an industry leader and its union.

The principle of management prerogatives left the authority to determine what, how, and when work should be done to management, but job control unionism gave labor some control over work at the point of production by defining workers' rights and obligations to specific jobs in the union contract. Disputes over work assignment and staffing were handled through an elaborate grievance procedure, also specified in the contract. For union workers, job control meant job security. For employers, however, it often meant a large number of job classifications with strict lines of demarcation that limited how labor could be used in production, and employers often saw it as a source of workplace inflexibility and inefficiency.

By regulating labor-management conflict, the New Deal industrial relations system brought a stability and order to labor relations for which employers were willing to pay a premium, at least initially. The presence of unions often had a "shock effect" on management, which had to make operations more efficient and productive to offset the increased labor costs associated with collective bargaining (Slichter, Healy, & Livernash, 1960).

There are different interpretations of why the unions accepted a law that limited the scope of their participation in organizational decision making to the labor exchange and left intact both management's authority to determine strategic and entrepreneurial decisions and to manage the shop and office floor. One argument is that the NLRA fit the values of both labor and management, merging the business unionism philosophy with management's desire for autonomy and control. The labor movement's political goal was not to overthrow capitalism but to improve workers' standard of living (Katz & Kochan, 1992). Others have claimed that labor traded political power, including a voice in company governance, for recognition (Reich, 1989).

The passage of pro-union legislation did not mean that U.S. employers willingly accepted unions. They tolerated the unions, but continued to discourage their employees from joining them. In contrast, most European employers accepted unions as the legitimate representatives of workers' interests and did not try to stop employees from unionizing. European employers formed their own national associations and collaborated with federations of unions and with government in establishing national wage and employment policies, adopting what is known as a *tripartite,* or *corporatist,* model of government (Slomp, 1996).

The U.K., however, differed from many of its European neighbors in not choosing a corporatist approach and from the United States by not enacting pro-union legislation. Public policy on trade unionism in the U.K. has, at different times, supported trade union recognition but not legal rights (Bain & Price, 1983; Waddington & Whitston, 1995).

It would be tempting to ascribe U.S. employers' opposition to unions to the characteristics of an individualist culture and to argue that European employers were more accepting because they lived in more collectivist societies. However, Hofstede's data show that Northern Europe and Great Britain are not collectivist societies, and Schwartz's more recent findings (1994) rank the United States below the European countries on affective and intellectual autonomy and above them on conservatism.

In an analysis of the European response to the rise of unionism, Adams (1981) rejected the hypothesis that value systems explained the differences in employer responses across countries. He argued that the attitudes and values of North American (that is, both Canadian and U.S.) and European employers are very similar, and that their initial responses to the emergence of the labor movement were much the same; they focused on destroying or containing the unions. However, from about 1880, the IR systems in North America and Europe went in very different directions. At that time European unions began to organize unskilled labor, adopt a political ideology of replacing capitalism with socialism, and forge links with labor and socialist political parties. Increased union membership, political power, and militancy in the form of large strikes made governments take up labor's grievances as major political issues and put pressure on the two sides to negotiate resolutions to the conflicts. The employers recognized that their open conflict with unions ideologically opposed to capitalism would bring government intervention and could be a threat to them as a class (Adams, 1981).

From about 1890, then, employers' confederations were formed in a number of European countries. The ensuing national-level negotiations and collaboration between federations of employers, the unions, and the state on issues of broad social concerns as well as employment relations have remained the most distinctive features of labor relations in Northern and Central Europe.

Challenges to Institutional Industrial Relations: The Nonunion System

In the United States the first serious challenge to the New Deal model came in the 1960s, with a rise in shop floor militancy brought on by the social and political upheaval of the decade, an economic upswing that created a tighter labor market, and the inability of centralized collective bargaining to respond to the local-level concerns of rank-and-file union members. Legal and illegal (wildcat) strikes increased significantly, as did grievance rates. However, neither management nor union leadership changed course from established policies and practices to respond to this obvious failure of the industrial relations system to manage conflict.

In contrast to the U.S. business-as-usual approach to industrial relations, employers, unions, and governments in some other countries looked for alternatives to their industrial relations systems when these ceased to function as expected. For example, the employers' confederations and central trade union organizations in Norway and Sweden interpreted the highly unusual outbreak of local union militancy and wildcat strikes that occurred there during the early 1960s as a rank-and-file protest against lack of local union control over collective bargaining and lack of employee involvement in workplace decision making. The unrest became the impetus for a series of joint union-employer-sponsored worker participation experiments with autonomous workgroups (Bolweg, 1976; Emery & Thorsrud, 1976), which became stepping stones toward passage of industrial democracy legislation in the 1970s (Gustavsen & Hunnius, 1981).

The seriousness with which the central organizations in these countries responded to the open conflict reflects the importance they accorded harmonious labor relations. A preference for solving conflicts as soon as possible, or better still for preventing them by compromise and negotiation, is part of the feminine cultural values that characterize Norway and Sweden. In the masculine and individualist culture of the United States, open conflict is not unusual, and its existence less likely to provoke a search for new methods of conflict resolution.

U.S. industrial relations did change, however. By the early 1980s, the rigid rule-based New Deal model was being replaced by local, company-based negotiations, employer-designed work and compensation packages, flexible job classifications, and direct worker participation in organizational decision making (Kochan, Katz, & McKersie, 1986). This transformation was employer initiated and run; it was a long-term business strategy to create a nonunion industrial relation system. It began with the development of a nonunion sector within traditionally unionized industries, as corporations closed or stopped investing in older unionized plants and instead built new nonunion facilities to which they transferred work. Management of these *greenfield* sites experimented with new human resource management programs such as employee involvement, job redesign, gain sharing, and employee stock ownership, copied from policies and practices of companies that had never been unionized to begin with. As this nonunion sector grew and union membership declined precipitously through the 1970s and 1980s (by 1984, only 19 percent of the nonagricultural private-sector workforce were union members), unions were forced to give up pattern bargaining and job control in favor of locally negotiated contracts and flexible work and staffing arrangements. In many cases they had to agree to wage and fringe benefit concessions to save plants and jobs (for example, Kochan, Katz, & Mower, 1984; Schuster, 1984; Gerhart, 1987; Whyte, Hammer, Meek, Nelson, & Stern, 1983).

This new corporate business strategy was not the only reason for the decline of union power. Union membership also decreased because the labor market was changing as employment shrank in the blue-collar manufacturing sector prevalent in the Northern industrialized, heavily unionized states and expanded in nonunion areas: the service sector, white-collar professional jobs, and the Southern states (Farber, 1985). This shift in employment away from traditional industries and locations was not felt only in the United States, of course; it was part of a global trend. But U.S. unions had always had a difficult time trying to organize white-collar workers, and they were prohibited by law (Taft-Hartley Act of 1947) from unionizing supervisory personnel, so the loss of membership could not easily be recouped from other constituents. In addition the unions had chosen not to organize aggressively in the service sector (McDonald, 1985).

A third reason for union decline, and a primary reason for the emergence of a nonunion industrial relations system, was management values. As we described earlier, U.S. managers' opposition to unions has always been strong, and it has not diminished much with time and experience. We attributed part of this opposition to individualist cultural values. In the 1980s, political climate and ideologies changed both in the United States and in Europe, becoming more favorable toward individualist values and a market-driven economy and more hostile to collectivist political movements and trade unions. Recent Gallup polls have shown that although the majority of Americans, executives included, believe that a free trade union movement is valuable in a democratic society, most managers do not want a union in their workplaces (Kochan & Osterman, 1994). Other recent national survey data show that a large majority (69 percent) of nonunion managers would oppose any unionization effort at their firms (Freeman & Rogers, 1995, p. 10).

In the U.K. the rise of the nonunion firm also became more obvious in the 1980s. In the 1970s, such firms had been regarded by many academics as an aberrant form that would disappear, or at least shrink, with a public policy concerned with union recognition. By the 1980s, the picture had changed considerably, and a majority of new start-ups were nonunion. In addition, when established firms moved to greenfield sites, some chose to operate nonunion (Bassett, 1986). The increase in the size and significance of the nonunion sector in Britain was attributed, in part and at least initially, to the development of human resource management (HRM). HRM defines employees as a strategic component of competitiveness and therefore emphasizes the recruitment, retention, and reward of individuals. Part of HRM's prominence—at least in rhetorical terms—is that it addresses an issue somewhat neglected in traditional industrial relations: how to motivate rather than simply control employees.

HRM policies and practices are anchored in a unitarist model of the employment relationship. In this model, unions are unnecessary. However, recent analyses of both nonunion organizations and HRM have shown that in the U.K. at least, the picture is not so simple. In many U.K. organizations HRM practices have spread much more slowly and inconsistently than was first predicted and are also more likely to coexist with trade unions than was predicted, and not always peacefully (Millward, Stevens, Smart, & Hawes, 1992; Sisson & Marginson, 1995). In contrast to U.S. employers, U.K. firms have had to incorporate HRM practices within an established set of trade union structures. Despite its individualist focus, HRM is therefore more likely to be found in the union than in the nonunion firm in the U.K.

Anti-union attitudes in the United States have economic roots as well. In a comparison of union wage effects in countries of the Organization for Economic Cooperation and Development (OECD), Blanchflower and Freeman (1992) found that unions have a greater effect on wages in the United States than in other countries, and that high union wage premiums contributed to the 1980s U.S. decline in union density. This wage premium was not offset by the higher productivity in union firms. Also, the difference between union and nonunion wages was substantially higher in the United States than it was in the U.K., the former West Germany, Austria, Australia, and Switzerland (a subset of the eighteen countries included in the study). This is not surprising, however, because wages are set, or bargained, centrally in some of these comparison countries and union wage agreements are extended to nonunion workers in others. In the United States, negotiations take place locally, which encourages wage rate dispersion.

Being a union employer has been associated with lower profitability, both in the United States and the U.K., because the increased labor costs (both wages and fringe benefits go up with unionization) exceed productivity increases (Blanchflower & Freeman, 1992). If these data are valid, they are a motivator for employers to move to nonunion operations. However, British industrial relations scholars have argued that the blame for Britain's industrial performance cannot be placed on the trade unions. A number of macro-economic variables, such as patterns of foreign investments, the predominance of labor-intensive low-value-added work firms and economic constraints created by the government's industrial and labor market policies, have been the main reasons for decline (Nolan & Walsh, 1995).

In the United States, anti-union values combined with pressures to contain labor costs and increase productivity not only spurred the development and growth of greenfield sites but also stiffened employers' resistance to union organizing of new worksites. Union organizing drives became highly confrontational, with more intensive employer use of both legal and illegal tactics to defeat unions in elections. The number of NLRB representation elections won by unions declined during the 1980s, and research suggests that about 40 percent of this decline came from management opposition (Freeman, 1985). Decertification elections, however, accounted for only 2 percent of union membership decline during the same period (Dickens & Leonard, 1985). In addition about one-third of the workplaces that voted for union representation did not manage to obtain a collective bargaining contract with the employer (Commission on the Future of Worker-Management Relations, 1994).

Not all U.S. employers tried to develop a nonunion industrial relations strategy, and of those who tried not all succeeded. Employers that were heavily unionized to begin with and dealt with powerful unions such as the automakers', were less likely to succeed with a "Southern strategy," and they ended up collaborating with their unions to develop innovative and quite effective programs to contain labor costs and increase organizational effectiveness (for example, Appelbaum & Batt, 1994; Kochan & Osterman, 1994). National survey findings have reinforced the data from individual case studies by showing that in unionized companies, managers are inclined to make the best of the situation, with 69 percent stating that they accept the union as a partner, and 24 percent reporting that they want to get rid of the union.

Researchers disagree on whether decentralized bargaining and increased employer power to rewrite union contracts and employment policies and practices have occurred in other countries. In a study of bargaining structures in Sweden, Australia, the former West Germany, Italy, and the U.K., Katz (1993) found that the intensity of local bargaining increased substantially in all these countries after 1980, and he argued that this downward shift in bargaining structure resulted from employer initiatives (in all the countries except Australia, where it came about through an accord between the unions and the government) primarily to accommodate new forms of work restructuring, such as teamwork and lean production manufacturing, which require flexible staffing, training, employee participation, and often also include performance contingent pay.

However, a more recent study by Wallerstein, Golden, and Lange (1997) of private-sector union concentration and centralization of bargaining in Austria, Belgium, Denmark, Finland, Germany, the Netherlands, Norway, and Sweden found considerable between-country difference in decentralization and union density. Decentralization of wage setting occurred only in the Netherlands, Denmark, and Sweden, but in different time periods, and appeared to be caused by a desire felt by some unions and employers to reverse excessive wage compression, not by recent changes in the global economic environment. Average union density in Northern and Central Europe fell about 3 percent in the 1980s but declined 10 percent in Austria and the Netherlands. In the four Nordic countries, union membership in traditional blue-collar union federations declined, but membership in white-collar and professional unions grew. Data from 1989 and 1990 showed that despite large differences in union density (from 23 percent in the Netherlands to 83 percent in Sweden), union coverage—the percentage of all wage and salary earners covered by a collective bargaining agreement regardless of their union status—was uniformly high in all eight countries, ranging from 71 percent in Austria to 95 percent in Finland. And contrary to Katz's arguments (1993), U.K. researchers have suggested that claims of decentralized industrial relations in the U.K. are an illusion. Wage bargaining may take place at the local level but wages are not necessarily decided there (Sisson & Marginson, 1995).

Although there have been some changes in bargaining structures in Europe and Australia, unions there, with the exception of those in the U.K., did not suffer the same decline in union power as the United States has witnessed. These unions' ability to maintain their power in shaping employment relations at the firm level, despite increased employer discretion in collective bargaining, has been due in part to their role in national politics. The unions' ties to ruling labor and social democratic parties have helped them secure an alternative route to power, through industrial democracy legislation.

The codetermination laws passed in a number of European countries (or expanded, in the case of Germany) during the 1970s gave nonmanagerial workers the right to a voice in corporate-level decision making through representation on boards of directors, works councils, company assemblies, or similar governance bodies. Quite often unions either appointed or elected, and trained, the worker representatives whose roles were defined as labor interest-group advocates (for example, IDE, 1981; Strauss, 1982; Streeck, 1984). This industrial democracy legislation did not have the substantial effect on the within-firm distribution of power that its proponents had hoped and its opponents feared (for example, IDE,

1981, 1993), but labor relations practices did change, and the role of the workforce and unions in organizational decision making expanded as a result of it (Streeck, 1984; Turner, 1993).

In particular, *codetermination* has come to mean union-management cooperation and consultation on multiple levels in the organizational hierarchy. It is a *partnership model* (Dølvik & Stokland, 1992), which has increased union power in the workplace by expanding the areas of decision making open to union representatives and letting them into the decision-making process early on. The partnership model allows for union participation in the creation of company policy not just in its implementation. It is the very opposite of the adversarial New Deal model, in which management acts, and the union reacts.

A union-management partnership in corporate governance has until recently been an effective mechanism for maintaining industrial peace, especially when firms have faced situations with high potential for labor-management conflict, such as large-scale organizational change (Hammer, Ingebrigtsen, Karlsen, & Svarva, 1994; Kochan & Osterman, 1994), but it is not without costs. For example, it has been argued that the industrial democracy legislation, with its emphasis on accommodating the different interests of capital and labor to ensure industrial peace, has made Scandinavian managers focus too much on maintaining internal harmony and too little on increasing their firms' competitive position in external markets (Reve, 1994). This may be a possible cost of feminine cultural values when the other dominant players in the market operate with a masculine value system.

European employers did not welcome either the prospect or the reality of codetermination (IDE, 1981), but they adapted to the requirements of the legislation in such a way that it does not seem to have diminished their ability to manage their firms. Decision-making processes have changed with the incorporation of labor interests, but the relative power of management and labor has not (IDE, 1993). This conclusion would not be sufficient to assuage U.S. managers' and trade unionists' fear of industrial democracy legislation, however. Even modest suggestions about the adaptation of some components of European codetermination have met with strong opposition (Kochan & Osterman, 1994). At stake for labor is the possibility of losing power if unions are coopted through the participation process (for example, Hammer, Currall, & Stern, 1991) while management strongly resists further union encroachment on its power.

In the U.K. the substantial defeats of trade unions at workplace, enterprise, and national levels during the 1980s led to new thinking about collective bargaining and about partnership approaches to industrial relations. Traditionally, both employers and trade unions in general had been opposed to industrial democracy or worker participation schemes on the grounds that they either interfered with free collective bargaining or did not go far enough to give workers control. And Britain has been the only European Union member state that has refused to sign the Social Chapter of the Treaty of Maastricht, which would have conferred both individual and collective rights within the workplace to British workers.

However, the political and industrial changes of the 1980s have exposed the weaknesses of trade unions' voluntarist traditions. Feminists have, in any case, argued for some time that traditional trade unions were unable or unwilling to cater to the interests of women workers who lacked the "industrial muscle" of employees organized in traditional industries in large organizations (Colling & Dickens, 1989; Liff & Aitkenhead, 1992). In addition the Labour Party's 1987 failure to gain power in a general election dashed union hopes of a more emollient industrial environment. British unions reversed their former antipathy to European codetermination. In particular, prominent trade union leaders have started to argue for the need for partnership-based rather than adversarial industrial relations. The Trades Union Congress (TUC), the national body for trade unions in the U.K., has promoted the need to build consensus between labor and management as a way forward for the U.K.

British employers have also softened their traditional implacability to workplace representation structures. Large organizations with establishments in several European countries are aware that employee representation (for example, through works councils) is likely to become a reality through U.K. membership in the European Union and the resulting application of European law (Gold & Hall, 1994).

Thus we see a shift in attitudes and values about employee representation occurring among both trade unionists and employers in the U.K. The change of heart is far from complete or uncontroversial and is more the result of economic and political forces than immediate cultural forces. However, there is still some way to go before any of these aspirational changes take shape in concrete practices and procedures.

The Future of Employee Representation

Given the present state of U.S. unions, one could conclude that they are no longer necessary in the U.S. private sector. Government regulations cover an ever expanding part of the employment relationship, and nonunion employers may already provide what the unions promise in terms of both voice and wages and benefits. Do U.S. workers still need union representation to get justice and equity in the workplace?

A number of national-level surveys and studies of labor market and working conditions have described the current employment situation facing the workforce (for example, Appelbaum & Batt, 1994; Freeman & Rogers, 1994; Lawler, Mohrman, & Ledford, 1992). The most comprehensive of these is the fact-finding study of the Commission on the Future of Worker-Management Relations (1994), established by President Clinton to investigate the current state of U.S. worker-management relations and then determine, first, how workplace productivity could be enhanced through labor-management cooperation and employee participation; second, what changes, if any, should be made in labor law and collective bargaining practices to enhance cooperation, improve productivity, and reduce conflict; and third, what should be done to increase the resolution of workplace problems by labor and management at the local level and to avoid using the courts and governmental agencies to solve disputes?

The commission's study of wage patterns showed that the real hourly compensation for U.S. workers has stagnated in the last two decades and actually fallen for male workers. Further, there is a growing gap in earnings between higher-paid and more educated or skilled workers and lower-paid and less educated workers. This widening earnings inequality—what the unions tried to overcome with pattern bargaining—reflects the current bifurcation of U.S. labor into a highly skilled technical and professional workforce and manual workers with few skills. Temporary, or contingent, work has grown at the expense of full-time jobs. In short, during the industrial relations transformation of the 1980s, both union and non-union employers in the United States adopted a "labor cheapening" strategy (Kochan & Osterman, 1994) that included cutbacks both in wages and in benefits such as pension coverage (Blanchflower & Freeman, 1992).

In contrast, manufacturing wages increased in each of the other large OECD countries during the same period, and all European countries except Great Britain experienced a much smaller wage inequality gap than the United States did (Bureau of Labor Statistics data from 1990 in Kochan & Osterman, 1994). Britain has shown similar trends in wage polarization and subsequent poverty even among the employed as the United States (Benington & Taylor, 1993).

U.S. job security, another traditional union issue, also decreased. The unemployment rate for the second quarter of 1996 was 5.3 percent, which is a considerable improvement after the 1980s decade when the average rate was 7.3, and it is lower than the rate in many European countries. However, after the financial market turbulence of the 1980s, with mergers and acquisitions, downsizing and reengineering (for example, Hammer & Champy, 1993; Tichy & Sherman, 1993), feelings of job insecurity are now widespread (*The Changing Workforce . . . ,* 1993). The majority of workers who lost their jobs found new ones but of lower quality. Department of Labor figures show that 74 percent of the 4.5 million workers displaced between 1991 and 1993 became worse off, ending up with either lower earnings, fewer benefits, or only part-time work or with continuing unemployment (AFL-CIO, 1995).

Lower wages, poor fringe benefits, wage inequalities, and job insecurity would suggest that unions could still have an important role to play in U.S. employment relations if unorganized workers believed that their interests would be protected by group action and that the union is the best form of collective voice for them.

The research on union voting in the United States and Canada has shown that wages, pay dissatisfaction, and perceived pay inequities predict intentions to vote for union representation (Barling, Fullagar, & Kelloway, 1992). Lack of trust in management and feelings of powerlessness also contribute to pro-union voting (for example, Hammer & Berman, 1981; Zalesny, 1985; Keaveny, Rose,

& Fossum, 1988). However, workers' general attitudes toward unions also influence their willingness to join (Barling, Kelloway, & Bremermann, 1991), as do perceptions of union instrumentality (Premack & Hunter, 1988).

Recent U.S. national-level survey data have shown that private-sector employees want to be represented by a group or an association when negotiating with management, and they want more involvement in and influence over workplace decisions than what they have at present, particularly with respect to benefits, pay raises, and training. There is a substantial *representation gap* among the unorganized, and there is a *participation gap* among both union members and nonmembers (Freeman & Rogers, 1994).

New evidence of a participation gap is not surprising. Research on participation in union and nonunion firms has found this gap consistently (for example, IDE, 1981, 1993; Hammer & Stern, 1980; Hammer, Currall, & Stern, 1991). It is also well documented that despite their higher wages and benefits unionized workers are not more satisfied than their nonunion counterparts with their jobs and working conditions (Freeman & Medoff, 1984). Union members are *on the whole* satisfied with their unions, however, and would vote to keep the union if there were a new election. They see the union as "a ticket to a good job with decent pay" (Freeman & Rogers, 1994, p. 34). This assessment is echoed by managers in unionized firms, a majority of whom credit the union with improving the work life of firm members.

But wanting a good job with decent pay is not a sufficiently strong reason for a pro-union vote among U.S. workers. The Freeman and Rogers (1994) data showed that only 32 percent of unorganized workforce would vote for union representation in an election. Part of the reason for these numbers is the belief that the employer would oppose a union, and there is fear of going against management. When management opposition to unionization is removed from consideration, 42 percent of the workers say they would vote for the union, which would still not be enough, however, for the union to win an election.

These findings suggest that U.S. workers want a new type of employee organization, one that will give them more influence in workplace decisions and will combine some characteristics of unions with those of the employee committees found in employee involvement programs. The new organization should be independent of management, have elected representatives, and include a grievance system with outside arbitrators to adjudicate disputes that cannot be solved internally. These features are part of the union legacy. However, the organization should have management support (workers want cooperative, not adversarial, labor-management relations), and it should rely on the company for its budget and staff. The model employee organization is not unlike a company union, which is an illegal entity under present labor laws.

Although there is both naïveté and lack of knowledge behind the definition of an ideal workers' association, there is a serious message to both trade unions and employers in workers' desire for increased involvement in workplace decisions. This desire echoes the arguments that psychologists and a small group of industrial relations researchers have made for the last two decades about the potential benefits of *job redesign, high-involvement management,* and *team-based manufacturing* for employee attitudes and performance (for example, Appelbaum & Batt, 1994; Cutcher-Gershenfeld, 1991; Hackman & Oldham, 1980; Hammer, 1988; Katz, 1985; Lawler, 1986).

Interestingly, the model employee association is similar in some respects to Japanese enterprise unions, which play a substantial role in the extensive consultative participation used in large Japanese firms. The role of these enterprise unions is to represent employees' interests in the workplace, but they are not independent voices. They negotiate with management over wages and employment conditions, but their primary function is to adapt workers' interests to employers' goals. The enterprise union is one of the "three sacred treasures" of the Japanese industrial relations system, the other two being lifetime employment (for men) and a compensation and promotion policy that rewards seniority and personal characteristics (Abo, 1994). Japan is a collectivist culture, however, in which the relationship between employer and employee is a family link as well as a contractual labor exchange. Mutual loyalty and commitment to one's in-group is, or at least has been in the past, a moral obligation. A collectivist culture demands from its members more adherence to norms, duties, and obligations and more submission to group interests than U.S. workers are probably prepared to give. Certainly, there is not much evidence that U.S. employers are psychologically prepared to view and treat employees as members of an employer-worker extended family. Thus the model employee association may fit U.S. cultural values as poorly as it fits U.S. labor laws.

We are not arguing that all U.S. unions have been unwilling or reluctant to respond to their members' preferences for more direct involvement in decision making. There are a number of well-documented case studies of extensive union-management programs where employee involvement has been used to boost productivity (for a good selection of recently updated cases, see Appelbaum & Batt, 1994; Kochan, Katz, & McKersie, 1986). However, national union leaders have been slow to recognize an unmet need among both members and nonmembers for greater involvement in workplace decisions and have failed to broaden unions' agendas accordingly. It was not until 1994 that the AFL-CIO went on record in support of workplace innovation (AFL-CIO Committee on the Evolution of Work, 1994). Although union leaders cannot ignore the possibility that empowerment can mean "doing more work in less time with fewer workers for lower pay" (Becon, 1994, p. 749), as even lean production manufacturing has been called empowerment (Womack, Jones, & Roos, 1990), a union presence would in all likelihood mean a more favorable labor exchange at least for those fewer workers.

In a discussion of possible future models of industrial relations, Kochan and Osterman (1994) argued for closing the representation gap for nonunion workers by adopting works councils adapted to U.S. work settings. The obvious objection to this proposal is that one cannot borrow a single component of a whole program of participation and expect the same results as those using the whole program have gotten. Works councils have been an effective voice at the workplace level for German employees precisely because they are linked to the trade unions, are coupled with other participation mechanisms stipulated in the codetermination laws, and are anchored in almost forty years of experience with national-level labor-management cooperation (Morris, 1995). There is no similar experience in the United States, and very little in the U.S. cultural value system that would sustain it.

That is not to say that management practices and work methods developed in one culture can never be transferred to another.

Research on the transfer of Japanese manufacturing methods has demonstrated that a company does not need to adopt the entire Japanese industrial relations system to use those methods successfully in other countries (Abo, 1994; MacDuffie & Krafcik, 1992; Womack, Jones, & Roos, 1990). But those components of an IR system that derive their effectiveness from their links to a dominant cultural value system cannot be expected to thrive in a culture that does not support them. The effective adoption of works councils as a form of representation for nonunionized workers in the United States would require, at the very least, such changes in national labor policy as making the government a more active proponent of and catalyst for workplace innovation and also changes in labor law. Kochan and Osterman (1994) advocate both these steps; however, neither change is likely to happen in the immediate future.

It is difficult to compare the future prospects for U.S. and British workplace representation. Although developments in employment relations in the two countries have been quite similar since the early 1980s, trade unionism in the U.K. has had a stronger political and social base. And even though a fair amount of that political power has been lost, union density remains much stronger in the U.K. The passage of legislation curbing U.K. union and employment rights (abolishing the wages councils responsible for setting minimum wage levels for low-skilled workers and protecting workers against unfair dismissal, for example), an increasing wage gap between the skilled and unskilled, and a dramatic increase in insecure and temporary employment in both the private and public sectors, has left the workforce more vulnerable than before (Hartley, 1983; Industrial Relations Services [Employment Trends], 1993). A major survey of industrial relations in Britain compared union with nonunion organizations and concluded that although managers reported better employee relations in the nonunion sector, the picture looked different with respect to representation. Employees in this sector had relatively few formal mechanisms for involvement in workplace decision making and were less likely to have opportunities to air grievances or resolve problems in a way designed to ensure fair treatment. There was no evidence that alternative models of employee representation had emerged as a viable substitute for union representation (Millward, Stevens, Smart, & Hawes, 1992, p. 365).

It is also difficult to make a general comparison between U.S. and European workers' attachments to unions because the research on union joining has followed different paths, each embedded in the very different social and institutional contexts that union recognition, membership, and participation have had in different countries. Cultural value systems have also shaped the research agendas. To a European eye, U.S. research on union joining has been overly focused on the individual employee's decision to vote for or against union representation, and theories of how employees come to belong to unions have been overly individualist (Hartley & Kelly, 1986). European research has been more focused on exploring socialization issues that lead an employee to join a union already established at the workplace, and to explain union commitment it has developed theories that combine individual rationality with social norms and pressures operating in the workplace (de Witte, 1996; Hartley, 1992a; Nicholson, Ursell, & Blyton, 1981).

The Psychology of Employment Relations

In North America the application of psychological theory and research designs to the study of employment relations has occurred in two separate streams. The prominent one is of course the analysis of the relationship between employers and employees, which has been the domain of industrial psychologists who have continued and refined the work of the personnel management school of industrial relations with the unitarist model as a guiding principle. The second stream has been the analysis of the relationship between employees and their unions, which has been carried out by a much smaller group of psychologists, some of whom, at least, understand that unions are political interest groups and that labor-management relations should be analyzed from a pluralist perspective.

In Britain the distinctions between these two streams of research is less apparent. Although there have always been those psychologists who have taken a unitarist perspective on relations between employer (or more often management) and employees, the second stream has been broader than a simple focus on trade unions. Psychologists interested in the processes of influence and control at work have examined the relationship between employees and their trade unions from both an organizational and an individual perspective (for example, Waddington, 1987; Hartley & Stephenson, 1992; Kelly & Kelly, 1991, 1992). Their research reflects the view that employment relations can be as much about the motivation to work as about control over work and the worker, and that issues of stress at work, organizational change, absenteeism and turnover, and so on can be considered from an industrial relations (that is, a pluralist) perspective.

Employment relations should not be viewed as sets of dyadic relationships. Employment relations have at least three parties, or sets of actors, and often four: employers, employees, unions, and the government. (We could also add a fifth party, employers' associations or confederations. Although employers' joining together in associations to bargain collectively is becoming less important in the U.K. and has never been significant in the United States, it has been and remains an important factor in Northern and Central Europe.) If researchers and practitioners concentrate their theoretical and empirical work on different combinations of dyads, it will lead to an incomplete understanding of complex processes. Two very good examples of this result are the psychological studies of union voting and union commitment.

We know that there are at least three parties with a psychological presence in union representation elections: the worker, the union, and the employer. The government is of course also involved through legislation governing the elections but may not exist as a player in the workers' consciousness. One early study of union elections based on psychological theory recognized and examined the importance of employer actions (Getman, Goldberg, & Herman, 1976), but most of the studies that followed left employer response to an organizing drive out altogether.

Yet the recent studies we have examined in this chapter have shown very clearly that employees' attitudes toward union representation are influenced by the employer's opposition to unions. This opposition happens to be especially strong in the United States for a number of reasons unique to the U.S. collective bargaining structure and to a society that values individualism and independence. It may be stronger in the private sector than in the public sector for economic reasons. These latter two arguments imply that studies of union voting should incorporate in their conceptual models not only the employer as an independent variable but also union characteristics and the social, political, or cultural context in which the union vote is embedded. It would be instructive for U.S.-trained researchers to examine the broader models of union joining proposed by European researchers, making the appropriate allowances for the very different legal, economic, political, and cultural contexts in which that joining occurs.

Part of the research on union commitment (for a list of North American and European studies, see Barling, Fullagar, & Kelloway, 1992) has paid some attention to the worker-union-employer triad by incorporating the relationship between the employer and the union in prediction models, on the assumption that, first, the union bears some of the responsibility for managing this relationship, and second, members prefer cooperative to adversarial labor relations. For example, one could argue that studies of dual commitment (that is, whether union members can be highly committed to both their employer and their union, and if so, what explains that phenomenon) recognize the three-way interaction. However, the dual commitment research has been very poor conceptually, leading Gordon and Ladd (1990) to argue that dual commitment is an epiphenomenon, a by-product of the labor relations climate. The very few cross-cultural studies available of union commitment and dual commitment have, unfortunately, focused more on answering questions about the dimensions of the commitment construct than on achieving a theoretical understanding of how different cultural contexts and industrial relations systems might shape commitment to the union (Kuruvilla & Iverson, 1993; Kuruvilla & Sverke, 1993).

Psychological research on employment relations should be guided by conceptual models that contain two levels of context. The first comprises the employer and/or the union. If both parties are included in the research, then their relationship will be part of the context as well. We believe that as long as researchers do not understand, or know, the employers and the unions that make up their research subjects' psychological environment, they will proceed with underspecified prediction models. Institutional industrial relations research always recognized this but have lost ground to cross-sectional econometric research models (Kaufman,

1993). When the individual is the unit of analysis, institutional characteristics should be a part of the conceptual model. For example, Hammer and Wazeter (1993) have shown that researchers need union-specific models to study union effectiveness because the conceptual definition of organizational effectiveness contains an evaluation of the extent to which the organization meets its goals, which of course are organization specific.

The second contextual level is the culture. Although some research at the workplace level need not take into account the forces that have created and are now maintaining existing employment relations, other research questions will require that the wider context be understood. This wider context may include governmental regulations and labor laws, the social and political climate, a national character (if there is one), and the values, beliefs, and norms of the key actors. For example, researchers and practitioners cannot solve the present problems of the representation and participation gap for the U.S. workforce without understanding, first, the boundaries that the U.S. cultural context places around the adoption of foreign employment policies and practices, and second, the extent to which effectiveness of the policies, practices, and programs that might be transferred from abroad depends on characteristics unique to the culture in which they originated. This is not only an interesting practical matter; it is also an issue of great theoretical importance.

Hartley (1992a, 1995) has argued that the political, economic, and social context of employment relations is crucial if psychology is not to overreach itself in the kinds of interpretations it makes about individual, group, and organizational behavior. For example, an analysis of the reasons why fewer people are joining trade unions over the last decade would be deficient—even irresponsible—if it focused solely on the individual employee's motivations and needs in the workplace. Although these employee characteristics play their part, they must be set in a legal and organizational context. For example, in the U.K. this research would have to recognize that the legal immunities of trade unions have narrowed, that unions' power vis-à-vis management has shrunk dramatically, and that the workplace and hence the workforce has been restructured to a degree not witnessed for a long time. The U.K. worker's decision to join a union (or express commitment to it) thus must be seen in this context of reduced employment rights, increased insecurity at work, and greater managerial readiness to ignore the union in the workplace. Some of this context will manifest at a psychological level; for example, worker perceptions of union effectiveness, an important predictor of union joining in both the United States and U.K., will be lower. However, it would be a mistake to presume that such psychological manifestation was the ultimate cause of a low level of union joining.

Conclusion

The idea of culture operates on several levels throughout this chapter; we see culture affecting both the way that industrial relations are enacted by employees, employers, unions, and governments and the way that industrial relations research is carried out. Given the large contextual differences we have described, even between countries with very similar cultural value systems, researchers and practitioners may wonder whether it is worth comparing the psychology of union-management relations across countries. Certainly, the differences argue for caution and for meticulous comparison prior to assertive comment. Nevertheless, we have seen several examples where national culture has provided some degree of understanding of intercountry differences.

We want to end this chapter on a note of caution, to warn against an overly enthusiastic embrace of cultural value systems as an all-powerful explanatory variable. Culture is certainly an appealing post hoc explanation for national differences in employment relations, but that explanation can easily lead to ignoring competing explanations, such as economic and legal structures. Indeed, our comparisons between the United States and the United Kingdom reveal that although these nations share certain cultural values, their IR systems have evolved to have many profound differences, which may well explain why employment relations operate in such different ways in the two countries. In this chapter we have tried to show how IR systems develop and function as a result of several factors, of which the cultural context is one. We believe strongly that cultural values belong in models of industrial relations but as additions to, not substitutes for, existing explanatory variables.

References

Abo, T. (Ed.). (1994). *Hybrid factory: The Japanese production system in the United States.* New York: Oxford University Press.

Adams, R. (1981). Theoretical dilemmas and value analysis in comparative industrial relations. In G. Dlugos & K. Weiermair (Eds.), *Management under differing value systems* (pp. 278–293). Hawthorne, NY: Walter de Gruyter.

AFL-CIO Committee on the Evolution of Work. (1994). *The New American workplace: A labor perspective.* Washington, DC: AFL-CIO Publication and Materials Office.

AFL-CIO. (1995). *Unemployment still a problem after four years of economic recovery: AFL-CIO reviews the issues* (Report No. 80). Washington, DC: AFL-CIO Publication and Materials Office.

Appelbaum, E., & Batt, R. (1994). *The new American workplace. Transforming work systems in the United States.* Ithaca, NY: ILR Press.

Bain, G., & Price, R. (1983). Union growth: Dimensions, determinants and destiny. In G. Bain (Ed.), *Industrial Relations in Britain* (pp. 3–33). Oxford, England: Blackwell.

Bamber, G. J., & Lansbury, R. D. (1992). *International and comparative industrial relations* (2nd ed.). New York: Routledge.

Barling, J., Kelloway, C., & Bremermann, E. H. (1991). Pre-employment predictors of union attitudes: The role of family socialization and work beliefs. *Journal of Applied Psychology, 76,* 725–731.

Barling, J., Fullagar C., & Kelloway, E. K. (1992). *The union & its members: A psychological approach.* New York: Oxford University Press.

Bassett, P. (1986). *Strike free: New industrial relations in Britain.* London: Macmillan.

Becon, D. (1994). Labor law "reform": Another sellout of the workers. *The Nation, 258*(21), 748–750.

Benington, J., & Taylor, M. (1993). Challenges and changes facing the UK welfare state in the Europe of the 1990s. *Policy and Politics, 21,* 121–134.

Blanchflower, D., & Freeman, R. B. (1992). Unionism in the U.S. and other advanced OECD countries. *Industrial Relations, 31*(1), 56–79.

Bolweg, J. F. (1976). *Job design and industrial democracy: The case of Norway.* Leiden: Martinus Nijhoff.

Brody, D. (1980). *Workers in industrial America: Essays on the twentieth century struggle.* New York: Oxford University Press.

The changing workforce: Highlights of the national study. (1993). New York: Families and Work Institute.

Colling, T., & Dickens, L. (1989). *Equality bargaining: Why not?* London: Her Majesty's Stationery Office.

Commission on the Future of Worker-Management Relations. (1994, May). *Fact finding report.* Washington, DC: U.S. Department of Labor.

Cullen, D. E., & Chamberlain, N. W. (1970). *The labor sector* (2nd ed.). N.Y.: McGraw-Hill.

Cutcher-Gershenfeld, J. (1991). The impact on economic performance of a transformation in workplace relations. *Industrial and Labor Relations Review, 44*(2), 241–260.

Dawley, A. (1989). Workers, capital, and the state in the twentieth century. In J. C. Moody & A. Kessler-Harris (Eds.), *Perspectives on American labor history* (pp. 166–200). De Kalb: Northern Illinois University Press.

de Witte, H. (1996). Are trade union members (still) motivated by ideology? A review of the importance of ideological factors as determinants of trade union participation in the (Flemish part of) Belgium. In P. Pasture, J. Verbeckmoes, and H. de Witte (Eds.), *The lost perspective? Trade unions between ideology and social action in the new Europe* (Vol. 2, pp. 326–352). Aldershot, England: Avebury Press.

Dickens, L., & Hall, M. (1995). The state: Labour law and industrial relations. In P. Edwards (Ed.), *Industrial relations: Theory and practice in Britain* (pp. 255–303). Oxford, England: Blackwell.

Dickens, W. T., & Leonard, J. S. (1985). Accounting for the decline in union membership. *Industrial and Labor Relations Review, 35,* 323–334.

Dlugos, G., & Weiermair, K. (Eds.). (1981). *Management under differing value systems.* Hawthorne, NY: Walter de Gruyter.

Dølvik, J. E., & Stokland, D. (1992). Norway: The "Norwegian model" in transition. In A. Ferner & R. Hyman (Eds.), *Industrial relations in the new Europe* (pp. 143–167). Oxford, England: Blackwell.

Dunlop, J. T. (1958). *Industrial relations systems.* New York: Holt.

Edwards, P. (1995). The employment relationship. In P. Edwards (Ed.), *Industrial relations: Theory and practice in Britain* (pp. 3–26). Oxford, England: Blackwell.

Emery, F., & Thorsrud, E. (1976). *Democracy at work.* Leiden: Martinus Nijhoff.

Farber, H. S. (1985). The extent of unionization in the United States. In T. A. Kochan (Ed.), *Challenges and choices facing American labor* (pp. 15–43). Cambridge, MA: MIT Press.

Ferner, A., & Hyman, R. (1992). *Industrial relations in the new Europe.* Oxford, England: Blackwell.

Flanders, A. (1974). The tradition of voluntarism. *British Journal of Industrial Relations, 12,* 352–370.

Foner, E. (1984). Why is there no socialism in the United States? *History Workshop, 17,* 57–80.

Fox, A. (1973). Industrial relations: A social critique of pluralist ideology. In J. Child (Ed.), *Man and organization* (pp. 185–233). London: Allen & Unwin.

Freeman, R. B. (1985). Why are workers faring poorly in NRLB representation elections? In T. A. Kochan (Ed.), *Challenges and choices facing American labor* (pp. 45–64). Cambridge, MA: MIT Press.

Freeman, R. B., & Medoff, J. L. (1984). *What do unions do?* New York: Basic Books.

Freeman, R. B., & Rogers, J. (1994). *Worker representation and participation survey: Report on the findings.* Princeton, NJ: Princeton Survey Research Associates.

Freeman, R. B., & Rogers, J. (1995, January). *Worker representation and participation survey: First report of findings.* Paper presented at the 47th annual meeting of the Industrial Relations Research Association, Washington, DC.

Frenkel, S. (Ed.). (1993). *Organized labor in the Asia-Pacific region. A comparative study of trade unionism in nine countries.* Ithaca, NY: ILR Press.

Frenkel, S., & Harrod, J. (Eds.). (1995). *Industrialization and labor relations: Contemporary research in seven countries.* Ithaca, NY: ILR Press.

Gerhart, P. F. (1987). *Saving plants and jobs: Union-management negotiations in the context of threatened plant closings.* Kalamazoo, MI: W. J. Upjohn Institute for Employment Research.

Getman, J. G., Goldberg, S. B., & Herman, J. B. (1976). *Union representations elections: Law and reality.* New York: Russell Sage Foundation.

Gold, M., & Hall, M. (1994). Statutory European works councils: The final countdown? *Industrial Relations Journal, 25,* 177–186.

Gordon, M. E., & Ladd, R. T. (1990). Dual allegiance: Renewal, reconsideration, and recantation. *Personnel Psychology, 43,* 37–69.

Gustavsen, B., & Hunnius, G. (1981). *New patterns of work reform: The case of Norway.* Oslo: Universitetsforlaget.

Hackman, J. R., & Oldham, G. R. (1980). *Work redesign.* Reading, MA: Addison-Wesley.

Hall, M., Carley, M., Gold, M., Marginson, P., & Sisson, K. (1995). *European works councils: Planning for the directive.* London: Industrial Relations Services.

Hammer, M., & Champy, J. (1993). *Reengineering the corporation: A manifesto of business revolution.* New York: Harper Business.

Hammer, T. H. (1988). New developments in profit sharing, gainsharing, and employee ownership. In J. P. Campbell, R. J. Campbell, &

Associates, *Productivity in organizations: New perspectives from industrial and organizational psychology* (pp. 328–366). San Francisco: Jossey-Bass.

Hammer, T. H., & Berman, M. (1981). The role of noneconomic factors in faculty union voting. *Journal of Applied Psychology, 63,* 415–421.

Hammer, T. H., Currall, S. C., & Stern, R. N. (1991). Worker representation on boards of directors: A study of competing roles. *Industrial and Labor Relations Review, 44*(4), 661–680.

Hammer, T. H., Ingebrigtsen, B., Karlsen, J. I., & Svarva, A. (1994, August). *Organizational renewal: The management of large-scale organizational change in Norwegian firms.* Paper presented at the Conference on Transformation in European Industrial Relations, Helsinki.

Hammer, T. H., & Stern, R. N. (1980). Employee ownership: Implications for the organizational distribution of power. *Academy of Management Journal, 23,* 78–100.

Hammer, T. H., & Wazeter, D. L. (1993). Dimensions of local union effectiveness. *Industrial and Labor Relations Review, 46*(2), 302–319.

Hartley, J. F. (1983). Ideology and organizational behavior. *International Studies of Management and Organization, 13*(3), 7–34.

Hartley, J. F. (1992a). Joining a trade union. In J. F. Hartley & G. Stephenson (Eds.), *Employment relations: The psychology of influence and control at work* (pp. 163–183). Oxford, England: Blackwell.

Hartley, J. F. (1992b). The psychology of industrial relations. In C. L. Cooper & I. Robertson (Eds.), *International review of industrial and organizational psychology* (Vol. 7, pp. 201–243). New York: Wiley.

Hartley, J. F. (1995). Job insecurity. In N. Nicholson (Ed.), *Encyclopedic dictionary of organizational behavior* (pp. 271–272). Oxford, England: Blackwell.

Hartley, J. F., & Kelly, J. E. (1986). Psychology and industrial relations: From conflict to cooperation? *Journal of Occupational Psychology, 59,* 161–176.

Hartley, J. F., Kelly, J. E., & Nicholson, N. (1983). *Steel strike.* London: Batsford.

Hartley, J. F., & Stephenson, G. (1992). *Employment relations: The psychology of influence and control at work.* Oxford, England: Blackwell.

Hofstede, G. (1980). *Culture's consequences: International differences in work-related values.* Thousand Oaks, CA: Sage.

Hofstede, G. (1991). *Cultures and organizations: Software of the mind.* London: McGraw-Hill.

Hyman, R. (1996). The geometry of trade unionism: A comparative analysis of identities and ideologies. In P. Pasture & J. Verbeckmoes (Eds.), *The lost perspective? Trade unions between ideology and social action in the new Europe* (pp. 60–89). Aldershot, England: Avebury Press.

IDE [Industrial Democracy in Europe] International Research Group. (1981). *Industrial democracy in Europe.* New York: Oxford University Press, Clarendon Press.

IDE [Industrial Democracy in Europe] International Research Group. (1993). *Industrial democracy in Europe revisited.* New York: Oxford University Press.

Industrial Relations Services [Employment Trends]. (1993). Fear of redundancy. *Industrial Relations Review and Report, 541,* p. 7.

Jacoby, S. (Ed.). (1990). *Masters to managers.* New York: Columbia University Press.

Katz, H. C. (1985). *Shifting gears: Changing labor relations in the U.S. automobile industry.* Cambridge, MA: MIT Press.

Katz, H. C. (1993). The decentralization of collective bargaining: A literature review and comparative analysis. *Industrial & Labor Relations Review, 47*(1), 3–22.

Katz, H. C., & Kochan, T. A. (1992). *An introduction to collective bargaining and industrial relations.* New York: McGraw-Hill.

Kaufman, B. (1993). *The origins & evolution of the field of industrial relations in the United States.* Ithaca, NY: ILR Press.

Keaveny, T. J., Rose, J., & Fossum, J. (1988, December). *Predicting support for unionization: Part time versus full time workers and professional/technical blue collar workers.* Paper presented at the annual conference of the Industrial Relations Research Association, New York.

Keenoy, T. (1985). *Invitation to industrial relations.* Oxford, England: Blackwell.

Kelly, J. E., & Kelly, C. (1991). Them and us: Social psychology and the new industrial relations. *British Journal of Industrial Relations, 29,* 25–48.

Kelly, J. E., & Kelly, C. (1992). The dynamics of intergroup relations. In J. F. Hartley & G. Stephenson (Eds.), *Employment relations: The psychology of influence and control at work* (pp. 246–268). Oxford, England: Blackwell.

Klandermans, B. (1986). Psychology and trade union participation: Joining, acting, quitting. *Journal of Occupational Psychology, 59,* 189–204.

Klandermans, B. (1992). Trade union participation. In J. F. Hartley & G. Stephenson (Eds.), *Employment relations: The psychology of influence and control at work* (pp. 184–199). Oxford, England: Blackwell.

Kochan, T. A., Katz, H. C., & McKersie, R. B. (1986). *The transformation of American industrial relations.* New York: Basic Books.

Kochan, T. A., Katz, H. C., & Mower, N. (1984). *Worker participation and*

American unions: Threat or opportunity? Kalamazoo, MI: W. J. Upjohn Institute for Employment Research.

Kochan, T. A., & Osterman, P. (1994). *The mutual gains enterprise.* Boston: Harvard Business School Press.

Kuruvilla, S. (1995). The linkages between industrialization strategies, national industrial relations policies, and workplace IR/HR policies in Southeast Asia. In K. Wever & L. Turner (Eds.), *Comparative political economy of industrial relations* (pp. 115–150). Madison, WI: Industrial Relations Research Association.

Kuruvilla, S., & Iverson, R. (1993). Union commitment in Australia. *Journal of Industrial Relations, 35*(3), 436–452.

Kuruvilla, S., & Sverke, M. (1993). Two dimensions of union commitment based on the theory of reasoned action: Cross-cultural comparisons. *Research and Practice in Human Resource Management, 1*(1), 1–16.

Lawler, E. E., III. (1986). *High-involvement management: Participative strategies for improving organizational performance.* San Francisco: Jossey-Bass.

Lawler, E. E., III, Mohrman, S. A., & Ledford, G. E., Jr. (1992). *Employee involvement and Total Quality Management: Practices and results in Fortune 1000 companies.* San Francisco: Jossey-Bass.

Legge, K. (1988). Personnel management in recession and recovery: A comparative analysis of what the surveys say. *Personnel Review, 17,* 1–72.

Liff, S., & Aitkenhead, M. (1992). Equal opportunities: An attempt to restructure employment relations. In J. F. Hartley & G. Stephenson (Eds.), *Employment relations: The psychology of influence and control at work* (pp. 271–290). Oxford, England: Blackwell.

Lipset, S. M. (1961). Trade unions and social structure. *Industrial Relations, 1*(1), 75–89.

Lipset, S. M. (1962). Trade unions and social structure. *Industrial Relations, 1*(2), 89–110.

MacDuffie, J. P., & Krafcik, J. (1992). Integrating technology and human resources for high performance manufacturing: Evidence from the international auto industry. In T. A. Kochan & M. Useem (Eds.), *Transforming organizations* (pp. 209–226). New York: Oxford University Press.

McDonald, C. (1985). Challenges to union organizing: Discussion. In T. A. Kochan (Ed.), *Challenges and choices facing American labor* (pp. 65–71). Cambridge, MA: MIT Press.

Millward, N., Stevens, M., Smart, D., & Hawes, W. (1992). *Workplace industrial relations in transition.* Aldershot, England. Dartmouth.

Montgomery, D. (1979). *Workers' control in America.* New York: Cambridge University Press.

Morris, C. J. (1995, January). *Section 8(a)(2) and the perception of reality.* Paper presented at the 47th annual meeting of the Industrial Relations Research Association, Washington, DC.

Nicholson, N., Ursell, G., & Blyton, P. (1981). *The dynamics of white-collar trade unionism: A study of local union participation.* Orlando: Academic Press.

Nolan, P., & Walsh, J. (1995). The structure of the economy and labour market. In P. Edwards (Ed.), *Industrial relations: Theory and practice in Britain* (pp. 50–88). Oxford, England: Blackwell.

Osterman, P. (1994). How common is workplace transformation and who adopts it? *Industrial & Labor Relations Review, 47*(2), 173–188.

Premack, S. L., & Hunter, J. E. (1988). Individual unionization decisions. *Psychological Bulletin, 103,* 223–234.

Reich, M. (1989). Capitalist development, class relations, and labor history. In J. C. Moody & A. Kessler-Harris (Eds.), *Perspectives on American labor history* (pp. 30–54). De Kalb: Northern Illinois University Press.

Reve, T. (1994, April). Scandinavian management: From competitive advantage to competitive disadvantage? *Tidsskrift for Samfunnsforskning,* pp. 568–582.

Salvatore, N. (Ed.). (1984). *Samuel Gompers, seventy years of life and labor: An autobiography.* Ithaca, NY: IRL Press.

Schuster, M. H. (1984). *Union-management cooperation: Structure-process-impact.* Kalamazoo, MI: W. J. Upjohn Institute for Employment Research.

Schwartz, S. H. (1992). Universals in the content and structure of values: Theoretical advances and empirical tests in 20 countries. In M. P. Zanna (Ed.), *Advances in experimental social psychology* (Vol. 25, pp. 1–65). Orlando: Academic Press.

Schwartz, S. H. (1994). Beyond individualism and collectivism: New cultural dimensions of values. In U. Kim, H. C. Triandis, Ç. Kagitcibasi, S.-C. Choi, & G. Yoon (Eds.), *Individualism and collectivism: Theory, method, and applications* (pp. 85–119). Thousand Oaks, CA: Sage.

Shalev, M. (1981). Theoretical dilemmas and value analysis in comparative industrial relations. In G. Dlugos & K. Weiermair (Eds.), *Management under differing value systems* (pp. 241–263). Hawthorne, NY: Walter de Gruyter.

Sisson, K., & Marginson, P. (1995). Management: Systems, structure and strategy. In P. Edwards (Ed.), *Industrial relations: Theory and practice in Britain* (pp. 89–122). Oxford, England: Blackwell.

Slichter, S. H., Healy, J. J., & Livernash, E. R. (1960). *The impact of collective bargaining on management.* Washington, DC: Brookings Institution.

Slomp, N. (1996). *Between bargaining and politics: An introduction to European labor relations.* New York: Praeger.

Strauss, G. (1982). Workers' participation in management: An international perspective. In B. M. Staw & L. L. Cummings (Eds.), *Research in organizational behavior* (Vol. 4, pp. 173–266). Greenwich, CT: JAI Press.

Streeck, W. (1984). Codetermination: The fourth decade. In B. Wilpert & A. Sorge (Eds.), *International yearbook of industrial democracy: Vol. 2. International perspectives on organizational democracy* (pp. 391–424). New York: Wiley.

Tichy, N. M., & Sherman, S. (1993). *Control your destiny or someone else will.* New York: HarperCollins.

Triandis, H. C. (1995). *Individualism & collectivism.* Boulder, CO: Westview Press.

Turner, L. (1993). *Democracy at work. Changing world markets and the future of labor unions.* Ithaca, NY: Cornell University Press.

Waddington, D. (1987). *Trouble brewing: A social psychological analysis of the Ansell's Brewery dispute.* Aldershot, England: Avebury Press.

Waddington, J., & Whitston, C. (1995). Trade unions: Growth, structure and policy. In P. Edwards (Ed.), *Industrial relations: Theory and practice in Britain* (pp. 151–202). Oxford, England: Blackwell.

Wallerstein, M., Golden, M., & Lange, P. (1997). Unions, employers associations, and wage-setting institutions in North and Central Europe, 1950–1992. *Industrial and Labor Relations Review, 50*(3), 379–401.

Whyte, W. F., Hammer, T. H., Meek, C., Nelson, R., & Stern, R. N. (1983). *Worker participation and ownership: Cooperative strategies for strengthening local economies.* Ithaca, NY: ILR Press.

Wilentz, S. (1989). The rise of the American working class, 1776–1877: A survey. In J. C. Moody & A. Kessler-Harris (Eds.), *Perspectives on American labor history* (pp. 83–151). De Kalb: Northern Illinois University Press.

Womack, J. P., Jones, D. T., & Roos, D. (1990). *The machine that changed the world.* New York: HarperCollins.

Zalesny, M. D. (1985). Comparison of economic and noneconomic factors in predicting faculty union vote preferences in a union representation election. *Journal of Applied Psychology, 70,* 243–256.

CHAPTER 18

A Conceptual Framework of Organizational Factors and Processes

An Application to International Human Resource Management

Helen De Cieri
Sara L. McGaughey
Peter J. Dowling

Since the 1950s, growth in international trade and investment has exceeded that in domestic economies (Czinkota, Ronkainen, & Moffett, 1994). Driven by the resultant opportunities and challenges, cooperative ventures, networks, and corporate structures that transcend national borders are no longer rare (Bartlett & Ghoshal, 1988, 1992; Lorange, 1986). This globalization of business increases the requirement for an understanding, both academic and practical, of ways in which multinational enterprises (MNEs) may operate most effectively now and in the future (Sundaram & Black, 1992). Critical to the successful operation of an international organization or alliance is the effective management of human resources (Black, Gregersen, & Mendenhall, 1992; Dowling, Schuler, & Welch, 1994; Edström & Lorange, 1984; Ferner, 1994). A prerequisite for that effective human resource management is recognition of the diverse factors and processes interacting in the organization's internal and external environments.

In this chapter we present a conceptual framework for these organizational factors and processes. Framework components include micro- and macro-level factors that are both endogenous and exogenous to the organization. We argue that these factors interact, either directly or via meso processes. Indeed, research efforts that do not recognize the interrelationships between micro- and macro-level factors and meso processes are not sustainable. Furthermore, these micro- and macro-level factors may be both initiators and outcomes of change. Our ultimate aim in this chapter is to make our general framework a guide to the development of context-specific research. We illustrate the functioning of the framework through an application to international human resource management.

The Development of International Human Resource Management

Research in international human resource management is relatively new and has its foundations in the domestic human resource management literature.

General Approaches

Schuler, Dowling, Smart, and Huber (1992) define human resource management (HRM) as "the recognition of the importance of an organisation's work force as vital human resources contributing to the goals of the organisation, and the utilisation of several functions and activities to ensure that they are used effectively and fairly for the benefit of the individual, the organisation and society" (p. 16). HRM embodies the comprehensive policies that govern human resource programs and practices (Schuler, 1992). Underpinning these policies is a philosophy that among other things, views people as organizational assets rather than costs.

The study of HRM has tended to focus on the organization as the unit of analysis (Beer, Spector, Lawrence, Mills, & Walton, 1984), with particular attention to specific functions and activities designed to enable organizations to achieve desired goals. The concepts and background of HRM have been discussed and debated in the literature (for example, Blyton & Turnbull, 1992; Storey, 1989). In particular, the conceptual framework of HRM offered by Beer, Spector, Lawrence, Mills, and Walton (1984), known as the

Harvard framework, has received much attention (Boxall, 1992; Guest, 1987; Hendry & Pettigrew, 1990; Poole, 1990; Storey & Sisson, 1993). This framework recognizes a wide range of stakeholder interests and contextual factors that influence the choice of human resource strategy. It identifies HRM policy choices relating to employee involvement, human resource flows (including recruitment and selection, training and development, and performance management), reward systems, and work systems. According to this framework, these policy choices result in such outcomes as organizational commitment and cost effectiveness that have long-term consequences for individuals, organizations, and society.

The dominant frameworks of HRM have assumed linearity and rational processes or flows. Subsequent research in the HRM field (for example, Hendry & Pettigrew, 1990) has extended the analytical elements of the Harvard framework and emphasized the need for contextual and processual rather than prescriptive approaches to HRM. The reciprocal relationship between organizational strategy and human resource strategy has been the subject of much attention throughout recent years (Butler, Ferris, & Napier, 1991; Dyer, 1984; Lengnick-Hall & Lengnick-Hall, 1988; Tichy, Fombrun, & Devanna, 1982; Wright & McMahan, 1992). Comprehensive and critical reviews of the developments in this literature have been provided by writers such as Boxall and Dowling (1990), Purcell and Ahlstrand (1994), and Storey and Sisson (1993). Recently, recognition of the importance of HRM in international management has also flourished (Dowling, Schuler, & Welch, 1994; Pucik, Tichy, & Barnett, 1992).

International HRM

Dowling, Schuler, and Welch (1994) argued that international human resource management (IHRM) involves the same elements as does domestic HRM but is more complex due to the employment of workers of different nationalities and the diverse national contexts of operation. The complexity of international operations is reflected in the definition of a multinational enterprise (MNE) provided by Sundaram and Black (1992): "any enterprise that carries out transactions in or between two sovereign entities, operating under a system of decision making that permits influence over resources and capabilities, where *the transactions are subject to influence by factors exogenous to the home country environment* of the enterprise" (p. 733, emphasis added).

Ricks, Toyne, and Martinez (1990) noted that IHRM research (which has largely concentrated on MNEs) is essentially concerned with the interactions of differing culture-based norms and value systems within a single organization that straddles national borders (Lorange, 1986; Shenkar & Zeira, 1987), the different ways of learning and responding to stimuli resulting from sociocultural differences (Pucik, 1992), and the cross-national transfer of management and management practices (Alkhafaji, 1990; Vance, McClaine, Boje, & Stage, 1992). The importance of such research should not be underestimated. As Duerr (1986) has stated: "Virtually any type of international problem, in the final analysis, is either created by people or must be solved by people. Hence, having the right people in the right place at the right time emerges as the key to a company's international growth. If we are successful in solving that problem, I am confident we can cope with all others" (p. 43).

The significance of both endogenous (internal to the organization) and exogenous (external to the organization) factors in MNE operations has been well recognized in the international management literature (Evans, 1992, 1993; Kobrin, 1992, 1994; Porter, 1990; Prahalad & Doz, 1987; Schuler, Dowling, & De Cieri, 1993). To achieve international competitiveness, MNEs must balance the often conflicting imperatives of global coordination (integration) and local responsiveness (differentiation) (Bartlett & Ghoshal, 1992; Doz & Prahalad, 1991; Nohria & Ghoshal, 1994). Although recognized in the classic organizational design literature (Lawrence & Lorsch, 1967; Pugh, 1973), these issues of integration and differentiation are far more complex in a global context, which brings a greater diversity of endogenous and exogenous forces to bear on the MNE.

Important exogenous country or regional elements that affect IHRM and necessitate varying degrees of differentiation include economic, political, historical, and legal environments (Begin, 1992; Jarvis, 1990; Ring, Lenway, & Govekar, 1990; Schuler, Dowling, & De Cieri, 1993; Sundaram & Black, 1992); workforce characteristics such as education levels and labor costs (Johnston, 1993;

Reiz, 1975; Teagarden, Butler, & Von Glinow, 1992); and employees' sociocultural characteristics (Laurent, 1983; Schuler, Dowling, & De Cieri, 1993). These sociocultural characteristics are often measured by employees' work-related needs, goals, and values, which may be referred to generically as *work-related preferences* (McGaughey, 1994).

In the face of these forces for differentiation, interunit integration or coordination in the MNE may be achieved through a variety of mechanisms, including bureaucratic control, centralization, normative integration, and critical flows. *Bureaucratic control* occurs through the systematic rules and procedures used in decision making (Ghoshal & Nohria, 1989). *Centralization* is the extent to which the locus of decision making lies in the higher levels of the organizational hierarchy (Child, 1973; Galbraith & Kazanjian, 1986; Pugh, Hickson, & Hinings, 1969). *Normative integration* refers to the building of common perspectives, purposes, and values amongst managers across different units (Edström & Galbraith, 1977; Ghoshal & Nohria, 1989, 1993; Kobrin, 1994; Martinez & Jarillo, 1991). *Critical flows* occur in capital, technology, and people (Bartlett & Ghoshal, 1987, 1989). The flow of people through staff transfers within and between MNE units affects the MNE corporate culture and disseminates knowledge, skills, and ideas (Welch, Fenwick, & De Cieri, 1994). The strategic and operational importance of effectively managed international staff transfers, that is, of the *management of expatriation,* has become a well-documented dimension of IHRM research (Black, Gregersen, & Mendenhall, 1992; Boyacigiller, 1990; Dowling, Schuler, & Welch, 1994; Ferner, 1994; Scullion, 1994).

Management of Expatriation

Reasons for staff transfers are to fill positions, to develop managers, and to develop the organization (Edström & Galbraith, 1977). An MNE's approaches to staffing and expatriation will be influenced by its strategic predisposition, the "way executives think about doing business around the world" (Perlmutter, 1969, p. 11). These predispositions may be ethnocentric, polycentric, regiocentric, or geocentric (Chakravarthy & Perlmutter, 1985; Heenan & Perlmutter, 1979; Perlmutter, 1969). The strategic predisposition of an

MNE is also associated with a range of organizational characteristics, including complexity, structure, communication flows, evaluation and control processes, performance management, allocation of resources, organizational culture, and staffing processes.

An *ethnocentric* approach to staffing fills all key management positions with parent country nationals. A *polycentric* staffing approach decentralizes HRM to each national location and fills management positions in the local units with host country nationals and positions at corporate headquarters with parent country nationals. *Regiocentric* staffing develops regional staff for key positions anywhere in that region; a *geocentric* approach seeks the "best" people for key positions throughout the organization, regardless of nationality. Kobrin (1994) argues that ability to compete globally may well depend on the development of a geocentric predisposition. An MNE may use any mix of these approaches, whether deliberate or ad hoc (Dowling, Schuler, & Welch, 1994; Ondrack, 1985). Indeed, although one strategic predisposition to staffing and expatriation may dominate, pure forms are seldom found (Chakravarthy & Perlmutter, 1985).

The expatriation process involves three major phases: predeparture, expatriation, and repatriation (De Cieri, McGaughey, & Dowling, 1996). The issues in each of the three phases require consideration of both organizational and individual needs, which are influenced by endogenous and exogenous factors. For example, the decision to select parent, host, or third-country nationals to be expatriates may be influenced by both exogenous factors such as host government requirements or cultural barriers and endogenous factors such as an individual's cultural tolerance, the impact on career paths of other employee groups, or the varying levels of control and coordination desired (Black, Gregersen, & Mendenhall, 1992; Dowling, Schuler, & Welch, 1994).

Key IHRM issues in the predeparture phase include determination of assignment objectives, development of selection and performance management systems based on these objectives, consensus on the compensation package for the expatriate, and the design and implementation of preparatory training and development programs. In the expatriation phase it is important to consider enhancement of the expatriate's adjustment to the new environment and conditions. Berry, Kim, and Boski (1988) define adjustment as a "process by which individuals change their psychological characteristics, change the surrounding context, or change the amount of contact in order to achieve a better fit (outcome) with other features of the system in which they carry out their life" (p. 66).

The expatriation adjustment process is multifaceted and affects both employees and family (Black & Gregersen, 1991b; De Cieri, Dowling, & Taylor, 1991). Several empirical studies have found a positive and significant relationship between spousal and expatriate adjustment (Black, 1988; Black & Stephens, 1989), and IHRM practices designed to facilitate expatriate adjustment, such as mentor systems (Fergus, 1990) and predeparture training (Brewster & Pickard, 1994), should cater for both the employee and his or her family (Black, Mendenhall, & Oddou, 1991). (Many of these issues of adjustment apply equally to domestic relocations, Fisher & Shaw, 1994.)

In the repatriation phase the MNE's goal is typically to return and retain an employee who can make valuable contributions to the organization in form of knowledge, experience, and networks gained overseas. Repatriation issues should be anticipated in the previous two phases. Although many organizations assume that reentry into the home country and operations is less traumatic than expatriation adjustment (Tung, 1982), repatriation adjustment may be the greater of the two (Black & Gregersen, 1991c). Repatriation programs have tended to focus on such tangibles as job allocation, compensation issues, and housing concerns and have lacked attention to the social and psychological problems confronted by many repatriates and their families. IHRM practices used to address repatriation adjustment include predeparture training and development (which includes repatriation planning), counseling, and sponsors or mentors for expatriates.

One review of the expatriation literature (De Cieri, McGaughey, & Dowling, 1996) suggests that MNEs could give greater attention to several areas of IHRM. These include offering predeparture training such as language instruction, providing clear performance criteria and appraisal information, establishing congruent expectations between home and local units, integrating relocations into career development, and providing support systems during the expatriation and repatriation phases. Organizations may also seek to develop such job characteristics as work role clarity and realistic expectations of the relocation destination and objectives. Of course IHRM policies and practices may vary somewhat in accord with an organization's specific intent or strategies.

Current Frameworks for IHRM

Acknowledging the complexity of MNE operations, Schuler, Dowling, and De Cieri (1993) have developed an integrative framework of strategic IHRM that recognizes that exogenous and endogenous forces interact and inform the choices of integration and differentiation between MNE units, ultimately affecting realization of MNE goals. Competitiveness, efficiency, local responsiveness, flexibility, and learning and transfer are included in Schuler, Dowling, and De Cieri's framework (1993) as typical MNE goals, although it is recognized that these concerns and goals will vary across specific organizations (Bartlett & Ghoshal, 1992; Porter, 1986, 1990). Hence, within the field of IHRM, as in domestic HRM, organizations have taken steps to develop integrative frameworks. It is, however, recognized that the "models offered are somewhat tentative and will require several iterations before their precision approaches the complexity of the explananda" (Redding, 1994, p. 335).

Although the field of international management research has made several important steps forward, inadequacies remain (Tayeb, 1994). Schöllhammer (1975) criticized the international and comparative management research field for being descriptive and lacking in analytical rigor, being ad hoc and expedient in research design and planning, acting self-centered in the sense that the existing research literature is frequently ignored, and lacking a sustained research effort to develop case material. In addition, theoretical development is scant, empirical research has suffered from oversimplification, and narrow perspectives have permitted parochialism to survive (Arvey, Bhagat, & Salas, 1991; Redding, 1994). Despite some evidence of progress in overcoming the limitations of previously held assumptions, these criticisms remain valid (Redding, 1994). It is well recognized that by definition, the development or iteration of previous conceptual models requires recourse to the extant literature and further attention to overcoming limitations.

A Conceptual Framework

As an iteration of previous models, a conceptual framework is offered here that builds on developments in the extant literature. As shown in Figure 18.1, this framework recognizes the need for integrative (Hendry & Pettigrew, 1990; Schuler, Dowling, & De Cieri, 1993) and multidisciplinary (Roberts, Hulin, & Rousseau, 1978; Rousseau & House, 1994; Sundaram & Black, 1992) approaches to examining the complex interactions of dynamic forces both endogenous and exogenous to the organization. The process of scientific inquiry "in practice typically involves an alternation between deduction and induction" (Babbie, 1992, p. 53). Thus theory testing and theory construction are closely interrelated. Indeed, the creative process of exploration and integration of concepts (Richards & Richards, 1993) is an important aspect of the overall process of scientific inquiry. Our framework has, therefore, been developed through an iterative process of revisiting the conceptual and empirical IHRM literature. And although in this chapter we focus on IHRM, the application of this framework is intended to be multidisciplinary.

Figure 18.1 can be contrasted with previous HRM frameworks. In the Harvard framework (Beer, Spector, Lawrence, Mills, & Walton, 1984), HRM policy choices result in human resource outcomes that in turn result in long-term consequences. These consequences influence stakeholder interests and situational factors. Although the Harvard framework has feedback links from the long-term consequences, it is worth noting that there is no feedback link from the human resource outcomes and previous elements of the framework. Hendry and Pettigrew's HRM model (1990) recognizes human resource outputs but does not explicitly identify organizational outcomes. Schuler, Dowling, and De Cieri's framework (1993) of strategic international HRM explicitly recognizes the range of MNE concerns and goals, including outcomes specific both to HRM and to the organization as a whole. This framework, however, tends to portray MNE concerns and goals as end points in a sequential process.

The process shown in Figure 18.1 reevaluates and extends earlier frameworks. First, like Hendry and Pettigrew's framework, it does not hold that relationships between variables form a unidirectional process. Second, it does not present outcomes as end

Figure 18.1. A Conceptual Framework of Organizational Factors and Processes.

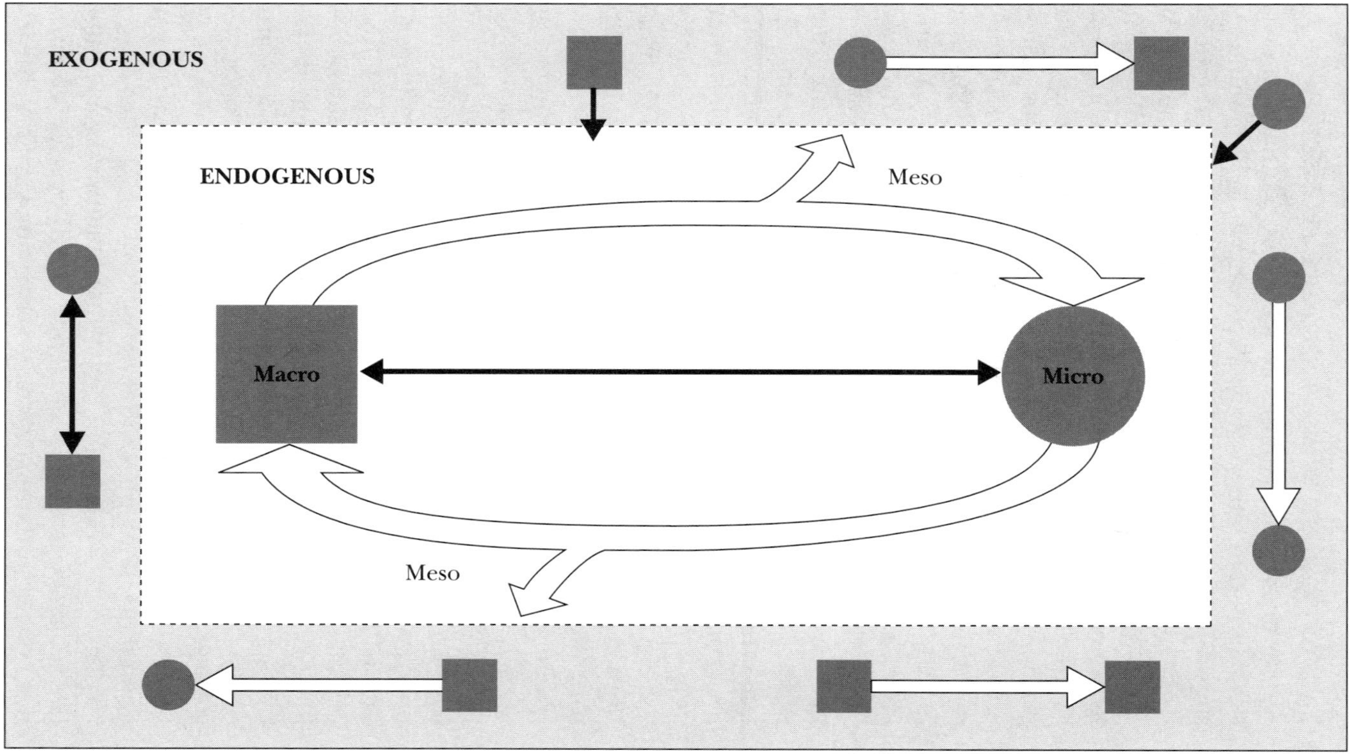

points in this process. Third, in a departure from the previous frameworks, it argues that outcomes are not intrinsically different from the other factors and processes in the MNE. Figure 18.1, a simplified framework of organizational factors and processes, shows the organization (the *endogenous* environment) embedded (Granovetter, 1992) in the surrounding (*exogenous*) environment. The intermittent line between the two environments reflects the ability of factors and processes to interact across this boundary, forming sets of relationships. The presence of *micro-* and *macro-level factors* and *meso processes* are shown in each environment. Micro and macro factors (black squares and circles) may interact indirectly via meso processes (white arrows) or directly (black arrows). Of course, not all factors in the endogenous environment will interact with the exogenous environment, and some relationships may be more tenuous or indirect than others.

Definition of Framework Terms

If IHRM research, or indeed management research in general, is to develop the much advocated integrative, multidisciplinary approach (Arvey, Bhagat, & Salas, 1991; Bhagat & McQuaid, 1982; Kochan, Batt, & Dyer, 1992; Redding, 1994; Schuler, Dowling, & De Cieri, 1993), precise articulation of terminology is of paramount importance (Klein, Dansereau, & Hall, 1994; McGaughey, 1994). The present literature lacks clear definitions of micro- and macro-level factors. The terms *macro* and *micro* have been discussed in the management literature simply in terms of their basic dictionary meanings: "large" and "small." Duberley and Burns (1993), for example, in linking HRM with organizational configurations relate micro to analysis of organization and management at departmental or subunit levels and macro to analysis at the organizational level. The organizational behavior literature, however, recognizes micro and macro factors as *qualitatively* different constructs: micro factors typically being considered "soft" or "intangible," and macro factors "hard" or "tangible."

Adler (1991) provides a nonspecific definition of micro-level factors as pertaining to the behavior of people in organizations and macro-level factors as pertaining to such issues as structure, size, and technology. According to Rousseau and House (1994), the micro level of analysis in organizational behavior is associated with psychological phenomena, focusing on individual work-related preferences, performance, and behaviors. The macro-level of analysis is associated with socioeconomic aspects of organizations, focusing on organizational outcomes such as structure-environment contingencies (Rousseau & House, 1994). Cappelli and Sherer (1991, pp. 55–56) refer to micro analysis of organizational behavior as "individual-based explanations of individual behavior" and macro analysis as "environment-based explanations of organizational characteristics."

Although a common understanding of micro and macro is often assumed, the definitions just discussed show how these terms may be open to different interpretations even within a single discipline such as organizational behavior. Those familiar with the writings of Leftwich and Eckert (1985) in the discipline of economics or of Czinkota, Ronkainen, and Moffett (1994) in the discipline of marketing could not be faulted if they misinterpreted these authors' use of the terms *micro factors* and *macro factors*.

Micro-level factors are defined here as psychological factors that have implications for organizational outcomes. *Micro-endogenous factors* (defined as micro-level factors internal to the organization) occur at different levels of analysis—individual, group, and organizational. For example, at the individual unit of analysis, micro-endogenous factors include individuals' work-related preferences (Hofstede, 1980; Ronen & Kraut, 1977; Ronen & Shenkar, 1985). At the level of subunit analysis, micro-endogenous factors include psychological aspects of group dynamics, such as groupthink (Janis, 1972). At the organizational unit of analysis, examples of micro-endogenous factors include organizational culture and human resource philosophy (Alvesson & Berg, 1992; Deal & Kennedy, 1982; Schein, 1985; Schuler, 1992). *Micro-exogenous factors* (defined as micro-level factors external to the organization) also occur at different units of analysis. Examples of micro-exogenous factors include subcultures, such as ethnic groups, in the population, industry cultures, national cultures, and the culture of an era (Hofstede, 1991; Sarasti, 1993; Tung, 1993). Although cultures may be manifested through tangible artifacts (macro-level factors), the *essence* of culture is argued to include psychological elements (micro-level factors) such as values and beliefs (Hofstede, 1991; Kluckhohn & Strodtbeck, 1961; Schein, 1985).

Macro-level factors are defined here as tangible factors that have implications for organizational outcomes. *Macro-endogenous factors* (defined as macro-level factors internal to the organization) also occur at different units of analysis. Examples of macro-endogenous factors include the production technology (Woodward, 1965), organizational structure (Chandler, 1980; Mintzberg, 1979), organizational strategy (Miles & Snow, 1984), human resource policy (Schuler, 1992), organizational size (Hickson, Hinings, McMillan, & Schwitter, 1974), and such internal labor market elements as skill levels and union density (Kochan, Batt, & Dyer, 1992). *Macro-exogenous factors* (defined as macro-level factors external to the organization) include economic systems (Child, 1981; Child & Markóczy, 1993), industry characteristics (Porter, 1990), national resources (Porter, 1990), political imperatives (Ring, Lenway, & Govekar, 1990), population education levels (Johnston, 1993), and local or cross-national legislation (Lockhart & Myers, 1993; Sundaram & Black, 1992).

There is an essential qualitative distinction between micro- and macro-level factors. Moreover, neither type of factor is bound to a single unit of analysis, nor is it static. Although fluctuations and changes in each type will occur, minimal fluctuations in micro-level factors may not always have repercussions for macro-level factors, and vice versa. This fact is represented in Figure 18.1 by the divergence of the white arrows. However, micro- and macro-level factors should not be considered in isolation of each other. As also shown in Figure 18.1, the micro- and macro-endogenous factors have direct and indirect interactions. An example of a direct interaction is the influence of philosophies and values held by individual managers (micro-endogenous factors) on organizational strategy (a macro-endogenous factor) (Purcell & Ahlstrand, 1994). Indirect relationships between micro and macro factors operate via meso processes.

The concept of *meso processes* is relatively new in the organizational behavior literature (Cappelli & Sherer, 1991; Rousseau & House, 1994). The term *meso,* with a basic meaning of "middle" or "intermediate" (*Living Webster Encyclopaedic Dictionary of the English Language,* 1977), in the context of research refers to "an integration of micro and macro theory in the study of processes specific to organizations which by their very nature are a synthesis of psychological and socioeconomic processes" (Rousseau & House, 1994, p. 14). This approach recognizes that macro- and micro-level factors should not be considered in isolation nor treated separately. Rousseau and House also argue that an approach to organizational behavior that assumes micro and macro are separate levels would be an oversimplification. The increasing complexity of business has created an imperative for an integrative meso approach.

HRM programs and practices provide fundamental examples of *meso-endogenous processes* (defined as meso processes internal to the organization) related to areas such as recruitment and selection, training and development (or human resource development), performance management, compensation practices, communication flows and information dissemination, and labor-management relations. *Meso-exogenous processes* (defined as processes external to the organization) include the implementation of legislation; interactions of customer and supplier networks; and political lobbying.

Factor and Process Interactions

Endogenous and exogenous factors and processes interact, as illustrated in the following discussion. First, the reciprocal relationship between micro-endogenous factors and meso-endogenous processes can be illustrated through the relationship between work-related preferences and human resource practices. Micro-level work-related preferences inform and are moderated by human resource practices (McGaughey, 1994). In designing compensation practices to meet organizational needs, for example, the question of what employees consider to be valued rewards—that is, their work-related preferences in this area—must be addressed (Rand, 1977; Vecchio, Hearn, & Southey, 1992). The findings can vary substantially across national groups. Hofstede (1983, cited in Hofstede, 1994) found that employees in the Netherlands and Scandinavia placed more importance on social needs and less on self-actualization than employees in the United States, Austria, and Switzerland. Individual job-enrichment may therefore be a motivating reward in the United States, and group activities may be considered more rewarding in Scandinavia (Daniels & Radebaugh, 1992). Similarly, Pennings (1993) found that executives in U.S. firms expressed a stronger belief than French and Dutch executives in the motivational power of variable pay based on performance. Group-based incentives are used more extensively in Japan than in the United States in part because of the Japanese emphasis on *wa* (harmony in interpersonal relations), which discourages the interpersonal competition that can arise from the individualist approach taken in the United States (Huo & Steers, 1993). In sum, the work-related preferences of employees (micro-endogenous factors) influence the human resource practices (meso-endogenous processes) in areas such as compensation.

Second, meso-endogenous processes moderate micro-endogenous factors. For example, performance-related pay (meso-endogenous) is an HRM practice that may facilitate change in organizational culture (micro-endogenous). Kessler and Purcell (1992) discuss the introduction of individual-based performance-related pay systems as mechanisms to facilitate an increase in entrepreneurial, performance-focused employee behaviors, with the intention of bringing about a changed organizational culture.[1]

Third, there is a reciprocal relationship between macro-endogenous factors and meso-endogenous processes. Moreover, macro-endogenous factors, such as production technology or organizational structure, may not only influence but also define meso processes. This is illustrated by the interaction between organizational strategy and structure (macro-endogenous) and work processes (meso-endogenous). In 1989, in what was known as Project 1990, British Petroleum (BP) began restructuring from a 11×70 matrix to a 4×3 matrix structure (Smart, 1992). Aligned with this restructuring was a move toward a more flexible organization based on teamwork rather than hierarchy (Humes, 1993). It follows then, that meso-endogenous processes such as human resource programs involving teamwork would have reciprocal influences on macro-endogenous factors insofar as the teamwork approach supported and reinforced factors such as a flatter organizational structure. Interestingly, the restructuring at BP involved not only changes in macro-endogenous factors (such as structure) and meso-endogenous processes (such as teamwork) but also changes in micro-endogenous factors. Indeed, an explicit aim of Project 1990 was to transform the corporate culture (Humes, 1993). The case of organizational change at BP illustrates the artificiality of examining macro, micro, or meso levels in isolation, as has been the trend in the organizational behavior literature (De Cieri & Dowling, 1995).

The factors and processes in MNEs are dynamic, and this is reflected in mechanisms of coordination. Traditionally, mechanisms such as formalization, standardization, and centralization have been considered part of organizational structure, a macro-endogenous factor (Pugh, Hickson, Hinings, & Turner, 1969). The complexity of MNE structures may necessitate alternative means of coordination. For example, implementation of a matrix structure designed to meet the dual imperatives of global coordination and local responsiveness may inadvertently also establish a complex bureaucratic hierarchy. Bartlett and Ghoshal (1990) therefore argue that a matrix structure must be dependent upon a frame of mind rather than a rule book. To achieve this mind-set, individuals must integrate the appropriate norms. It follows then, that such normative integration is an important control mechanism for MNEs operating in highly complex environments (Ghoshal & Nohria, 1993). Normative integration may not replace all centralization or formalization, but it acts as a complementary control mechanism that varies in importance depending on the MNE's dominant goals and operating environment (Bartlett & Ghoshal, 1987). The greater the emphasis placed on normative integration, the more control and coordination mechanisms will be influenced by micro-endogenous factors (for example, values) and meso-endogenous processes (for example, staff transfers) rather than macro-endogenous factors (for example, organizational structure).

Macro- and micro-level factors are not, however, confined to the organization as the broadest unit of analysis. Indeed, a common criticism of the organizational behavior literature is that it has ignored the potential influence of contextual elements (Cappelli & Sherer, 1991). As the HRM and organizational behavior literature has focused on the organization and the individuals within it as the units of analysis, there has been a tendency to consider micro-level factors only in terms of the internal organizational environment (micro-endogenous factors). The organizational behavior literature has largely neglected the existence of micro-level factors in the environment external to the organization (micro-exogenous factors), such as national cultures or the culture of the era (Sarasti, 1993). A multidisciplinary approach would encourage the recognition of both endogenous and exogenous factors.

The complexity of the interrelationships of endogenous factors and processes is mirrored by the respective exogenous factors and processes. The same levels and interrelationships found in the endogenous environment exist in the exogenous environment. In addition there are interactions between factors and processes in the exogenous and endogenous environments. For example, an interaction between macro-level factors involving human resource development (HRD) policies would occur when regional cooperation resulted in regional HRD policies (macro-exogenous) that influenced organizational HRD policies (macro-endogenous). A micro-level interaction is that organizational cultures and individual work-related preferences (micro-endogenous) are not divorced from national culture (micro-exogenous). For example, the collectivism of Japanese organizations is a reflection of collectivism in the broader Japanese society (Hofstede, 1994; Ohmae, 1983). In the same vein the individualism found by Hofstede (1980) in Australian and U.S. samples is argued to be a reflection of the broader society. In addition to culture this observation also applies to intranational diversity based on differences in factors such as gender, occupation, and education.

One HRM implication of the diverse work-related preferences present in MNE workforces is the need to balance integration and differentiation in MNEs operating across national borders (Gomez-Mejia & Balkin, 1991; Gomez-Mejia & Welbourne, 1991). For example, Tung (1993) discusses the HRM issues in managing cross-national and intranational diversity. Failure to appreciate the importance of micro-endogenous factors in each local unit of the organization is a major source of dissatisfaction in MNEs, due to inequity caused by nationality-based compensation systems. As Reynolds (1988) has noted, "There is no doubt that paying each expatriate according to his or her home country can be less expensive than paying everyone on an American scale, but justifying these differences can be very difficult indeed" (p. 320). This difficulty reflects the reciprocity between exogenous and endogenous factors and processes.

A further example of macro-exogenous factors is seen in International Labor Organization conventions and national legislation. These meetings and laws influence meso-exogenous processes such as the implementation of legislation. These processes in turn influence organizational human resource philosophies, policies, and programs and practices (respectively, micro- and macro-endogenous factors and meso-endogenous processes). Evidence of this process is found in occupational safety and health legislation and the concomitant requirements for HRM in countries such as the United States and Australia (Quinlan & Bohle, 1991). Although a less obvious link, it is evident that endogenous factors also enable an organization to influence its environment. For example, the managerial philosophies (micro-endogenous) of dominant employers in the United Kingdom has led to much resistance and political lobbying (meso-exogenous process) and has had a powerful impact on the progress of the Maastricht Treaty (regarding workers' rights), and proposed social and employment legislation (macro-exogenous factors) in the European Union (Bercusson & Van Dijk, 1995; Hyman & Ferner, 1994; Teague, 1993).

Applying the Conceptual Framework

Outcomes have an important relationship to the framework presented in Figure 18.1. Outcomes are intentional or unintentional results of interactions between the factors and processes in our framework. We argue that outcomes can be micro, macro, or meso level and are therefore not intrinsically different from the other factors and processes discussed above. This argument can be characterized by the application of the conceptual framework (Figure 18.1) to the example of factors and processes, including outcomes, related to human resource development, shown in Figure 18.2. HRD has been selected to illustrate this argument because it is a key organizational activity that underpins a number of other human resource functions. It should be noted that although the illustration presented in Figure 18.2 focuses on HRD in a multinational enterprise, it has application to meso processes other than human resource programs and practices, in both domestic and international organizations.

Like Figure 18.1, Figure 18.2 shows endogenous organizational factors embedded in the external environment. Outcomes are highlighted by dashed lines surrounding the micro (circular) and macro (rectangular) factors. Meso processes continue to be represented by white arrows, and direct relationships between factors

Figure 18.2. Application of the Conceptual Framework to IHRM.

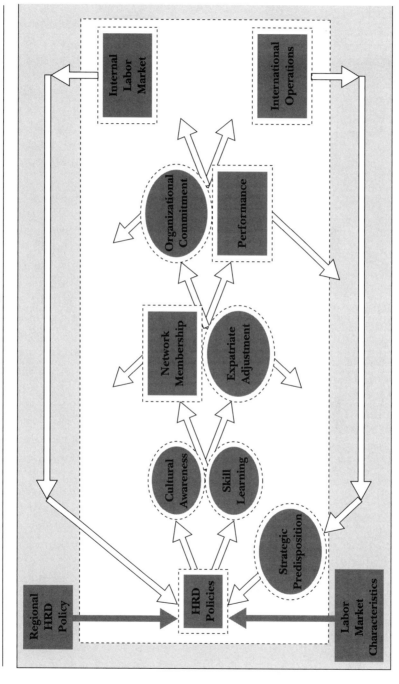

are shown by black arrows. The example in Figure 18.2 is not intended to represent a sequential flow of relationships but rather multiple interactions between factors and processes, including feedback relationships. That is, Figure 18.2 portrays one *possible* set of relationships, with the acknowledgment that they are interwoven with other factors and processes in the endogenous and exogenous environments. One purpose of Figure 18.2 is to show that outcomes are not intrinsically different from other organizational factors and processes. Furthermore, outcomes are not end points in themselves but may be viewed as measurable intermediate points in the ongoing organizational dynamics.

As depicted in Figure 18.2, HRD policies (macro-endogenous) in MNEs will be influenced by multiple factors, both exogenous and endogenous. One macro-exogenous influence is *regional or national HRD policies.* Dowling (1994) has observed, for example, that there are significant opportunities for Asia-Pacific Economic Cooperation (APEC) countries to cooperate to develop policies on human resource development. In particular, large organizations from industrialized economies could participate in an exchange program by accepting managers and human resource practitioners from small- and medium-sized organizations in newly industrializing countries for short-term assignments with the goal of transferring the HRD expertise of larger organizations to smaller ones. Such regional cooperation would influence HRD policies in multinationals. Knowledge transfer to host country nationals will also depend to some extent upon other macro-level factors such as host country *labor market characteristics* (Dowling, Schuler, & Welch, 1994). The propensity of the MNE to invest resources in training and developing host country nationals will be influenced by the *strategic predisposition* of MNE management (micro-endogenous). For example, insofar as the use of parent country expatriates is preferred, an ethnocentric mind-set will result. That predisposition is less likely than other predispositions to result in HRD policies that emphasize the development of host country nationals as managers (Welch, 1994).

A multinational's HRD policy will play a primary role in directing the implementation of HRD programs and practices (meso-endogenous processes). According to Black and Mendenhall (1990), HRD programs are designed to result, for example, in such psychological outcomes as improved *cross-cultural awareness* and *skills learning* (both micro-endogenous). These HRD outcomes have implications for all employees. Considering expatriates in particular, cross-cultural training in the predeparture phase may facilitate expatriate adjustment and network development in the host environment (Black & Mendenhall, 1990; McEnery & Des Harnais, 1990). Additional factors and processes will also play a role in the realization of outcomes such as *expatriate adjustment* (micro-endogenous) and *network membership* (which may be considered both macro-endogenous and -exogenous when it crosses organizational boundaries).

Expatriate adjustment and network membership will have implications for the individual and organization. For the individual, poor adjustment may result in decreased performance levels (Church, 1982), decreased organizational commitment (Gregersen & Black, 1992), and employee turnover (Naumann, 1992). For the organization, related outcomes include difficulty in finding suitably qualified candidates for expatriation (Black & Gregersen, 1991a). When less suitable candidates are sent on expatriate assignments, the problems associated with poor adjustment are exacerbated, and a "downward-spiralling vicious cycle" results (Black & Gregersen, 1992). This outcome has long-term consequences for international operations, possibly including changes in HRD policies and even organizational withdrawal from some international operations.

Changes in HRD policies reflect the messages coming from the feedback relationship between outcomes and other organizational factors and processes. Indeed, it could be said that a change in HRD policies is an outcome in itself. As shown in Figure 18.2, all factors and processes may be both initiators and outcomes, as they are integrated components of organizational dynamics. An artificial divide between factors and processes and outcomes therefore appears untenable. This is a fundamental assumption of the conceptual framework we presented in Figure 18.1 and developed throughout this chapter.

Conclusion

The dominant approach taken in previous IHRM research has been to distinguish between micro- and macro-level factors and meso processes and between initiators and outcomes of change.

Organizational behavior research has been criticized for tending to focus exclusively on micro-level factors (De Cieri & Dowling, 1995). Similarly, HRM research has been criticized for taking a prescriptive managerial approach, neglecting to some extent the micro level of organizational behavior (Ferner, 1994). We have argued that distinctions between micro and macro levels that do not recognize their interrelationships are not sustainable in any environment.

Understanding organizational dynamics necessitates recognition and consideration of relationships between factors and processes across levels and environments. Academics and practitioners must therefore recognize that these factors and processes are complex and act integratively in the endogenous and exogenous environments. Application of our conceptual framework in the development of context-specific studies will facilitate multilevel, multidisciplinary research. Thus our conceptual framework is not intended as an end in itself but as one step in an iterative process whereby conceptual frameworks are developed and new contributions offered. In this process a multidisciplinary approach is essential if substantive, or even incremental, progress is to be realized in research and practice.

Note

1.   We recognize that just how much influence such mechanisms have on employees' underlying values has been much debated in the HRM literature (Ogbonna, 1993).

References

Adler, N. J. (1991). *International dimensions of organizational behavior* (2nd ed.). Boston: PWS-Kent.

Alkhafaji, A. F. (1990). Comparative management in developed and developing countries. *Management Decision, 29*(6), 36–40.

Alvesson, M., & Berg, P. O. (1992). *Corporate culture and organizational symbolism.* Hawthorne, NY: Walter de Gruyter.

Arvey, R. D., Bhagat, R. S., & Salas, E. (1991). Cross-cultural and cross-national issues in personnel and human resource management: Where do we go from here? In G. R. Ferris & K. M. Rowland (Eds.), *Research in personnel and human resources management* (Vol. 9, pp. 367–407). Greenwich, CT: JAI Press.

Babbie, E. (1992). *The practice of social research* (6th ed.). Belmont, CA: Wadsworth.

Bartlett, C. A., & Ghoshal, S. (1987, Fall). Managing across borders: New organizational responses. *Sloan Management Review*, pp. 45–53.

Bartlett, C. A., & Ghoshal, S. (1988). Organizing for worldwide effectiveness: The transnational solution. *California Management Review, 33*(1), 54–74.

Bartlett, C. A., & Ghoshal, S. (1989). *Managing across borders: The transnational solution.* Boston, MA: Harvard Business School Press.

Bartlett, C. A., & Ghoshal, S. (1990, July-August). Matrix management: Not a structure, a frame of mind. *Harvard Business Review*, pp. 138–145.

Bartlett, C. A., & Ghoshal, S. (1992). *Transnational management: Text, cases, and readings in cross-border management.* Homewood, IL: Irwin.

Beer, M., Spector, B., Lawrence, P. R., Mills, D. Q., & Walton, R. E. (1984). *Managing human assets.* New York: Free Press.

Begin, J. P. (1992). Comparative human resource management (HRM): A systems perspective. *International Journal of Human Resource Management, 3*(3), 379–408.

Bercusson, B., & Van Dijk, J. J. (1995). The implementation of the protocol and agreement on social policy of the Treaty on European Union. *International Journal of Comparative Labour Law and Industrial Relations, 11*(1), 3–30.

Berry, J. W., Kim, U., & Boski, P. (1988). Psychological acculturation of immigrants. In Y. Y. Kim & W. B. Gudykunst (Eds.), *Cross-cultural adaptation: Current approaches* (pp. 62–89). Thousand Oaks, CA: Sage.

Bhagat, R. S., & McQuaid, S. J. (1982). Role of subjective culture in organizations: A review and directions for future research. *Journal of Applied Psychology, 67*, 653–685.

Black, J. S. (1988). Work role transitions: A study of American expatriate managers in Japan. *Journal of International Business Studies, 19*, 277–294.

Black, J. S., & Gregersen, H. B. (1991a). Antecedents to cross-cultural adjustment for expatriates in Pacific Rim assignments. *Human Relations, 44*(5), 497–515.

Black, J. S., & Gregersen, H. B. (1991b). The other half of the picture: Antecedents of spouse cross-cultural adjustment. *Journal of International Business Studies, 22*(3), 461–477.

Black, J. S., & Gregersen, H. B. (1991c). When Yankee comes home: Factors related to expatriate and spouse repatriation adjustment. *Journal of International Business Studies, 22*(4), 671–694.

Black, J. S., & Gregersen, H. B. (1992). Serving two masters: Managing the dual allegiance of expatriate employees. *Sloan Management Review, 33*(4), 61–71.

Black, J. S., Gregersen, H. B., & Mendenhall, M. E. (1992). *Global assignments: Successfully expatriating and repatriating international managers.* San Francisco, CA: Jossey-Bass.

Black, J. S., & Mendenhall, M. E. (1990). Cross-cultural training effectiveness: A review and a theoretical framework for future research. *Academy of Management Review, 15*(1), 113–136.

Black, J. S., Mendenhall, M. E., & Oddou, G. (1991). Toward a comprehensive model of international adjustment: An integration of multiple theoretical perspective. *Academy of Management Review, 16*(2), 291–317.

Black, J. S., & Stephens, G. K. (1989). The influence of the spouse on American expatriate adjustment and intent to stay in Pacific Rim overseas assignments. *Journal of Management, 15*(4), 529–544.

Blyton, P., & Turnbull, P. (Eds.). (1992). *Reassessing human resource management.* Thousand Oaks, CA: Sage.

Boxall, P. F. (1992). Strategic human resource management: Beginnings of a new theoretical sophistication? *Human Resource Management, 2*(3), 60–79.

Boxall, P. F., & Dowling, P. J. (1990). Human resource management and the industrial relations tradition. *Labour & Industry, 3*(2–3), 195–214.

Boyacigiller, N. A. (1990). The role of expatriates in the management of interdependence, complexity and risk in multinational corporations. *Journal of International Business Studies, 21*(3), 357–381.

Brewster, C., & Pickard, J. (1994). Evaluating expatriate training. *International Studies of Management and Organization, 24*(3), 18–35.

Butler, J. E., Ferris, G. R., & Napier, N. K. (1991). *Strategy and human resources management.* Cincinnati: South-Western.

Cappelli, P., & Sherer, P. D. (1991). The missing role of context in OB: The need for a meso-level approach. In B. M. Staw & L. L. Cummings (Eds.), *Research in organizational behavior* (Vol. 13, pp. 55–110). Greenwich, CT: JAI Press.

Chakravarthy, B. S., & Perlmutter, H. V. (1985, Summer). Strategic planning for a global business. *Columbia Journal of World Business,* pp. 3–10.

Chandler, A. D., Jr. (1980). The United States: Seedbed of managerial capitalism. In A. D. Chandler & H. Daems (Eds.), *Managerial hierarchies: Comparative perspectives on the rise of modern industrial enterprises* (pp. 9–40). Boston: Harvard Business School Press.

Child, J. D. (1973). Strategies of control and organizational behavior. *Administrative Science Quarterly, 17,* 1–17.

Child, J. D. (1981). Culture, contingency and capitalism in the cross-national study of organizations. In L. L. Cummings and B. M. Staw

(Eds.), *Research in organizational behavior* (Vol. 3, pp. 303–356). Greenwich, CT: JAI Press.

Child, J. D., and Markóczy, L. (1993). Host country managerial behavior and learning in Chinese and Hungarian joint ventures. *Journal of Management Studies, 30*(4), 611–631.

Church, A. T. (1982). Sojourner adjustment. *Psychological Bulletin, 9,* 540–572.

Czinkota, M. R., Ronkainen, I. A., & Moffett, M. H. (1994). *International business* (3rd ed.). Fort Worth, TX: Dryden Press.

Daniels, J. D., & Radebaugh, L. H. (1992). *International business: Environments and operations* (6th ed.). Reading, MA: Addison-Wesley.

De Cieri, H., & Dowling, P. J. (1995). Cross-cultural issues in organizational behavior. In C. L. Cooper & D. M. Rousseau (Eds.), *Trends in organizational behavior* (Vol. 2, pp. 127–145). New York: Wiley.

De Cieri, H., Dowling, P. J., & Taylor, K. F. (1991). The psychological impact of expatriate relocation on partners. *The International Journal of Human Resource Management, 2*(3), 377–414.

De Cieri, H., McGaughey, S. L., & Dowling, P. J. (1996). Relocation. In M. Warner (Ed.), *International encyclopedia of business and management* (Vol. 5, pp. 4300–4310). New York: Routledge.

Deal, T. E., & Kennedy, A. A. (1982). *Corporate cultures: The rites and rituals of corporate life.* Reading, MA: Addison-Wesley.

Dowling, P. J. (1994, November). *Human resource transformation through regional economic cooperation.* Paper presented at the Asia-Pacific Economic Cooperation (APEC) Business Conference, Djakarta.

Dowling, P. J., Schuler, R. S., & Welch, D. E. (1994). *International dimensions of human resource management* (2nd ed.). Belmont, CA: Wadsworth.

Doz, Y. L., & Prahalad, C. K. (1991). Managing DMNCs: A search for a new paradigm. *Strategic Management Journal, 12,* 146–164.

Duberley, J. P., & Burns, N. D. (1993). Organizational configurations: Implications for the human resource/personnel management debate. *Personnel Review, 22*(4), 26–34.

Duerr, M. G. (1986). International business management: Its four tasks. *Conference Board Record.* New York: The Conference Board.

Dyer, L. D. (1984). Studying human resource strategy: An approach and an agenda. *Industrial Relations, 23*(2), 156–169.

Edström, A., & Galbraith, J. R. (1977). Transfer of managers as a coordination and control strategy in multinational organizations. *Administrative Science Quarterly, 22,* 248–263.

Edström, A., & Lorange, P. (1984). Matching strategy and human resources in multinational corporations. *Journal of International Business Studies, 15*(2), 125–136.

Evans, P.A.L. (1992). Management development as glue technology. *Human Resource Planning, 15*(1), 85–106.

Evans, P.A.L. (1993). Dosing the glue: Applying human resource technology to build the global organization. In G. R. Ferris & K. M. Rowland (Eds.), *Research in personnel and human resources management* (pp. 21–54). Greenwich, CT: JAI Press:

Fergus, M. (1990, May). Employees on the move. *HRMagazine,* pp. 44–46.

Ferner, A. (1994). Multinational companies and human resource management: An overview of research issues. *Human Resource Management Journal, 4*(2), 79–102.

Fisher, C. D., & Shaw, J. B. (1994). Relocation attitudes and adjustment: A longitudinal study. *Journal of Organizational Behavior, 15,* 209–224.

Galbraith, J. R., & Kazanjian, R. K. (1986). Organizing to implement strategies of diversity and globalization: The role of matrix designs. *Human Resource Management, 25*(1), 55–54.

Ghoshal, S., & Nohria, N. (1989). Internal differentiation within multinational corporations. *Strategic Management Journal, 10,* 323–337.

Ghoshal, S., & Nohria, N. (1993, Winter). Horses for courses: Organizational forms for multinational corporations. *Sloan Management Review,* pp. 23–35.

Gomez-Mejia, L. R., & Balkin, D. B. (1991). *Compensation strategies, business policy, and firm performance.* Cincinnati: South-Western.

Gomez-Mejia, L., & Welbourne, T. (1991). Compensation strategies in a global context. *Human Resource Planning, 14*(1), 29–41.

Granovetter, M. (1992). Problems of explanation in economic sociology. In N. Nohria & R. G. Eccles (Eds.), *Networks and organizations. Structure, form and action* (pp. 1–56). Boston: Harvard Business School Press.

Gregersen, H. B., & Black, J. S. (1992). Antecedents to commitment to a parent company and a foreign operation. *Academy of Management Journal, 35*(1), 65–90.

Guest, D. (1987). Human resource management and industrial relations. *Journal of Management Studies, 24*(5), 503–522.

Heenan, D. A., & Perlmutter, H. (1979). *Multinational organization development.* Reading, MA: Addison-Wesley.

Hendry, C., & Pettigrew, A. (1990). Human resource management: An agenda for the 1990s. *International Journal of Human Resource Management, 1*(1), 17–43.

Hickson, D. J., Hinings, C. R., McMillan, C. J., & Schwitter, J. P. (1974). The culture-free context of organizational structure. *Sociology, 8,* 59–80.

Hofstede, G. (1980). *Culture's consequences: International differences in work-related values.* Thousand Oaks, CA: Sage.

Hofstede, G. (1991). *Cultures and organizations. Software of the mind.* London: McGraw-Hill.

Humes, S. (1993). *Managing the multinational. Confronting the global-local dilemma.* Upper Saddle River, NJ: Prentice Hall.

Huo, Y. P., & Steers, R. M. (1993). Cultural influences on the design of incentive systems: The case of East Asia. *Asia Pacific Journal of Management, 10*(1), 71–85.

Hyman, R., & Ferner, A. (Eds.). (1994). *New frontiers in European industrial relations.* Oxford, England: Blackwell.

Janis, I. L. (1972). *Victims of groupthink: A psychological study analysis of policy decisions and fiascos.* Boston: Houghton Mifflin.

Jarvis, S. (1990, June). Preparing employees to work south of the border. *Personnel,* pp. 59–63.

Johnston, W. B. (1993). Global work force 2000: The new world labor market. *Harvard Business Review, 69*(2), 115–127.

Kessler, I., & Purcell, J. (1992). Performance related pay: Objectives and application. *Human Resource Management Journal, 2*(3), 16–33.

Klein, K. J., Dansereau, F., & Hall, R. J. (1994). Levels issues in theory development, data collection, and analysis. *Academy of Management Review, 19*(2), 195–229.

Kluckhohn, F. R., & Strodtbeck, F. L. (1961). *Variations in value orientations.* New York: HarperCollins.

Kobrin, S. J. (1992). *Multinational strategy and international human resource management policy.* Unpublished manuscript. Wharton School, University of Pennsylvania.

Kobrin, S. J. (1994). Is there a relationship between a geocentric mindset and multinational strategy? *Journal of International Studies, 25*(3), 493–511.

Kochan, T. A., Batt, R., & Dyer, L. D. (1992). International human resource studies: A framework for future research. In D. Lewin, O. S. Mitchell, & P. D. Sherer (Eds.), *Research frontiers in industrial relations and human resources* (pp. 309–337). Madison, WI: Industrial Relations Research Association.

Laurent, A. (1983). The cultural diversity of Western conceptions of management. *International Studies of Management & Organization, 13*(1–2), 75–96.

Lawrence, P. R., & Lorsch, J. W. (1967). *Organization and environment.* Boston: Harvard Business School Press.

Leftwich, P. H., & Eckert, R. D. (1985). *The price system and resource allocation* (9th ed.). New York: Holt Saunders.

Lengnick-Hall, C. A., & Lengnick-Hall, M. L. (1988). Strategic human resource management: A review of the literature and a proposed typology. *Academy of Management Review, 13,* 454–470.

Lockhart, T., & Myers, A. (1993). The social charter: Implications for personnel managers. *Personnel Review, 22*(4), 3–16.

Lorange, P. (1986). Human resource management in multinational cooperative ventures. *Human Resource Management, 25*(1), 133–148.

Martinez, J. I., & Jarillo, J. C. (1991). Coordination demands of international strategies. *Journal of International Business Studies, 22*(3), 429–444.

McEnery, J., & Des Harnais, G. (1990, April). Culture shock. *Training & Development Journal*, pp. 43–47.

McGaughey, S. L. (1994). *Work related preferences of undergraduates in three nations: Implications for international management and research.* Unpublished thesis. Monash University, Australia.

Miles, R. E., & Snow, C. C. (1984). Fit, failure and the hall of fame. *California Management Review, 26*(3), 10–28.

Mintzberg, H. (1979). *The structuring of organizations.* Upper Saddle River, NJ: Prentice Hall.

Naumann, E. (1992). A conceptual model of expatriate turnover. *Journal of International Business Studies, 23*(3), 499–531.

Nohria, N., & Ghoshal, S. (1994). Differentiated fit and shared values: Alternatives for managing headquarters-subsidiary relations. *Strategic Management Journal, 15,* 491–502.

Ogbonna, E. (1993). Managing organizational culture: Fantasy or reality? *Human Resource Management Journal, 3*(2), 42–54.

Ohmae, K. (1983). *The mind of the strategist: The art of Japanese business.* Harmondsworth, England: Penguin Books.

Ondrack, D. (1985). International transfers of managers in North American and European MNEs. *Journal of International Business Studies, 16*(3), 1–19.

Pennings, J. M. (1993). Executive reward systems: A cross-national comparison. *Journal of Management Studies, 30*(2), 261–280.

Perlmutter, H. V. (1969, January-February). The tortuous evolution of the multinational corporation. *Columbia Journal of World Business*, pp. 9–18.

Poole, M. (1990). Editorial: Human resource management in an international perspective. *International Journal of Human Resource Management, 1*(1), 1–15.

Porter, M. E. (1986). Changing patterns of international competition. *California Management Review, 28*(2), 9–40.

Porter, M. E. (1990). *The competitive advantage of nations.* New York: Free Press.

Prahalad, C. K., & Doz, Y. L. (1987). *The multinational mission.* New York: Free Press.

Pucik, V. (1992). Globalization and human resource management. In V. Pucik, N. M. Tichy, & C. K. Barnett (Eds.), *Globalizing management: Creating and leading the competitive organization* (pp. 61–81). New York: Wiley.

Pucik, V., Tichy, N. M., & Barnett, C. K. (Eds.). (1992). *Globalizing management: Creating and leading the competitive organization*. New York: Wiley.

Pugh, D. S. (1973, Spring). The measurement of organization structures: Does context determine form? *Organizational Dynamics*, pp. 19–34.

Pugh, D. S., Hickson, D. J., & Hinings, C. R. (1969). The context of organizational structure. *Administrative Science Quarterly, 14,* 91–114.

Pugh, D. S., Hickson, D. J., Hinings, C. R., & Turner, C. (1969). Dimensions of organization structure. *Administrative Science Quarterly, 13,* 65–105.

Purcell, J., & Ahlstrand, B. (1994). *Human resource management in the multidivisional company.* New York: Oxford University Press.

Quinlan, M., & Bohle, P. (1991). *Managing occupational health and safety in Australia: A multidisciplinary approach.* South Melbourne: Macmillan.

Rand, T. (1977, September). Diagnosing the valued reward orientations of employees. *Personnel Journal,* pp. 451–454.

Redding, S. G. (1994). Comparative management theory: Jungle, zoo or fossil bed? *Organization Studies, 15*(3), 323–359.

Reiz, H. J. (1975). The relative importance of five categories of needs among industrial workers in eight countries. *Academy of Management Proceedings,* pp. 270–273.

Reynolds, C. (1988). Cost-effective compensation of expatriates. *Topics in Total Compensation, 2*(4), 319–326.

Richards, T., & Richards, L. (1993). *Using computers in qualitative analysis* (Technical report No. 8/93). Melbourne, Australia: Department of Computer Science & Computer Engineering, LaTrobe University.

Ricks, D., Toyne, B., & Martinez, Z. (1990). Recent developments in international management research and practice. *Journal of Management, 16*(2), 219–253.

Ring, P. S., Lenway, A. S., & Govekar, M. (1990). Management of the political imperative in international business. *Strategic Management Journal, 11,* 141–151.

Roberts, K. H., Hulin, C. L., & Rousseau, D. M. (1978). *Developing an interdisciplinary science of organizations.* San Francisco: Jossey-Bass.

Ronen, S., & Kraut, A. (1977, Summer). Similarities among countries based on employee work values and attitudes. *Columbia Journal of World Business,* pp. 89–96.

Ronen, S., & Shenkar, O. (1985). Clustering countries on attitudinal dimensions: A review and synthesis. *Academy of Management Review, 10*(3), 435–454.

Rousseau, D. M., & House, R. J. (1994). Meso organizational behavior: Avoiding three fundamental biases. In C. L. Cooper and D. M. Rousseau (Eds.), *Trends in organizational behavior* (Vol. 1, pp. 15–29). New York: Wiley.

Sarasti, J. (1993, April). *Aspects of corporate culture as a management tool for an MNC.* Paper presented at the European Institute for Advanced Studies in Management 8th Workshop on Strategic Human Resource Management, University of Toronto.

Schein, E. H. (1985). *Organizational culture and leadership: A dynamic view.* San Francisco: Jossey-Bass.

Schöllhammer, H. (1975). Current research in international and comparative management issues. *Management International Review, 15*(2–3), 29–40.

Schuler, R. S. (1992, Summer). Strategic human resources management: Linking the people with the strategic needs of the business. *Organizational Dynamics*, pp. 18–32.

Schuler, R. S., Dowling, P. J., & De Cieri, H. (1993). An integrative framework of strategic international human resource management. *Journal of Management, 19*(2), 419–459.

Schuler, R. S., Dowling, P. J., Smart, J. P., & Huber, V. L. (1992). *Human resource management in Australia* (2nd ed.). Sydney: Harper Educational.

Scullion, H. (1994). Staffing policies and strategic control in British multinationals. *International Studies of Management & Organization, 24*(3), 86–104.

Shenkar, O., & Zeira, Y. (1987). International joint ventures: Implications for organizational development. *Personnel Review, 16*(1), 30–37.

Smart, J. P. (1992, December). *Cultural change at BP.* Paper presented at the meeting of the Australian and New Zealand Academy of Management, Sydney.

Storey, J. (Ed.). (1989). *New perspectives on human resource management.* London: Routledge.

Storey, J., & Sisson, K. (1993). *Managing human resources and industrial relations.* Buckingham, U.K.: Open University Press.

Sundaram, A. K., & Black, J. S. (1992). The environment and internal organization of multinational enterprises. *Academy of Management Review, 17*(4), 729–757.

Tayeb, M. H. (1994). Organizations and national culture: Methodology considered. *Organization Studies, 15*(3), 429–446.

Teagarden, M., Butler, M. C., & Von Glinow, M. (1992). Mexico's *Maquiladora* industry: Where strategic human resource management makes a difference. *Organizational Dynamics, 20*(3), 34–47.

Teague, P. (1993). Towards social Europe? Industrial relations after 1992. *International Journal of Human Resource Management, 4*(2), 349–375.

Tichy, N. M., Fombrun, C. J., & Devanna, M. A. (1982). Strategic human resource management. *Sloan Management Review, 23*(2), 47–61.

Tung, R. L. (1982). Selection and training procedures of U.S., European and Japanese multinationals. *California Management Review, 25*(1), 57–71.

Tung, R. L. (1993). Managing cross-national and intra-national diversity. *Human Resource Management, 32*(4), 461–477.

Vance, C. M., McClaine, S. R., Boje, D. M., & Stage, H. D. (1992). An examination of the transferability of traditional performance appraisal principles across cultural boundaries. *Management International Review, 32,* 313–326.

Vecchio, R., Hearn, G., & Southey, G. (1992). *Organisational behaviour: Life at work in Australia.* Brisbane: Harcourt Brace Jovanovich.

Welch, D. E. (1994). HRM implications of globalization. *Journal of General Management, 19*(4), 52–68.

Welch, D. E., Fenwick, M. S., & De Cieri, H. (1994). Staff transfers as a control strategy: An exploratory story of two Australian organizations. *International Journal of Human Resource Management, 5*(2), 474–489.

Woodward, J. (1965). *Industrial organization.* New York: Oxford University Press.

Wright, P., & McMahan, G. (1992). Theoretical perspectives for strategic human resource management. *Journal of Management, 18*(2), 295–320.

CHAPTER 19

Complex Interactions Influencing International Human Resource Management
Putting Some Meat on the Bones

Richard D. Arvey
Neil Anderson

We begin our commentary on Chapter Eighteen by summarizing the basic framework that De Cieri, McGaughey, and Dowling provide for conceptualizing the complex interactions of dynamic forces that affect the strategic aspects of international human resource management (IHRM). This framework, built on an interactive process of "revisiting the conceptual and empirical IHRM literature," is an effort to provide an integrative and multidisciplinary approach to the understanding of IHRM. Essentially, it identifies the following six major classes of variables that interrelate with one another:

1. *Micro-level endogenous factors.* Psychological factors that "reside" within the organization and occur at different levels of analysis—the individual (such as work-related preferences), the group (such as group dynamics), or the organizational (such as HR philosophy).
2. *Micro-level exogenous factors.* Factors external to the organization,

such as subcultures of ethnic groups in the population, national cultures, and so on.

3. *Macro-level endogenous factors.* Factors internal to the organization that are considered relatively "larger" forces, such as technology, organizational structure, and HR policy.

4. *Macro-level exogenous factors.* External factors such as economic systems of governance, industry characteristics, population education levels, and so on.

5. *Meso-level endogenous factors.* Internal mid-level human resource processes, referring to traditional processes like recruitment and selection, performance management, compensation, and so forth.

6. *Meso-level exogenous factors.* External mid-level processes such as legislative actions, political factors, and so forth.

De Cieri, McGaughey, and Dowling outline the notion that these six classes of variables influence each other directly and indirectly, moderate or interact with each other, reciprocally influence each other, and otherwise operate in a dynamic manner. Finally, they suggest that many of these variables also influence a variety of outcomes but that it is the various micro and macro endogenous factors that represent the desired (or undesired) outcomes of interest.

Commentary: Opening Shots

If we have fairly characterized the framework offered by these authors, we offer the following observations and points of commentary.

First, it is appropriate (and we believe accurate) to recognize the variety of factors involved in IHRM settings. It is true that a variety of factors, both endogenous and exogenous, will influence how HRM practices are deployed, how effective they are in achieving desired outcomes, and what the impact is of such practices on employees.

Second, it also seems accurate to argue that these variables influence each other in complex ways. Multiple factors are at play at any one time; things change over time, outcomes are multiply determined, and so forth. What is perhaps more problematic is to develop and transpose these complex patterns of interrelationships into testable hypotheses of cause-effect relations. Whether the framework is as yet testable is open to some debate.

Third, the distinction between endogenous and exogenous factors is important to make and recognize. The authors propose a pretty clear typology of different types (endogenous and exogenous) and different levels (micro, meso, and macro) of factors. They propose a classic open systems model of organizations, and certainly this model is in accord with the meta-trends in organizational behavior theory and research that have emphasized the linkages between organization strategy and its wider environmental impact. Ultimately, of course, the organization has little or no control over exogenous factors, but it can indeed influence endogenous variables. This stated, the De Cieri, McGaughey, and Dowling typology is valuable in that it puts forward an easily understandable model, applicable to most if not all organizations and business environments, to classify and summarize factors of interest to human resource researchers and practitioners alike.

Having noted what in our opinion are the major contributions of this chapter, we now adopt a somewhat more constructively critical stance in order to suggest areas in which the model could be further developed and explicated.

Critique of the Model

First, we believe the framework is perhaps a little too broad and therefore loses some of its heuristic value. One is left with the impression that everything influences everything in this IHRM framework. Therefore the framework could be criticized for a lack of specificity and detail sufficient to permit precise predictions of relationships and outcomes. This in itself is not necessarily a fundamental weakness given that the model is at an early stage of development and as yet awaits empirical testing. The question is just how would one go about testing the De Cieri, McGaughey, and Dowling model in organizational settings? Further development of this model should focus upon fleshing out its component categories and interactions. As for any model of this kind, we would argue that it needs to fulfill two main functions. First, it should accurately describe prior data. That is, can a researcher or practitioner use this framework to analyze case studies, data bases, and the like that contain measurements of the various variables specified? Second, it should permit the prediction of future events, outcomes, relationships, and so on.

A second issue involves the somewhat arbitrary classification of variables into the categories of micro, macro, and meso factors. Because these types of distinctions are just beginning to be understood and made, it might be a little unfair to criticize De Cieri, McGaughey, and Dowling for not being particularly precise in their classifying definitions. In any case, although the conceptual underpinnings of these variables and processes are pretty clear, their precise meanings remain unclear. Indeed, there are distinct overlaps within and between the defined categories. Individual differences in workgroups will affect the climate and decision-making style of the group, group structures and intergroup relations will affect organizational functioning, and intersecting all of these strata of variables will be the human resource strategies and procedures of the organization. It is perhaps all the more interesting to explicate these interfaces between micro, meso, and macro factors than to limit one's field of vision to a particular level or stratum. Although these multidirectional cross-strata influences are noted in the De Cieri, McGaughey, and Dowling model, the classification (perhaps unavoidably) begins to creak at the seams in its attempt to pigeon-hole every conceivable variable present in organizational settings.

Third, we would raise the specter of measurement, which is inherent in but largely unexplored by the model. As a precursor to quantifying relationships between variables at different levels in organizational settings, it is first necessary to quantify the actual variables themselves. Practical difficulties in measurement of variables are not easily dismissed and, indeed, have over the recent years begun to receive substantial research attention, particularly from industrial-organizational psychologists and micro-industrial economists. Reiterating our earlier point, we find that the model puts forward generalized expectations of interactions; it does not specify precise hypotheses of cause-effect relationships in a manner that allows fellow researchers to operationalize the model through testable field study designs.

Finally, although the authors of Chapter Eighteen attempted to illustrate the meaning of this framework by building an example that used human resource development activities, the resulting discussion did not seem really to exemplify the model, partly because the example was rooted in rather macro-level concepts and research literature bases. For us, the example did not put much meat on the bones of the model.

An Illustrative Case Study

Perhaps we can provide an example that might illustrate the framework with a little more clarity. About two years ago the lead author of this chapter, Richard Arvey, visited a firm in South Africa that was experiencing a number of challenges. Although we will not relate organizational specifics here, we can still portray some of the issues and also convey some personal impressions to illustrate the case.

The organization is in the business of mining gold and has over 40,000 employees involved in its operations. Over 90 percent of the 30,000-member indigenous black South African employee population work as laborers down in the deep mine shafts over three shift periods. Virtually one hundred percent of the white employees occupy management positions. The organization has explicit policies prohibiting discrimination in hiring, promoting, and training individuals, and indeed, there are clear affirmative action targets to increase the representation of black employees in management levels. Efforts are being made to identify black employees with managerial potential, yet a substantial proportion of the black employee population has low literacy levels. Moreover, although the business of managing the firm is conducted in English, as many as eight different languages are spoken by the organization's employees. Current efforts to identify talent seem to involve white supervisors' personal knowledge and experience with employees. The organization is considering installing some kind of assessment center procedure, but again difficulties are encountered as a result of the different languages spoken by participants. (One of the interesting questions that surfaced concerned whether English, the required language for normal business operations in the firm, should be required of assessment center participants.) The firm is considering the use of other assessment devices such as psychological tests (for example, "culture fair" tests such as the Ravens Progressive Matrices) that place a lower premium on language skills compared to other verbally loaded assessment tools.

Training and development programs exist but focus exclusively on essential mining operations rather than managerial development. (We observed an ongoing training session where the trainer would shout out a number from one to ten, and the participants would respond in unison with the particular work rule that corresponded to that number.) The firm acquires highly technical skills and knowledge at the professional and managerial ranks by hiring people with those talents rather than by developing and using in-house training programs. Talented professionals with specific knowledge in the mining industry are difficult to find and, at least under Apartheid, quite difficult to recruit from abroad. The government is trying to develop and sponsor employee training programs, but these are not operational as of yet (to our knowledge). The University of South Africa has a number of outreach educational programs (most of them off site) that will eventually help businesses develop a cadre of talent, but the proportion of blacks who attend these classes and matriculate is still small.

The mining organization is extremely vulnerable to the market price of gold; below a certain price level the organization will not recover its costs of extraction. And the organization cannot simply increase the costs of the product to cover increased labor costs or inefficiencies. Moreover, middle- and higher-level management personnel are highly paid, especially relative to basic labor, and enjoy desirable perks (including company-provided vehicles). Such pay and perks cannot easily be withdrawn; lack of such incentives would make it difficult to recruit new management talent, and existing talent would leave. However, it seemed that the pay differentials between middle management and lower-level labor exacerbated feelings of inequity between the black and white employee populations. Union pressure is also high: strikes are common, and demands are regularly made for greater wage payouts, higher rates of promotion for black employees, and better working conditions. Regular stoppages shut down entire mining operations.

The external environment is also in great flux. A new government had been convened, Apartheid has been abandoned, and a new constitution has been debated and installed. One constitutional right being debated and voted upon has to do with equal rights. It states, "No person shall be unfairly discriminated against . . . on one or more of the following grounds in particular: race, gender, sex, ethnic or social origin, color, sexual orientation, age, disability, religion, conscience, belief, culture or language."

Violence in the community is rampant; the assault and murder rate is extremely high, cars are frequently hijacked (making nice company cars easy targets?), and organizational sabotage is also frequent. The perception of the visitor is that within the community there is an underlying rage and anger—a sense that the black population is saying, "It's our turn; Apartheid is over, a new government has been installed, and we want our share of the pie." The message is clear (at least it was to us): organizations better start aggressively moving black employees into management levels or much havoc might ensue.

This mining company is obviously facing a number of challenges, including how to orchestrate its human resource policies and practices so that more full integration of black employees into management ranks can be accomplished quickly, how to decrease management-labor compensation differentials, how to provide sufficient training and development opportunities for employees, how to respond to the external political and social environment, how to deal with union demands, and so forth. From the perspective of a visitor, it was difficult to see how the organization could respond effectively to these challenges, especially within a relatively short time frame.

This case example is rich in dynamics and challenges. But how does it relate to the model and framework offered by De Cieri, McGaughey, and Dowling? We believe it perhaps illustrates the framework in a slightly more comprehensible fashion. Here, briefly, is how the framework can be illustrated by the mining company case:

1. Exogenous and endogenous variables are represented in the case as well as micro-, meso-, and macro-level differences in these variable structures and processes. The political and economic environment represent clear macro-exogenous variables; the human resource reward, selection, and training and development systems represent meso-endogenous processes; and perceptions of equity and fairness by employees represent micro-endogenous variables. Meso-exogenous factors are represented by the legislative activities that are unfolding, macro-endogenous factors are defined

by the structures associated with the mining industry and ore extraction, and micro-exogenous factors are represented by the different cultures represented in the organization.

2. These micro, macro, and meso variables and processes interact dynamically with each other. It is clear that current and future human resource activities and practices (for example selection and promotion processes) will be heavily influenced by the current external demands and pressures (for example, demand for affirmative action, legislation, and so forth). Perhaps the firm will implement some kind of assessment center to diagnose talent more accurately and quickly and thus achieve faster rates of promotion for black employees. Changes in human resource practices (for example, reward systems) will likely affect micro-endogenous variables such as perceptions of equity and fairness. It could be that success in terms of meeting affirmative action goals (meso-endogenous factors) will change community perceptions of the organization (micro-exogenous factors). In a recent mining tragedy at another mining company, over a hundred miners were killed by a falling elevator. Most probably, government regulations will ensue and more stringent safety standards will be imposed (macro-exogenous), increasing the costs of operation but also increasing perceptions of security and safety among personnel (micro-endogenous factors).

3. In our case, multiple forces can be seen to operate. Outcomes and processes may be a result of multiple forces and variables. For example, a change in promotion practices may be a result of both meso-exogenous (legislation) and micro-exogenous (cultural) factors occurring simultaneously. Or a single source may have multiple outcomes.

4. Although the De Cieri, McGaughey, and Dowling model did not emphasize the strategic choices facing the members of management given the complexity of the different forces and variables, there are clearly a variety of strategy choices for management facing this environment. For example, the price of gold in the marketplace may simply increase and the ensuing profitability could spill over into such HRM activities as greater pay rates, increased safety training, more promotional opportunities, and so forth. It seems to us that management should carefully examine just how to allocate any increased profits. It would seem wise to allocate

such resources to human resource management activities in order to survive in the long term (as opposed to returning increased profits in the form of dividends to shareholders).

Thus the case study perhaps gives a little more interpretability to the framework provided by De Cieri, McGaughey, and Dowling. But the same issues pertain here as described earlier; that is, first, exactly which factors will lead to which outcomes and, second, what models or theories will help us explain the potentially infinite number of relationships that are possible within this framework? There are a number of more limiting economic, political, and psychological theories, ones that may help researchers and practitioners to limit the predictions and hypotheses made and therefore to contain the prediction space or to curtail the numerous pathways. Such theories may also help provide directionality to such posited paths. For example, equity theory predictions could be helpful in understanding and predicting relationships between pay practices (meso factors) and employee perceptions of fairness and satisfaction (micro factors). Human capital theory might be helpful in forming more precise predictions about the role of government-sponsored training programs (macro-exogenous) and firm specific training programs (meso-factors). Thus more information is needed to round out and expand the framework or model provided by De Cieri, McGaughey, and Dowling.

Conclusion

It is easy to be too tough on early efforts in IHRM model building and theory generation. We have therefore presented a constructively critical but balanced commentary on the De Cieri, McGaughey, and Dowling model, and in addition, we have illustrated the model by applying it to a real-life case study of an organization undergoing fairly radical change in endogenous and exogenous factors. The next stage in the development of this model, in our view, is for researchers to work up precise specifications of cause-effect relationships. If this is undertaken, the model will provide not only a useful general heuristic but also a framework of testable hypotheses of value for researchers in the undoubtedly burgeoning area of IHRM.

PART 4

Power
Relationships

Understanding the International Leader

Negotiation and Procedural Justice

CHAPTER 20

Cross-Cultural Research on Organizational Leadership
A Critical Analysis and a Proposed Theory

Robert J. House
Norman S. Wright
Ram N. Aditya

Consider the following statements taken from interviews with members of various countries.

> The Dutch place emphasis on egalitarianism and are skeptical about the value of leadership. Terms like leader and manager carry a stigma. If a father is employed as a manager, Dutch children will not admit it to their schoolmates.

> Arabs worship their leaders—*as long as they are in power!*

> Iranians seek power and strength in their leaders.

> The Malaysian leader is expected to behave in a manner that is humble, modest, and dignified.

Note: This chapter was written while the first author was the Unilever Visiting Professor at the Australian Graduate School of Management, The University of New South Wales, from June through August 1996. The authors are indebted to Tracey Dourley and Michelle Garcia-Navaro for searching for and obtaining references and obscure manuscripts to assist in the preparation of this chapter, and to Geoffrey Eagleson for his intellectual contributions to many of the substantive topics discussed in this chapter.

The French appreciate two kinds of leaders. De Gaulle and Mitterand are examples. De Gaulle is an example of a strong charismatic leader. Mitterand is an example of a consensus builder,
coalition former, and effective negotiator.

The Americans appreciate two kinds of leaders. They seek empowerment from leaders who grant autonomy and delegate authority
to subordinates. They also respect the bold, forceful, confident,
and risk-taking leader as personified by John Wayne.

Clearly, what is expected of leaders, what leaders may and may
not do, and the influence that leaders have vary considerably as a
result of the cultural forces in the countries or regions in which
the leaders function.

In this chapter we present a review of the scope and domain of
cross-cultural leadership research. We begin with a review of the
concept of culture and the definition of leadership. We then present a review of cross-cultural leadership research findings to date
and advance three empirical generalizations. Following the literature review we turn to a discussion of several theoretical issues relevant to the study of cross-cultural leadership. We then present a
preliminary theoretical framework intended to be a basis for guiding future cross-cultural leadership research. Finally, we advance
some methodological suggestions for the improvement of cross-
cultural leadership research and theory.

Definitions

As we shall show, in the extant literature, definitions of the terms
culture and leadership are varied and problematic. In the following sections we define these terms as they are used throughout this
chapter.

Culture

The following list contains the definitions of culture advanced by
several prominent social scientists. From this list it can be seen that
there is no consensually agreed-upon definition of culture. In the
most general sense, *culture* is a term used by social scientists to refer

to a set of parameters for social collectivities that differentiates among them in meaningful ways. Collectivities thus differentiated are regarded and referred to as cultures.

Selected Definitions of Culture

1. A patterned way of thinking, feeling, and reacting, acquired and transmitted mainly by symbols, constituting the distinctive achievements of human groups, including their embodiments in artifacts (Kluckhohn, 1951).
2. The collective programming of the mind that distinguishes the members of one human group from another (Hofstede, 1980).
3. The part of the environment that is created or modified by human beings (Herskovits, 1955).
4. Systems of shared meanings placed upon events (Smith & Peterson, 1994).
5. Norms, roles, belief systems, laws, and values that form meaningful wholes and that are interrelated in meaningful ways (Triandis, 1972).
6. A historically transmitted pattern of meanings embodied in symbols, a system of inherited conceptions expressed in symbolic forms by means of which men communicate, perpetuate, and develop their knowledge about and attitudes toward life (Geertz, 1973).
7. A learned, shared, compelling, interrelated set of symbols whose meanings provide a set of orientations for members of a society (Terpstra & David, 1991).
8. The cumulative deposit of knowledge; experience; meanings; beliefs; values; attitudes; religions; concepts of self, the universe, and self-universe relationships; hierarchies of status; role expectations; spatial relations; and time concepts acquired by a large group of people in the course of generations through individual and group striving (Samovar & Porter, 1976).

Culture is variously defined in terms of a number of commonly shared processes: shared ways of thinking, feeling, and reacting; shared meanings and identities; shared socially constructed environments; common ways in which technologies are used; and commonly experienced events including the history, language, and religion of their members. Definitions of culture are generally so broad that they include almost anything and everything in the environment of human beings that is not immutably determined by nature. For example, Herskovits (1955) defines culture as that part of the environment of humans that is made (or modified) by human beings. Hofstede (1980) anthropomorphizes culture as the collective software of the mind. Such broad definitions virtually preclude consensus among scholars on the way cultural variables can and cannot be appropriately operationalized. As a consequence, the empirical culture literature is inconsistent and confusing with respect to what has been discovered or verified and quite incoherent with respect to theoretical generalizations.

Some Essential Parameters of Culture

Despite lack of consensus among scholars, there are several essential common threads that run throughout the various conceptualizations and definitions of the construct generally referred to as culture.

First, culture represents some form and degree of collective agreement—cultures are collectively oriented phenomena. Second, culture refers to sharing of important interpretations of entities, activities, and events, that is, shared meanings. Third, cultural norms (agreed-upon values and beliefs that have prescriptive or proscriptive implications) and cultural forces are manifested linguistically, behaviorally, and symbolically in the form of artifacts. Fourth, common member experiences, most notably history, language, political and economic experiences, and religion are inherent in the notion of culture. Fifth, cultural variables take on the force of social influence largely because members of collectivities identify with an agreed-upon specific set of values and common social identities. Sixth, common experiences and agreed-upon norms have powerful socialization effects on the members of collectivities referred to as cultures. Seventh, cultural interpretations, symbols, artifacts, and effects are transmitted across generations. Eighth, the social influence of cultural forces is assumed to provide a set of compelling behavioral, affective, and attitudinal orientations for members of cultures. Finally, members of specific cultures are presumed to abide by a set of norms that reflect the above-mentioned commonalities.

Two Ways of Defining Culture

In the literature we discern at least two implicit ways of defining culture. First, as can be seen from the list of existing definitions, culture often refers to collectivities in which the members share several psychological commonalities—assumptions, beliefs, values, interpretations of events (meanings), social identities, and motives—and abide by a set of shared norms in a common manner. For simplicity we refer to these kinds of definitions as *normative definitions* of culture.

Normative definitions are difficult to operationalize. What is the standard by which one determines when there is sufficient commonalty among assumptions, beliefs, values, interpretations of events (meanings), social identities, and motives to assert that a collectivity indeed has a culture or that members of a collectivity are of a common culture?

Alternatively, culture can be defined in terms of distinctive common experiences and environmental forces. Many such experiences and forces are tangible, measurable, and objective, that is, empirically verifiable and not expressed as subjective opinions, beliefs, assumptions, perceptions, interpretations, or values. We refer to definitions of this kind as *experiential definitions*. Distinctive common experiences and environmental forces consist of, but are not limited to, a common history, physical climate and environment, ethnic origin, language, and religion. De facto, very many if not most cross-cultural studies operationalize culture on the basis of common experiences, using nations, geographic regions, religions, or ethnic origins as the units of analysis, *assuming* that the psychological commonalties included in normative definitions follow from such operationalizations.

Two Proposed Definitions of Culture

After consideration of the foregoing arguments, we propose two definitions of culture, in an effort at introducing clarity into the operationalization of the construct in cross-cultural research designs.

A normative definition of culture:

Cultures are distinctive normative systems consisting of model patterns of shared psychological properties among members of collectivities that result in compelling common affective, attitudinal, and behavioral orientations that are transmitted across generations and that differentiate collectivities from each other.

The *shared psychological properties* are those referred to previously: assumptions, beliefs, values, interpretations of events (meanings), social identities, and motives. When shared among collectivities, these psychological properties constitute cultural norms, that is, agreed-upon behavioral proscriptions and prescriptions.

An experiential definition of culture:

Cultures are distinctive environments of collectivities about which members share meaning and values, resulting in a compelling model pattern of common affective, attitudinal, and behavioral orientation that is transmitted across generations and that differentiates collectivities from each other.

Because our normative definition is consistent with traditional culture theory (Hofstede, 1980; Kluckhohn & Strodtbeck, 1961; Triandis, 1994), we do not elaborate on it here. We do elaborate on our experiential definition because it has some implications not explicitly recognized in the literature.

According to the experiential definition culture is neither the members of the collectivity nor the investigator. It is a select set of variables experienced by members of collectivities that provides compelling individual and group member orientations. To the extent that these variables are interpreted and valued in a common manner, they distinguish collectivities from each other. According to this definition the components of normative definitions—psychological commonalities such as shared values, beliefs, identities, and such—are viewed as *consequences* of the common external variables to which members of cultures respond and not as *defining attributes* of cultures.

This definition assumes that the reactions of the vast majority of members of collectivities to the common variables to which they are exposed are, though not uniform due to individual differences, very similar. The precise proportion of common experiences and common reactions required to declare that a "common culture" exists is of course an empirical issue. And that issue need not be posed as all or nothing. Whether a culture does or does not exist or whether the individuals in a group belong to a common culture is often not the main concern of researchers or practitioners. Rather the proportion of members who have common experiences and the intensity of their reactions may be considered indicators of *strength of culture.* A collectivity of newly arrived immigrants in Country X from *n* different ethnic and national backgrounds would thus form a very weak culture, having only the common experience of being immigrants and all that goes with that experience. However, several years after settlement this same collectivity would likely have more common experiences—political, economic, climatic, and the like—and similar reactions to such experiences. Thus they would be members of a stronger, or more intensive, culture.

The experiential definition can be objectively operationalized once one specifies the components of the environment that are relevant. For example, common history, religion, language, ethnic heritage, political experiences, and ecological variables are candidates for the operationalization of this definition of culture. The definition does not need to rely on individuals' subjective reactions, such as opinions, values, or beliefs. Further, the experiential definition can be quantified in terms of both commonalty (scope or percentage of individuals subjected to the common external variables) and strength (intensity of these experiences). If individuals react to common experiences differently, they will likely become members of subcultures within a larger pluralist culture. (We discuss pluralist cultures and subcultures further on.)

The experiential definition also allows for, accounts for, and is likely to more readily reflect cultural change—changes in specific environmental variables that have pervasive effects, such as changes in laws, the introduction of international competition, or widespread increase in the use of such technologies as television and electronic mail. Witness the change in Russia following the fall of Russian communism. Although substantial cultural change did not occur overnight, within a very few years a new subculture emerged—referred to as the New Russians—a class of entrepreneurs who take advantage of Russia's newly established free market. Also witness the change in the definitions of *haves* and *have nots.* The haves are now the economically advantaged; whereas before the haves were those politically favored by their position in the Communist Party. Clearly the political and economic systems, two external variables that can be objectively operationalized and verified, are strongly implicated in the changes that have taken place in Russia during the last several years.

Normative and experiential definitions of culture are not incompatible or mutually exclusive. In fact, veteran cross-cultural researchers will see these two definitions as two sides of a single coin. However, it is likely that different topics of investigation and different research settings will focus on one or the other of these definitions.

Monolithic Versus Pluralist Cultures

Cultures may be monolithic or pluralist. *Monolithic* cultures provide approximately common experiences for members of collectivities. The basic meaning of monolithic is "having a massive uniform structure that does not permit individual variations" (*Funk and Wagnalls Standard Dictionary,* 1958). This concept of culture is problematic for complex and diverse societies comprising multiple subgroups, commonly referred to as *subcultures.* Members of such societies experience *pluralist* cultures (Ronen & Shankar, 1985). According to the experiential definition, a pluralist culture contains two or more subgroups that share some common experiences but not others. For example, they may share the experience of a common form of government, common national borders, a common currency, and a common economic system but not share the same ethnic origin, religion, language, or history.

Members of pluralist cultures are influenced not only by the common norms and institutions of the pluralist culture (to which all subcultural entities are subjected) but also by normative pressures of other subcultural units *of which they are not members.* Thus one cannot speak of a single source of cultural influence in pluralist cultures.

Social influences emanating from multiple subcultural entities are complex, diverse, fragmented, and overlapping rather than monolithic because they originate from multiple experiences. These social influences may or may not be universally experienced or accepted by all members of pluralist cultural entities.

In our later review of cross-cultural theory and research on organizational leadership, because the overwhelming preponderance of studies is based on collectivities assumed to be cultural units, not subcultures, we will refer to these units of analysis as *cultural units* or *cultural entities* unless it is clear that the investigators consider them subcultural units. In that case we refer to them as *subcultural units* or *subcultural entities* as well as by their proper names. For ease of communication, we refer to the shared social influences in monolithic or pluralist cultures as *cultural influences* or *cultural forces*. We also use the terms *cultural values, cultural norms,* and *cultural effects*. When we do so, we explicate the source of the social influences, forces, values, and effects to which we refer. We eschew the use of the noun *culture* and substitute more precise terms (particularly the proper names, when possible) that refer specifically to the cultural or subcultural units under discussion. Finally, also for convenience and ease of interpretation, we refer to the body of literature on which this chapter is based as *cross-cultural leadership literature.*

Operationalization of the Culture Construct

The vast majority of cross-cultural leadership studies operationalize cultures by using national or regional political borders as proxies for the boundaries of cultures. This approach ignores the possible existence of subcultural units within political borders, extensions of cultural influences across national boundaries, the influence of international media, the effect of cross-border trading and mobility, and the increased globalization of markets and technology. However, it provides a quick and easy way of operationalizing culture. Of course, one can code several aspects of culture separately in the same study, as demonstrated by Mejia (1984). He found that in three measures of work orientation—job involvement, task related, and contextual scales—culture accounted for 25 percent, 27 percent, and 31 percent of the variance, respectively.

Another prominent approach to operationalizing cultural boundaries focuses on normative differences due to location of residence versus expatriates' country, ethnic heritage, or other origin. This approach involves selecting managers from two countries, the United States and China for example, and comparing them to each other as well as comparing them with a third group of immigrants (Chinese-American managers of Chinese descent, for example). Using this research design, Huo and Randall (1991) demonstrated that location of residence often has a more powerful effect on individuals than does Chinese heritage. They also found that Chinese living in Taiwan, Beijing, Wahan, and Hong Kong reported both similarities and differences in work values despite their common Chinese heritage. Similar effects of the local residence of expatriates were reported in studies by Kelly and Worthley (1981) with respect to Japanese working in the United States and by Zurcher, Meadow, and Zurcher (1965) and Zurcher (1968) with respect to Chicanos working in the United States. Conversely, Shackleton and Ali (1990) found no effect of relocation on Pakistani employees of a Pakistani-owned company in Britain.

A third approach to operationalizing cultural boundaries is to classify nations, groups, or other units of analysis that serve as proxies for cultures into empirically similar clusters. Ronen and Shenkar (1985) synthesized eight prior studies using this approach and concluded that the nations of the world can be clustered into eight distinct groups, each of which share many cultural similarities concerning work, personal, and interpersonal values and leadership practices. Four countries (Brazil, Japan, India, and Israel) did not fall into any cluster and were therefore considered "independents." The Eastern European countries were not included in the clustering scheme. As was consistent with the experiential definition of culture, geography, history, religion, technological development, and language strongly influenced the clustering.

On the one hand, using clusters of similar cultural units has at least five advantages. First, the effects of unique and irrelevant variables within any given collectivity are likely to be muted as a consequence of aggregating to the cluster level of analysis. Second, aggregation of cultural units minimizes the effects of outliers in the distribution of data. Third, comparison of clusters yields more parsimonious conclusions than does comparison of individual units. Fourth, the higher the level of aggregation, the more likely the indices reflecting independent clusters are to correlate with other indices. Fifth, as a consequence of the previous features, conclusions are more likely to be useful for inductive theory building.

On the other hand, clustering has the disadvantage of suppressing subtle differences among cultural units that might be of theoretical or practical importance. For example, clustering Chinese-speaking countries together would have muted the differences among the countries studied by Huo and Randall (1991).

A fourth approach to operationalizing cultural boundaries consists of identifying groups of individuals who have been exposed to common institutions, institutional practices, or institutionalized norms within specific nations. For example, Gallino (1975) identified among Italian managers distinct leadership orientations that depended on whether the managers worked in older private firms, newer private firms, or state-run organizations.

In the next section we describe the various methods of analysis used in cross-cultural research.

Three Methods of Cross-Cultural Analysis

Hofstede, Bond, and Luk (1993) argue forcefully that it is necessary to be clear about the level of analysis employed in quantitative comparisons among cultural entities. They distinguish four types of analysis based on the work of Leung and Bond (1989). We chose to refer to these types as *levels of analysis,* and we distinguish between *levels* and *methods* of analysis. In the following section we describe three basic methods of analysis that may be carried out at one or more levels of analysis.

Comparison of Group Means

The first and most frequently used method is comparison of group means, either in simple, descriptive form or through more formal procedures using tests of significance. The vast majority of comparative quantitative studies of cultural units examines mean scores of groups of individual scores based on numerical responses to questionnaires. Most frequently such mean data are taken to represent "cultural"-level variables defined a priori on the basis of theoretical or conceptual definitions. These group means scores are then compared across cultural units, generally using rank ordering and statistical methods, such as analysis of variance or paired comparisons. We refer to all such comparisons of means scores collectively as *group mean analyses*. The level of analysis here is the cultural group.

Correlations

A second method of analysis is the computation of correlations between variable. Correlations can be computed at several levels of analysis. One can obtain a correlation between two variables taking all individual observations regardless of the cultural unit to which the observation belongs. Following Hofstede, Bond, and Luk (1993), we refer to this as *pan-cultural analysis*.

A set of within-group correlations can also be computed between two variables. This results in as many correlations of the two variables as there are cultural units in the sample. Hofstede, Bond, and Luk refer to this as *within-group analysis*. The level of analysis here is the group. Since the correlations specify the relationships between variables within a group, we refer to such correlations as *within-group correlations*.

Correlations can also be computed between the two variables using group means scores (where the groups are cultural units) instead of individual scores. This has the effect of dampening individual variations and enabling one to work with scores that function as cultural indicators. Therefore, in this analysis we again obtain a single correlation for each pair of variables. The unit of analysis here, as in the previous case, is the cultural group, but in this case we obtain information on the relationships between variables across groups. Following Hofstede, Bond, and Luk, we refer to this as *ecological analysis*.

Finally, there is *individual analysis*, in which all individual scores are taken together but the cultural component of the score is eliminated by subtracting the group mean from each individual score or by standardizing the scores over the entire sample. This results in a mean of zero and standard deviation of 1.0. In either case, the result is a single correlation for a set of two variables. The level of analysis here is the individual.

Dimensionalization

A third method of analysis is aimed at extracting cross-cultural dimensions or factors and is based on some form of statistical procedure, such as factor analysis or multidimensional scaling. Dimensions may be extracted from individual-level as well as aggregate-level data. This method presupposes a large number of variables but is again based on correlations, thus the various levels of analysis discussed in relation to method two are applicable to this method as well. If all individual scores are used in the factor analysis in a pan-cultural approach, the factors extracted concern dimensions of individual character. If groups of individual scores are analyzed separately, we obtain dimensions of individual character within each cultural unit, but this does not tell us anything about the unit as a collective. That information can be obtained by using group means scores as individual observations; in short, groups are treated as individuals in the analysis.

It is worth noting that whereas the aforementioned first method is exclusively at the group (ecological) level of analysis, the second and third methods can be applied at any of the four levels. Ecological and individual analyses produce entirely separate and different information, and the correlations between the same two variables may differ, not only in magnitude by also in sign at these two levels.

Hofstede, Bond, and Luk (1993, p. 486) use the example of a study conducted by Lincoln and Zeitz (1980) to illustrate the differences in results of ecological and individual levels of analysis. Lincoln and Zeitz collected responses of 500 employees in twenty different social-service departments in a U.S. city. They found that the relationship between employees' professional accreditation and their amount of supervisory duties was positive across all employees but negative across departments. This finding is explained by the facts that employees with higher professional accreditation tended to be given more supervisory duties within departments and that departments with a higher overall level of accreditation have a smaller proportion of supervisory personnel.

Hofstede, Bond, and Luk (1993) further illustrate the difference between ecological and individual levels of analysis by comparing the results of data collected from twenty organizational units using the two method of analysis. Hofstede, Neuijen, Ohayv, and Sanders (1990) had previously shown that at the ecological level of analysis, respondent values correlated with other values, organizational practices correlated with other organizational practices, and the mean level of within-unit values rarely correlated with organizational practices. Organizations differed primarily in their practices. Organizational membership per se did not account for much variance in values.

At the individual level of analysis, Hofstede, Bond, and Luk found a mirror image of this conclusion. After eliminating aggregate effects uniquely associated with organizational units, they found that practices have a strong unit-level component, leaving less variance or difference in perceptions of practices among individuals within units. Thus practices that provided common member experiences differentiated "organizational cultures" at both the ecological and the individual level of analysis. Differences in practices thus are strong etic phenomena. If culture is taken to mean a concept that differentiates across large numbers of collectivities, we believe that the findings of Hofstede, Bond, and Luk meet this requirement and support the experiential-based definition of culture we stated earlier.

Leadership

At present there is no consensually agreed-upon definition of leadership among scholars. Definitions vary in terms of emphasis on leader abilities, personality traits, influence relationships, cognitive versus emotional orientation, individual versus group orientation, and appeal to self- versus collective interest (Bass, 1990; Yukl, 1994).

As part of the Global Leadership and Organizational Behavior Effectiveness (GLOBE)[1] international cross-cultural research project, a meeting of eighty-four scholars representing fifty-six countries from all regions of the world was conducted. In that meeting a consensus and universal definition of *organizational leadership* emerged: "the ability of an individual to influence, motivate, and enable others to contribute toward the effectiveness and success of the organizations of which they are members." Simonton (1994,

p. 411), speaking of *leadership in general* defines a "leader" as "that group member whose influence on group attitudes, performance, or decision making greatly exceeds that of the average member of the group." In keeping with the scope of this chapter, we address the phenomenon of organizational leadership, and not leadership in general.

We now turn to a review of prior empirical leadership literature. We take as our point of departure the review of cross-cultural leadership research that appears in *Bass and Stogdill's Handbook of Leadership Research* (Bass, 1990). After briefly summarizing Bass's review, we discuss two large sample studies conducted prior to that review, and then we summarize the major topics that emerged from our review of the cross-cultural leadership research conducted to date.

Empirical Research Reviewed by Bass

Bass (1990) reviews over 100 studies concerned with the effects of differences in cultural or subcultural units on managerial behaviors, attitudes, preferences, and motivations. National boundaries specify cultural units in almost all of these studies, and the method of analysis for almost all is the within-group mean of individual responses.

The review reveals two major trends in the cross-cultural leadership literature. First, substantial research has examined the applicability of Western leadership theory in multiple national settings. Second, a great deal of effort has been made to compare the leadership styles and requirements of small groups of nations. Usually the comparisons are made between the United States, Western European nations, Latin American nations, and/or Asian nations. Consequently, more is known about leadership in these regions than in South Pacific, African, Arab, and Eastern European countries.

Bass's review also reveals a number of shortcomings in the literature. First, the studies cited lacked theoretical cohesiveness. Although some investigators draw from well-established theories of leadership, many merely describe national differences and draw on rather atheoretical and unsystematic intellectual frameworks. Second, there was a dearth of studies based on more than three or four countries. As we shall show, this situation has improved considerably since Bass's review. Third, many studies made use of existing standardized U.S. instruments, which may not fully capture non-Western or non-U.S. conceptualizations of leadership.

Two studies that examined cross-cultural leadership based on twelve or more countries were reported before Bass's review. We review these studies here in some detail because of their substantial contribution.

Haire, Ghiselli, and Porter (1966) studied responses from 3,641 managers from fourteen countries: eight European countries and Argentina, Chile, England, India, Japan, and the United States. Sample sizes ranged from 92 to 101 managers per country. Although the study is not based on matched samples, respondents were drawn from a large number of industries, and controls for numerous individual demographic characteristics were included. Haire, Ghiselli, and Porter found that country differences accounted for an average of 28 percent of questionnaire response variance when calculated as the ratio of individual differences to national differences. They also found that countries could be clustered into five groups: a Nordic-European group, a Latin-European group, an Anglo pair, a developing countries group, and Japan, which stood alone. The number of managers in these groups ranged from 187 to 399. Within clusters (excluding Japan) the average correlation between countries was .57, and the average correlation of any one cluster with countries outside that cluster was −.39. Countries within clusters spoke similar languages, had similar religions, and had "many common elements in their cultural background" (Haire, Ghiselli, & Porter, 1966, p. 11).

Differences and similarities among cultures were identified by the method of within-group individual mean comparisons of questionnaire responses. Haire, Ghiselli, and Porter found some universal characteristics of managers. Across all countries studied, managers favored democratic styles of management. They also rather consistently felt that subordinates lacked the abilities necessary to be led democratically. Managers in all countries also endorsed egalitarian organizational structures and yet also responded in ways that indicated they saw themselves as a part of an elite group. Managers in all countries indicated that it is better to direct than to persuade. This conviction was much stronger among managers in Germany, Norway, Denmark, and Sweden. The general impact of country citizenship or cluster membership outweighed the effects of managers' age and the size of their firms. However, there was a modest tendency for younger high-level managers in large firms to endorse more democratic practices and to recognize the need for satisfying employee needs. Consequently it is possible that there is more emphasis on democratic practices today than there was in the 1960s when Haire, Ghiselli, and Porter collected their data. Managerial need fulfillment was very similar in all countries. Two needs stood out as unsatisfied, regardless of country: need for autonomy and need for self-actualization.

The second large sample study (Bass, Burger, Doktor, & Barrett, 1979) was based on multiple measures of observed behavior and questionnaire responses of 8,566 middle managers. The data were collected between 1966 and 1973. The samples consisted of middle managers from Austria, Belgium, Britain, France, Germany, Iberia, India, Italy, Japan, Netherlands, Scandinavia, and the United States. The managers were in government and in private businesses representing several industries. The sample sizes ranged from 104 to 235 per country; the samples were not matched and consisted almost exclusively of men. The managers completed a series of simulation exercises as part of a management training program and a series of introspective exercises relevant to their own behavior and their careers. They also provided observational data relevant to each other's behavior. The dependent variables consisted of a host of managers' responses to questionnaires, self-reports of their behavior in the exercises, and observations of each other's behavior. As in the Haire, Ghiselli, and Porter study, differences and similarities among cultures were identified by within-group individual mean comparisons of questionnaire responses. Mean scores on the dependent variables for the national samples were compared. Interactions of rate of advancement with mean country scores language groupings were also computed. Thus it was possible to detect differences in responses due to country citizenship. It was also possible to determine how rapidly advancing managers differed from less rapidly advancing managers in each country group.

There were strong main effects of national citizenship and modest main effects of rate of advancement on many of the dependent variables. These two variables also interacted in their effects on the dependent variables. Bass, Burger, Doktor, and Barrett (1979) present findings for each of thirty-four dependent variables. The relevant means and standard deviations are presented throughout that book, so one can analyze the data further if one wishes. In addition, profiles are presented for each nation.

The major contribution of this research is not only that it demonstrates that a large number of dependent variables are affected by national citizenship, which is a proxy for a host of "cultural" variables, but also that it demonstrates how cross-cultural research based on controlled observation of behavior and responses of subjects to controlled stimuli can be conducted. The findings are potentially useful for managerial assessment and for the design of management training programs in each of the countries studied.

Topics Studied

Investigators in cross-cultural leadership examine a number of topics. A computerized search identified seventy studies on cross-cultural leadership published since 1989, presumably the year in which *Bass and Stogdill's Handbook of Leadership* (1990) went to press. These seventy titles included approximately twenty empirical studies and Ph.D. dissertations. Approximately fifteen additional studies were identified by scanning fifteen relevant journals from January of 1989 to June of 1996. Space limitations prevent a thorough review of the empirical evidence revealed by all of these studies. Therefore in this section we briefly state the conclusions we have drawn after conducting an exhaustive review of the empirical evidence relevant to cross-cultural organizational leadership.

For illustrative purposes, selected studies are summarized in Table 20.1. These studies met one or more of the following criteria:

1. They are based on ten or more cultural units of analyses.
2. They address important issues.
3. They assess conventional organizational behavior dependent variables such as satisfaction, performance, stress, turnover, or degree of conflict.
4. They introduce important moderators of relationships between cultural dimensions or attributes and dependent variables.
5. They cover cultural units (countries, geographic regions, ethnic groups) not covered in the studies reviewed by Bass (1990).
6. They illustrate new, innovative, and especially useful methodology.

Prior to 1989, few studies reported in the social science literature met the criteria just listed. Unless otherwise indicated, the studies reviewed here and described in Table 20.1 were based on the second method of aggregation described earlier: within-group (cultural entities) means were compared across groups.

In order to review the relevant issues we call upon both the studies reviewed by Bass (1990) and selected studies published since then. We also discuss several selected studies published prior to 1990 and not reviewed by Bass that concern the measurement of cultural variables.

In the remainder of this section, we organize the discussion of our findings by the most frequent topics addressed in the cross-cultural leadership literature.

Leader Prototypes. Leadership prototypes are profiles of presumed typical or preferred leader attributes or behaviors (Lord & Maher, 1991). Prototypes may include leader behaviors, values, attitudes, and personality traits. Gerstner and Day (1994) identified three dimensions relevant to distinct leadership prototypes as expressed by university students from eight nations. These dimensions had rank-order correlations with Hofstede's measures (1980) of power distance, uncertainty avoidance, and individualism .81, 1.00, and .70, respectively. Several studies have also identified prototypical work-related preferences and value differences among managers from different countries. These include the importance placed on being systematic, careful, logical, resourceful, and sociable (Bass, Burger, Doktor, & Barrett, 1979); the value given to strength, intelligence, and supportiveness (Bigoness & Blakely, 1989); views as to what ought to determine pay (Bass, Burger, Doktor, & Barrett, 1979; Beatty, McCune, & Beatty, 1988); the degree of trust placed in coworkers (Senner, 1971); and the attitude toward taking risks and the emphasis on precedence over written rules (Terry, 1979).

Leadership Behavior Patterns. Modal leader behavior patterns differ widely across countries in their emphasis on individualism versus team orientation, particularism versus universalism (Dorfman & Howell, 1988; Smith, Dugan, & Trompenaars, 1996); performance versus maintenance orientation (Smith, Misumi, Tayeb, Paterson, & Bond, 1989, Smith, Peterson, Misumi, & Bond, 1992); authoritarian versus democratic orientation (Al-Hajjeh, 1984;

Table 20.1. Empirical Cross-Cultural Leadership Studies Conducted Since 1989.

Name of the Author(s) & Year Published	Method Employed	Units of Analysis & Sample Characteristics	Psychometric Properties	Findings
Chinese Culture Connection (1987)	Measure of values (Chinese Value Survey, CVS) developed to reflect unique cultural values of the Chinese administered to university students in 22 countries, of which 20 overlapped with Hofstede's sample (1980). Ecological factor analysis followed by nonmetric multidimensional scaling (MDS) to extract dimensions in the CVS.	Ecological factor scores. Subjects recruited from psychology undergraduate program, with at least 50 men and 50 women from any one class level.	None reported for reliability of the measures. Confirmed dimensions through ecological factor analysis and MDS, both of which produced closely matching dimensions (average correlation of the four MDS dimensions-factor scores judged to be corresponding was .68).	Found new dimension, Confucian work dynamic, which reflects cultural support for entrepreneurial behavior. Four dimensions extracted from study data (collected from a different type of sample than were Hofstede's data) were asserted to reflect Hofstede's dimensions (see text for counterargument). CVS moral discipline correlated: .55 with PD, .36 with UA, .54 with IC. This correlation is opposite from Hofstede's interpretation of masculinity. CVS integration correlated −.58 with PD, .65 with individualism. CVS human heartedness correlated .67 with masculinity. CVS Confucian work dynamic correlated .32 with IC.

Study	Description	Psychometric Properties	Results
Gebert & Steinkemp (1991)	Economic success of firms identified through three questionnaire responses: total number of staff, turnover, and profit. Leader behavior described using two dimensions: patriarchal and production orientation.	21 Nigerian and 24 Taiwanese small- and medium-sized manufacturing firms with 20 to 200 employees. Samples described as "similar"—a variety of manufacturing firms in each sample.	Construct validity inferred through performance-maintenance (P-M) correlations between the expectations of leader behavior and the dimensions of general entrepreneurship behavior.	Patriarchal care-taking (both within and outside the firm) was inversely related to economic success ($r = -0.39$ for Nigeria; $r = -0.67$ for Taiwan).
Gerstner & Day (1994)	Questionnaire with 59 attributes relevant to leadership given to students enrolled in a U.S. university.	University students representing eight countries: U.S., 35; China, 35; France, 22; Germany, 16; Honduras, 15; Japan, 10; Taiwan, 11; India, 18.	No psychometric properties reported. Used three dimensions derived by multidimensional scaling.	Results indicate that business leader prototypes vary systematically as a function of a particular country. Significant correlations between Hofstede's dimensions of culture and the present study dimensions for rank ordering of countries: r PD–dimension $1 = .81$; r UA–dimension $2 = 1.00$; r IC–dimension $3 = .76$. Demonstrated usefulness of Hofstede PD, UA, IC dimensions. Hofstede's masculinity scores correlated with dimension 1 $-.64$ and dimension 2 $.41$. Several masculine items failed to cluster yield an independent dimension.

Table 20.1. Empirical Cross-Cultural Leadership Studies Conducted Since 1989, Cont'd.

Name of the Author(s) & Year Published	Method Employed	Units of Analysis & Sample Characteristics	Psychometric Properties	Findings
Hofstede, Bond, & Luk (1993)	Used data obtained from an earlier survey of organizational cultures (Hofstede, Neuijen, Ohayv, & Sanders, 1990).	Comparison of individual and ecological levels of analysis. Sample in original study consisted of responses from nearly 1,300 employees from 20 organizational units in Denmark and the Netherlands; samples consisted of 33 percent managers, 33 percent college-educated nonmanagers or professionals, and 33 percent others, with about 25 of each category randomly selected from each organizational unit.	Psychometric properties not reported.	By reanalyzing the data from Hofstede, Neuijen, Ohayv, & Sanders at the individual level, showed that the dimensions of organizational culture found in the previous study completely disappeared at the individual level, and a new set of dimensions (termed *psychological culture*) emerged. These results focus attention on the importance of defining one's level of analysis to avoid ecological and reverse ecological fallacies.
Morris, Davis, & Allen (1994)	Questionnaires consisting of 24 items on IC and 15 on entrepreneurship, administered to executives in a variety of industrial firms in the U.S., South Africa, and Portugal. Portuguese version back-translated and pretested; other two samples responded in English.	Organizational unit of analysis. Senior marketing executives and heads of personnel/human resource departments and production/operations departments. In the case of Portugal, only one senior official from each firm. 225 surveys obtained from 75 firms in South Africa, 252	Individualism scale (IND1) consisting of 9 items adapted from Hofstede's Value Survey Module (VSM) (Cronbach alphas ranging from .67 to .81 for the three samples); second individualism scale (IND2) developed from Earley's measures (1989) of collectivism and social loafing (Cronbach alphas	Although Hofstede's country scores differed widely among the three countries, organizational scores showed negligible difference. Also, an exploratory analysis revealed a curvilinear relationship (as hypothesized) between levels of organizational individualism and entrepreneurship, with

	from 84 firms in the U.S., and 25 from 25 firms in Portugal.	ranging from .63 to .76 for the three samples). Entrepreneurship scale (IND3) (12 items) derived from three variations of Miller & Friesen's scale (1983) (Cronbach alphas of .65 to .74 for the three samples).	entrepreneurial activity peaking at moderate levels of individualism (whether measured by IND2 or IND3) and lower at the extremes.
Peterson et al. (1995)	House, Schuler, & Levanoni's role conflict and ambiguity measure (1983) and Pareek's role overload measures (1976) were used. Translated and back-translated. Data collected during training programs.	100 middle managers from each of 21 nations: Western and Eastern European nations and Japan, Brazil, India, South Africa, Nigeria, and Uganda.	Reliability coefficient for role conflict measure is less than 0.7, and for other measures coefficients are generally satisfactory, with a few exceptions. Used exploratory and LISREL confirmatory factor analysis.	Addressed what role stress issues are likely to arise in cultures that vary along Hofstede's cultural dimensions. Role stress varied more by country than by demographic or organizational characteristics. Contrary to the implications of Hofstede's UA measure, role stress was not associated with high UA. In ecological analysis high PD was related to high role overload and low role ambiguity. Although role stress appeared to be a universal (etic) feature, the study pointed to an emic quality in the interpretation of the construct across cultures.

Table 20.1. Empirical Cross-Cultural Leadership Studies Conducted Since 1989, Cont'd.

Name of the Author(s) & Year Published	Method Employed	Units of Analysis & Sample Characteristics	Psychometric Properties	Findings
Rahim, Kim, & Kim (1994)	Rahim's Leader Power Inventory and the Job Description Index (JDI) & compliances scale. Translated and back-translated.	Managers in U.S., 459, and S. Korea, 625.	Independence of constructs established in subsequent study of Bangladesh respondents (Rahim & Magner, 1995). Factor structure invariance found for U.S. managers. Alphas ~.73; test-retreat r_s ~.82; low r_s with Crown-Marlow Social Desirability scale.	Power bases of both samples remarkably similar. U.S. managers had greater position power; Korean managers had greater personal power bases. In both samples, referent power base explained highest percent of variation in satisfaction. Performance contingent coercive power least effective. Managers in both individualist and collectivist cultures most effective in inducing subordinate's compliance and satisfaction by enhancing personal power bases, such as expert and referent. Legitimate power may be used to gain compliance from subordinates, but may lead to reduction in satisfaction with supervisors.
Ralston, Gustafson, Elsass, Cheung, & Terpstra (1992)	Chinese Culture Connection's CVS administered to practicing managers in the U.S., Hong Kong (H.K.), and	Ecological factor scores. Sample of 36 men and 25 women from the U.S., 145 men and 37 women from H.K. and 75 men	Not reported. Used existing scales and translations developed by the Chinese Culture Connection (1987).	U.S. and H.K. managers scored equally but significantly higher than the P.R.C. sample on integration. All three scored

	and 7 women from the P.R.C. Approximately two-thirds middle managers and about 18 percent lower-level and 15 percent upper-level managers, with overall management experience of 5 to 7 years.	People's Republic of China (P.R.C.). Manova and WABA analysis performed.		about the same on moral discipline. In Confucian work dynamism, P.R.C. scored the highest, followed by H.K. and U.S., in that order. All ps based on paired comparisons ~.05. On human heartedness, U.S. scored highest, followed by H.K. and then by P.R.C. (all ps ~.05). This last finding is consistent with Hofstede's ranking of the U.S. and H.K. on the masculinity dimension.
Schmidt & Yeh (1992)	In Australia, 126 supervisors and managers; U.K., 121 supervisors; Taiwan, 231 managers; Japan, 355 managers. Samples belonged to different industries.	POIS (Profiles of Organizational Influence Strategies) used. In Australia and U.K., data collected during a training program. In Taiwan, a survey was conducted. Japanese data collected in prior study. Translated into Chinese and Japanese and back-translated.	Alpha reliability coefficients and factor loadings reported by nations. Approximately 80 percent of alpha coefficients >.60.	Explored structure of leader influence behavior toward subordinates. Results compared with results of the U.S. sample used in developing POIS. Interpretable 7-factor solution obtained for all nations except Australia, for which an interpretable 6-factor solution emerged. English leaders placed greater emphasis on appealing to higher authorities and assertiveness in subordinate relationships than did U.S. managers. Australians were more similar to U.S. managers

Table 20.1. Empirical Cross-Cultural Leadership Studies Conducted Since 1989, Cont'd.

Name of the Author(s) & Year Published	Method Employed	Units of Analysis & Sample Characteristics	Psychometric Properties	Findings
				in their emphasis on reasoning and bargaining with subordinates. U.S., U.K., and Australian leaders used friendliness in combination with reason. The leader influence processes used in Taiwan and Japan are more similar to each other than to those in Australia and U.K., that is, they reflect assertiveness and reasoning tactics. Although both Taiwan and Japan tend toward high PD, the Japanese emphasize sanctions less and bureaucratic channels more than the Taiwanese do. Scores consistent with Hofstede's PD scores.
Shackleton & Ali (1990)	Parts of Hofstede's VSM measuring PD and UA used. Translated and back-translated. Part of the sample was given questionnaires to take home to complete, the	Managers of 7 firms in Sudan, Pakistan (operating in U.K.), and U.K.; $n = 214$. All subjects male, with mean age of 34 years and 12 to 14 years of education.	No psychometric properties reported. VSM assumed to be valid.	Pakistan's managers, in spite of being in U.K., exhibited a substantial effect of country of origin rather than current country values. As hypothesized, Sudanese scores on PD and

Author (Year)	Method / Measure	Sample	Psychometric Properties	Findings
	remainder was given questionnaires during a training program. PD and UA subscales of Hofstede's country scores were plotted on PD and UA dimensions.			UA were found to lie between the scores of African and Arab nations reported by Hofstede, and the British scores were very close to those obtained by Hofstede. These results provided support for the relative rankings of Hofstede's UA and PD dimensions.
Shenkar & Ronen (1987)	Hofstede's 14-item work goals questionnaire was modified and administered during a training program. Translated and back-translated.	All Chinese societies: China, Taiwan, Singapore, and H.K.; 163 managers—officials of government and administrative staff. Samples for other countries taken from Hofstede's study.	No psychometric properties reported.	Examined the effects of traditional and modern ideologies and economic conditions influencing the importance of work goals. Results suggest shared cultural traditions of Chinese societies on one hand and variations due to modern ideologies and economic conditions on the other, especially between China and others. Findings suggest the emergence of 2 new concepts—*cultural pluralism* and *cultural disjunction*, that is, existence of multiple cultures in a society and differences in culturally derived expectations and economic, political, social, and organizational relations.

Table 20.1. Empirical Cross-Cultural Leadership Studies Conducted Since 1989, Cont'd.

Name of the Author(s) & Year Published	Method Employed	Units of Analysis & Sample Characteristics	Psychometric Properties	Findings
Smith et al. (1994)	Questionnaire translated and administered to middle managers in 14 countries. Scores standardized within subjects. Items required managers to rate each of 8 sources of meanings for each of 8 organizational events, on 5-point rating scales.	Country-level analysis, although adjustments for demographic differences made on individual scores. Middle managers drawn from several public- and private-sector organizations in the 14 countries; CEOs and frontline supervisors excluded.	Reliability coefficients (across events) for each source of meaning computed for each country, resulting in a total of 112 alphas; 88 (79 percent) were at .70 or above.	Related sources of meaning of critical incidents in each country to Hofstede's rankings of countries in terms of his four dimensions. Managers in countries Hofstede classified as high individualism and low PD report greater reliance on their own experience and their subordinates, whereas managers in low individualism and high PD countries report greater reliance on formal rules.
Smith, Dugan, & Trompenaars (1996)	Values of managers studied using many instruments originally collected by Trompenaars although not for this study. Convenience sampling. Translated and back-translated. Transformations of individual-level data to derive ecological measures analyzed through multidimensional scaling and regression analysis.	Data collected mostly during training programs. Anglo, European, Latin American, East Asian, S.E. Asian, and Middle Eastern nations. Nonrandom sample; sizes range from 29 to 1,212. Ecological (country) unit of analysis, derived from questionnaires with 39 items administered to 8,841 employees (at least 24	Country-level coefficient alpha for the 6-item achievement-ascription scale was .83; for the 4-item universalist-particularist scale, .91; for the individualism-collectivism scale, not reported.	Sample heterogeneity did not influence results. Two interpretable dimensions emerged: egalitarianism vs. conservatism and loyalty. These correlated with each other −.83. The first correlated .36 with Hofstede's IC dimension and −.30 with PD dimension. The second correlated −.51 and .44 with Hofstede's IC and PD dimensions. Results generally

	Method	Sample	Reliability	Findings
		percent lower-level workers, 54 percent managers or professionals, and 22 percent not known) in 43 countries. One-third were females.		consistent with Hofstede's country scores on these dimensions. Found support for national culture as source of variation in PD and Egalitarian Commitment, and Confucian Work Dynamism. UA and MF were included in study hypotheses without being included in measures. Emerged dimensions were associated with life expectancy, per-capita income, and socioeconomic status of subjects in samples.
Smith & Peterson (1994)	5-point questionnaire scale constructed to elicit responses about processes in 8 organizational critical events. Translated and back-translated. Used demographic data to control for sample heterogeneity.	Middle managers from 25 nations representing all regions of the world. Convenience sampling; samples consisted of both public- and private-sector employees. Hofstede's country scores used as independent variables.	Only reliability coefficients were reported. Alphas were generally acceptable (~.70).	Derived 3 factors describing managers' various combinations of reliance on rules and procedures, beliefs, unwritten rules, advice from subordinates, colleagues, and superiors, and own experience. Leader event management processes were consistently related to the differences in national cultures Hofstede identified. Relationships consistent with Hofstede's dimensions of PD, IC, UA, MF. No culturally

Table 20.1. Empirical Cross-Cultural Leadership Studies Conducted Since 1989, Cont'd.

Name of the Author(s) & Year Published	Method Employed	Units of Analysis & Sample Characteristics	Psychometric Properties	Findings
				consistent variation in event management is seen as more effective than another. Samples high on IC and low on PD reported great reliance on their own experience, training, and subordinates. Samples low on IC and high on PD relied on formal rules and procedures. Similarly, countries labeled high on dimensions of masculinity and UA were also found to be consistent with Hofstede's study. These results are consistent despite convenience sampling.
Smith, Misumi, Tayeb, Paterson, & Bond (1986)	Questionnaire, partly adapted from Misumi's performance (P) and maintenance (M) scales and partly developed for this study, assessed employees' perceptions about their supervisors in electronics industry in Britain, U.S., Japan, and H.K. Translated and back-translated.	Electronic plant shop-floor supervisors within a number of similar electronics assembly plants. Respondents predominantly young and middle-aged women, except in Japan. Demographics not indicated for U.S. N in U.K. 280; U.S., 197; H.K., 168; and Japan, 532. Ecological factor	Substantiated 2-factor structure of the general measure of leadership style through factor analysis. Alphas for all scales in all countries ~.72, except U.S., which was .62.	Both similarities and differences existed between general leadership styles across nations. In U.S. clear distinction seen between P and M behavior but not in any other countries. Identified several emic (culture-specific) items related to M and P constructs. Specific emic measures differentiated

	scores and factor structures of general and specific measures of leadership styles reported.		among countries better than measures of global leadership styles. Suggests importance of measuring the emic manifestations of more general etic descriptions of leader behaviors.
Yeh & Lawrence (1995)	Reanalyzed Franke, Hofstede, & Bond's data (1991) purporting to link cultural factors to economic growth; used regression analysis as used by Franke, Hofstede, & Bond but paid particular attention to outliers.	Data from Franke, Hofstede, & Bond.	Production orientation significantly correlated with economic success ($r = 0.35$ for Nigeria and $r = 0.51$ for Taiwan). Link between cultural dimensions and economic growth predicted by Franke, Hofstede, & Bond did not hold for Pakistan. Reanalysis after removing Pakistan from the data set found (1) the correlation between individualism and Confucian work dynamism changed from −.46 to −.70, becoming highly significant. The authors argue that in light of this correlation, the link between Confucian work dynamism and economic growth is suspect. (See chapter text for different interpretations.)
		Not applicable.	

PD = power distance; IC = individualism-collectivism; UA= uncertainty avoidance; MF = masculinity-femininity.

Stening & Wong, 1983); paternalism (Dorfman & Howell, 1988); reliance on personal abilities, subordinates, or rules (Smith, Peterson, & Misumi, 1994); leader influence processes (Rahim, Kim, & Kim, 1994; Schmidt & Yeh, 1992); and consensual decision making and service orientation (Bass, Burger, Doktor, & Barrett, 1979).

Differential Effects on Followers. Followers differ by nation in their preferences for and acceptance of different levels of communication intensity and different kinds of communication with leaders (Earley, 1984) and in their task versus person orientation (Blake & Mouton, 1970; Misumi, 1974), responses to organizational development efforts (Deyo, 1978), acceptance of close versus general supervision and democratic versus autocratic leader behavior, and performance responses to the use of participatory practices (Bass, Burger, Doktor, & Barrett).

Origins of Leaders. Individuals gain leadership through ascription or achievement. Differences in education, class, occupation, ownership, and technical expertise have all been cited as influential factors in determining who fills leadership roles in different countries (Boyd, 1974; Harbron, 1965; McClelland, 1961; Lee & Schwendiman, 1982). Leaders's origins also influence their behavior as expatriates. Shackleton and Ali (1990) found that managers of Pakistan origin working in England were differentiated from English managers by a substantial effect of origin. The effect of origin does not overwhelm the contexts of expatriate managers, however. Huo and Randall (1991), for instance, found that location of residence also often has a powerful effect on individuals.

Dependent Variables. Finally, few studies have examined the effects of culture on the generally accepted dependent variables in the discipline of organizational behavior (a U.S.-based discipline). One area of interest generating research is cultural influences on organizations' or nations' economic success. McClelland (1961) found that cultural emphasis on achievement motivation is predictive of country industrial development and economic success twenty-five years later. Gebert and Steinkamp (1991) found that manager patriarchal care-taking was inversely related to economic success and manager production orientation was positively related to economic success of firms in both Nigeria and Taiwan. Hofstede and Bond (1988) showed that the Confucian work dynamic (discussed later in this chapter) is related to Asian nations' economic growth. Smith, Dugan, and Trompenaars (1996) found that their three dimensions of culture (also discussed later) are related to national per-capita income and the socioeconomic status of country samples.

Scholars have also examined the effect of cultural influences on employee satisfaction, general welfare, and ability to perform effectively.

Dorfman and Howell (1988) found no relationships between Mexican and Taiwanese employees' cultural values and the dependent variables of work satisfaction, satisfaction with superiors, organizational commitment, and performance. However, employee identification with dominant societal values turned out to be a variable that influenced the relationship between leaders' directiveness and selected reward and punishment practices and also influenced the dependent variables just mentioned: the relationships were significantly higher for those employees who identified with the dominant values than for those who did not. This study nicely deals with one of the limitations of interpreting countries as monolithic cultures and shows the effect of differential degrees of socialization within countries.

There is some empirical evidence for cultural influences on employee stress. Hofstede (1980) found that questionnaire reports of employee stress are associated with uncertainty avoidance. Smith and Peterson (1994) found that role stress experienced by managers varies more across than within countries and is positively related to power distance and collectivism.

Antecedents to Preferred Leader Behavior

We now turn to a discussion of the antecedents to the differences in preferred leader behaviors among cultural entities.

Dominant Norms and Religion

Differences among cultural entities relevant to preferences for leader behaviors have been shown to result from the entities' dominant norms (Dorfman & Howell, 1988; Stening & Wong, 1983) and religious or ideological values such as Confucianism (Hofstede & Bond, 1988), Catholicism (Pelletier, 1966), and the Protestant work ethic of saving, sacrifice, hard work, and investment (Weber, [1924] 1947).

The Dominant Elite

McClelland (1961) and Boyd (1974) noted the role that the landed gentry played in the development of leadership traits in Confucian China and Victorian England. Specifically, leaders in both countries were expected to possess good manners, good physical conditioning, and classical training. Interviews conducted in France by the first author of this chapter indicate that French leaders are generally well educated and expected to be "cultivated," that is, classically educated.

Historical Leaders

Leaders considered to have made a major contribution to society are often not only revered but also often emulated, especially in societies with a highly stratified distribution of power. Qualitative research by the first author of this chapter disclosed a proliferation of public commemorations of macho-like military leaders in France and Russia and a marked absence of such commemorations in Australia, Canada, Ireland, the Netherlands, New Zealand, and the German regions of Switzerland. Hofstede (1980) reported no data on Russia but found France to be in the eighth highest country on power distance. The remainder of these countries were ranked twenty-eighth or lower on power distance among the forty countries Hofstede reported on in 1980.

Of course, a nation may also have strong norms against leaders who represent countercultural values. Lord Nelson's statue in Dublin was destroyed by the IRA and never replaced because of its pro-British symbolism. The statue of King Edward VII was removed from public view in Toronto due to resentment at its imperialist implications. Most of the statues in Moscow and Budapest of high-level communist leaders have been retired to "cemeteries of statues," where they are preserved for posterity but no longer revered or in public view. The institutions, streets, and cities renamed for communist leaders and events have reverted to their historical names in almost all former Soviet Union nations except Russia. Even in Russia, Leningrad is once again Saint Petersburg and Stalingrad is now Volgograd. In Budapest the former Karl Marx Institute of Economics is now the Hungarian Institute of Economics.

Highly assertive leadership is generally viewed as undesirable by individuals in societies previously dominated by dictators. Interviews and focus groups in the GLOBE research program revealed strong reservations, suspicions, and distaste for authoritarian leadership among German, Mexican, Spanish, and Portuguese managers and rather widespread distrust of managers in general in many of the countries of the former Soviet Union. This distaste for leadership and distrust of management are likely the results of their historical association with despotic leadership in these countries.

Modernization

Modernization also appears to be associated with differential expectations of and preferences for specific leader behaviors. For example, merit is more often expected to be the basis of performance evaluation and compensation in modernized nations. Leaders in the relatively tradition-bound countries more often take factors other than merit into account when deciding on salary increases (Bass, Burger, Doktor, & Barrett, 1979; Ryterbrand & Thiagarajan, 1968; Ulin, 1976). Managers in tradition-bound countries are also more likely to find bribery acceptable and to relegate women to lower-status positions (Davis, Ming, & Brosnan, 1986). In contrast, leaders from modern societies tend to focus more on issues of merit, orderliness, punctuality, intended rationality, and progress (Inkeles, 1966; Bass, Burger, Doktor, & Barrett, 1979).

Indices of modernization such as literacy rates and amount of electrical power used per capita are publicly available for most nations of the world and can be used by cross-cultural investigators as either control or explanatory variables.

Unique Role Demands on Leaders

The varying demographic composition of organizations and of national or regional political systems and the varying strategic requirements of organizations often place differential role demands on leaders (Anzizu & Nuenos, 1984; Bass, 1990; Granick, 1960;

Heller, 1958). In India, China, and Hong Kong, for example, management practices in small- and medium-sized organizations are often based on kinship relationships and involve obedience to elders, based on deference to the wisdom of experience. Many of the same behaviors can also be found in the management of large firms. Even today, for example, five of the largest business organizations in India—Reliance (managed by the Ambani family), Birla, Goenka, Kirloskar, and Tata—remain family managed (Chowdhry & Tarneja, 1961).

Cultural Convergence

It is often suggested that there may be a substantial amount of cross-national convergence of management practices, values, and beliefs as a result of the interactions between organizations engaged in cross-border trading and the widespread proliferation of management education programs that reflect Western assumptions, values, and practices.

The lack of historical baseline data makes it difficult to assess the extent of international convergence that may be taking place in leadership practices. However, a limited number of studies support the convergence hypothesis. Ralston, Gustafson, Elsass, Cheung, and Terpstra (1992) found that responses of Hong Kong managers reflected more Western values than did responses of Chinese managers and more Eastern values than did responses of American managers, suggesting cultural convergence as a result of Hong Kong managers' exposure to both Western and Eastern societies. Although studies that compare longitudinal data for a large number of cultural units are not available, two comprehensive, exhaustive studies based on historical analyses demonstrated that management practices in multiple industries in Korea (Amsden, 1989) and Taiwan (Wade, 1990) had become more similar to Japanese practices in the preceding decade.

It appears that global management practices may be converging, but not necessarily toward U.S. management styles (Alpander, 1973; Beechler & Yang, 1994; Craig, Douglas, & Grein, 1992). Further, some U.S. authors have proposed U.S. adoption of Japanese management practices (Ouchi, 1981; Pascale & Athos, 1981). There is no evidence of a single model of management practices or cultural values toward which all nations are converging. It is most likely that there is some convergence toward U.S. practices, some toward Western European practices, and some toward Japanese practices.

Although some convergence in management practices is likely taking place, there is also a great deal of stability in the fundamental cultural practices and psychological commonalties within cultural entities. Studies in many geographic regions show consistent results between earlier and subsequent studies even when as many as twenty years have elapsed between studies. As shown in Table 20.1, Hofstede's country rankings based on data collected between 1967 and 1973 have been replicated by several studies of selected countries conducted in the late 1980s and 1990s. Thus changes in the fundamental cultural values such as those studied by Hofstede (1980) appear to be very slow and likely resistant to convergence forces.

Cultural Influences on Leadership: Conclusions

Our review of empirical research clearly shows that cultural forces influence many aspects of the leadership phenomenon. These aspects include prototypical requisites for leadership positions, the degree to which leadership roles are filled by ascription or achievement, modal leader behavior patterns, preferences for and expectations of leaders, and followers' and subordinates' reactions to different kinds of leader behavior. Several antecedents to preferred leader behaviors were revealed including dominant norms, dominant elites, religious values, modernization, unique role demands, and historical experiences with leaders.

Issues Studied

In this section we look at the issues predominantly studied by cross-cultural leadership scholars.

Measurement of Cultural Dimensions: Some Problems of Inconsistency, Interpretation, and Labeling

The seminal study of cultural dimensions is Hofstede's work. Hofstede (1980) analyzed data collected between 1967 and 1973 by IBM headquarters staff to measure employee morale in forty nations distributed widely throughout the world. Sample sizes ranged from 37 to 4,691 respondents per country. Subsequently Hofstede added ten countries and three geographical regions to his data bank. The country scores on each cultural dimension for the fifty-three cultural units are reported in Hofstede and Bond (1988). The data sets consist of questionnaire responses relevant to the following four theoretical constructs.

Power distance is the degree to which less powerful members of a society accept a hierarchical or unequal distribution of power in organizations and in the society. *Uncertainty avoidance* is the degree to which members of a given society feel uncomfortable in unstructured, ambiguous, and uncertain situations and have created beliefs, norms, and institutions that are intended to minimize the occurrence of or cope with such situations. Individualism versus collectivism describes at its individualist pole the degree to which individuals function independently of each other and are expected to look after themselves and their immediate families and at its collectivist pole the degree to which individuals are integrated into groups that are expected to look after these individuals in exchange for loyalty to the group. High scores on this scale indicate an individualist orientation in cultural entities. *Masculinity versus femininity* is the final scale. High scores on this scale indicate the degree to which members of cultural entities look favorably on assertive, aggressive, competitive, and materialist behavior and striving for success. Low scores indicate the degree to which members value supportive behavior, nurturance, care, and service and endorse gender role differentiation and discrimination.

Hofstede selected these four dimensions because of their theoretical implications and relationships to organizational behavior phenomena. More specifically, the power distance construct was derived from prior research on power sharing and participative management. The uncertainty avoidance construct was derived from prior organizational studies that dealt with bureaucratization and formalization of organizational practices. The individualism-collectivism and masculinity-femininity constructs have a long-standing history in the theoretical, anthropological, and cross-cultural psychology literature (Kluckhohn & Strodtbeck, 1961; Triandis, 1995) and are fundamental to anthropological inquiry.

Hofstede formulated the power distance and uncertainty avoidance constructs on the basis of theoretical reasoning. The individualism-collectivism and masculinity-femininity constructs were derived statistically from ecological factor analysis of fourteen items drawn from the IBM questionnaire. Because the IBM morale survey had of course not been designed to provide measures of these four theoretical constructs, some compromises were necessarily made in the development of the scales.

Ecological factor analysis assumes that the mean of the individual responses is representative of the population studied in the respective cultural unit. Further, both the individual scores and their means are assumed to be normally distributed. Ecological factor analysis also assumes that the variance of individual scores within cultural units will be significantly lower than the variance of all individual scores and lower than the variance of the mean scores of the cultural units. To our knowledge, investigators who have used ecological factor analysis have not demonstrated that their data have met these assumptions.

Hofstede's power distance and individualism scales correlated $-.7$ ($p < .01$). Uncertainty avoidance correlated with power distance and individualism .28 and $-.35$, respectively ($p < .05$). Despite the fact that his scales were not independent, he chose to retain them as indicators of conceptually different constructs. He noted (1980, p. 316) that correlations among his scales varied widely depending on whether the countries sampled were wealthy or poor. These differential correlations support the argument for distinguishing between the constructs.

In *Culture's Consequences*, Hofstede (1980) reviewed thirteen survey studies that included between five and nineteen countries. The findings from each of these studies were shown to be significantly correlated, in the theoretically expected direction, with at least one of the four Hofstede dimensions. Hofstede also lists thirty country-level indicators such as country economic growth and population size. Many of these correlated significantly with at least one of his four dimensions. He showed that studies that dealt with constructs similar to those he measured were consistent with his findings, thus attesting to the validity of his measures. Subsequently Hofstede and Bond (1988) reported mean data relevant to the original four dimensions from another ten countries and three geographical regions as well as data relevant to a fifth dimension for nineteen of the countries in his fifty-three-country data set.

Hofstede advanced several theoretical interpretations that went well beyond mere description of his findings. With respect to leadership, Hofstede and Bond (1988) state:

> Both Power Distance and Individualism affect the type of leadership most likely to be effective in a country. The ideal leader in a culture in which power distances are small would be a resourceful democrat; on the other hand, the ideal leader in a culture in which Power Distances are large is a benevolent autocrat (or "good father"). In Collectivist cultures, leadership should respect and encourage employees' group loyalties; incentives should be given collectively, and their distribution should be left up to the group. In Individualist cultures, people can be moved around as individuals, and incentives should be given to individuals [p. 14].

Thus, in total, the major findings of Hofstede's first (1980) and subsequent (Hofstede and Bond, 1988) research concern the relative rankings of the fifty-three nations according to their scores on each of the four theoretical dimensions.

Hofstede's research has not escaped criticism. Although we do not agree with all of the criticisms, we review them here for the sake of completeness. First, the scales are criticized because of their item composition, because they are not independent, and because some critics believe they are inappropriately labeled (Dorfman & Howell, 1988; Jaeger, 1986; Robinson, 1983; Triandis, 1982).

Second, the face validity of the items is not always apparent, that is, some of the items do not appear to measure the constructs to which they were assigned. Dorfman and Howell (1988) note that the uncertainty avoidance (UA) scale is composed of items that reflect seemingly disparate constructs: level of perceived stress, length of time the individual believes he or she will work for the present company, and beliefs regarding whether rules should be broken. We see little relationship between stress and uncertainty avoidance as a parent construct—perhaps as a consequence, but not as a descriptor.

In our opinion the item composition of the individualism-collectivism scale is also suspect. This scale includes physical conditions, use of skills, and training opportunities as valued work goals. Because these items are not stated explicitly as *group* goals they reflect individualist more than collectivist job attributes, yet they are negatively related to individualism and used as indicators of collectivism. Consequently, it is difficult to determine what is measured by this scale.

Interestingly, the individualism-collectivism scale contains only items relevant to respondents' preferred job goals. The remaining three scales contain items describing employees' intentions of continuing in the company, fear of their supervisors, concerns about their job environment, or attitudes about various aspects of their organization or their work. It is not clear how these different questionnaire referents affected employee responses or whether they elicited unknown response biases, such as lenient, central, or extreme response tendencies.

A third criticism is that because the data are based on responses of predominantly middle-class male employees from one international firm, the representativeness and generalizability of the findings may be limited. The findings may tell us more about IBM than about the countries studied, more about IBM organizational practices than about the cultures of the nations in which the data were collected. Further, no tests of between-county functional equivalence of items or scales are reported.

However, the socioeconomic and organizational homogeneity of the sample is also a strength in that it provides some control for variations in organizational practices, assuming that IBM organizational practices are relatively uniform throughout the world. However, to attribute differences in national cultures to differences in scores based on IBM employee responses is to ignore the non-organizational components of national populations and possibly differences in the way the IBM units varied across nations. It is possible that presumed sample homogeneity may have been gained at the expense of having country score differences that do not represent true country differences. Thus Hofstede's findings are ambiguous due to possible inappropriate item composition of his scales and to data collected from a single firm.

Independent replications of Hofstede's country rankings would attest to the robustness of the four dimensions. This has been achieved to some extent by a number of studies (some of which are described in Table 20.1: Morris, Davis, & Allen, 1994; Ralston,

Gustafson, Elsass, Cheung, & Terpstra, 1992; Schmidt & Yeh, 1992; Shackleton & Ali, 1990; Smith, Misumi, Tayeb, Paterson, & Bond, 1989; Smith, Peterson, & Misumi, 1994; Smith & Peterson, 1994). Their findings not only replicate Hofstede's country rankings with relatively small samples of selected countries and selected dimensions but indicate substantial temporal stability (over more than twenty-five years) of the ranking of countries by cultural dimensions.

Hofstede's theory asserts that behavior of individual members of nations will usually be congruent with the values endorsed by the members as a group. Several independent studies conducted at approximately the same time or shortly after Hofstede's data were collected show that individuals in countries ranked high by Hofstede on power distance and collectivism accept and respond more positively to authoritarian leadership styles than do individuals from low power distance and high individualism nations (Al-Hajjeh, 1984; Bass, Burger, Doktor, & Barrett, 1979; Deyo, 1978; Dorfman & Howell, 1988; Kennis, 1977; Stening & Wong, 1983).

Members of countries that scored as collectivist have subsequently been shown in independent studies to engage in collectivist behavior, placing a high value on group maintenance, paternalism, in-group loyalty and harmony, treatment of in-group members with dignity, face saving among in-group members, and nonconfrontational and peaceful resolution of conflict (Beatty, McCune, & Beatty, 1988; Castaldi & Sorrentino, 1988; Leung, 1983; Smith, 1984; Weiss & Bloom, 1990). Of particular interest is the heavy emphasis placed by Asian managers on group maintenance activities (Bass, Burger, Doktor, & Barrett, 1979; Bolon and Crain, 1985; Fukuda, 1983; Ivancevich, Schweiger, & Ragan, 1986).

Hofstede's uncertainty avoidance scores are associated with less risky entry into foreign markets (Kogut & Singh, 1988). Zarzeski (1996) has shown countries ranked by Hofstede as low on uncertainty avoidance publish higher disclosure of financial data in general, even for domestic firms. Countries scoring high on Hofstede's individualism have been shown in independent studies to prefer individual- rather than group-based compensation practices (Bass, Burger, Doktor, & Barrett, 1979; Beatty, McCune, & Beatty, 1988; Dorfman & Howell, 1988) and to exhibit greater willingness to take risks (Bass, Burger, Doktor, & Barrett, 1979;

Hornstein, 1986; Ronen, 1986). Finally, several recent studies also have findings consistent with theoretical predictions given Hofstede's ratings (Gerstner & Day, 1994; Peterson et al., 1995; Smith et al., 1994; Smith, Misumi, Tayeb, Paterson, & Bond, 1989; Smith, Dugan, & Trompenaars, 1996; Smith & Peterson, 1994). Thus the ambiguity surrounding the representativeness of Hofstede's country samples is somewhat alleviated.

Two reasons are likely to account for the robustness of Hofstede's findings. First, the theoretical variables are well conceived and relate to four of the fundamental social problems of human beings. Second, the data are aggregated to the level of within-country means. The higher the level of aggregation the more likely scores are to have significant and high correlation with other aggregated variables such as those employed by almost all of the studies cited in this connection. Further, the higher the level of aggregation, the lower the effects of fluctuations of single environmental forces on the aggregated scores.

Some Lingering Doubts

Three studies have failed to demonstrate consistency with Hofstede's dimensions even through they included multiple items relevant to those dimensions (Ng et al., 1982; Chinese Culture Connection, 1987; Gerstner & Day, 1994). And the first two of these studies identified dimensions that correlate with Hofstede's dimensions in a manner opposite to theoretical expectations. Gerstner and Day (1994) failed to find a dimension analogous to the masculinity-femininity dimension, despite the fact that their questionnaire included many items that would be expected to form an independent dimension. Ng et al. (1982) used a modified form of the Rokeach Value Survey to obtain ratings of values endorsed by fifty female and fifty male psychology students in each of ten "cultural groups" in nine counties representing six languages. A discriminate function analysis of the students' responses yielded four functions.

Hofstede and Bond (1984) used the Ng et al. data in an attempt to validate the Hofstede dimensions. Taking the six countries in the Ng et al. data that overlapped with Hofstede's 1980 sample, they first examined the correspondence between the two studies. Three of the four discriminant functions found by Ng et al. correlated highly with Hofstede's four dimensions. Function 1 correlated with power distance, and function 3 correlated with individualism. However, function 2 correlated with uncertainty avoidance as well as masculinity. Function 4 did not correlate with any of the Hofstede dimensions. Thus, although Hofstede and Bond (1984) could show some support for individualism and power distance, the other two dimensions did not emerge as separate dimensions. Next, Hofstede and Bond performed several factor analyses on the Ng et al. data, and found a five-factor solution to be the most interpretable. Four of the five factors correlated strongly with Hofstede's four dimensions, serving to partially replicate Hofstede's extraction of those four dimensions.

The concurrence of Ng et al.'s data with Hofstede's dimensions is not without problems. First, in the discriminate analysis, the high correlation of function 3 with two of Hofstede's dimensions could be explained by a sizable correlation between these two dimensions (r(MAS × UAI) = .64 for the six countries, Hofstede & Bond, 1984, p. 423). This finding may be sample specific. However, it does suggest some possible ambiguity and confounding in the distinction between masculinity-femininity and uncertainty avoidance scales. Second, as Hofstede and Bond note, the positive loading of the item "independence" on a factor they label "femininity" is inconsistent with the theoretical expectation and prior findings that indicate that this item should load negatively on this factor. Hofstede and Bond (1984) attribute this anomalous finding to inaccurate translation. No evidence of faulty translation is provided however.

The most interesting contribution of Ng et al., however, is that their data consistently pointed to something beyond four dimensions, even though they had stopped with extraction of four discriminate functions. Hofstede and Bond's analysis (1984) showed that three of those four functions correlated with the Hofstede dimensions. What was the fourth? It is plausible that they would have found a four-factor solution to be the most interpretable, had it not been for the fact that the uncorrelated factor emerged as the first, and not the fifth, factor. The following values had high loadings on this factor: world of peace, equality, pleasure, accomplishment, self-determination, and freedom.

Because this factor is different from any of the four Hofstede dimensions, Hofstede and Bond (1984) suggested social desirability bias as an explanation—albeit not a satisfactory one—for its emergence. They observe correctly that turning a ranking task into a rating instrument, as Ng et al. did with the Rokeach Value Survey, makes response set bias possible, and they argue that a social desirability bias would come to the fore. They ignore the possibility that the same bias would likely be present in the other factors as a result of similar item formatting—ratings rather than rankings. If the items that loaded on the first factor are susceptible to response set bias, then why not "courageous," "capable" (second factor), "self-controlled," "self-respect" (third factor), "cheerful," "polite," "comfortable life" (fourth factor), and "world of beauty" (fifth factor) as well? In addition, Hofstede and Bond's explanation (1984) that social desirability bias may be reflected particularly in the case of the first factor establishes that factor as a legitimate dimension demanding a label, because as Hofstede (1980, p. 20) previously argued, social desirability is "part and parcel of the phenomena studied in cross-cultural research." The first factor, then, cannot be dismissed as a result of social desirability bias.

A third study relevant to the measurement of cultural entities is reported by the Chinese Culture Connection (CCC) (1987), organized by Bond. The CCC is a network of twenty-two social scientists interested in cross-cultural research. Bond's concern was that the Hofstede dimensions might not capture important values held by Asians because the IBM questionnaire that supplied Hofstede's data was developed by IBM headquarters staff who might have had a strong Western bias. Bond asked a number of social scientists to prepare a list of at least ten "fundamental and basic values for Chinese people." These social scientists were presumably China scholars, but this is not so indicated in the CCC's 1987 article. After substantial translation, review, editing, and rewording, a forty-item questionnaire was settled on. Entitled the Chinese Value Survey (CVS), it was administered to fifty male and fifty female students in each of the twenty-two countries represented by members of the CCC. Factor analyses of the responses produced four factors: *integration, human heartedness, moral discipline,* and *Confucian work dynamic* (CWD). Hofstede and Bond (1988) interpret the first three of these factors as corresponding to power distance, individualism-collectivism, and femininity-masculinity.

Of the twenty-two nations sampled, twenty were also represented in Hofstede's 1980 report. Consequently, it was possible to estimate the relationships among the CCC and the Hofstede dimensions. Table 20.2 lists these correlations, which have implications both for convergence of the two sets of dimensions and for interpretation of the Confucian work dynamic (CWD) dimension and its relationship to economic growth.

Hofstede and Bond (1988) imply some convergence among the findings of their two studies by stating that these studies "yielded dimensions that describe expected social behavior; behavior toward seniors or juniors, toward the group, and as a function of sex" (pp. 15–16).

Table 20.2 shows human heartedness positively related to masculinity ($r = .67$). According to Hofstede's earlier reasoning and findings (1980), supportive and nurturant behavior such as human heartedness should be a feminine attribute. The Chinese Culture Connection (1987) recognizes this relationship as anomalous: "What is perhaps surprising is that the CVS-III (Human Heartedness) content suggests 'feminine' rather than 'masculine' valuing" (p. 152).

These findings call into question the labeling and proper interpretation of either the masculinity-femininity or the human heartedness scale or of both scales because the correlations of the two scales are based on responses from the same twenty countries. Clearly, some reconciliation of the findings of these two studies, either theoretical, empirical, or statistical, is called for.

Despite these lingering doubts, it should be mentioned that it was never claimed by Hofstede that his four dimensions are complete or exhaustive dimensions of cultural values. Further, the apparent anomalies could be sample specific or due to a host of other uncontrolled variables. Nevertheless the human heartedness–masculinity-femininity correlation requires further investigation.

Cultural Determinants of Economic Development and Growth

Hofstede and Bond (1988) claim that the Confucian work dynamic (CWD) dimension is strongly related to economic growth over the

Table 20.2. Associations Among the Hofstede Dimensions; the Smith, Dugan, and Trompenaars Dimensions; and the CVS Dimensions Across Twenty Nations.

	Correlations							Beta (Direction Cosines)		
	2	3	4	5	6	7	8	9	10	11
1. (CVS-I) integration	.05	.06	.16	-.58	.06	.65	.11	.92	-.11	.70
2. (CVS-II) Confucian work dynamism		.02	-.11	.23	.22	-.32	.08	-.58	-.22	.35
3. (CVS-III) human heartedness			.07	.13	-.04	-.05	.67	n.a.	n.a.	n.a.
4. (CVS-IV) moral discipline				.55	.36	-.54	.22	-.39	-.09	-.11
5. (Hofstede) power distance					-.02	-.67	.09	-.30	.44	-.03
6. (Hofstede) uncertainty avoidance						-.22	.22	n.a.	n.a.	n.a.
7. (Hofstede) individualism-collectivism							.08	.36	-.31	.02
8. (Hofstede) masculinity-femininity								n.a.	n.a.	n.a.
9. (Smith) conservative-egalitarian									n.a.	n.a.
10. (Smith) utilitarian–loyal commitment										n.a.
11. (Smith) dimension$_{III}$ (not labeled)										

period from 1965 to 1985 across all twenty-two countries in the CCC sample. Four of the Five Asian Dragons—Hong Kong, Taiwan, Japan, and South Korea—held the top positions on the CWD scale, and these countries also enjoyed the most economic growth over the period under consideration. The CWD scale consists of eight items: persistence, ordering relationships by status and observing the order, thrift, having a sense of shame, personal steadiness and stability, protecting one's face, respect for tradition, and reciprocation of favors, gifts, and greetings. The first four items load positively on the CWD scale and the last four items load negatively. Thus for samples scoring high on this scale the positively loaded values are of most importance, and for samples scoring low the negatively loaded values are of most importance.

Although recognizing that the CWD values are also found in Brazil and India and are therefore not exclusively Confucian, Hofstede and Bond (1988) label this scale the Confucian Work Dynamic scale because the values expressed in the items can be traced back to the teachings of Confucius. They argue that this scale reflects support for entrepreneurship in the countries scoring high on it and that Westerners would find the values expressed in this scale foreign.

Hofstede and Bond (1988) go on to explain how each positively loaded item reflects cultural support for entrepreneurial behavior. Persistence and thrift facilitate entrepreneurial effectiveness, ordering relationships by status and observing the order makes it easier to be entrepreneurial, having a sense of shame supports interrelatedness through sensitivity to social contacts. They also argue that the items loading negatively on the CWD scale impede entrepreneurial behavior. Reciprocation of greetings, gifts, and favors places manners and politeness over business performance. Saving face inhibits business-oriented behavior, and stability and steadiness inhibits innovation and change. Respect for tradition inhibits innovation and change. This last item appears to contradict the assertion that ordering relationships by status and observing order facilitates entrepreneurial behavior.

Other than this latter apparent contradiction, their explanation is quite plausible. It is very likely that the CWD scale does reflect societal support of entrepreneurial behavior in the societies that score high on it. However, Hofstede and Bond do not report the correlation between CWD and annual growth of gross national product: rather, they show that the top few countries on the CWD scale also have high growth rates.

We computed this correlation. Taking CWD scores from Exhibit 2 in Hofstede and Bond (1988) and GNP and growth rate figures in their Exhibit 1, we first computed the rank order correlation between CWD score rankings and annual GNP growth rate (1965 to 1985) rankings. The rank order correlation is .69 ($p < .01$). This correlation is based on the thirteen countries for which Hofstede and Bond provided adequate data. However, growth rates are also influenced by baseline figures: high growth rates are easier to obtain when baseline values are low. The rank order correlation between baseline GNP (1965) and country economic growth rate is a significant −.52, as expected ($p < .05$). Also, the correlation between baseline GNP (1965) and CWD is −.74. To measure the association between CWD and GNP growth rate, we therefore need to partial out the association between CWD and the GNP base (1965). The semipartial correlation of growth rate with CWD, with the effect of base rate removed, is .45 (p slightly greater than .10). In other words, the incremental variance in annual GNP growth rate explained by CWD scores is about 21 percent (correlation squared).

McClelland (1961) found a very similar phenomenon—the achievement motive—which is also related to economic growth. Southwood has examined a host of variables and found four to be significantly related to economic growth, and a reanalysis of McClelland's original data by Southwood (McClelland, 1976) demonstrated that the achievement motive remains significantly predictive of economic growth even when these four additional variables are included in a prediction regression equation. The four variables are the population of the country in 1961, percentage of the population against which discrimination is practiced, occupational opportunity, and an index of open political competition. Achievement motivation enters the regression first and remains significant through the final step when other variables fail to contribute additionally to the variance accounted for in rates of growth. In the light of this evidence, it is interesting to explore the association between achievement motivation and CWD.

The achievement motive is characterized by the behavioral expression of setting challenging goals, risk taking, being persistent, and using feedback in the interest of performance. Highly achievement-motivated individuals tend to be entrepreneurial and not to be concerned with tradition or convention, protection of face, or social reciprocation. Thus the behavioral expression of achievement motivation is quite similar to the value syndrome described by the CWD scale. This similarity suggests that achievement motivation and CWD are tapping a similar phenomenon, an entrepreneurial societal orientation.

The achievement motive has traditionally been assumed to be a highly individualist motive reflecting constructive self-interest and described by Weber ([1924] 1947) as the Protestant work ethic. However, interestingly, CWD is not associated with the individualism pole of Hofstede's individualism-collectivism scale. In fact a recent study by Yeh and Lawrence (1995) rather strongly suggests that the opposite is true. These investigators related the CWD scores reported by Hofstede and Bond (1988) to economic growth data, paying particular attention to outliers. They found that the link between cultural dimensions and economic growth did not hold for Pakistan. After Pakistan was removed from the data set, the original correlation between individualism and CWD of $-.47$ was found to increase to a highly significant $-.70$ ($p < .01$). The CWD and GNP relationship must be considered with caution due to the limited sample size of thirteen countries. This finding does suggest, however, that CWD may be measuring a particular kind of societal achievement orientation—one that is collectively rather than individually based. This interpretation is intriguing in that it allows for diverse manifestations of achievement motivation: individualist in Western individually oriented societies and collectivist in Eastern collectively oriented societies.

Although the findings reported by Hofstede remain somewhat ambiguous due to the item composition of his scales and the three contradictory studies reviewed above, *Culture's Consequences* is a major contribution to the cross-cultural organizational behavior and leadership literature. Despite the criticisms of Hofstede's scales and their psychometric and interpretive limitations, the consistency of the findings reviewed here cannot be dismissed.

The facts that the findings of many independent studies are consistent with Hofstede's rankings, that several studies are consistent with his theoretical predictions, and that his findings have temporal stability are remarkable. The theoretical robustness of his constructs and the fact that he used aggregated scores of country values largely overcomes the interpretive and item composition limitations of his scales. As can be seen in Table 20.1 and from our review, despite the limitations discussed here his findings continue to have long-term predictive validity in a substantial number of studies conducted as long as twenty-five years after the IBM data were collected.

Hofstede is perhaps the most widely cited author in the cross-cultural organizational behavior literature. For example, he is the fourth most frequently cited in the *Journal of International Business Studies* from 1983 through 1993 (Chandy & Williams, 1994). Hofstede's research has stimulated many additional studies, so many in fact that his theoretical formulations and his research have stimulated the emergence of a new and important literature.

The Nature of Collectivism: The Smith, Dugan, and Trompenaars Forty-Three-Country Study

Another study that has relevance for the measurement of cultural values is that of Smith, Dugan, and Trompenaars (1996). This study is described here in modest detail because of its substantial contribution. This study is based on questionnaire responses of employees from forty-three countries. Sample sizes ranged from 29 to 1,212. Twenty-four percent of the employees studied were clerical or manual workers. Fifty-four percent were managers or professional employees, predominantly the former. The remainder could not be categorized for lack of information, making the sample composition ambiguous. In addition to many of the nations included in Hofstede's original work, this sample includes several Eastern European countries. The country samples were not matched; however, statistical analyses indicated that demographic heterogeneity of samples did not influence the findings.

The first set of questionnaire items was intended to measure various phenomena expected to yield information about individualist versus collectivist nations: universalist versus particularist obligations, status-based versus ascriptive achievement, paternalism versus nonpaternalism, utilitarian versus affective commitment to groups or organizations, and collectivist versus individualist ways in which individuals relate to work organizations and superiors.

The items took the form of dilemmas in a forced-choice format, except for the achievement-ascription items, which had a Likert-type format.

A second set of forty items referred to four additional dimensions postulated by Trompenaars (1985) to differentiate cultural units: locus of control, time perspective, affectivity-neutrality, and preference for specific versus diffuse social relationships. The dimensionality and psychometric properties of these items were not assessed.

Thirty-nine items were subjected to multidimensional scaling based on pooled individual responses. The results revealed two readily interpretable dimensions and a third dimension that is less interpretable though correlated with measures from previous research. The first dimension, *egalitarianism versus conservatism*, measures a tendency toward low paternalism, status based on achievement, and universalism. Countries that value ascription, particularism, and paternalism lie at the low end of the scale. The second dimension is *utilitarian versus loyal involvement*. Items composing this dimension describe contrasting bases of individual involvement in a group or organization: instrumental considerations versus affective considerations of loyalty. High scores on this dimension indicate high loyal-affective involvement and commitment to groups or organizations. These first and second dimensions correlated −.85. The third dimension, which is not labeled, consists predominantly of items that had high loadings on the other two dimensions and consequently is not interpretable and is not a psychometrically sound or useful dimension.

Smith, Dugan, and Trompenaars (1996) report multiple regressions in which their three dimensions are regressed on several variables. They find that life expectancy, literacy, per-capita income, socioeconomic status, percentage of agricultural workers, percentage of Christians, mean age, and percentage of men are country sample variables that have multiple correlations with the three dimensions ranging from .51 to .80. Clearly, mean country responses to the Smith, Dugan, and Trompenaars questionnaire are rather strongly associated with a number of important other variables.

Referring again to Table 20.2, it can be seen that countries scoring toward the egalitarian end of Smith, Dugan, and Trompenaars's first dimension enjoy a high degree of integration (CVS-I) —harmony, solidarity, trust, noncompetitiveness, and friendship. They also tend to be conservative, though not committed to family or ancestral piety, patriotism, or enforcement of female chastity. Egalitarian countries also tend to be somewhat low on CVS-II, the Confucian work dynamic. They do not endorse being thrifty, persistent, and steady, having a sense of shame, and maintaining orderly relationships, and they do endorse being concerned about tradition, face saving, and social reciprocation. Further, egalitarian countries are moderately low on CVS-IV, moral discipline— showing moderation, purity, suppression or avoidance of desires, and disinterest and being nonadaptable and not concerned with prudent judgment.

These associations suggest that people in countries with high egalitarian scores are likely to have less life stress because of the supportiveness and harmony likely found in their environments, the freedom from authoritarian control over their lives, and the lack of compulsion and rigidity likely associated with their low scores on the moral discipline dimension. Consistent with this speculation, Smith, Dugan, and Trompenaars (1996) found that the following variables had small but positive relationships with egalitarianism, as revealed by their multi-dimensional scaling solution: life expectancy (beta coefficient: .25), log of per-capita income (.32), literacy rate (.22), and percentage of sample having high socioeconomic status (.34).

On the whole, Smith, Dugan, and Trompenaars conclude that their results indicate a *great deal of replicability* in previous cross-cultural studies. They are referring to the recurring findings of various operationalizations of individualism versus collectivism, and they conclude that the greatest yield of cross-cultural research concerns the individualism-collectivism distinction. The uncertainty avoidance and masculinity dimensions were not revealed in their analysis, but that is not surprising given that their measures were not designed to tap these dimensions, though the dimensions had, curiously enough, been included in their hypotheses.

The major contribution of this study is that it provides information with which to better understand the nature of collectivism. It suggests that seven rather important constructs on which individually oriented collectivities are likely to differ from collectively oriented collectivities are integration, utilitarian versus affective commitment based on loyalty, Confucian work dynamism, status-based versus ascriptive achievement, particularism versus universalism, power distance, and collectivism. Smith, Dugan, and Trompenaars's findings suggest an integrative reconceptualization of the individualism-collectivism dimension that includes a number of constructs not previously incorporated in the same research design. We suggest that measures of these constructs be included in future large-sample studies and that for the sake of precision and parsimony second-order ecological factor analyses be conducted to determine the most appropriate grouping of these constructs into higher-order constructs.

Emic Versus Etic Leader Behaviors

Most cross-cultural leadership studies operationalize leadership with a set of questionnaire items. These items are assumed to reflect genotypic leader behaviors, that is, behaviors assumed to be genetic to leadership and to vary across cultural entities. Such behaviors are referred to in cross-cultural literature as *etic*—they are to some extent common to all cultural entities.

Misumi (1985) has argued that different genotypic behaviors need to be operationalized differently, according to the manner in which they are expressed in each culture. Thus he argues for both genotypic (*etic*) and phenotypic (*emic*) behaviors. Research by Smith, Misumi, Tayeb, Paterson, and Bond (1989) demonstrates the efficacy of following Misumi's suggestion with respect to leader behavior constructs oriented toward performance (P) and maintenance (M). These constructs concern task- and person-oriented behavior and are similar to the Ohio State Leader Initiating Structure and Consideration constructs, respectively. The study is based on questionnaire responses of supervisors from six electronics-producing companies in Britain, Hong Kong, Japan, and Korea. Smith, Peterson, Misumi, and Bond (1992) demonstrated that a select set of questionnaire items were etic in the sense that similar factor structures representing the P and M constructs emerged in each of the four countries. Several other items reflected emic (culture-specific) manifestations of the more general etic P and M constructs. Different emic items were shown to correlate differentially across countries with the etic P and M factors.

For example, these two questions were found to be etic M items in the sense that they were shown to load on M factors in all four countries: Does your superior try to understand your viewpoint? Does your superior treat you fairly? Specific items associated with the etic M factor in Japan described supervisors as speaking about a subordinate's personal difficulties with others in his or her absence rather than face to face and as sending written memos. In contrast, specific emic items associated with the etic M factor in the U.S. described supervisors as being consultative and participative and as *not* sending written memos. From these examples it can be seen that the specific behaviors viewed as person oriented (M) differ markedly but in ways that are understandable within each setting. Avoidance of direct confrontation by use of third parties and written memos reflect the emphasis in Japanese culture on harmony and face-saving. Consultation, participation, and avoidance of written memos reflect the egalitarian and informal culture of the United States. Smith, Peterson, Misumi, and Bond (1992) found both etic and emic items for the performance orientation (P) as well.

Using both etic constructs and emic measures has the advantage of more precise measurement. It allows investigators to relate emic items to etic constructs and to describe leadership as it is uniquely manifested in each cultural unit studied. Therefore it should be appropriate for applied purposes such as training or organizational development efforts.

Some Theoretical Propositions

Our review suggests three theoretical propositions that enjoy considerable empirical support.

The Cultural Congruence Proposition

The *cultural congruence* proposition asserts that cultural forces affect the kind of leader behavior that is usually accepted, enacted, and effective within a collectivity. Accordingly, behavior that is consistent with collective values will be more acceptable and effective than behavior that represents conflicting values. This hypothesis is taken as an article of faith among culture theorists. The empirical evidence strongly supports this hypothesis. Here are several examples.

As shown in our discussion of measuring cultural dimensions, when nations have high power distance and collectivism scores, individuals in those nations experience a tendency toward behaviors that are consistent with these high national scores. Highly collectively oriented cultures place a high value on group maintenance, paternalism, in-group loyalty and harmony, treating in-group members with dignity, and engaging in face saving among in-group members and nonconfrontational peaceful resolution of conflict. Of particular interest is Asian managers' heavy emphasis on paternalism (Dorfman & Howell, 1988; Farmer & Richman, 1965) and group maintenance activities (Bass, Burger, Doktor, & Barrett, 1979; Bolon & Crain, 1985; Ivancevich, Schweiger, & Ragan, 1986). These findings are consistent with Hofstede's rankings of countries on individualism-collectivism.

Hofstede's uncertainty avoidance scores are associated with less risky entry into foreign markets and fuller disclosure of accounting information. The level of achievement motivation reflected in grammar school books was found to be predictive of entrepreneurial behavior twenty-five years later. In individualist societies, people prefer individual rather than group-based compensation practices and exhibit greater willingness to take risks. Thus the cultural congruence proposition is well supported.

A corollary of the cultural congruence proposition is that violation of cultural norms by leaders or managers will result in dissatisfaction, conflict, and resistance on the part of followers or subordinates and, at times, lower performance of leaders, their work units, and their subordinates. Anecdotal examples from the literature on expatriate adjustment illustrate lower productivity and satisfaction when collective norms and expatriate values conflict (Lindsay & Dempsey, 1985; Weiss & Bloom, 1990). An illustration of this line of research concerns leadership requirements for implementing quality-control teams in the United States as compared to Japan. Japanese managers emphasize socioemotional orientation, involvement, loyalty, and cooperation. In contrast, U.S. managers are less inclined toward these behaviors and at times violate cultural norms to implement quality control practices (Miskin & Gmelch, 1985).

The Cultural Difference Proposition

Juxtaposed to the cultural congruence proposition is the *cultural difference* proposition. According to this proposition, increased task performance of followers, organizations, and institutions in societies will be induced by the introduction of selected values, techniques, and behavior patterns that are different from those commonly valued in the society. The rationale for this hypothesis is that by being different with *respect to some behaviors,* leaders introduce more changes of the kind required for innovation and performance improvement.

Several examples of minority groups leading the way to industrialization, business development, and entrepreneurship illustrate this hypothesis: consider the Methodists in England, the Protestant Huguenots in France prior to the Edict of Nantes, and the Cubans in the United States who fled from Cuban communism. These groups and their leaders acted and behaved in ways that were largely outside the cultural norms of their respective larger societies but were also effective in business development.

Thus it appears that leaders make a difference by being different with respect to *some* leader behaviors. No research has been conducted to determine the precise leader behaviors associated with such improvement. We hypothesize that the leader behaviors associated with breakthrough improvement in organizations and societies are often those also associated with the introduction of constructive change, such as articulating a vision of a different way of life and communicating high performance expectations and confidence in followers.

The Near Universality of Leader Behaviors Proposition

The *near universality of leader behaviors* proposition asserts that some leader behaviors are universally or nearly universally accepted and effective. Despite wide-ranging differences in cultural norms across countries studied, there is some support for this proposition.

Bass, Burger, Doktor, and Barrett (1979) found that managers from twelve culturally diverse countries indicated a desire to get work done while using less authority. Similarly, Smith and Peterson (1994) found that managers in twenty-five countries reported satisfaction with events for which they were delegated substantial discretion. Transformational leadership has been found to be acceptable and effective in Canada (Bass & Avolio, 1993; Howell & Frost, 1989), India (Pereira, 1987), Japan (Bass, 1997), the Netherlands (Koene, Pennings, & Schreuder, 1991), and Singapore (Koh, Terborg, & Steers, 1991) as well as the United States (Bass & Avolio, 1993). And Bass (1997) argues that the three components of transformational leadership are near universal: charisma, intellectual stimulation of followers, and individualized consideration toward followers. Bass reports that although some fine tuning may be required, on all continents people's ideal leader is transformational, not transactional. He asserts that transformational leadership is more effective than contingent reward which in turn is more effective than managing by exception, and that laissez faire leadership is contraindicated. It should be noted that Bass's measures operationalize leader behaviors as rather etic items. It is likely that his constructs will be enacted differentially in an emic manner from one cultural entity to another. For example, charismatic leader-ship may be enacted in a highly assertive manner, as in the case of John F. Kennedy, Martin Luther King Jr., Theodore Roosevelt, and Winston Churchill, or in a quiet, nonaggressive manner, as in the case of Mahatma Gandhi, Nelson Mandela, and Mother Teresa. All these leaders, however, displayed charisma, in that they articulated an ideological message, set a personal example of the values inherent in their message, conveyed a high sense of confidence in self, and were in turn highly respected and trusted by their followers.

Support for the near universality of future-oriented and inspirational leader behaviors is provided by interpretative interview and focus group research in thirty-eight countries and by questionnaire pilot study samples from fifty countries involved in the GLOBE study. The universality or near universality of these leader behaviors remains to be established with more rigorous research, larger samples, and emic as well as etic measures, however.

There is reason to suspect that several leadership behaviors that might be universally acceptable and effective have never been widely introduced to the members of many societies. When individuals have never experienced such leader behaviors, it may be difficult for them to express a preference for these behaviors and unrealistic of researchers to expect such preferences. This conclusion is supported Bass, Burger, Doktor, and Barrett (1979), who showed that despite the relatively high power distance orientation of the French (Hofstede, 1980), French managers who experienced democratically oriented management by their superiors expressed a desire to work for such managers again.

Some Unresolved Issues

In this section we discuss several controversial issues yet to be resolved.

Magnitude of Cultural Effects

The first issue concerns the magnitude of the effect of cultural influences. In traditional culture theory, differences in psychological commonalities between cultural entities are believed to account for significant amounts of variance in a wide range of individuals' behaviors (Hofstede, 1980; Kluckhohn & Strodtbeck, 1961; Triandis, 1995) and organizations' practices (Hall & Hall, 1987; Hofstede, 1980; Schein, 1985). Although the studies reviewed here provide support for this position with respect to leadership, it is not clear just *how much* variance is accounted for by differences in such psychological properties as assumptions, values, beliefs, meanings, social identities, and motives (Dorfman, 1996). A meta-analysis to address this question would be a useful contribution.

Further, despite the abundance of evidence in support of the cultural congruence proposition, there remains the question of how external forces such as international competition, military aggression, international political conflict, economic environment, technology, and physical climate influence cultural norms, artifacts, beliefs, individual behaviors, organizational practices, and other variables assumed to be reflections of cultural differences. It may well be that after controlling for such external variables, psychological commonalities may account for much less variance in other relevant variables such as leader attributes and behavior than is commonly assumed.

There also remains the question of how much variance in organizational practices and leader behaviors is accounted for by specific task and environmental influences. The strategic contingency theory of organizations asserts that organizational form is strongly influenced by the size of organizations, their technologies, their strategies, and the stability of their environments (Donaldson, 1993). Accordingly, it may well be that such variables directly influence leaders' strategic decision-making processes as well as their day-to-day behavior without influencing cultural norms, identities, motives, and shared meanings. The relative amount of variance in the emergence, acceptance, and effectiveness of leader behavior accounted for by psychological commonalties versus strategic contingency variables remains to be determined. Further, military, economic, technological, political, and competitive forces possibly influence organizations as much as psychological commonalities. Such forces may enhance, dampen, or nullify the influence of psychological commonalties among members of cultural units on some important organizational practices and leadership-related variables.

Relationships Among Critical Variables

A second issue to be resolved concerns the relationships between within-unit psychological commonalties, organizational structure and management practices, and leader behavior. There is substantial evidence that organizational structure and practices influence the behavior of organizational members (Mintzberg, 1979). We found only two studies that investigated the relationship between psychological commonalties and organizational structure, practices, form, or effectiveness: Hofstede, Neuijen, Ohayv, and Sanders (1990) and Morris, Davis, and Allen (1994). Neither revealed a significant relationship between country or organizational unit scores on Hofstede's dimensions of culture and respondents' descriptions of organizational practices. The possibility that externally imposed variables or strategic contingency variables mute the effects of shared cultural beliefs and values as measured by Hofstede's scales is given some credence by these two studies. It remains unclear how and for what kinds of management practices psychological commonalties within cultural entities have a non-trivial influence. It is also not clear how organizational structure and practices and psychological commonalties interact to influence leadership-related variables. Clearly, cross-cultural explanations of leadership and organizational behavior need to include consideration of the possibility that external forces directly affect behavior without the intervening influence of shared cultural psychological variables.

Culture and Leadership

A third issue requiring attention concerns the influence of cultural forces on local conceptions of leadership, the social status of leaders, and the amount of influence granted to leaders. In some nations, leaders are romanticized and glorified. For example, in the Arab countries and in France, Germany, Russia, and the United States one finds frequent public symbols such as statues and pictures of leaders or buildings and streets named in recognition and commemoration of leaders. Qualitative research conducted by the first author of this chapter suggests that in these countries leaders and managers are granted substantial influence over a wide variety of political and economic policies and practices. In contrast, in the Netherlands, Sweden, Austria, and German-speaking Switzerland, there is a marked absence of public symbols that attest to the greatness of leaders. In these countries, leaders and managers are granted relatively little influence. Thus within cultural entities psychological commonalties very likely enhance or constrain leaders and their influence and leadership-related variables differentially. Unfortunately, there is little systematic evidence that shows how such commonalties might evolve or the mechanisms by which cultural entities might enhance or constrain the exercise of leadership or the effectiveness of leaders.

Cultural Processes

The fourth issue concerns many scholars' assertion that cultural entities influence the values of their members and that these values, once internalized, influence members' behavior. However, the processes by which cultural entities affect member psychological states and behavior are not clear. Values are cognitively based judgments of the appropriateness or worth of entities, events, behaviors, and outcomes. As such, they are very similar to attitudes. In fact Smith, Dugan, and Trompenaars (1996) refer to values as attitudes. However, there is little substantial systematic evidence that demonstrates relationships between attitudes and generalized *global behavior patterns* such as leadership styles, friendship patterns, or child-rearing practices. Attitudes specifically related to specific behaviors are predictive of such behavior in the *short term* in response to very *specific stimuli and incentives* but often not predictive of *generalized stable global behavior patterns* such as leadership styles (Ajzen & Fishbein, 1970). For example, several interviewees expressed to the first author of this chapter the sentiment that "leadership" is a phenomenon that conflicts with Dutch egalitarian values and that charismatic leadership would be especially suspect and ineffective in the Netherlands. Despite these sentiments, Koene, Pennings, and Schreuder (1991) found in a longitudinal study of large supermarkets that charismatic leadership had positive effects on employee performance and more pervasive effects than either considerate or directive leadership.

It could be argued that research on attitudinal-behavioral relationships casts serious doubt on the assertion that values expressed in interviews or questionnaire responses influence behavior. There are at least three competing processes that might have produced the findings we reviewed for the cultural congruence and cultural difference propositions.

One explanation of the effects of cultural forces on individual behavior is that psychological commonalties influence the valence individuals place on behaviors and events. Valences in turn influence behavioral intentions, which influence manifest behavior. There is some evidence to support this explanation. Bond and Leung (1993) showed that country differences accounted for significant variance in the valence individuals place on selected outcomes and that valences in turn influence their behavioral intentions. Lee and Green (1990) found similar effects of country differences on behavioral intentions. This explanation is somewhat weak, however, because it is well established that behavioral intentions predict behavior primarily in the short run and that myriad circumstances can attenuate the relationship between behavioral intentions and enacted behavior. Further, as stated earlier, behavioral intentions predict discrete behaviors and not global behavior patterns such as leadership styles. Additionally, as the length of time between the formulation of behavioral intentions and action increases, or when environmental conditions change or interfere with behavioral enactment of intentions, the intention-behavior relationship is also attenuated (Ajzen & Fishbein, 1970).

A second explanation of the effects of cultural forces on individual behavior is that expressions of values in responses to questionnaires represent agreed-on norms rather than respondent attitudes. Thus it may be that important common experiences result in agreed-upon norms and that members are influenced by norm enforcement, resulting in the tyranny of the majority rather than individual volition. For example, at one time in Polynesian villages, individuals who had violated cultural norms were forced to stand before members of the village, who collectively decided the appropriate remedial action or punishment. The offender subsequently complied but as a result of the coercion of the majority, not as a result of internalized values.

A third explanation of the effects of cultural forces on individual behavior may be that common experiences affect nonconscious motivation and that it is such motivation that influences behavior rather than conscious values. As we stated, McClelland (1961) demonstrated that expressions of achievement motivation in children's literature are predictive of economic development of nations. Achievement motivation thus expressed was assumed by McClelland to be a collectively stressed nonconscious motive. Thus there is the question whether cognitive value orientation, coercive norm enforcement, nonconscious motivation, or all three of these processes are affected by cultural influences and account for differential behavior across cultural entities.

Sampling

The fourth unresolved issue concerns sampling. Of necessity most cross-cultural research uses convenience sampling rather than some form of systematic sampling. This often results in unmatched samples and samples of varying sizes, with, for example, as few as thirty-seven and twenty-nine respondents in countries studied by Hofstede (1980) and Smith, Dugan, and Trompenaars (1996), respectively. Heterogeneous samples and samples of unequal size reduce a study's ability to identify differences in cultural entities. We urge cross-cultural investigators to at least attempt to obtain comparable samples in terms of size and demographic variables. Smith and his associates in their large-sample country studies have successfully used demographic variables to control for cultural heterogeneity.

Unmatched samples may be affected by a host of possible confounds: informant demographic variables; subcultural variations; informants socialized to different degrees in cultural values and beliefs; varying exposure to international communication and competition; disparate organizational settings, industry types, and sectors (profit versus nonprofit); and different government regulations imposed on organizations. Although it is impossible to control for all of these confounding variables by matched sampling, it is advisable to attempt to randomize their effect by collecting data from a large number of cultural units and also by collecting data that can be used to statistically control for such confounds.

Surprisingly, when the number of samples is relatively large, unmatched samples appear to be sufficiently robust to overcome a nontrivial amount of variance due to differential confounding influences. Table 20.1 describes several studies based on unmatched samples that yielded significant country effects despite their sample heterogeneity. Smith, Dugan, and Trompenaars (1996) demonstrated that the substantial demographic heterogeneity of the forty-three samples they studied did not affect their results. Evidentially, confounding variables due to nonmatched samples and external influences can be canceled out in large-sample studies. Studies with smaller samples, in contrast, are especially susceptible to such confounds, and differences in dependent variables found by studies that compare only two cultural entities can never be attributed to cultural differences.

Limitations of Informants' Ability

The final unresolved issue concerns respondents' ability to provide valid interview or questionnaire information if they have not had relevant experiences. In some cultures it is likely that most individuals have experiences with only a limited range of leader behaviors. Asking them to select their preferences from broad range of leader attributes or behaviors may yield responses that have little to do with how these informants will actually respond to these kinds of leader behaviors. In contrast, it is possible that unobtrusive measures and aggregated measures of nonconscious motives may be better predictors of the kinds of leader behavior that will be commonly expected, accepted, and effective. We speculate that culturally different preferences for selected leader behaviors might diminish once the broad range of such behavior is introduced. We are reminded of this observation from Metro-Goldwyn-Mayer movie studio founder Louis B. Mayer: "The public cannot tell you what they want in a movie until they see it." Recall that a study by Koene, Pennings, and Schreuder (1991) showed that despite proclamations that charismatic leadership is not welcome in the Netherlands, charismatic leadership had greater positive effects on organizational performance than did leader support or initiating structure behavior.

Theoretical Perspectives

This section proposes a theoretical framework that we hope will be useful for investigators of cross-cultural leadership phenomena. The framework is an integration of several theoretical perspectives: implicit leadership theory (Lord & Maher, 1991), value/belief theory of culture (Hofstede, 1980), implicit motivation theory (McClelland, 1985), and strategic contingency theory of organizations (Donaldson, 1993). The relevant and essential features of each theory are briefly described in the following paragraphs. We then present an integration of selected aspects of each theory as our theoretical framework.

Implicit Leadership Theory

According to implicit leadership theory, individuals have implicit theories (stereotypes, beliefs, convictions, and assumptions) about the attributes and behaviors that distinguish leaders from nonleaders, moral from evil leaders, and effective from ineffective leaders. Implicit theories influence the values individuals place on selected leader behaviors and attributes and the motives of individuals relevant to acceptance and enactment of leader behavior. Implicit leadership theory asserts that individuals are attributed leadership qualities and then accepted as leaders on the basis of the degree of fit, or congruence, between the leader behaviors they enact and the implicit leadership theory held by the attributers. The better the fit, the more leadership ability is attributed to the individual and the more the leader is accepted by the attributers.

Implicit leadership theories jointly held by members of cultural entities are hypothesized to constrain, moderate, or facilitate the exercise of leadership, the acceptance of leaders, and the perception of leaders as influential, acceptable, and effective. There is substantial evidence in support of this hypothesis (Lord & Maher, 1991). Because members of cultural entities share values, beliefs, assumptions, social identities, meanings, and motives, they are likely to have very similar implicit theories of leadership. To the extent that implicit leadership theories vary across cultural units, they are likely to differentially constrain, moderate, or facilitate all aspects of leadership, including the status granted to leaders, the influence leaders are perceived to have, what is expected of leaders, the degree of compliance with leaders' influence attempts, and the general acceptance of the leaders and their behavior.

Value-Belief Theory

Value-belief theory is the theory favored by most cross-cultural scholars (Hofstede, 1980; Kluckhohn & Strodtbeck, 1961; Triandis, 1995). It asserts that the values and beliefs held by members of collectivities influence the behavior of individuals and the degree to which selected behaviors are viewed as legitimate, acceptable, and effective. Value-belief theory implies that external cultural forces influence individual values, which in turn influence behavioral intentions, which are then enacted behaviorally (Leung & Bond, 1993).

Implicit Motivation Theory

Implicit motivation theory is the theory of nonconscious motives originally advanced by McClelland, Atkinson, Clark, and Lowell

(1953). In its most general form the theory asserts that the essential nature of human motivation can be understood in terms of three implicit (nonconscious) motives: achievement, affiliation, and power (social influence). In contrast to behavioral intentions and conscious values, which are predictive of discrete task behaviors for short periods of time under constant situational forces (Ajzen & Fishbein, 1970), implicit motives are predictive of motive arousal in the presence of selected stimuli, spontaneous behavior in the absence of motive arousal stimuli, and long-term (as long as twenty years) individual *global* behavior patterns such as patterns of social relationships, citizenship behavior, family practices, and leadership styles.

Substantial evidence supports these assertions (McClelland, 1985; McClelland & Boyatzis, 1982; McClelland, Koestner, & Weinberger, 1989; Spangler, 1992). Further, McClelland (1961) has demonstrated the cross-cultural relevance of implicit motivation theory. And as already described, he has found that expressions of achievement motivation stressed in children's literature are predictive of the long-term economic development of nations measured twenty-five years later.

In addition to considerable supporting evidence concerning individual motivation (McClelland, 1985), the theory's relevance to leadership also has empirical support. Three concurrent correlational studies (House, Delbecq, & Taris, 1996; McClelland & Burnham, 1976; Messalum & House, 1996) and four longitudinal studies (House, Spangler, & Woycke, 1991; McClelland & Boyatzis, 1982; Winter, 1978, 1991) show that implicit motivation theory is predictive of managerial effectiveness or success. (The studies by McClelland and Boyatzis, 1982, and Winter, 1991, are based on the same sample.)

Strategic Contingency Theory of Organizations

The strategic contingency theory of organizations (Donaldson, 1993) asserts that four strategic contingencies affect organizational form. They are the strategy, size, and technology of an organization and the environment in which that organization functions. According to this theory organizational structure must be adapted to the demands of the organization's strategic contingencies.

Accordingly, for effective performance, structure must reflect the degree to which these strategic contingencies call for flexible or inflexible behavior, an integrated or fragmented response to environments, and a short- or long-term orientation. The choices made here become the strategic requirements of organizational behavior. Organizational forms that do not provide the resources and coordination needed by their strategic requirements will be ineffective. Further, according to strategic contingency theory, organizational formalization inevitably increases with size.

We integrate strategic contingency theory with the other leadership theories we have discussed by asserting that leader behaviors must be in accordance with the strategic requirements of organizations. Thus organizations with long-term, high-risk strategies require leaders with long-term orientation who take high-risk decisions. Organizations such as churches, political organizations, and organizations producing goods and services with implications for the welfare of their constituencies require strategies with strong ideological orientations and require leaders who behave in accordance with the value implications of these strategies. For example, pharmaceutical producers and producers of medical supplies require leaders whose behavior reflects the values inherent in health services. National military organizations require leaders whose behavior reflects national patriotism. Political organizations require leaders whose behavior reflects the values of their constituencies.

An Integrated Theoretical Framework

We have integrated the theoretical perspectives presented here into a theoretical framework intended to facilitate future cross-cultural development of theory and empirical investigation. Figure 20.1 shows the integrated framework in the form of a systems causal loop diagram. Our integrated theory describes the process by which cultural variables, leader behavior, and organizational practices interact to influence organizational effectiveness. Following are the major assertions of the theory.

1. Important common experiences involving history, religion, ethnic heritage, international competition, or physical climate result in common assumptions, values, beliefs, meanings, social identities, and motives shared by members of cultural entities.

Figure 20.1. Systems Model of Common Experiences, Cultural Norms, Leader Behavior, Organizational Practices, and Organizational and Leader Effectiveness.

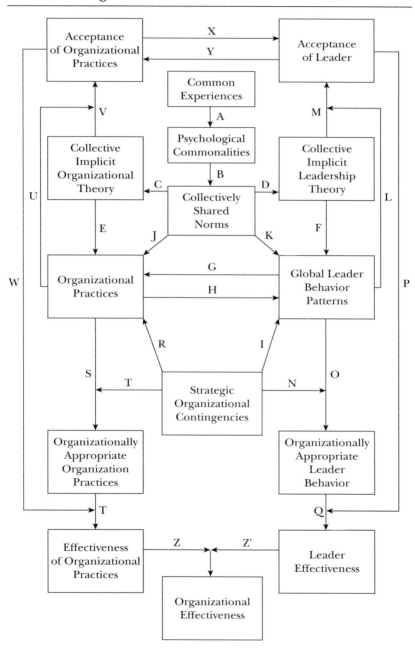

These are the shared variables we refer to as psychological commonalties (arrow A in Figure 20.1).

2. These psychological commonalties result in socialization of members and provide incentives, cues, guidance, constraints, and reinforcements for selected behaviors and organizational practices.

3. Joint psychological commonalties endorsed by members of cultural entities bestow shared meaning on leader attributes and behaviors and on organizational practices. They provide meaning in the sense that selected leader behaviors and organizational practices are understood in a particular way in each collectivity.

4. Psychological commonalties take on the status of collective norms, which are socially learned, communicated, and enforced by members of cultural entities. These norms are macro- (collectivity-) level variables that guide individual behavior and the evaluation of such behavior (arrow B).

5. The collective norms result in implicit theories of organizing and leadership held by members of the cultural entities (arrows C and D).

6. These implicit theories are predictive of differential organizational practices and global leader behavior patterns that are favored or disfavored within cultural entities. Cultural entities that favor achievement motivation, for example, will favor the patterns and practices that emphasize performance excellence, choice of challenging tasks, intermediate risk taking, use of information to measure progress toward goal attainment, and persistence in pursuit of goals (McClelland, 1985).

7. The leader behavior patterns and organizational practices favored in a collectivity will be those most frequently enacted and reinforced in that collectivity (arrows E and F).

8. Leaders will influence organizational practices by adjusting such practices to their preferred global leader behavior pattern and to the role demands imposed by organizational contingencies (arrow G).

9. Organizational practices will influence global leader behavior patterns by providing incentives, reinforcements, and constraints for selected leader behaviors (arrow H).

10. Strategic organizational contingencies will influence leader behavior by imposing role demands on leaders (arrow I).

11. The shared norms will be enforced by members of the collectivity (arrows J and K).

12. The greater the fit between leader behaviors enacted by persons in positions of authority and the implicit theory of leadership held by organizational members, the more the members will accept the leader (indicated by the joint interaction of arrows L and M).

13. The greater the fit between leader behaviors enacted by persons in positions of authority and the role demands of the strategic organizational contingencies these leaders manage, the more organizationally appropriate will be the leaders' behavior (indicated by the joint interaction of arrows N and O).

14. The greater the acceptance of the leader (in interaction with the appropriateness of the leader's behavior), the more the leader will be effective (indicated by the joining of arrows P and Q).

15–21. A similar process occurs with respect to organizational practices (indicated by arrows R through W).

22. Acceptance of leaders is in part a function of the acceptability of organizational practices because leaders represent their organizations to organizational members and enforce organizational practices (arrow X).

23. Acceptance of organizational practices is in part a function of the acceptability of the leader also because leaders represent their organizations to organizational members and enforce organizational practices (arrow Y).

24. Effectiveness of organizations is a function of the interaction of the organizational practices effectiveness and leader effectiveness (indicated by the joining of arrows Z and Z').

Some Further Comments on Methodology

Research methodology for cross-cultural research has been discussed competently by a number of authors (Adler, 1986; Adler, Campbell, & Laurent, 1989; Brislin, 1970: Brislin, Lonner, & Thorndike, 1973; Deutscher, 1973; England & Itzhak, 1983; Green & White, 1976; Hofstede, Bond, & Luk, 1993; Leung & Bond, 1989; Mitchell, 1973; Nasif, Al-Daeaj, Ebrahimi, & Thibodeaux, 1991; Nath, 1969; Peng, Peterson, & Shyi, 1991; Roberts & Boyacigiller, 1984; Ueno & Sekaran, 1992). Following is a brief discussion of some methodological issues that are relevant to cross-cultural investigations but that have been given little attention in the cross-cultural leadership literature.

Cross-cultural comparisons are greatly assisted when the variables under investigation are quantified. There are six measurement instruments designed specifically for this purpose: the Value Survey Module (VSM) (Hofstede, 1980), the Chinese Value Survey (CVS) (Chinese Culture Connection, 1987), the Culture Perspectives Questionnaire (CPQ) (Maznevski & DiStefano, 1995), the instrument used by Smith, Dugan, and Trompenaars (1996) and discussed previously, the Culture Dimension Questionnaire (Dorfman, 1988), and the GLOBE questionnaire designed to measure dimensions of values, beliefs, and practices at the societal and organizational levels of analysis and also valued leader attributes and behaviors.

In the study by Chinese Culture Connection (1987), the CVS yielded four factors, as described previously. As can be seen from Table 20.1, this scale discriminates between cultural entities (Chinese Culture Connection, 1987; Ralston, Gustafson, Elsass, Cheung, & Terpstra, 1992). The PD and UA scales of the VMS have been shown to discriminate between country samples (Shackleton & Ali, 1990). Although these two instruments appear to have face validity, to our knowledge to date no other psychometric properties relevant to them have been reported. Of course there may be reports we could not find or that are as yet unpublished.

The CPQ is designed to measure the dimensions of culture advocated by Kluckhohn and Strodtbeck (1961) at the organizational level of analysis. Maznevski and DiStefano (1995) argue that various combinations of cultural dimensions suggested by Kluckhohn and Strodtbeck can be combined to yield Hofstede's four dimensions. After substantial pilot testing and revision Maznevski and DiStefano administered a seventy-eight-item questionnaire to 355 respondents in four countries. They found that within each scale different configurations of items make the most internally consistent set for different countries. Nevertheless their most recent version of the questionnaire yielded promising within-country Cronbach alpha reliability coefficients, generally exceeding .60. They also found that thirty-three out of forty-four comparisons of eleven scales administered in each of the four countries significantly discriminated between countries. Finally, factor analyses showed that most of their scales were unidimensional. Thus these scales, although still in the developmental stage, show substantial promise for the measurement of cross-cultural phenomena and will likely become useful to predict organizational and leader-related phenomena cross-culturally.

Dorfman and Howell (1988) developed a questionnaire called the Culture Dimension Survey, which measures at the individual level respondents' identification with Hofstede's four cultural dimensions as well as a fifth dimension—paternalism. Successive refinements of the questionnaire have resulted in a twenty-nine item instrument with alphas over .70 for all subscales. The usefulness of this questionnaire is demonstrated in the study reported by Dorfman and Howell (1988).

The instruments developed as part of the GLOBE program measure Hofstede's four dimensions plus humane orientation, performance orientation, and long- versus short-term orientation. The humane orientation scale is likely to measure the same phenomena as the CVS human heartedness scale. The performance and long- versus short-term orientation scales combined are likely to be analogous to the CVS Confucian work dynamic scale, that is, measures of cultural support for entrepreneurship. Additionally, GLOBE scales were developed to measure the same constructs at the organizational and the leader levels of analysis. These scales measure practices as well as values and beliefs. Finally, several additional dimensions of leader attributes and behavior are also measured by the GLOBE questionnaire.

Extensive psychometric analyses based on samples of respondents in thirty-two countries were used to develop the scales. The findings were replicated on samples of respondents in an additional eighteen countries. Several goodness-of-fit indices demonstrated congruence between the first and second sample dimensions. These findings indicate that use of the scales as aggregate measures of cultural phenomena is justified. With the exception of three scales that require further development, all the GLOBE scales have been demonstrated to be unidimensional and to be scalable with generalizability coefficients (interclass ICC-KK correlations) of .86 or greater. The generalizability coefficients indicate combined inter-item scale reliabilities, within-country response agreement, and between-country differences. The psychometric properties of the GLOBE scales indicate that they can meaningfully measure differences between cultural units in terms of leadership behavior and societal and organizational practices, values, and beliefs.

Although additional instrument development is still required, it is clear that the study of cross-cultural leadership is becoming more rigorous and that psychometrically sound instruments are now available to measure many of the constructs we have discussed here.

The Need for Triangulation

Qualitative data can be collected through focus groups, interviews, participant observation, and unobtrusive measures based on cultural artifacts or media narratives. When such information is systematically content analyzed and coded into quantitative categories, or levels, it can either validate other measures or, with other measures, form an index of the dimensions under study.

One problem with existing cross-cultural comparisons is that most studies are based on a single measure of each of the variables investigated. With single variable measurement researchers can never be sure what biases are associated with a measure. The findings may be due to biases inherent in the method of data collection rather than to true variation of the variables under investigation. Further, reliance on a single method may make findings method bound, that is, reproducible only when the same method is used. To avoid these problems we strongly suggest that investigators use at least two and preferably three or more methods to assess the variables they investigate. Interview-, questionnaire-, focus group–, and participant observation–based data are subject to the biases of those who provide information and those who collect it. Unobtrusive measures are measures that do not rely on people to report data (Webb, Campbell, Schwartz, & Sechrest, 1966). When adequately operationalized, unobtrusive measures can be relatively free of such biases. Following are some interesting examples of unobtrusive measures of selected dimensions of cultures.

Individualism is likely indicated by the proportion of individuals in a society who are left-handed. This proportion varies across cultural units from about 8 to 15 percent (Triandis, 1995). Presumably, the lower percentages reflect less tolerance in parents for a child's individualism. Compared to parents in individualist countries, parents in collectivist countries are hypothesized to put more pressure on left-handed children to make them right-handed.

Power distance might be measured by the number of titles and hierarchical levels among domestic help hired by wealthy individuals. For example, researchers might find such titles as head cook, kitchen helper, butler, handyman (or -woman), chief housekeeper, housekeeper or maid, and the like in highly power stratified societies and few such titles in societies characterized by low power distance.

An unobtrusive measure of tolerance of uncertainty might be the average age of top executive officers in the industries studied. In organizations and societies that have low tolerance for uncertainty one would expect the average age of high-level managers to be quite high because age is revered and assumed to be associated with long experience and wisdom.

Three possible candidates for unobtrusive measures of achievement motivation are the proportion of entrepreneurial firms in each collectivity studied, the number of new business start-ups, and the relative amount of resources devoted to occupational education. Two unobtrusive measures of gender discrimination might be the percentage of women who drive automobiles and the percentage of women in high-level organizational positions in each cultural entity.

An unobtrusive measure of any major variable might be the number of words used in the cultural entity to describe that variable. This number might indicate the dimension's cultural importance. In Iran there are forty different words indicating different kinds of rice, for example. To measure some cultural dimensions, a researcher could select three or four key words for each one. For example power, authority, control, and dominance might be used as key words for the measurement of power distance. Uncertainty, vagueness, equivocality, and ambiguity might be used as key words for uncertainty avoidance. The investigator could consult a culture's two most prominent thesauruses and count the number of synonyms and antonyms for each key word. The total number of synonyms and antonyms could then be used to indicate the prominence of the dimension under consideration.

These few speculative examples give a flavor of how unobtrusive measures might be used to measure theoretical cultural dimensions. Some other candidates for unobtrusive measures of cultural dimensions appear in the following list.

Candidates for Unobtrusive Measures

- Intolerance of uncertainty
  - *Mean age of chief executive officers*
  - *Existence and enforcement of rules*
  - *Life insurance penetration controlling for level of disposable income*
  - *Eating practices (advance preparation and announcements)*
  - *Public transportation (adherence to schedule, publication of schedules)*
  - *Work practices (adherence to schedule, existence and enforcement of rules)*

- Power stratification
  - *Distribution of wealth*
  - *Number of job titles*
  - *Centralization of decision making*
  - *Public symbols of leaders*
  - *Eating practices (status-related eating places, who eats with whom)*
  - *Public transportation (reserved places for selected minorities)*
  - *Work practices (number of hierarchical levels, span of control, work space allocation, perquisite allocation, differential attire according to status, use of titles)*
  - *Modes of address reflecting status equality or differences*

- Individualism-collectivism
  - *Left-handedness (reflecting pressure toward conformity)*
  - *Prevalence of extended families*

- *Sports and entertainment practices*
- *Last child predominantly male (except China)*
- *Eating practices (collective food purchasing, communal dishes, and sharing)*
- *Transportation practices (shared versus individualized)*
- *Work practices (job design—team versus individual, allocation of responsibilities, collaborative effort)*
- *Gender-role differentiation*
- *Percentage of females in high positions*
- *Characteristics of national heroes*
- *Characteristics of heroes in myths and stories*
- *Work practices (gender distribution for high- and low-status positions, gender differentiation and discrimination, tolerance of sexual harassment)*
- *Female versus male literacy*

- Humane orientation
  - *Treatment of minorities*
  - *Prison practices*
  - *Treatment of poor*
  - *Quality of food and eating places for the elderly, poor, imprisoned*
  - *Public transportation (affordability or reduced rates for poor, elderly)*
  - *Work practices*

- Future orientation
  - *Research and development expenditures*
  - *Planning practices (short- versus long-term)*
  - *Investment practices*
  - *Tax incentives for investment*
  - *Eating practices (inverse of fat, sugar, alcohol consumption)*
  - *Work practices (planning, preparation, employee development)*

- Performance orientation
  - *New business start-ups per year*
  - *Tax incentives for new businesses*

- *Emphasis on occupational education*
- *Eating practices (inverse of time devoted to meals)*

[Source: House, R. J. (1997, February). Prospectus. The Global Leadership and Organizational Effectiveness Research Program.]

Some Criteria for the Use of Unobtrusive Measures

For unobtrusive measures to be useful they must reflect the construct for which they are considered to be an indicator. Thus it is necessary to validate such measures. Validation can be conducted by asking members of collectivities to interpret the meaning of the candidates for unobtrusive measures. Structured and coded (quantified) interviews and focus groups are appropriate for such investigation. Expert informants can also be asked to sort candidates for unobtrusive measures into theoretical classifications of cultural entities, a procedure known as Q sorting. In the GLOBE study approximately 80 percent consensus on the allocation of twenty-seven such measures was attained with respect to all of the cultural dimensions previously described except uncertainty avoidance. Expert informants agreed on only three indicators of uncertainty avoidance.

Another requirement for the use of unobtrusive measures is availability. Publicly available information is the most easily obtained. Unfortunately some countries do not make public the information necessary to operationalize a given unobtrusive measure.

A third requirement is that researchers must verify that unobtrusive measures reflect the current situation or the recent past. For example, using the number of public symbols that commemorate or recognize leaders as an indicator of power distance is valid only when these symbols reflect current sentiments toward leaders.

Other Sources of Information: Cultural Leaks

A major source of useful information is symbols. Language consists of symbols. Words, phrases, aphorisms, titles, or slogans can be used to gain cultural insights. Difficulties in word or phrase translations are also clues to unique aspects of cultural units. Words unique to a cultural entity say something about that collectivity. Words from one cultural unit that have no equivalent in another cultural unit say something about the differences between the two. Recurring incidents, routines, or commonly practiced activities that present difficulties or surprises to an outsider or that take on a different meaning in different cultural entities convey useful information for interpreting cultural norms and forces. Unique rituals, symbols, myths, and ceremonies also reveal differences. Another source of useful information, is history—history of leaders, history of the economy and political system, history of the industries studied, history of dominant organizations, and history of words, especially words that are unique to the particular society, industry, or organization studied.

Linguistic anthropologist Michael Agar refers to all these sources of information about collectivities as "cultural leaks." The meanings embedded in a cultural entity leak through in the form of unobtrusive measures, critical incidents, difficulties of translation, symbols, and history, making that entity understandable.

Conclusion

Cultural differences in societies and in organizations are asserted to account for significant amounts of variance in individuals' expectations and assumptions about their environment, attitudes toward others, modes of social interaction, expressions of emotions and global behavior patterns, and reactions to others. We refer to this assertion as the *cultural pervasiveness* proposition. It is this bedrock assumption on which the enterprise of cross-cultural research and theory building rests. In this chapter, we reviewed the evidence relevant to this proposition, with specific reference to individuals in positions of leadership and individuals who exert or try to exert leadership.

As we have shown, the evidence in support of this proposition is rather massive, even though the existing research to identify the variables and dimensions of cultures is far from complete and many unresolved issues remain. To start with, the construct of culture has eluded precise definition. Further, it is even arguable whether the construct known as culture is viable for the study of large complex social-economic-political collectivities consisting of multiple ethnic or religious subgroups with different histories, ethnic backgrounds, and languages. The processes by which cultural forces influence the members of collectivities, the appropriate ways of measuring cultural phenomena, the scope and domain of cultural effects, and the moderating influence of such external variables as international competition, military aggression, political pressures, and technological forces remain to be explicated theoretically and investigated empirically.

Our first conclusion with respect to the effects of cultural influences on leadership is that the magnitude of cultural influences varies by kind of leader behavior under consideration. As shown earlier, there are some classes of leader behaviors that are differentially influenced by cultural forces and some that are rather universal with respect to the frequency of their enactment (Smith, Misumi, Tayeb, Paterson, & Bond, 1989) and their effectiveness (Dorfman, Howell, Hibino, Lee, Tate, & Bautista, 1997). Additional research is needed to determine which leader behaviors are etic, which are emic, and how etic behaviors are manifested emically.

In this chapter we have suggested a theoretical framework to guide cross-cultural leadership theory and investigation. We have advanced a set of competing hypotheses and believe that tests of these hypotheses will shed light on many currently unresolved issues. We have also argued for a particular methodological approach for future empirical investigation—triangulation through multiple measures of cultural phenomena.

We are interested in both etic and emic phenomena. With respect to etic phenomena we seek to identify falsifiable nomothetic (law-like) statements on which theories of cross-cultural phenomena can be built. Nomothetic research is directed toward the discovery of behavioral regularities, global behavior patterns, and law-like relationships among important variables. We believe this approach will help explain and predict such phenomena and be useful in resolving many of the issues we have specified here.

We recognize the difficulties in establishing functional equivalences among meanings of words, symbols, and cultural artifacts. However, we chose to view these difficulties as challenges rather than insurmountable obstacles, believing that the recently developed statistical modeling methods we have discussed make it possible to assess degrees of convergence of meaning.

We recognize that not everything is subject to quantification and that there are other ways of knowing—poetry, ascetic appreciation, wisdom, experience, intuition, and empathy, for example. However, we choose the nomothetic approach because we believe it is a scientifically defensible way of understanding cross-cultural phenomena. We also believe that case studies, ethnographic research, and other qualitative research approaches can provide useful insights, enhance understanding of specific cultural entities, and generate theoretical hypotheses and prescriptive assertions to be tested qualitatively. And we have proposed both emic- and etic-directed research to further understanding of cultural differences. This issue is currently being investigated as part of the GLOBE research program. Finally, we believe that if cultural entities are understood, explained, and described in terms of both etic and emic variables it will be possible for researchers and practitioners to assist individuals in adjusting to cultural units other than their own and it will also be possible to make useful prescriptive contributions to the improvement of the quality of the human condition.

Note

1. The Global Leadership and Organizational Behavior Effectiveness Program (GLOBE) is a cross-cultural research program involving 154 investigators in research teams in sixty nations from all major geographical regions of the world. Although the present chapter is not a product of GLOBE, some of its contents will appear in subsequent GLOBE publications.

    Robert J. House, University of Pennsylvania, is the principal investigator of GLOBE. Paul Hanges, University of Maryland, and Antonio-Ruiz Quintanilla, Cornell University, are co-principal investigators. The GLOBE coordinating team consists of House, Hanges, Quintanilla, and the following members:

    Ram Aditya, Temple University, Philadelphia
    Staffan Akerblom, School of Economics, Stockholm, Sweden
    Joydeep Bhattacharya, New School for Social Research, New York
    Felix Brodbeck, University of Munich
    Jagdeep Chhoker, Indian Institute of Management, Ahmedabad, India
    Marcus W. Dickson, University of Maryland
    Peter W. Dorfman, New Mexico State University
    Mansour Javidan, University of Calgary
    Enrique Ogliastri, University of Los Andes, Columbia
    Marius van Wyk, University of South Africa

References

Aditya, R. N. (1994). Managing the multinational sales force: Cross-cultural exchange in the dyad. *Proceedings of the American Marketing Association Summer Educators' Conference.* American Marketing Association.

Adler, N. J. (1986). Cross-cultural management research: The ostrich and the trend. *Academy of Management Review, 8,* 226–232.

Adler, N. J., Campbell, N., & Laurent, A. (1989). In search of appropriate methodology: From outside the People's Republic of China looking in. *Journal of International Business Studies, 20*(1), 61–74.

Ajzen, L., & Fishbein, M. (1970). *Understanding attitudes and predicting social behavior.* Upper Saddle River, NJ: Prentice Hall.

Al-Hajjeh, A.-A. (1984). Managerial leadership and work-related values of American and Middle Eastern nationals: A cross-cultural study (Doctoral dissertation, United States International University). *Dissertation Abstracts International, 45,* 6A.

Alpander, G. G. (1973). Drift to authoritarianism: The changing managerial styles of the US. Executives Overseas, 1–14.

Amsden, A. H. (1989). *Asia's next giant: South Korea and late industrialization.* New York: Oxford University Press.

Anzizu, J. M., & Nuenos, P. (1984). *Leadership under sociopolitical change: Business enterprise in Spain.* Paper presented at the 75th Anniversary Colloquium, Harvard Business School, Boston.

Bass, B. M. (1990). *Bass and Stogdill's handbook of leadership: Theory, research and managerial applications* (3rd ed.). New York: Free Press.

Bass, B. M. (1997). Does the transactional-transformational paradigm transcend organizational and national boundaries? *American Psychologist, 52*(2), 130–139.

Bass, B. M., & Avolio, B. J. (1993). *Transformational leadership: A response to critiques.* In M. M. Chemers and R. Ayman (Eds.), *Leadership theory and research: Perspectives and directions.* Orlando: Academic Press.

Bass, B. M., Burger, P. C., Doktor, R., & Barrett, G. V. (1979). *Assessment of managers: An international comparison.* New York: Free Press.

Beatty, J. R., McCune, J. T., & Beatty, R. W. (1988). A policy capturing approach to the study of United States and Japanese managers' compensation decisions. *Journal of Management, 14,* 465–474.

Beechler, S., & Yang, J. Z. (1994). The transfer of Japanese-style management to American subsidiaries: Contingencies, constraints, and competencies. *Journal of International Business Studies, 25,* 467–491.

Bigoness, W. J., & Blakely, G. L. (1989). *A cross-national study of managerial values.* Paper presented at the meeting of the Academy of Management, Washington, DC.

Blake, R. R., & Mouton, J. S. (1970). The fifth achievement. *Journal of Applied Behavioral Science, 6*(4), 413–426.

Bolon, D. S., & Crain, C. R. (1985). Decision sequence: A recurring theme in comparing American and Japanese management. *Academy of Management Proceedings*, pp. 88–92.

Bond, M. H., & Leung, K. (1993). The relationship between culture, individual valences and behavioral intentions. *Journal of Cross-Cultural Psychology, 24,* 331–338.

Boyd, D. P. (1974). Research note: The educational background of a selected group of England's leaders. *Sociology, 8,* 305–312.

Brislin, R. W. (1970). Back-translation for cross-cultural research. *Journal of Cross-Cultural Psychology, 1*(3), 185–216.

Brislin, R. W., Lonner, W. J., & Thorndike, R. M. (1973). *Cross-cultural research methods.* New York: Wiley.

Castaldi, R. M., & Sorrentino, T. (1988). *Post-Confucianism management practices and behaviors: A comparison of Japan versus China and South Korea.* Paper presented at the meeting of the Western Academy of Management, Big Sky, MT.

Chandy, P. R., & Williams, T.G.E. (1994). The impact of journals and authors on international business research. *Journal of International Business Studies, 25,* 713–728.

Chinese Culture Connection. (1987). Chinese values and the search for culture-free dimensions of culture. *Journal of Cross-Cultural Psychology, 18,* 143–164.

Chowdhry, K., & Tarneja, R. (1961). India. In W. S. Wikstrom (Ed.), *Developing better managers: An eight-nation study.* New York: National Industrial Conference Board.

Craig, C. S., Douglas, S. P., & Grein, A. (1992). Patterns of convergence and divergence among industrialized nations: 1960–1988. *Journal of International Business Studies, 23,* 773–787.

Davis, H. J., Ming, L. W., & Brosnan, T. F. (1986). *The Farmer-Richman model: A bibliographic essay emphasizing applicability to Singapore and Indonesia.* Paper presented at the meeting of the Academy of Management, Chicago.

Deutscher, I. (1973). Asking questions cross-culturally: Some problems in linguistic comparability. In D. P. Warwick & S. Osherson (Eds.), *Comparative research methods* (pp. 163–186). Upper Saddle River, NJ: Prentice Hall.

Deyo, F. C. (1978). The cultural patterning of organizational development: A comparative case study of Thailand and Chinese industrial enterprises. *Human Organization, 37,* 68–72.

Donaldson, L. (1993). *Anti-management theories of organization: A critique of paradigm proliferation.* New York: Cambridge University Press.

Dorfman, P. W. (1996). International and cross-cultural leadership. In J. Punnitt & O. Shenkar (Eds.), *Handbook for international management research* (pp. 267–349). Cambridge, MA: Blackwell.

Dorfman, P. W., & Howell, J. P. (1988). Dimensions of national culture and effective leadership patterns. *Advances in International Comparative Management, 3,* 127–150.

Dorfman, P. W., Howell, J. P., Hibino, S., Lee, J. K., Tate, U., & Bautista, A. (1997). Leadership in Western and Asian countries: Commonalities and differences in effective leadership processes across cultures. *Leadership Quarterly.*

Earley, P. C. (1984). Social interaction: The frequency and use of valuation in the United States, England & Ghana. *Journal of Cross-Cultural Psychology, 15,* 477–485.

Earley, P. C. (1989). Social loafing and collectivism: A comparison of the United States and the People's Republic of China. *Administrative Science Quarterly, 34*(4), 565–581.

England, G. W., & Itzhak, H. (1983). Some methodological and analytical considerations in cross-national comparative research. *Journal of International Business Studies, 14,* 49–59.

Farmer, R. N., & Richman, B. M. (1965). *Comparative management and economic progress.* Homewood, IL: Irwin.

Franke, R. H., Hofstede, G., & Bond, M. H. (1991). Cultural roots of economic performance: A research note. *Strategic Management Journal, 12,* 165–173.

Fukuda, J. K. (1983). Japanese and Chinese management practices: Uncovering the differences. *Mid-Atlantic Journal of Business, 21,* 35–44.

Gallino, J. (1975). Three types of Italian top managers. *International Studies of Management & Organization, 5,* 43–70.

Gebert, D., & Steinkamp, T. (1991). Leadership style and economic success in Nigeria and Taiwan. *Management International Review, 31*(2), 161–171.

Geertz, C. (1973). *The interpretation of cultures.* New York: Basic Books.

Gerstner, C. R., & Day, D. V. (1994). Cross-cultural comparison of leadership prototypes. *Leadership Quarterly, 5*(2), 121–134.

Grannick, D. (1960). *The red executive.* New York: Doubleday.

Green, R. T., & White, P. D. (1976). Methodological considerations in cross-national consumer research. *Journal of International Business Studies, 7,* 81–88.

Haire, M., Ghiselli, E. E., & Porter, L. W. (1966). *Managerial thinking: An international study.* New York: Wiley.

Hall, E. T., & Hall, M. R. (1987). *Hidden differences: Doing business with the Japanese.* New York: Doubleday.

Harbron, J. D. (1965). The dilemma of an elite group: The industrialist in Latin America. *Inter-American Economic Affairs, 19,* 43–62.

Heller, T. (1958). Changing authority patterns: A cultural perspective. *Academy of Management Review, 10,* 488–495.

Herskovits, M. J. (1955). *Cultural anthropology.* New York: Knopf.

Hofstede, G. (1980). *Culture's consequences: International differences in work-related values.* Thousand Oaks, CA: Sage.

Hofstede, G., & Bond, M. H. (1984). Hofstede's culture dimensions: An independent validation using Rokeach's Value Survey. *Journal of Cross-Cultural Psychology, 15,* 417–433.

Hofstede, G., & Bond, M. H. (1988). The Confucian connection: From cultural roots to economic growth. *Organizational Dynamics, 16,* 4–21.

Hofstede, G., Bond, M. H., & Luk, C. L. (1993). Individual perceptions of organizational cultures: A methodological treatise on levels of analysis. *Organization Studies, 14,* 483–503.

Hofstede, G., Neuijen, B., Ohayv, D. D., & Sanders, G. (1990). Measuring organizational cultures: A qualitative and quantitative study across twenty cases. *Administrative Science Quarterly, 35,* 286–316.

Hornstein, H. (1986). Managerial courage: Revitalizing your company without sacrificing your job. New York: Wiley.

House, R. J., Delbecq, A., & Taris, T. W. (1996). *Value based leadership: An integrated theory and an empirical test* (Working paper). Philadelphia: Reginald Jones Center for Strategic Management, Wharton School, University of Pennsylvania.

House, R. J., Schuler, R. S., & Levanoni, E. (1983). Role conflict and ambiguity scales: Reality or artifacts? *Journal of Applied Psychology, 68*(2), 334–337.

House, R. J., Spangler, D., & Woycke, J. (1991). Charismatic leadership in the US presidency. *Administrative Science Quarterly, 36,* 364–396.

Howell, J. M., & Frost, P. J. (1989). A laboratory study of charismatic leadership. *Organizational Behavior and Human Decision Processes, 43*(2), 243–269.

Huo, Y. P., & Randall, D. M. (1991). Exploring subcultural differences in Hofstede's survey: The case of the Chinese. *Asia Pacific Journal of Management, 8,* 159–173.

Inkeles, A. (1966). The modernization of man. In M. Weiner (Ed.), *Modernization.* New York: Basic Books.

Ivancevich, J. M., Schweiger, D. M., & Ragan, J. W. (1986). *Employee stress, health, and attitudes: A comparison of American, Indian & Japanese managers.* Chicago: Academy of Management.

Jaeger, A. M. (1986). Organization development and national culture: Where's the fit? *Academy of Management Review, 11*(1), 178–190.

Kelly, L., & Worthley, R. (1981). The role of culture in comparative management: A cross-cultural perspective. *Academy of Management Journal, 24,* 164–173.

Kennis, I. (1977). A cross-cultural study of personality and leadership. *Group and Organization Studies, 2,* 49–60.

Kluckhohn, C. (1951). Culture and behavior. *Handbook of Social Psychology,* pp. 921–976.

Kluckhohn, F. R., & Strodtbeck, F. L. (1961). *Variations in value orientations.* New York: HarperCollins.

Koene, H., Pennings, H., & Schreuder, M. (1991). Leadership, culture, and organizational effectiveness. In K. E. Clark, M. E. Clark, & D. P. Campbell (Eds.), *The impact of leadership.* Greensboro, NC: Center for Creative Leadership.

Kogut, B., & Singh, H. (1988). The effects of national culture on the choice of entry mode. *Journal of International Business Studies, 19,* 411–432.

Koh, W. L., Terborg, J. R., & Steers, R. M. (1991, August). *The impact of transformational leaders on organizational commitment, organizational citizenship behavior, teacher satisfaction and student performance in Singapore.* Paper presented at the meeting of the Academy of Management, Miami.

Lee, C., & Green, R. T. (1990). Cross-cultural examination of the Fishbein behavioral intentions model. *Journal of International Business Studies, 91*(2), 289–305.

Lee, S. M., & Schwendiman, G. (1982). *Japanese management: Cultural and environmental considerations.* New York: Praeger.

Leung, K. (1983). *The impact of cultural collectivism on reward allocation.* Unpublished master's thesis. University of Illinois, Urbana.

Leung, K., & Bond, M. H. (1989). On the empirical identification of dimensions for cross-cultural comparisons. *Journal of Cross-Cultural Psychology, 20,* 133–151.

Lincoln, J. R., & Zeitz, G. (1980). Organizational properties from aggregate data: Separating individual and structural effects. *American Sociological Review, 45,* 391–408.

Lindsay, C. P., & Dempsey, B. L. (1985). Experiences in training Chinese business people to use U.S. management techniques. *Journal of Applied Behavioral Science, 21,* 65–78.

Lord, R. G., & Maher, K. J. (1991). *Leadership and information processing: Linking perceptions and performance.* London: Unwin Hyman.

Maznevski, M. L., & DiStefano, J. J. (1995). *Measuring culture in international management: The Cultural Perspectives Questionnaire* (Working paper No. 95–39). London, Canada: Western Business School, University of Western Ontario.

McClelland, D. C. (1961). *The achieving society.* New York: Van Nostrand Reinhold.

McClelland, D. C. (1976). *The achieving society* (with a new introduction). New York: Van Nostrand Reinhold.

McClelland, D. C. (1985). *Human motivation.* Glenview, IL: Scott, Foresman.

McClelland, D. C., Atkinson, J. W., Clark, R. A., & Lowell, E. L. (Eds.). (1953). *The achievement motive.* Englewood Cliffs, NJ: Appleton-Century-Crofts.

McClelland, D. C., & Boyatzis, R. E. (1982). Leadership motive pattern and long-term success in management. *Journal of Applied Psychology, 67,* 737–743.

McClelland, D. C., & Burnham, D. (1976, March-April). Power is the great motivator. *Harvard Business Review,* pp. 100–110, 159–166.

McClelland, D. C., & Clark, R. A. (1953). Antecedent conditions for affective arousal. In D. C. McClelland, J. W. Atkinson, R. A. Clark, & E. L. Lowell (Eds.), *The achievement motive.* Englewood Cliffs, NJ: Appleton-Century-Crofts.

McClelland, D. C., Koestner, R., & Weinberger, J. (1989). How do self-attributed and implicit motives differ? *Psychological Review, 96*(4), 690–702.

Messalum, A., & House, R. J. (1996). *Effects of Egyptian CEO leader behavior: A test of the value based theory of leadership* (Working paper). Philadelphia: Global Leadership and Organizational Behavior Effectiveness [GLOBE], Department of Management, Wharton School, University of Pennsylvania.

Miller, G., & Friesen, P. H. (1984). *Organization: A quantum view.* Upper Saddle River, NJ: Prentice Hall.

Mintzberg, H. (1979). *The structuring of organizations.* Upper Saddle River, NJ: Prentice Hall.

Miskin, V. D., & Gmelch, W. H. (1985). Quality leadership for quality teams. *Training & Development Journal, 39*(5), 122–129.

Misumi, J. (1974). *Action research on the development of leadership, decision-making processes and organizational performance in a Japanese shipyard.* Paper presented at the meeting of the International Congress of Applied Psychology, Liège.

Misumi, J. (1985). *The behavioral science of leadership: An interdisciplinary Japanese research program.* Ann Arbor: University of Michigan Press.

Mitchell, R. E. (1973). Survey materials collected in the developing countries: Sampling, measurements, and interviewing obstacles to intra- and international comparisons. In D. P. Warwick & S. Osherson (Eds.), *Comparative research methods* (pp. 204–226). Upper Saddle River, NJ: Prentice Hall.

Morris, M. H., Davis, D. L., & Allen, J. W. (1994). Fostering corporate entrepreneurship: Cross-cultural comparison of the importance of individualism versus collectivism. *Journal of International Business Studies, 25,* 65–89.

Nasif, E. G., Al-Daeaj, H., Ebrahimi, B., & Thibodeaux, M. S. (1991). Methodological problems in cross-cultural research: An updated review. *Management International Review, 31,* 79–91.

Nath, R. (1969). A methodological review of cross-cultural management research. In J. Boddewyn (Ed.), *Comparative management and marketing.* Glenview, IL: Scott, Foresman.

Ng, S. H., Akhtar-Hossain, A.B.M., Ball, P., Bond, M. H., Hayashi, K., Lim, S. P., O'Driscoll, M. P., Sinha, D., & Yang, K. S. (1982). Values in nine countries. In R. Rath, J.B.H. Sinha, & H. S. Asthana (Eds.), *Diversity and unity in cross-cultural psychology* (pp. 196–205). Lisse, Netherlands: Swets & Zeitlinger.

Ouchi, W. (1981). *Theory Z: How American business can meet the Japanese challenge.* Reading, MA: Addison-Wesley.

Pareek, U. (1976). Interrole exploration. In J. W. Pfeiffer & J. E. Jones (Eds.), *The 1996 annual handbook for group facilitators* (pp. 211–224). La Jolla, CA: University Associates.

Pascale, R. T., & Athos, A. G. (1981). *The art of Japanese management.* New York: Simon & Schuster.

Pelletier, G. (1966). Business management in French Canada. *Business Quarterly–Canada Management Journal,* pp. 56–62.

Peng, T. K., Peterson, M. F., & Shyi, Y. P. (1991). Quantitative methods in cross-cultural management research: Trends and equivalence issues. *Journal of Organizational Behavior, 12,* 87–108.

Pereira, D. (1987). *Factors associated with transformational leadership in an Indian engineering firm.* Paper presented at the annual meeting of the Administrative Science Association of Canada, Vancouver.

Peterson, M. F., Smith, P. B., Akande, A., Ayestaran, S., Bochner, S., Callan, V., Cho, N. G., Jesuino, J. C., D'Amorim, M., Francois, P.-H., Hofmann, K., Koopman, P. L., Leung, K., Lim, T. K., Mortazavi, S., Munene, J., Radford, M., Ropo, A., Savage, G., Setiadi, B., Sinha, T. N., Sorenson, R., Viedge, C. (1995). Role conflict, ambiguity and overload: A 21 nation study. *Academy of Management Journal, 38,* 429–452.

Rahim, M. A., Kim, N. H., & Kim, J. S. (1994). Bases of leader power, subordinate compliance, and satisfaction with supervision: A cross-cultural study of managers in the US and S. Korea. *International Journal of Organizational Analysis, 2*(2), 136–154.

Rahim, M. A., & Magner, N. R. (1995). Confirmatory factor analysis of the styles of handling interpersonal conflict: First-order factor model and its invariance across groups. *Journal of Applied Psychology, 80*(1), 122–132.

Ralston, D. A., Gustafson, D. J., Elsass, P. M., Cheung, F., & Terpstra, R. H. (1992). Eastern values: A comparison of managers in the United States, Hong Kong, and the People's Republic of China. *Journal of Applied Psychology, 77*(5), 664–671.

Roberts, K. H., & Boyacigiller, N. A. (1984). Cross-national organizational research: The grasp of the blind men. In B. M. Shaw & L. L. Cummings (Eds.), *Research in organizational behavior* (Vol. 6, pp. 423–475). Greenwich, CT: JAI Press.

Robinson, R. V. (1983). Review of *Culture's Consequences:* International differences in work-related values. *Work and Occupations, 10,* 110–115.

Ronen, S. (1986). *Comparative and multinational management.* New York: Wiley.

Ronen, S., & Shenkar, O. (1985). Clustering countries on attitudinal dimensions: A review and synthesis. *Academy of Management Review, 10*(3), 435–454.

Ryterbrand, E. C., & Thiagarajan, K. M. (1968). *Managerial attitudes toward salaries as a function of social and economic development* (Technical report No. 24). Rochester, NY: University of Rochester, Management Research Centre.

Samovar, L. A., & Porter, R. E. (1976). *Intercultural communication: A reader* (2nd ed.). Belmont, CA: Wadsworth.

Schein, E. H. (1985). *Organizational culture and leadership: A dynamic view.* San Francisco: Jossey-Bass.

Schmidt, S. M., & Yeh, R.-S. (1992). The structure of leader influence: A cross-national comparison. *Journal of Cross-Cultural Psychology, 23*(2), 251–264.

Senner, E. E. (1971). *Trust as a measure of the impact of cultural differences on individual behavior in organizations.* Paper presented at the annual meeting of the American Psychological Association, Washington, DC.

Shackleton, V.-J., & Ali, A.-H. (1990, March). Work-related values of managers: A test of the Hofstede model. *Journal of Cross-Cultural Psychology, 21*(1), 109–118.

Shenkar, O., & Ronen, S. (1987). Structure and importance of work goals among managers in the People's Republic of China. *Academy of Management Journal, 30*(3), 564–576.

Simonton, D. K. (1994). *Greatness: Who makes history and why.* New York: Guilford Press.

Smith, P. B. (1984). The effectiveness of Japanese styles of management: A review and critique. *Journal of Occupational Psychology, 57,* 121–136.

Smith, P. B., Dugan, S., & Trompenaars, F. (1996). National culture and the values of organizational employees: A 43 nation study. *Journal of Cross-Cultural Psychology, 27,* 231–264.

Smith, P. B., Misumi, J., Tayeb, M. H., Paterson, M., & Bond, M. H. (1989). On the generality of leadership styles across cultures. *Journal of Occupational Psychology, 62,* 97–110.

Smith, P. B., & Peterson, M. F. (1994). *Leadership as event management: A cross-cultural survey based on managers from 25 nations.* Paper presented at the meeting of the International Congress of Psychology, Madrid.

Smith, P. B., Peterson, M. F., & Misumi, J. (1994). Event management and work team effectiveness in Japan, Britain and U.S.A. *Journal of Occupational and Organizational Psychology, 67*(4), 33–43.

Smith, P. B., Peterson, M. F., Misumi, J., & Bond, M. H. (1992). A cross-cultural test of the Japanese P-M leadership theory. *Applied Psychology: An International Review, 41,* 5–19.

Smith, P. B., Peterson, M. F., Akande, D., Callan, V., Cho, N. G., Jesuino, J., D'Amorim, M. A., Koopman, P. L., Leung, K., Mortazavi, S., Munene, J., Radford, M., Ropo, A., Savage, G., Viedge, C. (1994). Organizational event management in 14 countries: A comparison with Hofstede's dimensions. In A.-M. Bouvy, F.J.R. Van de Vijver, P. Schmitz, & P. Boski (Eds.), *Journeys in cross-cultural psychology* (pp. 372–381). Lisse, Netherlands: Swets & Zeitlinger.

Spangler, W. D. (1992). The validity of questionnaire and TAT measures of need for achievement: Two meta analyses. *Psychological Bulletin, 112,* 140–154.

Stening, B. W., & Wong, P. S. (1983). Australian managers' leadership beliefs. *Psychological Reports, 53,* 274–278.

Terpstra, V., & David, K. (1991). *The cultural environment of international business* (3rd ed.). Cincinnati: South-Western.

Terry, P. T. (1979). The English in management. *Management Today, 1*(11), 90–97.

Triandis, H. C., with Vassiliou, V., Vassiliou, G., Tonaka, Y., & Shanmugam, A. V. (Eds.). (1972). *The analysis of subjective culture.* New York: Wiley-Interscience.

Triandis, H. C. (1982). Review of *Culture's Consequences:* International differences in work-related values. *Human Organization, 41,* 86–90.

Triandis, H. C. (1994). *Culture and social behavior.* New York: McGraw-Hill.

Triandis, H. C. (1995). *Individualism and collectivism.* Boulder, CO: Westview Press.

Trompenaars, F. (1985). *The organization of meaning and the meaning of organization: A comparative study on the conceptions of organizational structure in different cultures.* Unpublished doctoral dissertation, University of Pennsylvania.

Ueno, S., & Sekaran, U. (1992). The influence of culture on budget control practices in the USA and Japan: An empirical study. *Journal of International Business Studies, 23*(4), 659–674.

Ulin, R. D. (1976). African leadership: National goals and the values of Botswana University students. *Comparative Education, 12,* 145–155.

Wade, R. (1990). *Governing the market: The role of government in East Asian industrialization.* Princeton, NJ: Princeton University Press.

Webb, E. J., Campbell, D. T., Schwartz, R. D., & Sechrest, L. (1996). *Unobtrusive measures.* Skokie, IL: Rand McNally.

Weber, M. (1947). *The theory of social and economic organization* (A. M. Henderson & T. Parsons, Trans., T. Parsons, Ed.). New York: Free Press. (Original work published 1924)

Weiss, J. W., & Bloom, S. (1990). Managing in China: Expatriate experiences and training. *Business Horizons, 33,* 23–29.

Winter, D. G. (1978). *Navy leadership and management competencies: Convergence among tests, interviews, & performance ratings.* Boston: McBer.

Winter, D. G. (1991). A motivational model of leadership: Predicting long-term management success from TAT measures of power, motivation, & responsibility. *Leadership Quarterly, 2,* 67–86.

Yeh, R., & Lawrence, J. J. (1995). Individualism and Confucian dynamism: Note on Hofstede's cultural root to economic growth. *Journal of International Business Studies, 26*(3), 655–668.

Yukl, G. (1994a). *Leadership in organizations* (3rd ed.). Upper Saddle River, NJ: Prentice Hall.

Yukl, G. (1994b). A retrospective on Robert House's 1976 theory of charismatic leadership and recent revisions. *Leadership Quarterly, 4*(3–4), 367–373.

Zarzeski, M. T. (1996). Spontaneous harmonization effects of culture and market forces on accounting disclosure practices. *Journal of International Studies, 10*(1), 9–17.

Zurcher, L. A. (1968). Particularism and organizational position: A cross-cultural analysis. *Journal of Applied Psychology, 52,* 139–144.

Zurcher, L. A., Meadow, A., & Zurcher, S. L. (1965). Value orientation, role conflict & alienation from work: A cross cultural study. *American Sociological Review, 30,* 539–538.

CHAPTER 21

Cross-Cultural Leadership
A Path to the Goal?
Peter B. Smith

The preceding chapter on cross-cultural leadership research seeks to investigate etic aspects of the leadership process. It provides early indications of the structure of the GLOBE project, one of the most ambitious cross-cultural projects yet essayed in this field. The goal of escaping culture-bound formulations of leadership is one with which I have much sympathy, and I like the way that House, Wright, and Aditya read the priorities in setting their sights upon that goal. In essence, they see the need to stand back before they present their own model and to reexamine the usefulness of existing conceptualizations of the cultural and organizational contexts within which leadership occurs.

Positivism or Relativism?

There is much to applaud within this chapter and too many interesting and provocative ideas for me to have space to discuss them all. I choose to focus first upon a modestly positivist theme that surfaces periodically through the chapter. House, Wright, and Aditya acknowledge that specific behaviors can have different meanings or serve different functions within differing cultural entities, noting in particular the theoretical position of Misumi (1985). Nonetheless, as their "near universality of leader behaviors" propo-

---

Note: I am grateful to Michael Bond, Peter Dorfman, and Mark Peterson for comments upon an earlier draft of this chapter.

sition states, they read the existing literature as converging strongly upon certain leader behaviors as generally accepted and effective. In support of this view they cite a range of studies conducted in many nations and using measures of charismatic leadership, plus two research programs indicating that managers prefer to use less authority (Bass, Burger, Doktor, & Barrett, 1979) and feel that events are better handled when they rely more on their own experience and training (Peterson & Smith, 1996). I have no difficulty in accepting that these studies did come up with findings that showed a good deal of generality across national samples. My question is how do we interpret the meaning of these generalities? House, Wright, and Aditya illustrate the dilemma with reference on the one hand to Dutch interviewees who stated that they would not respond well to charismatic leadership and on the other hand to Dutch supermarket employees who did respond well to leaders whom they had described on questionnaires in ways the researchers deemed to be charismatic. The positivist (or as cross-cultural researchers would call it, imposed etic) position would conclude that charismatic leadership is after all effective in the Netherlands. The skeptical position would argue that there is indeed something in common between the questionnaire ratings and the leader effectiveness ratings but that there is room for a good deal of doubt whether that something should be called charisma. In studies using same-source ratings to measure leader style and leader effectiveness, some type of halo effect is a prime candidate as an explanation, although it is not clear whether this was the case in the supermarket study by Koene, Pennings, and Schreuder (1991).

So is a global definition of charisma possible? There does exist a substantial empirical literature (Bass & Avolio, 1993) suggesting that charismatic leadership is valued in many countries around the world. Furthermore it has been persuasively argued that charismatic leadership is particularly required in developing countries characterized by high power distance and collectivist values (Jaeger & Kanungo, 1990; Sinha, 1995). However, the Bass questionnaire is U.S.–designed and has been used in other countries in an imposed etic manner, with few checks made on the meanings imputed to it in other cultures. Dorfman (1996) notes that the factor structures it yields in Singapore, the Netherlands, and the Dominican Republic are quite different from those obtained with U.S.

samples. Charisma may be best thought of as a quality that is global but imputed to leaders on the basis of behaviors that are culture-specific.

To put the issue in a more general way, how can we be sure of cross-cultural generalities about leader behaviors before we have conducted in-depth studies of the local, or emic, meanings given to leader behaviors? The distinction between etic and emic studies has been drawn in a variety of ways, many of which conjure up a polarization between what is found to be universally true and what is found to be only locally true. However, what is universally true must by definition also be locally true. As Berry (1989) puts it, a derived etic can be constructed only out of a parallel series of emic studies. Studies that neglect local variations in the understanding of concepts or measures are likely to generate results better thought of as imposed etic. That is to say, if we assume that measures devised in one part of the world are clearly understood in all other parts of the world, we may be able to identify some global uniformities of response, but we will have few ways of estimating how much understanding of the process under study has been lost through measure invalidity. If we identify a globally consistent aspect of leadership that accounts for only a small fraction of the ways in which leadership is expressed in different cultures, then our imposed etic measure will have little value.

So how does this line of reasoning relate to the propositions advanced by House, Wright, and Aditya? Their leadership model is cast in terms of leader behaviors, and my question is, therefore, do we have sufficient evidence as to the ways in which leader behaviors are interpreted in different cultures for *behavior* to be the central concept in analyzing leadership processes? House, Wright, and Aditya themselves acknowledge that charismatic behaviors may vary by culture.

One might argue that even when the meanings of a given leader behavior vary a bit from culture to culture, the meaning held in common should allow us to consider those variations as some type of error variance that does not affect that indisputable central core of meaning. Giving an order is giving an order, isn't it? I was recently consulted by a British multinational with extensive subsidiaries within the United States. British management had asked these subsidiaries to "take a look" at their appraisal system.

The U.S. plant managers did indeed take a brief look but saw no reason to change anything. The British managers were dismayed because what they perceived as an order for a global overhaul of the appraisal system had been ignored by the U.S. managers. But in fact the British managers' low-key expression of that order had failed to communicate effectively to the U.S. managers. Although this example concerns a failure of leadership across cultures whereas House, Wright, and Aditya are primarily concerned with leadership processes within cultures, it underlines the point that even behaviors as central to most definitions of leadership as the giving of instructions do not necessarily carry the same nuances of meaning in different cultures.

The emphasis of House, Wright, and Aditya upon behavior as a central component of leadership is consistent with the approach of most North American leadership theory of the past half century. Note, however, that the definition of leadership that arose from the meeting of GLOBE project contributors refers to influencing, motivating and enabling rather than to behavior. Plainly, the process of influencing, motivating, and enabling will involve a range of different leader behaviors, but the question to address here concerns whether there is any preferable way of treating behavior if it is to remain the core concept in the analysis of leadership. Because we are seeking an account of leadership that has cross-cultural validity, it is prudent first to examine leadership theories that have been advanced in non-Western countries.

Leadership Functions

The most extensive program of non-Western leadership research is that conducted over the past forty years by Misumi (1985) in Japan. Misumi's model of leadership superficially resembles traditional U.S. conceptualizations of leader styles, such as the Ohio State studies, but a closer reading indicates some fundamental divergences. Misumi proposes that leaders in all settings must adequately provide two leadership functions: performance (P) and maintenance (M). The P function refers to the task requirements that have led to the existence of the group being studied, and the M function refers to the maintenance of satisfactory relationships among work team members. Where Misumi parts company with

Western theorists is in his emphasis that the leader functions are general functions and that these functions will be provided by effective leaders through specific behaviors that will vary according to context. Accordingly, he devises new measures of the ways leaders provide P and M functions, not just within each country but within each organization and even within each level of seniority within an organization. Thus the Western emphasis upon psychometrically valid situation-free measures of leader style is replaced by an emphasis on measures that are constantly recontextualized. Misumi's measures refer to leader behaviors but have a high probability of emic validity. The etic aspect of his model lies in his assertion that when these emically valid measures are factor analyzed, they will be found to fall into two clusters representing universal aspects of leadership. It is not wholly clear even within his Japanese data that there are just two leadership functions. Studies rather frequently yield three factors rather than two, dividing the P factor between items referring to pressure and items referring to planning (Misumi & Peterson, 1985). However, for the present purpose this is unimportant. Misumi's contribution lies in his demonstration that the emic-etic dilemma can be handled by distinguishing general leadership functions from specific leadership behaviors.

The fact that Misumi gives greater emphasis to the situational requirements of leaders than do Western theorists, even those who favor contingency theories, probably reflects the greater collectivism of Japanese society. Markus and Kitayama (1991) underline the degree to which the interdependent self-concept of many Japanese may lead them to give priority to adapting their behavior to circumstances rather than to asserting a trans-situational identity. Nonetheless, the concern here is not whether Misumi gives a good account of Japanese leadership but whether thinking of leadership in terms of functions can aid a global conceptualization of the leadership process.

Sinha (1995) is the other non-Western leadership theorist to have conducted a sustained program of research over several decades. His NT, or *nurturant-task,* theory, developed and tested in India, focuses upon the requirement that the leader must both attend to task and nurture subordinates. Sinha uses fixed measures of leader styles, but in other respects his theory has much in common with Misumi's approach. He emphasizes that in the context of Indian expectations of authoritarian leadership, the leader's task is to nurture subordinates' readiness for greater participation. If the leader provides both task-centered leadership and nurtures subordinates, an add-on effect occurs whereby NT leadership becomes more effective than the sum of the N and T styles. Misumi hypothesizes a similar interaction between his P and M functions. Sinha's more recent work lays increasing emphasis upon the way in which the leader's organizational context does not provide opportunities to choose between differing leader styles but forces the selection of a given style. For instance, Indian leaders may rather often find that they have very limited powers in facing an adversarial workforce. Indian organizations differ in numerous respects from Japanese ones; nonetheless leadership theorists from both these non-Western nations give a major role to context as a determinant of what will be good leadership and what will not.

Recontextualizing Western Conceptions

If differing cultural and organizational contexts elicit needs for differing leader behaviors, then, as I asserted earlier, our global understanding of leadership needs to be cast in terms of basic leadership functions rather than specific leader behaviors. Such thinking has by no means been wholly absent from the Western literature on leadership. For instance, Katz and Kahn noted back in 1966 the different requirements of leadership at the senior, middle, and junior levels of an organization. Many of the more recent formulations (for example, Bass, 1985) continue to seek specification of context-free effective leader behaviors, and other theories have continuing support for their focus upon environmental contingencies that may predispose leaders to a given choice between a fixed menu of specific behaviors or styles.

However, some approaches are more amenable than others to interpretation in terms of generalized leadership functions. Consider, for instance, models that focus upon the leader's use of rewards and punishments. Podsakoff, Dorfman, Howell, and Todor (1986) found that U.S. and Mexican workers respond equally positively to contingent rewards, despite marked cultural differences in values. Howell, Dorfman, Hibino, Lee, and Tate (1994) have extended that finding to several further countries. However, the concepts of reward and punishment do not have specified content. Like Misumi's leadership functions they may be fulfilled in different ways in different contexts. There may be a core of specific behaviors that are found rewarding in a wide variety of cultural contexts, but there will be many other behaviors whose reward value is restricted to particular settings. For instance, Jones, Rozelle, and Chang (1990) asked managers in the United States and China to rate sixty possible behaviors in terms of their utility as rewards. "Listens carefully to what you say" was seen as much more rewarding in the United States, whereas "praises you to others but not to you directly" was much more rewarding in China. Other behaviors seen as neutral in China were seen as having reward or punishment value in the United States. Some behaviors, however, were rated similarly in both countries, and it is an open research question whether the similarities or the differences are the more interesting and important in determining leader effectiveness.

Two other recent formulations of the leadership process viewed cross-culturally (Erez & Earley, 1993: Dorfman, 1996) also incorporate an acknowledgment that the meaning and effectiveness of leader behaviors will be culturally contingent. These models see leaders to be effective within a culture to the degree that leaders' actions articulate the values and priorities relevant to the context and address some of the cognitive processes a leader would typically employ in achieving this articulation. These models do not attempt to specify any more general types of leadership functions, and in that respect they reflect recent North American trends toward micro-level information-processing theories.

Cultural Congruence

Having put down one or two markers for my own favored position, I can now consider the other two general propositions advanced by House, Wright, and Aditya. The cultural congruence proposition provides the basis for the model of leadership formulated.at the close of Chapter Twenty. House, Wright, and Aditya describe the cultural congruence proposition as an article of faith among cultural theorists, and indeed I find it hard to envisage a world in which there was not substantial support for it. If leadership processes are defined in terms of their emergence from the common experiences, values, and norms of the members of particular cultural entities, the model becomes, at the general level, tautologous. It lacks only some feedback loops to represent cultural continuities, that is, the ways in which the performances of leaders and their organizations serve to influence and partially to define the experiences and commonalities of cultural entity members.

At a more specific level the model is indeed testable. How strong are the various arrows (in Figure 20.1), relative to one another and within different cultural entities? Research projects as imaginative as the GLOBE project can shed light upon this question if they succeed in mastering the problems of cross-cultural measurement validity. House, Wright, and Aditya discern strong support within the existing literature for at least the broadly stated cultural congruence hypothesis. However, this support is largely focused upon the congruence between national cultures as defined by aggregated values and various aspects of leadership and organizational practices. Studies of values have provided the basis for some of the most substantial advances in cross-cultural psychology during the past decade (Bond & Smith, 1996; Smith & Schwartz, 1997), and it is reassuring that links have been found between predominant value emphases and leadership practices. However, the House, Wright, and Aditya model reminds us of the need also to define the influence of beliefs and norms and of the broader environment.

It is worth pausing at this point to consider why so much attention has been paid by cross-cultural researchers to the study of values rather than the study of beliefs, norms, or organizational practices. The reasons may be partly fortuitous. Hofstede's study (1980) provided an impetus in that direction, and subsequent studies confirmed that despite the numerous reasons we might expect value indices to fail to predict a broad range of behavioral indices, they can in fact do so. However there are more substantive reasons why the focus on values has advantages. Because values can be expressed in more abstract terms than attitudes and behaviors, it is easier to determine whether or not they have equivalent meanings within different cultural entities.

Schwartz's ten-year program of research into cross-cultural variations in values tackles this problem head on. Schwartz (1992) argues that one can begin to compare values across cultures only if one first determines whether values interrelate with one another in the same way *within* each of the cultures to be studied. Having done a series of what are essentially emic studies, one may make valid comparisons of the values whose structure is consistent across cultures (Schwartz, 1994) and subsidiary analyses of values that are more idiosyncratically interpreted (Schwartz & Sagiv, 1995). Schwartz found adequate generality for forty-five of the fifty-six values included in his questionnaire and is now able to test hypotheses concerning their incidence in more than fifty countries. As Dorfman (1996) also concludes, we do not currently have a similar basis upon which to make valid comparisons of leader behaviors. Furthermore, it is not certain that the interrelations of behaviors within a given culture could be studied in the same way that Schwartz studied values. Descriptions of behaviors are much more situated, implicitly or explicitly, than are abstract statements of value. Endorsement of an abstractly stated value (equality, for example) may be compared with endorsement of other abstract values. The interrelated culture-specific meanings of such leader behaviors as participating, consulting, advising, teaching, and monitoring are likely to be much more varied.

A partial solution to this problem is to focus not upon the meanings placed on behaviors by leaders and others but upon the processes by which meanings are assigned. This way of getting at the problem rests upon the *event management* model that Peterson and I advanced (Smith & Peterson, 1988). As House, Wright, and Aditya note, we asked managers how eight relatively routine events in their immediate work environment are most typically handled. For instance, one of the events was the appointment of a new subordinate. Respondents were asked to what extent they handled this event by reliance on their own experience and training and to what extent they also relied on consultation with others including superiors, specialists, colleagues, and subordinates or on more impersonal sources of guidance such as formal rules, informal norms, or beliefs widespread in their country. Analyses of data of this type are now available from thirty-five nations (Peterson & Smith, 1996). Results continue to show that reliance on their own experience and training is most widely used by managers in all nations. However, the proportion of reliance upon each way of handling events varies markedly by nation. These variations are found to correlate significantly with country scores for values derived from the largest-scale existing studies (Hofstede, 1980; Schwartz, 1994; Smith, Dugan, & Trompenaars, 1996). Thus there is some empirically based evidence that day-to-day actions of managers in different nations do covary with the values prevalent in those nations. What cannot be described with confidence are the meanings placed upon those actions by the managers or by others. If the GLOBE project can make progress in this direction, it will be of great value.

Cultural Difference

House, Wright, and Aditya propose that although effective leadership rests primarily upon cultural congruence, there are circumstances under which leaders will be effective because they are different. Here I feel that House, Wright, and Aditya create a confusion between levels of analysis. The examples they cite of leadership through difference are entrepreneurial behaviors of members of ethnic or religious minorities living in what the authors term pluralistic cultures. Such leaders are indeed different from the majority culture of those among whom they live, but their success is most typically dependent on their continuing congruence with ethnically homogeneous organizations that they create. Immigrant ethnic Chinese in South East Asia, Indians in East Africa and elsewhere, and Cubans in Florida have created highly successful organizations whose structures and leadership are congruent with the entrepreneurs' culture of origin. Perhaps the best documented case is that of the overseas Chinese (Redding, 1990; Redding, Norman, & Schlander, 1994), whose spectacular current achievements are rather precisely delimited by the regions of the world in which they have been able to build businesses upon the requisite networks of region-of-origin and family connections.

However, when the level of analysis is changed from the culture to the individual, the idea of leadership through difference is entirely plausible. From Hollander's proposition (1958) of *idiosyncrasy credit* onwards, the idea that leaders are movers rather than simply expressions of the general will has been widely accepted. Western theorists of charisma suggest that leaders produce this movement by creating a shared vision of a desired end-state. In other cultural contexts the formulation may look rather different. For instance, Sinha (1995) provides instances of what he sees as the excessively relationship-oriented culture of many Indian organizations. As noted earlier, he finds evidence that effective leaders are those who nurture their subordinates toward greater emphasis upon the task. This effectiveness is not due to the leader's cultural congruence with the employee but to the leader's encouraging the employee toward a cultural value not strongly held by that employee. The frequency of finding such effects is probably heavily dependent upon the measure of leadership effectiveness that is employed. Subordinate ratings will favor cultural congruence, and other measures will give cultural difference a better chance.

Conclusion

House, Wright, and Aditya's chapter differs from others in this volume in that one of its key components (and the component upon which these comments have largely focused) is a description of a study still in a relatively early stage. The authors' emphasis upon conceptual clarity as a prerequisite for progress in understanding leadership cross-culturally is entirely welcome. The problem is to identify the most appropriate concepts with which to delineate leadership. My reading of the model presented in Chapter Twenty is that it retains behavior as the central leadership concept, albeit within a broad set of contextual variables. In testing this model, crucial choices are required: how should researchers operationalize the measurement of behavior, given likely local variability in assignment of meanings to behaviors? In practice the GLOBE project researchers have designed their behavior measures as a series of ratings concerning fifty-six possibly desirable qualities of an outstanding manager. Respondents are asked, for example, to rate how important it is for a manager to be sincere, ruthless, diplomatic, clear, and so forth. These qualities are derived from a series of dimensions drawn from the existing literature. This type of measure is much closer to existing cross-cultural studies of value differences and much further from traditional studies of leader style than one might expect from the Chapter Twenty discussion.

Treatments of cross-cultural research methods from Brislin, Lonner, and Thorndike (1973) to van de Vijver and Leung (1996) give considerable emphasis to the need to ensure the emic validity of measures used. Only where such validity is ensured can we be confident that conclusions arrived at can be considered derived etic rather than imposed etic. A recent content analysis of papers published in the *Journal of Cross-Cultural Psychology* (Öngel & Smith, 1994) assigned a derived etic coding to only 7 of 721 studies. How will the GLOBE project fare in relation to these criteria? The analysis procedures envisaged include analyzing each national sample separately, thereby permitting procedures analogous to those Schwartz (1992) used in determining whether his values had the same meanings in each culture sampled. Provided that the fifty-six qualities defined for the GLOBE project adequately represent the range of ways in which organizational members in a given cultural entity think about managers, the data should have good emic validity. I look forward to seeing the results.

References

Bass, B. M. (1985). *Leadership and performance beyond expectations.* New York: Free Press.

Bass, B. M., & Avolio, B. J. (1993). Transformational leadership: A response to critiques. In M. M. Chemers and R. Ayman (Eds.), *Leadership theory and research: Perspectives and directions.* Orlando: Academic Press.

Bass, B. M., Burger, P. C., Doktor, R., & Barrett, G. V. (1979). *Assessment of managers: An international comparison.* New York: Free Press.

Berry, J. (1989). Imposed etics-etics-derived etics: The operationalization of a compelling idea. *International Journal of Psychology, 24,* 721–735.

Bond, M. H., & Smith, P. B. (1996). Cross-cultural social and organizational psychology. *Annual Review of Psychology, 47,* 205–235.

Brislin, R., Lonner, W. J., & Thorndike, R. M. (1973). *Cross-cultural research methods.* New York: Wiley.

Dorfman, P. W. (1996). International and cross-cultural leadership. In B. J. Punnett & O. Shenkar (Eds.), *Handbook of international management research.* Oxford, England: Blackwell.

Erez, M., & Earley, P. C. (1993). *Culture, self-identity and work.* New York: Oxford University Press.

Hofstede, G. (1980). *Culture's consequences: International differences in work-related values.* Thousand Oaks, CA: Sage.

Hollander, E. P. (1958). Conformity, status and idiosyncrasy credit. *Psychological Review, 65,* 117–127.

Howell, J. P., Dorfman, P. W., Hibino, S., Lee, J. K., & Tate, U. (1994). *Leadership in Western and Asian countries: Commonalities and differences in effective leadership processes and substitutes across cultures.* Las Cruces: Center for Business Research, New Mexico State University.

Jaeger, A. M., & Kanungo, R. N. (Eds.). (1990). *Management in developing countries.* London: Routledge.

Jones, A. P., Rozelle, R. M., & Chang, W. C. (1990). Perceived punishment and reward values of supervisor actions in a Chinese sample. *Psychological Studies, 35,* 1–10.

Katz, D., & Kahn, R. L. (1966). *The social psychology of organizations.* New York: Wiley.

Koene, H., Pennings, H., & Schreuder, M. (1991). Leadership, culture, and organizational effectiveness. In K. E. Clark, M. E. Clark, & D. P. Campbell (Eds.), *The impact of leadership.* Greensboro NC: Center for Creative Leadership.

Markus, H. R., & Kitayama, S. (1991). Culture and the self: Implications for cognition, emotion, and motivation. *Psychological Review, 98,* 224–253.

Misumi, J. (1985). *The behavioral science of leadership: An interdisciplinary Japanese research program.* Ann Arbor: University of Michigan Press.

Misumi, J., & Peterson, M. F. (1985). The performance-maintenance theory of leadership: Review of a Japanese leadership program. *Administrative Science Quarterly, 30,* 198–223.

Öngel, U., & Smith, P. B. (1994). Who are we and where are we going? JCCP approaches its 100th issue. *Journal of Cross-Cultural Psychology, 25,* 25–53.

Peterson, M. F., & Smith, P. B. (1996, August). *Cross-cultural organisational studies beyond value comparisons: Managing work events.* In P. B. Smith (Chair), *The consequences of "Culture's Consequences."* Symposium conducted at the 26th International Congress of Psychology, Montreal.

Podsakoff, P., Dorfman, P. W., Howell, J. P., & Todor, W. D. (1986). Leader reward and punishment behaviors: A preliminary test of a culture-free style of leadership effectiveness. *Advances in International Comparative Management, 2,* 95–138.

Redding, S. G. (1990). *The spirit of Chinese capitalism.* Berlin: De Gruyter.

Redding, S. G., Norman, A., & Schlander, A. (1994). The nature of individual attachment to the organization: A review of East Asian variations. In H. C. Triandis, M. D. Dunnette, & L. M. Hough (Eds.), *Handbook of industrial and organizational psychology* (2nd ed., Vol. 4, pp. 647–688). Palo Alto, CA: Consulting Psychologists Press.

Schwartz, S. H. (1992). Universals in the content and structure of values: Theoretical advances and empirical tests in 20 countries. In M. P. Zanna (Ed.), *Advances in experimental social psychology* (Vol. 25, pp. 1–65). Orlando: Academic Press.

Schwartz, S. H. (1994). Beyond individualism and collectivism: New cultural dimensions of values. In U. Kim, H. C. Triandis, Ç. Kagitçibaşi, S. C. Choi, & G. Yoon (Eds.). *Individualism and collectivism: Theory, method and applications* (pp. 85–119). Thousand Oaks, CA: Sage.

Schwartz, S. H., & Sagiv, L. (1995). Identifying culture specifics in the content and structure of values. *Journal of Cross-Cultural Psychology, 26,* 92–116.

Sinha, J.B.P. (1995). *The cultural context of leadership and power.* Thousand Oaks, CA: Sage.

Smith, P. B., Dugan, S., & Trompenaars, F. (1996). National culture and the values of organizational employees. *Journal of Cross-Cultural Psychology, 27,* 231–264.

Smith, P. B., Misumi, J., Tayeb, M. H., Peterson, M. F., & Bond, M. H. (1989). On the generality of leadership style measures across cultures. *Journal of Occupational and Organizational Psychology, 62,* 97–109.

Smith, P. B., & Peterson, M. F. (1988). *Leadership, organizations and culture: An event management model.* Thousand Oaks, CA: Sage.

Smith, P. B., Peterson, M. F., Misumi, J., & Bond, M. H. (1992). A cross-cultural test of the Japanese PM leadership theory. *Applied Psychology: An International Review, 41,* 5–19.

Smith, P. B., & Schwartz, S. H. (1997). Values. In J. W. Berry, M. H. Segall, and Ç. Kagitçibaşi (Eds.), *Handbook of cross-cultural psychology: Vol 3. Social behavior and applications* (2nd ed., pp. 77–118). Needham Heights, MA: Allyn & Bacon.

van de Vijver, F.J.R., & Leung, K. (1996). *Methods and data analysis for cross-cultural research.* Thousand Oaks, CA: Sage.

CHAPTER 22

Negotiation and Reward Allocations Across Cultures
Kwok Leung

Globalization in businesses and migration patterns have led to workplace diversity in many countries. It is now common in many countries to find employees of various ethnicities or nationalities working together under the same roof. Given the prevalence of multicultural work teams, it becomes important to understand the dynamics of cross-cultural interaction. The aim of the present chapter is to review the literature on two important areas of group interaction: negotiation and reward allocation.

Negotiation from a Cross-Cultural Perspective

Disputes at the cultural interface are likely to be a major challenge in culturally diverse organizations. Despite the importance of cross-cultural knowledge about negotiation, research in this area seems to be inadequate and sometimes inconclusive (for reviews, see James, 1993; Leung & Fan, 1997; Leung & Wu, 1990). Although a number of books have been written on intercultural negotiation (for example, Fisher, 1988; McCall & Warrington, 1989), they take a how-to approach without much theoretical integration, and their materials are mostly based on speculations and personal experi-

Note: I would like to thank Michael Bond, Harry Triandis, and the editors for their critical comments on earlier drafts of this chapter.

ences rather than on results of systematic research. The field is in sore need of a coherent framework for integrating the wide array of findings in the literature and for guiding future research. This review begins with a broad framework that serves these purposes.

A Pan-Cultural Framework for Understanding Conflict Behavior

A number of theoretical frameworks have been proposed for understanding cross-cultural differences in human behavior (for a review, see Jahoda, 1980). These frameworks are by nature broad-brushed and hence limited in helping us understand specific behaviors such as negotiation across cultures. However, three major domains are identifiable in these frameworks, namely, the motivational, cognitive, and normative. This tripartite classification of the antecedents of cross-cultural differences seem to provide a simple framework useful for organizing the cross-cultural findings on negotiation.

The Dual Concern Model

It is helpful to understand a general model of conflict processing before looking closely at the relationship between culture and negotiation. The dual concern model that I discuss here is probably the more widely used scheme to classify strategies for handling a dispute (for example, Pruitt & Rubin, 1986). It is based on Blake and Mouton's conflict grid (1964), which has been adopted by many conflict researchers (for example, Thomas, 1976; Rahim, 1986). According to this model, negotiation behavior is influenced by two dimensions: concern about *own outcomes* and concern about *other's outcomes*. If concerns for own as well as other's outcomes are low, avoiding or inaction is likely. If concern for own outcomes is high and concern for other's outcomes is low, contending or competition is likely. If concern for own outcomes is low and concern for other's outcome is high, yielding is likely. If concern for both own and other's outcomes are high, problem solving is likely. Finally, if concern for own outcomes is moderate and concern for other's outcomes is high, compromise is likely (van de Vliert, 1990; van de Vliert & Prein, 1989).

Motivational Domain

The motivational domain concerns factors that direct, energize, and guide negotiation behavior; that is, it concerns the factors found in common definitions of motivation (for example, Bandura, 1991; Ford, 1992). The key issue here is to illuminate how cultural differences in motivational factors lead to cultural differences in negotiation behavior. My colleagues and I (Leung, Bond, & Schwartz, 1995) have observed that values are probably the more frequently used explanatory framework in cross-cultural research. In addition virtually all cross-cultural research on conflict is based on the value framework. Thus, the following analysis will focus on values in the motivational domain.

The now classic study on values by Hofstede (1980) has identified four value dimensions on which cultures can be located, and each dimension has been shown to relate to a variety of behaviors across cultures. Two of these dimensions have received considerable attention in conflict research: individualism-collectivism and power distance.

Individualism-Collectivism

Individualism refers to a tendency to be more concerned with one's own interests, needs, and goals, whereas collectivism refers to a tendency to be more concerned with the interests, needs, and goals of in-group members. The very distinction between in-group and out-group is also more marked in collectivist than individualist cultures (Kim, Triandis, Kagitçibasi, Choi, and Yoon, 1994). Individualist cultures are found in North America and Western Europe, and collectivist cultures are found in Asia, South America, and Southern Europe.

How might individualism-collectivism be related to conflict behavior? There have been two attempts thus far to link individualism-collectivism to conflict behavior: Ting-Toomey (1988) and Leung (1987). Ting-Toomey's approach is based on cultural differences in communication patterns. In her *conflict face-negotiation theory*, she argues that people high in individualist values should be inclined to employ a direct mode of conflict management; this mode includes problem solving (integrating), compromising, and contending (dominating or controlling) styles. In contrast, collectivists should be inclined to prefer an indirect mode of conflict management; this mode includes avoiding and yielding styles. However, this model received only partial support in a study involving Taiwanese Chinese and U.S. subjects (Trubisky, Ting-Toomey, & Lin, 1991). Consistent with the predictions of the model, Chinese subjects scored higher on yielding and avoidance. However, contrary to predictions, Chinese subjects also scored higher on contending. A closer examination of the data indicated that the Chinese subjects had higher scores than the Americans on all five styles. Thus, a response bias might be present in the data, preventing a direct comparison of the two cultural groups. To eliminate the cultural difference in response patterns, the scores of the two cultural groups should be adjusted by the difference in their overall average (Leung & Bond, 1989). When the means were thus adjusted, U.S. subjects scored much higher in contending, whereas Chinese scored much higher in avoiding. In any event, this pattern is still only partially consistent with the conflict face-negotiation framework. Thus, it seems that Ting-Toomey's concept of directness may not be crucial to an explanation of cultural differences in styles of conflict handling.

I have argued (Leung, 1987) that animosity reduction is a major goal in dispute resolution in collectivist cultures. Thus, individuals in collectivist cultures should prefer conflict resolution procedures likely to reduce disputants' animosity. I (Leung, 1987) showed that compared to U.S. subjects, Chinese subjects showed a stronger preference for negotiation and mediation and a weaker preference for adjudication. The explanation for this pattern is that negotiation and mediation are conducive to animosity reduction, whereas adjudication is less so because it binds parties to a resolution (for a review, see Leung & Wu, 1990).

My argument was tested with severe disputes, those likely to be handled formally, as in a court of law. In such situations, animosity between the disputants is usually at a high level, and animosity reduction becomes a major concern. However, in many everyday conflicts, animosity may be relatively low, and it is doubtful whether animosity reduction is still a major concern in such conflict. It is entirely possible that the emphasis in my study on animosity reduction is only applicable to disputes of high intensity. For disputes of low intensity, a different psychological process may take place. If animosity reduction is a central concern of collectivists in low-intensity disputes, it is difficult to explain why collectivists usually show a weaker preference for compromising and problem solving and a stronger preference for avoidance than do individualists (as described in a number of studies reviewed later). In the dual concern model, problem solving and compromising place equal emphasis on one's self-interest and on the interest of others. If a person's concern is animosity reduction, he or she should attempt to use these two modes to enhance the parties' interests simultaneously. In a similar vein, if collectivists' motive is animosity reduction, it is hard to explain why they would prefer avoidance, which does not enhance the interests of both sides.

To overcome this conceptual difficulty, this chapter proposes that a new concept, *disintegration avoidance,* be used to explain the conflict-handling strategies of collectivists in situations where the conflict is relatively mild. In the individualism-collectivism literature, it is widely accepted that collectivism is associated with a heightened concern for in-group harmony, and in-group harmony is understood as a unitary concept (for reviews, see Kim, Triandis, Kagitçibasi, Choi, & Yoon, 1994; Triandis, 1989). In the analysis here, however, it is posited that in order to explain the conflict behavior of collectivists fully, we need to make a distinction between harmony enhancement and disintegration avoidance. *Harmony enhancement* refers to engaging in behaviors presumed to strengthen the relationships among the interactants. Disintegration avoidance refers to avoiding actions that will strain a relationship and lead to its weakening and dissolving.

To understand the conflict behavior of collectivists, we need to classify conflict-handling strategies in terms of their likelihood of disintegrating an ongoing relationship. Contention or confrontation is obviously highly detrimental to any ongoing relationship. The result of problem solving is more complex. According to the dual concern model, problem solving attempts to promote the well-being of both disputing parties and should therefore be conducive to a harmonious working relationship. However, because integrative solutions are rare in the real world and well-intended discussions sometimes develop into hostile confrontations (for example, Bazerman & Neale, 1992; Pruitt & Carnevale, 1993), it is entirely possible that despite problem solving's potential to generate win-win solutions, collectivists will view it as a potential relationship threat. Compromising is another interesting case. Traditionally, this strategy is seen to promote the relationship between the disputing parties because it allows both sides to concede to a degree to arrive at a mutually acceptable solution. Many writers (for example, Gulliver, 1979; Leung & Wu, 1990; Nader & Todd, 1978) have used this logic to explain why collectivists favor mediation. However, the haggling and tough bargaining that are common in the process of arriving at a compromise may actually jeopardize the relationship between the disputants and cause ill-feelings between them. Viewed from this angle, compromising too may be a threat to the ongoing relationship. Thus, compromising may be seen to have either a positive or a negative impact on the ongoing relationship. Avoiding provides a temporary time-out for disputants, and collectivists may construe it as an effective strategy to avoid relationship disintegration, at least in the short run. The salient belief may be that over time the conflict may diminish on its own. Finally, yielding obviously should be least harmful to the ongoing relationship. It should be pointed out, however, that unlike the other strategies, yielding requires the sacrifice of one's interest and is costly to the individual.

Given the characteristic conflict styles prescribed by the dual concern model and the concept of disintegration avoidance, it is now possible to generate some predictions about cultural differences in conflict-handling strategies. The general prediction is that compared to individualists, collectivists will avoid behavior that may lead to the disintegration of the ongoing relationship. That is, collectivists should prefer yielding and avoiding more strongly, and problem solving and contending less strongly, than individualists. With regard to compromising, the pattern may be more complex because, as explained before, compromising has the potential to be harmony enhancing or to be disintegrating. There may not be a consistent pattern of cultural difference in the preference for compromising.

This hypothesis seems to provide a coherent account of the cross-cultural literature on conflict-handling behavior. After adjusting for the cross-cultural difference in the overall mean, Chinese college students in Taiwan reported a higher level of avoiding but a lower level of contending than did U.S. college students (Trubisky, Ting-Toomey, & Lin, 1991). Tang and Kirkbride (1988) and Kirkbride, Tang, and Westwood (1991) reported that Chinese employees preferred avoiding, yielding, and compromising more strongly, whereas British employees preferred contending and problem solving more strongly. Colleagues and I (Leung, Au, Fernández-Dols, & Iwawaki, 1992) found that compared with Canadian and Dutch college students, Japanese and Spanish college students preferred complying and negotiation more and accusing less in handling a conflict. Chua and Gudykunst (1987) found that college students from a number of collectivist countries showed a stronger preference for nonconfrontation, which involves avoiding or withdrawing from a disagreement and hiding ill-feelings. In contrast, students from a number of individualist countries showed a stronger solution orientation, which involves direct confrontation, problem solving, and compromising. Cushman and King (1985) found that Americans preferred competition in handling a dispute, whereas Japanese and Yugoslavians preferred compromises. Agee and Kabasakal (1993) found that in handling a conflict due to different working styles, Turkish students preferred competing less than did U.S. students, and a combination of competition, avoidance, and accommodation more than did the Americans. Ohbuchi and Takahashi (1994) found that when subjects were asked to describe their actual conflict-handling behaviors, Japanese subjects used avoiding and indirect methods (suggesting, ingratiation, impression management, and appeasing) more, whereas U.S. subjects used direct methods (persuasion, bargaining, and compromise) more. Compared with U.S. subjects, Japanese subjects were also more likely not to inform others when the actions of those others had negatively affected the subjects' daily life. The most frequently mentioned reason for this tolerance of transgression was the maintenance of the relationship. It is interesting that the dominant style for U.S. but not for Japanese subjects was compromising; this once again suggests that compromising, rather than producing harmony, may actually constitute a threat to the ongoing relationship.

Tse, Francis, and Walls (1994) studied the conflict management behavior of executives from mainland China and Canada. Two types of conflict were presented to subjects: task related and person related. In the task-related conflict, the problem was different production technologies, whereas in the person-related conflict, the problem was the arrogance and stubbornness of the other negotiator. Faced with task-related conflict, Canadian subjects were more likely to recommend discontinuation of negotiation and less likely to be friendly. In contrast, when dealing with conflict caused by personal styles, Chinese subjects were more likely to recommend discontinuation of negotiation, showed less satisfaction with the negotiation, and were less likely to be friendly. This pattern of results is consistent with the framework. In the task-related conflict, disintegration avoidance should be salient for the Chinese subjects, and hence they would prefer continuation of the negotiation and the maintenance of the relationship. However, when the conflict was caused by the difficult behavior of the other party, disintegration avoidance would become moot as there would be no reason to maintain a relationship with a difficult person who was not an in-group member. Chinese subjects would want to avoid this person, and this would explain why they were less friendly and less willing than the Canadian subjects to continue the negotiation with such a person.

Finally, Graham, Mintu, and Rodgers (1994) found that across eight countries, collectivism was correlated with a negotiation style characterized by cooperativeness and willingness to attend to the other party's needs, behaviors that can be interpreted as driven by an emphasis on disintegration avoidance.

To conclude, the concepts of harmony enhancement and disintegration avoidance may look similar at a glance, but they have very different implications for conflict-handling behaviors. As reviewed here, harmony enhancement should be associated with a stronger preference for problem solving or for procedures allowing compromises—such as negotiation and mediation—despite the potential of these procedures to generate strain in the relationship. Disintegration avoidance should be linked to a stronger preference for conflict avoidance. The usefulness of this more fine-grained analysis of the concept of harmony should be evaluated in future research.

Individualism-Collectivism and Negotiators' Social Relationship

In individualist societies, negotiation is seen more as a task than as a social process. The primary role of negotiators is to work out a solution that is acceptable to both sides. For instance, German negotiators tend to keep a distance from each other because they feel that a personal relationship with the opponent may hinder their performance in the negotiation (Schmidt, 1979). Similarly, U.S. negotiators are not concerned with establishing a close relationship with their opponents (Graham, 1981). In contrast, social relationships between the negotiators are seen to be as important as the negotiation itself in collectivist societies. Negotiators typically try to establish a close relationship with each other before and during the negotiation. See Moran (1985) for the case of Japan, Pye (1982) for the case of China, and Renwick (1985) for the case of Malaysia. Finally, Tse, Francis, and Walls (1994) found that compared with Canadian executives, executives from mainland China were more likely to negotiate using relational tactics such as attempts to influence and impress the other party.

Further, in collectivist cultures the preservation of a long-term relationship may be more important than maximizing short-term gain. For instance, in Japan buyers and sellers have a vertical hierarchical relationship in which buyers usually can get what they request (Graham & Sano, 1984). However, buyers are also expected to protect the interests of sellers and not to exploit them. In a simulation of a buyer-seller negotiation where the buyers had a structural advantage over the sellers, Harnett and Cummings (1980) found that U.S. and European (Belgian, Finnish, French, and Spanish) buyers were better at using their bargaining strength to obtain a larger profit, whereas Japanese and Thai buyers were more willing to settle on an equalitarian division of profit with the sellers.

Individualism-Collectivism and In-Group–Out-Group Relationships

It has been argued that members of collectivist societies make a sharper distinction than members of individualist societies do between in-groups and out-groups (for example, Triandis, 1989). For collectivists, the concern for harmony is much stronger with in-group than with out-group members. Based on the framework presented earlier, it can be posited that for collectivists, harmony enhancement should be salient with in-group members only. In line with this reasoning, a study I conducted (Leung, 1988a) found that compared to U.S. students, Hong Kong Chinese students were more likely to sue a stranger and less likely to sue a friend. In a negotiation experiment, Chan, Triandis, and Carnevale (1994) found that both U.S. and Chinese subjects made more concession to in-group members than to out-group members, but that Chinese subjects exhibited this pattern more strongly than did Americans. Consistent also is the observation that Greeks are more competitive with out-group members (Triandis, 1972), and so are Japanese (Kawashima, 1963).

Disintegration avoidance should be more prominent with members of a peripheral in-group, that is, with people with whom a stable, harmonious relationship is desired. For instance, Chinese are known for their desire to develop interpersonal connections (*guanxi*) with a wide range of people so that they can rely on these persons' help if the need arises. However, such connections can be a burden if the person who initiates the connections is not seen as an in-group member. King (1991) has provided a detailed account of the mechanisms Chinese can use to avoid connection-building attempts from acquaintances without creating strains in the relationship as it already exists. Consistent with the analysis so far, such tactics can be interpreted to be driven by the motive of disintegration avoidance. Empirical work is definitely needed to explore this possibility.

Individualism-Collectivism and Social Face

The role of *social face* (see Chapter Nine for details) in bargaining is well known in the negotiation literature (for example, Deutsch, 1961). Negotiators are assumed to desire a public image of strength and capability, and if their maintenance of this image is being threatened, they will engage in face-restoring behavior. For instance, Brown (1968) found that bargainers would retaliate severely against an exploiter if they believed that they had lost face by looking foolish in front of an audience.

Many authors generally regard face as more important in collectivist than in individualist societies (for example, Bond & Hwang, 1986; Ho, 1976; Ting-Toomey, 1988). Collectivists are generally more sensitive about issues of face and more concerned with maintaining face. The impact of this concern on their negotiation behavior has not been systematically investigated. However, anecdotal evidence abounds to support its importance in collectivist societies. Cohen (1991) describes how in the trade talks between the United States and Japan in the early 1970s, a symbolic concession made by the U.S. negotiators protected the face of the Japanese negotiators and hence was instrumental to the settlement of the trade dispute. Cohen provides similar stories involving China, India, Egypt, and Mexico and illustrating the concern people in these countries have for protecting their face during the negotiation process.

Concern for face has led to a number of interesting characteristics of collectivists' negotiation behavior. First, informal private discussions are often preferred, as the process and agreement are less likely to be scrutinized in these settings, and the chance of losing face is minimized. Pye (1982) has described in detail the preference of Chinese negotiators for private informal negotiations rather than public formal negotiations. Second, informal agreements are often preferred because an agreement that unexpectedly causes one side to lose face can then be easily revised to restore that party's face. When a binding agreement has been made, such flexibility for restoring face would not exist. Cohen (1991) presents an interesting discussion on how the United States and Mexico ran into negotiation stalemates because the United States insisted on a formal agreement but Mexico preferred an informal agreement.

This review of face has been based on anecdotal evidence rather than empirical results. It should be noted that face as a major determinant of social behavior has also been discussed by Western researchers (for example, Goffman, 1959). Yet it remains to be demonstrated that the analysis in this chapter is supported by empirical evidence, and to what extent face can explain cross-cultural differences in negotiation behavior.

Power Distance

Power distance refers to the extent to which social hierarchy is accepted in a culture. In high power distance societies, superiors are given more power and privileges, and subordinates are expected to comply with instructions and not challenge the superiors. In contrast, in low power distance societies, superiors and subordinates are assumed to have a more egalitarian relationship, and subordinates are given a freer hand in doing their work. Hofstede (1980) has shown that power distance and individualism-collectivism are highly correlated and that individualist societies are likely to be lower in power distance. Despite this overlap, Hofstede maintains that it is useful to separate these two dimensions and that they are conceptually distinct from each other.

Several studies have shown that power distance is systematically related to conflict behavior, and from this cultural dimension two predictions can be generated: first, conflict with superiors will be less frequent in high power distance societies than in low power distance societies; second, superiors will be more involved in settling disputes among subordinates in high power distance societies, whereas subordinates will have a stronger tendency to resolve disputes on their own in lower power distance societies.

James (1993) has reviewed a few studies that are in line with the first prediction. Gudykunst and Ting-Toomey (1988) correlated the data on anger and justice collected from seven European countries by Wallbott, Scherer, Babad, and their associates (Babad & Wallbott, 1986; Wallbott & Scherer, 1986) with power distance scores reported by Hofstede (1980). They found a strong correlation between the anger expressed in reaction to injustice and power distance. The higher the power distance in a society, the lower is the percentage of anger attributed to injustice. Gudykunst and Ting-Toomey argued that a higher acceptance of power differences in a society leads people to be more tolerant of unjust events. In contrast, a lower acceptance of power distance in a society makes people less receptive to power differences and hence less tolerant of unfair treatment.

Gudykunst and Ting-Toomey's conclusion is based on indirect evidence. Bond, Wan, Leung, and Giacalone (1985) were able to demonstrate the same pattern directly. Compared to U.S. subjects, Chinese subjects were more willing to accept insulting remarks from a high-status in-group person, whereas there was no cultural difference when the person giving the insults was of low-status. Graham, Mintu, and Rodgers (1994) also found results consistent with this pattern: across eight countries, power distance was related to the impact the bargainer (buyer or seller) had on the bargaining outcome. In other words, in high power distance societies the role of the negotiator showed a stronger impact on the negotiation outcomes.

A few studies in the legal arena have provided data that are in line with the second hypothesis—that superiors will be expected to help settle disputes among their subordinates in high power distance societies (for a review, see Leung & Wu, 1990). In high power countries like Hong Kong and Japan, litigants look to the judge to provide the facts about the case and ultimate justice, whereas U.S. litigants are more inclined to rely on their own efforts to argue for their case (Benjamin, 1975; Leung & Lind, 1986; Tanabe, 1963).

Three studies on organizational dispute resolution provide direct evidence for this second prediction. In a culture-level analysis based on over twenty national groups, Smith, Peterson, and I (Smith, Peterson, & Leung, in press) found that in countries with a lower power distance, subjects were more likely to rely on their peers and their subordinates to resolve a dispute within their work group. Tse, Francis, and Walls (1994) found that compared to Canadian executives, executives from China were more likely to consult their superior about a conflict. Finally, another study (Bond, Wan, Leung, & Giacalone, 1985) asked subjects to comment on the president of a company who chaired a meeting in which two of his subordinates broke into a dispute. Compared with U.S. subjects, Chinese subjects were more critical of the president and often described him as "unprepared," "lacking in leadership," "indecisive," and "incompetent." Clearly, Chinese subjects were more inclined to attribute the dispute to lack of ability on the part of the president.

Cognitive Domain

The recent years have seen rising interest in the impact of cognitive factors on conflict behavior. For instance, the impact of cognitive biases on conflict processing has been widely documented (Bazerman & Neale, 1992). Unfortunately, to the best of my knowledge, very few cross-cultural studies have employed a cognitive framework in their design. Such omission of cognitive factors in cross-cultural research is obviously unsatisfactory. This section reviews several cognitive variables that may prove useful in understanding cultural differences in conflict behavior.

Conception of Time

Hall (1983) has proposed that there are two major conceptions of time. A person with a *monochronic* conception of time believes that things should be done sequentially and that one thing should be the focus of attention at a time. Planning ahead of time is highly valued, and things are often done according to a preset schedule. A person with a *polychronic* conception of time, however, perceives time to be nonlinear; thus many things can happen at once. Improvisations are more common, and unexpected events and interruptions are more accepted. According to Hall, Western Europe and North America are more monochronic, whereas Asia, Africa, South America, and the Middle East are more polychronic. Foster's comparison (1992) of U.S. and Mexican practices provides substantial anecdotal evidence to illustrate the impact of the conception of time on negotiation processes. U.S. negotiators, because of their monochronic conception of time, preferred to organize the issues sequentially so that they could work on one issue at a time. They structured the negotiation process sequentially as well, and each negotiator spoke in turn. In contrast, Mexican negotiators discussed many issues simultaneously and often moved from issue to issue without any attempt to finish one issue before moving on to another. The negotiation process was also polychronic. Many people might speak simultaneously, and turn-taking was usually ignored. It was also common for the negotiation to be interrupted by unrelated events.

Styles of Persuasion

Glenn, Witmeyer, and Stevenson (1977) have observed that people use three major persuasion styles in negotiation: *rational, affective,* and *ideological.* Americans are likely to adopt the rational approach, and facts and logic play a dominant role in their negotiation processes. For instance, Kimmel (1994) observed that on the one hand U.S. negotiators regard expert opinions and facts as highly persuasive and value objective thinking highly. Arabs, on the other hand, use the affective approach, and facts are often based on feelings.

The affective approach is best illustrated by a traditional negotiation tactic in Japan. It is called the *naniwabushi,* and March (1988) provides a succinct summary of its three stages: "the opening, the *kikkake,* which gives the general background of the story and tells what the people involved are thinking or feeling; the *seme,* or a narrative of critical events; and the final *urei,* which expresses pathos and sorrows at what has happened" (p. 22). For example, a Japanese disputant adopting the *naniwabushi* approach will first remind the other party of the parties' long-established harmonious relationship. He or she will then focus on the disputed issues and describe how disastrous the situation is for him or her. As the person describes these sufferings resulting from the conflict, tears and emotional outbursts are common. The more tragic and moving the account of this suffering, the more likely it is that he or she will persuade the other disputant to accommodate his or her requests. Indeed, if the other disputant is not moved by the tragic suffering of the storyteller, he or she is often condemned as cold-hearted or mercenary.

Finally, in the ideological approach the first step in negotiation is to agree on general principles, or ideologies, and specific details can then be derived from these general principles. Russians, for example, are known for their concern with general principles in political negotiations (Glenn, Witmeyer, and Stevenson, 1977) and so are the mainland Chinese (Pye, 1982). Fisher (1980) offers some anecdotal evidence that suggests the French and Latin Americans also adopt the ideological approach in political negotiation.

Attribution

A number of studies have shown that some cultural groups are less likely than Americans to make dispositional attributions. For instance, Indians were found less likely to make dispositional attributions (Miller, 1984) and Koreans were found less likely to make internal attributions (Cha & Nam, 1985) than were Americans. In a series of studies, Morris and Peng (1994) showed that compared with Americans, mainland Chinese made more situational attributions for the behavior of others. Finally, Al-Zahrani and

Kaplowitz (1993) found that compared to Americans, Saudis made more external attributions for others' behavior.

The current data seem to suggest that internal attribution seems more prevalent in an individualist society like the U.S., whereas the tendency to make dispositional attribution seems to be weaker in several collectivist societies including India, Korea, Saudi Arabia, and China. At this point, it is unclear how this cultural difference in attributional patterns may be related to cultural differences in conflict behavior. One possibility is that if members of a given culture are more likely to make dispositional attributions for the behavior of others, this tendency may make conflict settlement more difficult (Morris, Leung, & Sethi, 1995). In conflicts, disputants' behaviors range from mildly confrontational (for example, argumentative and unwilling to concede) to hostile and aggressive. If on the one hand a disputant attributes such behavior in the other party to dispositional causes, he or she is likely to see that party as possessing negative personal traits, such as aggressiveness, uncooperativeness, and belligerence. Seeing the other person in this light should reduce the disputant's willingness to work with that person to settle the conflict in a way satisfactory to both parties. Who would want to work with an aggressive and rigid person? If on the other hand, a disputant attributes uncooperative behavior in the other party to situational forces, he or she may be more willing to work with the other party and cooperate to resolve the conflict. The disputant would not see the other party as difficult to work with, and as long as the situational forces could be removed, the conflict should be resolvable.

This reasoning suggests that the tendency to make dispositional attributions may prove to be a barrier to joint problem solving in conflicts. If so, joint problem solving should be more difficult in the United States and less difficult in societies less likely to make dispositional attributions. There is thus far no evidence to evaluate this conjecture. However, some anecdotal evidence exists to support its validity. For example, Kimmel (1994) reports that right before the 1991 Gulf War, U.S. Secretary of State Baker sent an ultimatum from President Bush to Iraqi Foreign Minister Aziz about the U.S. intention to engage in military action if Iraq did not withdraw from Kuwait. Aziz did not accept the letter. Kimmel (1994) suggests that Aziz's refusal to accept the letter probably triggered an attribution process in Baker and other U.S. senior officials that led them to conclude that Iraq was reluctant to negotiate and hence the dispute must be settled with force. The probability that U.S. decision makers viewed the behavior of their Iraqi counterparts in dispositional terms is further supported by the way senior U.S. officials compared Hussein to Hitler. Kimmel's analysis, however, is that the bluntness of the ultimatum probably violated the accepted protocol of Iraq. Thus, the ambassador's refusal to accept the letter was probably not based as much on its content as on its communication style. Obviously, the Americans did not adopt this situational explanation of the Iraqi behavior and ignoring that situational explanation led to the breakdown of the negotiation process.

Foster (1992) provides another illustration of how Americans have been quick to make dispositional attributions. When a Russian fighter plane shot down a South Korean passenger jet in Soviet airspace in 1983, "Americans, with the President and the Press in the lead, immediately attributed the motive to a trigger-happy and callous Soviet disregard for human life, assuming the action was taken with full knowledge that the plane being attacked was a passenger aircraft" (p. 34). Although this particular dispositional attribution was contradicted by subsequent analysis, this kind of attribution would obviously reduce Americans' willingness to consider the explanations offered by the Soviets and to work with them to resolve the crisis.

Probability Judgments

A number of studies show that compared with U.S. and British subjects, Asian subjects from several groups (including Chinese on the mainland and in Taiwan, Malays, and Indians in Malaysia) show a higher level of overconfidence in their probability judgments (for a review, see Yates & Lee, 1996). That is, these groups tend to overestimate the accuracy of their judgments. However, Japanese and U.S. subjects show a similar level of overconfidence (Yates et al., 1989). Yates, Lee, and Shinotsuka (1992) argue that a possible reason for the overconfidence of Chinese is that they do not recruit arguments counter to their initial judgments as frequently as do Americans and thus can maintain their initial confidence level.

Yates, Lee, and Shinotsuka (1992) tested this notion with U.S., Japanese, and Chinese subjects in the following manner. Subjects were asked to judge whether certain statements were correct or not. In one condition, subjects were asked to list as many arguments as possible that either supported or opposed the truth of each of the statements before they estimated the probability of the correctness of their judgments. In line with the hypothesis, Chinese subjects were found to generate fewer arguments that contradicted their judgment than did U.S. and Japanese subjects.

No study has looked at how this overconfidence of the Chinese may affect their conflict behavior. It is possible that it may be related to negotiation flexibility, which refers to the extent planned strategies are changed along the way as the negotiation proceeds. In a simulation of labor management disputes, Porat (1970) showed that negotiators from Spain turned out to be the most flexible, followed in descending order by those from the United Kingdom, Switzerland, Denmark, and Sweden. If Chinese are generally more confident of their judgment than Americans, they may show a lower level of negotiation flexibility, persist in a certain style of conflict handling longer, and be less likely to experiment with alternate modes of conflict handling. Thus it may be more difficult for Chinese to discover innovative solutions that are markedly different from their initial approach to disputes. And because of their overconfidence, Chinese may also be less willing to make an effort to collect objective evidence to evaluate their initial judgments. In other words, they are less likely to change positions, and this rigidity may result in more frequent stalemates.

Again, there are no empirical data available to evaluate these possibilities, although some anecdotal evidence can be cited. In an analysis of the commercial negotiation style of mainland Chinese, Pye (1982) observed that Chinese negotiators are often tenacious in holding onto their principles and are unwilling to compromise over them. The effects of overconfidence should definitely be evaluated in future research.

Normative Domain

A number of the cultural differences in negotiation behavior that have been documented in the literature are difficult to explain by pan-cultural frameworks, such as individualism-collectivism. These behaviors are probably best conceptualized as culture specific, that is, governed by behavioral norms unique to a culture.

Directness

Hall (1976) has proposed the concept *communication context* for classifying communication systems. According to Hall, "HC (high context) transactions feature preprogrammed information that is in the receiver and in the setting, with only minimal information in the transmitted message. LC (low context) transactions are the reverse. Most of the information must be in the transmitted message in order to make up for what is missing in the context" (p. 101). High-context cultures include Japan, China, Korea, and Vietnam, whereas low-context cultures include Germany, Scandinavia, Switzerland, and the United States.

Based on Hall's framework, Ting-Toomey (1985) argued that direct communication is more common in low-context cultures. In contrast, because implicit or restricted codes are used in high-context cultures, indirect communication is preferred. In line with this reasoning, Chua and Gudykunst (1987) found that in a conflict situation Taiwanese students were more likely to maintain silence, gloss over differences, and conceal ill feelings, and U.S. students were more likely to communicate about a dispute directly. In addition direct objections, heated debates, and confrontation are common in the negotiation process in a number of countries, such as France (Campbell, Graham, Jolibert, & Meissner, 1988), Brazil (Graham, 1985), and the United States (Moran, 1985), but a more subtle way of negotiation is preferred in other cultures. Japanese negotiators are famous for their polite manners, ambiguous rejections, and hidden emotions at the bargaining table (Graham & Sano, 1984; Goldman, 1994). Similar patterns are found in Malay negotiators (Renwick, 1985) and Chinese negotiators (Pye, 1982). For instance, Adler, Brahm, and Graham (1992) found that Chinese negotiators from the mainland used the word no less frequently than did U.S. negotiators.

In the absence of empirical research, it is unclear whether a framework based on communication context is able to explain cultural differences in the exhibition of direct communication in negotiation. This issue too awaits further empirical substantiation in the future.

Initial Positions

The initial offers made by negotiators seem to be influenced by culture. A number of cultural groups have been found to make extreme initial offers, such as Russians (Glenn, Witmeyer, & Stevenson, 1977; Ikle, 1964), Arabs (Glenn, Witmeyer, & Stevenson, 1977), Chinese (Pye, 1982), and Japanese (Graham & Andrews, 1987). U.S. negotiators, however, tend to make moderate initial offers.

Concession Patterns

Culture plays a significant role in influencing the concession rate of negotiators. Russians tend to view opponents' concessions as weak and seldom reciprocate (Glenn, Witmeyer, & Stevenson, 1977). In contrast, Americans and Arabs (Glenn, Witmeyer, & Stevenson, 1977) and Malays (Renwick, 1985) are likely to make concessions and to reciprocate the other party's concessions. In an experiment using the prisoner's dilemma game, Maxwell and Schmitt (1975) found that Norwegians were even more willing to reciprocate, more likely to respond to a cooperative choice with a cooperative choice than were Americans.

Nonverbal Behavior

Culture also affects the nonverbal behavior observed in negotiation. In an experimental simulation of negotiation behavior, Graham (1985) identified a number of differences among Japanese, U.S., and Brazilian negotiators. Japanese negotiators used silence most, followed by Americans, and then Brazilians. Japanese exhibited the least amount of facial gazing, and Brazilians exhibited the largest amount. Brazilians also exhibited a larger amount of touching and conversational overlaps than did Japanese and Americans. Adler, Brahm, and Graham (1992), however, found that Chinese negotiators from mainland China showed no difference from U.S. negotiators in terms of silent periods and facial gazing and touching behavior. Based on his observation of political negotiations, Cohen (1991) provides some anecdotal evidence to suggest that Indian negotiators often restrain from display of emotions and resort to silence in negotiation.

Directions for Future Research

This review has suggested three broad directions for future cross-cultural research on negotiation. First, although it has been recognized in the United States that animosity reduction is an important factor in conflict resolution (for example, Lissak & Sheppard, 1983), animosity reduction has not received much attention in the literature. In this current review, it is proposed that animosity reduction is a major variable in the negotiation process and especially important to understanding the negotiation behavior of collectivists. The two constructs of animosity reduction, harmony enhancement and disintegration avoidance, can explain why collectivists manifest certain negotiation behaviors. Future research should examine how these constructs are related to actual conflict-processing behavior and whether they are useful in understanding the conflict-processing behavior of individualists as well.

Second, I have treated individualism-collectivism and power distance as values when exploring their relationships with conflict behavior. This reflects the interpretation of these two constructs as values in the literature. Obviously, these constructs encompass cognitive and normative processes as well, and future work should look at these constructs' cognitive and normative implications for conflict-processing behavior.

Third, most cross-cultural works on negotiation rely on values as the explanatory framework. Many of the variables discussed in this chapter under the cognitive and normative domains have not been systematically investigated. Our understanding of negotiation behavior across cultures will benefit from a wider perspective that takes into account cognitive and normative processes.

Reward Allocation

This section reviews cultural influence on reward allocation. In any work group, a fair allocation of the group reward is crucial to that group's cohesiveness and efficiency. However, the notion of fairness is culture bound, and there are substantial cross-cultural differences in reward allocation (for reviews, see Leung, 1988b; James, 1993). Influenced by the seminal work of Homans (1961) and Adams (1963, 1965), early work in distributive justice is primarily concerned with evaluating *equity theory,* which stipulates that a person's share of a group reward should be proportional to that person's contribution. Subsequently, two more allocation norms were proposed: namely, *equality* and *need* (for example, Deutsch, 1975). It is generally agreed that equity is conducive to enhancing productivity, equality is conducive to harmony, and need is conducive to protecting members' well-being (for example, Deutsch, 1975; Leung & Park, 1986). A number of cross-cultural studies have been undertaken to find out how culture may influence the preference for these allocation norms. Although resources can take nontangible as well as tangible forms (Foa & Foa, 1974), cross-cultural research tends to focus on material resources. As might be expected, individualism-collectivism is the dominant theoretical framework used for interpreting the results obtained.

Individualism-Collectivism and Distributive Behavior

James (1993) has reviewed a number of studies on reward allocation and noted that equality is preferred in collectivist cultures, whereas equity is preferred in individualist cultures. However, as also noted by James, the relationship between culture and reward allocation may be complex and qualified by many situational variables. The current evidence suggests that the use of the individualism-collectivism dimension alone is inadequate to provide a coherent account of the empirical evidence and that a more complex model needs to be developed.

Bond and I (Leung & Bond, 1982) argued that cultural collectivism is related to the preference for the equality rule because equality is compatible with the emphasis on solidarity, harmony, and cohesion in collectivist cultures. In contrast, individualism is related to the preference for the equity norm because equity is compatible with the emphasis on productivity, competition, and self-gain in individualist cultures. Indeed, we found that collectivist Chinese subjects allocated reward in a more egalitarian fashion than did individualist U.S. subjects. Although the data also showed that Chinese subjects tended to see smaller differences among the contributions of group members, which may have led them to use a more egalitarian allocation than U.S. subjects did, this study provides initial support for a relationship between collectivism and the preference for equality.

A subsequent study (Bond, Leung, & Wan, 1982) examined the impact of collectivism on the allocation of two types of reward: task reward (assignment of a good grade to the recipient and willingness to work with the recipient again in the future) and socioemotional reward (willingness to make friends with the recipient). The results revealed that Chinese subjects again showed a more egalitarian tendency in allocating both types of reward than did U.S. subjects. Similar results were found by Kashima, Siegal, Tanaka, and Isaka (1988), who compared the allocation behavior of Japanese and Australian students. In the first study, subjects were asked to divide a bonus between two coworkers. Japanese subjects regarded an equal division as fairer and were more willing to change to an equality rule than were the Australian subjects.

Drawing upon previous theoretical work on the collectivism concept (for example, Hofstede, 1980; Triandis, 1972), Bond and I (Leung & Bond, 1984) argued that in collectivist cultures the recipient's group membership should affect the choice of allocation rules. With in-group members, collectivists should adopt a generosity rule that would give the recipients a bigger share. That is, collectivists would use the equality rule when their own input or contribution is high and use the equity rule when their own input is low. When out-group members are involved, however, collectivists should act like individualists and use the equity rule. We have obtained results in support of this more complicated relationship between collectivism and distributive behavior.

The argument we provided was consistent with several other studies comparing the allocation behavior of collectivists and individualists. Mahler, Greenberg, and Hayashi (1981) found no difference between Japanese and U.S. subjects in their allocation of a profit between two carpenters who invested together to buy a house. Marin (1981) found that Columbian subjects used the equity norm to a larger extent than did U.S. subjects in allocating a reward between two strangers who worked together in a psychological experiment. Aral and Sunar (1977) found that Turkish subjects used the equity norm to a larger extent than did U.S. subjects in allocating a reward between two architects who designed a project together. I (Leung, 1988b) have suggested that these several studies involved an out-group situation, and thus the collectivists were likely to use the equity rule in reward allocation.

The effect of collectivism on allocation behavior has been examined directly (Leung & Iwawaki, 1988) with subjects from the U.S., Japan, and Korea. Japan and Korea are collectivist according to Hofstede (1980, 1983). Because the Korean data had been collected before Hui's individualism-collectivism (INDCOL) scale (1984) was completed, only the collectivism level of Japanese and U.S. subjects was measured. Surprisingly, the three cultural groups showed no differences in their allocation behavior. Furthermore, contrary to Hofstede's result (1980), the collectivism level of the Japanese and U.S. subjects was found to be similar. Taking these two unexpected findings together, Iwawaki and I argued that because the Japanese and U.S. subjects were similar in their collectivism level, the lack of difference in their allocation behavior was actually consistent with the earlier results that Bond and I had reported (Leung & Bond, 1984). However, because the collectivism level of Korean subjects was not directly measured, it is unclear why their allocation behavior was also similar to that of the individualist U.S. subjects. It is possible that the Korean subjects, like the Japanese subjects, were more individualist than Hofstede's results have suggested.

Chen (1995) compared the allocation behavior of employees from mainland China and the United States. In this study, subjects were asked to allocate several rewards for the employees of a manufacturing company. Results showed that Chinese subjects actually preferred the equity solution more strongly than the U.S. subjects did. Chen (1995) argued that because China is moving toward a market economy, the desire to enhance productivity overrode the concern for in-group harmony, leading the Chinese subjects to prefer equity over equality. However, it can also be argued that the situation depicted in the study may involve an out-group situation and that the Chinese subjects' preference for equity in this situation is consistent with the argument Bond and I made (Leung & Bond, 1984).

The individualism-collectivism framework seems able to provide a coherent account of the reward allocation studies reviewed so far, but it fails to accommodate the following findings. Marin (1985) compared the allocation behavior of Indonesian and U.S. subjects. Regardless of the relationship between the allocator and the recipients (strangers, friends, or relatives), both cultural groups preferred equity over equality, and there were no cultural differences. Kim, Park, and Suzuki (1990) compared the allocation behavior of Korean, Japanese, and U.S. subjects. Subjects were instructed to allocate grades among classmates upon the completion of a group project. In contrast to earlier results (Leung & Iwawaki, 1988), Korean subjects in this study followed the equality rule more closely than did Japanese and U.S. subjects. Similar to the earlier results, however, there was no difference between the allocation patterns of U.S. and Japanese subjects. It seems difficult to reconcile the results of Leung and Iwawaki (1988) and Kim, Park, and Suzuki (1990).

The more disturbing result for the individualism-collectivism framework comes from a study by Hui, Triandis, and Yee (1991). They compared the distributive behavior of Chinese and U.S. subjects and obtained results consistent with those Bond and I had reported (Leung & Bond, 1984). Specifically, Hui, Triandis, and Yee found that Chinese subjects followed the generosity rule more closely and allocated a larger share to the recipient than did U.S. subjects when the reward to be divided was fixed. That is, they used an equality norm when their input was high and an equity norm when their input was low. In addition Chinese subjects were found to show a stronger preference for equality than U.S. subjects when the recipient was an in-group person. When the reward was unlimited, however, Chinese subjects were found to use equality to a larger extent than did U.S. subjects. This pattern of results makes sense because if the reward is unlimited, a person has no need to sacrifice his or her own share in order to give the recipient a larger share. The person can simply give the recipient a larger share without reducing his or her own allocation.

Using the INDCOL scale developed by Hui for measuring collectivism, Hui, Triandis, and Yee were able to see if in fact collectivism was related to the observed cultural differences in allocation behavior. When collectivism of the two cultural groups was equated in an analysis of covariance in which collectivism was treated as a covariate, the cultural difference in the use of equality disappeared in the case of unlimited resources. This result suggested that collectivism was indeed an adequate explanation in this condition. However, in the case of limited resources, even when the cultural difference in collectivism was statistically controlled, the cultural differences in allocation still remained significant. In other words, the tendency for Chinese subjects to follow the generosity rule and give the recipient a larger share was not adequately explained by collectivism. This pattern of results led Hui, Triandis, and Yee (1991) to conclude that the individualism-collectivism framework might be too global and nonspecific when it comes to explanation or prediction of specific allocation behavior.

The Contextual Model

It is clear from this review that even though the individualism-collectivism framework is able to account for quite an array of results, it has difficulty in accommodating several findings. To overcome this problem, the *contextual model* is proposed, which assumes that culture interacts with a number of situational variables to determine the allocation rule used. This model adopts a goal-directed view of allocation behavior (for example, Deutsch, 1975; Leung & Park, 1986). Interactional goals are hypothesized to be the immediate antecedent of allocation preferences, and the effect of culture is mediated by interactional goals. This assumption will accommodate the failure of Hui, Triandis, and Yee's study (1991) to find that individualism-collectivism directly accounted for cross-cultural differences in reward allocation. As individualism-collectivism is not the immediate determinant of allocation behavior in the contextual framework, its inability to provide a direct explanation for the use of the generosity rule by the Chinese subjects is no longer surprising.

In the contextual model, it is assumed that situational factors that have a strong impact on allocation behavior may override the effects of culture. For instance, Murphy-Berman, Berman, Singh, Pachauri, and Kumar (1984) and Berman, Murphy-Berman, and Singh (1985) both found that the need norm was followed more closely by Indian subjects than by U.S. subjects. In a 1988 report

(Leung, 1988b), I suggested that because resources are scarce in India, protecting the recipient's well-being is a more powerful goal than is maintaining a harmonious relationship. Thus the need norm would be more salient than the equality norm in India, despite that culture's collectivist tendency. In sum, it is hypothesized here that allocators will attempt to follow an allocation norm based on the interactional goal regarded as most appropriate for the situation.

Two situational variables are proposed to interact with culture to affect the allocation rule adopted. First, based on the individualism-collectivism framework, it is proposed that the relationship between allocators and recipients will affect the choice of interactional goal. The distinction between disintegration avoidance and harmony enhancement discussed before is again useful. With potential in-group members or members of a peripheral in-group, collectivists will regard disintegration avoidance as the goal, and equality will generally be favored in this situation. This prediction is in line with the finding that collectivists preferred equality over equity (for example, Kashima, Siegal, Tanaka, & Isaka, 1988). Furthermore, Hui, Triandis, and Yee (1991) and Leung and Iwawaki (1988) both found a positive correlation between collectivism and the preference for equality, and a negative correlation between collectivism and the preference for equity. Triandis, Leung, Villareal, and Clack (1985) have examined the relationship between individualism-collectivism with U.S. subjects. When the amount of money to be allocated was fixed, a higher level of individualism (or more precisely, idiocentrism, as the construct was used as an individual attribute in this study) was related to a stronger adherence to the equity rule. When the amount of money to be allocated was unlimited, individualism was correlated with a stronger deviation from an equality allocation. In sum, it seems that the relationship between collectivism and equality in U.S. subjects is consistent with the cross-cultural results of Hui (1984) and Leung and Iwawaki (1988).

In some situations, such as those involving core in-group members, collectivists may regard harmony enhancement as the interactional goal, and the generosity rule will be adopted to give the recipient a larger share of the reward (Leung & Bond, 1984). As in negotiation, the distinction between disintegration avoidance and harmony enhancement is crucial because these two goals lead to different allocation choices. Disintegration avoidance is associated with equality, and harmony enhancement is associated with generosity. With out-group members, it is predicted that like individualists, collectivists will adopt the equity rule. This prediction is in line with several studies that reported no difference between the allocation behavior of individualists and collectivists (for example, Leung & Iwawaki, 1988).

The second situational variable is the role assumed by the allocator. There are at least two of these roles. The first is actually a dual role in which the allocator is both an allocator and recipient. The second is a supervisory role in which the allocator is given the responsibility to allocate a group reward among the recipients, who are usually his or her subordinates. It is proposed that collectivists placed in the allocator-recipient dual role will be influenced by the harmony motive and show a stronger preference for either the equality rule or the generosity rule. In fact, in studies where subjects were placed in the dual role, the results are consistent with the predictions of the individualism-collectivism framework (for example, Leung & Bond, 1984; Hui, Triandis, & Yee, 1991).

In contrast, when subjects are placed in the supervisory role, the harmony motive should be less salient because the allocator is not tied to the recipients in a zero-sum situation. The allocation rule adopted should reflect the expectation the allocator has for the work group more than his or her personal relationship with the recipients. In a work setting, the dominant goal is productivity, and there is no reason to expect collectivists to emphasize it less when their interests are not tied to the recipients'. Thus collectivists should not show a stronger preference for the equality rule in this situation. In fact, Marin (1985) asked subjects to allocate a reward for two recipients and found that Indonesian subjects showed a stronger preference for equity than U.S. subjects regardless of the relationship between the allocator and the recipients. Chen (1995) asked subjects to role-play the president of a company and allocate several rewards for company employees. His results showed that Chinese subjects actually showed a stronger preference for equity than did U.S. subjects.

The contextual model seems to provide a reasonably coherent account of the current empirical results. However, direct tests of the model are needed to evaluate its usefulness in guiding future cross-cultural work in reward allocation.

Conclusion

Cross-cultural research on both negotiation and reward allocation tends to be incoherent, ad hoc, and atheoretical. Broad cultural dimensions or values are often used as the explanatory variables, even though mediating variables that may link these broad constructs to specific negotiation and reward allocation behaviors have not been explored (Bond, Leung, & Schwartz, 1992). Cross-cultural differences in negotiation and reward allocation are complex, and the use of broad cultural constructs as direct explanatory mechanisms may sometimes be inadequate (Leung, Bond, & Schwartz, 1995). A better strategy is to assume that cultural dimensions have an impact on a set of mediating variables and that it is these variables that are direct determinants of the behavior in question. Some initial models of this sort have been developed for understanding negotiation and reward allocation. It is hoped that they will stimulate future research and lead to the development of more powerful models.

References

Adams, J. S. (1963). Toward an understanding of inequity. *Journal of Abnormal and Social Psychology, 67,* 422–436.

Adams, J. S. (1965). Inequity in social exchange. In L. Berkowitz (Ed.), *Advances in experimental social psychology* (pp. 267–299). Orlando: Academic Press.

Adler, N. J., Brahm, R., & Graham, J. L. (1992). Strategy implementation: A comparison of face-to-face negotiations in the People's Republic of China and the United States. *Strategic Management Journal, 13,* 449–466.

Agee, M. L., & Kabasakal, H. E. (1993). Exploring conflict resolution styles: A study of Turkish and American university business students. *International Journal of Social Economics, 20,* 3–14.

Al-Zahrani, S.S.A., & Kaplowitz, S. A. (1993). Attributional biases in individualistic and collectivistic cultures: A comparison of Americans and Saudis. *Social Psychology Quarterly, 56,* 223–233.

Aral, S. O., & Sunar, D. G. (1977). Interaction and justice norms: A cross-national comparison. *Journal of Social Psychology, 101,* 175–186.

Babad, E. Y., & Wallbott, H. G. (1986). The effects of social factors on emotional reactions. In K. S. Scherer, H. G. Wallbott, & A. B. Summerfield (Eds.), *Experiencing emotion: A cross-cultural study* (pp. 246–255). New York: Cambridge University Press.

Bandura, A. (1991). Human agency: The rhetoric and the reality. *American Psychologist, 37,* 122–147.

Bazerman, M. H., & Neale, M. A. (1992). *Negotiating rationally.* New York: Free Press.

Benjamin, R. W. (1975). Images of conflict resolution and social control: American and Japanese attitudes to the adversary system. *Journal of Conflict Resolution, 19,* 123–137.

Berman, J. J., Murphy-Berman, V., & Singh, P. (1985). Cross-cultural similarities and differences in perceptions of fairness. *Journal of Cross-Cultural Psychology, 16,* 55–67.

Blake, R. R., & Mouton, J. S. (1964). *The managerial grid.* Houston, TX: Gulf.

Bond, M. H., & Hwang, K.-K. (1986). The social psychology of Chinese people. In M. W. Bond (Ed.), *The psychology of the Chinese people* (pp. 213–266). New York: Oxford University Press.

Bond, M. H., Leung, K., & Schwartz, S. H. (1992). Explaining choices in procedural and distributive justice across cultures. *International Journal of Psychology, 27,* 211–226.

Bond, M. H., Leung, K., & Wan, K. C. (1982). How does cultural collectivism operate? The impact of task and maintenance contributions on reward allocation. *Journal of Cross-Cultural Psychology, 13,* 186–200.

Bond, M. H., Wan, K. C., Leung, K., & Giacalone, R. A. (1985). How are responses to verbal insult related to cultural collectivism and power distance? *Journal of Cross-Cultural Psychology, 16,* 111–127.

Brown, B. R. (1968). The effects of need to maintain face in interpersonal bargaining. *Journal of Experimental Social Psychology, 4,* 107–122.

Campbell, N.C.G., Graham, J. L., Jolibert, A., & Meissner, H. G. (1988). Marketing negotiations in France, Germany, the United Kingdom, and the United States. *Journal of Marketing, 52,* 49–62.

Cha, J. K., & Nam, K. D. (1985). A test of Kelley's cube theory of attribution: A cross-cultural replication of McArthur's study. *Korean Social Science Journal, 12,* 151–180.

Chan, D.K.S., Triandis, H. C., & Carnevale, P. J. (1994). *A cross-cultural comparison of negotiation: Effects of collectivism, relationship between negotiators, and concession pattern on negotiation behavior.* Manuscript submitted for publication.

Chen, C. C. (1995). New trends in rewards allocation preferences: A Sino-U.S. comparison. *Academy of Management Journal, 38,* 408–428.

Chua, E., & Gudykunst, W. B. (1987). Conflict resolution styles in low- and high-context cultures. *Communication Research Reports, 4,* 32–37.

Cohen, R. (1991). *Negotiating across culture: Communication obstacles in international diplomacy.* Washington, DC: United States Institute of Peace Press.

Cushman, D. P., & King, S. S. (1985). National and organizational cultures in conflict resolution: Japan, the United States and Yugoslavia. In W. B. Gudykunst, L. P. Stewart, & S. Ting-Toomey (Eds.), *Communication, culture, and organizational processes* (pp. 114–133). Thousand Oaks, CA: Sage.

Deutsch, M. (1961). The face of bargaining. *Operations Research, 9,* 886–897.

Deutsch, M. (1975). Equity, equality, and need: What determines which value will be used as the basis of distributive justice? *Journal of Social Issues, 31,* 137–149.

Fisher, G. (1980). *International negotiation: A cross-cultural perspective.* Yarmouth, ME: Intercultural Press.

Fisher, G. (1988). *Mindsets.* Yarmouth, ME: Intercultural Press.

Foa, U. G., & Foa, E. B.(1974). *Societal structures of the mind.* Springfield, IL: Thomas.

Ford, M. E. (1992). *Motivating humans: Goals, emotions, and personal agency beliefs.* Thousand Oaks, CA: Sage.

Foster, D. A. (1992). *Bargaining across borders.* New York: McGraw-Hill.

Glenn, E. S., Witmeyer, D., & Stevenson, K. A. (1977). Cultural styles of persuasion. *International Journal of Intercultural Relations, 1,* 52–66.

Goffman, E. (1959). *The presentation of self in everyday life.* New York: Doubleday.

Goldman, A. (1994). The centrality of "ningensei" to Japanese negotiating and interpersonal relationships: Implications for U.S.-Japanese communication. *International Journal of Intercultural Relations, 18,* 29–54.

Graham, J. L. (1981). A hidden cause of America's trade deficit with Japan. *The Columbia Journal of World Business, 16,* 5–13.

Graham, J. L. (1985). The influence of culture on business negotiations. *Journal of International Business Studies, 16,* 81–96.

Graham, J. L., & Andrews, J. D. (1987). A holistic analysis of Japanese and American business negotiations. *Journal of Business Communication, 24,* 63–77.

Graham, J. L., Mintu, A. T., & Rodgers, W. (1994). Explorations of negotiation behaviors in ten foreign cultures using a model developed in the United States. *Management Science, 40,* 72–95.

Graham, J. L., & Sano, Y. (1984). *Smart bargaining: Doing business with the Japanese.* New York: Ballinger.

Gudykunst, W. B., & Ting-Toomey, S. (1988). Culture and affective communication. *American Behavioral Scientist, 31,* 384–400.

Gulliver, P. H. (1979). *Disputes and negotiations: A cross-cultural perspective.* Orlando: Academic Press.

Hall, E. T. (1976). *Beyond culture.* New York: Doubleday.

Hall, E. T. (1983). *The dance of life: The other dimension of time.* New York: Doubleday, Anchor Press.

Harnett, D. L., & Cummings, L. L. (1980). *Bargaining behavior: An international study.* Houston, TX: Dame.

Ho, D.Y.-F. (1976). On the concept of face. *American Journal of Sociology, 81,* 867–884.

Hofstede, G. (1980). *Culture's consequences: International differences in work-related values.* Thousand Oaks, CA: Sage.

Hofstede, G. (1983). Dimensions of national cultures in fifty countries and three regions. In J. B. Deregowski, S. Dziurawiec, & R. C. Annis (Eds.), *Expiscations in cross-cultural psychology* (pp. 335–355). Lisse, Netherlands: Swets & Zeitlinger.

Homans, G. C. (1961). *Social behavior: Its elementary forms.* Orlando: Harcourt Brace.

Hui, C. H. (1984). *Individualism-collectivism: Theory, measurement, and its relation to reward allocation.* Unpublished doctoral dissertation. Department of Psychology, University of Illinois.

Hui, C. H., Triandis, H. C., & Yee, C. (1991). Cultural differences in reward allocation: Is collectivism the explanation? *British Journal of Social Psychology, 30,* 145–157.

Ikle, F. C. (1964). *How nations negotiate.* New York: HarperCollins.

Jahoda, G. (1980). Theoretical and systematic approaches in cross-cultural psychology. In H. C. Triandis & W. W. Lambert (Eds.), *Handbook of cross-cultural psychology: Vol. 1. Perspectives.* (pp. 69–142). Needham Heights, MA: Allyn & Bacon.

James, K. (1993). The social context of organizational justice: Cultural, intergroup, and structural effects on justice behaviors and perceptions. In R. Cropanzano (Ed.), *Justice in the workplace: Approaching fairness in human resource management* (pp. 21–50). Hillsdale, NJ: Erlbaum.

Kashima, Y., Siegal, M., Tanaka, K., & Isaka, H. (1988). Universalism in lay conceptions of distributive justice: A cross-cultural examination. *International Journal of Psychology, 23,* 51–64.

Kawashima, T. (1963). Dispute resolution in contemporary Japan. In A. T. van Mehren (Ed.), *Law in Japan: The legal order in a changing society* (pp. 41–72). Cambridge, MA: Harvard University Press.

Kim, K. I., Park, H. J., & Suzuki, N. (1990). Reward allocations in the United States, Japan, and Korea: A comparison of individualistic and collectivistic cultures. *Academy of Management Journal, 33,* 188–198.

Kim, U., Triandis, H. C., Kagitçibasi, Ç., Choi, S.-C., & Yoon, G. (Eds.). (1994). *Individualism and collectivism: Theory, method, and applications.* Thousand Oaks, CA: Sage.

Kimmel, P. R. (1994). Cultural perspectives on international negotiation. *Journal of Social Issues, 50,* 179–196.

King, A.Y.C. (1991). Kuan-hsi and network building: A sociological interpretation. *Daedalus, 120,* 63–84.

Kirkbride, P. S., Tang, S. F., & Westwood, R. I. (1991). Chinese conflict preferences and negotiation behaviour: Cultural and psychological influences. *Organization Studies, 12,* 365–386.

Leung, K. (1987). Some determinants of reactions to procedural models for conflict resolution: A cross-national study. *Journal of Personality and Social Psychology, 53,* 898–908.

Leung, K. (1988a). Some determinants of conflict avoidance: A cross-national study. *Journal of Cross-Cultural Psychology, 19,* 125–136.

Leung, K. (1988b). Theoretical advances in justice behavior: Some cross-cultural inputs. In M. H. Bond (Ed.), *The cross-cultural challenge to social psychology* (pp. 218–229). Thousand Oaks, CA: Sage.

Leung, K., Au, Y. F., Fernández-Dols, J. M., & Iwawaki, S. (1992). Preferences for methods of conflict processing in two collectivist cultures. *International Journal of Psychology, 27,* 195–209.

Leung, K., & Bond, M. H. (1982). How Chinese and Americans reward task-related contributions: A preliminary study. *Psychologia, 25,* 32–39.

Leung, K., & Bond, M. H. (1984). The impact of cultural collectivism on reward allocation. *Journal of Personality and Social Psychology, 47,* 793–804.

Leung, K., & Bond, M. H. (1989). On the empirical identification of dimensions for cross-cultural comparison. *Journal of Cross-Cultural Psychology, 20,* 133–151.

Leung, K., Bond, M. H., & Schwartz, S. H. (1995). How to explain cross-cultural differences: Values, valences, and expectancies? *Asian Journal of Psychology, 1,* 70–75.

Leung, K., & Fan, R. M. (1997). Dispute processing: An Asian perspective. In H.S.R. Kao & D. Sinha (Eds.), *Asian perspectives in psychology* (pp. 201–217). New Delhi, India: Sage.

Leung, K., & Iwawaki, S. (1988). Cultural collectivism and distributive behavior: A cross-national study. *Journal of Cross-Cultural Psychology, 19,* 35–49.

Leung, K., & Lind, E. A. (1986). Procedure and culture: Effects of culture, gender, and investigator status on procedural preferences. *Journal of Personality and Social Psychology, 50,* 1134–1140.

Leung, K., & Park, H. J. (1986). Effects of interactional goal on choice of allocation rules: A cross-national study. *Organizational Behavior and Human Decision Processes, 37,* 111–120.

Leung, K., & Wu, P. G. (1990). Dispute processing: A cross-cultural analysis. In R. W. Brislin (Ed.), *Applied cross-cultural psychology* (pp. 209–231). Thousand Oaks, CA: Sage.

Lissak, R. I., & Sheppard, B. H. (1983). Beyond fairness: The criterion problem in research on dispute intervention. *Journal of Applied Social Psychology, 13,* 45–65.

Mahler, I., Greenberg, L., & Hayashi, H. (1981). A comparative study of rules of justice: Japanese versus Americans. *Psychologia, 24,* 1–8.

March, R. M. (1988). *The Japanese negotiator: Subtlety and strategy beyond Western logic.* Tokyo: Kodansha International.

Marin, G. (1981). Perceiving justice across cultures: Equity vs. equality in Columbia and in the United States. *International Journal of Psychology, 16,* 153–159.

Marin, G. (1985). The preference for equity when judging the attractiveness and fairness of an allocator: The role of familiarity and culture. *Journal of Social Psychology, 125,* 543–549.

Maxwell, G., & Schmitt, D. R. (1975). *Cooperation: An experimental analysis.* Orlando: Academic Press.

McCall, J. B., & Warrington, M. B. (1989). *Marketing by agreement: A cross-cultural approach to business negotiations.* New York: Wiley.

Miller, J. G. (1984). Culture and the development of everyday social explanation. *Journal of Personality and Social Psychology, 46,* 961–978.

Moran, R. T. (1985). *Getting your yen's worth: How to negotiate with Japan, Inc.* Houston, TX: Gulf.

Morris, M. W., Leung, K., & Sethi, S. (1995). Person perception in the heat of conflict: Perceptions of opponents' traits and conflict resolution choices in two cultures. Manuscript submitted for publication.

Morris, M. W., & Peng, K. (1994). Culture and cause: American and Chinese attributions for social and physical events. *Journal of Personality and Social Psychology, 67,* 949–971.

Murphy-Berman, V., Berman, J. J., Singh, P., Pachauri, A., & Kumar, P. (1984). Factors affecting allocation to needy and meritorious recipients: A cross-cultural comparison. *Journal of Personality and Social Psychology, 46,* 1267–1272.

Nader, L., & Todd, H. F. (1978). *The disputing process: Law in ten societies.* New York: Columbia University Press.

Ohbuchi, K., & Takahashi, Y. (1994). Cultural styles of conflict management in Japanese and Americans: Passivity, covertness, and effectiveness of strategies. *Journal of Applied Social Psychology, 24,* 1345–1366.

Porat, A. M. (1970). Cross-cultural differences in resolving union-management conflict through negotiations. *Journal of Applied Psychology, 54,* 441–451.

Pruitt, D. G., & Carnevale, P. J. (1993). *Negotiation in social conflict.* Bristol, PA: Open University Press.

Pruitt, D. G., & Rubin, J. R. (1986). *Social conflict: Escalation, stalemate and settlement.* New York: Random House.

Pye, L. (1982). *Chinese commercial negotiating style.* Cambridge, MA: Oelgeschlager, Gunn & Hain.

Rahim, M. A. (1986). *Management conflict in organizations.* New York: Praeger.

Renwick, G. (1985). *Malays and Americans: Definite differences, unique opportunities.* Yarmouth, ME: Intercultural Press.

Schmidt, K. D. (1979). *Doing business in France, Germany, and the United Kingdom* (pamphlets). Menlo Park, CA: Business Intelligence Program, SRI International.

Smith, P. B., Peterson, M. F., & Leung, K. (in press). Individualism-collectivism, power distance, and handling of disagreement: A cross-national study. *International Journal of Intercultural Relations.*

Tanabe, K. (1963). The process of litigation: An experiment with the adversary system. In A. T. van Mehren (Ed.), *Law in Japan: The legal order in a changing society* (pp. 73–110). Cambridge, MA: Harvard University Press.

Tang, S. F., & Kirkbride, P. S. (1986). Developing conflict management skills in Hong Kong: An analysis of some cross-cultural implications. *Management Education and Development, 17,* 287–301.

Thomas, K. W. (1976). Conflict and conflict management. In M. D. Dunnette (Ed.), *Handbook of industrial and organizational psychology* (pp. 889–935). Palo Alto: Consulting Psychologists Press.

Ting-Toomey, S. (1985). Toward a theory of conflict and culture. In W. B. Gudykunst, L. P. Stewart, & S. Ting-Toomey (Eds.), *Communication, culture, and organizational processes* (pp. 71–86). Thousand Oaks, CA: Sage.

Ting-Toomey, S. (1988). Intercultural conflict styles: A face-negotiation theory. In Y. Y. Kim & W. B. Gudykunst (Eds.), *Theories in intercultural communication* (pp. 213–235). Thousand Oaks, CA: Sage.

Triandis, H. C., with Vassiliou, V., Vassiliou, G., Tonaka, Y., & Shanmugam, A. V. (Eds.). (1972). *The analysis of subjective culture.* New York: Wiley-Interscience.

Triandis, H. C. (1989). The self and social behavior in differing cultural contexts. *Psychological Review, 96,* 506–520.

Triandis, H. C., Leung, K., Villareal, M., & Clack, F. L. (1985). Allocentric vs. idiocentric tendencies: Convergent and discriminant validation. *Journal of Research in Personality, 19,* 395–415.

Trubisky, P., Ting-Toomey, S., & Lin, S. L. (1991). The influence of individualism-collectivism and self-monitoring on conflict styles. *International Journal of Intercultural Relations, 15,* 65–84.

Tse, D. K., Francis, J., & Walls, J. (1994). Cultural differences in conducting intra- and inter-cultural negotiations: A Sino-Canadian comparison. *Journal of International Business Studies, 25,* 537–555.

van de Vliert, E. (1990). Positive effects of conflict: A field assessment. *International Journal of Conflict Management, 1,* 69–80.

van de Vliert, E., & Prein, H.C.M. (1989). The difference in the meaning of forcing in the conflict management of actors and observers. In M. A. Rahim (Ed.), *Managing conflict: An interdisciplinary approach* (pp. 51–66). New York: Praeger.

Wallbott, H. G., & Scherer, K. R. (1986). The antecedents of emotional experiences. In K. S. Scherer, H. G. Wallbott, & A. B. Summerfield (Eds.), *Experiencing emotion: A cross-cultural study* (pp. 69–83). New York: Cambridge University Press.

Yates, J. P., & Lee, J. W. (1996). Chinese decision-making. In M. H. Bond (Ed.), *Handbook of Chinese Psychology* (pp. 338–351). New York: Oxford University Press.

Yates, J. F., Lee, J. W., & Shinotsuka, H. (1992, November). *Cross-national variation in probability judgment.* Paper presented at the Annual Meeting of the Psychonomic Society, St. Louis.

Yates, J. F., Zhu, Y., Ronis, D. L., Wang, D. F., Shinotsuka, H., & Toda, M. (1989). Probability judgment accuracy: China, Japan, and the United States. *Organizational Behavior and Human Decision Processes, 43,* 147–171.

CHAPTER 23

Organizational Justice Across Cultures
Integrating Organization-Level and Culture-Level Perspectives
Boris Kabanoff

Leung's thoughtful review in Chapter Twenty-Two of the negotiation and reward allocation literature identified both the persisting problems and the beckoning opportunities that cross-cultural research in industrial and organizational psychology presents to researchers. The present chapter tries to realize some of those opportunities and demonstrate one approach for dealing with several of the problems. The two specific problems it addresses were clearly identified in the preceding chapter:

1. The use of individualist measures for describing collective phenomena
2. The need to identify mediating variables that link broad cultural constructs to micro-level psychological variables

The opportunities these problems provide are twofold: first, we can explore the contribution that cross-cultural research can make to our substantive understanding of organizational justice; second, we can demonstrate how the content, or text, analysis method can be applied to researching organizational justice cross-culturally and also demonstrate its applicability to cross-cultural research generally. Organizational justice (both its distributive and procedural elements) is the chosen area of exploration and application for three main reasons. In the first place, I suggest that justice is to be viewed not simply as just another organizational variable but as a framework for understanding the character or nature of organizations. This reflects the view about the central role of justice in organizations that I have described previously as follows: "[Justice is] an ever present, deep, and slowly-moving current that shapes people's relations with other organisational members and the nature and strength of people's attachments to organisations in general" (Kabanoff, 1991, p. 436). A second reason for discussing the issue of individualist and collectivist measurement in the context of organizational justice is that there is a striking parallel between the organizational justice and the cross-cultural literatures in their use of individualist measures to deal with collectivist phenomena. Although organizational justice research would seem to be concerned with a collectivist concept (the justice qualities of organizations), in fact what it almost invariably measures are individuals' perceptions of outcome and procedural fairness. In this chapter I argue that justice concerns and principles are in fact part of the *deep structure* of organizations (for example, Gersick, 1991) and that they help shape the structural and process features of organizational systems. Thus organizational justice needs to be studied at a more collective level than it currently is. Finally, justice is a good construct for drawing cross-cultural comparisons. As anthropologists Nader and Sursock (1986) noted, justice beliefs and behaviors and the justice motive are universal, but the meanings of justice vary across different social and cultural settings. For example, Wallbott and Scherer (1986) and Bahad and Wallbott (1986) have provided data from eight countries (Belgium, France, United Kingdom, West Germany, Italy, Spain, Switzerland, and Israel), showing that even though injustice was an important source of anger for people in all these countries, its absolute importance varied. Some other interesting evidence bearing on the importance of justice and its relation to conflict was provided by Martin, Scully, and Levitt (1988) who found that injustice was a major theme in the rhetoric of twenty-two leaders of violent twentieth-century revolutions across a variety of cultures, including Russia, China, Germany, and Cuba.

Measurement of Individualism and Collectivism

The issue of how we measure and compare aspects or dimensions of cultures is neither new nor simple to resolve, and it is not my intention to deal with it in detail here (detailed treatments are found in, for example, Rohner, 1984; Leung, 1989) but instead to provide a context for the approach this chapter adopts to making cross-cultural comparisons.

Survey research, a predominant method in social science in general, has been extremely important in cross-cultural research (for example, England, 1975; Hampden-Turner & Trompenaars, 1993; Hofstede, 1980; Lundbergh & Peterson, 1994; MOW International Research Team, 1987; Schwartz, 1992, 1994). It is arguable whether or not we should consider the paper-and-pencil experiments that have been fairly popular in cross-cultural research (for example, Bond, Leung, & Wan, 1982; Kim, Park, & Suzuki, 1990) as more akin to surveys than experiments because they gather opinions about hypothetical situations. Survey research has both advantages and disadvantages, but one intrinsic reason for actively seeking out and exploring other measurement approaches is the very degree of reliance that has been put on surveys. Namenwirth and Weber (1987), strongly critical of the use of surveys for measuring cultural differences, have also been pioneers in the development and application of an alternative approach to the problem of measuring culture—content, or text, analysis of cultural documents. We do not necessarily have to agree with their outright dismissal of the legitimacy of using surveys in cultural research, to recognize the importance of their observation that survey methodology has an inherent bias against "collective actors." Namenwirth and Weber described surveys as having what they termed a "democratic bias." That is, each individual surveyed is counted as an equal witness. However, in the creation, maintenance, and transmission of culture individuals are not of equal importance. Furthermore, survey research systematically excludes a whole class of collective actors, namely institutions such as churches, universities, governments, and other large organizations that are arguably more central to the creation, maintenance, and transmission of culture than any individual. Because organizations cannot be given a survey to complete, it is generally thought that organizational values are captured or represented by individuals' values; however, this is an assumption. This chapter proposes that organizational values are conceptually and empirically distinct from individuals' values and that organizations are one of the important links between cultural and individual values that researchers have been saying we need to identify and study.

In the next section, I begin to outline how researchers can derive collective measures that are not the averages of individual responses and that also can help bridge the gap between macro cultural values and the kinds of small-group and individual behaviors that are often of interest to organizational psychologists. The solution lies, I argue, in measuring organizational values. Values are usually defined as generalized enduring beliefs about the personal and social desirability of certain specific modes of conduct or end-states of existence (for example, Rokeach, 1979; Schwartz, 1992). One characteristic that has made the values concept of lasting interest to social scientists is that it is a multilevel concept that can be equally meaningfully applied across many different levels, ranging from the cultural to the individual. Organizations, as noted earlier, are important collective actors in the transmission, maintenance, and change of cultural values within virtually all contemporary societies. On a values continuum stretching from the cultural to the individual, organizational values represent an intermediate position between abstract cultural values and the small-group and individual values that can be seen as more proximal influences on small-group and individual behavior. Hofstede, best known of course for his description of cultural values, has also carried out one of the few cross-national comparisons of organizational values (Hofstede, Neuijen, Ohayv, & Sanders, 1990). Although Hofstede, Neuijen, Ohayv, and Sanders's equating of organizational values with the average of organization members' values does not concur with my own view of organizational values, their demonstration of a strong cultural influence upon organizational values at least suggests the kind of mediating role that organizational values can play between cultural values and organizational behavior and practices. Note also that the mediating role of organizations and institutions can be a two-way street, that is, the mediation is in principle bidirectional, and presumably one way changes in individuals' values can influence cultural values is via the impact of these changes upon institutional and organizational values. These are complex and intriguing issues beyond the scope of this chapter (see Namenwirth & Weber, 1987), nevertheless the main point remains—organizational values can be distinguished from individual values, and they may form a key linkage between cultures and individuals.

Organizational Justice as a Basis for Understanding Organizational Values

Mitchell and Scott (1990) argued that issues of trust, distributive fairness, and loss of sense of community constitute critical and growing problems for organizations. Their views have been proved correct if one judges by the growth of research into organizational justice, with several books (for example, Cropanzano, 1993; Sheppard, Lewicki, & Minton, 1992), major literature reviews (for example, Greenberg, 1990), and special journal issues all appearing in the last few years (for example, Baron & Cook, 1992). Sheppard, Lewicki, and Minton (1992) have described a simple "nested model" of organizational justice that has heuristic value for understanding the differences between a systemic and an individualist psychological view of organizational justice.

Sheppard, Lewicki, and Minton (1992) identified three "levels" at which organizational justice could be described: *system* (systemic), *procedures* (procedural), and *outcome* (psychological). Figure 23.1 defines and gives examples of variables that characterize each level, though the list is not meant to be exhaustive (incidentally, these definitions and examples differ somewhat from Sheppard, Lewicki, and Minton's, though they agree in spirit). The systemic (or as I termed it earlier, deep structure) level is not easy to define or describe (compare Gersick, 1991); it represents the relatively stable core of an organization's distributive system, where allocation "choices" and principles have implications for the whole system and for all organizational members. This level includes what Cohen (1986, p. 71) termed "the structure of allocative power" in that it helps define the broad allocation parameters of the whole system. It is a level whose workings are not easily perceived as it resides in both the implicit and explicit structure of the organization and includes such things as organizational members' shared

Figure 23.1. Three-Level Model of Organizational Justice.

Systemic Level ⟶	Procedural Level ⟶	Outcome (Psychological) Level
Core stable tendency toward equality/inequality of treatment and outcomes. Organizational members are only indirectly aware of this level.	Policies, procedures, and objectives that implement and can also moderate systemic priorities. This level is more modifiable and manageable, and there is greater awareness of it.	Psychological dimension of justice-perceptions, judgments, personal values, and beliefs about systems, procedures, and outcomes.
This level is reflected in	This level is reflected in	This level is reflected in
• Overall pattern of dispersion/inequality in all valued rewards and resources	• Nature and purposes of performance appraisal processes	• Perceptions of fairness of outcomes and procedures
• Power and role structures	• Socialization practices	• Types and levels of commitment (for example, compliance, identification, internalization)
• Demographic patterns and characteristics	• Form and degree of participation, consultation practices, for example, *ringi*)	• Frustration, satisfaction
• Shared assumptions and beliefs	• Styles of leadership, conflict resolution	• Feelings of injustice
• Forms and levels of task and interpersonal interdependence	• General styles of interpersonal interaction	• Sense of solidarity versus withdrawal
• And so forth	• And so forth	• Citizenship behaviors
		• And so forth

Source: Based on Sheppard, Lewicki, & Minton, 1992, p. 15.

assumptions (Schein, 1985). Put succinctly, it is the organization's *distributive culture*—a term that is perhaps best avoided at present, however, given the controversies associated with the organizational culture concept (for example, Martin, 1992).

The procedural level represents the policies, practices, and processes that implement system priorities and decisions—though as shown a little later, procedures need not simply replicate systemic priorities. The procedural level is more malleable than the systemic, and people more readily perceive its characteristics and workings. Finally, the outcome level represents primarily the psychological level, that is, people's perceptions and judgments about the other two levels rather than "actual" outcomes. For example, if the actual distribution pattern of rewards in an organization is primarily a system-level variable (see Figure 23.1) then people's perceptions, beliefs, and judgments about that distribution represent the outcome or psychological level. Although all three levels are important, this chapter focuses on the systemic level for three reasons.

In the first place, comparatively little research has been done at this level, thus it is a neglected topic. For example, James (1993) observed: "Justice principles, perceptions, and actions may be closely bound to the status, positional and power systems of organisations. These factors have not often been included in research or theory, however" (p. 39). Second, although research evidence about this level is scarce, there are clear indications of its importance. Hedström (1988) described his study in which the sample comprised employees of the whole of Sweden's manufacturing sector: 6,835 organizations and 732,465 individuals! He found that about 50 percent of the dispersion (that is, inequality) in people's earnings within and across organizations could be explained in terms of each organization's number of hierarchical levels. That is, the number of hierarchical levels had a massive impact on the level of inequality in people's earnings—the greater the number of hierarchical levels, the greater the overall level of inequality. Pfeffer (1990) reported broadly similar findings for U.S. samples. In short, if you wish to understand the sources of actual inequality in organizations, and presumably also an important influence on people's perceptions and beliefs about fairness, it is hard to ignore the nature and extent of the hierarchy. Finally, research that ignores the systemic level and concentrates on studying the reactions of recipients of allocation decisions rather than the nature of the allocation system itself cannot provide answers to some of the tough justice questions. Brockner and Weisenfeld (1994) provided a comprehensive integrative review of research into distributive and procedural justice and concluded that "resource allocators are likely to be forever grappling with how to make the 'tough choices,' in which decisions are seen as unpopular by significant numbers of people. . . . The present findings do not address, of course, the matter of whether the tough choices should be made at all. Moreover, they do not specify how 'tough' these choices should be" (p. 38). Why is it that the justice literature provides little insight into such issues? In brief, the reasons lie once again at the systemic level, where the most far-reaching resource allocation rules are shaped, and where the most powerful resource allocators operate. Focusing on the attitudes and responses of the recipients of allocation decisions does indeed provide few answers to the tough justice questions. At present few theories in organizational behavior address organizational justice at a collective or systemic level, and in the next section, I describe one recent attempt to develop such a theory.

A System-Level Theory of Organizational Justice

Figure 23.2 is a lightly modified representation of a theory of organizational types based upon the different *justice characters* of different organizations (described in previous publications: Kabanoff, 1991, 1993; Kabanoff, Waldersee, & Cohen, 1995). In describing differences between organizations in terms of systemic justice character, the theory seeks to describe general justice bias, the *orientation* of an organization as a whole, rather than focusing on whether a specific organizational decision or action is viewed as fair. I described this model first in Kabanoff (1991), and the main modification made here has been to give somewhat more abstract or broader interpretations to the two original dimensions of the model—power structure and process. As noted earlier, the extent of organizational hierarchy is one central influence on distributional outcomes. Thus the power structure dimension is reinterpreted here as reflecting an organization's general *outcome orientation,* that is, its tendency to produce among members outcomes that are more

Figure 23.2. Justice-Based Typology of Organizational Value Structures.

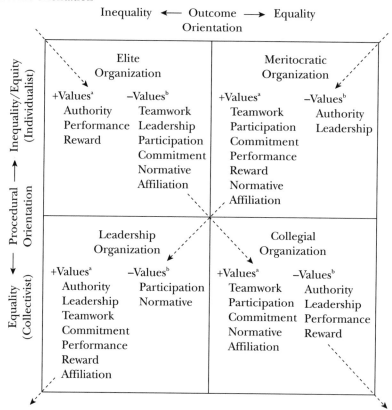

Procedures reinforce
outcome orientation

Procedures compensate for
    outcome orientation

---

[a]+ indicates values strongly or frequently espoused by organizations in the quadrant.
[b]− indicates values weakly or infrequently espoused by organizations in the quadrant.

Source: Based on Kabanoff, 1991, p. 431.

or less equal or unequal. Processes reflect an organization's *procedural orientation* for generating certain kinds of outcomes, and these processes also vary according to whether organizations are oriented to treating all people similarly or *equally* (that is, *collectively*) or differentially or *unequally* (that is, *individually*). In short, organizations have an underlying tendency toward producing equality or inequality of outcomes among organizational members, and they also have procedures oriented toward treating people more or less equally or unequally and producing outcomes that are more or less equal or unequal. The original conceptualization of the outcome dimension as a reflection of organizational power distribution (that is, degree of power inequality) is not discarded but rather subsumed within this broader interpretation; in the context of Figure 23.2, power distribution can be viewed as a core dimension reflecting an organization's outcome orientation. It is even easier to see how the renamed procedural orientation dimension represents a broadened version of the original process dimension—organizations' processes and policies are key reflections of their procedural orientations. Here is a summary of the model's key features.

A core assumption of the model is that organizations' allocation decisions and patterns inevitably reflect a trade-off between two competing principles—equity and equality. Although other principles such as need may also be important (for example, Meindl, 1989), equity and equality are the "big two" as far as this model is concerned, and the choice of these two principles is not arbitrary or a matter of convenience. It is based on the assumption that an inherent conflict between equality and equity is built into the deep structure of organizations. That is, even though other distributive principles may be important within the culture at large, they are not as central as equity and equality for understanding organizations' core distributive character. Organizations have two major goal-directed systems or functions that have been variously called *task* and *person, technical* and *social, production orientation* and *employee orientation,* and so on (for example, Katz & Kahn, 1978). The task system is oriented toward economic ends, such as productivity, performance, and efficient use of resources; the person system is oriented toward the maintenance of interpersonal solidarity, cohesion, and collaboration. Both are essential to organizations, but the two systems involve different psychological and distributive orientations (Deutsch, 1985), or *biases*. The task system involves an equity orientation, and the relational system involves an equality orientation. To the extent that all organizations have this dual task-person character, the theory applies in broadly the same way to organizations irrespective of their national culture; for the present, at least, there are no obvious theoretical or empirical reasons to question the validity of the general meta-theory of organizations, though future research and theorizing may lead us to alter this conclusion.

Organizations have to deal with the inherent tension between equity and equality in both their outcome and procedural dimensions, and the model says they do this in two different ways. Outcome and procedural orientations can *reinforce* one another, or the procedural dimension can *compensate* for the outcome dimension, producing four main organizational types. In the *elite* type both outcomes and procedures are inequality or equity oriented (that is, oriented toward differentiating between people, in the pursuit of economic outcomes). In the *collegial* type both dimensions are equality oriented (that is, oriented toward not differentiating between people, in the pursuit of solidarity). In the *leadership* type outcomes are inequality oriented, and procedures are equality oriented (that is, although oriented to inequality, the organization pursues some degree of balance via its procedures). And in the *meritocratic* type outcomes are equality oriented, and procedures are equity or inequality-oriented (that is, this organizational type also seeks balance between outcomes and procedures).

Value Structures Characteristic of the Four Organizational Types

One important way in which organizations demonstrate their different justice characters is through their values—different types have different value structures. Following Schwartz (1992) a value structure can be defined as the overall pattern of relations among a set of values, a pattern that can represent elements of both compatibility and conflict among values. The notion that the pattern contains conflict of course reflects the idea of an inherent conflict between equity and equality in organizations, but the notion of compatibility is also important because organizations can combine outcome values with compatible or compensatory procedural values, as explained earlier. A value structure is different from a value hierarchy because it allows for a mixture of compatibility and conflict among the values constituting a value system; it is not simply a priority-based ordering of values.

Figure 23.2 shows each organizational type's associated value structure, that is, the values it emphasizes and deemphasizes. Both are significant. For example, the elite organization is a "pure" unequal type, and it combines unequal outcome values with inequality-oriented procedural values. The elite value structure emphasizes unequal power relations (authority), deemphasizes egalitarian power values (participation, normative), and deemphasizes cohesion values (affiliation, teamwork, commitment, leadership) as it emphasizes performance and reward. The leadership type displays a mixed compensatory pattern that although it retains the elite organization's unequal outcomes orientation, superimposes on the elite value structure a set of cohesion-oriented procedural values that are nevertheless consistent with unequal outcome and power relations: namely, leadership, teamwork, commitment, and affiliation. As I observed in a previous essay, "Leadership has a paradoxical or dualistic quality—it both glorifies inequality and the differences between the leader and the led, while at the same time it creates identification and cohesiveness between the leader and his or her followers" (Kabanoff, 1991, pp. 433–434). In a parallel fashion, the meritocratic organization combines conflicting equity and equality concerns by superimposing a set of equity-oriented procedural values on a "pure" egalitarian collegial type. The collegial organization emphasizes equality in outcomes and procedures (participation, normative, affiliation, commitment, and teamwork values), and it deemphasizes inequality values (authority, leadership, rewards, performance).

This chapter reports some empirical data relating to these four value structures a little later; at this stage I explain how this typology of organizations can be related to several of Hofstede's key dimensions of cultural differences. One of the problems of cross-cultural research identified earlier was the use of broad cultural dimensions to explain behaviors and outcomes at the individual or small-group level. It was suggested that *mediating* variables that link these broad cultural constructs to micro, or psychological, variables need to be identified. The four organizational types constitute just such a potential mediating link between the cultural and psychological levels, and the remainder of this chapter shows how the values expressed in that organizational typology can be used to bridge culture-level values and lower-level values. To begin with, I discuss how Hofstede's typology and the present organizational typology can be integrated.

Integrating the Model of Organizational Types with Hofstede's Individualism and Power Distance Dimensions

Figure 23.3 shows how the theory of organizational types can be located within Hofstede's model of different culture types, or at least within two of its core dimensions: power-distance and individualism-collectivism. The outcome orientation dimension of the organizational typology, of which power centralization or power inequality is a key indicator, has an obvious parallel with Hofstede's cultural dimension of power distance—the greater the power distance at the cultural level, the greater the power inequality or centralization at the organizational level; this is a connection that Hofstede also made (Hofstede, 1980). The procedural dimension, which represents a tendency toward using individualist or solidaristic procedures, similarly can be seen to parallel at an organizational level Hofstede's individualism-collectivism dimension.

Figure 23.3 proposes that differences in the relative frequency of occurrence of different organizational types within different cultures is one important way in which differences are mediated from the cultural level to the individual level to produce differences in individuals' experiences, behaviors, and values at work (once again, it is assumed that mediation in the opposite direction is also feasible). That is, it is expected that all cultures will have examples of all four organizational types, but it is also expected that different organizational types will be *more or less prevalent* in different cultures, that is, some organizational types will have a higher density, or concentration, in some cultures relative to other cultures. This is a population-ecology explanation (Hannan & Freeman, 1977), which suggests that different cultural environments have common organizational or *species* types but that local conditions make dif-

Figure 23.3. Locating Kabanoff's Model of Organizational Types Within Hofstede's Model of National Culture Types.

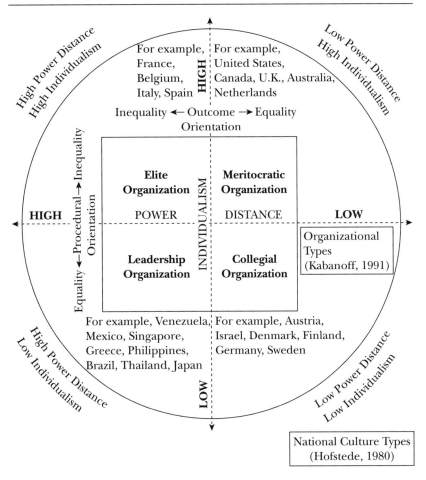

ferent types dominant. These local conditions include the values of the surrounding culture. Therefore more people within a particular culture will tend to have work experiences that reflect the practices, structures, and conditions associated with a particular organizational type and this will shape their values and attitudes as well as reinforce the values they have been socialized in. Schwartz (1994) explained why we should expect to find a meaningful relationship between individual- and culture-level values in the context of the conflict between values of *self-direction versus conformity:*

"Similar dynamics [to those at the individual level] are likely to find expression in the culture level organisation of priorities: Nations with institutional structures conducive to independence (e.g., widespread higher education, religious pluralism, occupations demanding nonroutine decision making, democratic political structures) will foster self-direction values in their citizens. Moreover, in the struggle to attain or maintain sway over cultural priorities, institutional structures that foster self-direction will come into conflict with those conducive to conformity (for example, limited educational opportunities, a single sovereign religion, routinised and closely supervised occupations, centralised political structures)" (p. 93).

Although the combined model has not been rigorously empirically tested, it makes some interesting predictions, and there are at least some suggestive empirical findings. For example, the combined model predicts that leadership-oriented teamwork-based organizations are more prevalent in Hofstede's high power distance, low individualism cultures such as Venezuela, Singapore, Mexico, Philippines, and to an extent, Japan. Evidence consistent with this prediction comes from an impressive study by Lincoln and Kalleberg (1990), who compared fifty-two U.S. and forty-six Japanese manufacturing organizations, surveying around 4,000 managerial and nonmanagerial respondents in each country. They studied both organization-level (for example, structure, centralization, span of control) and individual-level variables (job satisfaction, organizational commitment), and their work resulted in a number of interesting findings, but from the viewpoint of the present chapter the most interesting were those dealing with the balance between centralized structures and "consultative" or "inclusive" processes in Japanese organizations (Figure 23.2). For example, Lincoln and Kalleberg (1990) made these observations:

> In addition to teamwork being more pervasive in Japanese organizations, a very common observation is that styles of supervision are highly distinctive, with strong personal bonds developing between superior and subordinate. Japanese foremen have a wide mandate to involve themselves broadly in their subordinates' lives both on and off the job. . . . [I]ndications abound that such vertical dependency bonds have strong roots in Japanese culture. . . . [T]his kind

of broad, paternalistic leadership appears to be preferred by a very large segment of the Japanese workforce. . . . [T]here is also much evidence that the stress on consultation and consensus in Japanese decision-making tends to avert one-sided domination [by supervisors] [pp. 89–91].

The same sort of balance between centralized authority and decentralized participation processes is observed at management levels: "Participatory, consensus-oriented decision-making operates at both management and direct worker levels in Japanese organisations. . . . [Scholars] see Japanese authority structures combining high concentration of formal authority with decentralisation of *de facto* participation" (Lincoln & Kalleberg, 1990, p. 17).

Some further suggestive evidence comes from *The Seven Cultures of Capitalism* by Hampden-Turner and Trompenaars (1993). Their book is based upon a survey of 15,000 managers from around the world who attended seminars conducted by the Center for International Business Studies in Amstelveen in the Netherlands. An interesting feature of the study was the way it studied differences in managers' attitudes and beliefs. Managers were asked not simply a series of attitudinal or values questions but how they would deal with a number of universal managerial dilemmas, described in brief scenarios. For example, managers were posed this problem:

> Suppose you, as a manager are in the process of hiring a new employee to work in your department. Which of the two following considerations are more important to you:
>
> (a) The new employee must fit into the group or team in which he/she is to work.
> (b) The new employee must have the skills, the knowledge, and a record of success in a previous job [p. 42].

Hampden-Turner and Trompenaars' findings (1993) are interesting in relation to several of the quadrants in Figure 23.3. For example, what of the suggestions in Figure 23.3 that elite organizations are more prevalent in a high power distance, high individualism country such as France? Here is more evidence from Hampden-Turner and Trompenaars consistent with that view:

For the French the very structure of the organization is a competitive weapon with a chain of command already in place. It remains for those to whom status has been attributed to act out its rationale in practice, for the engineer from the Haute École Polytechnique to do the outstanding work for which he is qualified. The group's top leaders are propelled by the faith of their subordinates. Le Chef, le Patron, le Seigneur, "Monsieur le Directeur," senior qualified engineers, often use *tu* instead of *vous* when talking down to a mere technician. This was, until recently, the habitual form of address for servants, a mixture of familiarity and subordination. "To be an engineer in France," explained a manager at Saint Gobain, "doesn't mean you can fix a machine. It implies something about outlook, about professional self-esteem and national pride" [pp. 360–361].

The elitist nature of management in large French companies can be noted from the great number of overlapping board memberships. . . . Between them, [these overlapping members] can usually fend off takeover bids, and shareholders have little influence. Voting is very rare and is seen as an insult to, or lack of confidence in, *le président* [p. 361].

And the style of French organizations was recently labeled elitist and imperial by a *Business Week* story (Toy, 1995) that described senior corporate managers in France as acting often "like minor deities."

Hampden-Turner and Trompenaars's characterization of Swedish organizations as having *socialized individualism* at their core also fits quite well with the prediction in Figure 23.3 that collegial organizations should be characteristic of (relatively) less individualist, low power distance cultures such as Sweden, Austria, Norway, Israel. Socialized individualism is described as encompassing such qualities as seeking community through work, individualizing oneself by what one contributes to the workplace and to colleagues, having a deep sublimated affection at the root of the work ethic, putting great emphasis on the development of individuals, and holding a strong view that information, ability, and commitment are widely rather than narrowly dispersed among organizational members. Such beliefs clearly fit well with the collegial type of organization, with its emphasis on achievement through the action of equal and committed individuals. *Socialized individualism* may seem a rather paradoxical concept in that it combines individualist elements such as valuing individuals and individual development with collectivist elements emphasizing the importance of the group or at least the centrality of interdependence among group members. A somewhat similar cultural form was suggested by Triandis (1994) who called it horizontal collectivism. In Triandis's terms, *horizontal collectivism* emphasizes interdependence and oneness in voluntary solidarity among group members, and *vertical collectivism* emphasizes the individual who serves and complies with the group. Horizontal collectivism represents a form of balance between individual and group goals but does not make the individual secondary to the group, as tends to be the case in vertical collectivism.

In summary, this section has argued that different types of organizations can be recognized by the different values they possess. These values are shaped by (and in turn shape) the surrounding national culture. Therefore different types of organizations should be more or less prevalent in different national cultures. This argument also implies that organizational values form an important link between national values and the values and behavior of small groups and individuals in organizations. It is suggested that this linkage can be usefully described in terms of the combined model shown in Figure 23.3, which integrates a theory of organizational types (Kabanoff, 1991, 1993) with aspects of the dominant theory of culture types (Hofstede, 1980).

Measuring Organizations' Values and Value Structures

We could test the organizational typology I have described in several ways. We could, for example, collect survey data from members of a sample of organizations in different countries about the distribution of rewards, broadly defined, and the nature of allocation mechanisms and procedures. Apart from being very expensive, this research process lands us back in the domain of surveys; we would be back to studying what I have defined as the outcome level—people's justice perceptions—and using these perceptions to define the justice character of organizations. Instead, I have chosen the approach of studying organizations' justice characters through the values that organizations themselves espouse. But how can we measure the collective espoused values of organizations?

Measuring Collective Values

Rokeach (1973, 1979) is probably best known for his development of the Rokeach Value Survey, yet in a paper that has received comparatively little attention he explored five different methods for measuring values (Rokeach, 1979). In fact, in this paper Rokeach could not use his famous survey to measure the values of his "subject" directly, for in this case his subject was an institution—the institution of science.

Rokeach identified these five methods for measuring the values of science:

1. *Performing content analysis,* that is, extracting the values referred to and exhorted in institutional documents or publications (in this case editorials in the journal *Science*).
2. *Measuring personal values of institutional gatekeepers* (in this case the personal values of scientists).
3. *Measuring personal values of an institution's special clients* (in this case the personal values of graduate students in science).
4. *Measuring values of an institution as perceived by its gatekeepers* (in this case the values scientists attributed to science).
5. *Measuring values of an institution as perceived by general clients* (in this case the values university students attributed to science).

The next section considers how one of these methods identified by Rokeach—content, or text, analysis—provides us with a number of advantages for solving a problem similar to the one that Rokeach faced. In the present case, the problem is how to measure the values espoused by a relatively large number of different organizations.

Performing Text Analysis

Stone, Dunphy, Smith, and Ogilvie (1966) defined content analysis as "any technique for making inferences by systematically and objectively identifying specified characteristics within text" (p. 5).

Although content analysis is the traditional name for this process, I prefer the more limited and in most cases more accurate term *text analysis,* because the data for most of these analyses are words, text, and not picture, formats, or other forms of content discernable in many texts (compare Stone, in press). Weber (1985) states that the core process of virtually all forms of text analysis (TA) is data reduction, through which the many words of text are classified into many fewer content categories. Rokeach (1979) and others (for example, Simons, 1993) have described text analysis as a *trace methodology,* that is, it seeks evidence of the concerns of either individuals or collectives such as organizations in the physical or verbal behaviors, or traces, that they leave in documents they produce. Thus the core assumption underlying the use of text analysis for describing organizational values is that organizations leave traces of their distinctive value patterns in their documents and that these traces can be observed and measured by counting the frequency with which documents refer to different values. The relative frequency with which a value occurs is interpreted as an indication of its importance or cognitive centrality—values with high frequencies are seen as more important or salient (Huff, 1990).

In comparison to survey methods of value measurement, text analysis has a number of advantages: it is unobtrusive, uses naturally evoked verbal behavior as the source of value-data, is suitable for carrying out longitudinal research given the availability of different texts over long periods of time, and embodies a systematic and quantitative approach to measuring qualitative data. One of its major disadvantages traditionally has been that it is lengthy, labor intensive, and fundamentally boring. Coding even moderately long texts requires large amounts of rater time and money for paying raters. Burnout of both raters and researchers is a common outcome among text analysts. However, with the growing availability of computers and text analysis software, much of the drudgery and some of the time demands can be alleviated by employing *computer-aided text analysis* (CATA), in which a computer program checks the words in the text against a set of content categories stored in a content-analytic dictionary.

CATA has been extensively discussed in a number of sources (for example, Kabanoff, 1996; Gephart, 1993; Huff, 1990; Weber, 1985; Wolfe, Gephart, & Johnson, 1993), and that discussion need not be repeated here in detail; however, the main benefits of CATA should be emphasized. To the advantages offered by manual text analysis, CATA adds the following: *perfect reliability*—classification of text by multiple human coders permits the level of reliability achieved to be assessed, and classification by computer leads to perfect reliability because the coding rules are always applied in the same way; use of *standard dictionaries*—a number of generic dictionaries for content analysis have been developed and validated on different kinds of text; they contain categories useful in many social science contexts and enhance both comparability and validity; *efficiency and speed*—once a computer-based analysis dictionary has been developed, it works quickly, can be used efficiently with large text databases (the computer does not get bored), and applied to new data sets; the existence of standard dictionaries permits exploratory text analysis to be undertaken, which is inconceivable with a manual approach. Thus CATA offers a number of important advantages for studying organizational values both within and across cultures (with some limitations that I discuss a little later).

Empirical Evidence for Organizational Value Structures

The next two sections offer two examples of studies that have used CATA to study organizational values. The first study involved only one cultural setting and provides a general introduction to and description of the methodology. The second study demonstrates application in a cross-cultural research setting.

The Values Australian Organizations Espouse

Studies that I and my colleagues carried out (Kabanoff, 1993; Kabanoff, Waldersee, & Cohen, 1995) used CATA to measure differences in the kinds of values that Australian organizations espoused in certain documents. Specifically, we sought to show that differences between organizations' espoused values could be described in terms of the four main types of value structures, or value profiles, described earlier: elite, leadership, meritocratic, and collegial.

Annual reports, internal magazines, and mission statements from eighty-eight large Australian organizations were collected, and sections of these documents that dealt with or were likely to deal with organizational values, such as the CEO's annual letter to shareholders, were extracted for analysis. The annual report (AR) is the most visible and most publicized document that is produced regularly by publicly owned companies. It is the principal means by which corporations communicate explanations for past performance, expectations of future results, and other information that they feel it is important to convey (Staw, McKechnie, & Puffer, 1983). Because ARs are so important, top management plays a central role in determining their substantive content, even though internal or external public relations specialists may advise on stylistic issues (Goodman, 1980). Given their role and importance, ARs are an appropriate text to analyze for evidence of organizational values. This does *not* imply that all organizational members would subscribe to the values expressed in their organization's AR; nevertheless it is legitimate to consider that ARs indicate the publicly espoused "official" values that are expressed on behalf of organizations by senior managers. Analyzing additional types of text from sources such as internal magazines for a majority of the organizations represented an alternative, more internally focused source of information about organizational values.

A content analysis dictionary that included the nine core values specified by the theory (see Figure 23.2) was developed. Table 23.1 lists the nine core values, or categories, and some examples of the words included in each. Seven of the value categories were developed specifically to measure the values specified by the typological theory, using the text analysis software package Textpack 4 (Mohler & Zull, 1990). These categories were validated by using them to analyze samples of organizational text and then having staff retrieve and read sentences from the text that contained the target values, thereby checking that the words being tagged actually represented the targeted value. The other two value categories (affiliation and normative) came from two standard, or generic, content dictionaries that are contained in the General Inquirer III text analysis package (Zull, Weber, & Mohler, 1989); these categories have been used to analyze a variety of texts (Weber, 1985).

More than a million words of text were searched by the computer for references to these nine values. The relative density with which different values were referred to in a company's documents

Table 23.1. A Computer-Based Text Analysis Dictionary.

Category	Definition and Word Examples
Authority	Concerned with authority figures and relations: for example, "executive," "manager," "director."
Leadership	Concerned with leadership: for example, "leader," "leadership."
Team	Concerned with teams and teamwork: for example, "team," "teamwork," "cooperation."
Participation	Concerned with participation by nonmanagerial levels: for example, "participation," "consultation" co-occurring with reference to "employees."
Commitment	Concerned with organizational commitment and loyalty: for example, "commitment," "loyalty," "dedication."
Performance	Concerned with performance: for example, "achievement," "performance," "service," "efficiency."
Reward	Concerned with organizational reward system, especially remuneration: for example, "bonus," "compensation," "reward," "salary."
Affiliation[a]	All words with connotation of affiliation or supportiveness: for example, "share," "enthusiasm," "appreciate," "join together."
Normative[b] (rectitude ethics)	All rectitude values invoking in the final analysis the social order and its demands as justification: for example, "responsibilities," "fair," "rights."

[a]*Affiliation* comes from the Harvard IV dictionary.

[b]*Normative* is the same as the Rectitude (Ethics) category from the Lasswell dictionary.

was estimated by dividing the total number of references to each value by the total number of sentences analyzed from that company. These frequencies were standardized and then averaged across different types of documents. Thus each company received nine value scores based upon the relative frequency with which each of the nine values was referred to in its documents. Although it would be possible simply to compare organizations in terms of their scores on each single value, our aim was to discover whether organizations' value *profiles* could be characterized in terms of the limited number of different value patterns specified by the theory (Figure 23.2). That is, were there organizations whose espoused values matched each one of the four theoretical types of value structures: elite, leadership, collegial, and meritocratic?

A form of theory-based cluster analysis was used to identify organizations that had value profiles that resembled the value profiles we expected to find based upon the theory. The prototypical value profiles were used to define selection *templates* for the cluster program to use in assigning organizations to different clusters. For a relatively strong value, the selection criterion, that is the initial value-center for the cluster, was set at 1.0; because scores had been turned into Z-score form, the value score of organizations to be selected for that cluster was therefore initially set to be one standard deviation above the overall mean for organizations. Similarly, for a weak value, the initial center was set as −1.0; that is, one standard deviation below the sample mean. For example, the *selection template* for organizations with an elite value structure was: affiliation (−1.0), authority (1.0), commitment (−1.0), normative (−1.0), leadership (−1.0), participation (−1.0), performance (1.0), reward (1.0), and teamwork (−1.0) (The + values in Figure 23.2 were all translated as +1.0s for the selection templates and the − values were translated as −1.0s.) Figure 23.4 shows the average value profiles of four groups of organizations that were selected on the basis of the resemblance of their group's actual value profile to one of our theoretical value profiles. Seventy-two of the eighty-eight organizations were assignable to one of the four clusters, and sixteen were designated unclassifiable on the basis that they very infrequently mentioned any of the nine values.

It can be seen in Figure 23.4 that the four clusters of organizations have fairly distinctive value profiles that *approximate* the theoretical value profiles. We would not expect to find that organizations matched the theoretical types exactly because the theoretical types represent ideals that need not exist in the "real world" (see Doty & Glick's 1994 discussion of this issue). There was a collegial group that put strong emphases on affiliation, participation, and normative values and a low emphasis on rewards. We found that universities and governmental departments tended to cluster in this group. There was also a leadership group that put strong emphases on leadership, teamwork, and loyalty values and a meritocratic

Figure 23.4. Value Profiles of Four Types of Organizations.

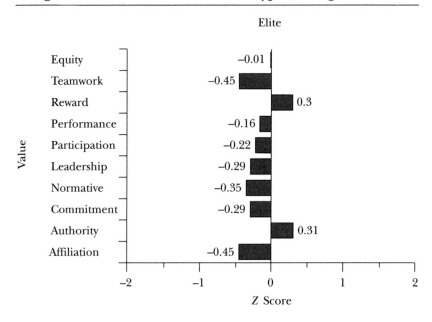

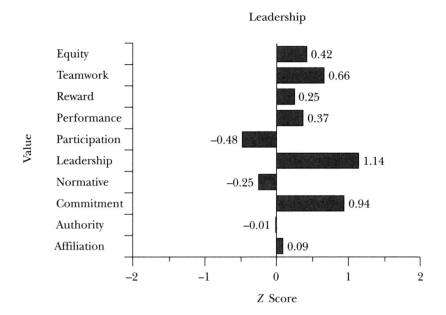

Figure 23.4. Value Profiles of Four Types of Organizations, Cont'd.

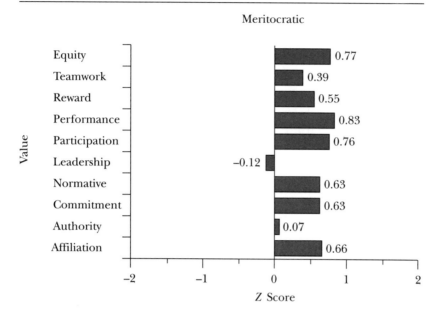

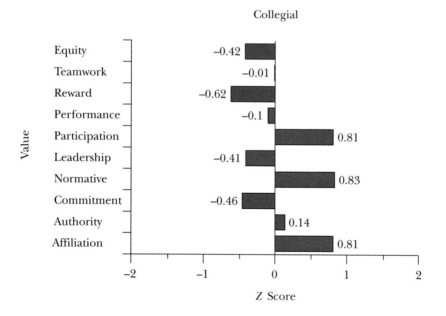

group that had the expected combination of cohesion and performance values. The profile for the elite group was less clear but still somewhat different from any of the other groups. On the whole the results were interesting and fairly supportive of the theory. The study suggested that CATA could be used to make meaningful comparisons among organizations in terms of their espoused values and to match organizations with different theoretical, organizational types. In the next example, I show that the same approach can be used to compare organizations cross-culturally as well.

The Values Australian and U.S. Organizations Espouse

Daly and I conducted a study (Kabanoff & Daly, 1995) that extended the approach just described to the cross-cultural setting. The sample comprised seventy-seven Australian and fifty-five U.S. organizations, all of them large and well known inside and in some cases outside their respective countries. They came from a range of industries and sectors, included a number of governmental departments, and were approximately matched by industry across the two countries. The fifty-five U.S. organizations were selected to match the Australian sample as well as possible by industry and size (total assets, number of full-time employees). Although it was not feasible to match the samples in terms of absolute size because the U.S. economy is more than twenty times larger than the Australian economy (*World Competitiveness Report,* 1995), the study compared leading companies in both countries. Mean rates of change in both total assets and full-time employees (calculated as the ratio 1991/1986) were not significantly different between the two countries, suggesting that general economic conditions were broadly similar over this period. Thus, as far as possible, the study selected comparable organizations in the two countries so that national differences could not be readily explained in terms of differences in the types of organizations sampled from the two countries.

We measured the same nine values as were used in the previous study, although in this study the text analyzed came from annual reports alone. Text from the ARs was selected as previously, to identify what should be value-rich portions of the reports. Five years of annual reports (1986 to 1990) were analyzed. As previously, to control for differences in the number of sentences analyzed for different organizations, the total frequency count for each value category was divided by the number of sentences analyzed from each organization. A total of 43,072 sentences (or 1,085,100 words) were analyzed.

When considered in the context of a number of other countries, Australia and the United States are often described as members of a specific group of "cultural allies" (Kanter, 1991)—the U.K., Canada, New Zealand, the United States, and Australia. Nevertheless, their assignment to the same broad cultural category does not mean they lack significant differences. Sociologists and social psychologists (for example, Encel, 1970; Feather, 1975) have suggested some important value differences between the United States and Australia, one being their different conceptions of social equality. Specifically, the two cultures appear to deal in different ways with the tension between equality and achievement, values important in both countries.

It has been said that the two core values of U.S. society are equality and achievement, where equality implies a respect for others simply because they too are human and also equality of opportunity (Lipset, 1963; see also Trice & Beyer, 1993). Equality of opportunity, however, does not imply equality of outcomes. As Potter (1954) put it: "The American ideal and practice of equality . . . [implies] for the individual . . . opportunity to make his own place in society . . . and emancipation from a system of status. . . . The American has traditionally expected to find a gamut running from rags to riches, from tramps to millionaires. . . . Equality did not mean uniform position on a common level, but it did mean universal opportunity to move through a scale which traversed many levels" (pp. 91–92).

Equality and individual achievement are also valued in Australia. However the emphasis on equality extends beyond equality of opportunity to a demand for a "fair and reasonable" standard of living for everyone and less tolerance of inequality in wealth. This emphasis on equality of outcomes also tends to be accompanied by a distrust of special excellence in many areas (Feather, 1975), one exception being sports. Encel (1970) summed up this version of equality as follows: "The conception of equality which prevails in Australia is one which places great stress on the enforcement of a high minimum standard of material well-being, on the outward show of equality and the minimisation of privileges due to formal rank, and almost by implication restricts the scope for the unusual, eccentric, or dissenting individual" (p. 56). Although a paradoxical outcome of the U.S. version of equality is considerable economic inequality, Encel (1970) also identified a paradox in the Australian version: "Constitutional liberalism, which thinks in terms of uniform general laws, would create a set of bureaucratic rules to enforce equal treatment. . . . Herein lies the paradox of egalitarianism in Australia: the search for equality of the redistributive kind breeds bureaucracy; bureaucracy breeds authority; and authority undermines the equality which bred it" (p. 57). The overt rejection of covert reliance on authority in Australian life has been noted by a number of writers (for example, Feather, 1994; Hughes, 1987).

On the basis of these cultural differences, what were expected to be the differences between Australia and the United States in terms of the four organizational types? One implication was that meritocratic value systems (which combine values of interpersonal equality with values of individual achievement and reward) should be more prevalent among U.S. than Australian organizations. However, the basis for making predictions about value structures among Australian organizations was less clear. There were reasons for expecting Australian organizations to be both more elite and more collegial. The elite type would represent the dominance of the authority-oriented bureaucratic theme in Australian life, and the collegial type would represent the emphasis on equality combined with the moral, normative concerns that England (1975) identified as characteristic of Australian managers. Therefore we advanced these two hypotheses:

Hypothesis 1: There is a higher incidence of meritocratic value structures among U.S. than among Australian organizations.

Hypothesis 2: There is a higher incidence of both elite- and collegial value structures among Australian than among U.S. organizations.

In order to test these two hypotheses, we first repeated the clustering procedure described earlier with the total sample of both

Australian and U.S. organizations. We then cross-tabulated the clusters organizations were assigned to by organizations' country of origin (Table 23.2).

The chi-square for Table 23.2 was highly significant ($\chi^2(4) = 18.22$, $p = .001$), indicating that there was a significant overall difference in the frequency with which U.S. and Australian organizations were assigned to the different clusters. It can be seen in Table 23.2 that a significantly greater proportion (80 percent) of the meritocratic cluster comprised U.S. organizations. Australian organizations were overrepresented in the elite cluster, where 70 percent were Australian. There were no significant country differences

Table 23.2. Organizational Type Cross-Tabulated by Country.

Value Cluster	Country		Row Total
	Australia	United States	
Elite	33[a]	14	47
	27.4[b]	19.6	
	2.1*[c]	−2.1*	
Leadership	9	10	19
	11.1	7.9	
	−1.0	1.0	
Meritocratic	4	16	20
	11.7	8.3	
	−3.8**	3.8**	
Collegial	18	11	29
	16.9	12.1	
	1.1	−1.1	
Nonclassifiable	13	4	17
	9.9	7.1	
	1.6	−1.6	
Total	77	55	132

[a]Observed frequency

[b]Expected frequency

[c]Standardized residual of observed minus expected frequencies and its associated significance level: * $p < .05$, ** $p < .01$

for either the leadership or collegial types although, as predicted, more Australian than U.S. organizations were classified as collegial. There was also a tendency for more Australian organizations to be assigned to the nonclassifiable group. Overall, these findings provided strong support for hypothesis 1 and partial support for hypothesis 2.

How well could a linear combination of these values distinguish between organizations from the two countries? This was examined by a discriminant analysis in which all nine values were entered simultaneously with the a priori likelihood of assignment determined by the group size. The value measures provided a highly significant degree of discrimination between countries, with a canonical correlation of .59 ($p < .000$), and a Wilks' lambda of .62 ($p < .000$). Another indication of the discriminating power of the measures was that they correctly assigned 78.7 percent (104/132) of organizations to their country of origin, with Australian organizations being somewhat more likely to be correctly classified than U.S. ones (86.8 percent versus 73.6 percent). Thus the nine theoretical values discriminated rather well between organizations from the two countries.

What is evident is that the approach adopted represents a quantitatively rigorous and simultaneously naturalistic approach to studying cross-cultural differences in organizational values. Another benefit of using this approach is that researchers can study values over extended time periods and therefore changes in values over time (for example, Kabanoff & Holt, 1996). Like any method, text analysis has its limitations, and it is by no means suggested to be a replacement for survey research, but it should be an important complement because it is good at things that survey research is not—generating unobtrusive naturalistic and longitudinal data.

Conclusion

Text analysis as a tool for cross-cultural research has one obvious limitation: it relies on language as its data source and most existing content dictionaries are in English. However, this is a practical problem rather than a problem of principle because text analysis dictionaries can be translated just as questionnaires can. For example, Martindale's Regressive Imagery Dictionary (RID) (Martindale, 1975, 1990) is available in a French version (Hogenraad & Orianne, 1985–1986), and the Lasswell Value Dictionary (LVD) (Namenwirth & Weber, 1987) has a German version. These and the other few existing translations show that it can be done. It is more time-consuming to translate a content analysis dictionary than a questionnaire, but it should also provide a greater return in that it opens up an entirely new universe of texts for analysis. The time and resources required by Osgood, May, and Miron (1975) to develop their world "atlas" of 620 words that were rated on the dimensions of evaluation, activity, and potency in a large number of cultures could be viewed as an indicator of the difficulties involved in developing text analysis dictionaries that are equivalent across cultures, yet I suspect that the reality will prove less daunting. I have several reasons for believing this. First, CATA typically involves the measurement of quite general themes using categories containing many words, and I would expect larger categories be to be less affected by the fact that some words have different connotations in different cultures. Second, I expect dictionaries will be translated in a thoughtful manner, with native speakers involved in the process to help guard against the problem of lack of equivalence in word usage. Whether these relatively optimistic expectations are fulfilled remains to be seen, nevertheless I expect to see text analysis dictionaries translated into a variety of languages in the future because of the possibilities for cross-cultural comparisons that they create.

Cross-cultural research has always been interesting, of late it has also become of urgent practical importance as a wave of globalization sweeps across nations, economies, and companies ("cascading globalization" Rosabeth Moss Kanter called it in her keynote address at the Academy of Management's National Meeting in 1994). The practical benefits of understanding differences in organizational types and values in different cultural contexts are highlighted by Jackson and Schuler's observation (1995) that

> globalisation may be the most potent catalyst for an explosion of research on HRM in Context: for those operating in a global environment, the importance of context is undeniable—it cannot be ignored. Multinational organizations strive for consistency in their ways of managing people on a worldwide basis and also adapt their

ways to the specific cultural requirements. . . . [T]hose responsible for design of globally effective HRM must shift their focus away from the almost overwhelming variety of specific practices and policies found around the world and look instead at the more abstract, fundamental dimensions of context, HRM systems . . . and employees' reactions [p. 257].

The organizational and cultural values discussed in this chapter and the relationships between them may provide at least some of the "fundamental dimensions" that Jackson and Schuler recommend we should seek.

References

Bahad, E. Y., & Wallbott, H. G. (1986). The effects of social factors on emotional reactions. In K. S. Scherer, H. G. Wallbott, & A. B. Summerfield (Eds.), *Experiencing emotion: A cross-cultural study* (pp. 246–255). New York: Cambridge University Press.

Baron, J. N., & Cook, K. S. (1992). Process and outcome: Perspectives on the distribution of rewards in organisations. *Administrative Science Quarterly, 37,* 191–197.

Bond, M. H., Leung, K., & Wan, K. C. (1982). How does cultural collectivism operate? The impact of task and maintenance contribution on reward allocation. *Journal of Cross-Cultural Psychology, 13,* 186–200.

Brockner, J., & Weisenfeld, B. M. (1994). *The interactive impact of procedural fairness and outcome favorability: The effects of what you do depend on how you do it.* Unpublished manuscript.

Cohen, R. L. (1986). Power and justice in intergroup relations. In H. W. Bierhof, R. L. Cohen, & J. Greenberg (Eds.), *Justice in social relations* (pp. 65–86). New York: Plenum.

Cropanzano, R. (Ed.). (1993). *Justice in the workplace: Approaching fairness in human resource management.* Hillsdale, NJ: Erlbaum.

Deutsch, M. (1985). *Distributive justice: A social-psychological perspective.* New Haven, CT: Yale University Press.

Doty, D. H., & Glick, W. H. (1994). Typologies as a unique form of theory building: Toward improved understanding and modelling. *Academy of Management Review, 19,* 230–251.

Encel, S. (1970). *Equality and authority: A study of class, status and power in Australia.* Melbourne: Cheshire.

England, G. W. (1975). *The manager and his values: An international perspective from the United States, Japan, Korea, India and Australia.* New York: Ballinger.

Feather, N. T. (1975). *Values in education and society.* New York: Free Press.

Feather, N. T. (1994). Values and national identification: Australian evidence. *Australian Journal of Psychology, 46,* 35–40.

Gephart, R. P., Jr. (1993). The textual approach: Risk and blame in disaster sensemaking. *Academy of Management Journal, 36,* 1465–1514.

Gersick, C.J.G. (1991). Revolutionary change theories: A multilevel exploration of the punctuated equilibrium paradigm. *Academy of Management Review, 16,* 10–36.

Goodman, R. (1980, Summer). Annual reports serving a dual marketing function: Report as survey. *Public Relations Quarterly, 36,* 21–24.

Greenberg, J. (1990). Organizational justice: Yesterday, today and tomorrow. *Journal of Management, 16,* 399–432.

Hampden-Turner, C., & Trompenaars, A. (1993). *The seven cultures of capitalism: Value systems for creating wealth in the United States, Japan, Germany, France, Britain, Sweden, and the Netherlands.* New York: Currency/Doubleday.

Hannan, M. T., & Freeman, J. (1977). The ecology of organizational founding: American Labor Unions, 1836–1985. *American Journal of Sociology, 92,* 901–943.

Hedström, P. (1988). *Structures of inequality: A study of stratification within work organizations.* Sweden: Kristianstads Boktryckeri.

Hofstede, G. (1980). *Culture's consequences: International differences in work-related values.* Thousand Oaks, CA: Sage.

Hofstede, G., Neuijen, B., Ohayv, D. D., & Sanders, G. (1990). Measuring organizational cultures: A qualitative and quantitative study across twenty cases. *Administrative Science Quarterly, 35,* 286–316.

Hogenraad, R., & Orianne, E. (1985–1986). Imagery, regressive thinking, and verbal performance in internal monologue. *Imagination, Cognition and Personality, 5*(2), 127–145.

Huff, A. S. (1990). *Mapping strategic thought.* New York: Wiley.

Hughes, R. (1987). *The fatal shore.* London: Pan Books.

Jackson, S. E., & Schuler, R. S. (1995). Understanding human resource management in the context of organizations and their environments. In J. T. Spence, J. M. Darley, & D. J. Foss (Eds.), *Annual Review of Psychology* (Vol. 46, pp. 237–264). Palo Alto, CA: Annual Reviews.

James, K. (1993). The social context of organizational justice: Cultural, intergroup, and structural effects on justice behaviors and perceptions. In R. Cropanzano (Ed.), *Justice in the workplace: Approaching fairness in human resource management* (pp. 21–50). Hillsdale, NJ: Erlbaum.

Kabanoff, B. (1991). Equity, equality, power and conflict. *Academy of Management Review, 16,* 416–441.

Kabanoff, B. (1993). An exploration of espoused culture in Australian organisations (with a closer look at the banking sector). *Asia Pacific Journal of Human Resources, 31,* 1–29.

Kabanoff, B. (1996). Computers can read as well as count: How computer-aided text analysis can benefit organizational research. In C. L. Cooper & D. M. Rousseau (Eds.), *Trends in organizational behavior* (Vol. 3, pp. 1–21). New York: Wiley.

Kabanoff, B., & Daly, J. P. (1995, August). *Values espoused by Australian and US organisations: A cross-national comparison using text analysis.* Paper presented at the National Academy of Management Meeting, Vancouver.

Kabanoff, B., & Holt, J. (1996). Changes in the espoused values of Australian organisations: 1986–1990. *Journal of Organizational Behavior, 17,* 201–219.

Kabanoff, B., Waldersee, R., & Cohen, M. (1995). Espoused organizational values and organizational change themes. *Academy of Management Journal, 38,* 1075–1104.

Kanter, R. M. (1991). Transcending business boundaries: 12,000 world managers view change. *Harvard Business Review, 69*(3), 151–164.

Katz, D., & Kahn, R. L. (1978). *The social psychology of organizations* (2nd ed.). New York: Wiley.

Kim, K. I., Park, H. J., & Suzuki, N. (1990). Reward allocations in the United States, Japan, and Korea: A comparison of individualistic and collectivistic cultures. *Academy of Management Journal, 33,* 188–198.

Leung, K. (1989). Cross-cultural differences: Individual-level vs. cultural-level analysis. *International Journal of Psychology, 24,* 703–719.

Lincoln, J. R., & Kalleberg, A. L. (1990). *Culture, control and commitment.* New York: Cambridge University Press.

Lipset, S. M. (1963). The value patterns of democracy: A case study in comparative analysis. *American Sociological Review, 28,* 515–531.

Lundbergh, C. L., & Peterson, M. F. (1994). The meaning of working in U.S. and Japanese local governments at three hierarchical levels. *Human Relations, 47,* 1459–1487.

Martin, J. (1992). *Cultures in organizations: Three perspectives.* New York: Oxford University Press.

Martin, J., Scully, M., & Levitt, B. (1988). *Injustice and the legitimation of revolution: Damning the past, excusing the present and neglecting the future* (Research paper No. 1011). Graduate School of Business, Stanford University.

Martindale, C. (1975). *Romantic progression: The psychology of literary history.* Washington, DC: Hemisphere.

Martindale, C. (1990). *The clockwork muse: The predictability of artistic change.* New York: Basic Books.

Meindl, J. R. (1989). Managing to be fair: An exploration of values, motives and leadership. *Administrative Science Quarterly, 34,* 252–276.

Mitchell, T. R., & Scott, W. G. (1990). America's problems and needed reforms: Confronting the ethic of personal advantage. *Academy of Management Executive, 4,* 23–35.

Mohler, P. P., & Zull, C. (1990). *Textpack P.C.* ZUMA. Mannheim, Germany: Centre for Surveys, Research and Methodology.

MOW [Meaning of Working] International Research Team. (1987). *The meaning of working.* Orlando: Academic Press.

Nader, L., & Sursock, A. (1986). Anthropology and justice. In R. L. Cohen (Ed.), *Justice: Views from the social sciences* (pp. 205–233). New York: Plenum.

Namenwirth, J. Z., & Weber, R. P. (1987). *Dynamics of culture.* London: Allen & Unwin.

Osgood, C. E., May, W., & Miron, M. (1975). *Cross-cultural universals of affective meaning.* Urbana: University of Illinois Press.

Pfeffer, J. (1990). Incentives in organizations: The importance of social relations. In O. E. Williamson (Ed.), *Organization theory: From Chester Barnard to the present and beyond* (pp. 72–97). New York: Oxford University Press.

Potter, D. M. (1954). *People of plenty.* Chicago: University of Chicago Press.

Rohner, R. P. (1984). Toward a conception of culture for cross-cultural psychology. *Journal of Cross-Cultural Psychology, 15*(2), 111–138.

Rokeach, M. (1973). *The nature of human values.* New York: Free Press.

Rokeach, M. (1979). From individual to institutional values: With special reference to the values of science. In M. Rokeach (Ed.), *Understanding human values* (pp. 47–70). New York: Free Press.

Schein, E. H. (1985). *Organizational culture and leadership: A dynamic view.* San Francisco: Jossey-Bass.

Schwartz, S. H. (1992). Universals in the content and structure of values: Theoretical advances and empirical tests in 20 countries. In M. P. Zanna (Ed.), *Advances in experimental social psychology* (Vol. 25, pp. 1–65). Orlando: Academic Press.

Schwartz, S. H. (1994). Beyond individualism and collectivism: New cultural dimensions of values. In U. Kim, H. C. Triandis, Ç. Kagitçibasi, S.-C. Choi, & G. Yoon (Eds.), *Individualism and collectivism: Theory, method, and applications* (pp. 85–119). Thousand Oaks, CA: Sage.

Sheppard, B. H., Lewicki, R. J., & Minton, J. W. (1992). *Organizational justice: The search for fairness in the workplace.* San Francisco: The New Lexington Press.

Simons, T. (1993). Speech patterns and the concept of utility in cognitive maps: The case of integrative bargaining. *Academy of Management Journal, 36,* 139–156.

Staw, B. M., McKechnie, P. I., & Puffer, S. M. (1983). The justification of organisational performance. *Administrative Science Quarterly, 28,* 582–600.

Stone, P. J. (in press). Thematic text analysis: New agendas for analyzing text content. In C. Roberts (Ed.), *Text analysis for the social sciences: Methods for drawing statistical inferences from texts and transcripts.* Hillsdale, NJ: Erlbaum.

Stone, P. J., Dunphy, D. C., Smith, M. S., & Ogilvie, D. M. (1966). *The General Inquirer: A computer approach to content analysis.* Cambridge, MA: MIT Press.

Toy, S. (1995, February 27). Will les affaires lead to reform in *la France? Business Week,* pp. 14–15.

Triandis, H. C. (1994). *Culture and social behavior.* New York: McGraw-Hill.

Trice, H. M., & Beyer, J. M. (1993). *The cultures of work organizations.* Upper Saddle River, NJ: Prentice Hall.

Wallbott, H. G., & Scherer, K. R. (1986). The antecedents of emotional experiences. In K. S. Scherer, H. G. Wallbott, & A. B. Summerfield (Eds.), *Experiencing emotion: A cross-cultural study* (pp. 69–83). New York: Cambridge University Press.

Weber, R. P. (1985). *Basic content analysis.* Thousand Oaks, CA: Sage.

Wolfe, R. A. (1991). The use of content analysis to assess corporate responsibility. *Research in Corporate Social Performance and Policy, 12,* 281–307.

Wolfe, R. A., Gephart, R. P., Jr., & Johnson, T. E. (1993). Computer-facilitated data analysis: Potential contributions to management research. *Journal of Management, 19,* 637–660.

World competitiveness report. (1995). Lausanne: Institute for Management Development.

Zull, C., Weber, P. W., & Mohler, P. P. (1989). *Computer-aided text classification for the social sciences: The General Inquirer III, ZUMA.* Mannheim, Germany: Centre for Surveys, Research and Methodology.

PART 5

Commentary

CHAPTER 24

Personal Reflections and Projections

International Industrial/Organizational Psychology at a Crossroads

Simcha Ronen

The following pages contain some reflections on the state of the art of comparative and cross-cultural industrial and organizational psychology and a few challenges for our scientific endeavors in the near future. Although I learned much from the chapters of this volume, they also provided triggers and examples for my reflection, criticism, and suggestions. These comments revolve around three critical methodological issues: (1) identification of relevant cultural dimensions for our analyses, (2) selection of the appropriate unit of analysis for cross-cultural I/O psychology, and (3) the often overlooked problem of defining and operationalizing cultural and organizational variables.

The existence of cultural differences that influence individual behavior is no longer in doubt and is therefore no longer the central question for research in cross-cultural I/O psychology. Such differences are well established and widely recognized in domains such as family relationships, organizational climate, team influence, and informal organization. But the issue of the identification of the cultural entity relevant to our field is still unresolved. Countries have been used because of practicality, local human resource and legal issues, and economic regulations and because often nations do indeed represent cultural units. Interacting closely with cultural parameters are such other parameters of nations as level of industrialization, religious affiliation, size, boundaries, economic wealth, literacy level, and recent history (Ronen & Shenkar, 1985). However, we should consider the possibility that certain states or nations will cease to serve as relevant cultural milieux, and that a well-defined subnation may be more appropriate. Indeed, in a few cases this course has been partially pursued.

Positivism and Culture

As psychologists whose primary scientific focus is on individual behavior, we have been trained to believe in individual differences and simultaneously in the usefulness of models and theories that attempt to generalize across individuals. On one hand the unique composition of an individual's dynamic processes is accepted as part of psychologist's reality. But on the other hand our entire endeavor can only succeed to the extent that we are able to establish general structures, variables, and relationships. Our commitment to a scientific discipline entails a belief that research will lead first to explanations for complex human phenomena and then to the ability to predict them.

Similar analytical issues arise in the study of cultures. Here a strong belief in the uniqueness of each individual culture is linked with a comparative paradigm using cross-cultural variables. Concern for understanding cultures on their own terms should be balanced by the need to develop constructs that are valid across cultures. The state of the art in cross-cultural industrial and organizational psychology therefore assumes that it is possible to devise research tools that are valid across cultures. Truly comparative data need to be gathered according to constructs that can be defined and operationalized universally. Accordingly, I will adopt a positivist perspective here and assume that there is an *objective reality* that can be studied and understood in terms of causal relationships between measurable variables. Following Brett and her colleagues (Chapter Four), I will recommend that we follow such a perspective and consider culture as a stable system in equilibrium.

The Attribution Paradigm

To justify the use of cultural factors as predictors of organizational phenomena, there must be a clear theoretical rationale for linking these two sets of variables. Members of all societies have implicit models in such areas as leadership and motivation, models that contain beliefs, convictions, and assumptions about effective and desirable attributes and behavior (Ronen, 1994). We need to ask if these implicit models are *culturally bound.* In cultures that differ in some distinguishable societal dimensions, will individuals make different attributions about organizational phenomena studied in the domain of I/O psychology? If indeed *members* of various collectivities are sufficiently homogeneous in terms of shared values, beliefs, social identities, shared meanings, and motives, they may demonstrate similar implicit assumptions about such organizational phenomena as leadership and motivation. They may hold *common implicit theories* and thus, in comparison to members of other societies, agree more among themselves in terms of the attributes and behaviors that distinguish, for example, desirable and effective leaders. House, Wright, and Aditya (Chapter Twenty) refer to such a set of shared beliefs as an implicit, collectively endorsed theory of leadership. These culturally bound implicit models may associate different attributes with effective leadership and may assign preferred processes such as enactment by a leader and acceptance by followers.

House, Wright, and Aditya (Chapter Twenty) suggest that certain leaders' attributes, in contrast to attributes that vary across cultures, are *universally* endorsed, such as value-oriented leadership, leader integrity, generalized managerial competence, visionary and inspirational leadership abilities, and humanist orientation toward subordinates (Bass, 1990). Still, we cannot help but realize that cross-cultural evaluation and *classification* of motivational and leadership manifestations have been reported for over thirty years. This is no longer sufficient. *A concerted effort to link attributions in these areas with specific cultural variables is long overdue.*

Identifying Cultural Variables

By introducing cultural variables into our models and theories, we have assumed that the scope of industrial and organizational psychology would be extended and deepened. These variables can serve either as predictors or mediators, but they are expected to add to the variance accounted for in dependent variables measuring relevant organizational features. The rationale was simple enough: if humans are socialized in more or less homogeneous societies or collectivities, the predispositions of individuals in such populations will be similar; and the more unique the socialization process of each society, the greater will be the levels of differences among individuals from different societies. Accordingly, *culture* has been defined in the industrial and organizational psychology literature and discussed in various chapters in this volume in terms of such socializing processes: culture is a system in which individuals share meanings and common ways of viewing events and objects. Those socialized within the same culture are therefore likely to interpret and evaluate situations and events in a consistent and similar fashion. Variation in the socializing milieu, such as differences in family structures, are likely to effect values related to other social domains, such as job performance or business negotiations.

It remains for us to tend to the task of developing a conceptual framework for understanding the interrelationships between cultural dimensions and organizational actions. This task is not as trivial as it may seem at first. One reason for the current inability of I/O psychology to develop a compelling cross-cultural paradigm may be the fact that not enough cultural variables integral to the field have been identified and conceptualized. When evaluating the multitude of publications attempting to investigate such models, one cannot avoid noticing two phenomena:

1. Often there is no distinction between the variables and constructs that describe the socializing milieu—the culture—and those that characterize the products of socialization—work values, norms, and individual behavior.
2. Even more alarming is the poverty of cultural dimensions used. Somehow we have relieved the appropriate scientific disciplines of their responsibility to provide dimensions for our models. The anthropologists, the political sociologists, the economists, the theologians, the geographers, the historians, and the legal experts have all been ignored by industrial and organizational psychology. The references that do exist to ge-

ography, religion, and level of industrialization (Hofstede, 1980; Ronen, 1986; Ronen & Shenkar, 1985) are rare at best and have been introduced as a posteriori explanations of cultural and national categorizations.

The task of isolating additional dimensions is not easy, and this difficulty is compounded by our neglect of cultural dimensions investigated in other sciences. Nonetheless, we have at times developed organizational dependent variables such as those which Sinha (Chapter Three) describes under role value conflict and that seem to be conceptualized in terms of such cultural norms as truth versus saving face, public versus private behavior, accommodating versus confronting, consideration of organizational effectiveness versus consideration of the individual and his or her family.

I have not conducted a thorough survey, but the number of additional innovative proposals for cultural dimensions in our research literature remains quite limited: Confucian work dynamism (Hofstede & Bond, 1988), abstractive versus associative, field dependent versus field independent, and universalism versus particularism (Glenn & Glenn, 1981). The more traditional dimensions such as space and time have rarely been applied in our research. But identification of the relevant cultural dimensions would *still* leave an additional challenge: namely, *the identification of the processes by which cultural dimensions affect attitudes and behavior in the work environment.*

Level of Analysis

The question of the appropriate level of analysis has become a challenge for the field of organizational behavior in all its areas of interest, including leadership, decision making, organizational climate, and organizational learning. It remains an open question whether organizational processes can be adequately studied through the conceptualizations used in explaining *micro* organizational behavior and drawn from the scientific discipline of psychology or whether these processes might be better understood through *macro* organizational behavior dimensions and socioeconomic models developed in other social-scientific fields (House, Wright, & Aditya, Chapter Twenty; House, Rousseau, & Thomas-

Hunt, 1995; Rousseau & House, 1994). Yet a third position claims that most organizational phenomena are better characterized as belonging to the *meso* level (De Cieri, McGaughey, & Dowling, Chapter Eighteen), and calls for research that integrates micro and macro paradigms. This approach, if applied effectively through appropriate research methodologies will allow a simultaneous analysis of the variables that best represent most organizational phenomena. Research at the meso level examines the relationships and interactions between variables at several levels of analysis.

This perspective is worth emphasizing due to its potential contribution to investigations of the cultural antecedents of organizational phenomena. For instance, many of the cross-cultural and cross-national dimensions refer to *associational* and *relational* norms. These dimensions, which are expected to account for certain behaviors (or predispositions to behavior) manifested in work organizations, would probably be best analyzed at the meso level. Another potential contribution of meso-level analysis is the ability to differentiate between the contribution of team climate and the contribution of cultural variables to organizational behavior.

But the potential of research at the meso level can be realized only if we are able to identify a set of cultural dimensions that do not overlap conceptually with the dimensions of organizational behavior we would like to explain. Using the *same* constructs for studying culture and organizations empties the potential causal effect of its meaning by equating the two environments. The model of cultural antecedents of organizational behavior requires for example that a culture-level variable may cause (or account for) various organizational (macro, meso, or micro) effects. For example, to explain high collectivist work values of teams in an organization as the result of the relatively high collectivist orientation of their national culture is trivial, although typical of 1970s I/O handbooks. To move beyond this sort of unenlightening conclusion, a few methodological requirements must be met:

The constructs defining different levels of variables should themselves be carefully differentiated.

Our investigation should be focused on the unique contributions of cultural variables to the organizational constructs that really matter.

The need to distinguish the unique contribution of culture from the contribution of organizational climate on individual and team behavior calls for multi-organizational studies.

Gibson (Chapter Thirteen) provides a good example of a study that meets most of these requirements as she predicts organizational communication style from the cultural value system. In particular, she claims that Hofstede's cultural dimension of masculinity-femininity (1980) (which she suggests should be renamed with the more gender-neutral terms communal-agenetic, Eagly, 1987), can predict communication style within organizations. More specifically, the degree to which the message content contains rational material based on facts or highly emotional material based on intuition and personal perspectives is predicted to be determined by the degree to which the culture emphasizes values associated with masculinity or femininity. It is expected, says Gibson, that in interpersonal communication, members of cultures that emphasize agenetic values will tend to construct messages with more rational than emotional content. In addition, power distance is predicted to have an effect as a cultural dimension that reflects the extent to which a society accepts an unequal distribution of power in organizations. Thus the degree of power distance will determine whether a formal or informal communication channel is used.

Another level of analysis dilemma with implications for industrial and organizational psychology and organizational behavior is exemplified here in the work of De Cieri, McGaughey, and Dowling (Chapter Eighteen). Research on human and social aspects of organizations has been plagued by separations, compartmentalization, and distinctions between micro- and macro-level factors (and now also meso processes). On one hand it is a reasonable methodological principle to focus on a relatively small number of variables when developing causal models of very complex processes. On the other hand the human resource management research proposed by De Cieri, McGaughey, and Dowling, in its effort to deal with a management approach, neglects to some extent the micro level of organizational behavior. In addition it seems to me at times that in its effort to encompass integrated policies and practices, the human resource management literature has to sacrifice rigor by employing a multitude of variables, meta-dimensions, or composite criteria (overall job satisfaction and overall job behavior, for example).

Teams: The Diversity-Consensus Dilemma

The work of Ilgen, LePine, and Hollenbeck reported in Chapter Fifteen raises an important issue pertaining to effective team performance. It has been suggested, for example, that in multinational companies, multinational or multicultural teams will contribute to effective decision-making processes by decreasing redundancy of operations across countries. Intuitively appealing as this proposal may be, we have not yet resolved the dilemma of the conflicting findings surrounding the desirability of diversity in team composition. It seems clear that organizations in a multicultural milieu would benefit to the extent that their diversity of employees, operations, and expertise is represented in decision making. But this observation seems to be contradicted by the fact that efficient communication and effective results are more likely to occur in homogeneous teams. And indeed, the effectiveness of teamwork in collectivist and thus largely Eastern societies is often highlighted in Western societies. It raises the question whether a team of diversified composition could reach the desired consensus as effectively and whether such a team could perform on a *long-term* basis.

Still, we are also sufficiently aware of the potential drawbacks of the cohesive homogeneous team, including its tendency toward the groupthink phenomenon. Cohesiveness, and the corresponding tendency to preserve harmony, may inhibit disagreement or critical evaluations in these teams. It may engender a perception of isolation from the outer world. Cohesive and homogeneous teams can also inhibit the emergence of effective team leadership. This unresolved dilemma clearly indicates that we should withhold judgment on the relative merits of a highly cohesive collectivist as opposed to a diversified team. The team domain remains the site of our greatest research challenge and has the greatest need for cross-cultural data.

Work-Family Relations

There is no doubt that with the growth in research dealing with discrimination and gender, the cross-cultural study of these issues has become a source of new insights. But the work-family area is also plagued by a confusion between observations that describe cultural norms and those that describe organizational phenomena. If an exhaustive listing of cultural and organizational features is the desired product (and such a catalog is useful for various purposes, such as training a departing expatriate; Ronen, 1989), then the distinction between the two levels of variables is immaterial. If, however, the goal is to develop models in which cultural features are among the predictors of organizationally relevant phenomena, then the constructs describing cultural norms pertaining to work-family relations should be distinct from the constructs used to assess organizational criteria and work-related variables.

For example, Watanabe, Takahashi, and Minami (Chapter Eleven) report the counterintuitive finding that Japanese fathers, although they spend less time at home than their counterparts in such other countries as Germany and the United States, are perceived by their children to be more central in the family and are more often named as the most reliable figure at home. In other words, in spite of long working hours and being physically absent, Japanese fathers are psychologically present at home in the form of an authority figure, or symbol of authority, more often than are the U.S. and German fathers who spend less hours at work and more time at home.

Behavioral and attitudinal manifestations of this kind are often interpreted as cultural characteristics. I wish to emphasize the theoretical poverty of such claims and the need to relate these manifestations to more fundamental cultural dimensions and norms. For example, what values and norms prompt the mother to promote the father's image? How extensive and how deeply rooted are traditional norms of gender? To what extent are mothers in dual-career families still responsible for the family duties, and why?

These questions are all related to a more basic question, why are certain societies more egalitarian or traditional than others? In order for industrial and organizational psychology research to be effective, the anthropological investigation must first identify the relevant cross-cultural dimension. For example, the extent to which societies display traditional versus egalitarian norms may result from their location on the individualist-collectivist dimension, presuming that individualist societies are more egalitarian (Berry, Poortinga, Segall, & Dasen, 1992). Alternately, these norms might be related to such constructs as the masculinity versus femininity dimension of social values, defined through a variety of observable characteristics such as being assertive or competitive (Hofstede, 1980). However, we should be careful not to apply a circular logic by which the masculinity versus femininity dimension is defined operationally by manifestations of work-family role differentiation, the very variables that we would like to explain.

It is legitimate to ask why some societies are more egalitarian or traditional than others. But the more important questions for industrial and organizational psychology have to do with the dimensions that describe traditionalism (for example, a clear division between gender roles) and with the implications of these dimensions for applied issues such as conflicts between obligations of home and work. The important implication for industrial and organizational psychology is the degree to which societies with more traditional role differentiation are more likely to assign the responsibility for work-family domains not dually but to women. Further implications of concern are the effects of traditional cultural norms in limiting women's opportunities for participation in the workforce.

Zedeck (Chapter Twelve) sheds some light on the distinction I am trying to make when he insists that "the meaning of work" to an individual should be expanded to encompass the various organizations in which a person works and should include both employing organizations and family organizations. Because work values and their importance are determined by the process of socialization, there are at least two main sources of variation in these values: within-group differences and variation across groups. Furthermore, Zedeck suggests that in these domains there are cultural universals and cultural variables. Still, the distinction between the cultural dimensions and the industrial and organizational constructs must be made in order to benefit from cross-cultural research findings.

Hofstede's Contribution

No review of the literature of the past decade, particularly when focused on the development of cultural variables, should omit an evaluation of Hofstede's contribution. There is no doubt that the four cultural dimensions extracted by Hofstede in 1980 and then developed further in additional countries with the addition of a fifth dimension (Hofstede & Bond, 1988) have together formed a cornerstone of cross-cultural industrial and organizational research. The contribution is even more remarkable in the face of the scarcity of other useful cultural dimensions for cross-cultural research. Furthermore, these cultural dimensions indeed predict organizationally relevant criteria. For example, the degree to which cultural orientation is individualist or collectivist effects the relationship between training methods and individual efficacy and performance (Earley, 1994), and collectivist managers performed poorly in out-groups compared to in-groups (Earley, 1994).

The impact of Hofstede's comparative research was the result of a combination of methodological and conceptual innovations. First, the original study (1980) was based on a survey with a very large sample comprising 116,000 cases from forty countries, and it thereby attained high levels of reliability and face validity (credibility). It should be pointed out, however, that data for each country were averaged for the factor analysis, yielding a sample size of $n = 40$. Second, the factors extracted were defined in broad cultural terms, despite the fact that the original survey items dealt with the mainstream of I/O psychology, namely job attitudes. The derived dimensions were therefore very appealing as a set of cultural independent variables to be used in accounting for various organizational dependent variables. Third, the ecological cultural dimensions proposed by Hofstede enabled him to rank thirty-nine nations on each, assuming that the average score captured the shared orientations of members of each of these societies. The analysis was carried out with a sensitivity to the ecological fallacy and to the hazards of drawing individual-level generalizations from nation-level analyses.

The dimensions developed by Hofstede have inspired a large and important body of research. Studies aimed at cross-validating, refining, and expanding the original dimensions (Hofstede & Bond, 1988) have proliferated. In addition, many confirmatory studies have related the various dimensions, as independent variables, to organizationally relevant attitudes, behaviors, and policies, such as preferred forms of compensation, leadership behaviors, and team decision-making processes. The general adoption of the five dimensions over almost two decades raises the possibility that these dimensions may indeed represent the best conceptualization of cultural antecedents of organizational behavior.

Individualism-Collectivism as a Cultural Dimension

The individualism-collectivism dimension has been given extensive treatment in comparative and cross-cultural studies. But a few ambiguous issues remain and are worth emphasizing here. Hui and his associates (Hui, Triandis, & Yee, 1991; Hui & Yee, 1994; Hui, Yee, & Eastman, 1995) have attempted to show that individuals as well as entire cultures vary in terms of individualism-collectivism. The existence of individual variation on this dimension allows researchers to show, for example, that collectivists across various cultures are more similar to each other than they are to individualists from their own cultures (Hui, 1988; Hui, 1989).

More relevant to our discussion is the extent to which variation across cultures on the individualism-collectivism dimension has indeed been found to be related to organizational features such as communication (for example, Gudykunst, Yoon, & Nishida, 1987) or bargaining style (Leung, 1987). These relationships are additional to the well-established relationship between a culture's location on the individualism-collectivism dimension and behaviors such as team collaboration, compromising, consensus building, and conformity that exemplify a value of harmonious relations.

Despite the explanatory power of the individualism-collectivism cultural dimension, we need to be aware of the pitfalls of drawing cross-cultural conclusions from research using individuals as the unit of analysis. For example, individualism-collectivism as measured by the INDCOL scale (Hui, 1988) can be used to study individual differences within cultures and—by averaging individual scores—to characterize entire societies. However, construct validity at the individual level does not ensure that the same validity exists at the cross-cultural level. Even the operational definition of the phenomenon itself may change when analysis moves from the individual to the aggregate level. Despite these caveats, as pointed out by Sego, Hui, and Law (Chapter Six), the practice of aggregating individual perceptions to infer collective cultural values occurs all too often in research in such areas as organizational culture and climate (for example, Schneider, 1972).

The dangers of transferring generalizations from one level of analysis to another are underscored by cases where apparently contradictory values are found at different levels of analysis within the same society. Kabanoff (Chapter Twenty-Three) reminds us of one such case, which initially seemed to defy industrial and organizational models. In Japan, organizations exhibit what seem to be manifestations of two contradictory paradigms. On one hand organizational members internalize the organization's status hierarchy and are acutely aware of each member's position in that hierarchy. This awareness in turn informs all of their interactions within the organization. Even when meeting a representative of another organization, a Japanese manager will be sure to determine in advance the counterpart's status. On the other hand this respect for status inequalities seems to be contradicted by the participatory and democratic style of behavior at the lateral level and a degree of egalitarianism rarely found in more individualist societies. Triandis (1995) refers to this phenomenon as horizontal collectivism.

Sinha (Chapter Three) reports an instance of the coexistence of collectivist and individualist norms in India as well. There is strong evidence that Indian managers internalize both types of norms, creating a duality that indeed may cause a dilemma for the individual. Moreover, the values are internalized sequentially: managers acquire collectivist norms during early socialization and only as adults learn to emulate individualist values that they associate with the West.

In response to the evidence that a unidimensional conception of individualism-collectivism is too limited, Triandis and Bhawuk (Chapter Two) have suggested adopting the further distinction of vertical versus horizontal dimensions. The result is a typology consisting of four categories (Triandis, 1995; Chen, Meindl, & Hunt, 1997): horizontal collectivism, horizontal individualism, vertical collectivism, and vertical individualism. Triandis and Bhawuk identify specific national cultures as examples of each of these categories and generate an extensive list of hypotheses relating the four categories to various organizational outcomes.

Unfortunately, this typology seems to exhibit some of the methodological problems that I mentioned earlier. In particular, the authors do not distinguish between culture-level norms and organization-level variables when assigning societies to each of the four categories. Without distinct constructs for the cultural level, their scheme is of limited value in explaining or predicting organizational phenomena. For instance, a characteristic that is found in a range of domains, such as work, family, and recreation, can be treated as a cultural phenomenon and can then be related to its specific manifestations within organizations. However, a characteristic that is found primarily in work organizations will be redundant and useless for predictive models of those organizations. For example, when the characterization of Americans as vertical individualists is based primarily on their acceptance of inequality in organizational settings, the researcher cannot then use this ostensibly cultural characteristic to predict organizational behavior. These problems, however, are not *inherent* to efforts to cross individualism-collectivism with other variables, and such efforts may be quite useful, depending on the research question.

Researchers investigating the horizontal-vertical distinction also need to be sensitive to the possibility that perceptions of hierarchy may shift in content but maintain the same intensity. Thus the decline of a particular hierarchy within a society does not necessarily mean that the society overall has changed its horizontal-vertical orientation. India may move away from the caste system, but it is more likely to move toward other hierarchical structures rather than toward horizontal values.

The individualism-collectivism distinction will serve cross-cultural research better if it is unburdened of some of the moral connotations attached to it. These are often implicit in the assumed connection between collectivism and relatedness and between individualism and rational calculation (Triandis & Bhawuk, Chapter Two). This assumption is typical of a kind of latent preference for collectivist norms over individualist ones that associates collectivism with affective ties and individualism with cold, impersonal calculation. The implication is that collectivists give priority to relationships and take into account the needs of others and that individualists do the opposite. I cannot help but reflect that the misery suffered by members of collectivist societies at the hands of others in the same society is not less than that inflicted in individualist societies. Again, when we examine collectivism at the micro level, as it relates to team work or organizations, we find that there is nothing in collectivism to rule out rational calculation. New members of teams in these societies are fully aware of the privileges to which they will be entitled upon joining the group.

Alternatively, individualism is associated with modernization and development, and collectivism with a traditionalist past. For example, the tentative suggestion is made, using Greece and India as examples, that affluence is shifting most cultures toward individualism (Triandis and Bhawuk, Chapter Two). But this proposition is contradicted by a number of well-known phenomena: the kibbutz movement is threatened by bankruptcy rather than affluence, Japan has sustained affluence while preserving collectivist orientation, and collectivist symptoms are beginning to appear among the North Americans. The challenge now is to ascertain whether collectivism that results from ingrained traditional sources, as in the Japanese case, can be equated with that found in collectives such as the kibbutzim that are deliberately established in accordance with an ideology.

Conclusion

Culture and cultural variation present a unique challenge to any science that endeavors to analytically isolate and measure the causal influence of psychological traits on social behavior. But we should not be forced to choose between a positivist approach, which emphasizes the external, generic features of cultures, and an interpretive approach, which insists on studying each culture from the perspective of those immersed in it. Our analyses should be as sensitive as possible to cultural differences; they should take advantage of the rich anthropological literature on these differences and also remain focused on the goal of developing and testing causal hypotheses that can be validated across cultures. The basic confirmatory model (which could apply either the one-way or n-way approaches delineated by Brett and her colleagues in Chapter Four) does not have to be insensitive to the subtleties of each unique culture.

Cross-cultural research in industrial and organizational psychology pose more than practical and scientific challenges. It is also linked to the social and intellectual movement that can be defined as a *new multiculturalism* whose aim is to promote "the value of diversity as a core principle and insist that all cultural groups be treated with respect and as equals" (Fowers & Richardson, 1996, p. 609). Similarly, the scientific value of our cross-cultural generalizations can only be enhanced by each person's refusal to use his or her culture's values as the yardstick for all other cultures and by greater sensitivity to all differences.

References

Bass, B. M. (1990). *Bass and Stogdill's handbook of leadership: Theory, research and managerial applications* (3rd ed.). New York: Free Press.

Berry, J. W., Poortinga, Y. H., Segall, M. H., & Dasen, P. R. (1992). *Cross-cultural psychology: Research and applications.* New York: Cambridge University Press.

Chen, C. C., Meindl, J. R., & Hunt, R. B. (1997). Testing the effects of vertical and horizontal collectivism: A study of reward allocation preferences in China. *Journal of Cross-Cultural Psychology, 28,* 44–70.

Eagly, A. H. (1987). *Sex differences in social behavior: A social-role interpretation.* Hillsdale, NJ: Erlbaum.

Earley, P. C. (1994). East meets West meets Mideast: Further explorations of collectivistic and individualistic work groups. *Academy of Management Journal, 36,* 319–348.

Earley, P. C. (1994). Self or group? Cultural effects of training on self-efficacy and performance. *Administrative Science Quarterly, 39,* 89–117.

Fowers, B. J., & Richardson, F. C. (1996). Why is multiculturalism good? *American Psychologist, 51*(6), 609–621.

Glenn, E. S., & Glenn, C. G. (1981). *Man and mankind: Conflicts and communications between cultures.* Norwood, NJ: Ablex.

Gudykunst, W. B., Yoon, Y. C., & Nishida, T. (1987). Perceptions of communication in ingroup and outgroup relationships. *Communication Monographs, 54,* 295–306.

Hofstede, G. (1980). *Culture's consequences: International differences in work-related values.* Thousand Oaks, CA: Sage.

Hofstede, G., & Bond, M. H. (1988). The Confucian connection: From cultural roots to economic growth. *Organizational Dynamics,* Spring, 4–21.

House, R. J., Rousseau, D. M., & Thomas-Hunt, M. (1995). The meso paradigm: A framework for the integration of micro and macro organizational behavior. In L. L. Cummings and B. M. Staw (Eds.), *Research in organizational behavior* (Vol. 17, pp. 71–114). Greenwich, CT: JAI Press.

Hui, C. H. (1988). Measurement of individualism-collectivism. *Journal of Research in Personality, 22,* 17–36.

Hui, C. H. (1989). Psychological collectivism: Self-sacrifice or sharing? In J. P. Forgas & J. M. Innes (Eds.), *Recent advances in social psychology: An international perspective* (pp. 521–528). Amsterdam: Elsevier.

Hui, C. H., Triandis, H. C., & Yee, C. (1991). Individualism-collectivism and psychological needs: Their relationships in two cultures. *Journal of Cross-Cultural Psychology, 20,* 310–323.

Hui, C. H., & Yee, C. (1994). The shortened individualism-collectivism scale: Its relationship with demographic and work-related variables. *Journal of Research in Personality, 28,* 409–422.

Hui, C. H., Yee, C., & Eastman, K. L. (1995). The relationship between individualism-collectivism and job-satisfaction. *Applied Psychology: An International Review, 44*(3), 277–282.

Leung, I. (1987). Some determinants of reaction to procedural models for conflict resolution: A cross-national study. *Journal of Personality and Social Psychology, 53,* 898–908.

Ronen, S. (1986). *Comparative and multinational management.* New York: Wiley.

Ronen, S. (1989). Training the international assignee. In I. L. Goldstein & Associates, *Training and development in organizations* (pp. 417–453). San Francisco: Jossey-Bass.

Ronen, S. (1994). An understanding of motivational need taxonomies: A cross-cultural confirmation. In H. D. Triandis, M. D. Dunnette, and L. M. Hough (Eds.), *Handbook of industrial and organizational psychology* (2nd ed., Vol. 4, pp. 241–270). Palo Alto, CA: Consulting Psychologists Press.

Ronen, S., & Shenkar, O. (1985). Clustering countries on attitudinal dimensions: A review and synthesis. *Academy of Management Review, 10*(3), 435–454.

Rousseau, D. M., & House, R. J. (1994). Meso organizational behavior: Avoiding three fundamental biases. In C. L. Cooper and D. M. Rousseau (Eds.), *Trends in organizational behavior,* (Vol. 1, pp. 13–29). New York: Wiley.

Schneider, B. (1972). *Culture and social behavior.* New York: McGraw-Hill.

Triandis, H. C. (1995). *Individualism & collectivism.* Boulder, CO: Westview.

CHAPTER 25

Reassessing What We Know
Critical Commentaries and New Directions

P. Christopher Earley
Miriam Erez

Tradition and inertia often inhibit the creation of fresh new perspectives on organizational behavior; the authors of the chapters in this volume have overcome these inertial bonds and have developed new models of cross-cultural psychology for exploring an employee's relationship to his or her organization. Theory development is a critical first stage in the series of steps taken by researchers as they create new knowledge. This first stage is stimulated by a recognition of the inherent limitation in transferring research findings across national and cultural boundaries. From a psychological perspective this recognition has directed attention to the construct of nationality and culture. Organizational practices common in one country are often ineffective in other countries, and researchers lack explanations. The next stage is to look to the newly formed models as lenses for understanding cultural effects. Unfortunately, many existing models of organizational behavior do not take the cultural dimension into consideration. They are based on theories that stemmed from the traditional stream in psychology, which focused heavily on individual difference characteristics and their effects on behavior.

Situational effects have often been ignored, and in studies of validity generalization, situational effects have often been treated as artifacts; hence their effects were attributed to individual differences.

Kurt Lewin used to argue that there is nothing more practical than a good theory. The major guiding force in the construction of this edited volume was the development of useful, and interesting, theory. A good theory starts with an explicit diagnosis of a problem—in the present instance, a recognition that individual and organizational phenomena occur within a cultural context. From a theoretical perspective, this fact of contextual richness pertains to issues of validity generalization and thus to organizations' failures in effectively transferring organizational practices across cultures.

Without question I/O researchers of the past two decades have taken seriously the relevance of culture and nation, as evidenced by the plethora of studies using cultural values, dimensions, and the like. However, these studies typically use culture, or cultural dimensions, in an ipsative fashion. Even worse, a number of studies evoke cultural values or dimensions as post host explanations. For example, some researchers have observed differences between, say, conflict management styles in the United States (confrontational and aggressive) and conflict management styles in Japan (indirect and conflict avoiding). Next a cultural variable such as individualism is evoked to explain the observed difference. That is, people in an individualist culture such as the United States are argued to be direct and challenging of others, and people from a collectivist culture such as Japan are argued to be group oriented and facilitative of social interaction. However, this approach fails to provide a means for establishing discriminant validity because other cultural explanations for the same empirical observations are possible (for example, differences in conflict style are as easily explained by high versus low power differentials or context differentials). This approach is revealed as even more problematic when we examine conflict style in Israel, another country commonly labeled collectivist. There we would observe a preponderance of the confrontational style of conflict and we would learn about the Israeli value of *dugri,* or candid, speech (Erez & Earley, 1993). Thus the next step in conducting meaningful research is to take a fresh look at the latest theoretical developments in the field of I/O psychology, in order to understand the potential contribution of nation or culture.

The often demonstrated limitations to generalization concerning our current practices have called into question the external validity of present theories in I/O psychology. A number of researchers have criticized I/O models because they have not shown a full appreciation for the potential impact of the situation, or context, in which organizational activities occur. Writers including Cappelli and Sherer (1991) and House and Rousseau (1990), to name a few, have argued that organizational behavior and psychology studies demonstrate a consistent lack of regard for the contextual richness in which behavioral phenomena occur. Ironically, some of these researchers are quick to relish the importance of macro organizational variables such as governance structure or control systems without extending that importance one step further to the general cultural, or societal, context for organizational phenomena. In order to overcome this challenge and limitation, James, Mulaik, and Brett (1982) suggest that a theoretical framework is necessary before researchers can proactively identify potential situational moderators, and with the contributions of the authors in the present volume such models and frameworks are within our grasp.

The various frameworks described and defined in this volume are a major attempt to jump-start or ignite empirical research in the field of industrial and organizational psychology and organizational behavior. (We do not say *cross-cultural* or *international* industrial and organizational psychology and organizational behavior because research frameworks and empirical work *must* be cross-cultural or international if they are to satisfy the test marker of validity generalization. This is not to say that within-culture, or emic, frameworks are without merit. However, it is critical that a researcher choose ex ante to establish either within-culture or across-culture assumptions and not confuse the two approaches.) The ideas presented by this volume's contributors can be broken into three general categories: culture-as-construct, culture-as-method, and culture-in-framework. In tackling the first category, Chapters Two and Three address a new way of thinking about several specific aspects of cultural values. A somewhat complementary approach is presented in Chapter Ten as well. These chapters suggest that cultural research requires a fine-grained and well-constructed notion of specific aspects of culture and a movement away from black-box treatments of culture. This theme is expanded further in Chapter Four inasmuch as Brett and her colleagues formulate an important and interesting multifaceted methodology for better understanding culture as a construct, a methodology to which Sego and his colleagues respond in Chapter Six.

The second category, culture-as-method, is also addressed in Chapters Four, Five, and Six and in Chapter Seven. Both Brett and her colleagues and Berry present interesting approaches to the study of culture through specific frameworks. Berry, drawing from his general ecological framework, provides the organizational researcher with a general style of conducting research by tracing cultural antecedents to historical and environmental considerations. Sego and his colleagues provide some useful structural modeling considerations. Finally, Graen and his colleagues examine culture-as-method as they advocate a particular and unique approach to conducting cross-cultural research, specifying a research alliance in which cross-cultural collaboration becomes cultural discovery.

Culture-in-framework is the approach taken by the meta-organizational models presented in this volume that create links among such macro-level factors as culture and such meso-level factors as organizational management practices and employee behavior (including attitudinal and performance outcomes). In many of the models presented in this volume, culture serves as the macro-level external stimulus and organizational phenomena as the meso-level influences of individual behavior. Using the general organizing principle of examining an employee's relationship to his or her organization across cultural and national boundaries, the contributors to this book have helped us better understand the moderating and main effects influence of culture on behavior.

The type of conceptualizing exhibited in this volume is a change from the concern many organizational researchers have shown with the nature of culture per se. To meet this concern, a number of typologies of culture were developed during the 1970s and 1980s (for example, Hofstede, 1980; Ronen, 1986; Ronen & Shenkar, 1985; Schwartz & Bilsky, 1987; Triandis, Bontempo, Villareal, Asai, & Lucca, 1988). Cultural typologies contributed to our understanding of cross-cultural differences in work values and preferences, but they did not help us understand the causal relationship between culture and employees' behavior or the moderating effect of culture on the relationship between managerial and motivational techniques and work behavior. In the present volume, general typologies of culture have been supplanted by the thinking of Triandis and Bhawuk and of Sinha, authors who explicitly link cultural context to organizational context, and by the explorations of Brett and her colleagues, Berry, and Sego and his colleagues into the nature of the construct of culture itself. Through these advances, we are now in a position to incorporate culture when we build specific midrange models of organizational phenomena. This theme is developed further in Bond's analysis and critique of the I/O field's excessive reliance on cultural values as a surrogate for cultural context.

Where should we go from here? There are several meta-strategies we can derive from these chapters over and above their specific content. First, all the contributors seek to understand the processes through which cultural context operates on various organizational phenomena. Second, relying on nation and culture as unitary, unidimensional explanations is no longer an acceptable research strategy. Third, relying on a specific dimension, or facet, of culture such as individualism underestimates the complexity of the cultural milieu. And finally, multilevel models help us understand culture in both its macro- and micro-level manifestations. That is to say, culture can be conceived through its presence in a general social system as well as through its presence in an individual's psyche. Our understanding that there is a mediating and moderating effect of culture on the relationship between organizational phenomena and employee behavior is also benefited by the exemplary contributions of the authors in this volume.

The value and potential contribution of the present models can be measured using Campbell's guidelines (1990) concerning theory: namely, that theories should (1) tell us that certain facts among the accumulated knowledge are important, and others are not, (2) give old data new interpretations and new meaning, (3) identify important new issues and prescribe the most critical research questions that need to be answered to maximize understanding of the issue, (4) provide a means by which new research data can be interpreted and coded for future use, (5) provide a means for identifying and defining applied problems and for prescribing and evaluating solutions to applied problems, and (6) provide a means for responding to new problems that have no previously identified solution strategy.

Using these criteria, it is obvious that the contributors to this volume have created a unique basis for future research in this arena. It is our hope that this volume will have a lasting impact on organizational researchers who investigate international and cross-cultural industrial and organizational psychology and organizational behavior. More specifically, we hope that regardless of each reader's research agenda, the chapters in this book will sensitize each reader to the centrality of nation and culture in understanding the fundamental processes underlying an employee's relationship to his or her work organization.

References

Campbell, J. P. (1990). The role of theory in industrial and organizational psychology. In M. O. Dunnette & L. M. Hough (Eds.), *Handbook of industrial and organizational psychology* (2nd ed., Vol. 1, pp. 39–73). Palo Alto, CA: Consulting Psychologists Press.

Cappelli, P., & Sherer, P. D. (1991). The missing role of context in OB: The need for a meso-level approach. In B. M. Staw & L. L. Cummings (Eds.), *Research in organizational behavior* (Vol. 13, pp. 55–110). Greenwich, CT: JAI Press.

Erez, M., & Earley, P. C. (1993). *Culture, self-identity, and work.* New York: Oxford University Press.

Hofstede, G. (1980). *Culture's consequences: International differences in work-related values.* Thousand Oaks, CA: Sage.

House, R. J., and Rousseau, D. M. (1990). *On the bifurcation of OB or if it ain't meso it ain't OB* (Working paper). Philadelphia: Wharton School, University of Pennsylvania.

James, L. R., Mulaik, S. A., & Brett, J. M. (1982). *Causal analysis: Assumptions, models, and data.* Thousand Oaks, CA: Sage.

Ronen, S. (1986). *Comparative and multinational management.* New York: Wiley.

Ronen, S., & Shenkar, O. (1985). Clustering countries on attitudinal dimensions: A review and synthesis. *Academy of Management Review, 10*(3), 435–454.

Schwartz, S. H., & Bilsky, W. (1987). Toward a universal psychological structure of human values. *Journal of Personality and Social Psychology, 53,* 550–562.

Triandis, H. C., Bontempo, R., Villareal, M. J., Asai, M., & Lucca, N. (1988). Individualism and collectivism: Cross-cultural perspectives on self-ingroup relationships. *Journal of Personality and Social Psychology, 54,* 323–338.

Name Index

Poortinga, Y. H., 81, 92, 108, 126, 129, 132, 133, 139, 141, 146, 290, 312, 321, 331, 721, 730
Popper, K. R., 128
Porat, A. M., 657, 674
Porter, L. W., 2, 9, 163, 189, 217, 235, 618
Porter, M. E., 496, 500, 505, 520
Porter, R. E., 537, 623
Potter, D. M., 703, 711
Powell, B., 281, 315
Powell, M. C., 15, 47
Power, S., 269, 271
Pradham, P., 197, 226, 227, 242
Prahalad, C. K., 496, 517, 520
Prasad, S. B., 347, 361
Prein, H.C.M., 641, 675
Preissle, J., 75, 128
Premack, S. L., 476, 491
Price, R., 464, 485
Priestly, K., 284, 312
Prieto, J. M., 8, 410, 440, 444
Prokesch, S., 224, 240
Pruitt, D. G., 641, 674
Pucik, V., 495, 496, 521
Puffer, S. M., 697, 712
Pugh, D. S., 496, 497, 508, 521
Purcell, J., 495, 505, 507, 519, 521
Putnam, R. D., 152, 159
Pye, L., 648, 650, 654, 657, 658, 659, 674

Q
Quinlan, M., 510, 521
Quinn, R. P., 297, 317

R
Radebaugh, L. H., 506, 517
Ragan, J. W., 576, 590, 619
Rahim, M. A., 558, 566, 622–623, 641, 674
Ralston, D. A., 558–559, 570, 575–576, 606, 623
Ramanujan, A. K., 61, 72
Ramon, M., 413, 444
Rand, T., 506, 521

Randall, D. M., 544, 545, 566, 619
Redding, S. G., 244, 255, 278, 317, 500, 503, 521, 635, 638
Redmond, M., 355, 360
Reed, S., 377, 406
Reich, M., 464, 491
Reischauer, E. O., 279, 317
Reiz, H. J., 497, 521
Renwick, G., 648, 658, 659, 674
Resnick, L. B., 226, 239
Retschitzky, J., 134, 146
Reve, T., 472, 491
Reykowski, J., 15, 49
Reynolds, C., 509, 521
Rice, R., 437, 444
Rice, R. W., 305, 317
Richards, L., 501, 521
Richards, T., 501, 521
Richardson, F. C., 730
Richman, B. M., 590, 618
Richtand, C. N., 325, 332
Richter, J., 276, 277, 287, 292, 299, 317
Ricks, D., 496, 521
Rimmer, L., 284, 314
Ring, P. S., 496, 505, 521
Rivero, J. C., 15, 46–47
Roberts, H., 229, 240
Roberts, K. H., 2, 4–5, 9, 156–157, 159, 501, 521, 605, 623
Robinson, J. P., 285, 317
Robinson, R. V., 292, 313, 574, 623
Robinson, W. S., 149, 159
Rodgers, W., 647, 651–652, 670
Rogers, J., 468, 474, 476, 487
Rohner, R. P., 79, 128, 678, 711
Rokeach, M., 13, 21, 23–25, 27, 46, 49, 201, 204–205, 240, 308, 317, 337, 361, 679, 694, 695, 711
Roland, A., 58, 61, 69, 73
Ronen, S., 8, 35, 49–50, 201, 240, 504, 521, 522, 542, 544, 561, 577, 623, 715, 716, 717, 719, 723, 731, 735, 737
Ronis, D. L., 675
Ronkainen, I. A., 493, 504, 517

Subject Index

Role stress, cultural influences on, 557, 567
Roper Organization poll, 193
Russia: leadership in, 541–542, 568–569; negotiation in, 654, 659

S

Safety policy, 89–91, 121–122, 510
Sampling: of behaviors, 142; of individuals, 141–142; issues of, 597–598; and level of theory, 119, 141–142; populations for, 141
Satisfaction/dissatisfaction: and attitudes research, 301–309; cultural differences in, 567; employee, 193–194; individual differences and, 296–298; measures of, 302–303; and three-dimensional matrix of individuals, situations, behaviors, 304–309; triangular work/family/life model of, 301–304; values and, 205–208; work-family relationship and, 294–300, 301–309
Scandinavia, unionism in, 461, 466, 470–471. *See also* Sweden
Schwartz's theory of universal values, 25–26, 27, 149–151, 458
Scientific management, 214
Segmentation model of work-family relationship, 295
Segregation, 151–152
Self, same versus different, 16–17. *See also* Horizontal-vertical relationships
Self definition, in individualistic versus collective cultures, 15, 27
Self-evaluation, 199, 200, 206; and face, 244–245
Self-monitoring, 199
Self-presentation, and face, 243–247. *See also* Face
Self-reaction, 199
Self-regulation, and proximal motivation processes, 199–200, 206–208, 209

Self-representation. *See* Cultural self-representation
Self-respect, 202
Sensory-perceptual cognitive processes, 205–206
Seven Cultures of Capitalism, The (Hampton-Turner and Trompenaars), 691–692
Shared meaning, 2–3, 148–149, 154. *See also* Culture; Values, cultural
Similarities perspective, 81–82; and cultural dialogue, 123, 124
Singapore, 26
Situation-disposition interaction, 28–30, 60–61
Slovakia, 26
Smith, Dugan, and Trompenaars study, 581, 585–588
Social behavior, Fiske's theory of, 21–23, 24, 27
Social conflict, 390
Social construction perspective, 135
Social desirability bias, 578–579
Social exchange: and face in organizations, 250–253; horizontal-vertical individualism-collectivism typology applied to, 35–36
Social judgment theory, 438
Social loafing, 102, 115, 226–227, 384
Social service organizations, professional status in, 117–118
Social ties, 250; and face in organizations, 250–253
Social values, Indian, 58–60, 70
Socialism, 460–460
Socialization: and culture, 718; in history, 400; inclusionary dimension of, 398; language, 399; as multinational team homogenizer, 398–400; people, 399; in performance proficiency, 399; political, 399
Socializing synthesizers, 170–171, 173
Socially Oriented Achievement Scale, 34

148–155, 726–729; and motivation, 193–235, 642; and negotiation, 642–650; neutrality of, in ecological approach, 138; and organizational behavior, 53–71; psycho-spiritual, Indian, 56–58; as representation of culture, 201–204; Rokeach's typology of, 23–25, 27; Schwartz's theory of universal, 25–26, 27, 149–151, 458; and self-evaluation, 200; social, Indian, 58–60, 70; study of, value of, 257–271, 633–634; typologies of, 23–27; typologies of, and industrial relations, 456–459; typologies of, and motivation, 201–204; typologies of, value of, 257–260, 571–580, 595–597; and unionism, 461, 465, 467–468, 472, 477–479; and work-family relationship, 276–311, 319–331. *See also* Confucian work dynamic; Hofstede's cultural values typology; Horizontal-vertical individualism-collectivism typology; Individualism-collectivism; Masculinity-femininity; Power distance; Uncertainty avoidance

Values, individual: as cognitive representations of needs, 204–205; in cross-cultural context, 265, 268; linking, to individual behavior, 264–268; measurement of, aggregation biases in, 149–151, 156; measurement of, and change over time, 151–152; measurement of, when collective/individual values are not equal, 152–153; in organizations, 262–264, 678–680; using mean of, to operationalize cultural values, 148–155, 726–729; and personality, 263–264. *See also* Values, cultural

Values, organizational, 260–264; computer-aided text analysis

(CATA) to study, 695–706; and individual values, 262, 678–680; and justice-based typology of organizations, 680–708; measurement of, 693–696; profiles of, 699–706. *See also* Organizational culture; Organizational justice

Values, work, 327. *See also* Work ethic

Vertical collectivism, 17–19, 203, 693. *See also* Collectivism; Horizontal-vertical individualism-collectivism typology; India

Vertical dimension: and authority ranking, 23; defined, 16. *See also* Horizontal-vertical individualism-collectivism typology; Horizontal-vertical relationships

Vertical individualism, 17, 19–21, 204. *See also* Horizontal-vertical individualism-collectivism typology; Horizontal-vertical relationships; Individualism

Vertical solidarity, 59. *See also* Vertical collectivism

Victorian England, and leadership, 568

Volvo, 223–225

W

West Germany, 26

West Lake Center for Joint-Venture Management, 185

Wiring mentality, 423, 426–427

Within and Between Analysis (WABA), 198

Within-group analysis/correlations, 546

Women employees. *See* Gender roles; Mothers

Work: defined, 323–324; meaning of, 324–329, 724

Work councils, 478–479

Work ethic: Confucian, 554, 567; and cultural influences on economic growth, 580, 582–585; in India, 63–64; religious values